Mysterium & Medulla Bibliorum
THE
Mystery and Marrow of the B I B L E
NAMELY:

God's Covenants

WITH MAN

In the *First Adam* before the Fall, and in the *Last Adam*, JESUS CHRIST, after the fall, From the beginning to the end of the world:

Unfolded & Illustrated

In positive *Aphorisms* & their *explanations*.

WHEREIN

The general nature, several kinds, gradual discoveries, sanctions and administrations of all God's *holy COVENANTS*, fr*om* first to last, throughout the whole *Scriptures*: together with their peculiar terms, occasions, author, federates, matter, end, properties, agreements, disagreements, and many other their noted excellencies are largely and familiarly expounded: the blessed person and office of *JESUS CHRIST*, the *soul of all the Covenant of Faith*, and sole *Mediator* of the *NEW COVENANT*, is described: many choice fundamental points of Christianity, are explained, sundry practical questions, or cases of conscience are resolved; various puzzling controversies about the present occasionally elucidated; and in all, the great supernatural MYSTERY of the whole Sacred BIBLE, touching God's most wise, gracious, merciful, righteous, plenary, wonderful, and eternal salvation of sinners by *JESUS CHRIST through faith*, sweetly couched and gradually revealed in his *covenant-expressions* in all ages of the church, is disclosed and unveiled.

---

by F R A N C I S R O B E R T S, *M. A.*
Pastor of the Church at Wrington, in the County of Somerset

Berith Press
P.O. Box 861, Kansas, OK 74347
(918) 896-2055
www.berithpress.com

God's Covenants: The Mystery & Marrow of the Bible was first published in 1657. This Berith Press reprint, in which spelling, grammar, and formatting changes have been made, is 2024 by Berith Press, is a public domain work, as are now considered all volumes published by Berith Press.
Printed in the U.S.A.

ISBN 978-1-963516-07-4

But ye are come unto Mount Sion,—and to JESUS the Mediator of the NEW COVENANT, Hebrews 12:22-24

"I will be, says God, their God, and they shall be my people. What is better than this good, what is happier than this happiness?!" Augustine, On The Spirit and Letter, Chapter 22, Tome 3

London, Printed by R.W. for George Calvert, and are to be sold at his shop at the sign of the half-moon in Paul's Church-yard. 1657.

THIS is THE COVENANT that I will make with the House of Israel after those days, saith the LORD; I will give my Laws into their mind, and write them in their hearts. And I will be to them a God; and they shall be to me a people, etc.
Hebrews 8:10-12, Jeremiah 31:33-34

4

BOOK IV

OF

God's Covenant

OF

PERFORMANCE,

made and confirmed in JESUS CHRIST actually performed and exhibited in our flesh, according to the Covenants of Promise, *namely:*

THE

New Covenant:

BEING

The last and most excellent covenant expressure, which shall continue NEW, *from Christ's death, until the world's end.*

Contents

~~~

Chapter 5 – Of the matter, or substance of the New Covenant. *15*

Section 1: First, as to the brief analytical explication of the apostle's recited words, consider that the New Covenant is here set forth, with a note of excellency, and attention: Behold. And is described by the (1) time, (2) author, (3) federates, (4) name, and (5) nature thereof. *17*

Section 2: Generalities to be noted and observed diligently concerning the matter or substance of the New Covenant. *25*

Section 3: Thirdly, having analytically explained the words wherein the prophet and apostle describe this New Covenant, and having unfolded such generals as much conduce to the right understanding of the matter of the New Covenant; now in the last place I shall proceed to the opening of the matter of the New Covenant; more particularly, and this with the greater evidence and perspicuity. *61*

Aphorism 1: The matter of the New Covenant on God's part consists in certain New Covenant mercies or blessings promised by him to his federates. *63*

Article 1: Of God's writing his laws in their mind and hearts. *64*
    Question 1: What is here meant by {*mind and hearts*}? *65*
    Question 2: What laws of God are here intended to be written in their mind and heart? *68*

Question 3: What sort of writing is this, whereby God writes his laws in the mind and hearts of his federates? And how does he write his laws therein? *71*

Question 4: Were God's Laws not written in his People's minds and Hearts before the time of this New Covenant? *89*

Question 5: Why will the Lord write his laws in the minds and hearts of his federates, now under the New Covenant? And why does God covenant thus to do? *95*

Question 6: How may we know whether God has given his laws into our minds, and written them upon our hearts? *98*

Article 2: Of God's federate people's more excellent and more universal knowledge of the Lord, than under the Old Covenant. *117*

Question 1: Wherein does the nature of this New Covenant knowledge more especially consist? *119*

Question 2: How, and in what way, does God furnish his New Covenant people with such a knowledge of himself? *135*

Question 3: Do all God's New Covenant people attain to this Promised Knowledge of God, and so on? *141*

Question 4: Does God by this promise intended to take away, vacate, annul, and make void all human teaching, private and public, as altogether useless and needless now under the New Covenant, seeing he says: {*And they shall not teach, every man his neighbor, and every man his brother, saying, Know the LORD*}; and John says elsewhere: {*Ye need not that any man teach you*}? *149*

Question 5: Why has God promised this blessing in his New Covenant, that all shall know him, from the least of them to the greatest of them? *165*

Question 6: How may we discover that we so know the Lord, as God here intends in this his New Covenant promise? *173*

Article 3: Of God's mercy or propitiousness to them in his utter remission and oblivion, forgiving and forgetting all their sins forever. *185*

Proposition 1: That, under the New Covenant, the LORD God, in and through Jesus Christ, will freely, fully and utterly remit all his true federates' sins whatsoever. *188*

Question 1: What is the nature of sin, which is the subject of remission? *191*

Question 2: What is the remission of sins, which is here promised and covenanted in this New Covenant? *200*

[Position 1]: That remission of sins, here promised in this New Covenant, is not intended of any human remission fraternal or ministerial, but of divine remission of sins – and that not particular, but universal. *214*

[Position 2] That remission of sin is a distinct blessing and grace from mortification of sin, and not to be confounded therewith. *216*

[Position 3] That remission of sins strictly and properly taken, is not the all, but only a part of our justification before God; but more largely and improperly it is all. *217*

[Position 4] That remission of sins – strictly taken, most properly and especially – consists in the removal of the offense done to God, and in the acquittal or absolution of the sinner from the guilt of sin, that is: from his obligation, or being bound over, to endure the punishment of death, due for such offense. *219*

[Position 5] That God alone remits sin. *222*

[Position 6] That God pardons sin freely of his own mere grace, without any the least merit or desert of the pardoned sinner. *225*

[Position 7] That God remits sin only upon and for the satisfaction made to his justice for sin by the obedience and death of Jesus Christ. *228*

[Position 8] That God actually remits sin to all truly believing and repenting sinners, and (in his ordinary dispensation) to them only. *232*

[Position 9] That when God actually and savingly pardons sin to the believing and repenting sinner, he pardons fully and finally all his sins past and present, but not his sins to come. *238*

[Position 10] That God's elect, whose sins are pardoned, do daily need renewed pardons, for future and renewed sins. *244*

[Position 11] That pardon of sin, though full without exception, and final without revocation, yet is not complete and consummate in this present life until the very Day of Judgment. *246*

[Position 12] That in persons savingly pardoned sin may remain, yet those persons are in the account of God no longer sinners, but righteous. *248*

[Position 13] That sometimes sin may be universally and savingly pardoned, when yet the sense of that pardon may be suspended, and the contrary sense of God's displeasure for sin may be continued. *249*

[Position 14] That wherever God remits sin, not imputing it to the sinner unto condemnation, there he accepts the person as righteous, imputing Christ's righteousness to him unto justification. *251*

Question 3: May those who have their sins remitted, may know that they are remitted, and how may this be known? *253*

Question 4: Wherein does God's remission of sins under the New Covenant differs from and excel the remission of sins that was under the Old Covenant? *259*

Proposition 2: That God will therefore bestow upon his sincere federates all other the promised benefits of the New Covenant, because he will so freely, fully and utterly remit all their sins in and for the satisfaction of Jesus Christ. *267*

Article 4: Of the grand New Covenant relation, interest, and communion, mutually, between God and his sincere federates. *279*

    [Matter 1]: Information *284*
    [Matter 2]: Probation & Examination *288*
    {Question 1}: Has the LORD become our God in covenant? *289*
    {Question 2}: Have we become God's people in covenant? *311*
    [Matter 3]: Exhortation *313*
    [Matter 4]: Consolation *321*

Aphorism 2: The matter of this New Covenant, on the part of God's New Covenant federates, consists in certain New Covenant duties, implicitly here required from, and restipulated by his New Covenant people. *387*

Chapter 6 – Of the blessed Messiah, our Lord Jesus Christ God-man; the only Mediator, Testator, and Surety of the New Covenant between God and man. *401*

Aphorism 1: Of the necessity of a Mediator between God and man, in general. *404*

Aphorism 2: Of the person of Christ; and of his mediatory office, more generally. *412*

    Position 1: That Jesus, the only Son of God, and the son of the virgin Mary, is God and man in one person. *414*
    Position 2: That this Jesus, God-man, is the Christ, the promised Messiah; and he alone. *433*
    Position 3: That Jesus Christ, God and man, is the only true, fit and sufficient Mediator, Testator, and Surety of the New Covenant between God and man. *445*

Position 4: That Jesus Christ is Mediator, Testator and Surety of the New Covenant between God and man, as he is God-man. *452*

Aphorism 3: Of Christ's execution of his mediatory office, more particularly. *461*

Section 1: Whence it may be evinced, that Christ executes his Mediatory office, in a prophetical, priestly and kingly way. *462*

Section 2: Wherein the nature of Christ's prophecy, priesthood, and kingship consists. *468*
- [Part 1 of Christ's priesthood]: Of Christ's satisfaction. *476*
- [Part 2 of Christ's priesthood]: Of Christ's intercession. *495*
- [Part 3 of Christ's priesthood]: Of Christ's kingly office. *504*

Section 3: What are those two states of Christ's humiliation and exaltation, wherein he, as prophet, priest and king, thus executes his mediation between God and man? *523*

Aphorism 4: Of Christ's establishment of his New Covenant, and application of it to God's elect: that Jesus Christ, by virtue of this his prophetical, priestly and kingly mediation, Surety-ship and Testator-ship, has established his New Covenant forever; and is continually bringing all those whom the father hath given him into this New Covenant with God, to partake all the mercies, and perform all the duties thereof. *533*

Chapter 7 – Of the form of the New Covenant. *587*

Aphorism: The form of this New Covenant consists inwardly, in the mutual obligation between God and his New Covenant federates in Jesus Christ the Mediator thereof: outwardly, in the way and manner of this New Covenant's manifestation, confirmation and administration. *587*

Chapter 8 – Of the intended scope, or end of the New Covenant. *619*

Chapter 9 – Of certain General Inferences resulting from the whole of this New Covenant. *627*

A general synopsis of the subject matters in all these four books [*five volumes from Berith Press*]. *669*

Chapter 5

Of the matter, or substance of the New Covenant.

The substance or matter of the New Covenant comes next in order under consideration. Herein the very marrow and kernel of the New Covenant is comprised. The matter of the New Covenant is laid down: (1) partly, in the body of the New Covenant, promised by Jeremiah[1] and recited by Paul;[2] (2) partly, in the explanations of the nature of this New Covenant in the holy Scriptures, especially those of the New Testament. In opening of this matter of the New Covenant, I shall have recourse to both (as occasion shall require) for the fuller clearing and unfolding thereof, but primarily to the former, namely: To the body of the New Covenant, as promised and recited; and then secondarily to such explanations thereof, as are more necessary and apposite to explicate, illustrate, and unfold the same. And this I must be forced unto the rather, because the matter of the New Covenant is expressed so concisely in words, but comprehensively in sense, both by the prophet and apostle.

The matter of the **New Covenant** is chiefly laid down in the body of the Covenant: *Behold the days come, saith the LORD,*[3] *when I will make a new covenant with the house of Israel and the house of Judah.*[4] *Not according to the covenant that I made with their fathers in the day when I took them by the hand, to lead them out of the land of Egypt, because they continued not in my covenant, and I regarded them not, saith the Lord.*[5] *For this is the covenant that I will make with the house of Israel after those days, saith the Lord: I will give my laws into their mind, and I will inscribe them upon their hearts* {και επι

---

[1] Jeremiah 31:31-34
[2] Hebrews 8:8-12
[3] Συντελεσω: I will finish, I will perfect, or I will consummate. So properly; very significantly; for by this New Covenant God did perfect, finish and consummate all his Covenant administrators: this the last and most complete of them all.
[4] Hebrews 8:8-12
[5] Εποιησα: I made.

καρδιας αυτων επιγραψω αυτους}: *And I will be to them for a God* (εις θεον), *and they shall be to me for a people. And they shall not teach every one his neighbor, and every one his brother, saying: Know thou the Lord: for all shall know me from the least of them to the greatest of them. For I will be merciful* (ιλεως εσομαι ταις αδικιαις αυτων: *I will be propitiatorily-pacified*, or, *I will be propitious*) *to their unrighteousnesses, and their sins and their transgressions I will remember no more* (ου μη μνησθω ετι: *I will not remember again*, or, *anymore*) *that is: I will never remember them again.*[6] In these words, according to the emphasis and propriety of the Greek original, the matter of the New Covenant is declared to us. The parallel between the words of Paul and Jeremiah, see in chapter 1.

For the more clear delineation and description of the matter of this New Covenant, I shall do three things, namely: (1) I shall analytically explain these words briefly. (2) I shall lay down (*notanda quaedam generalia*) certain generals [generalities] to be noted and diligently observed touching the matter of the New Covenant, as represented in this narrative thereof. (3) Lastly, I shall descend to the unfolding of the matter of this New Covenant particularly, both promised by God to his federates, and restipulated by them unto God. And these I shall digest into three distinct sections.

---

[6] διαθηκη ην διαθησομαι: *The covenant which I will covenant*; or: *The covenant which I will dispose*. It may have reference both to a federal establishment, and to a testamentary disposal. And so it agrees well with this New Covenant, which is a Federal Testament or a Testamentary Covenant.

Section 1

First, as to the brief analytical explication[7] of the apostle's recited words, consider that the New Covenant is here set forth, with a note of excellency, and attention: Behold. And is described by the (1) time, (2) author, (3) federates, (4) name, and (5) nature thereof.

(1) **By the time when it should be made and established.** *The days come, saith the Lord, when I will make,* etc. (Hebrews 8:9). The apostle alleges this out of Jeremiah: Jeremiah herein prophesied of future days, namely: the days of Christ, when this New Covenant should begin to commence. These days were already actually come and fulfilled in Paul's days: Christ had established his New Covenant *preparatorily* by his public ministry and *completely* by his death, resurrection, ascension, and effusion of his Spirit, as I have formerly evidenced.[8]

(2) **By the author, or efficient cause of it,** the Lord: *saith the Lord, when I will make a New Covenant*, etc. (Hebrews 8:9-10) – of this formerly.[9]

(3) **By the federates with whom the Lord would make this New Covenant**: with the house of Israel, and with the house of Judah (Hebrews 8:9-10). Even with all professed believers, Jews and Gentiles, and with their children, as I have already proven.[10]

(4) **By the denomination or name given to this Covenant**: *I will make a new covenant* (Hebrews 8:8). In what sense it is called a {New Covenant}, I have heretofore explained at large: as also the nature of it more generally.[11]

---

[7] See this done, but much more briefly in my *Key of the Bible* on Hebrews, Section 6.
[8] In this 4th Book, Chapter 1.
[9] In Chapter 3
[10] In Chapter 4
[11] In Chapter 2

(5) **By the nature of this New Covenant**, which is laid down: [1] negatively and [2] affirmatively. [1] Negatively, he declares what manner of covenant this New Covenant should not be, namely: not such a covenant as was the Sinai Covenant, that Old Covenant. *Not according to the covenant that I made with their fathers*, etc (Hebrews 8:9). This New Covenant should not be according to that Covenant, not like that Covenant, but very different from it, and far before it. In all this negative, the Holy Spirit seems to have respect to the form and administration (of which I shall speak when I come to the form of this New Covenant), not to the matter and substance of the New Covenant, which is after laid down in the affirmative, that this may the better appear. He sets forth that Old Covenant in various ways, namely:

{1} **By the author of it**: God – *which I made*.

{2} **By the federates with whom God made it**: *That I made with their fathers*, namely: with the Israelites at Mount Sinai, after they were brought out of Egypt.

{3} **By the time when this Old Covenant was made with them**: *In the day when I took them by the hand to lead them out of the land of Egypt*. The word {*day*} here is not to be taken properly, precisely and strictly for the very day when God brought Israel out of Egypt, for in that day this Covenant was not made, but about fifty days after: but synecdochically, for that time that was a time of God's special love to their fathers, redeeming them strangers from Egypt, conducting them wonderfully towards Canaan, and by the way bringing them into Covenant with himself, and therefore by God's commemoration of these his great favors and kindnesses to them, he notably aggravates their unkind covenant-breaking with him after mentioned.[12]

---

[12] "By saying that the covenant was made in the day when he laid holds on their hand to rescue them from bondage, he enhanced the sin of defection by thus reminding them of so great a benefit."
[https://www.studylight.org/commentaries/eng/cal/hebrews-8.html]
<Accessed 4/2/2024>

{4} By the evil event of this Covenant as to their fathers, which is given in here as a reason why God would afterwards make a New Covenant. This ill event is twofold:

(i) **Their sinful breach of this Covenant**: *Because they continued not in my covenant*. This has reference, not only to that notorious breach of this Covenant at first in the golden calf in Exodus 32, but also to all their [reiterated] and aggravated idolatries afterwards until their captivity in Babylon. They promised to do all that God in this Covenant required in Exodus 24, but they did not know their own weakness and the law's exactness. They did not attain to God's righteousness, because they sought it as it were by the deeds of the law. This Covenant required duty, but furnished them not with ability, etc, so that, this Covenant becoming faulty, defective, and insufficient, through their infirmity and faultiness, this was one cause why there was place sought for the Second Covenant (Hebrews 8:7-8): this First Covenant becoming so weak, unprofitable and ineffectual to them (Hebrews 7:18-19). (ii) God's just displeasure and judgment upon them for this breach of Covenant: *And I regarded them not, saith the Lord*. Under God's disregard of them, all sorts of punishments, judgments and afflictions that afterwards came upon them for their idolatries and breach of covenant with God from generation to generation, are comprised. The Hebrew phrase in Jeremiah is somewhat different from this of the Greek: *Although I was an husband to them*, or, *should I have continued an husband to them?* – both our translation. But the Hebrew {וְאָנֹכִי בָּעַלְתִּי בָם} is better rendered by Pagnin and Montanus, *Et ego dominatus sum in eos*, "And I lorded it over them," that is, "I used my husbandly and lordly authority over them, and so disregarded them."[13] For this phrase, the Septuagint has, {καὶ ἐγὼ ἠμέλησα αὐτῶν} *and I disregarded them*, which the apostle also follows in Hebrews 8:9. So then, God's lordly and husbandly authority not only obliges to covenant-keeping, but also afflicts for covenant-breaking. And, when God puts forth his authority against covenant

---

[13] David Dickson on Hebrews 8:9

breakers, he disregards them, counts them as not in covenant with him – which disregard from God comprises in it, as it were, all sorts of God's judgments. Thus, though the phrases in Jeremiah and Paul differ, yet the sense agrees.

(ii) **Affirmatively and positively, he shows what this New Covenant should be.** *For this is the covenant that I will make with the house of Israel, after those days, saith the Lord* (Hebrews 8:10). The words import a surpassing eminence and excellence in this New Covenant, beyond what was in the Old. {*For this is the covenant*}:[14] the expression in the Hebrew and Greek is very emphatic. But what is this Covenant? Or wherein does the nature and matter of it consist? Principally in four exceeding great and precious promises of God laid down here altogether (Hebrews 8:10-12), namely – here God promises:

(a) *His donation and inscription of his laws in their inwards, mind, and hearts. I will give my laws into their mind, and write them upon their hearts* (Hebrews 8:10). I will give my law into their inward-part, and upon their heart will I write it (Jeremiah 31:33). Here note: (1) the agent, God: *I will give, I will inscribe*; (2) the twofold act: giving: *I will give*; inscribing: *I will inscribe*; (3) The object of this act, about which this act shall be exerted and put forth: God's laws – {*my laws*} distributively, as Paul has it; {*my law*} collectively, as Jeremiah has it, both importing the same thing, namely: God's moral law especially, formerly written in stony tables, and the whole word of God generally, wherein the moral law is expounded. The moral law is the abridgement of the Word of God; the Word of God is the explanatory enlargement of the moral law. (4) The subject whereinto this law of God shall be given, and wherein it shall be written by God: in their mind, or inward

---

[14] כִּי זֹאת הַבְּרִית; οτι αυτη η διαθηκη

part:[15] the mind being most inward; and in their hearts: that denoting the understanding: this, the will and affections.

(b) *The great federal relation, union, communion, and interest between God and his federates reciprocally*. *And will be unto them for a God, and they shall be to me for a people* (Hebrews 8:10), namely: I will be to them all, whatsoever, a God can be, or can need to be, to his covenant people, and they shall be to me all, whatsoever, a people in covenant can or should be to their God. *I will*; *they shall* – God here promises both, undertakes for both for himself, and for his federates. O sweet and blessed New Covenant!

(c) *His federate people's more excellent and more universal knowledge of the LORD, than formerly under the Old Covenant*. This has in it two things, namely:

(1) The surpassing excellency of the New Covenant knowledge of the Lord, beyond that of the Old: *And they shall not teach everyone his neighbor, and everyone his brother, saying, know the Lord* (Hebrews 8:11). The word {*not*} here, is not a simple and absolute negative, as if hereby the New Covenant excluded all human teaching, for that is most repugnant to New Covenant doctrine, as elsewhere I have shown, and shall afterwards manifest further.[16] But it is rather a comparative (as it is times used in Scripture several times – see John 9:41 and 1 Corinthians 1:17), importing that the former teaching under the Old Covenant should be comparatively as no teaching at all, as nothing to the divine teaching of God's federates under his New Covenant. Then they were taught the elements, first principles, and ABC of divine knowledge, as a people in minority; but now God's federates shall be instructed in the abstruse and more perfect mysteries of God, as a people in maturity. Under the New Covenant, the divine revelation is more clear and

---

[15] Hebr. בְּקִרְבָּם This word קרב is significant. Medium, venter, Sic appellatus, quod sit in medio corporis; & Metaphorice nonnunquam Cogitatio. Sic appellatur quicquid est propinquissimum & intimum, ut Cor, & exta, ac viscera; unde ad mentem & Cogitationem humani cordis, quae in homine intima est, significandam tranfertur sicut & autor epist. ad Hebr. vertit διαθηκη. Pagnin. Thesaur. ad verb.

[16] In my *Key of the Bible* on Hebrews, Section 5

complete, the donation of the Spirit more full, and proportionably, the spiritual illumination of their minds more perfect and accurate.

(2) The generality of this knowledge of the Lord among all sorts under the New Covenant: *For all shall know me from the least of them to the greatest of them* (Hebrews 8:11). God will indifferently illuminate small and great: One as well as the other must be beholding to him herein. Some particular persons under the New Covenant may be grossly ignorant, through natural incapacity or want of ministerial instruction, or contempt of the New Covenant, but here the Holy Spirit intends the whole New Covenant dispensation, which generally shall introduce such a knowledge of the Lord as the generality of federates never had under the Old Covenant.[17] Now this promise, though it have wonderful accomplishments under the New Covenant, yet shall not have (as Pareus well advertises)[18] its plenary accomplishment until we come to heaven, when we shall all be perfectly taught of God, being beyond all human instruction public and private, when we shall know as we are known, and see God as he is (1 Corinthians 13:12; 1 John 3:2-3).

(d) *Finally, God promises (as a foundation, ground or cause of all the former benefits) his own gratuitous propitiousness in Christ to them in the utter remission and oblivion, forgiving and forgetting all sorts of their sins*: *For I will be propitiously-merciful to their unrighteousnesses, and their sins and their transgressions will I remember no more* (Hebrews 8:12). Here note:

(1) The agent or author of this benefit, God; *I will be propitiously merciful*; *I will not remember* – God alone is the God of Pardons (Nehemiah

---

[17] John Calvin's commentary on in Hebrews 8:9
[18] "Tertia Promissio: cujus complementum etsi futurae vitae: [reservatur], quando omnes erimus perfecti [... διδαξωσιν], nec opus erit Ministerio publico vel institutione privata; sed omnes intuebimur Deum sicuti est; tamen etiam in hac vita illustria [futuri complementi] initia & incrementa [appellantur] Ecclesiae novae; quoniam non ut olim paucis, sed pluribus; uno omnibus Ecclesiae civibus Deus luculenter in Christo sepatefacit. Neque ut olim in primis fidei rudimentis subsistunt Novi Testamenti cives, sed intima Fidei Mysteria praeclare intelligunt, gratia uberiore Spiritus Sancti super omnem carnem effusa."
D. Pareus in Com. ad Heb. 8. 11.

9:17). *Who can forgive sins like him?* (Micah 7:18) Or *besides him?* (Mark 2:7, Luke 5:21). Pardon of sin is God's peculiar prerogative.

(2) The act of grace expressed in two phrases, namely: [1] *I-will-be-propitiously-merciful*, ιλεως εσομαι, the Greek word (as also the Hebrew word, סלח (Jeremiah 31:34), denotes such a mercy in God as has respect to Christ's propitiation, propitiatory expiation of, and satisfaction for sin; who is called ιλασμος {*a propitiation for our sins*}, etc. (1 John 2:2), and ιλαστηριον: {*a propitiation*} or {*mercy-seat*} (Romans 3:25), whose offering up of himself once was so satisfactory to God, that it was an odor of a sweet smell to God (Ephesians 5:2). And that thereby *he hath forever perfected them that are sanctified* (Hebrews 10:13-14). [2] *I will not remember again*, ου μη μνησθω ετι, that is: I will never remember again to them, so as to impute them to them. I will forgive and forget. I will pass an act of utter oblivion upon them forever. This is God's free pardoning and remission of sin in and for Christ's meritorious satisfaction.

(3) The object about which this act of grace shall be exercised, which is expressed by two Hebrew words, namely: עֲוֺנָם *gnavonam*, signifying properly, *perversenesses, crookednesses, perverse iniquities*, etc.; and חַטָּאתָם *chattatham*, properly *errors, stray sins*, wherein they miss the mark – both these are in Jeremiah 31:34. But this object is expressed in three words in the Greek, αδικιαις, αμαρτιων, and ανομιων, which properly signify, *unrighteousnesses, sinful errors*, and *unlawfulnesses*. The words are very comprehensive, they take in all sorts of sins whatsoever: God will forgive and forget them all.

(4) The connection of this promise to the promises foregoing, in the causal particle כִּי – *for, because*. This lets us know that God's gratuitous mercy in purging away and pardoning all the sins of his people in Christ, is the foundation of all the fore-covenanted benefits.

Thus I have analytically explained in brief the words wherein the **New Covenant** is described to us both by Jeremiah and Paul. Oh, how significant, how comprehensive, how emphatical, how proper and suitable, how sweet and comfortable are these words for a New Covenant expressure! Hence we shall easily borrow much light for the clearing of all ensuing particulars.

Section 2

Generalities to be noted and observed diligently concerning the matter or substance of the New Covenant

Secondly, as for those generals to be noted and observed diligently, in this narrative or description of the **New Covenant** by the prophet and apostle, touching the matter or substance of this New Covenant, I shall clearly and briefly represent them in this ensuing aphorism.

In general, touching the matter of the New Covenant, as here described by the prophet Jeremiah and the apostle Paul, we are diligently to note and observe these things, namely: (1) that the matter of the New Covenant is here set forth very compendiously in words, but most comprehensively in sense; (2) that the whole matter of the New Covenant is represented only in promises; (3) that all these New Covenant promises, in their express terms, run wholly upon spirituals; (4) that these New Covenant promises have a sweet harmony and correspondence with the priesthood, prophecy, and kingship of Christ's mediatory office in actual performance of which promises to us, we also are made unto God priests, prophets, and kings by Jesus Christ; (5) that the matter of the New Covenant is so contrived in these promises, as may sufficiently remove all the principal doubts, discouragements, and objections which either a bleeding heart-wounded sinner, or a distressed saint, may make against his salvation; (6) that these New Covenant promises are so expressed, as virtually to contain in them the agreement and difference between the Old and New Covenant, yea, the preeminences of the New above the Old; (7) that all these New Covenant promises are wholly grounded upon the mere grace and good pleasure of God's will in Jesus Christ alone.

I shall explain a little these seven generals, because the right and clear understanding of them is very necessary and advantageous to the true understanding of the **New Covenant**.

(1) That the matter of the New Covenant is here set forth very compendiously in words, but most comprehensively in sense.

This was one excellency of the Old Covenant promulgated at Mount Sinai by God himself: that it comprised all duties of religion towards God, and righteousness towards man, in ten words, or ten sayings.[19] Proportionably, this is a great excellency of the New Covenant: that it comprehends all saving mercies and blessings from God to his federates, and all answerable duties of his federates to him, in four sententious sayings, in four precious promises. The words are very few, but the meaning much: mountains of sense under molehills of sentences. These sentences are but as four drops; the sense under them is as a very sea. The very first article comprises in it the whole law of God, not only the letter, but the spirit of the law: *I will give my laws into their mind*, etc.[20] Who then can [fathom] what is comprised in all the rest?

[1] Here we have a secret and mysterious discovery of the blessed cooperation of Father, Son, and Holy Spirit to the felicity of the New Covenant federates, Jews and Gentiles:[21] the Father promising pardon of their sins, for the Son's expiation of them, whereby the wrath of God is pacified (Hebrews 8:12); the Holy Spirit effectually applying Christ in the Renovation, (Hebrews 8:10).

[2] Here we have the mere free grace of God and good pleasure of his will displayed, as the prime origin and fundamental cause of all the federal happiness here promised.[22]

[3] Here the mediatory office of Jesus Christ is tacitly implied, in the proper and peculiar fruits of his priesthood, prophecy and kingship, namely: remission of sins, wrought by his priesthood; knowledge of the Lord, by his

---

[19] Hebrew: עֲשֶׂרֶת, הַדְּבָרִים (Deuteronomy 4:13)
[20] Hebrews 8:10
[21] Hebrews 8:10-12
[22] Hebrews 8:10, 12

prophecy; and conformity of mind and heart to the law of God, by his kingship.[23]

[4] Here the plentiful donation and effusion of the Spirit upon all sorts Jews and Gentiles is discovered by the many effects of the Spirit upon their minds, wills, and hearts here promised.[24]

[5] Here the sacred knot of saving benefits and spiritual blessings in heavenly things in Christ is assured to the federates: namely: conviction, illumination, conversion, regeneration, effectual vocation, sanctification, conformity to God's law, cordial sincerity, adoption into the number of God's people and children, justification, union, and communion with God; and consequently all good things for the life present, and all glory for the life to come.[25] What is not promised, when God himself is promised?

[6] Here, consequently, all answerable New Covenant duties, dispositions, inclinations, affections, endeavors, actions, deportments, and performances of these federates towards God, are virtually, yet vigorously enjoined.[26]

[7] Here, finally, in few words are couched all [things] necessary to sinners' happiness and eternal salvation.

(2) **That the whole matter of the New Covenant is represented here only in promises.**

This New Covenant is so described by Jeremiah and Paul, that the matter and substance thereof is set forth in nothing but promises. Mark it well: here is not one threatening expressed, not one commandment or precept expressed, but all that is expressed is only promises. It runs all upon promises; it consists all in promises. This New Covenant is a knot, a bundle of promises, a rich chain or jewel made up of nothing but promises. Here are four grand articles of promises – and that is all the matter and substance of the New Covenant

---

[23] Hebrews 8:10-12
[24] Hebrews 8:10-11
[25] Hebrews 8:10-12
[26] Hebrews 8:10-12

here expressed.[27] No wonder, that the New Covenant is said to be established upon promises, for we find it in nothing else.[28] All the New Covenant mercies and blessings which God stipulates to his federates, and all the New Covenant duties which his federates restipulate and condition with God; they are all digested into promises, contained in promises, and to be extracted out of promises, either formally or virtually, directly, or consequentially – explicitly or implicitly. Yea all New Covenant duties required or restipulated are proportionably to be collected from New Covenant mercies promised: all our duties, as well as God's mercies are founded in his promises. God promises that his federates shall generally know the Lord; proportionably it is their duty to know God. God promises many blessings; proportionably it is their duty to believe these promises. The promises and faith are relatives. God promises remission and obliteration of all their sins; proportionably they are to repent of these sins, and accept that promised remission by faith. God promises to write his laws in their hearts; proportionably it is their duty to love and observe sincerely the laws of God in newness of life. God promises he will be their God, they shall be his people; proportionably it is their duty to accept him, and demean themselves every way towards him, as to their God, and wholly to devote and resign up themselves to in him soul and body, in life and death as his people. O what an admirable dispensation of grace is this! That all our duties should flow from God's blessings, all God's blessings from his promises; and all his promises from the mere grace and good pleasure of his will in Jesus Christ! Who can sufficiently value this New Covenant administration in this regard? For:

[1] Hence how far does this New Covenant excel the Old! The Old Covenant ran chiefly upon precepts and commands, requiring duties from the federates; this New Covenant runs altogether upon promises, imparting mercies and blessings to the federates.[29]

---

[27] Hebrews 8:10-12, Jeremiah 31:33-34
[28] Hebrews 8:6
[29] Exodus 20:1-18, Deuteronomy 5:1-22

[2] Hence God in this New Covenant affords ability, as well as requires duty. he requires duty only implicitly and virtually; but he assures of ability for that duty expressly and formally; yea he first assures them of ability, before he calls for any duty. This is a sweet dispensation indeed, according to which all our duties take their first rise from God's mercies. It was not thus in the old covenant dispensation: there was much duty required, little ability promised or afforded, but in case of failing the dreadful curse denounced. Hereupon the apostle, entering a parallel between that old and this new ministration of God's Covenant,[30] highly prefers this before that in many particulars – two whereof are observable here, namely:

{1} That Old was a ministration of the letter; this New, a ministration of the Spirit. That is, in that Old Covenant, there was a strict law promulgated by God, written in tables of stone, and repeated by Moses, there was precept upon precept, commandment upon commandment, but there was not any inward ability, inclination, disposition or aptness promised for the performance of these commands. All this was but a ministration of the letter, a dead, lifeless, spiritless ministration. But In this New Covenant, here is ability, fitness, and disposedness to perform God's law. Here is a law within the heart answering to that law without, inclining and enabling to observe and perform. Here is the Spirit of the law as well as the letter. This is a ministration of the Spirit.

{2} That Old was a ministration of death and condemnation; this New, a ministration of life and righteousness.[31] That is, the Old Covenant holding forth many strict commandments, and a severe curse in case of failing, but giving no ability or sufficiency to the performance, discovers man's sin, together with his deserved death and condemnation: so it terrifies him, fights with him, condemns him, kills him; thus it is a ministration of death and condemnation. Thus, it is all clothed with fire, fills with terror and

---

[30] 2 Corinthians 3:6 to the end; see my *Key of the Bible* on that chapter, Section 5.
[31] 2 Corinthians 3:7, 9

amazement; so that Israel was affrighted and fled back, and Moses himself did exceedingly fear and quake.[32] The fault is not in the law, which is a perfect rule, but in the infirmity of our flesh, we are not able to keep it.[33] As a brittle glass or potsherd dashed against a rock is broken, the fault is not in the rock. A rock should be hard and strong, but the glass or potsherd is weak. On the other hand, this New Covenant discovers to us a way of satisfying divine justice and fulfilling the law by the death and obedience of our surety Jesus Christ, for all our transgressions against the law, so that these transgressions shall not be imputed to us, but Christ's righteousness (Hebrews 8:12). It also assures us of an inward principle and ability by the inscription of the law in our hearts, whereby the righteousness of the law may in uprightness be fulfilled in us who walk not after the flesh but after the Spirit.[34] Thus it is a ministration of life and righteousness.

[3] Hence in this New Covenant, God in effect undertakes all: not only for himself, but for his federates also: he will, and they shall. In the Old Covenant, God undertook his part, Israel their part; but in this New Covenant God undertakes both parts; his own, that he will perform such mercies; his federates, that they shall perform such duties. Why? Because he has digested and molded this New Covenant only into promises, which formally assures of mercies from God, virtually assures of duties from us, which derives all our duties from promised mercies and abilities. In all other Covenants between husband and wife, master and servant, man and man, nation and nation, each party undertakes only for himself; but this Covenant of God is herein altogether singular and extraordinary that God undertakes all both for himself and his federates. O this is a sweet foundation of comfort to us against all our infirmities, frailties, insufficiencies and failings; that though we can do nothing, God will do all. Let God enable us to do what he commands and then let him command us what he pleases.

---

[32] Hebrews 12:18-21 with Exodus 20:18 to the end
[33] Romans 8:3
[34] Romans 8:4

[4] Hence in all our defects, impotencies, inabilities, etc. unto spiritual performances, as repentance, mortification of sin, vivification of grace, new obedience, walking with God in communion, self-resignation, etc., we see here whither to have recourse for supplies: namely: to the promises, and promised mercies in this New Covenant. Here God undertakes for our ability: he has implied and wrapped up all our strength and sufficiency in his promised mercies. Therefore we must not think to subdue this sin, to increase this grace, to dispatch this duty, etc. upon our own interest, by our own endeavors, resolutions, wrestlings, etc. but we must go to work upon God's interest, upon his promise-interest in this New Covenant. Lord, you have undertaken for me in thy New Covenant; I have no power against all these strong lusts and corruptions, etc., but my eyes are to you, I rest on you; do perform all for me.

[5] Hence faith is of greatest importance and necessity for extracting all influences from the New Covenant, and appropriating them to ourselves. All our salvation and happiness is contained in this New Covenant; all this New Covenant is contained in promises, and nothing but promises; God's mercies are promised expressly, our duties are promised in those mercies virtually and implicitly. Now wherewithal shall we extract all the virtue, strength and sweetness from these promises. and make all our own, but only by faith? What the law of works commands by threatening, the law of faith obtains by believing.[35] Faith is the hand whereby we milk these promises; faith is the arms, whereby we clasp and embrace these promises;[36] faith is the mouth, whereby we suck the breasts of these promises; faith is the bucket, whereby we draw waters out of these wells of the promises; faith will reach though this well be deep; in a word, faith is the spiritual fire whereby we extract the celestial spirits and quintessence of these promises. If this New Covenant were laid down in threatenings and menaces only, then fear and trembling would be of chief use. If it were set forth in precepts and commandments only, then love

---

[35] Romans 8:3
[36] Hebrews 11:13

and obedience would be of chief use. But since it is represented in promises only, therefore faith, the daughter of the promises is of chief use. Bring faith to these promises, and then take all that is in these promises, and I am sure that is enough. Faith was of principal necessity and utility in all covenant expressures since the fall, but most eminently in this New Covenant, which is all promises, yea comparatively faith (the doctrine of faith, of life and righteousness by faith, etc) is not said to come, or to be revealed until this New Covenant came and was revealed.[37] Before, faith did but sparkle like a twinkling star, but now faith shines out gloriously like the sun.

(3) **That all these New Covenant promises in their express terms, run only upon spirituals.**

View all these articles and bundles of promises: here is not one express promise about temporals, about the outward good things of this present life, but every of them is about spirituals. I know that all the good things of this life are virtually, implicitly, and consequentially included in spirituals, as the lesser in the greater; but here is no express mention of anything but only of spirituals, namely: of the knowledge of God, the law in the heart, the covenant interest in God, the remission of sins, etc.[38] Temporals are too low a subject for the New Covenant to insist upon and be expressive in: it delights to soar aloft towards heaven, and to raise up the church (now come to ripeness and maturity)[39] from things below to things above – from carnals to spirituals; from perishables to eternals.

[1] Hence the New Covenant is deservedly said to be *established upon better promises*,[40] namely: upon better promises than the Old Covenant was established upon. Why? For this reason especially; because the Old Covenant did principally run upon promises of outward and temporal blessings, as the

---

[37] Galatians 3:23
[38] Hebrews 8:10-12
[39] Galatians 4:1-3
[40] Hebrews 8:6

inheritance of the land of Canaan, long life there, honor, wealth, peace and all outward prosperity there, etc.[41] Now and then, there were some few drops of spiritual promises sparingly sprinkled among them, but the main stream of the promises ran upon temporals; but here the whole current of the New Covenant runs only upon spirituals. That was a more carnal; this a more spiritual Covenant. That had more of earth in it; this, more of heaven. That bred low, earth-creeping principles; this breeds sublime, high, heaven-aspiring principles. The Old Covenant-people were happier than all other people, but the New Covenant people far happier than the Old Covenant people.

[2] Hence, as the New Covenant promises, for the express terms thereof, were wholly of spirituals; so the New Covenant federates proportionably should tend chiefly (yea, if it were possible, only) to spirituals. Shall the New Covenant be only spiritual; and shall the covenanters be only carnal? Shall the New Covenant be only above, and shall the covenanters be only below? Shall the New Covenant be all for heaven, and shall the covenanters be all for earth? When we come to the New Covenant, whither are we come? To a touchable Sinai, to a visible fire, to an earthly Canaan, to an earthly Jerusalem? etc. No, No. We are *come unto Mount Zion; and unto the city of the living God, the heavenly Jerusalem; and to an innumerable company of angels; to the general assembly and church of the firstborn, which are enrolled in heaven; and to God, the judge of all; And to the spirits of just men made perfect; and to Jesus the Mediator of the new covenant; and to the blood of sprinkling, that speaketh better things than that of Abel.*[42] Behold, all things here are sublime, spiritual, heavenly; and shall not we be elevated? Shall not we be spiritualized by all this federal spirituality? Has God, under and by this New Covenant dispensation, quickened us together with Christ, and raised us up together, and made us sit together in heavenly places in Christ Jesus;[43] and shall not we be elevated above

---

[41] Exodus 20:12, Deuteronomy 5:16 with Ephesians 6:2, Deuteronomy 7:12 to the end & 8:7-9 & 11 & 28:1-15
[42] Hebrews 12:18-25
[43] Ephesians 2:5-6

this earth; shall not we seek and set our affections on things above?[44] Shall not we have our *conversation* (our πολιτευμα: *whole business*) in heaven?[45] Oh! Let our minds, wills, and affections be all spiritual; let our inward furniture, principles and dispositions, be all spiritual; let our thoughts, words, and actions be all spiritual; let our designs, tendencies and intentions be all spiritual; let us be wholly swallowed up with spirituality. Then shall we be covenanters answerable to this New Covenant and promises thereof, which are wholly spiritual.

(4) That these New Covenant promises have a sweet harmony and correspondence with the priesthood, prophecy, and kingship of Christ's mediatorial office. In actual performance of these promises to us, we also are made unto God priests, prophets, and kings by Jesus Christ.

The greatest and most eminent public blessings which God in ancient time was pleased to confer upon his church and people, were most usually imparted to them by priests, prophets, and kings, those three renowned sorts of officers. By a priest and a king, Melchizedek, was Abraham the father of all the faithful blessed.[46] By a priest, a prophet, and a king was Israel brought out of Egypt, conducted through the Red Sea on dry ground, espoused to God at Mount Sinai by covenant, governed as a church in the wilderness, and as the commonwealth of God, by administration of morals, ceremonials, and judicials,[47] and led as a flock through the wilderness, by the hand of Moses and Aaron[48] – Aaron being priest, and Moses both priest, prophet, and king in Jeshurun.[49] By a priest and a king was Israel brought to inherit the land of Canaan, and it was divided to them by lot – even by Eleazar the priest, and

---

[44] Colossians 3:1-2
[45] Philippians 3:20
[46] Genesis 14:18-20, Romans 4:11-12, 16
[47] *By a prophet the LORD brought Israel out of Egypt, and by a prophet was he preserved* (Hosea 12:13).
[48] Exodus 6:13, 27 & 19:14 & 24:1, etc, Psalm 77:20
[49] Psalm 99:6, Deuteronomy 18:15, 18; 34:10 & 33:4-5

Joshua the successor of Moses, who was a mighty prince in Israel.[50] By priests were all the affairs of religion managed in the tabernacle and temple from the days of Moses until the death of Christ.[51] By the prophets and prophetic persons were all the Holy Scriptures revealed from God, and recorded for the church.[52] By kings and kingly rulers was the commonwealth of Israel guided and governed until Shiloh came. Now all these and such like dispensations were but types and shadows of better things in Christ, who is the priest of priests, the prophet of prophets, the king of kings – by whose mediatory priesthood, prophecy, and kingship, all sorts and degrees of blessings and mercies are procured, revealed and effectually applied to his church and people for their happiness in this and in the world to come.[53]

This profound and excellent mystery is very observably suggested to us in this body of the New Covenant and promises thereof. For:

[1] The mercies here promised are such, and so answerable to these mediatory offices of Christ, that we may evidently conclude them to be the proper fruits and effects of his priesthood, prophecy, and kingship, namely: {1} remission of sins, upon the pacifying of God for them, promised in the fourth article (Hebrews 8:12), is the proper fruit of his priesthood; {2} the supernatural and saving knowledge of the Lord promised in the third article (Hebrews 8:11) is the proper effect of his prophecy; {3} the powerful conforming of our hearts to the will of God in all things, by his inscribing of his laws in our inwards, mind, and hearts, efficaciously applying his graces and benefits to the soul, promised in the first article (Hebrews 8:10) is the proper influence of his kingly office; {4} and the federal relation, interest, union and communion between God and his New Covenant federates reciprocally, which is promised in the second article (Hebrews 8:10) is the common and blessed result of all these three together, namely: of his priesthood, prophecy, and

---

[50] Joshua 14:1
[51] Numbers 17:13 & 18:1-8
[52] Luke 16:16, 29, Acts 3:18, 21, Ephesians 2:20
[53] Genesis 49:10 with Matthew 1:1-18

kingship. Thus in the matter of the New Covenant, as here expressed, we have an observable idea, model or representation of Christ's mediatory office in all the three primary branches thereof.

[2] These promised New Covenant mercies, being actually performed to us, do also imprint a holy image and resemblance of all Christ's offices upon us, So that we also are made unto our God priests, prophets, and kings, by Jesus Christ. The character and print of these offices is engraven upon us: when once this matter of the New Covenant is actually applied to us, and effectually fulfilled in us. For: {1} when Christ, as our great high priest, has washed us from our sins in his own blood, and purged our consciences from dead works to serve the living God, having forgiven us all our trespasses (Hebrews 8:12), he makes us kings and priests, or a royal priesthood to our God, to offer up spiritual sacrifices, acceptable to God by Jesus Christ.[54] {2} When Christ as our prophet has brought us savingly to know the Lord (Hebrews 8:11), he makes us also prophets, by giving us an anointing that teacheth us all things necessary to salvation, whereby we are also enabled to teach and instruct others.[55] {3} When Christ as our king has subdued our minds and hearts so far as to make them conform and answerable to his law (Hebrews 8:10). Thereby he makes us also spiritual kings, to rule over and subdue our corruptions more and more, and conquer our spiritual enemies.[56]

[1] Hence the matter of the New Covenant, these spiritual promises, are an excellent glass wherein we may see the beauteous face of our Mediator Christ Jesus, and an excellent map delineating forth unto us his officers of mediatorship: yea the vigor, force and efficacy of those offices. What greater discovery can we have of their excellency and efficacy than {1} in the fruits and effects thereof upon us, remitting our sins, as a priest: making us know the Lord as a prophet, and writing his laws in our minds and hearts, as a king (Hebrews 8:10-12). {2} In transforming us hereby into the similitude of his

---

[54] Revelation 1:5-6, Hebrews 9:14, Colossians 2:13; 1 Peter 2:5
[55] 1 John 2:27, Colossians 3:16
[56] Revelation 1:5-6, Galatians 5:24, Colossians 3:1-12

offices, to become priests, prophets, and kings by him unto our God. All the expressures of the Covenant of Faith, were as so many draughts and portraitures [descriptions] of **Jesus Christ**. The first Covenants with Adam and Abraham, declare his natures, namely: that he should be man, expressly: the seed of the woman – the seed of Abraham: that he is God, implicitly: being able to bruise the serpent's head, and to bless all the nations of the earth.[57] The after-Covenants with Israel, David, and the captives, declare his offices of priesthood, prophecy and kingship: his priesthood under the type of Aaron's, his prophecy under the type of Moses, and his kingship under the type of David's. But this New Covenant with Jews and Gentiles declares the influences, virtues, and efficacy of all these his offices of priesthood, prophecy, and kingship, in remission of sins and justification, in knowledge of the Lord and supernatural illumination, in conversion, regeneration and sanctification. So that as Jesus Christ and his mediation can never be rightly understood without the sound knowledge of the Covenants of Faith, especially of this New Covenant, so no expressures of the Covenant of Faith, least of all this New Covenant, can ever be judiciously understood without the solid knowledge of Jesus Christ and his mediation.

[2] Hence the effects of Christ's offices applied unto us, and conforming us according to our measure unto Christ, are singular evidences of our good New Covenant state, for the spiritual mercies promised in this New Covenant are the proper or common effects of Christ's priesthood, prophecy, and kingship. When therefore Jesus Christ is become our priest, our prophet, and our king actually, then we are become God's New Covenant federates, not formally but effectually. Hereby then, let us examine whether we have a saving interest in the New Covenant.

(5) **That the matter of the New Covenant is so contrived in these promises, as it may most sweetly and sufficiently remove all the principal**

---

[57] Genesis 3:15 & 12:2-3 & 27:18

doubts, discouragements and objections, which either a bleeding heart-wounded sinner, or a distressed saint, may make against his own salvation.

For better clearing of this particular, which is of very great consequence, I desire these three things may be seriously considered, namely:

[1] That when God converts a sinner to himself, most usually he prepares the sinner for that great work of conversion by previous conviction of his mind and conscience of his sin and misery, and contrition of heart and spirit for that sin and misery; so that the heart is wounded deeply and bleeds exceedingly. He first breaks the heart, then binds up the broken-hearted. He first captivates the soul, and brings it into a spiritual prison or dungeon under chains of guilt and horror, then he *proclaims liberty to the captives, and the opening of the prison to them that are bound, and the acceptable year* (even the spiritual jubilee year) *of the LORD:* He first makes him mourn, and fills him with a spirit of heaviness; and then *appoints to him that mourns in Zion, to give unto him beauty for ashes, the oil of joy for mourning, the garments of praise for the spirit of heaviness.*[58] He first burdens the soul; and then gives ease and rest of soul to the weary and heavy laden.[59] He first pricks him in the heart, and then brings him to gladness and singleness of heart in Christ.[60] He first gives him *the spirit of bondage to fear*, and then *the Spirit of adoption, whereby we cry Abba Father.*[61] This is God's ordinary way in a sinner's conversion – thus he dealt with the prodigal son (Luke 15:13 to the end), with the sinful woman (Luke 7:37, etc), with Peter's hearers (Acts 2:36-37, 41, 46), with persecuting Saul (Acts 9:3-20). And thus he will do with the Jews when their families shall more fully return unto the Lord and be called (Zechariah

---

[58] Isaiah 61:1-3 with Luke 4:18-19
[59] Matthew 11:28-29
[60] Acts 2:36-37, 41, 46
[61] Romans 8:15-16

12:10-13 and 13:1).[62] This is God's usual way to bring sinners towards heaven by the very gates of hell.

[2] That even after conversion, God's people oft times meet with many sad and dangerous plunges, that greatly distract and distress them about their spiritual state, and eternal salvation. Especially in these three cases, namely: {1} In case of some sinful relapse. As it was, with David: his very bones were broken, the joy of God's salvation was removed, and his sin was ever before him;[63] with Peter's denial of Jesus Christ, cost many bitter tears.[64] {2} In case of some violent temptation of the flesh, world or Satan, which sometimes staggers the servants of God, and makes them call into question their condition towards God, just as David – beholding the prosperity of the wicked, and his own adversity – was almost gone, had almost condemned the generation of the righteous, and concluded that he had washed his hands in vain, etc.[65] {3} In case of some sad desertion, some passive desertion, when God himself seems to hide his face, withdraw himself from them, and forsake them, in withholding the sweet gleams and influences of his wonted grace, favor and consolations from them. Whence they are apt sometimes to conclude, that God has utterly cast them off, and will never more be merciful unto them, etc. – as it was with Asaph,[66] with Heman the Ezrahite,[67] with Mr. Peacock in his last sickness until within a little before his dissolution;[68] and with many others of the dear servants of the Lord.[69]

[3] That the Lord (to whom a broken heart is sacrifices indeed, who will not despise a broken and a contrite heart, Psalms 51:17), who delights to dwell

---

[62] See Mr. George Hutcheson's judicious exposition on Zechariah 12:10, etc.
[63] Psalm 51 throughout with 2 Samuel 12
[64] Matthew 26:69 to the end
[65] Psalm 73:1 to the end
[66] Psalm 77 throughout
[67] Psalm 88 throughout
[68] See a narrative of Mr. Peacock's grievous visitation and desertion (London, 1641)
[69] See, The story of Mr. Robert Glover, in *Acts and Monuments*, Volume 3. pp. 420-429 (London, 1641), and the discourse of *The Christian Life and Death of Mrs. Katherine Bretterg* (London, 1617).

with him that is of a contrite and humble spirit, to revive the spirit of the humble, and to revive the heart of the contrite ones, etc (Isaiah 57:15-16, and 66:2) – the Lord, I say, that is the Father of tender mercies, and the *God of all consolations* (2 Corinthians 1:3) has sufficiently provided against all these spiritual distress of wounded sinners and perplexed saints in his **New Covenant**. For the Lord has so wisely contrived the matter of the New Covenant in a sweet conjunction of promises: that, all the principal, considerable and most dangerous doubts, discouragements or objections, which a bleeding sinner, or a distressed saint, may commonly make against their own present comfort or future salvation, may hence receive very satisfactory resolutions. Their most perplexing and puzzling doubts, discouragements, and objections are about: {1} their sins, {2} the wrath of God, {3} their gross ignorance of God, and all the things of God, {4} the deadness, hardness, deceitfulness and manifold vileness of their own hearts, {5} the lack of all spiritual abilities, excellencies and duties which might commend them to God, {6} the great distance between them and God between them and Christ, and {7} the difficulty and seeming impossibility of ever obtaining any assurance of their salvation. Now you shall see, what an antidote this New Covenant is against all these. God, that knows the troubles of all men's hearts, hath such pertinent, fit and sufficient cordials against all these faintings of soul in his New Covenant promises, as if they had been devised for this and no other purpose in the world.

{Doubt 1}: About sin.

Oh (thinks the wounded sinner, and the distressed saint) Mine iniquities are increased over mine head, and my guiltiness is grown up unto the heavens. They are more than the hairs of mine head, they are heavier than the sand.[70]

---

[70] Ezra 9:6

The acts of them in thought, word, and deed, are innumerable; the venom, poison, and sinfulnesses of them are unutterable; the circumstances and black aggravations of them are intolerable. I have sinned against the God that has made me curiously, and preserved me to this day graciously;[71] I have kicked against the bowels of mercy, that should pity me; I have trampled upon the precious blood that should wash me, I have grieved the Holy Spirit, that should comfort and sanctify me; I have despised the riches of free grace, that should save me. Oh my sin is ever before me![72] In the morning, in the evening, in my house, in the field, in society, but especially in my solitude. Oh how it grates upon my spirit, how it flashes in my conscience, how it kills and murders my soul! Are there any sins in the world, like my sins? Is there any possibility they should be forgiven? Is there any mercy, any pardon, any cure, any comfort, any hope, any salvation, for such a wretch, such a miscreant, such a monster of wickedness as I am?

Resolution: Stay a little, you sin-bruised soul, yet there is hope in Israel concerning all this. O hark [listen to] what the blessed God has said, has promised, has covenanted, has confirmed by the irrevocable death of Jesus Christ: *I will be propitiously-merciful to their unrighteousnesses, and their sinful-errors and their unlawfulnesses will I remember no more.*[73] Read this act of divine grace, ponder upon it deliberately, mark it heedfully: if you can believe it and apply it to yourself, here is enough against all thy sins. We had better lose the sun and moon out of God's firmament; then this glorious promise out of God's Covenant. Here's pardon – divine pardon, free pardon, full pardon, final pardon – for all your iniquities; now draw near, and touch the top of this golden scepter, and you shall live.

(i) Here is pardon and remission of sin offered: *I will be propitiously-merciful, – I will remember their sins*, etc., *no more.*[74] This

---

[71] Psalm 139:14-16
[72] Psalm 51:3
[73] Hebrews 8:12
[74] Hebrews 10:16-18

non-remembering of sins, the apostle interprets to be *remission of sins*. What can be more seasonable, more suitable, more acceptable to a guilty self-condemned sinner than pardon? Pardoned sin shall not be anymore imputed;[75] the pardoned sinner shall not be condemned, has peace with God, and is a blessed soul.[76] O grasp this pardon tendered, and then all your sins shall be as if they had never been.

(ii) Here is God's pardon: *I will be merciful, – I will remember no more, – saith God*. Your sins that distress you, your great sins that kill your heart, are in their utmost extremity but the sins of a finite man; but the pardon here promised is the pardon of an infinite God. There is some proportion between one drop of water, and the whole ocean; or between one grain of dust and the whole earthly globe; but between God's pardons and your sins, there is no proportion or comparison. He is a God of pardons, can create and give pardons, not as a man, not as judge, not as a king, but as a God.[77] Do not dishonor this God of pardons by doubting his pardons. Do not be merciless to your own soul, when God will be merciful to your unrighteousnesses. Do not still pore upon thy sins, when God will remember them no more. What creature can charge you, if God will clear you and discharge you? *Who shall lay anything to the charge of God's elect? It is God that justifieth; who is he that condemneth?*[78]

(iii) Here is free pardon. God says: *I will be merciful, – I will remember their sins no more*. Why will God do it? Here is no other reason given, but he will do it. He does not say, "You must bring so many sighs, so many tears, so much contrition, so much repentance, etc., or else here's no remission," but: *I will be merciful, I will remember no more*; that is, "I will do all this freely for mine own sake." You must repent,[79] but God pardons the penitent for his own

---

[75] Psalm 32:1-2
[76] Romans 8:1 & 5:1, Psalm 32:1-2
[77] Nehemiah 9:17
[78] Romans 8:33-34
[79] Acts 5:31

sake.[80] Your pardon cost Christ dearly – his liberty, his blood, his life – and herewith God was fully satisfied and pacified; but your pardon shall cost you nothing; come, believe, repent, and take it freely.

(iv) Here is full pardon. God will not only pardon this or that sin, but all sin: unrighteousnesses, sinful errors, and unlawfulnesses. Where God forgives one sin, he forgives all without exception.[81] Do not these three words reach all your sins of whatsoever sort, degree, or aggravation?

(v) Here is final pardon also. God will not remember their sins anymore. God will not only forgive, but forget, and that forever. God will pass an everlasting act of oblivion upon all your unrighteousnesses forever, which no tract of time shall repeal. Men may remember your sins to reproach and upbraid you for them; you yourself may remember your sins again and again to sigh and mourn for them, to loathe and abhor yourself for them, but your God will remember them no more; he will not mention them anymore to you,[82] he will not upbraid you with them, you shall never hear of them from him, to your shame, confusion, or condemnation, but he will hide them from his face, under Christ thy true mercy seat forever – he will bury them out of his sight in the grave of oblivion forever.[83] Therefore, O you sin-burdened soul, prop up your fainting spirit with these reviving consolations.

{Doubt 2}: About the wrath of God.

Alas (thinks the bruised sinner and perplexed saint), by my audacious rebellions against God, Christ, and the Spirit of Grace, etc, I have woefully plunged myself into God's deep displeasure. I have been such a desperate enemy to God, that I have provoked God to be an utter enemy to me.[84] I have made myself a target for all the arrows of his threats, curses and judgments

---

[80] Isaiah 43:25
[81] Larga Dei bonitas veniam non Dimidiabit: Aut nihil, aut totum, te lachrymante, dabit.
[82] Ezekiel 18:21-23
[83] Psalm 51:9
[84] Psalm 5:5

which are denounced in his book.[85] I cannot look up to him, but as to an angry sin-revenging judge, as to a consuming fire. I am consumed with the burning heat of his indignation, *for the arrows of the Almighty are within me, the poison whereof drinketh up my Spirit: The terrors of God do set themselves in array against me.*[86] *His wrath lieth hard upon me, and he afflicteth me with all his waves.*[87] My conscience is full of horror! I tremble day and night; I am afraid of darkness and solitude, lest God should turn Satan loose upon me; when I sit down to eat, when I lie down to sleep, when I bow down to pray, etc. methinks the wrath and curse of God is still pursuing me and ready to overtake me. O wretch that I am, while I suffer his terrors, I am distracted.[88]

Resolution: O why do you thus cast yourself down? And why is your heart thus disquieted within you? Once more cast an eye upon the former consolation: *I will be propitiously-merciful to their unrighteousnesses, and their sinful-errors, and their unlawfulnesses will I remember no more.*[89] Here you art assured:

(i) That the Lord himself will freely, fully and finally pardon and obliterate all sorts and degrees of your sins, if you will but accept this pardon, this promise. And if sin is pardoned, the storm of God's wrath is over. Where God remits the sin, he remits also the punishment. *Comfort ye, Comfort ye, my people. Speak ye to the heart of Jerusalem, and cry unto her, that her war-fare is accomplished, that her sin is pardoned.*[90] Where sin is pardoned, God's wrath is removed: *I will heal their backsliding, I will love them freely, for mine anger is turned away from him.*[91] Where sin is pardoned, the sinner is justified and at peace with God: *Being justified by faith, we have peace with God through our*

---

[85] Galatians 3:10
[86] Job 6:4
[87] Psalm 88:7
[88] Psalm 88:15
[89] Hebrews 8:12
[90] Isaiah 40:1-2
[91] Hosea 14:4

Lord Jesus Christ.[92] Can you believe God's pardon here promised? Then all God's wrath is turned into love.

(ii) That God will pardon thy sins, upon satisfaction of his wrath and justice for them in Christ. *I will be propitiously-merciful to their unrighteousnesses*: ιλεως εσομαι, *I will be propitious, I will be pacified*, etc. The word (as was formerly noted) has reference to Christ's propitiation, whereby God is so fully satisfied and appeased forever, that there needs no more offering for sin while the world stands.[93] This one sacrifice of Christ has more pleased and pacified God than all the Levitical sacrifices whatsoever. The stream of Christ's most precious blood has quenched the flame of God's wrath forever, to all that will accept Christ by believing. Be of good cheer therefore, your provocation of God's wrath is great, but Christ's pacification of God's provoked wrath is greater, for (by reason of the infiniteness of his person) it is infinite. Oh grasp this infinite satisfaction, and then God cannot choose but have all thoughts of love, and peace, and fatherliness towards you.

{Doubt 3}: About their gross ignorance of God, and of all the things of God.

Alas! How should I be saved? I, who knows, nothing of God, nor of his ways – I am altogether blind, sottish, inapprehensive, incapable of discerning spirituals: they are hidden mysteries, riddles, paradoxes to me; I know not what they mean. O what shall I do, when the Lord Jesus *shall be revealed from heaven, with his mighty angels, in flaming fire, taking vengeance of them that know not God*?[94]

Resolution: O you ignorant and dark soul, God has promised here also to open your eyes, and give sight to the blind. Look into this New Covenant: there is a sufficient remedy: *And they shall not teach every man his neighbor, and every man his brother, saying, know the Lord; For all shall know me from*

---

[92] Romans 5:1
[93] Romans 3:24-26; 1 John 2:1-2, Ephesians 5:2, Hebrews 10:5-19
[94] 2 Thessalonians 1:7-8

the least, to the greatest.[95] O what an antidote against a blind, dark, blockish understanding! What an admirable knowledge of God, for sort, for degree, for extent, is here promised! Wash the eyes of your understanding daily with the spirits of this promise, and see if the scales of ignorance shall not by little and little fall away.

(i) The sort of the knowledge of God here promised is more than human. It is not such as everyone may teach his neighbor or brother touching God, therefore it must needs be divine, such as God teaches, touching himself.[96] God will teach you,[97] God will anoint you with eye-salve that you may see, God will open your understanding: he will anoint you with the Holy Spirit, that *anointing that shall teach thee all things.*[98] He will so teach you as man cannot teach you, as flesh and blood cannot teach you. He will illuminate you, he will shine into your heart;[99] he will give you a saving experimental knowledge of himself.[100] He will so teach you, as to make you come to him, and come to Christ, and taste how pleasant the Lord is.[101] No knowledge in the world can compare with such knowledge of God, and of the things of God, as God himself will vouchsafe you. And usually when God first converts a sinner to himself, he then most observably opens his eyes and turns him from darkness to light;[102] then he rubs off the scales of ignorance, recovers sight to the blind touching God and spirituals, that (like a prisoner brought out of a most darksome dungeon into the bright sunshine) he thinks himself as in another world.[103] Then a man begins to know God and the things of God, to

---

[95] Hebrews 8:11

[96] "For God does not promise what is in our own power, but what he alone can perform for us." John Calvin's commentary on Hebrews 8:11
[https://www.studylight.org/commentaries/eng/cal/hebrews-8.html]
<Accessed 4/2/2024>

[97] John 6:45

[98] Revelation 3:18; 1 John 2:27

[99] Hebrews 6:4; 2 Corinthians 4:6, Ephesians 1:18

[100] Philippians 1:9-10

[101] John 6:45; 1 Peter 2:3

[102] Acts 26:18

[103] Luke 4:18

his own and others admiration. Here God assures such a sort of knowledge unto thee.

(ii) The degree of the knowledge of God here promised, is not only an initial, elementary, ABC-knowledge of God, according to first principles and fundamentals; as the Jews knowledge for the most part was, the church being then till Christ, as a child under age, under elements and rudiments: but a more ripe, perfect and plenary knowledge of God, penetrating into the abstruse, secret and excellent mysteries of godliness.[104] This is notably insinuated (thinks Calvin)[105] in that phrase {*know the Lord*}, which seems to denote the first rudiments of faith, or celestial doctrine, taught to them by others, in the time of the Old Testament. But now the federates under the New Covenant shall comparatively need no such elementary instruction, their knowledge shall attain such maturity and perfection; God will make them scholars in a higher form, etc. As for kind, so for degree, they shall be taught more perfectly.

(iii) The extent of this knowledge to all the federates: *All shall know me from the least to the greatest.* That is, this New Covenant knowledge shall be very general and universal to all sorts and degrees of federates, small, and great,

---

[104] Galatians 4:1-3
[105] "And that we may no farther seek an explanation, let us carefully weigh the words; for it is not simply and without exception said {*No one shall teach his neighbor*}, but it is added, {*Saying, Know ye Jehovah*}. We hence see that the prophet promises knowledge, so that they might be no longer alphabetarians; for these words, {*Know ye Jehovah*}, point out the first elements of faith, or celestial doctrine. And, doubtless, if we consider how great was the ignorance of the ancient people, they were then only in the elements. He who is at this day the least among the faithful, has so far advanced, that he knows much more clearly what pertains chiefly to salvation than those who were then the most learned."
And a little before:
"Here is mentioned another difference between the old and the new covenant, even that God, who had obscurely manifested himself under the Law, would send forth a fuller light, so that the knowledge of him would be commonly enjoyed. But he hyperbolically extols this favor, when he says that no one would have need of a teacher or instructor, as every one would have himself sufficient knowledge."
John Calvin's commentary on Jeremiah 31:34
[https://ccel.org/ccel/calvin/calcom20/calcom20.iii.xliv.html]
<Accessed 4/4/2024>

in comparison of the knowledge that was under the Old Covenant, which was but narrow and confined to the Jews, a handful of people to the Gentiles. As to this knowledge, no man's greatness shall help him, no man's meanness shall hinder him. The Spirit of God shall be poured forth so plenteously, that *the knowledge of the Lord shall cover the earth, as the waters cover the sea.* Here then God undertakes to instruct all sorts of his federates, even the meanest of them, and consequently to teach you who are so ignorant and incapable, to give them a sort of knowledge more than human, to afford them a degree of knowledge more than elementary, usual in former times; wherefore yield up yourself to God to be his disciple. Despise not his word, grieve not his Spirit; then that *God, that caused light to shine out of darkness, will shine into thine heart, with the light of the knowledge of the glory of God in the face of Jesus Christ.*

{Doubt 4}: About the deadness, hardness, deceitfulness and manifold vileness of their own hearts.

Ah (thinks the wounded and perplexed soul), I have a most vile and naughty heart: it is as hard and dead, as intractable and inflexible, to any good, as a very stone. How deceitful, how crooked, how rebellious, how unbelieving, how impenitent, how abominably wicked is it? Is it possible that any in the world should have so bad a heart as I have? How can any of my thoughts, words or works; how can any of my prayers or religious services, be good or acceptable in the sight of God, which flow from so corrupt a fountain?

Resolution: It is most true, an unbelieving impenitent, rebellious, dead, hard stony heart, is a very vile heart; and naturally every man has such a heart.[106] But in this New Covenant, God has provided an excellent and effectual cure for such a distempered heart: *I will give my laws into their mind, and write them upon their hearts* (Hebrews 8:10). Note here three things, namely: (i) God's inscription of his laws in their mind and hearts, (ii) his

---

[106] 1 Timothy 1:13, Romans 2:5, Ephesians 2:1-2, 5, Ezekiel 36:26

preparation of the mind and heart for such Inscription, and (iii) the heart's temper and disposition after such inscription.

(i) God's inscription of his laws in their mind and heart. The minds and hearts of all by nature are vile and naught: but the laws of God are holy, and just, and good;[107] and these laws of God (who has absolute command, sovereignty and dominion over all men's minds and hearts) will inscribe in these hearts and minds. Mark: God does not write his laws in their minds and hearts because they are good, but that they may be made good. A holy law shall be written in an unholy heart, to make it holy; a just and straight law, in an unrighteous and crooked heart, to make it straight and righteous; a good law in a bad heart, to make the bad heart good. The laws of God shall be given and written in the mind and heart, that the mind and heart may have better principles, rules, and directions supernaturally, than ever they had naturally. And God's writing will be: (a) most gratuitous, without, yea contrary to desert [merit]: *I will give – I will write*; his own mere will and good-pleasure is the cause why it shall be done; (b) most efficacious: he can make the heart take what inscription and impression he pleases; (c) most advantageous: there shall be a draught of his own laws delineated upon them.

(ii) God's preparation of the mind and heart for this inscription. This is implied and presupposed. When God says {*I will write my laws*}, he implies that he will fit and prepare the heart for this writing. Man's heart by nature is extremely incapable of God's writing, being so blurred and blotted with contrary laws, so stony and obdurate. God therefore prepares the heart for his own laws: (a) Partly, by obliteration of all contrary laws. The law of sin, the law of the members, the law and lusts of Satan, etc – these are contrary laws to the laws of God, they cannot be written both at once on the same hearts therefore, as in table books.[108] We first wipe out the old writing before we can write new; so God first wipes out these old abominable laws and principles out

---

[107] Romans 7:12
[108] John 8:44

of the heart, by self-denial and repentance, and then writes his own blessed laws there.[109] (b) Partly, by mollification and softening the heart, that it may take God's impression. Until the heart is softened it will take no spiritual stamp, but afterwards it will receive any. God therefore takes away the heart of stone, and gives a heart of flesh.[110]

(iii) The heart's temper and disposition after such inscription of God's laws therein, is universally conform to God's laws written therein: there is a law within answerable to God's law without: the temper and disposition is now holy, just, good, spiritual, heavenly. As the wax answers to the seal, as the printed characters answer to the stamp; so the heart and mind answer to God's laws, to act or omit, as God shall please. Then the heart bends towards the will of God, willingly, delightfully, sincerely, universally, constantly. If the heart was never so bad before, now all is mended by God's writing his laws there. And therefore put your heart into God's hand; beseech him to prepare it for this writing by obliteration, by mollification, to write his laws therein; to make it conform every way to his laws and will – and then you shall have a holy, a good heart indeed. And all this, God has covenanted to do.

{Doubt 5}: About the want of all spiritual excellencies, abilities, and duties which might commend them to God.

Alas (says the bruised soul), if I had any spiritual beauty and loveliness, if I had any true worth and excellency in me, if I had any strength or ability to believe, to repent to love and obey him, to resign up myself sincerely unto him, then I might draw near to him, then I might lay hold of his New Covenant and of Jesus Christ therein, then I might hopefully wait for his acceptation of me: but I have no such thing in me, a poor, worthless, useless, strengthless creature. Ah, what shall I do, that I may be saved?

Resolution: To this I reply several things, namely:

---

[109] Titus 2:11-12
[110] Ezekiel 36:26

(i) You think that you might come to God and accept his Covenant, his Christ, etc., if you had a spiritual excellency and worth in you, etc. Alas, poor soul! Do you think that you may not draw near to God and to this Covenant, without a bribe? Do you think that Christ Jesus will not be had, without money and without price? You are quite mistaken. Do you thirst after him, do you earnestly desire him, and long for him? Then you are one whom he bids: {*come to the waters*} – yea, though you have no money, yet you may come, buy and eat, yea come buy wine and milk without money and without price.[111] God does not sell himself, his Christ, his Covenant, his favors, his salvation to the sinner; but he gives all these freely. He does not bring a sinner into Covenant with himself, because he finds him excellent and worthy; but by bringing him into Covenant, of vile and unworthy he makes him excellent and worthy. If you stay away from God and his Covenant until you are worthy, then you shall never come while the world stands. Accept and lay hold of this Covenant, and this Covenant assures you that God will write his laws in your heart, will make you know the Lord, will forgive and forget all your sins, will be your God, and you shall be one of his people – and all this because he will do it, not for anything in you, but for his own sake, for his Christ's sake.[112] And these, these are the things that will make thee excellent and worthy indeed. Does the patient come to the physician because he is sound? or nor rather because he is sick: that he may be sound? Does the beggar cry at the rich man's door, because he is full and well clothed, or not rather because he is hungry and naked: that he may be fed and clothed? And have you forgotten Christ's saying: *The whole need not the physician, but they that are sick*; *I came not to call the righteous, but sinners to repentance?*[113]

(ii) This New Covenant, embraced by you, will furnish you with all spiritual sufficiency and ability for duties, as well as with spiritual excellencies. Hence you shall be enabled to believe, to repent, to obey, to do and be

---

[111] Isaiah 55:1-6
[112] Hebrews 8:10-12
[113] Matthew 9:12-13

anything that God shall please. In his explicit promises of mercy and sufficiency of spirituals to you, you have his implicit promises of your duties and performances to him. He undertakes for both parties: for himself, to give you mercy and ability; for you, that you shall perform duty to him from that mercy. As: (a) that you shall know him because his laws shall be in your mind, and all shall know him;[114] (b) that you shall believe in him and in Christ; (c) that you shall repent sincerely of all your sins; (d) that you shall love and obey him uprightly – and all because he will write his laws in your mind and heart;[115] which act of grace will abundantly furnish you and incite unto all these performances, that you cannot choose but to do them delightfully, because his law is in your heart, in your inwards;[116] and (e) that you shall resign up yourself unto him acceptably because you shall be one of his people.[117] Thus you are not to contrive so much to bring ability and duty to this New Covenant as to fetch and derive all ability and duty from this New Covenant. Though this New Covenant finds you empty, it will send you away full and rich.

{Doubt 6}: About the great distance between them and God; them and Christ.

For thus thinks the bruised and perplexed heart: although I am now somewhat satisfied and quieted with all this that has been spoken, yet there is such an infinite distance and disparity between God and me, Christ and me, that I tremble and quake to think of approaching near unto him, or his Covenant. For, he is the holy, holy, holy **Jehovah**;[118] I am a sinful lump of defiled dust and ashes. He is all light, and *in him is no darkness at all*;[119] I am

---

[114] Hebrews 8:10-11
[115] Hebrews 8:10
[116] Psalm 40:8
[117] Hebrews 8:10
[118] Isaiah 6:3
[119] 1 John 1:5

all darkness, and in me is no light at all, *in me dwelleth no good thing*.[120] He is all life; I am all deadness, sinful deadness. He is all beauty; I am all deformity. He is all majesty; I am all meanness. He is all might; I am all weakness. He is all justice; I am all guiltiness. He is a consuming fire,[121] and I as dry stubble before a devouring fire, and will this great, this glorious, this infinite God cast an eye upon such a worm, such a dead dog, such a filthy dunghill of corruption as I am? How should I expect it?

Resolution: True, the distance, the disparity between God and a sinner, between Christ and a sinner is infinite, and God knows this most exactly; yet notwithstanding all this distance which he perfectly observes, God tells all poor sinners that will embrace his New Covenant and promises thereof: *And I will be to them for a God, and they shall be to me for a people.*[122] As if God had said: I will not stand upon any terms of distance and disparity between myself and poor sinners, though it be infinite: but I will pass by it all, it shall not come into consideration with me, to exclude them from my New Covenant, for, I will not disdain to be theirs, Nor will I be ashamed to account them mine, I will condescend to them, I will deal familiarly with them in a covenant way, I will contract and marry them unto myself, there shall be an indissoluble relation established between us; all that I am and have shall be theirs, And all that they are and have shall be mine. And all this, because so it pleases me. O glorious promise! O blissful enjoyment! What can God promise beyond himself: what can a poor soul enjoy beyond, or equal to God? "Oh," said Augustine, "What is better than this goodness? What is happier than this happiness?"[123] If God will not object this distance against afflicted sinners, then why should they object it against themselves? Close then with God, O trembling soul, and say to him: *Behold the servant of the Lord, be it unto me even according to thy word.*

---

[120] Romans 8:18, Ephesians 5:8
[121] Hebrews 12:29
[122] Hebrews 8:10
[123] Augustine, *D. Spir. & Litera*

{Doubt 7}: About the difficulty and seeming impossibility of ever obtaining any assurance of their salvation.

But alas (says the wounded sinner and perplexed saint) though God should forgive my sins, remove his wrath, heal the blindness of my mind, cure the vileness of my heart, furnish with spiritual sufficiency and ability, and become a Covenant-God unto me; though I say, God should do all this for me; yet if I have no assurance hereof unto myself, if I have no evident discovery hereof within myself, what comfort or advantage can I have thereby? If Christ would audibly say to me as once to Zacchaeus: *This day is salvation come to this house*;[124] or as once to the palsy-man,[125] and to the penitent woman:[126] *Thy sins are forgiven thee*; Or if Christ would disclose the certainty of my salvation unto me by an angel, by some voice from heaven, by revelation, or by some miracle: then I should walk sweetly and cheerfully in the joy of his salvation, then I should run with patience and triumph the race that is set before me.[127] But alas, I am wholly swallowed up with doubts, fears, jealousies, and sad apprehensions, that I am still in a lost and reprobate condition; I would not care what I did do, or endure: what I should gain, or lose; whether I should live or die: so I might but have a certain assurance of my eternal salvation. But is it ever possible that such assurance should be rooted in my staggering and unbelieving soul?

Resolution: To this also I reply:

(i) That this New Covenant is so laid down in these promises, as (being judiciously improved) may be a strong foundation of this desired assurance to a perplexed soul. For: (a) In his New Covenant, here are four excellent topics or common places of assurance,[128] namely: (1) the divine inscription of God's

---

[124] Luke 19:9
[125] Mark 2:5
[126] Luke 7:48
[127] Hebrews 12:1
[128] Hebrews 6:10-12

laws in the heart, (2) the supernatural knowledge of the Lord, (3) the gratuitous remission of all sin, (4) and the grand covenant relation unto God. He that upon good grounds can discover these laws of God written in his heart by the finger of God, This knowledge of the Lord shining in the mind by supernatural instruction, This remission of sin through the blood of Christ sprinkled upon the conscience by faith, and this covenant relation and mutual interest established between God and the soul. He, I say, that can solidly discover in himself these things, may undoubtedly assure himself of his own eternal salvation, forasmuch as these New Covenant benefits are in effect one and the same with effectual vocation, sanctification, and justification, which unquestionably determine in glorification.[129] (b) These promised blessings of the New Covenant, are the peculiar and saving effects of Christ's mediation, which as priest, prophet and king he enriches all his members also.[130] Now the enjoying of these peculiar and saving fruits of Christ's mediation, is an undoubted evidence of the enjoyer's endless salvation. (c) All these grounds of assurance and evidences of happiness promised in this New Covenant are therein most infallibly ascertained to every sincere federate. Not by revelation, miracle, voice from heaven, or testimony of an angel (all of which Satan might counterfeit, and so undo the soul forever), but by God's own immutable promise and Covenant upon record in writing both in Old and New Testament,[131] in which *it is impossible for God to lie*,[132] which is ten thousand times more sure, infallible, and unquestionable than all. Would you believe an angel or a voice from heaven? And will you not much more believe unto all assurance, the ever-living God himself, and this his more sure word of prophecy?[133]

---

[129] Romans 8:29-30
[130] See in this Section 2, General 4
[131] Jeremiah 31:31-34, Hebrews 8:10-12
[132] Hebrews 6:13, 17-18
[133] 2 Peter 1:17-19

(ii) That sometimes the elect of God, in the pangs of their new birth (when their own sins and the wrath of God have lain heavy upon their souls), have so intensively desired, so fervently longed for this blessed assurance of their salvation, that they have wished earnestly for some extraordinary and miraculous expressure from God to that end, that their assurance of their salvation might be past all possibility of doubt or question.[134] But this desire of theirs might possibly arise: (a) Partly, from their ignorance of, and unacquaintedness with, the holy Scriptures, and the ways of God: they not understanding (in their infancy of grace) what abundant unquestionable and infallible foundations of assurance are treasured up and provided for God's people in the Scriptures, and how the Lord is never wont to work extraordinarily in temporals or spirituals, when his ordinary provisions are

---

[134] I knew a Christian over thirty years ago, who in the infancy of his Christianity so vehemently panted after the infallible assurance of God's favor in Christ, of his own election and salvation, that for a long time together he most earnestly desired some voice from heaven, yea, some miraculous voice from trees or flowers in the field, or some other extraordinary testimony, for establishing and confirming his spirit in the undoubted assurance of his eternal happiness. This after many desires and longings, was denied; but a better grounded Assurance was afterwards afforded:

(1) Partly, by the sweet attestation and obsignation of the Spirit of God, and that especially vouchsafed in his prayers and tears, persuading him of his comfortable and saving condition towards God (Romans 8:15-16, Ephesians 1:13-14), which testimony of the Spirit of God did so abundantly fill and satisfy the thirstings of his soul, that not only his former desires after extraordinary and miraculous ways of assurance did cease, through the surpassing sweetness of the Spirit's certioration secretly refreshing him at his heart-root, but also whilst that activity of the Spirit's witness remained upon his soul, whilst this sacred fire was burning, and this heavenly light shining there, he was so powerfully possessed of the love of God shed abroad in his heart, that he could have done and endured any thing for God, yea could have been contented (if it had been possible, and if God had so pleased) to have been dragged through the very torments of hell for the immediate vision and fruition of Christ.
(2) Partly, by an experimental argumentation from the holy Scriptures. The Scriptures dictating to him the proposition, in some characteristics and discoveries of a gracious and saving condition, as he that believes shall be saved (Mark 16:16). He that truly loves his brother (a Christian for his Christianity) is passed from death to life (1 John 3:14): his conscience furnishing him out of his own experience with the assumption, from his agreement with the Scripture characteristics: But I believe – But I truly love my Christian brother for his Christianity, etc; whereupon the heart was able to make a comfortable conclusion touching his own good spiritual estate. And this discourse and reasoning from Scripture evidence and his own experience joined together, he found to be a very convincing, comfortable, and continuing ground of assurance to his soul.

sufficient and abundant. (b) Partly, from the subtlety of Satan, who might cunningly put young beginners in grace, to seek for assurance by miracle or extraordinary unwarranted ways: that so he might take the advantage of their disappointments, to drive them to despair, saying, "You see, God will give you no miracle, no voice from heaven to assure you of your salvation, and therefore you are but reprobates and castaways, only to expect damnation." But at last they have comfortably overcome these infirmities and temptations, upon further experience in the mysteries of Christianity: and by judicious comparing the holy Scriptures and their own hearts experiments together, have been invincibly established in assurance of their salvation, and in sweet peace with God in Jesus Christ.

---

(6) **That these New Covenant promises are so expressed as virtually to contain in them, the agreement and difference between the Old and New Covenant – yea, the pre-eminences of the New above the Old. This agreement, difference, and preeminence may thus in brief be evinced, from the words of the Covenant.**

[1] *The agreement between the Old and New Covenant*, for the substance of them, is expressed in two particulars especially, namely:

{1} In the sum and glorious abstract of the Covenants: *I will be to them a God, and they shall be to me a people.*[135] This is the sum of both Old and New Covenant in express terms.

{2} In the laws of this Covenant promised to be written in their hearts: *And I will give my laws into their minds, and write them in their hearts.*[136] What laws? Even the same moral laws which were given for a Covenant to Israel at Mount Sinai, which was the Old Covenant.[137] "God does not say (as

---

[135] Compare Hebrews 8:10 & Jeremiah 31:33 with Deuteronomy 5:2, 6-7 & Leviticus 26:12
[136] Hebrews 8:10
[137] Deuteronomy 5:2, 5-6, etc.

Calvin excellently observes),[138] "I will give another law," but "*I will write my law*," namely: the same which was anciently given to the fathers." He speaks of a law of his that was famous, eminent, well-known amongst them: which best agrees to that moral law, which is as an abridgement of the Scripture.

[2] ***The difference also between the Old and New Covenant*** is here purposely expressed, and this, more generally, and more particularly:

{1} More generally, in those words: *I will make a new covenant with the house of Israel and with the house of Judah: not according to the covenant that I made with their fathers in the day when I took them by the hand to lead them out of the land of Egypt*, etc.[139] Here the Lord plainly declares in the general, that he would make a New Covenant with them, which should be another manner of covenant, a very different covenant from that Old Covenant.

{2} More particularly, he states this difference in three points expressly, as Calvin has very well noted,[140] namely: (i) In the inscription of God's laws. In both Old and New Covenant there is a writing of God's laws; but, in the Old Covenant they were written in tables of stone,[141] in this New Covenant upon the fleshy tables of their mind and heart.[142] *That* was only a literal and ineffectual writing, that showed duty but gave no ability; *this* is a spiritual and efficacious writing, that affords ability for the required duty. (ii) In the instruction of the federates. In that Old Covenant, they had mostly a human instruction, and that but in principles of the knowledge of the Lord; they were alphabetarians, children under age, capable only of elements and rudiments.[143] But under this New Covenant, the generality of the federates have a more-than-human – even a divine – teaching promised them touching the Lord. They are come to age, shall be put up into a higher form, and have in sight into higher mysteries. (iii) In the ablation or taking away of sins. In the

---

[138] John Calvin's commentary on Jeremiah 31:33
[139] Hebrews 8:8-9
[140] John Calvin's commentary on Jeremiah 31:33-34
[141] Deuteronomy 4:13
[142] Hebrews 8:10
[143] Hebrews 8:11, Galatians 4:1-3

Old Covenant there were many sacrifices for expiation of sin which were repeated every year, every day, being unable to take away sin, but rather becoming renewed remembrances of sin, year by year, day by day;[144] but in this New Covenant, Christ by that one sacrifice of himself once offered, and never to be repeated, has purged away the sins of his elect forever, so that they shall need no more sacrifice for expiation, and that God will remember them no more.[145]

[3] *The preeminence of the New Covenant also above the Old, does stand in all those three points of difference fore-expressed: in all which this New Covenant far excels.* But of this more hereafter in the general inferences.

(7) **That all these New Covenant promises are wholly grounded upon the mere grace and good pleasure of God's will in Jesus Christ alone.** The covenant expressions evince: [1] That all these promises are founded upon the mere grace and good-pleasure of God's will. Because God's will is still declared as the cause of God's making them: *I will give my laws. – I will write them. – I will be their God. – They shall be my people. – All shall know me. – I will be merciful, – I will remember no more.*[146] Here is no cause, no reason, no motive at all drawn from the house of Israel or Judah, from the federates themselves, but all from God. [2] That all these promises are also gratuitously made in Jesus Christ alone, and with reference to his meritorious mediation. Partly, because all these promised blessings have an excellent suitableness and answerableness to Christ's priestly, prophetic, and kingly offices – as has been already shown.[147] Partly, because remission of sins and justification here freely promised by god to his federates, and laid down as a ground why God will perform all the fore-promised blessings, hath a special reference to Christ's

---

[144] Hebrews 10:1-3
[145] Hebrews 8:12 & 10:10-19
[146] Hebrews 8:10-12
[147] In Section 2 General 4

plenary satisfaction of God's justice for the sins of all his elect, whereby God is appeased and pacified towards them forever.[148]

Thus far of the generals which are more necessary and helpful to the clear understanding of the matters of the New Covenant, as here described by the prophet and apostle.

---

[148] Hebrews 8:12 ιλεως εσομαι: *I will be merciful*, etc.

Section 3

Thirdly, having analytically explained the words wherein the prophet and apostle describe this New Covenant, and having unfolded such generals as much conduce to the right understanding of the matter of the New Covenant; now in the last place I shall proceed to the opening of the matter of the New Covenant; more particularly, and this with the greater evidence and perspicuity.

The matter or substance of the **New Covenant**, as here described by Jeremiah and Paul, is wholly contained in promises.[149] Here is nothing else expressed, not one precept or commandment, not one threatening; but all promises, and those promises from God unto his federates. Yet these promises are not mere absolute promises, as some others are; but conditional promises, having implicitly in them certain conditioned duties which the federates should perform towards God, answerable to his blessings promised unto them. Explicitly, these promises contain God's covenant mercies to his federates; implicitly, they also contain the federates' duties towards God. This must needs be so:

(1) Because these promises here laid down are covenant promises. God calls them, his New Covenant: *I will make a new covenant. – But this shall be the covenant that I will make with the house of Israel, after those days, saith the LORD: I will give my laws into their mind*, etc.[150] And what is this Covenant, but these promises? Now all covenant promises, in the nature of them, are conditional: either expressly conditional, when the condition is expressed, as Genesis 6:18, etc., 17:1-2, etc., Deuteronomy 5:2-4, 6, etc. Psalm 132:11-12; or

---

[149] Jeremiah 31:31-34, Hebrews 8:8-12
[150] Jeremiah 31:31-34, Hebrews 8:8-12

implicitly conditional, when the condition required and expected on the part of the federates is only implied, as in Genesis 3:15, and here in Hebrews 8:10-12. For in covenants, there is still a mutual agreement between the federates upon certain terms to be performed by each party. It cannot rationally be imagined, that God should be tied by his promises, and his federates altogether remain at liberty unobliged, for that would destroy the very nature of a covenant.

(2) Because the explanations of this New Covenant in the books of the New Testament, do express the conditions required and to be performed by us towards God, which in this description of the New Covenant are only implied: as, knowledge, faith, repentance, new obedience, self-resignation to God, etc – as hereafter in the second aphorism of this section will more at large appear. Now God's explanations of his New Covenant, are (next unto the description of the body of the Covenant itself) the best discovery and indication of the nature of the Covenant, both in regard of God's promises and stipulations, and of his federates' restipulations.

Now therefore, **the matter** of this **New Covenant** consists: (1) in certain mercies or blessings therein promised expressly on God's part to his New Covenant federates, and (2) in certain duties therein implicitly here required from, and restipulated by the New Covenant federates unto God. These two I shall lay down and explain in two distinct aphorisms.

Aphorism 1

The matter of the New Covenant on God's part consists in certain New Covenant mercies or blessings promised by him to his federates.

[These mercies or blessings promised are] namely: (1) God's giving and inscribing of his laws in their mind and hearts. (2) His federate people's more excellent and more universal knowledge of the Lord than formerly under the Old Covenant. (3) His mercy or propitiousness unto them, in his utter remission and oblivion, forgiving and forgetting all their sins forever. (4) The grand federal relation, union, communion, and interest established between God and his federates reciprocally: he being their God and they his people.

These are the four great articles of agreement in this New Covenant, and the four great New Covenant blessings which God promises on his part. I shall handle them in this order as I have here propounded them, wherein I shall only in one particular vary from the order of the text, namely: in putting the second article last, because it is the general sum of the Covenant,[151] comprehending in it all the rest. All the other particulars follow one another in a clear natural order of their dependence one upon another.

---

[151] "Here God comprehends generally the substance of his Covenant" John Calvin's commentary on Jeremiah 31:33 [https://biblehub.com/commentaries/calvin/jeremiah/31.htm] <Accessed 4/2/2024>

Article 1

Of God's writing his laws in their mind and hearts.

The first particular, but more complexive, New Covenant blessing promised by God, wherein this New Covenant differs from, and excels the Old Covenant, is; his giving his laws into their mind, and writing them upon their hearts. *I will give my laws into their mind, and write them upon their hearts.*[152] This article has in it illumination, effectual calling, regeneration, renovation, new-creation, sanctification, and such like leading mercies, initiating blessings, in the kingdom of God, and therefore this very properly comes first under consideration.

For clearing whereof, I shall chiefly unfold these questions, namely: (1) what is here meant by {*mind and hearts*}; (2) what laws of God are here intended; (3) what sort of writing this is, whereby God writes his laws in the mind and hearts of his federates: and how he writes them there; (4) whether God's laws were not written in his people's hearts before the time of this New Covenant; (5) why the Lord will write his laws in the mind and hearts of his federates, now under the New Covenant; (6) how we may know, whether God hath written his laws in our mind and hearts? These questions (several whereof are cases of conscience) being unfolded and resolved, this first article will be very clear.

---

[152] Hebrews 8:10, Jeremiah 31:33; see the explanation of these words in Section 1 of Chapter 5.

Question 1: What is here meant by {*mind and hearts*}?

Answer: For resolution herein, note:

(1) That, what Paul calls διανοιαν: *mind*,[153] Jeremiah calls קֶרֶב: *kereb* – {*inward part*}.[154]

The Hebrew word properly signifies the middle of anything, that which is most near, most intimate, most inward: as the heart, intrals, bowels, etc.[155] And thence it is metaphorically translated to signify the mind, thought, reason or understanding of man, which is most intimate and inward to him. And so here Paul renders it, according to the meaning of the Holy Ghost, διανοιαν {*mind*}.

This word, {*mind*} in Scripture has many various acceptations. It is used: [1] for the soul: *Gird up the loins of your mind.*[156] That is, let your souls be in a fitted and prepared posture to walk on in ways of grace to glory. [2] For the intellectual faculty, the reason, the understanding, etc. whereby we think, know, reason, discourse, etc. *The peace of God – shall keep your hearts and minds through Christ Jesus.*[157] That is, that you do not think, reason not anything unfitly against God's justice and providential dispensations. So: *He opened their mind to understand the Scriptures.*[158] And in this sense (to mention no more acceptations of the word {*mind*} in Scripture), the Lord here says: *I will give my laws into their mind, and write them in their minds.*[159] For {*mind*} is here contradistinct from their hearts, and therefore imports the whole intellectual faculty: the superior powers in the turret of the soul.

---

[153] Hebrews 8:10
[154] Jeremiah 31:33
[155] See Pagnin's Thesaurus: ling. Sanct. in verb קרב
[156] 1 Peter 1:13
[157] Philippians 4:7
[158] Luke 24:45
[159] Hebrews 8:10 & 10:16 from Jeremiah 31:33

(2) **That the word *{heart}* also is used in Scripture in many several senses, as:**

[1] Sometimes, properly for the corporal heart, that fountain of vital spirits, that first lives and last dies;[160] *Wine that maketh glad the heart of man, – and bread which strengtheneth man's heart.*[161] [2] Sometimes, metonymically, for the soul, which (according to some) is principally seated in the heart: *The hidden man of the heart – Even the ornament of a meek and quiet spirit.*[162] *– Which is an honest and good heart having heard the word, keep it*: that is, keep it in an honest and good soul.[163] *Circumcise the foreskin of your heart*, i.e., of your soul.[164] [3] Sometimes, for the mind and understanding, as: *the eyes of the heart being illuminated*, etc.[165] *– That every imagination of the thoughts of his heart was only evil continually.*[166] [4] Sometimes, for the conscience, as: *David's heart smote him*, namely: his conscience checked him, etc.[167] *If our heart* (namely: our conscience) *condemn us, God is greater than our heart, and knoweth all things.*[168] [5] Sometimes, for the memory, which is as the treasury of the soul where we lay up and keep things that we would not forget. *– But his mother kept all these sayings in her heart.*[169] [6] Sometimes, for the will and affections, because the heart is the special seat and receptacle of the affections, as: *Whose heart the Lord opened, that she attended unto the things which were spoken of Paul*;[170] that is, whose will and affections the Lord efficaciously bowed, moved, inclined, etc. to hear and believe. And in this sense the word *{heart}* is often used in Scripture. Now, as the mind takes in the understanding and all the superior faculties of

---

[160] Primum vivens et ultimum moriens.
[161] Psalm 104:15
[162] 1 Peter 3:4
[163] Luke 8:15
[164] Deuteronomy 10:16 & 30:6
[165] Ephesians 1:18
[166] Genesis 6:5
[167] 1 Samuel 24:6
[168] 1 John 3:20-21
[169] Luke 2:51
[170] Acts 16:14

the soul: so the heart, here contradistinguished from it, takes in the will and affections, and all the inferior faculties. But both mind and heart are here mentioned, because God by this his New Covenant intends the whole soul and all the faculties, powers, affections and capacities thereof to be the subject or receptacle of his laws. All of them, according to their manner and measure of receiving, shall have the characters, impressions, image, portraiture, and counter-pane of God's Laws within them.

(3) That, probably all the faculties, powers and affections of the soul are here reduced to two heads, mind and heart, in allusion to the former tables wherein the law was written: that as under the Old Covenant, God's laws were literally written in two tables of stone, so under this New Covenant, God's laws shall be spiritually written in two new tables of flesh: the mind and heart.[171]

---

[171] Deuteronomy 4:13

Question 2: What laws of God are here intended to be written in their mind and heart?

Answer: For resolution herein, note:

(1) That {*the law of God*} has many several acceptations in holy Scriptures (as I have heretofore at large manifested),[172] but as to our present purpose, consider some few:

[1] Generally, it is used for any or all divine doctrine or instruction revealed by God, especially in his written word, as Psalm 1:2, 19:8-9, and 119:70, 72, 77, etc., Romans 3:27, Isaiah 2:3 and 42:4, and Galatians 2:20.

[2] Particularly, it is taken, {1} sometimes, for the whole law given by Moses: morals, ceremonials, and judicials, as Exodus 24:12, Deuteronomy 33:2, 4 and 4:44-45. (2) Sometimes, more strictly for the moral law which God wrote in two tables of stone: *I will give thee tables of stone, and a law, and commandments which I have written.*[173] Now God thus wrote only the moral law, the ten commandments (Deuteronomy 4:13). Thus {*law*} in Malachi – contradistinguished from statutes and judgments – denotes the moral law (Malachi 4:4). But of these and other acceptations of {*the law of God*}, I have spoken more fully in the place forementioned, to which I refer the reader for his fuller satisfaction.

(2) That by {*God's law*}[174] or {*laws*}[175] here promised in the New Covenant to be written in the hearts of God's New Covenant federates, God's moral law or laws seem (in my judgment) most especially to be intended.

---

[172] In Book 3, Chapter 4, Aphorism 1, Question 2
[173] Exodus 24:12
[174] Jeremiah 31:33
[175] Hebrews 8:10 & 10:16

I will not exclude God's whole doctrine and instruction revealed in his written Word, which is a large commentary upon God's moral law that abstract epitome and abridgement of the Holy Scriptures; but more especially and peculiarly, the moral law seems here to be intended by the Holy Spirit. And this I judge for these reasons:

[1] Because this promise here – {*I will give my laws*}, or {*law*}, and {*I will write them*}, etc.[176] – does not import any new, strange, unknown, unheard of, or obscure law of God; but some ancient, familiar, well-known, noted and famous law of God. And what law or laws of God, were ever more famous, eminent, noted, known, etc. among the people of God than his moral laws? Calvin has well observed: "He says afterwards: {*I will put my law into their inwards*}. By these words, he confirms what I have said, namely that the newness which he before mentioned is not placed in the substance, but only in the form. For God does not here say {*I will give another law*}, but {*I will write my law*} – namely: the same which was anciently delivered to the fathers."[177]

[2] Because this writing of his laws in their hearts, cannot have reference either to God's ceremonial or judicial laws, but to his moral laws. Forasmuch as this writing of his laws here promised, was to be performed to the house of Israel after those days (Hebrews 8:10 and 10:16, Jeremiah 31:33), namely: after those days of the Old Covenant, for this New Covenant was not to be according to that Old, but to succeed, supersede and vacate that Old Covenant; which was done at the death of Jesus Christ, whereby he established this New Covenant in his own blood. Now after the death of Jesus Christ, and the commencing of the New Covenant, the ceremonials vanished, and the judicials, together with the Jewish commonwealth ceased, and therefore these dying and vanishing laws of God could never be intended to be written in their hearts, but some other law that was not vanishing and decaying – and what law is that but the moral law?

---

[176] Jeremiah 31:33, Hebrews 8:10 & 10:16
[177] John Calvin's commentary on Jeremiah 31:33

[3] Because this writing of God's laws in their minds and hearts, is here laid down as one great difference and preeminence of the New Covenant, from and above the Old, namely: not in essence or substance, that there should be a new law given under the New Covenant; but in accidents and circumstance, that there should be new tables for this old law to be written in, and a new form or manner of writing this law therein.[178] Then, God's law was written literally in two dead and hard tables of stone; but now, this law should be written spiritually in two living and fleshy tables of the mind and heart. Herein this New Covenant should not be according to that Old Covenant which they brake, but far differing and far excelling.[179]

[4] Because God's writing of his moral law in his people's minds and hearts by Christ the second Adam, recovers them nearest to the perfection which they at first had, but speedily lost in the first Adam. The first Adam was made in the image of God, upright and straight, every way conformed and answering to his will and law, without any crookedness or deviation;[180] so that the moral law for substance was written in his heart perfectly, as appears by the imperfect remains and relics thereof written in the very hearts of pagans, who never had God's written law imparted to them.[181] Now God – recovering lapsed man out of his lost condition in Adam – raises him up to as good and a better condition in Christ; who as man's surety, has God's law perfectly written in his heart, which he perfectly fulfilled in his whole life, and satisfied the penalty of the law by his death for our breach thereof;[182] so redeeming us from it; and who conforms his elect unto himself, writing this law effectually in their hearts by his Spirit, that the righteousness of the law may (in integrity and uprightness) be fulfilled also in them, not walking after the flesh but after the Spirit (Romans 8:2-4).[183]

---

[178] Consider well Hebrews 8:8-9 with verse 10
[179] Deuteronomy 4:13
[180] Genesis 1:26-27, Ecclesiastes 7:29
[181] Romans 2:14-15
[182] Psalm 40:6-8 with Hebrews 10:5-8, etc.
[183] Galatians 3:10, 13-14

Question 3: What sort of writing is this, whereby God writes his laws in the mind and hearts of his federates? And how does he write his laws therein?

Answer: God's writing of his laws in their minds and hearts that are his covenant people, is an excellent mystery, and worthy of most diligent consideration. For, this is a primary blessing of the New Covenant, and one excellent way whereby we may certainly discover that we are God's New Covenant people. God's writing his laws in our minds and hearts is an improper, metaphorical form of speech, borrowed from men's writing of their laws and edicts in books or upon tables, or from God's writing his laws of old in tables of stone.[184] Now for the clearing and opening hereof more particularly, note these things, namely:

(1) **That God here in his New Covenant useth two expressions to one and the same effect:** *I will give my laws into their mind, and write them in their hearts.*[185] He contents not himself to say only {*I will give my laws*}, or only, {*I will write my laws*}, but he uses both words, {*I will give*} and {*I will write*}. Hereby he seems to denote unto us the difficulty, efficacy, and excellency of this work.

---

[184] Deuteronomy 4:13
[185] Hebrews 8:10 & 10:16, Jeremiah 31:33

[1] The difficulty of this work of bringing man's heart and life to be conformed to his law and will.[186] God's law is so razed out of man's heart by the fall, the prints thereof are so obliterated, dimmed and defaced, and so few relics thereof remaining; yea naturally there is so much enmity, contrariety and repugnancy in man's heart against the law of God, the φρονημα της σαρκος: *the wisdom of the flesh, the high excellency of the flesh, is enmity against God, and is not subject to the law of God, nor indeed can be* (Romans 8:6-7). That it is a very great and hard work to bring man's refractory heart to agree with God's law. God must give his law into his heart – yea, that is not enough, God must write it in his heart, printing and fixing it there, or else this work will not be done.

[2] The efficacy and excellency of this work. God himself will give it, and he will write it: God will both convey his law into their minds and hearts, that is: his giving; and confirm, root, and establish his law in their hearts, that is: his writing of it. Here is power and divine efficacy indeed, that brings mind and heart into sweet conformity to the law of God. This is an excellent work, beyond the creatures activity: and as Calvin says, "it is a kind of renovation of the world, when men suffer themselves to be governed by God." They cannot give or write God's laws in their own hearts by any power or free will of their own, but God alone will do all, this belongs only to him."

---

[186] "But he states the same thing in two ways, and says that he would put his law in their inward parts, and that he would write it in their hearts. We indeed know how difficult it is that man should be so formed to obedience that his whole life may be in unison with the Law of God, for all the lusts of the flesh are so many enemies, as Paul says, who fight against God. (Romans 8:7) As then all our affections and lusts thus carry on war with God, it is in a manner a renovation of the world when men suffer themselves to be ruled by God. And we know what Scripture says, that we cannot be the disciples of Christ, except we renounce ourselves and the world, and deny our own selves. (Matthew 6:24; Luke 14:26, 27) This is the reason why the Prophet was not satisfied with one statement, but said, I will put my Law in their inward parts, I will write it in their hearts."
John Calvin's commentary on Jeremiah 31:33
[https://biblehub.com/commentaries/calvin/jeremiah/31.htm]
<Accessed 4/3/2024>

(2) **That God, by this giving and writing his laws in their minds and hearts here promised, intends a far better and more excellent inscription of his laws now under the New Covenant than he had ever made before under any Covenant foregoing (Hebrews 8:8-10, Jeremiah 31:31-33).** The New Covenant is the last and most excellent of all Covenants, therefore God's writing of his laws for his federates under this New Covenant must answerably be the most excellent writing. The Scriptures signify to us God's threefold writing of his moral laws, namely: [1] in the soul of Adam by his creation, under the Covenant of Works. For if pagans since the fall, that never had the written law of God made known to them, do by nature the things contained in the law, thereby showing the work of the law written in their hearts: how much more had Adam before the fall this law perfectly written in his heart?[187] [2] In two tables of stone at Mount Sinai, under the Old Covenant, or Old Testament.[188] [3] In two spiritual tables of the mind and heart now under the New Covenant: the first writing was natural, or connatural. The second writing was literal; this third writing was spiritual and supernatural. The first writing was, to enable Adam to keep the Covenant of Works, the second writing was, to enable Israel to keep the Old Covenant, and the third writing is to enable the spiritual Israel of Jews and Gentiles to keep the New Covenant. The first writing was in the heart of man, without Christ; the second was in tables of stone, without man, but leading to Christ.[189] The third is in the spiritual tables of their mind and heart that are brought to Christ, and actually partakers of him. The first writing was not continuing, but quickly obliterated by the fall; the second writing was not effectual, but only discovered their sin and duty, yet neither enabling them against the one nor unto the other; the third writing is both effectual and continuing; effectual in furnishing with ability for duty discovered; and continuing, in enabling them to persevere in

---

[187] Romans 2:14-15 with Genesis 1:26-27, Ecclesiastes 7:29
[188] Deuteronomy 4:13; 2 Corinthians 3:7
[189] Deuteronomy 4:13; Galatians 3:24-25

well-doing continually. So that this last inscription of God's laws in the minds and hearts of the New Covenant federates, does far excel all that went before.

(3) **That God's most excellent giving and writing of his laws in his people's minds and hearts according to this New Covenant, comprises in it several things, namely:** [1] God's preparing of their minds and hearts for this writing; [2] God's manner and way of writing his laws in the mind and heart so prepared; and [3] the consequences and effects upon the mind and heart, when God's laws shall be thus written upon them.

[1] *God's preparing of men's minds and hearts, for his giving and writing his laws in them.* When God would write his law naturally in Adam's heart, there was first a kind of preparation for it: a divine consultation to create man in God's own image.[190] And when God was about to write his law, his ten words in the two tables of stone, he first prepared the tables by his own immediate workmanship, he made them apt and fit for that purpose, and then wrote his laws upon them with his own finger;[191] so proportionably, when God does actually go about the writing of his laws in the minds and hearts of his New Covenant people, he first previously prepares, fits and disposes their minds and hearts for such inscription. Now God prepares and fits their minds and hearts for his own writing of his laws in them: by hewing them, by razing all other writings out of them, and by mollifying them to receive this better writing of his holy laws.

{1} God hews these tables of mind and heart by the Spirit of bondage working fear and terror.[192] Men's minds and hearts are naturally like stones in the quarry, rough, rugged, uneven, crooked, etc: very unfit to have anything engraven or written upon them, until they are hewn, squared, polished and their ruggedness be taken away.[193] God therefore comes with his Spirit of bondage, which lays their sins and the aggravations thereof before their naked

---

[190] Genesis 1:26
[191] Exodus 32:15-16
[192] Romans 8:15
[193] Ezekiel 36:26

consciences,[194] and lays the curse, the wrath of God, and the wages of sin, death, before their eyes.[195] Hereupon their hearts are pricked, and punctually wounded in every part, like the hearts of Peter's hearers (Acts 2:35-36). They are full of fear, horror, trembling and astonishment, like the jailor in Acts 16:29, and like Saul in Acts 9:5, 9. They are in excessive bitterness for their sins against God and Jesus Christ, like those in Zechariah 12:10 to the end. Thus this Spirit of bondage rough-hews their minds and hearts, takes down their pride and exalting imaginations,[196] takes off the knobbedness, ruggedness, and crookedness of their Spirits, and brings them unto some more smoothness, evenness and fittedness for this writing than naturally they had. Thus God hews the tables.

{2} God obliterates and razes all other laws and writings out of their minds and hearts, repugnant to, and inconsistent with his laws, As the law of sin in their members,[197] the lusts of Satan,[198] the lusts and wills of the flesh,[199] self-opinion, self-love, self-righteousness, and all manner of self-fullness.[200] All these vile law and writings wherewith the mind and heart is naturally blotted and blurred, God wipes out by a spirit of self-denial, as men wipe out the old writings in their table books, or pare off the old letters in a stone before they can write new therein. Without this self-emptying, self-denial none can be Christ's disciple, as Christ himself has often intimated.[201] This is a primary preparative unto Christianity. Thus the disciples left all for Christ (Mark 10:28-30). Thus Paul suffered the loss of all things which were formerly gain to him, accounting all things but loss and dung that he might win Christ (Philippians 3:4-10). When a man's mind and heart is thus razed, when contrary laws and writings are thus expunged and defaced out of them, then

---

[194] Acts 2:35-36
[195] Galatians 3:10, Ephesians 2:3, Romans 6:23
[196] 2 Corinthians 10:4, etc.
[197] Romans 7:23
[198] John 8:44
[199] 1 John 2:16 & Ephesians 2:1-3
[200] Romans 7:9, Matthew 10:37-39, Philippians 3:4, etc.
[201] Luke 9:23, Matthew 10:37-39, Luke 14:26-34, Titus 2:11-12

these tables are in an excellent degree of preparedness for God's writing of his laws therein. For until this is done, there is no room for God's laws: different laws, contrary laws cannot both at once be there written. This is that which God notably intimates in his excellent promise: *And the LORD thy God will circumcise thine heart, and the heart of thy seed, To love the LORD thy God with all thine heart, and with all thy soul, that thou mayest live.*[202] Mark, God will first circumcise the heart of them and their seed, that is, he will raze out all other laws of sin, the world and Satan, he will pare [cut] off the old blots and blurs of corruption, he will wipe out and deface the old writing, etc. And then they shall *love the LORD with all their heart, and with all their soul* – that is, when the heart shall be thus circumcised, thus razed, then it will be prepared for the inscription of the law therein, then the sincere and entire love of God which is the great commandment of the law shall be graven there, shall be acting there, and shall have dominion there.

{3} Finally, God mollifies and softens the mind and heart, he makes them pliant and flexible to receive this better writing of his laws upon them. God turns the heart's stoniness into fleshiness.[203] A stony heart will take no impression of God's laws; a fleshy heart will receive any. Now God most kindly melts and thaws the heart of a sinner by his Covenant of Faith, and especially by his New Covenant, through the cooperation of his Spirit applying it. For the Covenant of Faith lets him see the riches of God's free grace in Jesus Christ as the sinner's surety, enduring the curse, appeasing God's wrath, fulfilling all righteousness, etc. for the sinner, that the sinner may be adopted into God's family in the right of Christ, may be justified in the sight of God by Christ's righteousness through faith, and may be eternally saved by Christ's merits. The Covenant of Faith tells him that God will inwardly frame his heart with grace, to observe all his laws; will supernaturally instruct him in the knowledge of the Lord; will in Christ be pacified towards all sorts and degrees of his sins,

---

[202] Deuteronomy 30:6
[203] Ezekiel 36:26

so as to remember them no more, but forgive and forget them forever – yea, that he will be his God, and he shall be one of his people.[204] Now when the poor sinner perceives such a door of hope opened for him, such a flood of mercy and grace flowing in upon him, that God will do all this because he will, because it is his mere pleasure; Oh how this infinite goodness of God in Christ, laid to heart by the Spirit's assistance, melts, softens and even overcomes the soul. Now his mind and heart – his opinion, his affection, his disposition – are wonderfully altered towards God, towards Christ, towards his law, and towards all his ways. Now he does not count God as formerly, an enemy or a hard master, but a friend indeed, a most gracious and compassionate God, not only requiring duty, but giving ability; not only discovering misery, but assuring of the eternal and all-sufficient remedy against it. Now he looks not upon the law of God, as a rigorous, harsh and heavy yoke: but as holy just and good, as a sweet and easy yoke in Christ, and as a comfortable rule of life and obedience. Now when the mind and heart are thus prepared by hewing, by razing, by softening them: Then comes the Spirit of God and gives his laws into their minds, writes them in their hearts. This is very observable, if we compare this clause of this New Covenant: *I will give my laws into their mind, and write them upon their hearts*;[205] together with that passage of Paul elsewhere: *Ye are our epistle, written in our hearts, known and read of all men. Forasmuch as ye are manifestly declared to be the epistle of Christ, ministered by us, written not with Ink, but with the Spirit of the living God: not in tables of stone, but in fleshly tables of the heart.*[206] Hereby he intimates to us: (i) that the heart must first be prepared as tables to write on; (ii) that these tables of the heart are then especially prepared for this writing, when they are not hard, stony, but soft fleshly tables. Then the Spirit writes God's laws there; then they become Christ's own epistle. Thus of God's preparing their minds and hearts, for writing his laws therein. This is the first thing.

---

[204] Hebrews 8:10-12 & 10:16-7, Jeremiah 31:33-34
[205] Hebrews 8:10 & Jeremiah 31:33
[206] 2 Corinthians 3:2-3

[2] *God's way and manner of writing his laws in their minds and hearts thus prepared for it.* The apostle – alluding (as Calvin well observes)[207] to the promise of the New Covenant in Jeremiah: *I will give my law into their inwards, and write it in their hearts*; and to the promise in Ezekiel: *I will take away their heart of stone, and will give them an heart of flesh* – shows that this New Covenant promise was fulfilled upon the Corinthians by means of his ministry among them, and that therefore, he was a minister of the New Testament, not of the old; of the Spirit, not of the letter unto them: saying: *Ye are our epistle written in our hearts, known and read of all men. Forasmuch as ye are manifestly declared to be the epistle of Christ, ministered by us, written not with ink, but with the Spirit of the living God: not in tables of stone, but in fleshly tables of the heart.*[208] In which words also he tacitly gives us to understand, God's ordinary way and manner of writing his laws in his people's hearts, now under this New Covenant, namely: {1} That the tables whereon this law is written, are not tables of stone, but fleshly tables of the heart. The epithet {*fleshly*} is not here taken in a bad but in a good sense, and signifies a soft, flexible, tractable heart, here opposed to stony, that is, an hard, stubborn, contumacious heart, as man's heart by nature is till it be subdued by the Spirit of God.[209] Man's heart must first become fleshly and flexible before God's law can be written therein. {2} That the pen or instrument wherewith usually God's law is written in the heart, is the minister of Christ. *The epistle of Christ, ministered by us.* Ministers are the instrumental mean, the pen in the hand of God, in the hand of Christ, in this writing; they can do nothing of themselves, they cannot print this writing upon the mind and heart, but as Christ guides them, acts them, uses them, and accompanies their ministry by his Spirit to make it pierce into the heart, and render it effectual there.[210] {3} That the spiritual ink wherewith this writing is

---

[207] John Calvin's commentary on 2 Corinthians 3:3
[208] 2 Corinthians 3:2-3 with Jeremiah 31:33 & Ezekiel 36:26
[209] John Calvin's commentary on 2 Corinthians 3:3
[210] 2 Corinthians 3:6 & 1 Corinthians 3:5-7

immediately drawn, is the Spirit of the living God. What ink does upon the paper, that the Spirit of God does upon the mind and heart. It is ink that makes the characters, the lines, the words, the writing: and leaves them remaining upon the paper that they may be read: if there be no ink in the pen, there can be no writing, though the pen be used never so much. It is the Spirit of God that effectually writes the prints and characters of God's laws upon the mind and heart. Without this Spirit, the ministry of man can write nothing there, not one law there. They are but ministers by whom men believe, but it is God only that gives the increase.[211] The instruments in this point are nothing; all the power, virtue and efficacy thereof is only of God by his Spirit.[212] {4} That the writer, the efficient of this writing, is God in Christ by his Spirit. They are all three here mentioned: the writing is the epistle of Christ, written by the Spirit of the living God; they all three co-operate, and ministers co-operate with them all, and all to produce this great work of writing God's laws in these fleshly tables. Whensoever therefore this blessed writing is delineated upon any man's heart, he is to look upon it as a mighty work of God, and not as the work of man upon his heart. He cannot write these laws upon his own heart; nor can the most excellent ministers in the world, no not apostles themselves, do it without God; and ordinarily, God will not do it without his ministers. Hence, ministers are necessary instruments, as pens in the hand of Christ, for this writing. To despise them, will be to deprive ourselves of this inscription, and to despise God's way of giving his laws into our minds and hearts. Thus, the laws of God are the writing, fleshly hearts are the tables, ministers of the gospel are the pens, the Spirit of God is as the ink, and God in Christ the writer. There is much of Christ in the mind and heart when the laws of God are written there. This is God's usual way.

[3] *The consequences and effects of this writing of God's laws upon the mind and heart, are distinct, and very considerable*, such as: {1} the

---

[211] 1 Corinthians 3:3, 5-7
[212] 2 Corinthians 4:6-7

universal answerableness of the heart within, to God's law without; {2} the renovation of the whole soul; {3} true knowledge of the will and all the ways of God, and unfeigned love to God and man; {4} sincerity of obedience from right principles; {5} a cheerful delight in the law of God; {6} legibleness of the writing; and {7} firmness and durableness of the impression. Let me open these particulars a little.

{1} A universal answerableness of the mind and heart within, to God's laws without. Mark, he does not say, "I will write this law or that law, this table or that table," but indefinitely, {*I will give and write my laws*} – that is, all my laws: here, none are excepted. Again, he does not say, "I will write them in their minds alone, or wills alone, or affections alone," but {*in their mind and hearts*} – that is, in their whole souls and all the powers or faculties thereof. As under the Old Covenant, when God's laws were written on tables of stone, *the tables were written on both their sides, on the one side and on the other were they written*;[213] the tables were written all over, they were all full of the law, there was no vacant space; so here under the New Covenant, the spiritual tables shall be written on every side, on every faculty and affection, the whole law shall be written all over them, the mind and heart shall be full of the law. Before this writing, there was an universal contrariety; but since then, there is a universal correspondence, between God's laws and their hearts. Now there is a spiritual law within, called {*the law of the mind*},[214] answering in every point to the literal law without: as the counterpain answers to the original deed, as the print answers to the stamps, as the impression in the wax answers to the seal, as the image in the glass answers to the face, eye for eye, part for part, proportion for proportion, color for color. There is such a general conformity, compliance, and tendency of the mind and heart to and with the laws of God, that they have a sweet aptness and disposition to have

---

[213] Exodus 32:15
[214] Romans 7:23

respect to them all. *Then shall I not be ashamed, when I have respect to all thy commandments.*[215]

{2} **The renovation of the mind and heart, even of the whole soul by the Holy Spirit, according to the image of God in knowledge, righteousness, and true holiness.**[216] This is another consequent or concomitant of God's writing his law in the heart. Whilst Adam had the law of God in his heart, he retained the image of God in his heart wherein he was created; and when man receives the law of God supernaturally written in his heart, he receives the image of God also into his heart, wherein he is newly created. There cannot be a supernatural writing of the law in the heart, and conformity of the heart to the law, but also there must needs be the image of God renewed there, wherein this conformity consists. Holiness conforms the heart to the whole first table, righteousness conforms it to the whole second table, and knowledge completes this conformity to both. This renewing of the whole soul, mind, and heart after the image of God, is (as I said) another consequence following, or a concomitant accompanying God's writing of his law in the mind and heart. It may be accounted a consequence following upon it, forasmuch as this inscription of God's laws in the heart leaves this renewed state behind it upon the heart, the image of God remains there, and abides there ever after. It may also be counted a concomitant accompanying it, forasmuch as God's writing his law in the heart and mind, and his renewing the whole soul, are effects of divine grace wrought both at once in the soul; yea for substance they are both one, this renewing of the Holy Spirit being the heart's conformity to the law of God.[217]

By this, it is evident that this promised blessing of writing Gods' laws in their minds and hearts, is very comprehensive. It comprises in it: (i) God's giving of his Spirit into their hearts, whereby this writing of the law shall be

---

[215] Psalm 119:6
[216] Colossians 3:10, Ephesians 4:24, Titus 3:5
[217] Romans 7:22-23

delineated there;[218] (ii) The supernatural principles and habits of saving grace infused into the soul: which are called {*the image of God*} (Ephesians 4:24, Colossians 3:10), {*the new man*} (Ephesians 4:24), {*the law of their mind*} (Romans 7:23), {*the life of God*} (Ephesians 4:18), {*the divine nature*} (2 Peter 1:4), {the law of the Spirit of life in Christ} (Romans 8:2-3), as also the original and fundamental actings of the Spirit to the infusion of these principles, which acts are styled {*renovation*} (Titus 3:5), {*regeneration*} (Titus 3:5, John 3:3, 5 and 1:12), {*new creation*} (2 Corinthians 5:17), {*vocation*}, namely: {*effectual vocation*} (Romans 8:30; 1 Peter 2:9), and {*sanctification*} (1 Peter 1:2; 1 Corinthians 6:11). All of these and such like particulars are comprehended in this sweet promise of God's writing his laws in his people's minds and hearts. So that this is a very pregnant, full and rich promise.

{3} **True knowledge of God's will and all his ways, in Christ: and unfeigned love to God and man.** (i) God's laws are given into their mind, hence, the mind must needs have a true knowledge of God's will and all his ways, in Christ. For God's laws do summarily comprise in them the will and ways of God wherein we should walk, namely: all his ways of religion towards God, in the first table, and all his ways of righteousness towards man, in the second table. When the laws of God are within the mind, there is a true, inward, radical and infallible principle of knowledge there – and this a knowledge in Christ; forasmuch as, when men have the laws of God thus written in their minds and hearts, they are the epistle of Christ, this writing there is the special work of Christ by his Spirit, this is part of Christ's New Covenant work.[219] This knowledge is an excellent inlet into obedience, and consequently unto happiness: *If ye know these things, happy are ye if ye do them.*[220] (ii) God's laws are written in their hearts, hence unfeigned love to God and man (which is the very sum and abstract of all God's laws)[221] must needs

---

[218] 2 Corinthians 3:3
[219] 2 Corinthians 3:3, etc.
[220] John 13:17
[221] Matthew 22:36-41

be deeply engraven in their hearts also. For love is the life of the law, the end of the law,[222] the fulfilling of the law, the substance and abridgement of the whole law.[223] Love to God with all the heart, soul, mind and might, is the first and great commandment, namely: the sum of the first table; and love to our neighbor as to ourselves is the second like unto it, namely: the sum of the second table.[224] So that the law of God cannot be written in any heart: but consequently the love of God and man must needs be deeply engraven upon that heart. Now this twofold love must be unfeigned, for what is written in the mind and heart, is real, cordial, unfeigned, without dissimulation, formality or hypocrisy. By the sincerity of this love in the heart, we may notably discover that the laws of God are written there also.

{4} Sincerity of obedience from right principles of true knowledge and unfeigned love. This is another excellent effect of God's writing his law in the mind and heart: It makes him sincerely obedient from right principles. Before God's law is written in the heart, a man may perform many acts of obedience to the law, as, Herod *did many things*;[225] so the Pharisees performed many things; and Paul before his conversion, was touching the law a Pharisee, touching the righteousness of the law blameless;[226] but all that they did was from wrong principles, from fear of men, hope of popular applause, carnal expectation of justification by the work done, etc. These are but odd accidental and carnal principles to act upon; and all such actions are but forced and violent motions, as of a stone cast upwards, which is contrary to its natural motion and inward principle, they are unsound and hypocritical, therefore God disregards and abhors them. But after the law of God is written in a man's heart, then he obeys sincerely from a right inward and cordial Principle which is in his heart. The law of God is within, therefore he

---

[222] 1 Timothy 1:5
[223] Romans 13:8-10
[224] Matthew 22:36-41
[225] Mark 6:20
[226] Matthew 5 & 6, Luke 18:11-12, Philippians 3:5

cordially, inwardly, connaturally obeys this law. His motion is not a violent and forced, but a natural motion. His obedience springs out of his heart, He obeys in knowledge, He knows, and then does;[227] he obeys in love, *out of a pure heart and a good conscience, and faith unfeigned*[228] – here are right principles: such obedience is sincere, the heart and the act, the inward principle and the outward practice do agree. Here is no hypocrisy, no counterfeit deportment in such obedience. That is the purest honey that drops from the comb freely without squeezing, that is the purest and most generous wine that flows from the grape freely with the least pressing, that is the purest and most genuine motion that comes from an innate inward principle of nature, without external forcing; so that is the most sincere pure obedience to God that naturally flows from the principle of the law within, from the image of God, true grace, and love within the heart and soul. These principles breed an aptness, a proneness, a familiar, habitual, connatural disposition in the soul to obey, and it cannot choose but incline to such obedience from this supernatural bias that is set upon the heart.

{5} **A cheerful delight in the law of God, and in the obedience thereof.** This is another effect of God's law in the heart: it makes a man delight exceedingly in it, delight to know it, delight to meditate in it, delight to be conform to it, delight to do it, and perform the will of God in it. Paul said: *I delight in the law of God after the inward man.*[229] The truly godly and blessed man has this property: *His delight is in the law of the LORD, and in that law will he meditate day and night.*[230] David also acknowledged that from God's law written within – he had a delight to do God's will: *I delight to do thy will, O my God: yea thy law is in the midst of my bowels*, or *within my heart.*[231]

---

[227] John 13:17
[228] 1 Timothy 1:5
[229] Romans 7:22
[230] Psalm 1:1-2
[231] Psalm 40:8

Herein David was a special type of Jesus Christ, whose meat was to do the will of him that sent him, and to finish his work.[232]

When God's law is in the heart, then the very bent, disposition, inclination, tendency, and whole stream of the heart and affections is towards this law of God, and the observance of it, and that cheerfully, pleasantly, delightfully. Whatsoever a man does from this inward principle of God's law and engrafted propensity of the heart, he does not only in uprightness, but also with great alacrity and delightfulness. It is his meat and drink to be doing it, and beyond his appointed food. He delights in it, as the fish in the water, as the foul in the air, which is their proper element; so the law of God is his element, he would still be and live in this element. He delights to know God, to believe in him, to love him, to observe him, to worship him according to his will, to honor his name, to sanctify his sabbaths, to be doing all good to his brother: He is never well, but when he is dutifully walking with God, and using means to further his obedience. If there were no heaven to reward obedience, no hell to punish disobedience, yet he would fear the Lord, and delight greatly in his commandments.[233]

Oh what high esteem had David of the laws of God, beyond honey and honey-comb, beyond rich spoils, beyond thousands of gold and silver, beyond all riches; he counted them his counselors, his heritage forever, and the rejoicing of his heart. His spirit was endeared to them, and ravished with them exceedingly: *I love them exceedingly. – Oh how love I thy law, it is my meditation all the day, – My soul breaketh for the longing that it hath unto thy judgments at all times.*[234] But now on the contrary when God's law is not written in the heart, there is an extreme antipathy, averseness and enmity to it.[235] A man counts it as a hard, rigorous law, an intolerable yoke, could wish there never had been any such law to chain him up, and restrain him from his

---

[232] Hebrews 10:7, John 4:34
[233] Psalm 112:1
[234] Psalm 119:10, 3, 162, 127, 14, 14, 24, 111, 167, 97, 20 – read diligently the whole psalm.
[235] Romans 8:7

lusts and corruptions. he hates it, and the obedience thereof, it is very bitter, burdensome, and gravaminous [grievous] to his spirit.

{6} **The legibility of this writing.** When God writes his laws in men's hearts, he makes them legible and discernible there: they may be seen and read there: as when he wrote the law upon the two tables of stone – it was legible there; Moses was able to read it.[236] Now this law written in their hearts is legible – of God, of themselves, and of others.

(i) *Legible of God.* The Lord exactly discerns and reads his own writings in the heart. He fully knows what is in man,[237] he searches the reins and hearts of all men,[238] but he specially beholds with favorable acceptation such persons hearts as have his law in them, his image, his graces, his sanctifying endowments, etc. to such will he look;[239] such are men after his own heart (as David was), to fulfill all his will.[240]

(ii) *Legible of themselves.* They that have the law of God written in their hearts, can read it and discern it there, as David did: *Thy Law is within my heart*; Hebrew: {*Thy law is in the midst of my bowels*}.[241] There is a white stone given by Christ to some, and in the stone *a new name written, which no man knoweth* (namely: certainly and infallibly) *but he that receiveth it.*[242] Now a man may discover the law of God that is written in his heart: partly, by the apprehensiveness of his own spirit and conscience – *What man knoweth the things of a man, save the spirit of man which is in him?*[243] – partly, by the evidence and discoveries thereof by the Spirit of God. *Now we have received, not the Spirit of the world, but the Spirit which is of God, that we might know the things that are freely given to us of God.*[244] Partly, By the light of the law

---

[236] Deuteronomy 4:13
[237] John 8:25
[238] Revelation 2:23
[239] Isaiah 66:2
[240] Acts 13:22
[241] Psalm 40:8
[242] Revelation 2:17
[243] 1 Corinthians 2:11, Romans 8:16
[244] 1 Corinthians 2:12

written in the heart. The law put in the heart brings a spiritual light with it, whereby it may be discovered, as a diamond set in gold brings an orient sparkling with it, whereby it may be discerned. *The commandment of the LORD is pure, enlightening the eyes.*[245] – *The entrance of thy words giveth light, it giveth understanding unto the simple.*[246] When the sun or a star arises, they bring their natural light with them, and thereby discover themselves to the world; so when the day-star of grace and law of God arise in a man's heart, they bring their spiritual light with them, and so manifest themselves unto the soul. Partly, by the great and wonderful alteration which is made in the heart and soul by the writing of the law therein. It was stony, it is fleshly; it was rebellious, it is obsequious; it was full of hatred and enmity against God, it is full of amity and love to God, etc. There is a mighty change. Now great alterations of state are great demonstrations; a passage from one contrary state to another is very conspicuous.

(iii) **Legible also to others**. Though others cannot infallibly read the law of God written in their hearts, yet charitably and probably, they may read it, by the preparatives, properties, and consequences of such writing. Hence said Paul to his Corinthians: *Ye are our epistle, written in our hearts, seen and read of all men; forasmuch as ye are manifestly declared to be the epistle of Christ ministered by us*, etc.[247] Thus the law of God written in the heart is legible. And yet it is true that it is not always alike legible to ourselves and others. Sometimes, as in infancy of grace, the characters are very small; sometimes, they are so blurred and rubbed off by lapses and infirmities, that it is much ado to discover the writing, although there be a true writing there.

{7} **Finally, the firmness and durableness of the laws impression upon the mind and heart.** God gives it; God writes it in mind and heart.[248] By these two expressions, he intimates how firmly and strongly he conveys his laws into

---

[245] Psalm 19:8
[246] Psalm 119:130
[247] 2 Corinthians 3:2-3
[248] Hebrews 8:10

the mind and heart, that they may never be obliterated or worn out. Writings in the dust may be blown out with a puff of wind, writings in paper may be fetched out by art, yea writings in marble or dead materials may wear away; but God will write his laws in lasting tables: in mind and heart. There they shall be engraven deeply and indelibly more deeply than any acquired habits, they shall become connatural to the heart, they shall be incorporated into the very frame of the soul, they shall make such impression as shall never out, nay death itself shall not be able to deface this record; but the laws of God – once written by God upon the mind and heart – shall remain as long as those spiritual tables shall remain, that is, forevermore. These are the excellent fruits, effects or consequences of God's writing his laws in his federates' minds and hearts.

Question 4: Were God's laws not written in his people's minds and hearts before the time of this New Covenant?

The reason of this question is, because this New Covenant is here said to be *not according to the covenant made with the fathers*, etc,[249] and this is laid down as the first particular point wherein the New Covenant should differ from the Old, namely: that now God would give his laws into their mind, and write them in their hearts, which seems to import that his laws were never so written in the heart before – which to assert, seems very strange; especially seeing the New Covenant is substantially one and the same with former Covenants, and God's federates of Old were partakers of renovation in and after the image of God, as well as since the New Covenant.

Answer: For clear resolution to this question, these two things are to be heedfully considered, namely:

(1) That before the time of this New Covenant there was some kind and manner of God's writing his laws in the hearts of his people, as:

[1] *A natural writing of the substance of his moral laws in the heart of Adam in his innocence, under the Covenant of Works.* This is evident, partly by the integrity and uprightness of man in his first creation in the image of God: which was his conformity to God's law;[250] partly, by the work of the law in some measure written upon the hearts of pagans, who never had the written law.[251] If so much of the law remains in man's corrupt nature, how completely was it written in man's perfect nature? Now this writing of the law in Adam's heart, was only natural and concreated: it was such a writing as belonged and was agreeable to the pure primitive state and constitution of

---

[249] Hebrews 8:8-10, Jeremiah 31:31-33
[250] Ecclesiastes 7:29, Genesis 1:26-27
[251] Romans 2:14-15

man in his very creation. He had it only naturally from God as Creator, not supernaturally from God as Redeemer.

[2] *A supernatural writing of God's moral law, for the substance of it in the hearts of his people, after the fall, under the Covenant of Faith.* This is evident: partly, because God's people under the Covenant of Faith and before the time of the New Covenant had in effect some such thing promised to them, as God's circumcising their hearts to love him,[252] his putting his fear into their hearts that they should not depart from him,[253] his giving of his Spirit into their hearts, together with many excellent influences of the Spirit,[254] formerly explained.[255] What were these supernatural blessings, but principles of grace conforming them to the law of God, and the writing of God's laws in their hearts? Partly, because before the time of the New Covenant God's people experimentally received such an inscription of God's laws upon their hearts, as appears by their renovation, their inward principles, their holy practises, and sometimes their express acknowledgements hereof.

Thus: [1] under God's Covenant with Adam: Abel was a believer, and his works righteous;[256] Enoch a believer, and walked with God.[257] [2] Under God's Covenant with Noah: Noah was a believer, upright in his generations, walked with God, and moved with fear, and by God's warning obediently made an ark.[258] [3] Under God's Covenant with Abraham: Abraham believed in the Lord, walked before God, was perfect; most obedient to God's call and commands, to follow him (even *ad coecam obedientiam*) although he knew not whither; and commanded his children and household after him to keep the way of the Lord.[259] So Isaac, a believer, feared God.[260] Jacob, a believer,

---

[252] Deuteronomy 30:6
[253] Jeremiah 32:39-40
[254] Ezekiel 36:26-27, etc.
[255] In Book 3, Chapter 6, Aphorism 2, Section 1
[256] Hebrews 11:4; 1 John 3:12
[257] Hebrews 11:5-6, Genesis 5:22, 24
[258] Hebrews 11:7, Genesis 6:9
[259] Hebrews 11:8-20, Genesis 15:6 & 17:1 & 18:19
[260] Hebrews 11:80, Genesis 31:53

wrestled with God in prayer and prevailed, etc.[261] [4] Under God's Sinai Covenant with Israel: Moses an eminent believer and an excellent self-denier;[262] Caleb and Joshua, men of another spirit, followed the Lord fully;[263] and Gideon, Barack, Jephthah, Samson, etc, were also renowned believers.[264] [5] Under God's Covenant with David: David himself was a man after God's own heart,[265] and himself confesses: *I delight to do thy will, O my God, yea thy law is within my heart*; Hebrew: {*in the midst of my bowels*}.[266] [6] Finally, under God's Covenant with the captives, God assured them of a new heart and a new spirit, promising to take away their heart of stone, and to give them an heart of flesh, that they might walk in his statutes, and keep his ordinances, and do them.[267] By all this, it is very evident that in some sort, God did supernaturally write his laws in the minds and hearts of his people before the time of this New Covenant. I say, *supernaturally*, because whatsoever writing of this sort is savingly printed upon any man's heart since the fall under the Covenant of Faith in any administration thereof, is wrought by Christ the Redeemer, by the supernatural efficacy of his Spirit. Every such writing is the epistle of Christ: his grace, his Spirit, his efficacy, his image, is illustriously evident therein. This is the first thing to be considered, by way of concession.

(2) **That notwithstanding all this, thus granted, until the time of this New Covenant God's Laws were not so written in his people's hearts as since they have been.** This is very evident, if we take notice how far the manner, efficacy and extent of this New Covenant administration, differed from, and transcended all federal administrations that went before it –

---

[261] Hebrews 11:21, Genesis 32:24 to the end
[262] Hebrews 11:23-29
[263] Numbers 14:6, 24, 38
[264] Hebrews 11:31-32
[265] Acts 13:22
[266] Psalm 40:8
[267] Ezekiel 36:26-27, etc. & 11:19-20

answerable unto which is God's manner, efficacy, and extent of writing of his laws, especially under the Old and New Testament.

[1] The manner of God's former covenant administrations was more carnal and external, and ran for the most part upon carnal and outward blessings, as to the letter of them. As, bruising the serpent's head by the seed of the woman;[268] preservation in the ark from the flood of waters that drowned all the world;[269] the inheritance of Canaan, long life and prosperity there;[270] the continuance and glory of David's throne and kingdom to his seed;[271] the redemption of the captives out of Babylon and restitution of them into their own land, etc.[272] And proportionably, God's manner of writing his laws was more carnal and external, namely: in two tables of stone (Deuteronomy 4:13; 2 Corinthians 3:3, 7). But the manner of God's New Covenant administration is more spiritual and internal, mostly consisting of inward spiritual blessings. Yea as to the letter of the Covenant, it wholly runs upon spirituals altogether (Jeremiah 31:31-34, Hebrews 8:8–13). And proportionally, God's manner of writing his laws is spiritual and inward: not in tables of stone, but in the soft fleshly tables of the mind and heart (Jeremiah 31:33, Hebrews 8:10; 2 Corinthians 3:3). This different form and manner of the Old and New Covenants' administration is much to be noted, which eminently holds forth such a different writing of God's laws: *that*, in literal tables of stones; *this*, in spiritual tables of the mind and heart.

[2] The efficacy of former administrations was very weak and small, in comparison to this New Covenant administration which is great and powerful. *Under those*, the Holy Spirit was but as it were sparingly sprinkled upon them.[273] Their knowledge and love of God was dark, feeble, childlike;[274]

---

[268] Genesis 3:15
[269] Genesis 6:14-22
[270] Genesis 15:18-21 & 17:1-9, Exodus 20:12 & 28:1-15
[271] 2 Samuel 7:12-13, etc, Psalm 89:2-3, etc & 132:11-12, etc
[272] Ezekiel 37:1 to the end
[273] John 7:37-39
[274] Galatians 4:1-3

their hearts were very stony, hard, and inflexible, as God intimated to them in writing his laws upon stones, etc. But *under this*, the Holy Spirit is plentifully poured forth as in streams and rivers upon them; and into them.[275] Their knowledge and love of God is clear, strong, ripe, man-like; their hearts very fleshy and flexible to God and his will, etc. Hence, the Old Testament ministration is called {*the ministration of the letter*} that condemns and kills, namely: an ineffectual ministration, showing the letter of the duty and death in case of non-performance, but affording no ability for that duty; but the New Testament ministration is called *the ministration of the Spirit that quickeneth*, and is a *ministration of righteousness*, namely: an effectual and powerful ministration, that affords sufficiency of ability for the duty which it requires.[276] Hence, the Spirit is said not to be given until Christ was glorified – not as if it had not been given at all, but because it was bestowed so sparingly and slenderly, in comparison to what is now, that it might seem not to be given at all.[277]

[3] The extent of former covenant administrations, was but to particular families, as of Adam, Noah, Abraham, David; or to some particular tribes, as to the captives of Judah and Benjamin; or to a select nation, as to the Jews at Mount Sinai. Alas, how few, what a small handful were all these to the rest of the world! And yet of this small number, how few were there that had any saving inscription of God's laws upon their hearts at all? And we say, *Minimum in magne nihil*: a small thing in that which is great is as nothing; a drop is as nothing in the sea, a grain of sand is as nothing in the earth; so the writing of God's laws in the hearts of so few, is as nothing in the world But the extent of this New Covenant administration is universal, to all nations in the whole world, and consequently, God's writing of his laws in men's hearts is proportionably extended to all God's people in all those nations:[278] to many

---

[275] Isaiah 44:3-5, Joel 2:28-29, etc, John 7:39, Acts 2:2-3, etc.
[276] 2 Corinthians 3:6 to the end
[277] John 7:39
[278] Matthew 28:19-20

thousands and ten thousands more than under all former covenant expressures.

Thus the Lord under this New Covenant writes his laws in his people's hearts: {1} not *naturally*, as at first in Adam's heart in his state of creation, under the Covenant of Works; but *supernaturally*, by the Spirit of Jesus Christ, restoring them from their state of corruption under the Covenant of Faith: And this {2} not so imperfectly as under foregoing covenant administrations, but much more perfectly and completely in efficaciousness and extensiveness. The chiefest of former Covenants – the Old Covenant holding forth, in the public and open administration of it – only a writing of God's laws in stones; this New Covenant, in the open and manifest administration of it, revealing only a writing of God's laws in the minds and hearts of God's federates.

Question 5: Why will the Lord write his laws in the minds and hearts of his federates, now under the New Covenant? And why does God covenant thus to do?

Answer: The Lord does covenant this, and will accordingly thus write his laws in the minds and hearts of his covenant people now under the New Covenant:

(1) **Because he will.** The mere good pleasure of his will, and his free commiserating grace is the only original moving cause inclining him hereunto. *I will give my laws into their mind, and I will write them in their hearts.*[279] God's federates cannot deserve this blessing of themselves more than others, but God will peculiarly confer it upon them of the riches of his mere grace, which he now under the New Covenant displays more eminently and gloriously than ever (Ephesians 2:4-11).

(2) **Because God intended this New Covenant to be a far more perfect and excellent expressure than the Old Covenant.** *Behold – I will make a new covenant – not according to the covenant which I made with their fathers.*[280] Why? Wherein shall this New Covenant excel and be more perfect? Herein God says: "My Old Covenant was but written in tables of stone, but my New Covenant shall be engraven upon better tables, upon the mind and heart."[281] This better writing, these better tables, will make this a better Covenant. God's Covenants were so ordered in their revealing, that the later was still better than the former; and the last, this New Covenant, the best of all.

(3) **Because God would more effectually provide against his people's breach of Covenant than formerly.** God brought all Israel into an excellent

---

[279] Jeremiah 31:33, Hebrews 8:10 & 10:16
[280] Jeremiah 31:31-33, Hebrews 8:8-10
[281] Deuteronomy 4:13; 2 Corinthians 3:3, 7

Covenant at Mount Sinai – that Old Covenant – and after he had published it to them by his own immediate voice, he wrote it upon two tables of stone; but presently they broke this Covenant by their idolatry in Aaron's calf, as Moses signified by breaking the tables before their eyes. Why did they so soon break this Old Covenant? Because it was not written in their minds and hearts, but only upon tables of stone: they had an outward rule, but they had not the inward principle of obedience, therefore they broke it. *Which my covenant they brake* (Jeremiah 31:32) *Because they continued not in my covenant, and I regarded them not, saith the Lord. For this is the Covenant that I will make with the house of Israel after those days saith the Lord: I will give my laws into their mind, and write them upon their hearts.*[282] As if he had said: "I will take a more effectual course in my New Covenant, to prevent their breach of covenant; their inconstancy and unsteadfastness in, and their apostasy from my Covenant is very offensive to me, therefore I will give them inward principles and abilities for performance of, and perseverance in my Covenant, I will not engraven my laws anymore in stones without them, but upon their minds and hearts within them, so that they shall be no more able to forget and forsake my laws and Covenant, then they can forget and forsake their own minds and hearts; thus they shall be constant, steady, and steadfast in my New Covenant."

(4) Because God had reserved the most plenary and efficacious donation of his Spirit, and all his gracious influences, until the days of Christ, and times of the New Covenant, as the Scriptures often intimate.[283] Hence God's most eminent, excellent, efficacious, complete and extensive writing of his laws in the minds and hearts of his federates (which is the immediate and special work of his Spirit,[284] and has in it complexively very many of the gracious influences, endowments, effects, and operations of the

---

[282] Hebrews 8:9-10
[283] See Isaiah 35:6-7 & 44:3-5, Joel 2:28-29, etc., John 7:37-39, Acts 2:16-21, 33
[284] 2 Corinthians 3:3

Spirit of God, as I have already manifested)[285] is also reserved till these days of Christ and of his New Covenant. The plenary donation of the Spirit is the fruit of Christ's actual exaltation and glorification. Then he himself *received from the Father the promise of the Holy Ghost*, that is: the promised Holy Ghost, and upon that receipt, shed forth the same upon his people – answerably, the Spirit's most plenary and perfect inscription of God's laws in his people's hearts, is the proper fruit of the Spirit's plenary donation.[286] Both of these are the glorious trophies of Christ's triumphant ascension into heaven, and exaltation at God's right hand – and by both of these, Christ is exceedingly extolled and magnified in his church.

(5) Finally, God will under his New Covenant write his laws in his people's minds and hearts, that the spiritual consequences and effects of such his writing of his laws therein may rest upon them, and really make them God's covenant people indeed.[287] This is eminently intimated in the connection of those two promises together: *I will put my laws into their mind, and write them upon their hearts: And I will be to them a God, and they shall be to me a people.*[288] As if he had said: "Hereby I will effectually declare and demonstrate myself to be their God in covenant, and will effectually make them my covenant people indeed – even by giving my laws into their minds, and writing them upon their hearts. Until this writing is drawn upon their souls, I and the sons of men are at a distance; there is no saving covenant relation, nor covenant interest between us, etc., but when this shall be once actually done upon the minds and hearts of any, then all this distance shall be removed from between me and them, then I will be theirs, and they shall be mine effectually and savingly, according to my New Covenant."

---

[285] In Question 3, the consequences and effects of this writing.
[286] John 7:39, Acts 2:33
[287] These consequences and effects, see in Question 3
[288] Hebrews 8:10

Question 6: How may we know whether God has given his laws into our minds, and written them upon our hearts?

Answer: We may know this: (1) by the antecedents, (2) by the manner, and (3) by the consequences of God's writing his laws in our minds and hearts, as has already been explained.

(1) **By the antecedents foregoing and preparing the mind and heart for God's writing his laws there.** As: [1] Has God hewn the tables of mind and heart by his spirit of bondage? (Romans 8:15). [2] Has God razed and obliterated out of the mind and heart all other laws, writings, and impressions which are inconsistent with these laws of God? Has he circumcised your heart, cutting off your natural corruptions?[289] Has he taken away the stone out of your heart?[290] Has he stripped you naked, and emptied you of yourself by self-denial?[291] [3] Has God mollified and softened these tables of thy mind and heart to receive the impression of his laws, by the heart-melting discoveries of the gospel, laying open the riches of divine wisdom, grace, and mercy in Christ for saving of sinners?[292]

(2) **By the way and manner of God's writing his laws in mind and heart**, namely: [1] by Christ, as his hand, his writer; [2] by his ministers, as his pens in the hand of Christ; [3] by the Holy Spirit, as his ink that immediately makes the characters; and [4] in fleshly, soft, flexible tables of mind and heart.

[1] Has Christ made his supernatural draught upon mind and heart? Is he the writer? Is the epistle Christ's,[293] or another's? Sin's? The world's? Satan's? Whose image and superscription is it, that is upon the heart? Are you new

---
[289] Deuteronomy 30:6
[290] Ezekiel 36:26 & 11:19-20
[291] Luke 9:23
[292] Ezekiel 36:26 & 11:19-20
[293] 2 Corinthians 3:3, etc.

creatures in Christ Jesus?[294] Are you *the workmanship of God created in Christ unto good works*, etc? Have ye *put on the Lord Jesus*? (Romans 13:14, Galatians 3:26-27). Christ is close at work in the soul, when God's laws are [written] there.

[2] Are the ministers of Christ his pens to delineate God's laws in your minds and hearts?[295] Do you prize, love, obey, and submit to them in the Lord in their ministrations, as instruments in the hand of Christ (1 Thessalonians 5:12-13, Hebrews 13:17; 1 Thessalonians 1:5-6, Galatians 4:14-15; 1 Corinthians 4:1). The Corinthians overvalued their ministers (1 Corinthians 1:12-13 & 3:4-6); the Galatians removed from theirs, and undervalued them (Galatians 1:6, etc). *Those* by accounting them above instruments; *these* by debasing them below instruments, and rejecting them for false teachers (the epidemic disease of these our times). But then we shall rightly value them, when we shall account them as ministers, as instruments, as pens in the hand of Christ. Are they ministers of the Spirit, or only of the letter to you?[296] Has their gospel come unto you, *not in word only; but also in power, and in the Holy Ghost, and in much assurance*?

[3] Has the Holy Spirit been the blessed ink that has immediately written God's laws upon your minds and hearts?[297] Has this ink been put by Christ into his pens? Has this Spirit co-operated with his ministers? Has he left his marks; his characters behind him upon your souls, or not?

[4] Have your minds and hearts been found fleshly, not stony tables, when Christ – by his Spirit and ministers – was going to write God's laws upon them?[298] Have they rejected, or received his impressions? Have they yielded to, or rebelled against his inscriptions? Have they been like melted metal, ready to run into the mold of God's laws, and to receive any impression thereof?

---

[294] 2 Corinthians 5:17
[295] 2 Corinthians 3:2-3, etc.
[296] 1 Thessalonians 1:5
[297] 2 Corinthians 3:3
[298] 2 Corinthians 3:3

(3) **By the consequences and effects, resulting from, and remaining after God's writing his laws in the mind and heart.** After writing, there are characters and words remaining, wherein the mind, meaning, and will of the writer is represented; so after God's writing his laws in the heart, God's mind and will remain upon the heart, in many particulars, as in:

[1] A universal answerableness of the heart to God's laws. Do you have a law within, fully answering to God's laws without? Is there a universal counterpain [bedspread] of God's laws delineated in your hearts?[299] Is there an entire conformity to all his laws? Where God savingly writes one, he writes all his laws in the heart: his laws of religion and his laws of righteousness.[300] There is nothing God prescribes, but the heart is disposed to do it; nothing God prohibits, but the heart is careful to decline it. Herod, the Pharisees, hypocrites, and pagans may have some partial conformity to God's laws in some things, but because it is only in some things, or in many things, and not in all things – God's laws are not savingly written there.

[2] A renovation of the whole soul according to God's image.[301] There cannot be in the mind and heart an entire conformity to the law of God, but by a transformed renovation of the whole soul according to the image of God in knowledge, righteousness, and true holiness. The old frame is so full of pravity, malignity, and enmity against God and his laws that there must be a renovation, regeneration, new-creation, conversion, sanctification, etc., or else there can be no conformity to God's laws. Are you thus renewed, regenerated, etc? Where is this image of God in the soul?

[3] True knowledge of the will and all the ways of God, and unfeigned love both to God and man. Gross ignorance cannot remain in the soul, when the law of God comes to be written there, any more than gross midnight darkness can remain in the hemisphere when the sun appears in the sky. Nor can true love to God and man be absent from the heart, wherein the law is

---

[299] Psalm 119:6
[300] Hebrews 8:10, Jeremiah 31:33
[301] Titus 3:5, Colossians 3:10, Ephesians 4:24

present: because such love is the law of God, and the law of God is love.[302] What light now of true knowledge of all God's will and ways shines in your minds? What life and holy flames of true love to God and man burn in your hearts?

[4] Sincere, cordial and entire obedience to God's laws from right principles of knowledge and love. Where God's laws are in the heart, the soul is strongly bowed, inclined, disposed and persuaded to all cordial, sincere, entire obedience, because it knows what is to be done, and because it loves to do what it knows.[303] Do you obey knowingly, understandingly?[304] Do you obey lovingly?[305] Then you cannot choose but obey cordially, sincerely, entirely. For Knowledge says: "Everything is to be done that God requires," and Love says: "I am heartily willing to do everything that is to be done."

[5] Cheerful delight in the law of God. Such as is the inscription in the heart, whether of the law of sin, or law of God, etc. Such is the disposition and genuine temper of the heart; now such as is the temper and disposition of the heart, such is the delight of the heart. The heart delights most in that which is most homogeneal and connatural to it; so when the law of God is made homogeneal and connatural to the heart, by being written therein, the heart cannot choose but delight therein exceedingly. What delight now does your inner man have in the law of God, to meditate therein and do it?[306] Are the commandments of God joyous, or grievous?[307] Read David's affections to, and delights in God's law in Psalm 119, and see if yours are parallel.

[6] The legibility of this writing – not only by God, but also by themselves, and others.[308] Is God's law so written in your mind and heart that you yourself can read it within, in your constitution, so that both you and

---

[302] Matthew 22:36-41
[303] Psalm 40:8
[304] John 13:17
[305] 1 John 5:2-3
[306] Romans 7:22, Psalm 1:2 & 40:8
[307] 1 John 5:3
[308] 2 Corinthians 3:2-3

others can read it; without, in your conversation, that both yourself and others can see and read a general conformity and answerableness of your heart and life to God's whole law? If there be nothing, or nothing to the purpose, to be read of God's law in thine inward principles and outward practises; but rather the laws of sin and Satan, heaps of unmortified corruptions, scandals, and abominable offenses; then how can it be imagined that God's law is written in your mind or heart? If your own conscience and others' observation can behold no saving knowledge, but gross ignorance; no faith, but infidelity; no repentance, but impenitency; no fear of God, but audacious impiety; no love to God, but utter enmity; no true obedience, but notorious rebellion; no spirituality at all, but mere carnality; no regeneration, renovation and sanctification, etc. but an old, unregenerate, sinful state; then the law of God has as yet made no saving impression at all upon your soul.

[7] Finally, the permanency and durability of this impression. What is written by God in mind and heart will never out. No time, no temptation, no tribulation, no persecution – no, not nature's dissolution, can utterly obliterate or expunge the same. The writing may be slurred, dimmed, defaced, and obscured by these things: but can never be totally razed and blotted out. Is the impression of God's law upon your heart vanishing, or continuing; fading or flourishing: dying, or living? Is the tincture of your heart in grain? Does your soul break for the longing that it has unto God's judgments at all times?[309] Is your delight in the law of the Lord, and do you meditate therein day and night?[310]

---

[309] Psalm 119:20
[310] Psalm 1:2

Inferences

Will the Lord thus give his laws into their minds, and write them upon their hearts; as has been explained and evidenced? Then hence these things follow, namely:

(1) **That God's moral law is the law of Christ.** How does this appear from what has been spoken? Thus: the law which God promises here to write in their hearts, is God's moral law formerly written upon tables of stone, as I have already proven.[311] Now God writes this moral law in their hearts by Christ and his Spirit, as I have also manifested:[312] whereupon they that have God's laws written in their hearts, are called {*the epistle of Christ – written not with ink, but with the Spirit of the Living God*}.[313] Forasmuch then as it is Christ, who by his Spirit writes God's moral laws in his people's hearts, these moral laws may justly be denominated {*the laws of Christ*}. Christ is the Author, and effectual writer of them in their hearts by his Spirit: therefore they are his. If the moral law is called the law of Moses because Moses was the instrument by whom God gave and revealed it;[314] then how much more may it be called {*the law of God*} because God gave it, published it on Mount Sinai, and wrote it with his own finger on tables of stone, and {*the law of Christ and of his Spirit*} because by them it is written upon the fleshly tables of the mind and heart. So that Jesus Christ, and the moral law are not (as some weakly imagine) inconsistent, incompatible, and irreconcilable: but most consistent, suitable, and sweetly agreeable one to another. Since man's fall, God never gave his moral law but in his Covenant of Faith in Christ. In Christ typified and promised under the Old Covenant, it was given in tables of stone; in Christ

---

[311] In this Aphorism 1, Question 1
[312] In Question 3
[313] 2 Corinthians 3:2-3, etc.
[314] Malachi 4:4, John 1:17

performed and exhibited under the New Covenant, it is given in fleshly tables of mind and heart; but in both there is much of Christ, much of his wisdom, much of his merit, much of his justice, much of his goodness, mercy, free-grace, and love, much of his power, much of his Spirit, etc. Christ in both predominates. Hence: [1] the more of God's moral law is supernaturally engraven in the mind and heart, the more of Christ is in the mind and heart. When Christ comes into the soul, he brings this law with him thither. If this law is effectively there, then Christ is actually there also. [2] Christ *came not to destroy the law, but to fulfill it*[315] – to fulfill it in his own person, actively doing for his elect all the duty required in it, which they could not do; passively enduring for them all the curse and penalty threatened in it to the transgressors thereof, which otherwise they could not avoid nor endure; to fulfill it also in his members, by writing it in their hearts, that they might be able in sincerity and integrity to observe it. [3] They that set Christ and the moral law at odds irreconcilably, do neither understand the mystery of Jesus Christ, nor of the moral law solidly.

(2) **That God's moral law is not abolished, but established by his New Covenant.** Why? Because God's writing of his laws in the hearts of his federates, is a primary promise, yea the very first article of his New Covenant: *I will give my laws into their mind, and write them in their hearts.*[316] Had God intended by his New Covenant to have abolished his moral law, he would not have New written it, but utterly have expunged it. But in that God undertakes to write his laws again, and to write them more durably and indelibly than they were written before, not in the long-lasting tables of stone, but in the everlasting tables of mind and heart; hereby he eminently confirms and establishes the moral law, as that which shall never be reversed or repealed until the end of this world – yea, the substance and soul thereof in love to God and man shall continue forever in the world to come. Hence:

---

[315] Matthew 5:17-18; see this expounded in Book 3 Chapter 4 Aphorism 1.

[316] Jeremiah 31:33, Hebrews 8:10 & 10:16 with Romans 3:31; this last place, see expounded in Book 3 Chapter 4 Aphorism 1.

[1] That grand antinomian error touching the utter abrogation of the moral law (that the law given by Moses at Mount Sinai is of no use at all for matter or form to Christians now under the New Testament) is to be abhorred and abandoned, as repugnant and destructive to the very substance and nature of this New Covenant. But I have already spoken at large to this effect: {1} In handling that intricate question, whether the law of God given by Moses on Mount Sinai to Israel, be abrogated to us now under the New Testament or not? And how far it concerns or obliges us, if not abrogated?[317] {2} In unfolding in general, how useful it is to all sorts: in particular, of what use it is to carnal persons, and of what use it is to the regenerate.[318] {3} In answering such material objections from Scriptures wrested and misunderstood, as antinomians make against the establishment and use of the moral law now under the New Covenant. And therefore for satisfaction in all these particulars, I refer the reader to the places here alleged in the margin, that I may not go over the same things again.[319]

[2] All detractive and reproachful speeches derogatory from the continued obligation force and use of the moral law to believers and regenerate persons now under the New Covenant, ought by all intelligent and conscientious Christians, especially ministers, to be utterly forborne and avoided. As those ignorant and unsavory expressions of some: "legal preachers," "legal Christians," "literal duty men," "Old Testament spirits," "Mosaical justiciaries," etc. For by such rotten, railing, and reviling language as this, they not only discover their gross ignorance in the mysteries of Old and New Covenant, and of the moral law, but also blasphemously traduce and calumniate both Jesus Christ and his New Covenant, and the infinite wisdom of God, who in them both has contrived to establish and perpetuate the use of his most perfect moral law to all his Old and New Covenant people.

---

[317] In Book 3, Chapter 4, Aphorism 1, Question 7
[318] In the same Question 7
[319] In Book 3, Chapter 4, Aphorism 1

(3) **That the New Covenant agrees with the Old in matter and substance, although they differ in manner and circumstance**, for: {1} the matter and substance of them both, is God's moral law, and that moral law written, and that writing made only by the Lord himself. Herein these two Covenants do plainly agree, and are materially one. {2} The manner and circumstance of writing this moral law by God is very different under these two Covenants. In the Old Covenant, God wrote it in tables of stone; in the New Covenant he writes in the fleshly tables of mind and heart. In the Old Covenant it was written without; in the New within. In the Old Covenant it was written more imperfectly, weakly, literally, and ineffectually. Though the people's hearts had some impression thereof upon them, yet they remained very stony, stubborn, and intractable notwithstanding; but in the New Covenant, it is written more perfectly, strongly, spiritually, effectually. The people's hearts are more mollified, flexible, tractable, and transformed into the image of the law of God.

(4) **That the moral law is a most excellent law.**[320] This is evident, by the singular care that God has taken in this his most excellent Covenant, the New Covenant, to hide, treasure up, and fixedly engrave his moral law upon the minds and hearts of his people. These are holy, heavenly, spiritual, lasting, and everlasting treasuries. Consequently, God's moral laws – written and laid up there – are choice, rich, and precious jewels, and so to be accounted by us. Oh what an invaluable estimate did holy David (that man after God's own heart, who had the law of God in his heart) set upon them![321] And most deservedly. Read and mark and imitate his affections and estimations of the laws of God.

It is very observable that the Lord has taken care to write his moral law, for the perpetuating thereof, three several ways, namely: [1] naturally, in the heart of Adam before his fall, under the Covenant of Nature, or of Works.[322] [2] Literally, upon tables of stone – and that twice under the Old Covenant

---

[320] See Book 3, Chapter 4, Aphorism 1, Question 7
[321] Acts 13:22, Psalm 40:8 with Psalm 19:7 to the end & 119 throughout
[322] Genesis 1:26-27, Ecclesiastes 7:29, Romans 2:14

given at Mount Sinai.[323] [3] Spiritually and most efficaciously, upon the spiritual fleshly tables of his people's minds and hearts, under the New Covenant.[324] The first writing was perfect, but not durable; the second was complete, but ineffectual; the third is entire, efficacious, and permanent. Now how high and excellent is this moral law of the Lord, which God has so often written with his own finger upon so many tables before and since the fall, and before and after Christ!

(5) **That naturally, since and by the fall of Adam, the laws of God are obliterated or blotted out of men's minds and hearts.** God's new writing his laws in the mind and heart supernaturally, shows that his old writing of his laws is blotted out of all men's hearts naturally. God's laws were once in man's heart before the fall so perfectly, that he was able fully in every point to keep it, and by his own actual keeping of it, completely to have wrought out and completed his own righteousness and life eternal in the sight of God;[325] but by man's fall and sin (which makes havoc of all blessings and mercies), God's law was so extremely wiped out of the heart of Adam and of all his posterity, that nothing at all thereof remains sufficient for man's justification, but only so much as to leave him without excuse and aggravate his condemnation.[326] Hereupon God provides for lapsed man a savior, a surety: Jesus Christ (in whose heart God's laws should be perfectly written,[327] and in whose death the penalty of the law broken by man's sin should be perfectly satisfied),[328] by and in whom the obliterated law should, first be revived and recorded in tables of stone under the Old Covenant, that hereby man might behold:[329] [1] what integrity he once had before he fell, [2] what sin and misery he was now naturally enwrapped in by his fall, [3] what exact righteousness and

---

[323] Deuteronomy 4:13 & 31:18 & 34:1, 28
[324] Hebrews 8:10; 2 Corinthians 3:3, etc.
[325] Genesis 1:26-27, Ecclesiastes 7:29, Romans 2:14
[326] Romans 2:14-16
[327] Psalm 40:8 with Hebrews 10:6-7, etc.
[328] Galatians 3:10, 13-14
[329] Deuteronomy 4:13

satisfaction according to this law is required in and from man's surety, Jesus Christ, for lapsed sinners' restoration to life and righteousness, as also [4] what entire, sincere and cordial conformity of heart and life to the law of God is expected from those that accept Jesus Christ for their Surety and Savior. Secondly, be given and written in spiritual tables of mind and heart under the New Covenant, that by this supernatural efficacy, the heart might be furnished with ability, for the performance of all duty which the law requires.[330] So then, sin has expunged God's law out of all men's hearts and minds by nature, until God again inscribes and engraves it there. Hence flows all the impiety and irreligion of man's heart and life against God, all his unrighteousness against man, all his intemperance and insobriety against himself, even from this: that God's law is razed and expunged out of his mind and heart by nature. Whereupon carnal man is naturally become the most savage, wild, brutish, unruly, rebellious, malicious, mischievous, and miserable creature that is on earth. Ah! how cursed and abominable is the nature of sin, that so woefully robs and despoils the hearts of the sons of Adam of this blessed and perfect law of God!

(6) That the renewing of the mind and heart – even of the whole soul, according to God's image, by effectual vocation, conversion, regeneration, new creation, and sanctification – is not a natural, but a mere supernatural work. It is not at all from man himself, but wholly from God alone. Why? Because it is not man, but God alone that gives his laws into their minds; not man, but God alone that writes his laws in their hearts.[331] Now this effectual vocation, conversion, regeneration, new-creation, sanctification, etc. is that wherein this his writing his laws in their minds and hearts according to the image of God, especially consists. The carnal mind is nothing but darkness, blindness, ignorance and sottishness;[332] the carnal heart is hardness, stoniness,

---

[330] Jeremiah 31:33, Hebrews 8:10 & 10:16; 2 Corinthians 3:3, etc.
[331] Jeremiah 31:33, Hebrews 8:10 & 10:16
[332] Ephesians 5:8, Acts 26:18, 2 Peter 1:8-9

impenitency, unbelief, deadness, senselessness; and both of them,[333] even the whole soul is enmity and malignity against God and his laws,[334] so that there remains nothing at all in mere carnal man that may contribute the least saving influence, efficacy or assistance to the writing of God's laws in mind or heart. This must be let alone, and wholly left to God forever. He alone prepared the first tables of stone, and he alone wrote thereon, the whole workmanship was his;[335] so here, he alone prepares the mind and hearts, he alone in Christ by his Spirit makes the inscription of his laws on the heart so prepared, and he alone leaves the effectual fruits and consequences of this inscription upon the soul: the preparatives, acts, and effects of this writing are all his. Man could obliterate God's laws out of his heart, but it is the peculiar and proper work of God only to write them again in the heart. This thing in effect I have formerly cleared, in answering that question: whether God alone can give a new heart, and put a new spirit into us – there see.[336]

(7) **God first gives his laws into the mind, and then writes them in the heart.** In this New Covenant promise, the mind is still put before the heart.[337] Naturally, the mind must first be informed with the light of truth, and knowledge of duty, before the heart can be conformed to the love of truth and performance of duty. Natural light was the first particular distinct creature which God made, when he created the world, and supernatural light is the first particular grace which God infuses into the soul, when he new-creates the heart.[338] To turn them from darkness to light, there is God's first work upon the mind,[339] namely: illumination; and from the power of Satan unto God, there is his next work upon the heart, will and affections, namely: effectual liberation, or actual restitution out of bondage into spiritual liberty: in both

---

[333] Ezekiel 36:26, Romans 2:4-5; 1 Timothy 1:13, Ephesians 2:1, 5
[334] Romans 8:7, Colossians 1:21, James 4:4; 1 John 2:15
[335] Exodus 32:15-16
[336] In Book 3, Chapter 6, Aphorism, Section 1
[337] Jeremiah 31:33, Hebrews 8:10 & 10:16
[338] Genesis 1:1-4, etc.
[339] Acts 26:18

their conversion, effectual vocation, regeneration, etc, and sanctification. Though God's acts of grace are *supernatural*, yet are they not *contranatural*, or *unnatural*: they excel nature, but do not destroy nature. The mind must still precede, to direct and guide the heart; and then the heart, the will and affections, will orderly follow and obey. The will naturally follows the ultimate direction and command of the understanding: as the rest of the body follows the guidance of the eye.[340] If God has illuminated your mind, there is good hope that he will bend and bow your heart. But if your mind is darkness, your will and affections can be nothing but crookedness.

(8) That God's giving his laws into our minds, and writing them in our hearts, is an eminent and manifold privilege. Forasmuch as every article of the New Covenant (and consequently this first) contains an eminent and manifold privilege for God's New Covenant people above all other people in the world, namely: not only above all pagans and heathens whatsoever, that are mere strangers to this, and to all God's Covenants of Faith; but also above all God's covenant people under all former covenant expressions whatsoever – this New Covenant in many regards far excelling and transcending them all, as hereafter in the general inferences will appear. Now the eminency and multiplicity of this privilege, of God's giving his laws into our minds, and writing them upon our hearts, herein particularly appears: namely:

[1] *In the eminent preparation of mind and heart to be fit spiritual tables for the writing of God's laws therein.* The very preparing of the heart hereunto is an eminent and manifold privilege, for:

{1} Hereby, the stony mind and heart are hewed away by the spirit of bondage, filling them with fear and terror, because of sin, the wrath and curse of God.[341]

---

[340] Voluntas sequitur ultimum dictamen intellectus.
[341] Ezekiel 36:26, Romans 8:15, Acts 2:35-36, etc.

{2} Hereby, the contrary laws and writings of sin, world, and Satan are obliterated and razed out of the mind and heart, to make way for the better inscription of the laws of God therein.[342]

{3} Hereby, the mind and heart are sweetly mollified and softened, at the evangelical discovery of God's rich grace, mercy, loving-kindness, compassions, goodness, wisdom and justice whereby the sinners salvation by Jesus Christ through faith is so admirably and all-sufficiently contrived and tendered.[343] Now these spiritual tables of mind and heart are prepared.

[2] *In the eminent and joint operation of Father, Son, and Holy Spirit to this inscription of his laws in the mind and heart by the instrumental subserviency of his New Testament ministers thereunto.*[344] This is his ordinary way – so infinite, glorious, and excellent an agent, as God blessed forever, denominates this act most excellent. What manner of privilege also is this, that the ever-living God should stoop so low as to write his laws in the minds and hearts of poor sinful dust and ashes! What familiar condescension to our frailty, that God should make use of the ministration of weak mortal men as instruments in this writing?

[3] *In the eminency and transcendent excellency of God's laws, namely: his moral laws, which he writes in mind and heart.*[345] No laws in the world can compare with God's laws, and no laws of God can compare with his moral laws, for all manner of excellency. How high an advantage then must it needs be to have so choice, rich, and precious a treasure as these laws put so effectually into these mean and despised cabinets!

[4] *In the eminent and intensive efficacy of God's giving his laws into our minds, and writing them in our hearts.*[346] The divine efficacy of this operation shines forth most illustriously in all those perfective alterations,

---

[342] Romans 6:23, John 8:44, Deuteronomy 30:6, Ezekiel 36:26, Luke 9:23
[343] Ezekiel 36:25-32, Zechariah 12:10-13; 2
[344] Hebrews 8:10 & 10:16; 2 Corinthians 3:3, etc.
[345] See in Book 3 Chapter 4 Aphorism 1 at large
[346] See formerly in Question 3 of this present Chapter

which thereby are wrought upon the minds and hearts of God's sincere New Covenant people, namely:

{1} An universal answerableness of the mind and heart within, to God's laws without.

{2} The renovation of the whole soul according to the image of God in knowledge, righteousness and true holiness.

{3} True knowledge of the will and all the ways of God, and unfeigned love to God and man.

{4} Sincerity of obedience from right inward principles.

{5} A cheerful delight and pleasure of soul in the laws of God.

{6} The legibleness of this writing, and the impressions thereof – not only to the omniscient eye of God, and charitable eye of man, but also to the experimental and discerning eye of every particular soul in some good measure, upon whose mind and heart God's laws shall be effectually and supernaturally written.

{7} The firmness and durability of this sacred impression of God's laws upon the soul – against all danger of its backsliding from God, or from his ways.

[5] *In the sweet and comfortable provision* which hereby God lays [down] for bruised sinners and distressed saints, against sundry of their puzzling and perplexing doubts and scruples, especially about the blindness of their minds, vileness of their hearts, and extreme inability to do anything in spirituals as God requires.[347] His law given into their mind, removes the blindness and gross ignorance of their mind; his law – written in their hearts – cures the abominable vileness, badness, and viciousness of their hearts; his laws engraven in both, supplies them with a sufficiency of ability sincerely to act what God expects.

[6] *Finally, in the extensiveness of this promise*, which is exceeding large and broad – even of God's writing: {1} His whole law, not only some part of it;

---

[347] In this 5th Chapter, Section 2, Doubts 3-5

{2} in the whole soul, mind and heart, not mind, or heart alone; [3] and that of all his true federates in all nations of the world, and not only (as under the Old Covenant) in the Jewish nation.

Thus, God's giving his laws into our minds, and writing them in our hearts, is a very eminent and manifold privilege.

(9) **That, all such as would know whether they are God's New Covenant people indeed – inwardly as well as outwardly, in power as well as in profession – should diligently examine whether God has given his laws into their minds, and written them upon their hearts, or not?**

For all those, and those only, that have God's laws thus effectually planted within them by the Spirit of the living God, are savingly partakers of an inward New Covenant state and interest in God through Jesus Christ.[348]

Question: But how may we know this, that God has given his laws into our minds, and written them in our hearts?

Answer: This I have discovered already, in answering the sixth question – there see.

(10) **Finally, that God's sincere New Covenant people have – above all other people in the world – the greatest cause to live and walk according to the laws – the moral laws of God, in that the Lord has more excellently and obligatorily given and written his laws for them, than for any other.** For:

[1] His moral law was written in Adam's heart under the Covenant of Works, *naturally*;[349] but now it is written in his people's hearts, under the New Covenant, *supernaturally*.

[2] The work of his moral laws, remains written upon the very hearts of pagans and heathens that have not the law by other writing or preaching revealed to them, brokenly, maimedly, confusedly;[350] those characters of the law being only some dark, dim, shattered, broken, confused, maimed relics and

---

[348] Hebrews 8:10, 10:16; 2 Corinthians 3:3, etc.
[349] Ecclesiastes 7:29, Genesis 1:26, Romans 2:14
[350] Romans 2:14-16

remains of the law which was naturally written in Adam's heart at his first creation; but now it is written upon the minds and hearts of God's people under the New Covenant, distinctly, clearly, integrally, in all the parts and integral perfections thereof, so that they have an universal answerableness to all, and an entire respect to all the commandments of God.[351]

[3] The moral law, under the Old Covenant, as to the apparent visible administration thereof, was written only in dead tables of stone literally;[352] and as to the inward application and operation thereof, it was written in the hearts of the truly believing Jews more obscurely, weakly, and imperfectly, according to the *minority* of the church in those times.[353] But now under the New Testament, as to the very administration thereof, it is promised to be written in the living tables of mind and heart, spiritually; and as to the application and operation thereof, it is written in the hearts of all believers – Jews and Gentiles – much more clearly, powerfully, efficaciously, and perfectly, according to the *maturity* of the church in those times. Thus God's laws are given and written for his people now under this New Covenant, every way more excellently, than ever they were before for any other: not naturally, but supernaturally; not maimedly, but integrally; not literally, but spiritually; not more weakly and imperfectly, but more powerfully and perfectly.

Now the more excellently God has given and written his laws for his sincere New Covenant people, the more strongly has he thereby laid his obligations upon them to live and walk according to those laws. The greater the mercy is, received from God, the greater and stronger is the tie for all answerable duty to God. Pagans are bound much, Jews much more, but Christians most of all, to the observance of God's laws, for Christians have, not only the natural relics of the law in them, which pagans have; not only the very letter of the law, which the Jews had; but also the spirit of the law more

---

[351] Psalm 119:6
[352] Deuteronomy 4:13
[353] Galatians 4:1-3

than either of them had.[354] If therefore the Christian walks contrary to God's laws, his sins will, of all others, be most heinous; and his condemnation will, of all others, deserve to be most grievous. Certainly their error is very gross, who think their Christianity absolves them from the observance of the moral law of God: for true Christianity, in the power of it, most forcibly obliges, and even compels them above anything else to the observance of God's moral laws. Therefore, O you regenerate soul, you Israelite indeed, you sincere Christian, think seriously: how strong an obligation God has laid upon your soul and conscience to live and walk uprightly according to all his moral laws, by giving them effectually into your mind, and writing them powerfully upon thine heart. You, of all others, ought to be a law to yourself;[355] you of all other ought to delight in the law of God in your inward man,[356] and meditate therein day and night;[357] you, of all others, should forbear what God forbids, and perform what God prescribes in his holy laws, etc. For furtherance and encouragement of every true-hearted Nathaniel herein, let these two things be heedfully considered, namely:

{1} Gospel directions for Christians' right observing, performing, and walking according to the moral law. These I have at large heretofore proposed.[358]

{2} Gospel grounds or motives inciting to this evangelical observance of the moral law. These also I have already abundantly urged.[359] And if antinomians themselves, whether in opinion or in practice, will but lay aside prejudice against the law of God so far, as deliberately, advisedly and seriously to read, consider and weigh (as in the presence of the living God, and great Lawgiver of Israel) those gospel directions for walking according to the moral law; and those gospel motives inciting thereunto, then I hope through the

---

[354] In the Hebrew text of Exodus 20:1, etc.
[355] Romans 2:13-14
[356] Romans 7:18
[357] Psalm 1:2
[358] In Book 3, Chapter 4, Aphorism 1, Inference 5
[359] In the same place

blessing of the heart-ruling God, who alone can effectually give and write his laws in his people's hearts, they may be a convincing, persuading and prevailing means to reduce the one from the error of his opinion unto truth, and to reclaim the other from the error of his way, unto godliness and righteousness.

Thus of the first article: God's giving his law into his people's minds, and writing them in their hearts.

Article 2

Of God's federate people's more excellent and more universal knowledge of the Lord, than under the Old Covenant.

The second particular (but more distinct) New Covenant blessing here promised, wherein this New Covenant differs from, and excels the Old Covenant, is; his federate people's more excellent, and more universal knowledge of the Lord than under the Old Covenant. *And they shall not teach every man his neighbour, and every man his brother, saying: Know the LORD; For all shall know me from the least to the greatest.*[360] This is a second particular wherein the New Covenant shall not be according to the Old Covenant which God made with the fathers, etc., but shall much differ from it, shall far surpass and transcend it, namely: in the federates' more excellent and more extensive knowledge of the Lord than was under the Old Covenant.[361]

This is evidently the scope and intent of the Holy Spirit in his promise of this mercy, as is unquestionably clear by the tenor and current of the New Covenant laid down both by Jeremiah and Paul. And unless this be heedfully and judiciously marked. This promised blessing of the federates' knowledge of the Lord cannot be rightly expounded and understood; nor the abusive wrestings of this promise by the unlearned and unstable, so clearly and convincingly refelled.[362] Therefore I advertise again and again, that the direct and plain scope of the Holy Spirit, here may be diligently marked, which that judicious Calvin has excellently observed, saying [concerning the words]: {*And they shall teach no more*}, etc. "Here is laid down another difference between the Old and New Testament, namely: that God – who had more obscurely

---

[360] Hebrews 8:11, Jeremiah 31:34
[361] Jeremiah 31:31-33, Hebrews 8:8-11
[362] 2 Peter 3:16

manifested himself under the law – will send forth his full brightness, that the knowledge of him shall become familiar. But he hyperbolically extols this grace when he says that none shall need teacher or master, because everyone shall be taught enough. Therefore we have in sum the purpose of the prophet, namely: that the light of the gospel should be so great, that it may sufficiently appear God would deal more liberally with his people because his truth should shine as the sun at noon-day. This same thing Isaiah promises when he says {*They shall all be taught of God*} (Isaiah 54:13). That was true even under the law, but then God afforded only a slender taste of celestial doctrine. But at the coming of Christ, he opened the treasures of wisdom and understanding, so that in the gospel, there's the perfection of the beginning, because we know the old people were like unto children, and therefore God kept them under rudiments. Now because we are become ripe, he vouchsafes us fuller doctrine, as it were, and comes near to us."[363] So he; very pertinently.

The words of the New Covenant containing this promised blessing, I have analytically explained already in brief – there see.[364] But now for the fuller and clearer understanding of them, I shall further open these particulars, with all possible brevity, namely: (1) wherein the nature of this New Covenant knowledge of God more especially consists; (2) how and in what way God furnishes his New Covenant people with such a knowledge of himself; (3) whether all God's New Covenant people attain to this promised knowledge of God, seeing as experience testifies that very many under the New Covenant within the visible church remain most grossly ignorant of God and all his ways; (4) whether God by this promise intended to take away, evacuate, and annul all human teaching private and public as altogether useless and needless now under the New Covenant; (5) why God has promised this blessing in his New Covenant; (6) How we may discover that we so know the Lord, as God here intends in this his New Covenant promise; and (7) inferences.

---

[363] John Calvin's commentary on Jeremiah 31:34
[364] In this 5th Chapter, Section 1

Question 1: Wherein does the nature of this New Covenant knowledge more especially consist?

Answer: This New Covenant promise in Jeremiah 31:34 and Hebrews 8:11: *And they shall not teach every man his brother, and every man his neighbor, saying; Know the LORD, for all shall know me*, etc., evidently states this New Covenant knowledge of God in these two particulars especially, namely: (1) in the excellence of the knowledge, and (2) in the extensiveness and universality thereof.

(1) **In the excellence of the New Covenant knowledge of the Lord, beyond that which was vouchsafed under the Old Covenant.**

This I collect thus, namely:

[1] *Partly from the nature of this New Covenant laid down more generally, by way of negation*: *I will make a new covenant with the house of Israel and with the house of Judah: Not according to the covenant which I made with their fathers*, etc[365] – that is, "I will make a New Covenant, but very unlike to, and different from, and excelling above my Old Covenant."

[2] *Partly from the nature of this New Covenant laid down more particularly, by way of affirmation and explication*: *But this shall be the Covenant which I will make with the house of Israel, after those days, saith the LORD; I will give my law*, etc. *And they shall teach no more every man his brother, and every man his neighbor, saying; Know the LORD: for they shall all know me from the least of them to the greatest of them, saith the LORD.*[366] That is, "My people, under the Old Covenant made with their fathers, had many of

---

[365] Jeremiah 31:31-32, Hebrews 8:8-10; see the words expounded in Section 1 of this chapter.
[366] Jeremiah 31:33-34, Hebrews 8:10-11

them, some sort, some measure, of the knowledge of the Lord – they did teach one another every man his neighbor, and every man his brother, to know the Lord, according to their capacity; but my people under the New Covenant shall all of them generally have a far other and more excellent knowledge of the Lord, a knowledge far surpassing and transcending man's teaching, for I myself will instruct them; I will teach them to know the Lord. Thus, there shall be an excellence in the New Covenant knowledge of the Lord, beyond the Old Covenant knowledge."

[3] **Partly from such Scriptures as explicating the nature of that knowledge of God and his ways**, which God vouchsafes his covenant people under the New Covenant, declare that, in many regards, it is a knowledge far excelling and outstripping the knowledge which his people formerly had of him under the Old Covenant, as is evident:

{1} In the Old Testament promises, as in Joel: *And it shall come to pass afterwards, that I will pour out my Spirit upon all flesh, and your sons and your daughters shall prophesy; your old men shall dream dreams, your young men shall see visions: and also upon the servants, and upon the handmaids in those days, will I pour out my Spirit*, etc.[367] In that evangelical Isaiah: *I will pour out water upon him that is thirsty, and floods upon the dry ground; I will pour my Spirit upon thy seed, and my blessing upon thine offspring*, etc.[368] And elsewhere: *And all thy children shall be taught of the LORD.*[369]

{2} In the New Testament performances, witnessed by the apostles, such as by John: *But ye have an unction from the Holy One, and ye know all things. – But the Anointing* (namely: the Holy Spirit; compare Acts 10:38 with 2 Corinthians 1:21-22, John 16:13) *which ye have received of him, abideth in you: and ye need not that any man teach you; But as the same anointing teacheth you of all things, and is truth, and is no lie; and even as it hath taught you, ye shall abide in him.* By Paul: *The Spirit searcheth all things, yea, the deep*

---

[367] Joel 2:28-29, etc. & Acts 2:16-22
[368] Isaiah 44:3-5, John 7:37-39
[369] 1 John 2:20, 27

things of God. For what man knoweth the things of a man, save the spirit of man which is in him? Even so the things of God knoweth no man, but the Spirit of God. Now we have received not the spirit of the world, but the Spirit which is of God, that we might know the things that are freely given to us of God.[370] And elsewhere he prefers the New Covenant ministration far before the Old, upon this very point of the excellency of the New Covenant knowledge beyond that of the Old, saying: *We use great plainness of speech. And not as Moses which put a veil over his face, that the children of Israel could not steadfastly look to the end of that which is abolished. But their minds were blinded: For until this day remaineth the same veil untaken away, in the reading of the Old Testament: which veil is done away in Christ. – But we all with open face, beholding as in a glass the glory of the Lord, are changed into the same image, from glory to glory, even as by the Spirit of the Lord.*[371] In these and like passages, the excellencies and extensiveness of New Covenant knowledge, above that of the Old, is highly magnified, and particularly expounded, which may give much light to this New Covenant promise, touching the federates' knowledge of the Lord.

Particularly, the excellency of this New Covenant knowledge of the Lord, beyond that under the Old Covenant, does in many ways appear and manifest itself. And especially in that the federates' knowledge of God under the New Covenant is: (i) more divine, (ii) more spiritual, (iii) more clear, (iv) more evidential, (v) more complete, (vi) more efficacious, and (vii) more glorious.

(i) **More divine.** The knowledge which the federates had of God under the Old Covenant, was more human: there was more of man that appeared in it when it was taught to them. The parents taught their children, and their children taught the succeeding generation.[372] Moses and the prophets taught them in extraordinary;[373] the priests and Levites in ordinary: *the priest's lips*

---

[370] 1 Corinthians 2:10-13
[371] 2 Corinthians 3:12-18
[372] Genesis 18:19, Deuteronomy 6:7-9, Exodus 12:26-27, Psalm 78:4-7, etc.
[373] Isaiah 44:3-5, John 7:37-39

should keep knowledge, and they should seek the law at his mouth, for he is the Messenger of the Lord of Hosts.[374] They had very much of this teaching which was more outward and human, as this New Covenant promise intimates: *And they shall teach no more every man his neighbor, and every man his brother, saying; Know the LORD: for they shall all know me from the least of them to the greatest of them* (Jeremiah 31:34, Hebrews 8:11). Hereby God intimates that under his Old Covenant, his people were taught to know him by human instruction for the most part. They had comparatively very little of his immediate divine instruction, because his Spirit was very sparingly given until Christ's glorification.[375] But under his New Covenant, the knowledge which his federates should have of God should be more divine, God himself would more immediately teach them: *all their children should be taught of God.*[376] Not that God ever intended by this promise to lay aside all human teaching, public or private, under his New Covenant;[377] for God commands and calls for such teaching frequently and vehemently now under his New Covenant administration. Ministers must teach the church and people of God publicly (Matthew 28:18-20, Ephesians 4:11-13; 1 Timothy 5:17; 2 Timothy 4:1-5). Parents must teach their children, and Christians must teach one another, privately (Ephesians 6:4, Colossians 3:16, Hebrews 3:13).

But under the New Covenant his people should have more of the Spirit of God poured forth upon them, and more teaching immediately from God than under the Old Covenant. Under the New Covenant, God's own immediate teaching should so predominate and bear sway, that all human teaching should comparatively be eclipsed and become as nothing. To this effect, that of the apostle is very observable: *God who commanded the light to shine out of*

---

[374] Malachi 2:7
[375] John 7:37-39
[376] Isaiah 54:13 with John 6:45
[377] "Atqui propheta hic non designat entheusiasmum, qui excludat usum doctrinae; sed [...] tantum promittit clariorem fore evangelii lucem. Sicuti Deus sub lege non ita perfecte populum suum docuit, sicut nos hodie."
John Calvin's commentary on Jeremiah 31:34

darkness, hath shined in our hearts, to give the light of the knowledge of the glory of God in the face of Jesus Christ.[378]

In these words, Paul sets forth the light of the knowledge of God under that New Covenant ministration, as far surpassing that of the Old: (a) by the Author of it, God. God that at first commanded light to shine out of darkness, has shined in our hearts, in his ministers' dark hearts. (b) By the instrumental means which God makes use of for imparting the knowledge of God to men, namely: his ministers, to give the light, etc., that is, God has illuminated his ministers, that they may give light to others that they may teach others to know God in Christ: not in his own immediate essence, that they cannot endure; not only in the creature: that is not salvific; but in the face of Christ: that'is most saving and comfortable. Christ's face is open and unveiled; Moses' face was veiled.[379]

(ii) **More spiritual.** Under the Old Covenant, the knowledge which God's people had of God and of the things of God, was more literal and carnal. God, Christ, and divine mysteries were made known to them in the letter of the ten commandments written in two tables of stone, in the letter of the ceremonial law, etc.[380] Thus God was revealed to them as a God that made heaven and earth in six days, resting the seventh; that brought them out of a literal Egypt; that promised them a literal and earthly Canaan; that sat between the earthly cherubims, etc. And so Christ was represented literally, under the tabernacle, altar, table of showbread, ark, mercy-seat, manifold sacrifices, and such like carnal ordinances; so spiritual mysteries were taught that people by weak and carnal elements; as, redemption, by deliverance out of Egypt; justification, by the sprinkling of blood; sanctification, by many ceremonial washings: communion with God in Christ, by the shewbread on the holy table before

---

[378] 2 Corinthians 4:6
[379] "Illuxit cordibus nostris (i.e. eorum qui propter Christum vestri servi sumus) ut eam postea vobis imperti remus" Beza's Annotation on 2 Corinthians 4:6
[380] Exodus 20, Deuteronomy 5 & 4:13

the Lord continually; pardon of sin, by the mercy-seat covering the tables in the ark: the eternal rest in heaven, by Canaan's rest, and the holy of holies, etc.

All this was a kind of literal and carnal teaching, and for the most part raised up that people to a kind of carnal apprehension and literal knowledge of God, Christ, and spirituals – they generally resting in the letter and carnality of the ordinances. But under the New Covenant, the knowledge which God's people have of God, Christ, and the things of God, is more spiritual and heavenly. (a) They have the spiritual mysteries themselves, which were dimly represented in those earthly and carnal ordinances: they have not only the patterns of the things in the heavens, but the heavenly things themselves.[381] (b) They have not a ministration of the letter, but of the Spirit: abundance of Spirit being now poured forth, which was but sprinkled heretofore under the law.[382] (c) Hereby, their knowledge and apprehensions of God, Christ, and things spiritual are elevated unto a high pitch of spirituality. They do not rest in the letter, the shell, the carnality of manifestations; but they penetrate and dive into the spirit, life, kernel, and mystery of things. *He that is spiritual discerneth all things. – The Spirit searcheth all things, even the deep things of God*.[383]

(iii) **More clear**. Under the Old Testament, though the federates had a true and saving knowledge of God, etc. yet it was very dim, dark, obscure; they were taught by types and shadows of good things to come, by prophecies and promises which were to have a future accomplishment. All things were very remote and at a great distance from them. Now prophecies and promises of future blessings are usually very dim and dark in comparison with performances, and types are very obscure in comparison of the truth and substance of those shadows. And all things at a great distance are beheld darkly, in comparison of things at hand. Hence, Moses spoke to the people with a veil upon his face, which denoted: partly, the darkness of the Old

---

[381] Hebrews 9:23
[382] 2 Corinthians 3:6-8, John 7:38-39
[383] 2 Corinthians 3:13, etc.

Covenants ministration; partly, the darkness and blindness of the people's hearts, the veil of ignorance and unbelief predominating exceedingly there.[384]

The ministration was veiled, and their apprehensions veiled – all was under a dark veil. But now under the New Covenant, prophecies and promises are accomplished, types and shadows are fulfilled: *the veil is done away in Christ.*[385] All that remote distance is removed: *And we all with (unveiled) open face, beholding as in a glass the glory of the Lord, are changed into the same image from glory to glory, even as by the Spirit of the Lord.*[386] Now the shadows of the night are over, and the day is at hand, and *the Sun of Righteousness is risen with healing in his wings,*[387] as Malachi prophesied. "Jews," (as Calvin notes) "had some light, but we have the sun himself."[388] They had skylight, starlight, moonlight, as it were; but we have sunlight. They had the morning; we the noontide of light. Notable is that of our Savior's: *Blessed are the eyes which see the things that ye see: For I tell you, that many prophets and kings*

---

[384] 1 Corinthians 2:10, 15
[385] 2 Corinthians 3:14
[386] 2 Corinthians 3:18
[387] Malachi 4:2
[388] *Blessed are the eyes which see the things which ye see, and the ears which hear the things which ye hear; for many kings and prophets*, etc. (Luke 10:23)
"Christ, then, is the best interpreter of this passage, even that God would cause the truth to shine forth more fully under the gospel; and hence Christ is called by Malachi {*the Sun of Righteousness*} (Malachi 4:2), for the prophet there intimates that the fathers had indeed some light, but not such as we have. In short, we ought to bear in mind the comparison, of which mention was made yesterday, even that God held his people in suspense with the hope of a better state.
And that we may no farther seek an explanation, let us carefully weigh the words; for it is not simply and without exception said {*No one shall teach his neighbor*}, but it is added, {*Saying, Know ye Jehovah*}. We hence see that the prophet promises knowledge, so that they might be no longer alphabetarians; for these words, {*Know ye Jehovah*}, point out the first elements of faith, or of celestial doctrine. And, doubtless, if we consider how great was the ignorance of the ancient people, they were then only in the elements. He who is at this day the least among the faithful, has so far advanced, that he knows much more clearly what pertains chiefly to salvation than those who were then the most learned."
John Calvin's commentary on Jeremiah 31:34
[https://ccel.org/ccel/calvin/calcom20/calcom20.iii.xliv.html]
<Accessed 4/4/2024>

have desired to see those things that ye see, and have not seen them; and to hear those things which ye hear, and have not heard them (Luke 10:23-24). "Hereby, as Calvin observes, Christ intimates that God has shined out more fully by the doctrine of the gospel than formerly. In like sort, Christ said that he that is least in the kingdom of heaven is greater than John the Baptist (Matthew 11:11), who yet excelled all the prophets. John the Baptist in his office was more excellent than all the prophets, and surpassed them in understanding, and yet Christ says that the least professor and witness of the gospel is greater than he. This is not only referred to their persons, nor ought only to be restrained to them, but rather to the clear and plain manner of teaching, which is found in the gospel. "Now, he that is least among the faithful, much more clearly understands whatsoever belongs to the sum of salvation, than those which were not vulgar among the Jews" – as Calvin expresses himself.

(iv) **More evidential and ensuring, both in regard to itself, of spirituals, and consequently of our state towards God.** This evidentialness of New Testament knowledge, beyond that of the Old, necessarily follows from the former surpassing clearness thereof. That which is most clear, resplendent and perspicuous, is most evidential, and best discovers both itself and other things unto us. *Whatsoever maketh manifest is light.*[389] As in the celestial bodies, the more light any of them have in themselves, the more clear they are, the more they do discover, evidence and manifest themselves and all things visible to us: the moon more than the stars, and the sun far more than the moon. Thus the New Covenant knowledge of God – having in it much more shining brightness and clearness in the open face of Christ than the Old Covenant knowledge had in the veiled face of Moses – must needs proportionably evidence itself and spirituals much more to us, than the former could do unto the Jews.[390]

---

[389] Ephesians 5:13
[390] 2 Corinthians 4:6 & 3:18, 13-14

Now this New Covenant knowledge of God does not only behold God more clearly and conspicuously in the face of Jesus Christ, but also more evidently discovers to us, and assure us of three things: namely:

(a) That itself, even this knowledge of God which we have, is a right knowledge of him. *Hereby we do know that we know him, if we keep his commandments. He that saith, I know him, and keepeth not his commandments, is a liar, and the truth is not in him.*[391] We, by our knowledge of God, do know that we know God: partly by the fruits and right effects of the true knowledge of God, as here by obedience, etc.; partly by the reflex act[392] of knowledge looking back upon itself, and perceiving itself knowing.

(b) What spirituals we have from God. God has given us such a Spirit of knowledge in Christ, that we thereby assuredly know what things the Lord has done for us by Christ. *Now we have received, not the Spirit of the world but the Spirit which is of God, that we might know the things that are freely given to us of God.*[393] We know that Christ is in us (2 Corinthians 13:5), that we are of the truth (1 John 3:19), that we love the children of God (1 John 5:2), that we are regenerate, converted, quickened (1 John 3:14, etc.)

(c) That consequently, our spiritual estate towards God is good. This we may discern by an assurance of knowledge, as that *we are passed from death to life* (1 John 3:14), that *we have eternal life* (1 John 5:13), that *when God in Christ shall appear, we shall be like him, for we shall see him as he is* (1 John 3:2). Hereupon, full assurance of spirituals is ascribed – not only to faith and hope, but also to knowledge or understanding.[394]

(v) **More complete, full, and perfect.** Under the Old Covenant, the federates were as children under age, brought up and instructed in rudiments and first elements of divine doctrine, in the ABC or alphabet of religion. They had but an imperfect and childlike understanding of God and divine things.

---

[391] 1 John 2:3-5
[392] Original reads: "reflect act"
[393] 1 Corinthians 2:12
[394] Hebrews 10:22 & 6:11, Colossians 2:2

They understood as children; they were but alphabetarians in knowledge.[395] There were many mysteries which they knew not at all, and what they knew was very darkly, weakly, imperfectly. There was much darkness and ignorance upon them. Their knowledge was extremely imperfect; both extensively in regard to spiritual mysteries known, which were but few comparatively; and intensively, in regard to the degree and measure of their knowledge, which comparatively was but very small. Touching Christ and his priestly office, the Hebrews were dull of hearing, needed milk, not strong meat, were as babes that had need of instruction in first principles, etc.[396] Touching regeneration, what a mystery and paradox was it to Nicodemus, a master and teacher among them? etc.[397] But under the New Covenant, the federates are as grown men come to maturity, put up to a higher form and harder lesson, having a more ripe and complete knowledge of God, and the things of God: both extensively for sorts of things known, and intensively for measure and degree of knowing them. They have more complete revelations in the word, touching God and divine things to be known;[398] they have more perfect, donations and operations of the Spirit of God, illuminating them unto all gradual excellencies in knowledge,[399] and consequently: their knowledge is full, ripe, and much more perfect; they are *men in understanding*;[400] they know more than the kings and prophets of old;[401] they are greater than even John the Baptist in knowledge;[402] they have by reason of use *their senses exercised to discern both good and evil*;[403] they have such an anointing as teaches them all things, namely: all things necessary to their salvation, to their present New

---

[395] Galatians 4:1-4
[396] Hebrews 5:11-14
[397] John 3:1-14
[398] Ephesians 3:3-6, 10
[399] John 7:38-39, Ephesians 1:17-18
[400] 1 Corinthians 14:20
[401] Luke 10:23-24
[402] Matthew 11:11
[403] Hebrews 5;12-14

Testament state, to their spiritual being and well-being;[404] they penetrate into the most abstruse and hidden mysteries of religion, with acute, well-exercised senses; they have not weak glimmerings, but the full sunshine of light without clouds and shadows, wherein they are still increasing;[405] they look not upon the veiled face of Moses, but the unveiled face of Christ.[406]

(vi) **More efficacious and powerful.** Under the Old Testament, as the federates' knowledge of God was less clear and less perfect, so it was less efficacious. The power and efficacy thereof was proportionable: they rested much in a literal and notional knowledge; few of them had a spiritualized knowledge. Consequently, the efficacy of their knowledge upon them was either none at all, or very slender. Literals and mere notionals have no efficacy; weak spirituals have but weak efficacy upon the hearts and lives. But under the New Covenant, the federates' knowledge of God, etc, is much more powerful, strong, and efficacious. The apostle signifies this excellently, saying: *But we all with open face, beholding as in a glass the glory of the Lord, are changed into the same image from glory to glory, even as by the Spirit of the Lord.*[407] The intent of the apostle in this chapter, is principally to demonstrate the surpassing excellency of the New Testament ministration beyond that of Moses in many particulars, as I have elsewhere shown, and at last in regard of the perspicuity thereof.[408] The efficacy of this perspicuity of ministration and knowledge of God, is most notably set forth in verse 18, wherein note: the perspicuity, efficacy, progress and universality of our New Covenant knowledge of God.[409]

---

[404] 1 John 2:20, 27
[405] 2 Corinthians 3:18
[406] 2 Corinthians 4:6 & 3:13-14, 18
[407] 2 Corinthians 3:18
[408] In my *Key of the Bible* on 2 Corinthians 3
[409] "He points out, however, at the same time, both the strength of the revelation, and our daily progress. For he has employed such a similitude to denote three things: (1) that we have no occasion to fear obscurity, when we approach the gospel, for God there clearly discovers to us his face; (2) that it is not befitting, that it should be a dead contemplation, but that we should be transformed by means of it into the image of God; and (3) that the one and the other are not accomplished in us in one moment, but we must be constantly making progress both in the knowledge of God, and in conformity to his image, for this is

(a) The perspicuity of it: in that, *we with open face behold as in a glass the glory of the Lord*. Here note the object beheld, namely: {*the glory of the Lord*}. namely: The glorious excellencies and perfections of God in himself, as also his glorious manifestations of his grace, mercy, wisdom, etc., in the gospel towards his people under the New Covenant. The means whereby we behold this object, {*the glory of the Lord*}, namely: {*as in a glass*}. Christ Jesus is this glass, thinks Beza,[410] in whom as in a most pure crystal glass the glorious image of God shines forth to us most illustriously and sweetly unto salvation. In Christ, in the face of Christ, it is that God offers himself to be seen savingly (2 Corinthians 4:6). and not elsewhere. The manner of beholding God's glory in this glass, namely: with open face, without any dark veil or covering – this is elegantly opposed to the veil on Moses' face.

(b) The efficacy of it: in that this beholding the Lord's glory in this glass does not frighten us away from it, as Moses shining face frighted away the Israelites, but rather attracts and allures us to it through the intensive beauty of it; yea, transforms us into the same image, as it were by the reflection of its rays upon us. Here is the efficacy and virtue of the New Covenant knowledge of God: it is a transforming knowledge, the more we behold God and know God, the more we become like God, the shine and glory of God beheld, makes us shine and become divinely glorious. This is a powerful change indeed. The glory of Moses his face had no such efficacy in it: Israel were not – could not be

---

the meaning of the expression {*from glory to glory*}."
John Calvin's commentary on 2 Corinthians 3:18
[https://ccel.org/ccel/calvin/calcom40/calcom40.ix.iii.html]
<Accessed 4/4/2024>

[410] *Detecta* [...], etc.] Non potuit Paulus aut brevius aut Divinius in nobis gratiae Dei progressus explicare [...] [p]rimum omnium igitur gratia Dei in Christo n[o]bis velamen adimit; id est, Tenebras illas densissimas quibus undi{que} obsepti eramus. Deinde receptis jam oculis ad tantam lucem minime caligantibus sed ultro etiam eam appetentibus, offertur nobis Christus; in quo, non sicut olim in Mose, sed tanquam in [limpidiffiero] speculo, & vera Patris imagine, Deum ad salutem intueamos Neque vero splendor istius speculi effendimur, sed contra alicimur, magis ac magis in illud intuentes, donec in eam ipsam imaginem transformemur, id est, fiamus & ipse ejus splendoris participes, ac Tanquam Secundariae quaedam imagines, ex illorum radiorum veluti reflexione, &c. Beza Annotat. in 2 Cor. 3. 18.

transformed into the same image by beholding it, because this efficacy is wholly from the Spirit of the Lord.

(c) The progress of this efficacy by degrees. It is not put forth all at once, but *from glory to glory*. We are still increasing in knowledge and the image of God, from one glorious measure and degree to another.

(d) The universality of it: in that we all behold this glory of God in Christ, and are thus transformed – that is, all we that are inwardly and effectually his federates indeed, but more eminently this belongs to his faithful New Covenant ministers, of whom he is here especially discoursing.

Now this efficacy of the New Covenant knowledge of God is such, and so great upon God's true federates, that (a) it makes them come to Christ by faith: *Every man therefore that hath heard and learned of the Father, cometh unto me.*[411] (b) It is the beginning of life eternal in Christ. *This is life eternal, that they might know thee the only true God, and Jesus Christ whom thou hast sent.*[412] (c) It is of eminent note in the sacred list or catalog of sanctifying graces, that make the saints spiritually fruitful (2 Peter 1:5-8). (d) It powerfully puts upon universal obedience to God's commands. *Hereby we do know that we know him, if we keep his commandments.*[413] (e) It mightily incites unto bitter lamentings, and penitential mournings for sin, especially as acted against Christ (Zechariah 12:10 to the end). (f) It is such a universal and well-rooted knowledge, that it makes men persevere in truth and godliness, against all erroneous and ungodly defections. *But as the same anointing teacheth you of all things, and is truth, and is no lie: and even as it hath taught you, ye shall abide in him.*[414] (g) It transforms them that rightly thereby behold God in Christ, into the same image of God, gradually day by day.[415] The reflection of the divine rays as it were upon us, do make like perfective alterations and

---

[411] John 6:45
[412] John 17:3
[413] 1 John 2:3-4
[414] 1 John 2:27
[415] 2 Corinthians 3:18

impressions in us. It is so efficacious that it transforms the whole soul, and conforms the whole conversation unto God.

(vii) **More glorious.** The Old Testament ministry had some kind of glory, but it was glory under a veil (2 Corinthians 3:13, etc). Proportionably, the Old Covenant knowledge of God had some sparkles of glory in it, but the New Covenant ministration excels in glory – and that, not an outward literal and vanishing glory to be done away, but an inward spiritual and lasting glory that shall remain (2 Corinthians 3:6 to the end). Proportionably, the New Covenant knowledge of God is a far more glorious knowledge, more inwardly, spiritually and permanently glorious; yea the glory, splendor and luster of this knowledge is continually increasing, from glory to glory by the Spirit of the Lord,[416] until it be swallowed up in immediate vision of God face to face, when we shall see him as he is, and know as we are known, and then it shall be completely glorious.[417]

Thus of the surpassing excellency of the New Covenant knowledge of God and divine things, being more divine, spiritual, clear, evidential, complete, efficacious and glorious than the Old Covenant knowledge of him. This is the first thing wherein this promise places this New Covenant knowledge, etc. namely: in the singular excellency of it, beyond that of the Old Covenant.

(2) **In the extensiveness and universality of it.**

And therefore this knowledge of God under the New Covenant, is promised not only to some few, or to some chief and great ones, or to many; but to all. *For, they shall All know me, from the least of them to the greatest of them, saith the LORD.*[418] This knowledge, none, no not the greatest, can have, but from God and his promise: and God communicates it to small, as well as great, without respect of persons. In like extent and generality, both the

---

[416] 2 Corinthians 3:18 & 4:6
[417] Matthew 5:8; 1 Corinthians 13:12; 1 John 3:2
[418] Jeremiah 31:34, Hebrews 8:11

promise and performance of this knowledge of God, etc. is elsewhere mentioned.

[1] The promise: *And all thy children shall be taught of the LORD.*[419] They all shall be the Lord's disciples or scholars. *I will pour out my Spirit upon all flesh, and your sons and your daughters shall prophesy, your old men shall dream dreams, your young men shall see visions: and also upon the servants and upon the handmaids in those days will I pour out my Spirit* – that is, under the times of the New Covenant, God will so plentifully pour out his Spirit upon all flesh, upon all sorts of persons, male and female, old and young, free and bond, that they shall be furnished with such knowledge of the mysteries of salvation, that they shall equalize the very prophets themselves in knowledge.[420] Yea, they all shall be as so many prophets, as so many doctors, etc., as Calvin has observed.[421]

[2] The performance also of this promise is expressed very generally: *But we all with open face, beholding as in a glass the glory of the Lord, are changed into the same image, from glory to glory, even as by the Spirit of the Lord.*[422] Note here the extent of this New Covenant-knowledge: {*we all*}, etc. This has general reference to the whole body of the church, but specially to the ministers of the New Covenant.[423]

Now, this promise of New Covenant knowledge is propounded in such general and large terms: {*all flesh*}, {*all thy children*}, {*all we*}, etc., to let us see how far it shall go beyond the Old Testament knowledge, not only in the degree and measure of it, but also in the extent and compass of it. Not only

---

[419] Jeremiah 31:34, Hebrews 8:11
[420] Joel 2:28-29 with Acts 2:16-17, etc.
[421] "Promittit omnes passim fore prophetas & doctores: quia scilicet uberior hodie sit Dei gratia & semper comparative haec intelligi debent"
Calvin's commentary on Joel 2:28
[422] 2 Corinthians 3:18
[423] "{*We all*} says he, for he takes in the whole body of the church."
John Calvin's commentary on 2 Corinthians 3:18
[https://biblehub.com/commentaries/calvin/2_corinthians/3.htm]
<Accessed 4/4/2024>

some sorts, but all sorts of persons, great and small, young and old, bond and free, male and female, shall be endued with it – and those not only in that one nation of the Jews, but in all nations of the world.

Nevertheless, this universal extensiveness necessarily admits of sundry limitations, as: {1} it is to be limited to God's federates, to the church of God. For all these New Covenant promises are peculiarly directed to the house of Israel, and to the house of Judah.[424] They then that are out of the church, have actually no part in this promise of knowing the Lord. {2} It is to be limited to all sorts of persons in covenant – great and small, young and old, bond and free, male and female – as both the words of this promise, and the express terms in Joel do evince, and is not to be extended to every individual person of any of those sorts.[425] It is evidently to be understood *de generibus singulorum, non de singulis generum*: of the kinds of all, not of all those kinds. {3} It is to be limited to all sorts of sincere believing federates as touching that sort and measure of New Covenant knowledge which is salvific. False, hypocritical federates may have such notional knowledge, beyond what was under the Old Covenant, but not any saving knowledge. Thus our blessed Savior limits it: *It is written in the prophets, And they shall be all taught of God. Every man therefore that hath heard, and hath learned of the Father, cometh unto me.*[426] Therefore all they, and they only, that come to Christ by believing in him, are taught of God, and have heard and learned of the Father. That is, all they, and they alone, are under the New Covenant taught of God savingly, who come unto Christ believingly. Hypocritical professors may obtain the bark, the shell, the carcass of knowledge; may go as far in notionals as the sincere, but only sincere believers gain the substance, the kernel, and the soul of knowledge, which is experimental and efficacious to salvation.

Hitherto of the first question: **Wherein does the nature of this New Covenant knowledge of God and divine things more especially consist?**

---

[424] Jeremiah 31:31-34, Hebrews 8:8-13; 2 Corinthians 3:18, Isaiah 54:13
[425] Jeremiah 3134, Hebrews 8:11, Joel 2:28-29
[426] John 6:45 with Isaiah 54:13, Jeremiah 31:34

Question 2: How, and in what way, does God furnish his New Covenant people with such a knowledge of himself?

Answer: This may be resolved very briefly. God furnishes his New Covenant people with such a knowledge of God, etc., as has been described, in this way: namely: (1) in Jesus Christ; (2) by his Spirit and New Covenant ministry; and (3) in a continual progress and gradation, from their gracious conversion until their glorious consummation.

(1) **In and through Jesus Christ**. *God – hath shined in our hearts, to give the light of the knowledge of the glory of God,*[427] *in the face of Jesus Christ.*[428] So that in the face of Jesus Christ, the light of the knowledge of the glory of God is communicated to us under the New Covenant. We know God in Christ actually exhibited and performed, clearly revealed: In the face of Christ, the open, evident, unveiled face of Christ; whereas the Jews under the Old Testament knew God only in the veiled face of Moses, or in the shadowed veiled face of Christ. Hence, Christ is said to be: the brightness of his Father's glory, and the express character or image of his person;[429] the image of the invisible God;[430] the glass wherein we behold the glory of the Lord,[431] which – though by some it be interpreted *{the glass of the gospel}*, yet – seems peculiarly to be intended of Jesus Christ, because in the beginning of the next chapter, that phrase is used, of giving *the light of the knowledge of the glory of God in the face of Jesus Christ*. And God has so notably revealed, manifested and made known himself in Jesus Christ: his properties, his purposes and counsel, his

---

[427] 2 Corinthians 4:6
[428] "Namely: in Jesus Christ, who is as it were the great sun, and is revealed and made fully known in the gospel." John Diodati
[429] Hebrews 1:3
[430] Colossians 1:15
[431] 2 Corinthians 3:18 with 4:6

riches of free grace, mercy, love, etc, his will and ordinances, etc, that Christ says: *He that hath seen me, hath seen the Father;* and: *Believe me, that I am in the Father, and the Father in me.*[432] The knowledge of God immediately in his essence, is so high, that we cannot reach it, but be swallowed up with it; the knowledge of God remotely in his creatures, is so low, that we cannot be saved by it; but the knowledge of God in the face of Christ (that is, as he has made himself plainly, clearly, and familiarly known to us in and by Christ, as one man is exactly known to another by his face), is of all other the most safe, suitable, profitable and comfortable way of knowing God. In Christ, the invisible God has rendered himself visible to us; in Christ, the most majestical and glorious God has rendered himself familiar and near unto us; in Christ, the most holy and infinitely offended God has represented himself most sweetly and comfortably appeased towards us. Oh! To know God effectually, in Christ already revealed, and exhibited actually, is a knowledge next unto the beatific vision, wherein we shall see God gloriously.

(2) **By his Spirit, and New Covenant ministry**. Ordinarily, God brings his people to the saving knowledge of himself only this way: [1] efficiently, by his Spirit; more plentifully poured forth under the New Covenant than ever. God's Spirit is the principal and immediate efficient cause of this New Covenant knowledge of God: *I will pour my Spirit upon all flesh, and your sons and your daughters shall prophesy, etc.*[433] – *We all beholding as in a glass the glory of the Lord, are changed into the same image from glory to glory, even as by the Spirit of the Lord.*[434] If God's Spirit acts not, moves not, to the producing of this effect, it cannot be wrought at all. Now God's plentiful and powerful Spirit becomes the Author of this knowledge of God, etc. under the New Covenant, especially these three ways. namely:

[1] ***Partly, by his revelation***. He reveals God and the things of God, more clearly and fully now under the New Covenant, than ever formerly

---

[432] John 14:9-11
[433] Joel 2:28-29, Acts 2:16, etc.
[434] 2 Corinthians 3:18

under the Old. He makes the object of knowledge more plain and conspicuous, and that mightily furnishes knowledge itself. The mystery of the Trinity, of Christ, of free grace, of faith, of justification, of the Gentiles' calling, etc., were never before so manifested as now they are in the New Testament by the Spirit (Ephesians 3:4-5). Christ has now brought life and immortality to light, through the gospel.[435] Why? Had he never done it before? Yes, but never so fully and clearly.

[2] *Partly, by his illumination.* Having revealed more perfectly the object to the understanding, in the next place he more completely enlightens and opens the eye of the understanding to discern that object (2 Corinthians 3:18, Hebrews 6:4; 2 Timothy 1:7). The brightest sun affords no light to us until our eyes are opened and cured. Now the Spirit is that Anointing, which teaches us all things.[436] He creates a light within, receptive of the light without, and then we see clearly.

[3] *Partly, by his attestation.* God's Spirit attests, witnesses, and evidences to us whatsoever we have from God, and so our true knowledge of him (1 Corinthians 2:12). *Hereby we know that he abideth in us, by his Spirit that he hath given us* (1 John 3:24). *The Spirit witnesseth with our spirits, that we are the sons of God* (Romans 8:16). Thus God works this true and saving knowledge of himself, etc., in us by his Spirit, [1] efficiently revealing the object, illuminating the eye of the mind, and attesting to us what we have of God; and [2] instrumentally, by his New Covenant ministry. God has appointed all his New Testament ministry to disciple all nations: teaching them to observe all things whatsoever Christ has commanded;[437] to turn them from darkness to light;[438] *for the perfecting of the saints, for the work of the ministry, for the edifying of the body of Christ, till we all come in the unity of the Faith, and of the knowledge of the Son of God*, etc. *That we henceforth be no*

---

[435] 2 Timothy 1:10
[436] 1 John 2:20, 27
[437] Matthew 28:19-20
[438] Acts 26:17-18

more children, tossed to and fro, and carried about with every wind of doctrine.[439] Hence Christ calls his ministers {*the light of the world*}[440] and {*the stars in Christ's right hand*},[441] shining forth unto the church. But that they may shine forth instrumentally in their doctrine, and exemplarily in their life to others. God first shines into their hearts, and dispels their natural darkness, shines away their darkness and ignorance; that, making use of such frail earthy instruments, all the efficacy of their ministry may palpably appear to be of God, and not of them. *For God, who commanded the light to shine out of darkness, hath shined in our hearts, to give the light of the knowledge of the glory of God in the face of Jesus Christ.*[442] *But we have this treasure in earthen vessels* (namely: this treasure of divine light in us as earthen vessels, as Gideon and his men had their lamps in earthen pitchers: Judges 7) *that the excellency of the power may be of God, and not of us.*[443] God could have given his federates under the New Covenant this knowledge of God immediately by his Spirit only, without the ministry of man, but he would not: he gains to himself the more glory, upon occasion of the weakness of his instruments. They then that cast off the ministry and their teaching now under this New Covenant, do cast off God and his ordinance, for breeding New Covenant knowledge, and put themselves quite out of the way of the Spirit's operation: remaining still in gross darkness and blindness under a spirit of delusion, through God's just judgment. Witness the many horrid, prodigious and blasphemous errors against Jesus Christ, and almost all the fundamentals of Christianity,[444] published in print,[445] and otherwise by such as have in these days forsaken the Scriptures and way of truth, and separated from the true churches and

---

[439] Ephesians 4:11-14
[440] Matthew 5:14
[441] Revelation 1:20
[442] Hebrews 1:3
[443] 2 Corinthians 5:6-7
[444] See the catalog of errors in the *London Ministers' Testimony to the Truth*, pp.5-23 (London, 1648).
[445] See a catalog of popish books lately printed in England, in Francis Cheynell's *The Beacon Flaming with a Non-Obstante* (1652).

ministry of Christ unto popery, pretended revelations, enthusiasms, fabulous dreams, and damnable heresies, *even denying the Lord that bought them, and bringing upon themselves swift destruction. Many following their pernicious ways, by reason of whom the way of truth is evil spoken of* (2 Peter 2:1-2).[446]

(3) **In a continual progress in the knowledge of God, etc. by degrees, from their gracious conversion, till their glorious consummation.** Under this New Covenant, the promised knowledge of God is not given all at once in a moment to any of his federates, but gradually, and step by step, according to his people's capacities. *We know but in part, and prophesy in part; we see now through a glass darkly.*[447] Knowledge, as well as the grace of Christ in us, is not in complete maturity, but only in their growth thereunto.[448] For the completing and perfecting of this knowledge,[449] Christ has given all his New Testament ministry until the world's end. Hence it is said that: *We all beholding as in a glass the glory of the Lord, are changed into the same image from glory to glory,*[450] namely: from one glorious measure and degree of knowledge and the image of God, to another. And to this effect some understand those expressions in Joel, of prophesying, dreams, and visions, because so distinctly applied to sons and daughters, old men, and young men, to imply the gradual increase of knowledge in God's federates under the New

---

[446] See Mr. Ralph Farmer's treatise called *Quakerism in its Exaltation*, pp.1-45 (London, 1657).
[447] 1 Corinthians 13:9, 12
[448] 2 Peter 3:18
[449] Ephesians 4:11-14, Matthew 28:19-20
[450] 2 Corinthians 3:18

Covenant.[451] This New Covenant knowledge of God, etc. is radically and initially planted in us at our conversion (Acts 26:18; 1 Peter 2:8-9). Gradually increased in us day by day, whilst we are in our progress of grace in this life (2 Corinthians 3:18; 2 Peter 3:18), completely perfected and consummated in us, when we come to be perfected in heaven by full and immediate vision of God face to face (1 Corinthians 13:10-12; 1 John 3:2, Hebrews 13:23). God's federates therefore are not to be discouraged because their knowledge of God, and of the things of God in them, is very weak and small: but rather they are to make it clear and sure to themselves, that the little knowledge which they have is true saving knowledge, and then they may conclude it will be daily increasing to more and more perfection, and at last become complete in glory.

---

[451] Joel 2:28-29, Doctrine 10:
"As for those ways of revealing the will of God of old, by prophecy, visions, and dreams; albeit they point all at one thing, and seem to be named all here, to set out the fullness of gospel-knowledge answering to all of them; and therefore seem to be comprehended all under prophesying, as it is attributed to his servants of all sorts and ages (Acts 2:28). Yet seeing they are distinctly named, and attributed to several sorts of persons, as prophesying to sons and daughters; visions to young men, and dreams to old men; we may from it take up some steps and degrees of the knowledge of God, wherein they grow up who are under the Spirit's teaching, as (1) by prophesying, attributed to sons and daughters, we may understand simply, the knowledge of divine things; (2) by visions, attributed to young men, we may understand, their clearer insight, and taking up of these mysteries, then they had in their younger days: for vision does represent the thing revealed more sensibly; and (3) by dreams, wherein men have their senses shut up from the world, and which are attributed to old men, we may understand a further degree of illumination, when light received takes hold on the affections, to sanctify and subdue them; so that men's hearts are taken off the world, and filled with the things of God. And so this gradation will teach, that the knowledge of God which is communicated unto men by the Spirit, will be on the growing hand, until from a common notion and remembering of it, it come to be more seriously pondered and laid to heart, and until it take hold of the affections, and conquer the whole heart to God."
Mr. George Hutcheson in his exposition on Joel 2:28-29.

Question 3: Do all God's New Covenant people attain to this Promised Knowledge of God, and so on?

[This question is raised] seeing as sad experience seems to speak the contrary, that very many in the visible church remain most grossly ignorant of God, and of all his ways now under the New Covenant.

Answer: This question may be resolved by way of concession, explanation, and limitation.

(1) **By way of concession.**

It is granted that even under this brightest noontide and glorious sunshine of New Covenant light, many, alas very many, within the visible church of Christ, do still remain in gross darkness and ignorance of God and divine things. This comes to pass:

[1] Partly, from natural stupidity, incapacity, and unteacheableness in some,[452] who are so dull, blockish and unapprehensive of divine mysteries, that though they are ever learning, yet (like those silly women) they are never able to come to the knowledge of the truth.[453]

[2] Partly, from the sinful pravity and corruption in many, who {1} either like swine basely neglect and contemn the pearls of instruction, admonition, reproof, etc., trampling them under their feet, contenting themselves in an affected ignorance, and despising all endeavors and means of knowledge;[454] {2} or like dogs, bark, revile, turn again and rend those that would inform, teach and admonish them – not enduring, but utterly hating the light, because their deeds are evil.[455] *And this is the condemnation, that light is come into the world,*

---

[452] Ex quovis ligno non sit Mercurius.
[453] 2 Timothy 3:7
[454] Matthew 7:6
[455] Matthew 7:6

and men loved darkness rather than light, because their deeds were evil. For everyone that doeth evil, hateth the light; neither cometh to the light, lest his deeds should be reproved, etc.[456]

[3] Partly, from the carnal state and unregenerate condition of most, even in the visible church, who have no more Christianity than a blade, or lamp, or form of profession, or some common gifts of the Spirit whereby they reach only to some notional knowledge and speculations about God and spirituals, but, know nothing as they ought to know, experimentally, affectively, savingly, etc.[457] Carnal professors, though of the highest rank, lacking true spiritual senses, cannot perceive or discern the things of God, because they are spiritually discerned.[458]

[4] Partly, from the just judgment of God upon some, even reprobates and lost persons, whom God has smitten with judicial blindness, because they loved not, nor obeyed the truth of God tendered to them.[459] That forasmuch as, seeing, they would not see; therefore they shall never see (John 12:40, Acts 28:26-27).

[5] Partly, from the defect of Christian instruction, nurture and admonition in their first education, want of family duties. This is a grand and general sin of parents, that they bring up their children like pagans, not diligently catechizing, principling, and teaching them in the fundamentals of Christianity, as the Lord requires, and as the godly tend to do (Genesis 18:19; 1 Chronicles 28:9; 2 Timothy 3:14-15).[460]

[6] Partly, from the great neglect or insufficiency of church-government and discipline: when church government is not at all established, or if established, not duly managed for the healing of this evil, by catechizing and other ways.[461]

---

[456] John 3:19-21
[457] Matthew 13:18-24 & 25:3; 2 Timothy 3:5
[458] 1 Corinthians 2:14
[459] 2 Corinthians 4:3-4; 2 Thessalonians 2:10-12, Romans 1:21-24, etc.
[460] Ephesians 6:4, Deuteronomy 6:6-9
[461] Galatians 6:6

[7] Partly, from people's casting off the churches, ministry, and ordinances of Christ, wherein and whereby Christ ordinarily conveys to his New Covenant people the solid and saving knowledge of himself, and of all his ways (Ephesians 4:11-14, Matthew 28:19-20; 2 Corinthians 4:6-7).[462] I have diligently observed that, as ignorance in fundamentals is the mother of separation, causing it; so a further ignorance therein is the daughter of separation, being caused and increased by it; whilst such do usually lay out all their thoughts and studies, not about the substantials of Christianity, but about such odd newfangled conceits and opinions as they have entertained. From these bitter fountains, the great ignorance of people now under the New Covenant flows. Oh that there were some effectual remedy, some speedy healing of these great evils in England! When shall it once be?

(2) **By way of explanation.**

Although in the visible church there remains much gross ignorance in many now under the New Covenant, so that they attain not to this promised knowledge; yet notwithstanding, this promise, that *all shall know the Lord*, has its due and intended accomplishment. For clearing of this:

[1] *We must distinguish God's federates under the New Covenant.*

{1} Some are his federates or covenant people only outwardly, by visible profession, etc., as Simon Magus, who upon his profession of faith was baptized;[463] so Ananias and Sapphira[464] – so all hypocrites and formalists. And a great part of the visible church is only of such: of the four sorts of hearers, there were three naught.[465]

{2} Some are his federates inwardly, as well as outwardly; really, as well as formally; by invisible power of faith and grace, as well as by visible profession,

---

[462] Jude 17-23; 2 Timothy 4:3-4
[463] Acts 8:13, 23
[464] Acts 5:1, etc.
[465] Matthew 13:18-24

as Paul,[466] some of the Corinthians,[467] some of the Thessalonians,[468] and as all sincere converts effectually called from darkness to light, and from the power of Satan unto God.

[2] ***We must distinguish of the term {all}, which may be taken:***

{1} Sometimes, more restrainedly, for all sorts of persons, great and small: *All shall know me from the greatest to the least* (Hebrews 8:11, Jeremiah 31:34); *I will pour my Spirit upon all flesh*, namely: all sorts, male and female, young and old, bond and free (Joel 2:28-30).

{2} Sometimes, more largely and universally, for every individual person of all sorts: *We have before proved both Jews and Gentiles, that they are all under sin* – that is, all and singular, all and every individual person of Jews and Gentiles are by nature under sin.[469]

[3] ***We must distinguish of the knowledge of God.*** The knowledge which men may have of God is twofold, namely:

{1} Notional only and ineffectual, consisting in the mere swimming notion and speculation touching God and things of God, without any powerful sanctifying efficacy upon heart and life: *They profess that they know God, but in works they deny him, being abominable, disobedient*, etc.[470] All the knowledge which mere carnal unregenerate men have of God, is merely notional, and in the head.

{2} Real, effectual, cordial, and experimental also: when the heart and affections know God as well as the head; when they so know God as to believe in him, love, desire, esteem, delight in him, obey him, etc. *I know my sheep, and am known of mine.*[471] When they have experimental sense, and spiritual feeling of things: *I pray that your love may abound more and more, in*

---

[466] 1 Timothy 1:13-17
[467] 1 Corinthians 6:9-11
[468] 1 Thessalonians 1:4-5
[469] Romans 3:9
[470] Titus 1:16
[471] John 10:14

knowledge, and in all sense, παση αισθησει.[472] It intends spiritual sense and experience. God's people have spiritual senses, and those senses exercised unto experimental discernings.[473]

[4] ***We must also distinguish between the public administration of God's New Covenant; and the private condition and constitution of some particular persons in the visible church under the New Covenant.***

These distinctions premised, we may briefly thus resolve touching the extent of this promise: *All shall know me from the least to the greatest,*[474] namely:

{1} That in this promise, God does not intend only a notional and ineffectual knowledge of himself under the New Covenant, but also and most especially, a real, effectual, cordial and experimental knowledge of God, and the things of God. For all the rest of these New Covenant promises, and so consequently this of knowing God, are so laid down, as evidently and chiefly to intend true effectual and saving mercies to the federates, such as are proper and peculiar to the elect only.

{2} That therefore the federates, to whom this knowledge of God under the New Covenant is especially and peculiarly promised, are not the federates outwardly by mere visible profession, but the federates inwardly by invisible power of faith and other graces, as well as by outward profession. The outward federates may know God notionally, far more under the New Covenant than ever the like federates knew God notionally under the Old Covenant; but it is only the inward federates also that now know God really, effectually, cordially, experimentally – and herein they shall far excel the inward federates of the Old Covenant.

{3} That under this New Covenant, all that is, all God's inward federates, living till years of discretion, even all and everyone of them individually and numerically; and those of all sorts of people, Jews, or gentiles, male or female,

---

[472] Philippians 1:9
[473] Hebrews 5:14
[474] Hebrews 8:11

young or old, bond or free, great or small; shall know the Lord, not only with a notional, but also with a real, cordial, experimental saving knowledge, much more generally universally, and perfectly than God's people knew him under the Old Covenant.[475] Even the least of God's true New Covenant people shall have so much spirit, and knowledge, etc. That they shall so far excel God's Old Covenant people therein, that (as Calvin notes)[476] they shall comparatively be {*doctores et magistri*}: even doctors and masters, and as it were, all prophets. Hitherto that of Joel 2:28-29, and that of our Savior – *he that is least in the kingdom of heaven, is greater than John the Baptist* (Matthew 11:11) – are especially to be referred. Yea (as one has well noted)[477] believers under the New Covenant shall not only equalize, but in some sense excel all the prophets of old.

{4} That, finally, in this promise we are not so much to consider the private condition and constitution of some particular persons – visible federates under the New Covenant – as the public economy and administration of the New Covenant. The private condition of many particular persons may possibly be very dark and ignorant, having little knowledge of God or his ways, by reason of the occasions of their ignorance forementioned: and yet the public administration and current of the New Covenant is for a universal knowledge of God, *All shall know him*, etc. as has been explained; in comparison of which knowledge, that under the Old

---

[475] Jeremiah 31:34, Hebrews 8:11, Joel 2:28-29
[476] John Calvin's commentary on Jeremiah 31:4
[477] "The knowledge of the mysteries of salvation, which is communicated by the Spirit under the gospel, is comparable to any measure of knowledge attained by ancient prophets of old: Not only does extraordinary revelation under the New Testament in the primitive times parallel what they had then, but even the gifts of light and knowledge, conferred in ordinary upon men, and the saving knowledge conferred upon believers, may be compared therewith; for whereas these revelations were but at fits and times only, this is constant; and these, albeit they were singular in the manner of communicating, yet the truth conveyed thereby, was but more darkly held out, and under a veil, whereas now truths are seen with open face; Therefore as is before cleared, are the names of prophecy, visions and dreams, given to this knowledge. So that the ignorance of men under the gospel, speaks but little enjoyment of the Spirit."
Mr. George Hutcheson in his exposition of Joel 2:28-29 (London, 1655).

Testament (being very imperfect in degree, very dark and obscure for manner, and very much restrained to the Jews only and some few proselytes for extent) was as nothing; was gross ignorance rather than knowledge, comparatively. These things ought still to be understood comparatively, as Calvin notes in his commentary on Jeremiah 31:34.

(3) **By way of limitation.**

Though God in this New Covenant promises: *All shall know me, from the least even to the greatest of them*[478] – and though this promise is performed upon God's New Covenant people, as has been explained; yet all this is to be understood with some caution and limitation, as:

[1] That under the New Covenant, all those that thus know God come not to this knowledge of him in one and the same way. For, in the primitive churches, whose state and condition was somewhat extraordinary, God gave unto his apostles and to many others a knowledge of him and his affairs in an extraordinary way, namely: by prophecy (1 Timothy 1:18, 4:14, Acts 21:9), by visions, as to Peter (Acts 10:10-11) and to Paul (2 Corinthians 12:1-2, etc.), by dreams, as to Joseph (Matthew 1:20), by immediate infallible inspiration, as to the penmen of the books of New Testament (2 Timothy 3:16), and by peculiar revelation (Galatians 1:11-12, 2:2, Ephesians 3:5, Acts 27:23-25). But in the successive churches; whose state and condition is more ordinary, God gives unto his ministers and people a knowledge of himself in an ordinary way, as by illumination of the Spirit (Hebrews 6:4; 1 Corinthians 2:10-14), by preaching the gospel (Acts 26:18; 2 Corinthians 4:6); by searching the Scriptures (John 5:39; 2 Timothy 3:16-17); and by study, meditation, reading, etc. (1 Timothy 4:13, 15).

[2] That all God's sincere New Covenant-people do not have the same equal measure of knowledge, but *every one according to the measure of the gift*

---

[478] Hebrews 8:11, Jeremiah 31:34

of Christ,[479] and *as God has dealt to every man the measure of faith.*[480] Some are babes, and children in understanding, needing milk;[481] some are more ripe, grown men in understanding, able to digest strong meat, etc – but yet even the knowledge of the weakest and meanest, surpasses the knowledge of those under the Old Testament, in distinctness, integrality, and perspicuity.

---

[479] Ephesians 4:7
[480] Romans 12:2-3, etc.
[481] Hebrews 5:12-14

Question 4: Does God by this promise intended to take away, vacate, annul, and make void all human teaching, private and public, as altogether useless and needless now under the New Covenant, seeing he says: *And they shall not teach, every man his neighbor, and every man his brother, saying, Know the LORD;*[482] **and John says elsewhere:** *ye need not that any man teach you?*[483]

Answer: For resolution to this question, I shall offer various things: (1) by way of concession, that thus some have thought; (2) by way of negation, that God never intended this by these or any other like Scriptures; (3) by way of vindication of those Scriptures particularly objected.

(1) **By way of concession.**
I grant that in these our times some of unsound judgments[484] (who decry the New Covenant Ministry and ordinances of Christ, would lay all things in the church in a level, cry up the absolute gradual perfection of the saints in this life, are for enthusiasms, infallibilities, immediate revelations, and for a christ within them as their only savior, etc.) have ignorantly perverted and wrested these Scriptures – Isaiah 54:13, Jeremiah 31:34, Hebrews 8:11; 1 John 2:27, & Joel 2:28-29 – to the voiding of all human teaching as to the saints; but especially to the abolishing of the public ministry now under the New Testament, as useless and needless, yea as abrogated by God. Knowing well that the public ministry of Christ, set for the defense of the gospel, is the

---
[482] Jeremiah 31:34, Hebrews 8:11
[483] 1 John 2:27
[484] As is evident in various erroneous pamphlets printed of late, with whose names I think not fit to blur my margin.

hammer of their heresies to break them, and stands most in their way. And thus they revive the old rotten errors of former times. For, as Calvin observes upon this text {*they shall teach no more every man his neighbor, and every man his brother, etc*}:[485] "[I] have said, here the prophet amplifies the grace of God. And hence we collect that certain fanatic persons have ignorantly abused this testimony, when they would take away all use of doctrine, as in our time some of the Anabaptists have rejected all doctrine. And when they pleased themselves in their ignorance, yet they proudly boasted they were endued with the Spirit; and that it was an injury done to Christ if we should yet be disciples, because it is written among the encomiums and praises of the gospel: {*They shall teach no more every man his brother*}. Hence also it came to pass that they became drunk with horrid dotages. For the devil, when they did swell with so great pride, could bewitch them at his pleasure. Then each one's pride did move him, to feign dreams to himself. And many knaves have drawn this place to private profit. For when they boasted themselves to be prophets, and persuaded this to the simple ones, they obliged many to themselves, and made a gain of that boasting, etc."

(2) **By way of negation.**

God never intended by these or any other like Scriptures to destroy human teaching, private or public, or the office of the public ministry in the church of God. God's New Covenant promises do not at all tend to lay aside any such human teaching, for:

[1] Under the New Covenant, God's federates have but at best an imperfect knowledge of God and the things of God. They *know but in part* – they *see through a glass* (as it were a prospective) *darkly*.[486] Their knowledge is but growing (2 Peter 2:18): not fully grown up to exact perfection. Therefore, in order to their edification and salvation, they have still need of teaching, even

---

[485] John Calvin's commentary on Jeremiah 31:34
[486] 1 Corinthians 13:9, 12, Philippians 3:10, 12-13

of all kind of teaching, both divine and human, for removing of the remains of ignorance in them: now God will not deprive them of such necessaries for their edification and salvation.

[2] Under the New Covenant, {1} God often commands private teaching one of another; as, that husbands teach their wives (1 Corinthians 14:35), parents their children (Ephesians 6:4), and Christians one another (1 Thessalonians 5:11; 2 Thessalonians 3:15, Colossians 3:16). {2} God also promises in reference to the kingdom of Christ under his New Covenant that: *it shall come to pass in the last days that the mountain of the LORD's house shall be established in the top of the mountains, and shall be exalted above the hills: and all nations shall slow unto it. And many people shall go and say, come ye and let us go up to the mountain of the LORD, to the house of the God of Jacob, and he will teach us of his ways, and we will walk in his paths; for out of Zion shall go forth the law, and the word of the LORD from Jerusalem.*[487] Here note: (i) the glorious exaltation and enlargement of the church of God under the New Testament; (ii) the great zeal of many, not only themselves to repair to the house of the Lord, but to incite and instruct others also to go with them to be taught of God; and (iii) the way how they shall be taught: by God's law and Word going out of Zion and Jerusalem, namely: by the apostles' preaching the gospel first at Jerusalem, and then all over the world. Thus God's New Covenant people should privately provoke and instruct one another to repair to the gospel ordinances, especially to the word preached, that they may thereby be taught. This is a teaching both divine and human.

[3] Under the New Covenant, Jesus Christ – having dedicated the New Covenant in his own blood[488] – has taken most effectual order for establishing the public ministry, and teaching of his church thereby in all the nations of the world, from his own resurrection and ascension until the very end of the world, for:

---

[487] Isaiah 2:2-3
[488] Hebrews 9:14-18, Matthew 26:28, Luke 22:20

{1} When he ascended up on high, he gave gifts to men, namely: all his New Testament ministry; extraordinary, apostles, prophets, evangelists; ordinary, pastors and teachers. For what end? *For the perfecting of the saints, for the work of the ministry, for the edifying of the body of Christ.* For how long? *Till we all* (even all the elect of God) *come in the unity of the faith, and of the knowledge of the Son of God, unto a perfect man, unto the measure of the stature of the fullness of Christ.*[489] And that will not be until the world's end, when all the elect of Christ shall be called, and the mystical body of Christ fully completed.

{2} Jesus Christ, immediately before his ascension, gave commission to his ministers for discipling, baptizing and teaching all nations, promising to be with his ministers in this their ministerial work all days, even till the end of the world.[490] Therefore, the ministerial office must continue until the world's end, and the ministerial work of teaching all nations (namely: both the primitive and fundamental work of teaching them, that they may be disciples of Christ, which is here called *discipling* them; and the successive superstructive work of teaching them after they are discipled and baptized, how to walk as Christ's disciples, observing all his commands) is to continue until the end of the world. By these two full and clear Scriptures it is palpably evident beyond all contradiction, that Jesus Christ himself under his New Covenant has ordained, instituted, and commanded his public ministry and their public ministerial teaching of the church and people of God, still to continue and remain from his resurrection and ascension till the very end of the world. And therefore neither this passage in the New Covenant, nor any other in all the Scripture, can rationally and solidly be urged for vacating, voiding, or laying aside the office of Christ's public ministers, or their duty of public teaching the church of God.[491]

---

[489] Ephesians 4:8-13
[490] Matthew 28:18-20 compared with 2 Timothy 2:2
[491] Jeremiah 31:34, Hebrews 8:12

{3} Jesus Christ under his New Covenant has so fixedly settled this way of ministerial preaching and teaching for gaining sinners to himself by believing, that ordinarily none can come to him by believing but through his ministers instrumental teaching and preaching – the Spirit of God ordinarily working to the conversion of sinners, only by the preaching of the word. *Whosoever shall call on the name of the Lord, shall be saved; How then shall they call on him, in whom they have not believed? And how shall they believe in him of whom they have not heard, and how shall they hear. without a preacher? And how shall they preach, except they be sent?*[492] [This intimates] to us, that in God's ordinary course these things are impossible.

(3) **By way of vindication of those particular Scriptures, which usually are wrested, perverted, and ignorantly objected against all human teaching public and private, and against the very ministerial office, now under the New Covenant.**

[1] ***The first objected Scripture****: And all thy children shall be taught of the LORD* (Isaiah 54:13). Then what need is there of any human teaching, public or private, anymore?

Answer: What need? Great need of human teaching, even to all the church's children *that shall be taught of the LORD*, for:

{1} Human teaching both public and private is necessary – *necessitate medii*: by necessity of instrumental means, this being God's ordinary way and means whereby he teaches, namely: by the ministry of men. God teaches immediately, primarily, and efficiently by his Spirit (John 16:13; 1 Corinthians 2:10-13; 1 John 2:20, 27); mediately, secondarily, and instrumentally by men, by Christians privately (Colossians 3:16; 2 Thessalonians 3:15); by Christ's ministers publicly and privately (Matthew 28:19-20, Ephesians 4:8-14,

---

[492] Romans 10:13-15

Romans 10:13-15; 2 Timothy 2:2, Acts 20:20).[493] The position of the principal cause, and of the end, takes not away the less principal and instrumental causes of our teaching, but rather infers them and implies them, as means appointed by God to that end.[494] God will judge the people righteously, and govern the nations upon earth (Psalm 95:4). Is there therefore no more need of judges, governors, and magistrates? God will bless his people so, that the earth shall yield her increase (Psalm 95:6-7). Is there therefore no more need or use of sun, rain, husbandry, tillage, etc? So here, the Lord will teach all the children of the church. Is there therefore no more use of ministers, preaching, or public and private teaching? How absurd such inferences! When men teach by God's appointment, the Lord himself teaches by those men. Yea, because God has promised: *all the children shall be taught of the LORD*; therefore there is necessity and utility of human teaching, that being one special way of the LORD's teaching.

{2} Human teaching is also necessary – *necessitate praecepti*, by necessity of command: Christ having commanded both ministers to teach *ex officio*: publicly, and Christians to teach one another *ex charitate*, privately, as has been proven. Now God's promises do not overthrow his precepts, nor ought they to be made to fight one against another.[495] Scripture reveals both, and both have their use in their place.

[2] ***The second objected Scripture***: *I will pour out my Spirit upon all flesh, and your sons your and daughters shall prophesy, your old men shall*

---

[493] Matthew 28:19-20, Ephesians 4:8-14, Romans 10:13-15; 1 Thessalonians 5:11; 2 Thessalonians 3:15, Colossians 3:16

[494] Posito fine ponuntur omnia Media ad Finem. Arist. 2. Phis. tex. 69. Keck. Eng. c. l. 1. c. 1 [c.18] Canon 6.

[495] "Utrum{que} docet Scriptura: Omnes Doceri a Deo; Et omnes debere audire, legere, & meditari Scripturas & verbum dei. ita{que} Promissiones non evertunt praecepta; ne{que} posita causa prima tolluntur mediae; Vt enim non sequitur, Deus omnia pascit; ergo non opus est pane & agricultura, per haec enim media Deus pascit. Ita non sequitur Deus omnes docet; ergo non opus est verbo; per verbum enim auditum & praedicatum omnes docet." D. Pareus in comment. ad Heb. 8:11.

dream dreams, your young men shall see visions, etc. (Joel 2:28-29). Therefore under the New Covenant, all shall be so taught by the Spirit, that they shall be prophets, not needing any further human teaching.

Answer:

{1} The substance of the answer to the former objected Scripture is also applicable here, and enervates utterly this inference, from that of Joel.

{2} This passage in Joel has special reference to the times of the New Covenant; the scope whereof is, to show that God will more plentifully for measure, and more generally for extent, bestow his Spirit and the effects thereof upon his people under the New Covenant, than he did under the Old. For measure, they should have his Spirit in prophecy, visions, and dreams: that is, they should have all sorts of the manifestations of the Spirit upon them, and this should not be as formerly an extraordinary, but an ordinary and common thing. For extent, {*all flesh*}, that is, all sorts of God's people, male, female, young and old, bond and free (as here Joel expounds himself) should partake of this Spirit of God. So that they shall equalize, yea in some sort excel the ancient Old Covenant prophets themselves, much more the ordinary sort of people, in knowledge; in regard of the ordinariness, distinctness, clarity, and perfection thereof. This promise was most [singularly] and eminently fulfilled by God's miraculous pouring forth his spirit upon the apostles on the feast of Pentecost, and afterwards by his extraordinary and ordinary shedding forth of his Spirit upon others.[496]

{3} This promise of the Spirit was never intended to make everyone a prophet to himself, and to exclude all teaching by men: (i) partly, because the Spirit was usually performed to people at the hearing of the word preached by men, as to Peter's hearers at his sermon;[497] to Cornelius and his company at Peter's sermon;[498] to the Gentiles, at the preaching of Paul and Barnabas; to

---

[496] Acts 2:38, 41-42 to the end
[497] Acts 10:44, etc. & 11:15-17
[498] Acts 10:44, etc. & 11:15-17

the Galatians,⁴⁹⁹ by the ministry and preaching of Paul: *This only would I learn of you, received ye the Spirit by the works of the law, or by the hearing of faith?*⁵⁰⁰ – that is, by the hearing of the doctrine of faith preached. (ii) Partly, because several, having received the Spirit, did presently fall upon preaching the word to others. As the apostles at Pentecost – having received the Holy Spirit – began to speak with other tongues, as the Spirit gave them utterance the wonderful works of God,⁵⁰¹ and Peter so preached at that time as to convert three thousand souls.⁵⁰² So Saul converted and – having received the Holy Spirit – *straightway preached Christ in the synagogues, that he is the Son of God.*⁵⁰³ So that the receiving of the promised Holy Spirit, is so far from rendering human teaching useless and needless, that it contrariwise greatly confirms and establishes the same.

[3] **The third objected Scripture**: *And they shall teach no more* (Greek: *and they shall not teach*) *every man his neighbour, and every man his brother, saying; Know the LORD: for they shall all know me, from the least of them to the greatest of them* (Jeremiah 31:34, Hebrews 8:11). Therefore, it is most plain that under the New Covenant, all shall so know the Lord, that all man's teaching shall cease and be laid aside as needless. After Christ's coming, none ought to teach his neighbor: away therefore with the external ministry, and let it give place to God's internal inspiration – as Calvin recites the objection.⁵⁰⁴

---

⁴⁹⁹ Acts 13:46-49, 52
⁵⁰⁰ Galatians 3:2
⁵⁰¹ Acts 2:4, 11
⁵⁰² Acts 2:38-39, 41
⁵⁰³ Acts 9:17-20
⁵⁰⁴ "'Their objection is this: "After the coming of Christ every one is to teach his neighbor; away then with the external ministry, that a place may be given to the internal inspiration of God."'"
John Calvin's commentary on Hebrews 8:11
[https://biblehub.com/commentaries/calvin/hebrews/8.htm]
<Accessed 4/4/2024>

Answer: Much has been already spoken in this article of the New Covenant, whereby this objection may be refelled. But yet for the sake of clarity, note:

{1} First, that the intent and purpose of the Holy Spirit is here especially to be observed for the removal of this objection. His scope and intent herein is, to show in particular, what a different Covenant this New Covenant should be from the Old, and how far the New should excel the Old. That this is his scope is plain from the series of the context: *I will make a new covenant – not according to the covenant that I made with their fathers*, etc.[505] Here in general, he shows that the New Covenant should be different from, and excel the Old Covenant. Then he descends in particular to show wherein this difference and excellency of the New Covenant from, and above the Old shall consist: *But this shall be the covenant*, etc.[506] As if he had said: In these three points especially the New Covenant shall differ from, and far excel the Old, namely: (i) in the inscription of God's laws in the spiritual tables of their mind and heart; (ii) in the federates' more excellent and more universal knowledge of the Lord; (iii) in the utter forgiving and forgetting of all their sins forever. Whereas: (i) the Old Covenant was written in tables of stone;[507] (ii) the federates' knowledge of God under it was very sparing, small, dark and veiled; and (iii) in their sacrifices there was still a renewed remembrance of sin every year, every day.[508] Now we have the clear intent and purpose of the Holy Spirit in this Scripture. And this gives us a notable ground and light for discovering the vanity and impertinency of the objection, for:

{2} Secondly, hence it is plain that those words {*They shall not teach every man his neighbor, and every man his brother*, etc.} are not to be understood negatively, that under the New Covenant there shall be no more human teaching, public or private at all, but that all such teaching should absolutely

---

[505] Jeremiah 31:31-32
[506] Jeremiah 31:33-34
[507] Deuteronomy 4:13
[508] Hebrews 10:1-3

and utterly cease forever, and give way to immediate inspirations, revelations, etc., but are to be understood only comparatively, that they shall not so teach everyone his neighbor and brother under the New Covenant, as they did under the Old; there shall be such a surpassing, excellent, perfect, clear and general knowledge among all sorts of the federates: small and great.

And it is usual in Scripture in various places to take the word {*not*} comparatively rather than negatively: as, *If ye were blind ye should have no sin*; Greek: *Ye should not have sin*.[509] It cannot be taken negatively, that they should not absolutely have any sin at all: but comparatively, that they should not have so much sin, they should have no sin in comparison. For ignorance excuses sometimes *a tanto* from the greatness of the sin: and knowledge adds always an aggravation to sin. So Paul said: *Christ sent me not to baptize, but to preach the gospel.*[510] {*Not*} cannot here be an absolute and simple negative, as if Christ did not at all send him to baptize; for this is contrary to Christ's commission, authorizing his apostles and ministers both to preach and baptize;[511] nor did Paul himself so understand it; for he did baptize several; and did he do it unsent, or without a call?[512] But it must needs be here only a comparative particle. {*Not*}, that is, Christ sent me not so much to baptize, as to preach; he sent me principally and especially to preach, rather than to baptize. To this effect, the Old Covenant ministration, though glorious, is said to have no glory: not none *absolutely*, but none *comparatively*, in regard to the exceling glory of the New Covenant: *For even that which was made glorious, had no glory in this respect, by reason of the glory that excelleth.*[513]

So here: {*they shall not teach*}, etc. that is, they shall not so teach, so slenderly, so weakly, so sparingly, so darkly, so literally, so imperfectly, etc. under the New Covenant, as they did under the Old. Our godly and learned

---

[509] John 9:41 ουκ αν ειχετε αμαρτιαν
[510] 1 Corinthians 1:17
[511] Matthew 28:19-20
[512] 1 Corinthians 1:14-16
[513] 2 Corinthians 3:10

interpreters do very generally understand this phrase, not in the negative, but in this comparative sense, but they somewhat diversely explain themselves herein.

(i) Some thus, that: "whereas in the former Covenant, Moses and the prophets taught only literally; in this New Covenant, they shall all be taught of God, shall come to Christ, and having the Spirit's anointing, they shall know all things." So Junius.[514] But yet that Moses and the prophets taught only literally, must be warily understood: they taught more literally than spiritually (2 Corinthians 3:6 to the end). There was little Spirit then given, in comparison of what is given now: then, drops; now, rivers of the Spirit (John 7:37-39).

(ii) Some thus, that God does not here quite deny men's teaching one of another, but these are the words: *They shall not teach, saying: Know the LORD* – as if he had said, "Such ignorance shall not possess men's minds as heretofore, that they knew not who God was. They shall not be so grossly ignorant of principles and fundamentals, as alphabetarians in religion, etc. So

---

[514] Non autem solum docebunt amplius quisque, &c.] Vide Jescha. 11. 9. id est, In priore Foedere docuerunt Mosche & Prophetae Litera tantummodo: In posteriore vero erunt omnes Docti a Deo, venient ad Christum quos Pater traxerit, & unctionem habentes a Sancto illius Spiritu cognoscent omnia, Ioan. 6. 44, 45. 1 Cor. 1. 7. & 2. 10. & sequent. 1 Ioh. 2. 20. Est autem in his verbis Eclipsis apud Hebraeos frequens, ut observavimus, Gen. 32. 28. & 1 Shem. 8. 7.
Franciscus Junius' Annotation on Jeremiah 31:34

Calvin[515] and Diodati[516] much to that effect, although in another place he thinks that "the divine teaching is here preferred before all human teaching,"[517] which falls in with that of Junius.

(iii) Some thus: that "the New Covenant teaching shall not be restrained to a few of one nation, but to all sorts of all nations; shall not be only in fundamentals, but also in more perfect and abstruse mysteries of religion; shall not be with a servile coaction, but with a voluntary inclination to obedience," etc. So Pareus.[518]

But surely we may well put them all together. For this is a highly hyperbolic expression whereby God intends to magnify the New Testament knowledge above the Old, that it shall be far different, and much more extensive and excellent (as I have already shown): more divine, more spiritual,

---

[515] "But they pass by this, that the prophet does not wholly deny that they would teach one another, but his words are these, They shall not teach, saying {*Know the Lord*}; as though he had said, "Ignorance shall not as heretofore so possess the minds of men as not to know who God is." "for these words, "Know ye Jehovah," point out the first elements of faith, or of celestial doctrine. And, doubtless, if we consider how great was the ignorance of the ancient people, they were then only in the elements"
John Calvin's commentary on Hebrews 8:11 & Jeremiah 31:34
[https://www.studylight.org/commentaries/eng/cal/hebrews-8.html]
<Accessed 4/15/2024>
[https://ccel.org/ccel/calvin/calcom20/calcom20.iii.xliv.html]
<Accessed 4/15/2024>

[516] "{*Shall not teach*} – namely: men shall not be so ignorant, as they were when they knew not what belonged to God, for the prophet intends not here to take away the ministry of the church."
John Diodati's Annotation on Hebrews 8:11

[517] See also John Diodati's Annotation on Jeremiah 31:34: "{*Teach no more*} that is to say, all the true members of Christs Church shall be lively illumi|nated by God's Spirit, so that all human instruction and persuasion, after that divine and internal, shall be of small virtue; as without it, it has no force at all, but is altogether unprofitable. Or, he speaks of the infusion of the supernatural light, and of the motion of the heart, which are the true beginnings of faith created by the Spirit, and not framed by any humane precepts or authority. {*For I will*} that is to say, I will give them my Spirit, for I shall have received them into favor. As by the sine of man God's gifts had been taken away from him, see Romans 11:27."
[https://quod.lib.umich.edu/e/eebo/A36033.0001.001/1:29.31?c=eebo;c=eebo2;g=eebogroup;rgn=div2;view=fulltext;xc=1;rgn1=author;q1=diodati]
<Accessed 4/17/2024>

[518] David Pareus' commentary on Hebrews 8:11

more clear, more evidential, more complete, more efficacious, and more glorious. And yet all this by the instrumentality of the more excellent New Covenant ministry (2 Corinthians 3:4-5 to the end & 4:6-7). Therefore this promise does not at all seclude the New Covenant public ministry, nor Christians' mutual, private instruction one of another. The note in the Large London Annotations is excellent: therefore see it in the margin.[519]

---

[519] "{*And they shall teach no more*}, etc. This passage is not to be conceived, as if the meaning were that they should need no teaching at all in those times, or that the office of teachers should then cease as superfluous, [f]or while men live in this world, they know but in part, nor exactly indeed ought (1 Corinthians 8:2 & 13:19), nor can any while they live here, attain to such a height of perfection either in knowledge or in grace, but that they may still grow in either (Philippians 3:12-15, 2 Peter 3:18). And the office of teaching therefore is to continue to the world's end (Matthew 28:20, Ephesians 4:11, 13). Yea, it is expressly said, in the prophecies of the very same times here intended, that people should call one upon another to repair together unto God's house, there to be taught: by whom, but by his Ministers? (Isaiah 2:3, Micah 4:2). But the question is then: how are these words to be understood? For answer whereunto, some render the words: "they shall not only teach one another;" as the like defect of the restrictive term is often found omitted (Genesis 32:28, 1 Samuel 8:7), and so the meaning should be, that they shall not be taught by their teachers alone, but God should cooperate together with their teaching, and instruct them inwardly by his Spirit (Isaiah 54:13 & 59:21, John 6:5, Isaiah 54:13 & 59:21, John 6:45; 1 John 2:20, 27). Others conceive it to be understood that none should ordinarily be so silly and ignorant, as not to have some competent measure of knowledge of the main grounds at least, and the first principles of saving truth, though having need further to be built up in the same (Hebrews 6:1-2). Others, that they should not need to be urged and pressed upon the fear and service of God, they should be prone and forward to it of themselves: by the knowledge of God, after the Chaldee paraphrase, understanding such a knowledge of him as works in the heart a reverent dread and regard of him, and care to serve and obey him (chapter 22:16; 1 John 2:4). Others, that men shall not need to take so much pains and travel about teaching of the elect, as they had been constrained to take with people in former times, and all to no purpose (Isaiah 28:9-13). The like manner of speech they suppose to be found (John 16:26). I conceive in this form of speech to be intimated: (1) the great measure of clear light that should in those times be revealed (2 Corinthians 4:3, 6); (2) the great measure of knowledge that should by reason thereof abound (Isaiah 11:9, Habbakuk 2:14); (3) the clearness of understanding, that many should so be possessed with, that they might seem rather to have been taught by some immediate irradiation, than by any means of instruction, as Galatians 3:12; and (4) the generality or numerosity at least of knowing persons, far above that that had been in former times, and that even amongst the meaner sort. See Acts 18:25-26."
Large London Annotations on Jeremiah 31:34.

[4] ***The fourth objected Scripture***: *But the Anointing which ye have received of him, abideth in you, and ye need not that any man teach you* (1 John 2:27). Therefore after people receive this anointing from Christ, they need no more any man's teaching, etc.

Answer: For removal of this objection, as quite besides the apostle's intent, consider:

{1} First, that the scope and intent of this context from verse 17 to verse 29 is to exhort them to beware of the dangerous antichrists and heretical seducers, that should come, yea were in part come already, as Cerinthians, Ebionites, etc. against whom he arms them, encouraging them to persevere in the truth upon nine considerations, as I have elsewhere shown.[520] The eighth is this: that though he had written these things to them, concerning them that seduce them; yet he had propounded therein no new or strange doctrine to them, but such as for substance they knew already, by the Holy Spirit, that Anointing teaching them all things, namely: all things necessary to salvation, whose abiding in them should enable them to abide in the truth (1 John 2:26-27). This is the direct purpose of the words.

{2} Secondly, that therefore this phrase {*Ye need not that any man teach you*} does not at all import, that they were now past all need of man's teaching, being so taught by that Anointing: for John himself was now teaching of them, in writing this very epistle to them, and that very many ways, and particularly in this context he was teaching them to persevere in the truth against all seducements[521] – and will any one say that what here John taught them was more than needed? But this phrase does imply:

(i) That they were most thoroughly and solidly taught by the best teacher, the Anointing, namely: the Holy Spirit, received by them, and remaining in them (1 John 2:20, 27). They that are taught by this divine teacher, comparatively need not that man should teach them. The Spirit teaches most

---

[520] In my *Key of the Bible* on 1 John 2:18-29
[521] 1 John 2:13-29

convincingly, clearly, fully, powerfully, persuasively, efficaciously, etc. – beyond all man's teaching. Not that man's teaching is hereby simply and absolutely excluded, but that the Spirit's teaching is magnified and preferred above it. So that man's teaching (though necessary and useful in its place, yet is as no teaching, in comparison of the Spirit's teaching that excels.

(ii) That they needed not that man should teach them: (a) either any fundamental principles of faith or of the doctrine of the anointing, having so well grounded them, and taught them all things necessary to salvation; (2) or any new doctrine of a more exquisite and perfect stamp, as yet strange and unknown to them for they knew all things, and needed no new gospel, no new light or doctrine for kind and substance, though the best had need of man's teaching in order to growth and further degrees of knowledge (1 Corinthians 13:9-10, 12; 2 Peter 3:18).[522]

(iii) That here, John himself propounds no other doctrine to them, than what the holy anointing within them would approve and give attestation to, having written the effect and substance thereof in their hearts already by his own finger.[523] Thus he excellently confirms and establishes them against seducers, in the doctrine and truth which they had already received, showing that what now he inculcates unto them, they for substance knew already, and had long since not only heard it from their teachers, but learned it also effectually by the Holy Spirit within them.

{3} Thirdly, that what here John speaks of their anointing, of their knowing all things, and that they needed not that any man should teach them, being chiefly matters of fact, is specially and peculiarly to be understood of them to whom he wrote this epistle. They were so thoroughly and soundly instructed by the Spirit, that they knew in a sort all things requisite to salvation and sufficient to keep them from seducements, that they

---

[522] According to John Calvin in his commentary on 1 John 2:27, and Beza's annotation upon the same place.
[523] According to John Calvin in his commentary on 1 John 2:27, and Beza's annotation upon the same place.

comparatively and in some respects had not need that any man should teach them. But this cannot be the case of all, not of most in the visible church under the New Covenant. How few are there of whom ministers can affirm these things? How many children, babes, and infants are there in knowledge, but how few adult, ripe, and grown men in understanding? Therefore this cannot be drawn into a precedent or general rule for all under the New Covenant, as not needing human teaching.

Thus it is plain that God, by this promise of excellent knowledge under the New Covenant, never intended to deprive his church and people of so sweet and rich a blessing, as public and private teaching, or the public ministry.

Question 5: Why has God promised this blessing in his New Covenant, that all shall know him, from the least of them to the greatest of them?

Answer: These reasons especially may be given, why God has covenanted to confer such eminent knowledge upon all sorts and degrees of his New Covenant people, namely:

(1) **Because, none in all the world, besides God alone in Christ by his Spirit can furnish the soul with right saving knowledge of himself, and his affairs.**

For consider:

[1] There may be a natural knowledge of God and religion, such as pagans may have by the dim light of nature remaining in them, and by the book of the creature.[524] This may be sufficient to leave them without excuse in their damnation: though not sufficient for their salvation. For nature cannot elevate the soul above nature.

[2] There may be a literal or notional, and an acquired knowledge of God and religion by education, reading, hearing, public or private instruction, meditation, etc., such as hypocrites may have by common illumination; or as reprobates may have from the mere capacity of elevated reason.[525] But this literal, notional and acquired knowledge will not effectually save the soul. They that are most exquisite herein, may at last utterly fall away and perish.

[3] There is beyond all these a spiritual, supernatural, infused knowledge of God and religion, which God alone in Christ by his Spirit teaches to his elect, namely:

---

[524] Romans 1:18-21, 28
[525] Hebrews 6:4-6; 2 Peter 2:20-22

{1} God the Father of Lights (namely: of all lights natural, spiritual, and celestial) he is the fountain of this light of saving knowledge, he is the first teacher, it originally comes all from him.[526] *All thy children shall be taught of the LORD.*[527] This, Christ thus alledges and interprets: *And they shall be all taught of God. Every man therefore that hath heard and hath learned of the Father cometh unto me.*[528]

{2} In and by Jesus Christ the Son, our Mediator, God the Father reveals himself and ways savingly to his people. *No man knows the Son but the Father; neither knoweth any man the Father, save the Son, and he to whomsoever the Son will reveal him.*[529] Again, it is said of Christ: *That was the true light, which lighteth every man that cometh into the world.*[530] How? *Either* naturally with the light of natural reason and human understanding, so Christ the Word, as Creator, enlightens every man created with this principle of natural light (see John 1:1-10); *or* supernaturally with saving knowledge, So Jesus Christ as our Mediator and great Prophet, enlightens every man that comes into the world that is enlightened. Every man in the world that is savingly enlightened, is enlightened by him.[531] Christ is the express character and most perfect image of his Father (Hebrews 1:3). So that he who sees and knows the Son, knows the Father also (John 14:9). Hence it is said that the light of the knowledge of the glory of God is given in the face of Jesus Christ (2 Corinthians 4:6). As a man reads the father's countenance in the face of his son that is most like him, so God represents himself most lively, sweetly and savingly in Jesus Christ to his elect. In Christ, he reveals himself as their Redeemer, their Savior, their

---

[526] James 1:17
[527] Isaiah 54:13
[528] John 6:45
[529] Matthew 11:27, John 6:46
[530] John 1:9
[531] "It is another kind of teaching, when the Lord teaches us knowledge, than that is that we can have from the hands of men; Christ is another kind of prophet, you come not to hear him speak, to hear him teaching, as a man hears other lectures, where his understanding is informed; But he is such a prophet as enlightens every man within, that comes into the world; that is, Every man that is enlightened, is enlightened by him."
D. Preston of the New Covenant, Sermon 12. p 375. (London, 1634).

Father, their Husband, their God in Covenant, merciful, gracious, longsuffering, abundant in lovingkindness and truth, pardoning iniquity, transgression and sin, etc. All knowledge of God out of Christ is dead, vanishing, fruitless, ineffectual; but the knowledge of God in Christ is quickening, effectual, lasting and saving.

{3} God gives the saving knowledge of himself in Christ, by his Spirit. His Spirit is that unction, that anointing which immediately teaches them all things necessary to salvation.[532] *God hath revealed them unto us by his Spirit: For the Spirit searcheth all things, even the deep things of God, – The things of God knoweth no man but the Spirit of God. Now we have received not the Spirit of the world, but the Spirit which is of God, that we might know the things that are freely given to us of God.*[533] The Spirit makes use of the ministry of men, co-operates with the preaching of the gospel, to work this knowledge of God into the hearts of his elect at their conversion, and to increase it afterwards there; but all the efficacy and enlightening virtue is only from the Spirit – men are but only instruments.[534] Thus it is God in Christ by his Spirit, and he alone that can furnish and fill his people with saving knowledge of himself; he only can rub off the scales of blindness, he only can savingly open the understanding, he only can anoint us with such eye-salve, that we can supernaturally see: and therefore he promises and covenants to do this for his people, which himself alone can do.

(2) **Because it is most congruous and agreeable to the nature of the New Covenant to bring in a more transcendent and excellent knowledge of God and his ways, than was brought in by the Old Covenant.**

For: [1] this New Covenant is the last and best Covenant, the most perfect of all covenant administrations. [2] The condition of the church under the

---

[532] 1 John 2:20, 27
[533] 1 Corinthians 2:10-12
[534] Acts 26:18; 1 Peter 2:8-9, Philippians 1:9; 2 Corinthians 4:6-7

New Covenant is more ripe and perfect than ever it was before.[535] The church under the Old Covenant was as a child in minority, under age: but under the New Covenant, is as a man in maturity, of full age. [3] The New Covenant knowledge and fruition of God, is gradually the very next unto the immediate glorious vision and fruition of God in heaven face to face.[536] Consequently, this most excellent and complete knowledge of God is promised in this New Covenant, as being most congruous to the excellent nature of the New Covenant.

(3) **Because, gross ignorance of God and his ways, is very sinful, mischievous, and dangerous: but especially under the New Covenant.**

[1] *Gross ignorance of God and his ways, is*:

{1} Very sinful. (i) Partly, because the original root of it was Adam's great sin: his first apostasy from God. Hereby he deprived himself and all his posterity of the image of God, which did partly consist in knowledge.[537] Ignorance then is a rotten branch of a rotten root. (ii) Partly, because ignorance, in the nature of it, is the soul's darkness and blindness in spirituals.[538] A miserable and deformed sinfulness. Knowledge in the soul is as the eye in the body, or sun in the sky;[539] ignorance is contrariwise as a face without eyes, or the sky without a sun. Oh, how misshapen, dark, and deformed! (iii) Partly, because ignorance has a stubbornness and enmity in it against the light:[540] *Men loved darkness rather than light*, etc. (John 3:19-20). (iv) Partly, because ignorance is the cause, occasion and inlet to many other sins. It has a very train of sin at its heels (Isaiah 1:3-4, Hosea 4:2-3). Through ignorance, men crucified Christ (1 Corinthians 2:7-9). Through ignorance, Paul was a persecutor, blasphemer, and injurious (1 Timothy 1:13-14).

---

[535] Galatians 4:1-3
[536] 2 Corinthians 3:18; 1 Corinthians 13:12; 1 John 3:2-3
[537] Colossians 3:10
[538] Ephesians 5:8 & 4:18
[539] Ephesians 1:18
[540] Job 21:14-15, Ephesians 4:18

Through ignorance, men idolatrously worship they know not what (Acts 17:23). Oh into what extremities of wickedness will not a blind ignorant creature precipitate himself!

{2} Very mischievous and dangerous. The mischief and danger of ignorance is great and manifold, as: (i) ignorance makes people a prey to all manner of seducers (2 Timothy 3:6-7). (ii) Ignorance makes men wander in by-paths of error and ungodliness they know not whither (John 12:35). (iii) Ignorance hides the gospel from men, that the light thereof shines not in upon them, to their conversion (2 Corinthians 4:3-4, Acts 26:18, John 3:19-20). (iv) Ignorance alienates men from the life of God, that neither God nor godliness lives in them, or by them (Ephesians 4:18). (v) Ignorance involves men in senseless security (Hosea 7:9). (vi) Ignorance destroys a people: *my people are destroyed for lack of knowledge.*[541] It destroys them both corporally and spiritually (Isaiah 5:13; 2 Timothy 2:25-26). (vi) Ignorance is the highway to hell, and will at last bring upon men the vengeance of God in their everlasting destruction (2 Thessalonians 1:8-9).

[2] **This ignorance of God and his ways is most sinful under the New Covenant.** Because against the greatest light and most complete means of knowledge and fullest effusions of God's illuminating Spirit, which the New Covenant brings in above all former Covenants. Ignorance under such light, such means, such effusions of the Spirit is deeply aggravated, and more exceedingly sinful (John 15:22 & 3:19-20). Therefore seeing as gross ignorance of God is so sinful and dangerous, especially in this noontide of light now under the New Covenant, God has now covenanted to furnish his people with more excellent knowledge of himself than ever his people had formerly, that the sin and danger of such ignorance may not undo his New Covenant people.

---

[541] Hosea 4:6

(4) Because such New Covenant knowledge of God as is here intended, is of general necessity, influence and utility to God's New Covenant people about all the affairs of the Christian religion.

The light of this supernatural knowledge is as necessary and useful in the church, as the light of the natural luminaries – sun, moon and stars – is in the world. Now this knowledge of God is useful and necessary these ways especially, namely:

[1] As a discoverer of God, Christ, and of all the mysteries of Christian religion to the soul.[542] The right knowledge of God manifests all those; but gross ignorance leaves us wholly in the dark about them all.

[2] As a detector of all our sins and corruptions. The right knowledge of God and his infinite purity, in the exactness of his Word and law most notably lays open unto us the sinful impurity and pravity of our hearts and ways, repugnant to God and his will. Thus in Paul;[543] thus in Job of old.[544]

[3] As an inlet and open door to all sanctifying graces. As natural light was the first particular distinct creature when God made the world (Genesis 1:3), so supernatural light is the first distinct grace when God new-creates the soul (Colossians 1:10; 2 Peter 1:5-7), and is an introduction to the rest – as, to faith (Isaiah 53:11, Hebrews 11:2), to affiance, trust, and confidence (Psalm 9:10), to repentance (Job 42:5-6, Jeremiah 31:19), to temperance, patience, godliness, brotherly-kindness, and love (2 Peter 1:5-7), to obedience (John 13:17), etc. Knowledge and illumination still lead the way to all distinct graces in order of nature.

[4] As a guide to all our faculties and affections. Light in the bodily eye guides all the bodily parts and members; so light in the understanding guides all the faculties of the soul: there being a natural subordination of the affections to the will, of the will to the understanding, and of the

---

[542] Ephesians 1:17-21, John 17:3, Ephesians 3:19
[543] Romans 7:7-12, Philippians 3:4-12
[544] Job 42:5-6

understanding to the light therein only violence of corruption ofttimes inverts this orderly subordination.[545]

[5] As a pilot to all our Christian duties and actions. Knowledge sits at stern in every well-managed action and service. Whatsoever we do, we should do it knowingly, understandingly; we should preach understandingly (1 Corinthians 14:19; 1 Timothy 1:7 & 3:2, Titus 1:9), we should pray understandingly (1 Corinthians 14:15), we should give thanks understandingly (1 Corinthians 14:15), we should read and hear understandingly (Acts 8:30, John 13:17), we must manage all our actions and service of God understandingly (1 Chronicles 28:9); otherwise, all we do are but blind services and sacrifices of fools (Ecclesiastes 5:1).

[6] As an evidence of all that God has given us, and done for us in Christ.[546] True knowledge lets us see what we have from God, and so doubles our enjoyment.

[7] Finally, as an espial [noticing] of our better condition and state reserved for us in the world to come. *Knowing in yourselves that you have in heaven a better and more enduring substance.*[547] These, and many such like, are the advantages and benefits of true knowledge in the soul. The Lord therefore knowing how necessary and useful true knowledge is unto his people (in whose prosperity he exceedingly delights), has promised this knowledge in abundance to his people in this New Covenant.

(5) Finally, because such universal and eminent knowledge of God under the New Covenant, exceedingly advances the glory of Christ and of his New Covenant.

Before Christ came, the knowledge of God and divine things was restrained to a few – a handful of Jews and proselytes – and it was imparted to

---

[545] Luke 11:34-36, Matthew 6:22-23
[546] 1 Corinthians 2:10 to the end; 1 John 5: [13]; 2 Corinthians 13
[547] Hebrews 10:34

those few under a veil very darkly and obscurely.[548] Then Christ and his Covenant comparatively had but little glory. But since Christ's coming, this knowledge being extended generally to all sorts in all nations, and imparted to them eminently for measure and degree with a noontide-light and sunshine of irradiation, the knowledge of the Lord covering the earth as the waters cover the sea, and filling the church as the light of the sun fills the whole world. Hereby the glory of Jesus Christ is most highly advanced, bringing all this glorious light with him, and the glory of his New Covenant is notably exalted above the imperfect, dark, veiled administrations of God's fore-going Covenants.[549] Now God had a singular intent to glorify his Christ and his New Covenant in these latter days.

---

[548] 2 Corinthians 3:4 to the end
[549] 2 Timothy 1:9-10; 2 Corinthians 3:4 to the end

Question 6: How may we discover that we so know the Lord, as God here intends in this his New Covenant promise?

Answer: So much has been spoken to this effect already, that I need not add much more than briefly to point at the particulars, which more specially tend to the resolving of this question.

(1) **In general**, it is plain:

[1] *That such as know God aright, may know that they know him*: *Hereby we do know that we know him, if we keep his commandments*, etc.[550] The discerning of the truth of our knowledge of God is not a thing impossible or unfeasible.

[2] *That very many do think they know God aright, and the things of God aright, when as yet they know nothing as they ought to know.*[551] We all have knowledge – knowledge is an easy attainment – but how few have such knowledge as they ought to have, how hard is it to know God or religion as we ought to know? A man may know much of God theoretically or notionally – that he is, that he is one, that he subsists in three distinct persons, that he is all-sufficient, infinite, eternal, etc., that he has eternally ordained all things, in beginning of time created all things, etc. – and yet notwithstanding all this, not knowing him so as to believe in him, admire him, adore him, love him, fear him, delight in him with all his heart, with all his soul, with all his mind, with all his might, obey him sincerely, etc. Such a man knows nothing of God as he ought to know. So a man may know much of Christ – of his natures, person, offices, effects, and fruits of his offices, etc. – and yet not knowing him so as to deny a man's self for him, to forsake all for him, to hate father, mother, and dearest relations for him, to count all things loss and dung

---

[550] 1 John 2:3-4
[551] 1 Corinthians 8:1-2

for the excellency of the knowledge and righteousness of Christ, to believe and rest upon him alone for salvation, to be acted and ruled by him, his Spirit and Word, etc. Such a man knows nothing of Christ as he ought to know. So a man may know much of God's will, and of the things of God and of Christ, of his commandments, of his prohibitions, of his Covenant and promises, of his ordinances, of the fundamentals and other deeper mysteries of religion, etc. He may be able to describe them, to teach them to others, to defend them by dispute against all gainsayers, etc. Yet if after all this knowledge, he goes on still in his wickedness, he casts God's commands behind his back, walks contrary to the principles of religion, despises the Covenant and promises of God, profanes and pollutes all his ordinances, contradicts the will of God by fulfilling his own will and ways, etc. this man knows nothing of religion and of the things of God as he ought to know. The like is to be said in other cases. And therefore, there is great need of searching whether we know God aright, seeing we may have much knowledge of him, and yet know nothing of him as we ought to know.

(2) **In particular** we may discern that our knowledge of God is such as he intends in this New Covenant, especially these four ways, namely:

[1] *By the nature of our knowledge*. If it answers the nature of the New Covenant knowledge, which is more excellent than the Old Covenant knowledge of God, in {1} divineness, {2} spiritualness, {3} clarity, {4} evidentialness, {5} completeness, {6} efficaciousness, and {7} gloriousness. All of this, I have formerly opened in Question 1.

[2] *By God's way and method of bringing and working this knowledge in us*, if God: – {1} in Jesus Christ, {2} by his Spirit and public ministry – has wrought it in us, and {3} increasing it more and more in us by degrees, as has been explained in Question 2.

[3] *By the properties of true saving knowledge*. It has these more special properties: {1} It is affective. It works not only upon the head, but also upon the heart: not only upon the understanding, but also upon the affections (1

John 4:7-8, Philippians 1:9), as I have elsewhere shown.⁵⁵² It makes a man so know God, as to love him, fear him, obey him, etc. {2} It is experimental.⁵⁵³ It affords a man a spiritual sense, taste and experimental relish of God, Christ, and their sweetness, goodness, pleasantness, etc (Philippians 1:9, Hebrews 5:14, Psalm 34:8 with 1 Peter 2:2-3). This is far beyond all empty notions, though never so subtle and acute. {3} It is effective. It is not an idle, but a working knowledge;⁵⁵⁴ it is not ineffectual and weak, but very efficacious; it is not only contemplative, but active also. It especially produces these effects, namely: (i) humbles the soul for sin (Job 42:5-6), (ii) purifies the heart from sin (James 3:17, 1 John 3:6), (iii) makes obedient to God and his commands, is a practical knowledge (1 John 2:3-4 & 4:6, John 10:4), and (iv) disposes a man to serve the Lord sincerely and willingly (1 Chronicles 28:9). {4} It is very pregnant and fruitful in all goodness (2 Peter 1:5-8, James 3:17). A barren, empty, dry, fruitless, useless knowledge that ends only in knowing, and does good neither to a man's self nor others, etc., is a bad knowledge.

[4] *By the associates or companions, which the Scripture joins with true knowledge, and which actually do accompany true knowledge in the sanctified heart.*⁵⁵⁵ The companions of a man's delight, are notable indications of his principles, constitution, and disposition. The companions of true knowledge of God are: faith, virtue, temperance, patience, godliness, brotherly-kindness, charity⁵⁵⁶ – yea, knowledge, righteousness, and true holiness are co-partners in the image of God renewed in us.⁵⁵⁷ Where these sacred concomitants are indeed, there true saving knowledge is in some good measure.

---

⁵⁵² In my *Communicant Instructed*, p.105 (London, 1651)
⁵⁵³ See there, pp.99-100
⁵⁵⁴ See there, pp.101, 107-108
⁵⁵⁵ Noscitur ex comite qui non dignoscitur ex se
⁵⁵⁶ 2 Peter 1:5-7
⁵⁵⁷ Colossians 3:10, Ephesians 4:23-24

Inferences

Shall God's federates have generally a more excellent knowledge of God, etc., under the New Covenant than they had under the Old Covenant? *Shall not every man teach his neighbor and brother, saying; know the LORD? For that all shall know him from the least to the greatest of them*: Then:

(1) Hence the Old and New Covenant essentially and substantially agree, though accidentally and circumstantially they differ, about the knowledge of the Lord.

[1] Essentially they agree as to the essence and substance of this knowledge. Both of them teach their federates to know the Lord God – yea, and to know God in Christ in some sort.

[2] Accidentally they disagree, as to the accidents and circumstances of this knowledge of the Lord. For: {1} that knowledge of God under the Old Covenant was restrained to one sort of people the Jews; but this under the New Covenant is extended to all sorts of people of all nations. {2} That was more human; this more divine. {3} That was more literal and carnal; this more spiritual and celestial. {4} That was more dark and veiled; this more clear and revealed. {5} That was consequently much less; this much more evidential and ensuring. {6} That was more imperfect and childlike; this more perfect, complete, and manlike. {7} That more weak and ineffectual; this more powerful and efficacious. [8] That having some sort of glory; but this being far more excellently glorious. As in all these particulars has been formerly manifested. So then, though Old and New Covenant substantially do agree, yet accidentally they much disagree: the New Covenant far transcending and excelling [the Old].

(2) **Hence the chief perfection of knowledge, is to know God aright, for the most perfect light and knowledge, is that which is in the church of God, surpassing all pagan-knowledge** – the most perfect knowledge in the church, is that knowledge which the church has in her most ripe grown and perfect state, now under the New Covenant,[558] and the perfection of this New Covenant knowledge is wholly placed in this: that all his covenant people know the Lord,[559] for:

[1] The Lord God is the highest and most perfect object knowable, and therefore the right knowledge of the Lord is the height of knowledge.

[2] The Lord cannot be rightly and savingly known but in Jesus Christ, and in his face:[560] {1} in whom the divine perfections are most resplendent;[561] {2} in whom the whole mystery of sinners salvation was contrived and decreed before all time;[562] {3} by whom the redemption and reconcilement of sinners to God was wrought and effected in fullness of time;[563] {4} through whom the redemption, reconcilement and salvation of sinners is actually applied and appropriated to the elect in due time;[564] and {5} with whom the everlasting happiness and salvation of sinners shall be consummated in heavenly glory after all time.[565] So that the right knowledge of God comprehends in it all saving knowledge whatsoever; it is the center where it all meets; it is the circumference wherein it is all contained. know God aright, and know all things.

[3] The right knowledge of God, inchoate in this world, is life eternal, in the root and foundation;[566] the knowledge of God consummate in the world to come, shall be eternal life and happiness in the complete consummation

---

[558] Galatians 4:1-3, etc.
[559] Jeremiah 31:34, Hebrews 8:11
[560] 2 Corinthians 4:6-7 & 3:18
[561] 2 Corinthians 3:8, John 14:9-11
[562] Ephesians 1:4-6
[563] Ephesians 1:7, Romans 5:8-10
[564] Romans 8:29-30, Ephesians 1:3
[565] John 17:24 & 14:2-3
[566] John 17:3

thereof.[567] So then, to know God aright is the chief perfection of all knowledge. Would you have the chief perfection of all knowledge? Labor then to know God aright. All light is but darkness; all knowledge is but ignorance, which is besides, or without the true knowledge of God. And all dangerous damning darkness and ignorance vanishes away, as a morning's mist before the sun, when the true glory of this knowledge of God in Christ begins to shine into the soul.

(3) Hence the right and saving knowledge of God is a very great and eminent mercy.

Why? Because this, and this alone of particular graces, is expressly promised in this New Covenant.[568] And nothing is expressed in the New Covenant, but what is a very great and eminent mercy. As the sun and moon are great mercies to the world, the eye to the body, and reason to the mind; so the true knowledge of God is a very great and eminent mercy to the soul. All other graces of sanctification are implicitly promised, in God's promise of writing his laws in mind and heart: But besides that, the knowledge of the Lord is explicitly promised. Oh, there is a singular excellency in this true knowledge of the Lord, as I have formerly manifested.[569] Then let all that are ignorant of God, press after the right knowledge of him. And let all that know him aright, rejoice in him, and magnify him exceedingly who hath so opened their eyes.

(4) Hence all true saving knowledge of God is only from God.

Why? Because God promises it in his New Covenant. If we might have it by nature or by art, from ourselves or from the creature, or from any other fountain than from God alone the Father of lights,[570] God might have directed

---

[567] Matthew 5:8; 1 John 3:2-3, John 17:24
[568] Hebrews 8:11, Jeremiaih 31:34
[569] In 5, Question 4
[570] James 1:17

us to repair thither for supply; but promising this knowledge to his federates, he declares himself the only fountain of this light, and tacitly directs all that want it to come unto him alone for it. He promises what himself alone can perform. He shines unto all his federates by the instrumental light of his gospel and New Covenant.[571] He shines into all his federates, even into their minds and hearts by the effectual light of his Spirit.[572] He shines away all their gross sinful darkness, and brings light out of darkness The god of this world, Satan, can blind men's minds;[573] but it is only the Lord our God in Christ can recover sight to the blind, and open their eyes.[574] Therefore, you who are blind or weak-sighted, anoint your eyes with his eye-salve that you may see.[575] Beg him to open your eyes. Remember his promises to this effect: *If any of you lack wisdom, let him ask of God that giveth to all men liberally and upbraideth not, and it shall be given him.*[576] And here in this New Covenant: *All shall know me from the least to the greatest.*[577]

(5) Hence, as the greatest and highest ought not to despise; so the least and lowest need not despair of the true knowledge of God now under the New Covenant.

Why? Because the promise of this knowledge of the Lord is directed, not only to the greatest but to the least also.[578] God's promises are without respect of persons. The least shall know God as well as the greatest. The least had need to know God, because they know him not, or very little: The greatest had need to know him, because they know him not enough. The least shall know God by knowledge implanted into them; the greatest shall know God, by knowledge augmented in them. The least shall know God, that they may be

---

[571] 2 Corinthians 4:4-6
[572] 2 Corinthians 3:18
[573] 2 Corinthians 4:3-4
[574] Luke 4:18
[575] Revelation 3:18
[576] James 1:5
[577] Hebrews 8:11
[578] Hebrews 8:11, Jeremiah 31:34

God's disciples; the greatest shall know God, because they are but God's disciples. The least shall know God, because their meanness cannot debase them too low for God's illumination; the greatest shall know God, because their greatness cannot advance too high for God's illumination. The least shall know God, that they may not despair of knowing him enough; the greatest shall know God, that they may not presume of knowing him too much. All shall know God, because both great and small have their knowledge from God. Come hither, O ye least of God's people, and be comfortable; come hither, O ye greatest of God's people, and be humble. The least are not so ignorant, but God will make them know him; and the greatest are not so intelligent, but God will make them know him more. All knowledge of God in this world is but in part, and all knowledge in part needs to be increased.[579]

(6) Hence, God's federates now under the New Covenant should not content themselves to know only fundamentals and first principles touching God and his ways.

Under the Old Covenant they seemed to stick to principles and first elements; they taught one another, saying, *know the Lord*; they were but alphabetarians, as children in their ABC or primer of religion. But under the New Covenant, they have come of age.[580] They should know the Lord more perfectly. They should not stick to plain principles, but proceed to profound and abstruse mysteries. The New Covenant light is far greater, and proportionably, their knowledge of God and his ways should be greatened also. They *should be no longer children but men in understanding* of Christ's highest form, taking out his deepest and hardest lessons.[581] Away with that lazy, sluggish stupidity in many professed Christians, who in the knowledge of God take so little pains, that they therein come short of the very Jews. Shall

---

[579] 1 Corinthians 13:9-10, 12
[580] Galatians 4:1-3, etc.
[581] Ephesians 4:14; 1 Corinthians 14:20

Jews under veils and shadows of the Old Covenant know more of God then Christians under the sunshine and open face of the New Covenant?

(7) Hence all such ways and means of knowledge as God has ordained under his New Covenant, ought to be made use of in subservience to, and for accomplishment of, this promise of knowing the Lord in his New Covenant.

God's New Covenant precepts and institutions, must not thwart and cross his New Covenant promises and obligations: nor may his promises be urged to evacuate his precepts. God's promises set forth the end, which God will bring his federates unto: God's precepts set forth the means whereby God is pleased to bring them unto that end. The means must be subordinate and subservient to the end and consequently our observation of his precepts unto our expectation upon his promises. He that despises God's prescribed means, despises also God's promised end. The contempt of his precepts inevitably infers the contempt of his promises. Private Christian teaching, and public ministerial instruction until the world's end are (as has been formerly shown)[582] God's ordinary New Covenant way,[583] prescribed of God for breeding and increasing the right knowledge of God and his ways among his people; and by which his Spirit efficaciously works in them that effect: they therefore that despise and would destroy Christ's New Covenant ministry, preaching and other ordinances, or private Christian and domestic instruction, do therein despise the true knowledge of God, the New Covenant promising it, and the authority of Jesus Christ in his New Covenant ordinances and institutions as his ordinary fixed means for the attainment of it.

---

[582] Hebrews 8:11, Jeremiah 31:34

[583] In Question 2 especially; in question 4 throughout

(8) **Hence, so long as men remain grossly ignorant of God and the things of God under the New Covenant, so long they are without the excellent blessing, influence, and saving efficacy of the New Covenant.**

Hence, so long as men remain grossly ignorant of God and the things of God under the New Covenant, so long they are without the excellent blessing, influence and saving efficacy of the New Covenant. For the true saving knowledge of God and his ways, is the very first distinct particular blessing promised in the New Covenant, and performed accordingly: the writing of God's laws in their hearts, and the grand covenant interest mutually between God and them, formerly expressed in the New Covenant, being more general, large and complexive mercies. If therefore you do not as yet truly and savingly know the Lord in some degree, then you are partaker of the New Covenant's saving mercy, virtue and efficacy in no degree. As yet you are darkness, and not light in the Lord;[584] as yet you are not taught of God by his Spirit and ministry, so as to come to Christ;[585] as yet the gospel is hidden to you, as to one that is lost, the god of this world having blinded your mind;[586] as yet you are a child of the night, and not of the day:[587] the day has not savingly dawned upon you, nor is the day-star risen in your heart;[588] and lacking this first New Covenant mercy, consequently you lack all the rest. God's laws are not in your mind and heart.[589] Your unrighteousnesses, sins, and transgressions remain still unpardoned, the Lord is not your God, nor are you one of his New Covenant people. Oh how sinful and dangerous is this your dark, blind and ignorant condition![590] How should you lament the causes thereof![591] How can you eat,

---

[584] Ephesians 5:8
[585] John 6:45
[586] 2 Corinthians 4:3-4
[587] 1 Thessalonians 5:4-6
[588] 2 Peter 1:19
[589] Hebrews 8:10-11, Jeremiah 31:33-34
[590] See Question 5 Reason 3
[591] See Question 3.1

drink, or sleep quietly and contentedly in this God-less, Christ-less, covenantless and hopeless condition for a week together?[592]

(9) Hence as we desire to approve ourselves to be God's New Covenant people; so we should strive after the having and evidencing to ourselves that we have this New Covenant knowledge of the Lord.

Consider seriously:

[1] They that do not truly and savingly know the Lord according to his New Covenant, are none of God's New Covenant people, which are all a knowing people in some good measure, and yet there are very many now under the New Covenant extremely ignorant of God, as I have shown from many grounds.[593]

[2] They that are most grossly ignorant of God and his ways now under the New Covenant, may possibly (if the fault be not their own) attain to a sufficient measure of the saving knowledge of the Lord. For the Lord in his New Covenant has faithfully promised: *All shall know me from the least even to the greatest.*[594]

[3] The only ordinary way whereby dark, ignorant souls may come to the knowledge of God savingly is in and through Jesus Christ alone–fundamentally, by his Spirit efficaciously, by his New Covenant ministry and other more private instruction instrumentally, and all this in a continual progress gradually, as I have formerly evidenced.[595] Hither therefore, all must repair, and here all must attend, that want and desire true saving knowledge of God and his ways.

[4] When any person has gained saving knowledge of God in Christ, he may possibly discover and evidence to himself that he has such a knowledge. He may know that he knows God – and that in such ways, as I have already

---

[592] Ephesians 2:12
[593] In Question 3.1
[594] Hebrews 8:11, Jeremiah 31:34; see also Question 3.2 & 3.3.
[595] In Question 2.1, 2.2 & 2.3

indigitated [declared].⁵⁹⁶ If the seeing body may see that it sees, why then should not the knowing soul know that it knows? Now then, would we be assured of our good New Covenant state? Let us diligently in God's way press after this New Covenant knowledge. And that we may have the Comfort of such knowledge once attained, let us strive upon undeceiving grounds to evidence to our own hearts that we have such knowledge of the Lord and of his ways.

(10) Hence finally, the better we know the Lord, and the things of God now under the New Covenant, the more the glory of Christ and of his New Covenant are exalted and magnified in us.

God intended to display the glory of Christ now under his New Covenant more than ever before, and to that end he has clothed his New Covenant with far greater excellency and glory than all foregoing Covenants.⁵⁹⁷ Their glory was as no glory in comparison to the New Covenant's glory that excels. Consequently, when the true light and knowledge of God efficaciously shines in our hearts, the glory of Christ and of his New Covenant resteth upon us and is magnified in us exceedingly, while we are changed into the same image from glory to glory by the Spirit of the Lord.⁵⁹⁸

Thus of the second article: the federates' more excellent and more universal knowledge of the LORD under this New Covenant than under the Old. Of this, Jerome says: "The knowledge of one God is the possession of all virtues" – in such latitude he understands it.⁵⁹⁹

---

[596] In Question 6 throughout
[597] 2 Corinthians 3 throughout
[598] 2 Corinthians 3:18
[599] "Notitia{que} unius Dei, omnium virtutum possessio est." Hieron. Com. in Ier. 31. 34. p. 345. A. Tom. 5. Basil. 1553.

Article 3

Of God's mercy or propitiousness to them in his utter remission and oblivion, forgiving and forgetting all their sins forever.

The third particular, and distinct New Covenant blessing here promised, wherein this New Covenant differs from, yea far excels the Old Covenant, is God's mercy or propitiousness to his federates in his utter remission and oblivion, in his forgiving and forgetting all their sins for ever. *For, I will be merciful* (Hebrew: *I will pardon*, or *I will remit*, or *I will be propitious*; Greek: *I will be propitious*, or *I will be propitiously-merciful*) *to their unrighteousnesses, and their sinful errors, and their transgressions* (or *unlawfulnesses*) *I will remember no more* (Hebrew and Greek: *I will not remember again*, or, *anymore*).[600]

These words I have already in brief explained both analytically and grammatically; let the reader look back a little, for his satisfaction, to that explanation.[601] Here the Holy Spirit points out a third difference between the New Covenant and the Old; and a third excellency of the New Covenant above the Old. "God here promises," as Calvin well observes, "to be propitious to his people in another manner, and more perfectly, than of old."[602] Of old, under the Old Covenant (as the apostle most excellently makes the parallel)[603] they had many sacrifices, as bulls, goats, etc., whose bodies were offered, and whose blood was sprinkled year by year continually – the repetition of which sacrifices again and again so often, did evidence. Partly, the utter inability and insufficiency of those sacrifices to purge the conscience, take away sin, or to

---

[600] Hebrews 8:12, Jeremiah 31:34
[601] In Section 1 of this 5th Chapter
[602] Hebrews 10:[18-19]
[603] "Promittit Deum fore propitium suis alio modo & perfectius, quam olim fuerat." John Calvin's commentary on Jeremiah 31:34

make the comers thereunto perfect (Hebrews 10:1, 2, 4 & 9:9). Partly, that those sacrifices of the Old Covenant were so far from removing sins away, that in those sacrifices there was rather a remembrance again made of sins every year. The renewed sacrifices were a renewed accusation, arraignment, and condemnation of the sacrificers for their sins still un-purged away. But now under the New Covenant, instead of all those many weak and ineffectual sacrifices, yearly repeated; we have only one propitiatory sacrifice: Jesus Christ himself blessed forever, whose blood being shed and his body offered once for sins forever, *hath for ever perfected them that are sanctified*; that is, has forever expiated and purged away their sins that there needs no more sacrifice for sin forever (Hebrews 10:1-3 with verse 18), and has forever perfected his people as pertaining to the conscience, having purged their conscience from dead works, that they should have no more conscience of sins (Hebrews 9:9, 14 & 10:1-2).

And that thus Christ's one sacrifice has taken away our sins forever, He proves by three arguments, namely: (1) from the prophetic testimony of David (Hebrews 10:5-11); (2) from Christ's sitting down at God's right hand, presently after he had sacrificed himself: an evident demonstration of the perfect satisfaction given by that one sacrifice to God's justice for sins forever (verse 11-15); and (3) from the testimony of the Holy Spirit in this New Covenant, assuring that their sins and their iniquities God will remember no more (verses 15-19). In the Old Covenant, sins were remembered again every year; but in this New Covenant their sins should be remembered no more, etc. Herein the New shall differ from, and far excel the Old. So that this is a noted point of difference between the New Covenant and the Old, and wherein the New far excels the Old, namely: in this blessed, sweet, and heart-reviving mercy – **the remission of sins**.

Now in this precious article or promise of the New Covenant touching remission of sins (that we may proceed to a more theological consideration thereof) there are especially these two promissory propositions couched, which comprise the whole substance and intent of this promise in them:

namely: [1] that under the New Covenant the LORD God, in and through Jesus Christ, will freely, fully and utterly remit all his true federates' sins; [2] that therefore, God will bestow upon his federates all the other promised benefits of the New Covenant, because he will so freely, fully, and utterly remit all their sins, in and for the satisfaction of Jesus Christ. All that shall need to be spoken for the unfolding and clearing of this cordial article about remission of sins, may be easily referred to these two propositions, which I evince and explain as follows.

Proposition 1

That, under the New Covenant, the LORD God, in and through Jesus Christ, will freely, fully and utterly remit all his true federates' sins whatsoever.

In this proposition (for clearing the deduction of it from the words of the promise), note:

(1) **The efficient cause or author of this mercy, the LORD God**: *I will be merciful*, etc. *I will remember no more*, God says.

(2) **The meritorious means in and through whom this mercy is promised, namely: in and through Jesus Christ**: *I will be propitious, or I will be propitiously merciful*. This has reference to Christ's propitiation, whereby God's justice is appeased and pacified, touching their sins.[604] Christ is ιλασμος: *the propitiation for our sins*, etc.[605] Christ is ιλαστηριον: *the propitiatory through faith in his blood*, etc.[606]

(3) **The act of grace, wherein the special nature of this promised blessing is comprised, namely: remitting of sins**. The text expresses this in two words: {*I will be merciful*} and {*I will remember no more*}.[607] The first word in the Hebrew חָלַס {*eslach*} properly signifies, *I will remit, I will pardon*, etc. And the later phrase of remembering their sins and iniquities no more, the apostle himself interprets of remission of sins, so that in both phrases, remission of sins is the act of grace and mercy here intended.[608] This act of remitting sin is in this proposition amplified by three properties or excellencies thereof in these three terms, freely, fully, and utterly: [1] **Freely**: because it flows merely from God's will and good pleasure in Christ. *I will be*

---

[604] Ephesians 5:2
[605] 1 John 2:3
[606] Romans 3:25
[607] Jeremiah 31:34, Hebrews 8:12
[608] Hebrews 10:17-18

merciful – I will remember no more. [2] **Fully**: because such full and comprehensive terms are used; unrighteousnesses, sinful-errors, and unlawfulnesses, all in the plural number, and all very extensive, that is, all sorts, all degrees, and all aggravations of sin (except that sin against the Holy Ghost, which Scripture elsewhere declares unpardonable) shall be remitted.[609] For what kind, degree, or aggravation of sin can be named that comes not within these three words? [3] **Utterly**: that is – absolutely, finally, and forever. *Their sinful errors and unlawfulness will I remember no more*: that is, "I will not remember them anymore forever, so as to impute them to them, or charge them upon them to their condemnation."

(4) **The object on whom this act of grace, this free, full and utter remission of sin shall be conferred, namely: all God's true federates** – {*their unrighteousness*}, {*their sinful errors*}, and {*their unlawfulnesses*}.[610] Here's {*their*} thrice over: whose? Theirs of the house of Israel and Judah, of his whole church of Jews and Gentiles, that shall become God's true federates indeed, that shall be Israelites indeed, that shall be effectually called indeed according to God's purpose.

(5) **The season of this promised blessing, when it shall be otherwise and more excellently vouchsafed to God's federates, than of old, namely: under the New Covenant.** Sin was pardoned formerly under the Old Covenant, and before it; but now under the New Covenant, it shall be more excellently pardoned, as hereafter will appear.

Thus the deduction is clear – the proposition fully containing the true sense and substance of this promise of the New Covenant.

Now, for the more satisfactory explication of this great and excellent blessing, namely: **remission of sins**, contained in this first proposition, and covenanted here in this sweet New Covenant promise, I shall – as briefly and clearly as I can – resolve these four particular questions; namely:

---

[609] Matthew 12:31-32; 1 John 5:16
[610] Hebrews 8:12

(1) What is the nature of sin, which is the subject of remission?

(2) What is the nature of remission of sins, which is here promised and covenanted?

(3) May those that have their sins remitted, know that they are remitted, and how they may know this?

(4) Wherein does God's remission of sins under the New Covenant, differ from and excel the remission of sins under the Old Covenant?

To some of these particulars, the chief things to be known touching **pardon** and **remission of sins**, may be easily referred.

Question 1. What is the nature of sin, which is the subject of remission?

Resolution: In remission of sins (sin being the subject; remission the adjunct), this adjunct, remission, cannot well be explained, without explication also of this subject thereof, sin. Touching sin, I shall especially open: (1) the denominations of it here in this promise, (2) the description of it, and (3) the particulars in it: which come under pardon, and which do not.

(1) **The denominations of sin here in this promise, are in the Greek three:**[611] **all of them very comprehensive, all of them in the plural number, all of them for substance intending the same thing, but differing in the precise notion, way or manner of signifying the same thing.**

Answerable unto this, there are three other words in the Hebrew, namely: two in this promise in Jeremiah,[612] and one elsewhere.[613]

[1] The first denomination is αδικιαι,[614] properly it denotes injustices, unrighteousnesses, injuriousnesses, etc. (Hebrews 8:12), whatsoever is without, besides, or repugnant to the rule of righteousness, equity, etc. even that just law of God, (Romans 7:12), is styled {*unrighteousness*}; and is a wrong or injury against God and his law. Answerable to this is the Hebrew word עֲוֹנָם {*gnhavonam*} (Jeremiah 31:34). It properly signifies: their crookedness, their wryness, their perverseness, their iniquity, etc. from עוה {*gnhavah*}, which (as Mercerus notes)[615] properly signifies: to be crooked, or bowed, or writhen, etc.; metaphorically to be unjust, perverse, etc. or to do

---

[611] Hebrews 8:12
[612] Jeremiah 31:34
[613] Exodus 34:7
[614] Ab a privativ. & δίκη jus, justitia, fas, &c.
[615] Mercer. In Pagn. Thesaur. ad verb. עוה

perversely, frowardly, unjustly, etc – their perverse-iniquity; their crooked-iniquity; a metaphor from things crooked, that warp or bend away from the straight rule, when they are compared and laid together.

[2] The second denomination is, αμαρτιαι. Properly it signifies errors, wanderings, strayings, missings-of-the-mark, straying-sins, sinful-errors, etc. (Hebrews 8:12). It is derived from αμαρτεω, or (which is now in use for it) from αμαρτανω. To err or wander-away, namely: either out of the way, or from the intended scope, mark, or white, as Henricus Stephanus shows by many instances.[616] Thence by a metaphor it signifies to sin, because to sin is to err or wander out of God's way, from the paths of his Word and laws, etc. Answerable to this is the Hebrew חַטָּאָה *chattath* (Jeremiah 31:34)[617] which properly signifies error, namely: either by missing the scope or mark aimed at; as it is said of those 700 left-handed men, *every one could sling stones at an hair-breadth, and not miss*. Hebrew: {*not err*} (Judges 20:16), or by wandering out of the way, which error it more usually denotes. Hence it is metaphorically translated to signify sin, or sinful error, or sinful straying, etc., from the ways and laws of God.

[3] The third denomination is ἄνομαι, which properly signifies, illegalities, unlawfulnesses (Hebrews 8:12), which elsewhere is translated {*the-transgression-of-the-law*}.[618] This word is derived from a privative, without, or against, and νόμος, law: and so ἄνομος signifies not only one that is without law, as 1 Corinthians 9:21, but also one that is against law (2 Thessalonians 2:8; 1 Timothy 4:9; 2 Peter 2:8). Answerable to this word there is not a third Hebrew word in Jeremiah's narrative of the New Covenant (Jeremiah 31:34) but yet there is one elsewhere,[619] namely: פֶּשַׁע *peshaugh*, properly defection, prevarication, transgression of the law, precept, or

---

[616] Hen. Stephanus in Thesaur. Ling. Graec. Ad verb αμαρτεω
[617] Compare Psalm 32:2 with Romans 4:7-8.
[618] 1 John 3:4
[619] Exodus 34:7

covenant through perfidiousness, etc., as Mercer observes.[620] All these three Hebrew words are together in that one text: *pardoning iniquity and transgression and sin*; properly: lifting-up, crookedness, defection and error (Exodus 34:7). Now why does God use all these terms and comprehensive expressions, but thereby to assure his people of the largeness, fullness, completeness, and comprehensiveness of his pardons, sins of all sorts, of all notions, of all degrees and aggravations which his people shall be guilty of, he will fully pardon.

(2) **The description of sin, I offer thus in brief: sin is any evil habit**[621] **or act,**[622] **against the law of God,**[623] **and offensive to him,**[624] **drawing away from God,**[625] **depriving of righteousness and innocence,**[626] **defiling the person and action,**[627] **deserving death,**[628] **and making guilty of the curse of God.**[629]

In this description note: [1] the genus, or general nature of sin: any evil habit or act. Or more exactly, the pravity, viciosity, or evilness of habit or act. At first in Adam's apostasy, the evil acts bred evil habits in him; but ever since the evil habits produce evil acts. [2] The *differentia*, or specific difference that distinguishes sin from all other things, consisting in that heap of properties, fruits, and events of sin enumerated – all of which are evinced by the Scriptures annexed.

---

[620] John Mercer in Pagn. Thesaur. Ad verb פשע
[621] Psalm 51:5, Romans 7:17, 23-24
[622] Romans 7:7; 2 Samuel 24:10 & 12:13
[623] 1 John 3:4
[624] Romans 5:16-18, 20; 2 Samuel 11:27, Habakkuk 1:13-14
[625] James 1:14
[626] Ecclesiastes 7:29, Romans 3:23 {*come short of the glory of God*}, that is: come behind, come short of that glorious image of God wherein they were created – Colossians 3:10, Ephesians 4:24
[627] Titus 1:5, James 1:21, Revelation 1:3; 1 Corinthians 6:11, Psalm 51:2, Haggai 2:14
[628] Romans 6:23
[629] Romans 3:19, Galatians 3:10, Exodus 34:7, Ephesians 2:2-3

(3) Hence there are many particulars considerable in sin: that we may see what it is in sin, that is properly capable of, or curable by remission, and what is not.

For remission is not a fit and proper cure for everything in sin. Especially take notice of these particulars in sin, namely:

[1] ανομιαν: an unlawfulness, an anomy, a swerving, warping or discrepancy from the law, as John describes it: ανομιαν – *Sin is the transgression of the law*; or, *Sin is unlawfulness*.[630] This anomy is both in habituals, and in actuals, and these in defect or excess, in omission or commission, etc. This anomy, this unlawfulness, this discrepancy from, or repugnancy to the law of God, is most essential and intrinsical to sin: And this is healed: partly by remission, when it is not imputed, or reckoned to us, but put upon the account and head of Jesus Christ, our true scapegoat;[631] partly by sanctification and inscription of his laws in our minds and hearts (Jeremiah 31:33, Hebrews 8:10), whereby both inward faculties and outward acts – constitution and conversation – become conform and sweetly answerable to the laws of God, as has been explained.

[2] **Offensa**: the offense or offensiveness of sin unto God, whereby God is provoked, angered, displeased, grieved, etc. against the offender. Thus: *Forty years long was I grieved with this generation, and said, it is a people that err in their hearts*.[632] – *They angered him also at the waters of strife*.[633] – *Thus they provoked him to anger with their inventions*.[634] So, when David had involved himself in those two heinous sins of murder and adultery, it is said: *But the thing that David had done, displeased the LORD*.[635] Hebrew: *was evil in the eyes of the LORD*. Contrary hereunto, Paul's exercise was to have always an inoffensive conscience (απροσκοπον συνειδησιν), towards God and towards

---

[630] 1 John 3:4
[631] Psalm 32:2, Isaiah 53:6; 2 Corinthians 5:19, Leviticus 16:20-22
[632] Psalm 95:10 & 78:40
[633] Psalm 106:32
[634] Psalm 106:29
[635] 2 Samuel 11:27

men.[636] This offense, anger and displeasure of God for sin, is in some sense removed by remission of sin, namely: in regard of the enmity, hatred, punitive and vindictive nature thereof, properly so taken: *I will heal their backsliding, I will love them freely, for mine anger is turned away from him.*[637] So that properly, God does not, as a sin-avenging judge, punish his pardoned people: Yet notwithstanding, as a Father, he is offended and displeased at them for their sins, and sometimes severely chastises them for their iniquities, as he dealt with Moses,[638] Aaron,[639] David,[640] the Corinthians,[641] etc.

[3] **Aversio**: a withdrawing, recess, departure, or turning-away from God, from godliness, from his law, etc: *Every man is tempted, when he is drawn-away* (εξελκομενος) *of his own lust and enticed.*[642] Drawn away, from God; enticed, to evil. Thus, Adam at first turned away from God by eating the forbidden fruit; Israel turned aside quickly (Exodus 32:7-8). And in every sin, more or less, there is some aversion from God, some turning of the back upon God, and their face upon sin, etc. Now this aversion is not properly relieved by remission of sins, but by the returning or conversion of the sinner again unto God.[643]

[4] **Privatio**: a privation, a loss, etc., of righteousness, rectitude, innocency, integrity, etc. in whole or in part. So, when Adam first sinned, he wholly lost his concreated rectitude, innocency, and uprightness in the image of God.[644] When David, Peter, or other saints of God sinned, they lost their rectitude and innocence in part, namely: that innocence which they had before in respect of those particular gross offenses, whilst uncommitted. Now this privation of innocence and integrity, cannot properly be so cured by remission

---

[636] Acts 24:16
[637] Hosea 14:4
[638] Psalm 106:32-33
[639] Numbers 20:23-24
[640] 2 Samuel 11:27 & 12:13-14 & 24:10-13
[641] 1 Corinthians 11:32
[642] James 1:14
[643] Jeremiah 3:1, Hosea 6:1-2 & 14:1-2, Acts 26:18
[644] Ecclesiastes 7:29, Genesis 1:26-27, Romans 5:12

of sin, as that the nocent party should be made innocent again; innocence lost, is like virginity lost, can never be recovered. It cannot be said, such a one has not fallen, has not sinned, has not broken the law, etc. Herein, this cannot be repaired properly. But yet such innocence lost may so far be regained by remission of sin, as that sin shall not be imputed to them, to make them nocent and guilty before God;[645] and their persons may be reputed, accounted and accepted of God as innocent, as the righteousness of God in Christ.[646] By sanctification also, God brings in an integrity into a man's spirit, which is answerable in the sight of God to that innocence lost, whereupon God's people are accounted pure and holy (Ephesians 4:24, Psalm 18:22, Titus 1:15; 1 Peter 2:5, 9; 1 John 3:6-9).

[5] **Macula**: a stain, spot, pollution, defilement, etc. whereby the person or action is blemished, slurred, made foul, filthy and deformed.[647] This stain and foulness of sin, the Scripture represents by similitudes of most filthy things: as original uncleanness, by the uncleanness of a menstruous woman (Zechariah 13:1); actual uncleanness by many other legal defilements (Leviticus 5, 11-15), by the filth under the nails or arm-holes (James 1:21), skin of an Ethiopian, and spots of a leopard (Jeremiah 13:23), vomit of a dog, and filthy mire wherein a sow wallows (2 Peter 2:22). This inherent stain, spot, and defilement of sin, is efficaciously and most properly cleansed and washed out by the pure water of the renewing and sanctifying Spirit, by that infused purity and cleanness which abides in the people of God.[648] The guilt of which sin is meritoriously washed away and cleansed by Christ's blood unto justification (Revelation 1:5, Zechariah 13:1), by merit of whose blood the Holy Spirit also is procured for his members' sanctification.

[6] **Meritum**: the merit, desert, or due wages of sin, of all sin, yea of all the sin of God's elect, is eternal death and condemnation. *The wages of sin is*

---

[645] Psalm 32:1-2; 2 Corinthians 5:19
[646] 2 Corinthians 5:21
[647] Revelation 22:11 & 1:5, Haggai 2:14, Titus 1:15
[648] 1 Corinthians 6:11, Titus 3:5, Ephesians 5:26-27

death, but the gift of God is eternal life through Jesus Christ our Lord;[649] namely: eternal death (as appears here by the antithesis of eternal life) is the most proper adequate wages of sin, of all sin. And although deserved death and damnation are not actually inflicted upon God's elect, yet in strictness of justice, they do in themselves by their sins deserve it, as well as others. In this regard, men are said to be worthy of death for sin.[650] This desert [merit] of death is not taken away by remission of sins.

[7] Finally, **reatus**, guilt, or guiltiness of God's curse, namely: of death. This guilt is the actual obligation or binding-over of the sinner to the enduring or undergoing of the penalty denounced and threatened to sin. *In the day thou eatest thereof thou shalt die the death.*[651] And: *Cursed is everyone that continueth not in all things written in the law to do them.*[652] As therefore everyone that sins is guilty of death; that is, obliged to endure the punishment of death; so, in regard of the truth of God's threatening, and the vindictive justice of the most righteous judge, it is necessary that in one way or another, the sinner should undergo that punishment (Genesis 2:17, Galatians 3:10, Romans 1:32, 3:19, 5:12, 6:23, James 1:15) Hence those phrases: {*guilty of hellfire*},[653] {*guilty of eternal judgment*},[654] {*that every mouth may be stopped, and all the world may become guilty before God*},[655] υποδικος – τω θεω {*under judgment to God*}, or {*subject to the judgment of God*}. Hereupon, sins are called {*debts*} οφειληματα, *And forgive us our debts, as we forgive our debtors.*[656] They are debts to God. Not that we owe them to God, or ought to sin against God; but metonymically, because they render them that sin obnoxious to God's punishment, even as pecuniary debts oblige him (that has not

---

[649] Romans 6:23
[650] Romans 1:32
[651] Genesis 2:17
[652] Galatians 3:10
[653] Matthew 5:22
[654] Mark 3:29
[655] Romans 3:19
[656] Matthew 6:12

wherewith to pay) unto punishment.[657] Hence also (as that learned Gomarus has well observed)[658] the name {*sin*} is used by way of a double metonymy, namely: {1} by a metonymy of the cause for the effect, when sin is put for the punishment of sin, as Genesis 19:15 and 1 Peter 2:24. {2} By a metonymy of the adjunct for its subject, when sin is put for the sacrifice of sin, which bears the punishment of sin to expiate it. As, {*he was made sin*} – that is: a sacrifice for sin (2 Corinthians 5:21). {*Thou wouldst not have sin*} (Psalm 40:7) that is, thou wouldst not have legal sacrifice for sin, which the apostle by an ellipsis renders, περι αμαρτιας, *for sin* – that is: a sacrifice for sin (Hebrews 10:8). Now guilty sinners must undergo death and curse one way or other, as I said: either in their own persons, according to the express letter of the law (Deuteronomy 27:26, Galatians 3:10, Genesis 2:17), thus all reprobates shall endure the punishment forever (Matthew 25:41, 46, Daniel 12:2); or in their surety, according to the tacit intent of of the law, manifested to be the mind of the lawgiver in the whole current of the gospel, in Christ promised (Genesis 3:15 and 22:18, Acts 10:43) and in Christ exhibited (Galatians 3:13-14, Hebrews 2:14, Acts 3:25). Thus Christ died and became a curse for his elect (Isaiah 53:4-6, Romans 4:25, Galatians 3:13), whose temporal death was of eternal and infinite value, by reason of the infiniteness of his person, being God as well as man, purchasing his church with his own blood (Acts 20:28, Hebrews 9:14).[659] This sacrifice of Christ dying was fully accepted by God as a ransom for all his elect (Ephesians 5:2, Hebrews 10:6-20; 1 John 2:1-2, Hebrews 9:12-14, Matthew 20:28; 1 Peter 1:18). Now remission of sins most properly relieves a sinner against this guilt of death, curse, and condemnation – not by abolishing the desert of his guilt, or the merit of his sin, but by releasing him from his actual obligation and ordination to death, curse and damnation; that though it be deserved by him, yet it never shall be inflicted upon him.

---

[657] Matthew 18:34
[658] From Gomarus *in illustrat*. Luke 1:77, p.277. a. Tom. 1.
[659] John 1:14; 1 Timothy 3:16

Thus we see, what the nature of sin is, which is the subject of remission; and what it is in sin that more properly is cured and removed by remission.

Question 2: What is the remission of sins, which is here promised and covenanted in this New Covenant?

Resolution: Remission of sins is a most sweet and comfortable blessing, especially to a poor sin-bruised soul.

This blessing is more often spoken of than well understood, and yet it is better understood by many than experimentally enjoyed. This question, as it is difficult, so it cannot but be very delightful to be resolved. For satisfaction herein, Consider: (1) the expressions or phrases by which the Holy Spirit in Scripture sets it forth to us. He best knows how to signify and make known his own mind to us, touching this choice mercy, and (2) the nature of this blessing, of remission of sins.

(1) **The expressions, names, or phrases whereby the Holy Spirit describes this precious and excellent blessing to us, are very many both in the Hebrew of the Old Testament and Greek of the New – and those very emphatic and comfortable.** I shall briefly note some of the more observable expressions, as:

[1] **Remission, pardon,** or **forgiveness of sins.** Greek: αφεσιν αμαρτιων, *That they may receive forgiveness of sins.*[660] – *Repent and be baptized every one of you in the name of Jesus Christ, for the remission of sins.*[661] This word is most frequently used for this purpose in the New Testament. The origin of this word is ιεω or [ιεμι], to send: whence ἀφίημι, to dismiss, let-go, send-away, remit, permit, or suffer, leave, etc. And thence the noun ἄφεσις: dismission, remission, releasing, namely: of debts, or of bonds for debts, or of captives out of prison. And so its translated to signify the pardon and forgiveness of sins, because when God pardons sins, he dismisses them, he releases them, he lets

---

[660] Acts 26:18
[661] Acts 2:38

them alone, meddles not with them, so as to impute them to condemnation, he remits their debts, he sets the offender at liberty breaks their bands, and brings them out of prison, etc. By this metaphor, pardon of sin is sweetly set forth in that of Isaiah: *to proclaim liberty to the captives, and the opening of the prison to them that are bound*;[662] which in Luke is thus expounded: *to preach* (αφεσιν: dismission, remission, release) *deliverance to the captives – to set at liberty* (η ἄφεσις: in remission, etc.) *them that are bruised.*[663] Παρεσις is from the same origin, and is used for remission of sins (Romans 3:25). The Hebrew word answering properly to this Greek word is סָלַח {*salach*}: to remit, or forgive, or be merciful to – as here it is used in this promise: *For I will forgive their iniquity.*[664] This same word is also often used in this sense elsewhere, as Leviticus 4:20; 2 Chronicles 6:27, Exodus 34:9, Jeremiah 33:8, Psalms 130:4, and Daniel 9:9. Hence God is styled אֱלוֹהַּ סְלִיחוֹת {*Eloah selichoth*}: *a God of pardons* (Nehemiah 9:17) that can create, command, give and apply pardons, as a God. So then, before remission of sin, the sinner is in debt, in danger, in bonds, in prison, etc, but after sin is pardoned, his debt is released, his bonds are canceled, his prison is opened, and he is dismissed at liberty. God will have no more to say to him in regard to his pardoned sins; God now accounts of him as if he had not sinned. This is a great expression, and very frequent both in Old and New Testament.

[2] **Free-forgiveness; gratuitous-pardon of sin**. So it is in the Greek in the New Testament. Χαρισαμενος υμιν παντα τα παραπτωματα: *Having freely-forgiven us all our sins*. And again: *Even as Christ* – ἐχαρίσατο – *freely forgave you, so also do ye.*[665] The word {χαρίζομαι} does properly signify a gratuitous-forgiving, not only without, but even contrary to all our desert.[666] This denotes to us that pardon of sin originally flows from that blessed

---

[662] Isaiah 61:1
[663] Luke 4:18
[664] Jeremiah 31:34
[665] Colossians 2:13 & 3:13
[666] "χαρίζομαι significat, praeter meritum, imo contra quam quis meritus sit, ex gratia condonare." Chemnitz.

fountain of God's free grace. He pardons because he will pardon. He forgives freely for his own sake (Isaiah 43:25).

[3] **Propitiousness, or propitious-mercifulness upon pacification for sin.** The Greek ιλασκειν to expiate, pacify, and render propitious; and ιλεως: pacified, propitious, favorable, etc, are used for this purpose. As ιλεως εσομαι ταις αδικιαις αυτων: *I will be propitiously-merciful to their unrighteousnesses*; or, *I will be pacifiedly-favorable to their unrighteousnesses* (that I may so speak to express the emphasis of the word).[667] The like word is in the publican's prayer: ιλάσθητί – *O God be merciful to me a sinner*; properly: *O God be pacified*, or, be *pacifiedly-merciful to me a sinner*.[668] These are excellent expressions indeed, whereby God promises pardon, and the publican begs pardon of sin. These Greek words are for substance the same.

Now ιλασκειν has two principal significations in the New Testament, namely: {1} to expiate, or make-reconciliation for sins with God. So it is used only once, of Jesus Christ: *That he might be a merciful and faithful high priest, in things pertaining to God* – ιλάσκεσθαι – *to make reconciliation for the sins of the people*; or *to expiate the sins of the people*.[669] {2} Hence consequently it is drawn to signify, to pacify God, or to render him propitious, favorable, merciful. Because, when sins are expiated, when reconciliation is made for them, when the penalty is endured fully that is due to them, etc, then God is appeased, pacified, and becomes propitious, favorable, merciful to the sinner. And in this sense the word is often used in Scriptures, as Luke 18:13, Hebrews 8:12, and Matthew 16:22, and in profane authors – and this latter is the most usual and common signification of the word.

So that as the former word χαριζειν, freely to forgive, denotes the springhead and fountain whence pardon of sin arises, even the riches of God's free grace: So this word ιλασκειν intimates the meritorious means, or procuring-cause of pardon, namely: Christ's meritorious expiation of sin by

---

[667] Hebrews 8:12
[668] Luke 18:13
[669] Hebrews 2:17

his own death and blood, whereupon God is pacified and appeased touching sin, and becomes propitiously merciful to the sinner. Hence Christ is called, ἱλασμός, *the propitiation*: If *any man sin, we have an advocate with the Father, Jesus Christ the righteous, and he is the propitiation* (ἱλασμός) *for our sins*.[670] And ἱλαστήριον, the propitiatory or mercy-seat, whom *God hath set forth to be* ἱλαστήριον – *a propitiatory through faith in his blood, to declare his righteousness for the remission of sins that are past*, etc.[671] How excellently do God's gratuitous mercy and his justice meet in this great blessing of remission of sins! His gratuitous mercy, in that he remits freely, without any desert [merit] of the sinners, yea against all his desert, his justice, in that he remits righteously, upon expiation made by Christ's blood, and satisfaction given to God's justice for sin by his death.

Answerable to this Greek word, is also the Hebrew word סָלַח *salach*, in one of its significations, for it signifies not only to remit and forgive, but also to be propitious. And therefore for this, the apostle puts ἵλεως ἔσομαι: *I will be propitiously-merciful*, or *I will be pacifiedly favorable to their unrighteousnesses*.[672]

More fully answerable is the word חָטָא *khit*, to expiate, cleanse, purge. This word חָטָא *chata* in the kal conjugation is called signifies to sin, to err-away, to err from the scope; but in the piel conjugation: to expiate sin, to cleanse, or to purge away sin. So David uses it: *Thou shalt purge me with hyssop, and I shall be clean*, etc., or: *Thou shalt expiate me, or cleanse me with hyssop*, etc.[673] Herein David alludes to the ceremonial rite of cleansing the leper or other unclean persons under the law: the priest took a bunch of hyssop, and therewith sprinkled blood upon them (Leviticus 14:4-8), and sometimes a clean person with hyssop sprinkled water upon the unclean (Numbers 19:17-19). This was a type of Christ's blood and water sprinkled upon the

---

[670] 1 John 2:1-2
[671] Romans 3:25
[672] Compare Jeremiah 31:34 with Hebrews 8:12
[673] Psalm 51:7

hearts and consciences of sinners by faith for remission of sins (Romans 3:25, Hebrews 9:13-14). *The blood of Jesus Christ his Son cleanseth us from all sin* (1 John 1:7). In this phrase therefore, David begged pardon of sin in the blood of Jesus Christ, whereby God's justice was satisfied for sin. He could easily have had the literal ceremony: but he wanted and earnestly desired this spiritual mystery.

[4] **Not remembering sin anymore**. This is another expression for pardon of sin in this New Covenant: *And their sinful error* (לֹא אֶזְכָּר־עוֹד – *Lo escar guhod*) *I will not remember anymore*.[674] For which the Greek has it: *And their sinful errors and their unrighteousnesses I will not remember again, or anymore* – ου μη μνησθω ετι.[675] Here are two negatives, which do more vehemently deny, according to the propriety of the Greek language. That is: "I will never remember them again, I will in no case remember them anymore. I will so forgive, as to forget." Not that in propriety of phrase, God either remembers, or forgets; for all things are present to him, he knows and beholds them in one act all at once; but it is an allusion to the manner of men, who when they forgive injures fully and heartily, do also forget them, blot them out of mind, so as neither to upbraid and reproach them for them, nor seek reparation, satisfaction, etc. by way of revenge. Or rather, it is an allusion to the manner of the Old Covenant's administration, in the sacrifices, whereof there was a remembrance again of sins every year, they were a fresh indictment and arraignment of the people for sin continually;[676] but under this New Covenant, Christ *by one offering of himself once offered, hath forever perfected them that are sanctified* – has forever taken away the sins of his elect; there needs no more expiatory sacrifice for them, they that are sprinkled with the blood of this sacrifice shall have their sins no more remembered against

---

[674] Jeremiah 31:34
[675] Hebrews 8:12
[676] Hebrews 10:1-3, etc.

them,[677] or mentioned to them to their confusion and condemnation.[678] An act of everlasting oblivion shall be passed upon them.

[5] **Not imputing sin to the sinner**. By this expression, David describes the forgiveness of sin: *Blessed is the man whose transgression is forgiven, whose sin is covered. Blessed is the man unto whom the Lord imputeth not iniquity.*[679] Paul also has the same expression for substance, alleging that of David's.[680] The Hebrew word חָשַׁב *chashab* here used by David, and the Greek λογιζειν here used by Paul, have – both of them – great variety of acceptations in Scripture, and there is an imputation of evil, and an imputation of good to one (as elsewhere I have already at large manifested);[681] but to our present purpose, they signify: to impute-to, attribute-to, ascribe-to, to account-to, to charge-upon, etc. Thus when God forgives sin, he does not impute sin to such a man,[682] he does not attribute, account, or ascribe it to him; he does not charge it or lay it as a debt upon him; he does not lay it to his charge to his condemnation.

Why? Because he has imputed all his sins already unto Christ; he has laid them all upon him,[683] as his Surety, and – Christ having paid the debt as the sinner's Surety – it is no more to be charged upon the principal. *For he hath made him to be sin for us* (by imputation) *who knew no sin* (by inherent pollution or perpetration): *that we might be made* (by imputation) *the righteousness of God in him*.[684] So that this non-imputing of sin to us, leads us to Christ our Surety to whom they were imputed, *who himself bare our sins upon his own body on the tree*.[685] The expression seems to be a metaphorical allusion to an arithmetical accounting, when upon casting up various sums, a

---

[677] Hebrews 10:5-20
[678] Ezekiel 18:22
[679] Psalm 31:1-2
[680] Psalm 31:1-2
[681] Romans 4:7-8
[682] 2 Corinthians 5:19 {*not imputing their trespasses unto them*}.
[683] Isaiah 53:4-6; 2 Corinthians 5:19, 21
[684] 2 Corinthians 5:21
[685] 1 Peter 2:24

man at last comes to the total result and accounts, or charges so much debt upon one, so much upon another, etc; but where he will freely forgive the debt, he does not impute, reckon or account any debt to such an one at all. Thus God in pardoning sin, imputes not sin to us, reckons it not to us, puts it not upon our account, but as it were, crosses all out of his debt book. Oh he is a blessed man to whom the Lord will not thus impute sin!

[6] **Covering of sin, hiding it, or hiding God's face from it.** This expression is often used for the pardon of sin. The Hebrew has three words especially to this purpose:

{1} חָסָה *Chasah*: to cover, or hide out of sight. It is applied to any object or thing that is covered by something interposed between it and the eye: as the body is covered with garments (Ezekiel 18:16), the tabernacle was covered with the cloud (Numbers 9:15 & 16:42), and the waters of the Red Sea covered the Egyptians (Exodus 15:10). Thus when sin is pardoned, it is covered from God's eye. Not that God does not see it at all, but that he does not see it to punish it and require it with condemnation. So: *O the blessedness of the man whose transgression is forgiven, and whose sin is covered.*[686] And elsewhere: *Thou hast forgiven the iniquity of thy people, thou hast covered all their sin, Selah.*[687]

{2} כָּפַר *Caphar*. Our English word {cover} is very near to it. This word generally signifies to cover, to hide, to cover with pitch, etc,[688] as Genesis 6:14: the ark was covered with pitch. Hence in piel, it signifies to expiate, cleanse, purge, etc, which is to hide sin or uncleanness: to remove wrath, that it may not appear. Thus the seraphim – laying a live coal from the altar upon the mouth of Isaiah – said: *Thine iniquity is taken away, and thy sin purged*, or *covered.*[689] And again: *Surely this iniquity shall not be purged from you* (or,

---

[686] Psalm 32:1 with Romans 4:7
[687] Psalm 85:2
[688] Mercer in Pagn. Thesaur. ad verb.
[689] Isaiah 6:7

covered) *till ye die.*⁶⁹⁰ From this root that word כַּפֹּרֶת *kaphoreth* is derived, which signified the covering of the ark, called the mercy-seat or propitiatory, which was a special type of Christ (Exodus 25:17. to 23, Romans 3:25). For as the law in the ark, by which is the knowledge of sin, was covered with the mercy-seat: so Christ by his death expiates, remits, and covers our sins, that the law shall not accuse or condemn us for them.

{3} סָתַר *Sathar*: to hide, conceal, etc. when God Pardons sins, he hides his face from them, He will not look upon them in wrath or revenge; he looks as it were another way. So David prayed: *Hide thy face from my sin, and blot out all mine iniquities.*⁶⁹¹ It seems to be a metaphor, from a guilty person, that cannot endure the face of a strict judge; or from an offending child that cannot bear the fathers frown. When God pardons, he hides his face. Oh what comfortable words are these to a penitent, sin-bruised soul! You uncover all your sins before God, confessing them, lamenting them, and ripping them up; but God covers them all, he puts them out of his fight. Your sins are ever before you (Psalm 51:3), you are still pouring upon them, etc., but God hides his face from them; he will not look upon them anymore.

[7] Taking away sin, removing it, etc. When God remits sin to us, he Removes sin from us. Here are two Hebrew words:

{1} נָשָׂא *Nasa*: to lift up, to take-away, to spare, to remit, etc.⁶⁹² This word is very comprehensive in significations, if any other. When God remits sin, which is a heavy burden to the soul (Matthew 11:28), he lifts it up off the soul, he takes away this heavy, troublesome load that presseth it down and oppresses it, he gives lightning and ease to the soul, he unburdens it. Oh this is sweet to the heavy laden! Thus God proclaims himself: *Keeping mercy for thousands, forgiving* (נֹשֵׂא עָוֹן – *nose*: *lifting up, taking away*) *iniquity, and transgression, and sin.*⁶⁹³ That is: all sorts of sin. Here the participle is used: {*taking away*}. It

---

⁶⁹⁰ Isaiah 22:14
⁶⁹¹ Psalm 51:9
⁶⁹² See Pagn. Thesaur. ad verb.
⁶⁹³ Exodus 34:7

is God's constant, daily and continual act to be pardoning; though we are still sinning, yet he is still pardoning. So elsewhere: *Who is a God like unto thee, pardoning* (נֹשֵׂא עָוֹן – *nose*: *lifting up, taking away*) *iniquity*? etc.[694] There is no God like our sin-pardoning God: no god but he can pardon sin. – *Take away all iniquity, and receive us graciously*.[695] – *O the blessednesses of that man whose transgression is pardoned*, or *taken away!*[696] This taking away, or bearing away of sin noted by this word, was excellently shadowed out in the scapegoat, upon whose head Aaron was to lay both his hands, confessing over him all Israel's iniquities and transgressions, putting them upon his head, and then to send him away into the wilderness, never to return or be found more.[697] *And the goat* (נָשָׂא *nasa*: *shall take away*) *shall bear away upon him all their iniquities unto a land of separation, and he shall let go the goat in the wilderness*. So Christ bears away our sins, far from us, never more to return to us, or be charged upon us.

{2} מוּשׁ *Mosch*: to remove; properly, to remove from handling. *And I will remove* (Jerome renders it *auferam*: *I will-take-away*) *the iniquity of that land in one day. In that day, saith the LORD of hosts, shall ye call every man his neighbor, under the vine and under the fig tree*.[698] The pardon and removal of sin, is here discovered to be the sweet foundation of all peace, tranquility, and prosperity. Sin unremoved, like Jonah in the ship, storms and disturbs all; but sin removed, like Jonah cast out, calms and quiets all.

[8] **Blotting out, or wiping out, or razing out**, etc. מָחָה *Machah* properly and principally it signifies to blot out by wiping, and so to remove away from its place, that shall not anymore appear.[699] David prays: *Blot out, wipe out all mine iniquities* (Psalm 51:9). God says: *I, I am he that blotteth out*

---

[694] Micah 7:18
[695] Hosea 14:2
[696] Psalm 32:1
[697] Leviticus 16:20-22
[698] Zechariah 3:9-10
[699] Abstergendo-delere: & ita loco amovere ne ultra appareat. Mercer. in Pagn. Thesaur. ad verb.

thy transgressions for mine own sake, and will not remember thy sins (Isaiah 43:25), and again: *I have blotted out as a thick cloud thy transgressions, and as a cloud thy sins* (Isaiah 44:22). When a cloud is blotted out of the air, it is so utterly dissipated and dissolved, that it never returns thither again; there's nothing but serenity, clearness and brightness in the heavens; and when a writing is blotted out of a table book, it is so defaced that it can never be read any more; or, when a debt is wiped out of an account book or debt book, it is never called for or exacted anymore. So when God pardons sin, he so utterly blots and wipes it out by the blood of Christ, that it shall never be exacted more from that soul, never be found there more unto condemnation.

[9] **Casting behind God's back**. King Hezekiah said: *And thou hast loved my soul from the pit of corruption, for thou hast cast* (הִשְׁלַכְתָּ *hishlacta*: *thou hast cast away*) *all my sins behind thy back*[700] – a metaphor from the action of man, who casts behind his back such things as he cares not for, regards not, looks not after, minds not, etc. So God deals with all our sins which he pardons, and for which he will not condemn us. Contrariwise, when God punishes for sin, he is said to set our sins before his face: *For we are consumed by thine anger, and by thy wrath are we troubled. Thou hast set our iniquities before thee, our secret sins in the light of thy countenance.*[701]

[10] **Removing our sins from us as far as the east is from the west**. רָחַק *Rachak*: properly it signifies, to be far distant, to be afar off, to be far remote. David used this word for pardon of sin: *He hath not dealt with us after our sins, nor rewarded us according to our iniquities. For as the heaven is high above the earth: so great is his mercy towards them that fear him. As far as the east is from the west: so far hath he removed* (הִרְחִיק *Hirchic*, *has made far distant*) *our transgressions from us.*[702] Here God's pardoning mercy is magnified three ways, namely: {1} By his forbearance of deserved punishment, {2} by the incomparable transcendency of his mercy above our sins higher than

---

[700] Isaiah 38:17
[701] Psalm 90:7-8
[702] Psalm 103:10-12

heaven is above the earth, and {3} by his far removal of our sins from us, as east is remote from west – a proverbial speech. East and west are far distant, and never meet; so we and our pardoned sins shall never meet more: our true scapegoat Christ has carried them quite away from us into the wilderness. Augustine here says: "When sin is remitted, your sins set; your grace rises. Your sins are as it were in the west; the grace whereby you are freed is in the east. – Your sins set forever; and grace remains forever."[703] Oh, it is well for us when our sins are not rising, but setting.

[11] **Finally, the pardon of sin is most excellently set forth even in a knot or cluster of choice expressions in the prophet Micah:** *Who is a God like thee, pardoning* (Or, *lifting-up,* or *taking-away*) *iniquity, and passing by over the transgression of the remnant of his heritage? He retaineth not his anger forever, because he delighteth in loving-kindness. He will return, he-will-tenderly compassionate-us, he will subdue our iniquities: and thou wilt cast-away* (or *fling-away*) *all their sins into the depths of the sea.*[704]

In this glorious Scripture, the singular and incomparable goodness of God is magnified over all gods in his pardoning mercy. The true God is altogether matchless in his sin-pardoning mercy. *Who is a God like thee?* etc. This his sin-pardoning mercy is:

{1} ***Emphatically propounded*** by way of interrogation: *Who is a God like thee, pardoning,* (נֹשֵׂא *Nose*: lifting-up, taking-away) *iniquity?* Of this term formerly;[705]

{2} ***Elegantly amplified*** by many sweet and comfortable expressions, as:

(i) *Passing by over the transgression* (עֹבֵר עַל פֶּשַׁע *guhober guhal peshaugh*) *of the remnant of his heritage.* When God pardons sin, he passes over it, he passes by it, he so sees it that will not see it, he will have nothing to say or do to it or for it, as to the point of curse and condemnation, but only his heritage, that little remnant in the world shall share in this mercy. Thus God passed by the

---

[703] Augustine on Psalm 103
[704] Micah 7:18-19
[705] In the 7th Denomination or Expression of Pardon.

Israelites in Egypt, whose houses were sprinkled with blood, when he fell upon the Egyptians for their sins and destroyed them.[706]

(ii) *He retaineth not his anger forever*, etc. God may be angry with his people, and sore displeased at them for their sins so as to chastise them severely, though he pardon them graciously: yet he will not be ever angry, he will put off and lay aside his displeasure from them.

(iii) *He delights, takes-pleasure in loving-kindness*. חֶסֶד *Chesed* properly notes benignity, loving-kindness. Loving-kindness has these three special properties, namely: (a) to impart tokens and testifications of kindness to the object loved, (b) to accept the smallest upright performances or manifestations of duty, and (c) to cover and pass by all weaknesses and infirmities, as if there were no such things. God excels in all these; loving-kindness is his delight.

(iv) *He will return, he will tenderly-compassionate us*. The word רָחַם *racham* properly denotes to commiserate, intimately to tender with inward yearning bowels of compassion, tenderly to embrace, as the matrix the child.[707] Though sin drive God away sometimes, yet he will not utterly depart, he will return again to us – yea, though we have sinned against his mercy, kicked against his bowels, yet his very bowels yearn over us. When God pardons a sinner, Oh how he tenders him, how dearly he clasps and embraces him, how he puts him as it were into his very inward and dearest bowels! etc.

(v) *He will subdue our iniquities*. When God pardons sin, he subdues sin, he conquers the enmity of sin. Partly, he subdues the great and strong provocation of sin, that rises up against God. God's pardons prevail against, and overcome our sins provocations: his pardons are above our sins exasperations and aggravations. They are great, but God's pardons are infinitely greater. Partly, he subdues the great power of sin, that rises up

---

[706] Exodus 12
[707] "Sunt qui a visceribus factum verbum existimant, quasi Inviscerare dicas, hoc est intimo affectu qui visceribus inditus est, tangi, & commoveri erga aliquem. Intimo commiserationis affectu quempiam prosequi, quo scilicet Matrix quae רחם dicitur, fetum complectitur tuendo & fovendo."
Mercer. in Pagnin. Thesaur. ad verb.

against us. Where God pardons the guilt, he kills and mortifies the power of sin.

(vi) *He flings away all his people's sins into the depths of the sea.* That is, God so pardons their sins, that he pardons all, and that forever. As that which is flung into the sea, into the deepest places of the sea, can never again he seen or found: Or as the Egyptians were all swallowed up in the Red Sea, and never troubled, terrified or afflicted Israel anymore after that day; God could as easily drown all Pharaoh's army therein, as one man.[708] So their pardoned sins shall be all drowned in the sea of God's mercy and Christ's merit forever; they (though never so huge an army) shall never trouble, terrify or afflict them anymore to their condemnation; in that sense they shall never be found anymore at all, or heard of in God's wrath anymore at all.

Thus I have opened a box of rich and precious ointment. O how fragrant and refreshing are these expressions to a sin-bruised foul! How appositely and suitably are they accommodated against all the saddening considerations and apprehensions of sin!

{1} Our sins are debts, but God does freely remit them. {2} Our sins are offenses, but God in Christ expiates them, and is propitious to them. {3} Our sins are upon record in God's book, but God will not remember them, impute them to us, or charge them upon us; but wipe them quite away. {4} Our sins are foul and deformed, but God will hide and cover them. {5} Our sins are heavy burdens, but God will lift them off us, and take them away. {6} Our sins have been acted all in God's sight, and they are ever before us. but God will cast them all behind his back, and remove them as far away from us as the east is distant from the west. {7} Our sins are great provocations against God, and strong enemies to our salvation, but our matchless, sin-pardoning God will pass them by, will not still retain his anger against them, takes pleasure in loving-kindness, will return to us, will reembrace us with tenderest bowels of commiserations, will subdue our iniquities, and will fling away all our sins, as

---

[708] Exodus 14 & 15

once the Egyptians, into the depths of the sea. O think of these things, you penitent souls, that lie bleeding under your sins and the wrath of God: and lift up yourselves herewith out of the doleful pit of your despondencies and disconsolations.

Thus of the Scripture names and expressions touching remission of sin: the *quid nominis*.

(2) **The nature of remission of sins; the *quid rei*, what the thing of remission of sins is, has been very much discovered in all the former excellent expressions whereby the Holy Spirit points it out unto us in the Scriptures.**

But yet, because this is such a fundamental article of faith; upon which the consolation of believers so much depends, and against which it is very dangerous to err, on the right hand or on the left, I shall, for the more distinct and clear discovery of the nature of remission of sins, propound and explain these positions following, namely:

[Position 1]: That remission of sins, here promised in this New Covenant, is not intended of any human remission fraternal or ministerial, but of divine remission of sins – and that not particular, but universal.

We must rightly distinguish, before we can clearly and duly define or describe. Remission of sins, according to Scripture is twofold:

{1} *Human*, whereby man forgives man, according to God's appointment. This human remission is also twofold, namely:

(i) **Fraternal remission**, which every private Christian ought to perform to his brother sincerely and heartily, as he desires and expects pardon from God: *Forgive, and ye shall be forgiven.*[709] *– And forgive us our debts, as we forgive our debtors. – For if ye forgive men their trespasses, your heavenly Father will also forgive you. But if ye forgive not men their trespasses, neither will your Father forgive your trespasses.*[710] Thus Joseph forgave his brethren.[711] Nor must we forgive one another, until seven times, but *until seventy times seven*;[712] even as often as there is need: as our Savior teaches by his parable.

(ii) **Ministerial and ecclesiastical remission**, which *either* the ministers pronouncing doctrinally according to the word unto every true believing and repenting sinner, which is partly intended in that: *whosoever sins ye remit, they are remitted unto them; and whosoever sins ye retain, they are retained*;[713] or the church, the governing church,[714] pronouncing orderly, in a way of discipline and censure, to a penitent after ecclesiastical punishment inflicted. But none of these remissions are here intended; but rather, such a remission as is the immediate act of God (Hebrews 8:12, Jeremiah 31:34).

---

[709] Luke 6:37, Matthew 18:35
[710] Matthew 6:12, 14-15, Mark 11:25-26
[711] Genesis 50:16-17, etc.
[712] Matthew 18:21 to the end
[713] John 20:23
[714] Matthew 18:15-22, John 20:23, Matthew 16:18-19; 2 Corinthians 2:6-11

{2} ***Divine***, whereby God himself forgives man. And is likewise twofold, namely:

(i) **Particular or partial**, when God remits the punishment of sin in part, or for a time only. As when God remits temporal punishment, even unto reprobates: Thus God pardoned the murmurers, in not bringing the pestilence upon them, according to Moses' request: *Pardon I beseech thee the iniquity of this people, – as thou hast forgiven this people from Egypt even until now*;[715] and yet he afterwards shut them all out of the promised rest for their unbelief. Thus God in part pardoned wicked Ahab, in respiting the threatened judgment.[716] But however God may pardon wicked persons in regard to temporal punishment: he will never pardon them in regard to eternal (Matthew 25:46, Psalms 92:7).

(ii) **Universal or total**, when God gratuitously remits[717] unto truly penitent and believing sinners,[718] all punishment and curse of sin properly so called, both temporal and eternal,[719] for and through the meritorious satisfaction of Jesus Christ,[720] apprehended by faith.[721] I say "all punishment properly so called," for even those who are actually pardoned and justified, are not exempted from God's fatherly chastisements, judgments, and trials in this life, and those inflicted sometimes upon occasion of their sins – witness David, the Corinthians, and many others (2 Samuel 12:13-14, etc; 1 Corinthians 11:32, Hebrews 12:6-10). And this universal remission of sin, is that which is properly and plainly intended in this New Covenant.

---

[715] Numbers 14:12-26, 19, Hebrews 3:18-19 & 4:3
[716] 1 Kings 21:27-28
[717] Colossians 2:13 & 3:13
[718] Acts 2:38, Romans 3:25; 1 John 1:9
[719] Ephesians 1:7, Colossians 1:14, Galatians 3:13, Romans 8:1
[720] Isaiah 53:4-6, Romans 3:24 & 5:8; 2 Corinthians 5:21
[721] Romans 3:25

[Position 2] That remission of sin is a distinct blessing and grace from mortification of sin, and not to be confounded therewith.

For:

{1} **Remission of sin is a branch or part of justification** (Romans 3:24-26 & 4:6-8). But mortification of sin is a branch of sanctification (Colossians 3:5-11 & 2:11-12, Romans 6:4-15).

{2} **Remission of sin properly takes away the guilt of sin, the obligation to condemnation** (Ephesians 1:7, Hebrews 8:12). But mortification of sin takes away the filth, power, and dominion of sin, and at last by degrees destroys the very inherence and being of sin in us, that there shall be neither spot, nor wrinkle, nor any such thing (Romans 6:4-16, Ephesians 5:27). Remission makes a man no guilty sinner before God, but mortification tends daily to make a man no sinner at all. It is true: remission of sin and mortification of sin, are divine blessings, cast at the same time upon the same persons; but yet they are distinct blessings.[722]

---

[722] Colossians 2:11-13

[Position 3] That remission of sins strictly and properly taken, is not the all, but only a part of our justification before God; but more largely and improperly it is all.

For remission of sin is taken properly or improperly:

{1} **More strictly and properly, it denotes an absolution of the sinner from the guilt of sin, namely: from his just obligation unto due punishment** (2 Samuel 12:13, Matthew 6:12, Luke 11:4). And in this sense, remission of sins is not the all and whole nature of justification, but only a part thereof. For none are just before God perfectly, but such as perform the whole debt due to God. The debt due to God is twofold, namely: one directly and *per se*; that is, perfect and perpetual obedience to God's law;[723] the other indirectly and *per accidens*, by accident and occasion of sin, that is: undergoing the punishment due to the transgression of the law.[724] Both of these are necessarily to be performed for us; the latter, for obtaining remission of sins, that is, absolution from the curse and punishment of eternal death deserved: the former, for imputation of righteousness to us unto eternal life. Hereupon Jesus Christ, becoming our Mediator and Surety, paid and performed both these debts due to God; namely: The debt of punishment, for obtaining remission of sins, or acquittal from death and curse, for us (Isaiah 53:4-6, Ephesians 1:7; 2 Corinthians 5:21). The debt of perfect obedience, for justification of life (Romans 5:17-18).

{2} **More largely and improperly, by a synecdoche of the part for the whole, it comprehends in it the imputation also of righteousness.** As in that passage which Paul alleges out of the Psalms: *Even as David also describeth the blessedness of the man unto whom God imputeth righteousness without works: saying, Blessed are they whose iniquities are forgiven, and whose*

---

[723] Deuteronomy 27:26
[724] Romans 1:32 & 6:23, Deuteronomy 27:26

sins are covered. Blessed is the man unto whom the Lord will not impute sin.[725] David's words expressly mention not a word of the imputation of righteousness: but run only upon God's forgiving, covering, and not imputing sin, and yet Paul says: *David describes the blessedness of the man to whom God imputeth righteousness.*

Here therefore, a synecdoche must needs be acknowledged, and that remission of sins (here expressed by forgiving, covering, and not imputing sin) plainly imports and implies also an imputation of righteousness. And seeing as remission of sins is sometimes used in the New Testament synecdochically to comprise in it the whole of justification, why should it be thought strange to understand it in this extent and latitude here in this body of the New Covenant, the promises and blessings whereof are so complexive, extensive, and fundamental?[726] Surely I see no inconvenience contradicting. And certainly, If we may understand this federal article so largely, it will so much more advance the rich grace of the New Covenant, and advantage the consolation of the New Covenant federates.

---

[725] Psalm 32:1-2 with Romans 4:6-8
[726] Hebrews 8:12, Jeremiah 31:34

[Position 4] That remission of sins – strictly taken, most properly and especially – consists in the removal of the offense done to God, and in the acquittal or absolution of the sinner from the guilt of sin, that is: from his obligation, or being bound over, to endure the punishment of death, due for such offense.

I have already shown that,[727] among other particulars considerable in sin, these are two especially to be noted, as to the present subject in hand; namely: *offensa* and *reatus*.

{1} **The offense or provocation against God, as it were stirring up his anger and displeasure.** The act of sin may be transient and speedily pass away: but the offense against God remains and continues, until the sin is pardoned. God lays it to heart, when the sinner is pleased with it; God is displeased at it, when the sinner is pleased at it; God books it down, and remembers it, when the sinner forgets it, etc. And God ofttimes testifies his deep displeasure because of such offense, before the offender obtain repentance or pardon. But when sin is remitted, God ceases his conceived anger and displeasure;[728] blots the sinners offenses out of mind and memory, will remember them to him no more (Hebrews 8:12).

{2} **The guilt of sin, or the obligation of the sinner to the punishment of death and damnation, appointed by God.**[729] As soon as a man has sinned, he immediately falls into the hands of God, who has right and power over him as a supreme and righteous judge to take vengeance upon him, having already adjudged the sinner unto death: and he is also presently fallen into the hands (as it were) of his own conscience, his own guilty conscience. God and his own conscience bind him over to eternal condemnation, as the proper appointed

---

[727] In Question 1
[728] Micah 7:18
[729] Genesis 2:17, Romans 1:32, Deuteronomy 27:26

wages of sin.[730] While this guilt, while this obligation to death lies upon the soul and conscience, there's no remission of sin there; but in this guilt, sin still lives, still represents itself with horror to the awakened soul: *my sin is ever before me*;[731] still cries aloud for vengeance, as if it were but newly acted, etc. When sin therefore is remitted, this guilt removes, this obligation to threatened and deserved punishment ceases; the soul is now set at liberty, this dreadful bond is canceled, the pain, fear, trouble and terror of conscience is over, and the sinner begins to find some spiritual rest and ease unto his soul.[732] Herein principally and especially remission of sin stands: not in removal of the stain and power of sin, that is done by sanctification: nor in removal of the desert of punishment, for even in a pardoned person, as well as in an unpardoned, sin deserves eternal death and condemnation, this is the proper and adequate wages of sin wherever it is;[733] but in removal of the guilt of sin, and that obligation to everlasting death and condemnation, when this guilt is removed, when this obligation is canceled; then sin is pardoned. This is evident:

(i) Partly, by the metaphors used to express pardon of sin, which peculiarly intend acquittal from the guilt of sin, or disobligation from the punishment of sin, as *hiding God's face from them*, and blotting them out:[734] a similitude from creditors that blot debts out of their books, so as not to exact them to be paid. *Remembering sin no more*: not remembering them to punish them and damn for them:[735] a metaphor from judges that punish not offenses forgotten or unknown. If God punishes sin, he still remembers it. *Covering of sin*: not simply and absolutely that God cannot see it, but that God will not see it to condemnation, etc.[736]

---

[730] Romans 6:23
[731] Psalm 51:3
[732] Matthew 11:28-29
[733] Romans 2:32 & 6:23
[734] Psalm 51:9, Isaiah 43:25
[735] Hebrews 8:12, Jeremiah 31:34, Isaiah 43:25
[736] Psalm 32:1

(ii) Partly, by the expressions used about the pardoning of the sins of such as have been forgiven. As of David: *The LORD also hath put away thy sin* (Hebrew: *has made-to-pass-away thy sinful-error*), *thou shalt not die.*[737] In the former phrase, pardon of sin is assured: in the latter phrase, this assured pardon is explained, in acquitting him from the obligation to punishment. So of Hezekiah: *Thou hast loved my soul from the pit of corruption: For thou hast cast all my sins behind thy back.*[738] See also, Psalm 103:9-12.

(iii) Partly, by the method that God takes about pardoning the sins of his elect. Of his free grace he gave Christ to be our surety and savior (Hebrews 7:21, 22 & 9:15). Upon this our surety Christ, he lays all the punishment of our sins, that by his satisfaction, we may be acquitted from our guilt or obligation to punishment (Isaiah 53:6, Romans 3:24 & 5:8, Matthew 20:28, Hebrews 9:26; 1 Timothy 2:2; 2 Corinthians 5:21). As Christ was made sin for us, by having the punishment of our sins charged upon him: so we are discharged from our sins and pardoned, by being released and discharged from our obligation unto due punishment deserved by our sins.

---

[737] 2 Samuel 12:13
[738] Isaiah 38:17

[Position 5] That God alone remits sin.

Remission of sins is God's peculiar prerogative. Herein he is alone, and none with him, for:

{1} Remission of sins is in Scripture peculiarly ascribed to God, as belonging properly and only to him alone: *The LORD – pardoning iniquity and transgression and sin.*[739] *– I, even I, am he that blotteth out thy transgressions for mine own sake, and will not remember thy sins.*[740] *– A God of pardons.*[741] *– Who is a God like unto thee, pardoning iniquity,* etc.[742] Who can forgive sins save God only? And hence Christ declared himself to be God, that he was able to forgive sins to the palsy man; and he evidenced himself to be able to forgive sins by curing him of his palsy by his word.

{2} Our Savior teaches us daily to direct our prayers to our heavenly Father, and to none other for remission of sins.[743] And penitent, sin-bruised souls repair to God and him alone for pardon – see Psalms 51. 1, 2, 3, etc., Hosea 14:2 – because they know well that this blessed alms comes only from the bosom of God's love.

{3} It is God alone that justifies (Romans 8:33, 3:24-26, 4:5 & 8:30). And therefore it is God alone that remits sin, for remission of sin is one part of justification – as has been manifested.

{4} Our sins are debts primarily, properly and peculiarly against God alone; as being against his will, his laws, his authority, his purity, etc.[744] Hence David: *Against thee, thee only have I sinned,* etc.[745] Sins are only secondarily, and in reference to God, against others, as thereby his moral laws or law of nature, etc, are violated. Now who can remit the debt, but the

---

[739] Exodus 34:7
[740] Isaiah 43:25
[741] Nehemiah 9:17
[742] Micah 7:18
[743] Matthew 6:12, Luke 11:4
[744] Matthew 6:12, Luke 11:4
[745] Psalm 51:4

creditor? Who can remit the sin, but God against whom it is committed primarily, and in some sense only?

{5} **Remission of sins in every notion and cosideration, both *in foro coeli*, and *in foro soli* – in the court of heaven, and in the court of a man's own heart and conscience – belongs only to God.**

(i) *In the court of heaven*, remission belongs only to him, for against him only the offense is done (Psalm 51:4). And he only can save from hell, and destroy both soul and body in hell – and that forevermore.[746]

(ii) *In the court of a man's own conscience.* He only that is God and Father of spirits, having immediate sovereignty and power over the hearts and spirits of all men, can upon remission of sins calm, still and pacify the conscience, and give experimental persuasion, sense, evidence and assurance of pardon. Men, ministers may use arguments, apply promises, comforts, and many means to compose a troubled heart; but all to very little purpose, until the Lord himself by his Spirit comes in. Then if he does but say {*peace*} and {*be still*}, there is a perfect calm. So true is that of Elihu: *When he giveth quietness, who then can make trouble? And when he hideth his face, who then can behold him?*[747] Whether it be done against a nation, or against a man only. Nathan told David that God had put away his sin, he should not die;[748] but all this did not set David's broken bones in joint, nor restore to him the joy of God's salvation, until God himself began to smile upon him and speak peace to him.[749]

{6} **All human pardons are small matters, are as nothing to God's pardons.** Fraternal pardons between man and man, Christian and Christian, are only caritative passing by of private personal injuries, without seeking or meditating upon revenge.[750] But these cannot at all reach to remove the offense

---

[746] Matthew 10:28
[747] Job 34:29
[748] 2 Samuel 12:13
[749] Psalm 51 throughout
[750] Matthew 6:12, 14-15, Mark 11:25-26 with Matthew 5:38-42, Romans 12:17, 19-21

against God, or the guiltiness of God's judgment, or the trouble of conscience thereupon. Ministerial and ecclesiastical pardons, are only subordinate and declarative: whereby either the spiritual censure and punishment inflicted by the church upon an offender, is upon testification of his repentance removed in a way of discipline;[751] or God's own remission of sin to the truly penitent and believing sinner is – according to the holy Scripture – doctrinally assured.[752] Both of these remissions, or loosings of sin are only so far authentic and prevalent, as they are conform to the word, and are ratified in heaven (as for popish pardons, they are either wicked tolerations, protections and licenses of sinning, or abominable delusions and mockeries of sinners: mere Antichristian nets for catching of money, and enslaving souls under the papal tyranny). But God's pardons are absolutely supreme, authoritative and all-sufficient to take away all the offense against God, all the guilt of deserved punishment in this and the world to come, and all the trouble of conscience thereupon. He fully pardons in the court of heaven, and the court of conscience. His pardons are the only pardons.

Hence therefore: (i) all that have their sins pardoned, may see to whom alone they are to ascribe them; and (ii) all that lack pardons, may learn from whom alone they are to expect them.

---

[751] Matthew 18:15-22; 2 Corinthians 2:6-8, 10-11
[752] John 20:23

[Position 6] That God pardons sin freely of his own mere grace, without any the least merit or desert of the pardoned sinner.

This is most evident, for:

{1} **The impulsive or moving cause inclining the Lord to pardon sin, is not anything at all, in the creature, without himself; but only his own rich and free grace, within himself**, as the Scriptures abundantly testify: *Being justified freely by his grace.*[753] Therefore pardoned freely by his grace – remission being part of justification, as is there after intimated. *Having freely-forgiven {χαρισαμενος} you all trespasses.*[754] – *Even as Christ {εχαρισατο} freely forgave you, so also do ye.*[755] – *In whom we have redemption through his blood, the forgiveness of sins, according to the riches of his grace:*[756] – *I, even I am he that blotteth out thy transgressions for mine own sake, and will not remember thy sins.*[757]

{2} **Though God forgive sins only in Christ and for his merit and satisfaction: as after shall be shown, yet, in regard to the pardoned sinner, that also is of mere grace:**

(i) Partly, in that God pleased to contrive this way of saving sinners by a surety, Jesus Christ, to provide and accept the satisfaction of this surety by his death for the sins of his elect, which he might justly have demanded and exacted of the principals themselves (1 Timothy 2:5-6, Hebrews 10:10, Matthew 19:28, Daniel 9:24, 26, Isaiah 53:4-6, 10-12, Hebrews 7:22, Romans 8:32; 1 Peter 1:18-19).

(ii) Partly, in that God pleases actually to apply the blood and death of Jesus Christ unto the hearts and consciences of such or such sinners, by his Spirit and faith, for actual remission of sins, when he might justly have left

---

[753] Romans 3:24-25
[754] Colossians 2:13
[755] Colossians 3:13
[756] Ephesians 1:7
[757] Isaiah 43:25

them to perish with others in their sins and unbelief (Hebrews 9:14-15, Romans 3:22-26, Hebrews 10:22; 1 Corinthians 6:11, Acts 15:9, Revelation 1:5, Colossians 2:11-13; 1 Corinthians 4:7, Romans 9:15-16, 18, 20-25).

{3} **Although God remit sins to none, but to penitent and believing sinners only, yet that remission even upon such terms also is merely gratuitous – and not at all for any merit or desert of such faith or such repentance.** For both repentance[758] and faith[759] are the mere gifts of his free grace.

{4} **That God might most clearly evidence to all the gratuitousness and freeness of his pardoning mercies, he has singled out most notorious sinners, most undeserving – yea, most ill-deserving wretches as subjects and receptacles of his pardons.** Hereby his pardoning grace appears to be exceedingly gracious.

He pardoned David's murder and adultery (2 Samuel 12:13); the sinful woman, her many sins (Luke 7:37, 47); Manasseh his many horrid impieties (2 Chronicles 33:2-18); Peter, his triple denial of his Master, and every time worse than others (Matthew 26:70, 72, 74-75, John 21:15-20); Paul his persecutions, injuries, and blasphemies (1 Timothy 1:13, etc) – yea, the Jews, their betraying, crucifying and murdering of Jesus Christ the Son of God (Acts 2:23, 36-38, 41).

To this effect said Chrysostom elegantly: "Great is the tumult of my sins: but much is the security of my Lord's love to man. He became man: this was of mercy. He came into the virgin's womb: this was of love to man. He became what you are so that you might become what you are not. This was of mercy. And coming, whom did he immediately call? The wise men. After them, whom? The publican. After him, the whore. After her, the thief. After him, whom? The blasphemer. O new and strange things! The first-fruits of calling is the tyranny of sin," etc. "Are you impious? Call to mind the Magi, the wise

---

[758] Acts 11:18; 2 Timothy 2:25
[759] Ephesians 2:8, Philippians 1:29

men. Are you rapacious? Call to mind the publican. Are you unclean? Call to mind the whore. Art you a manslayer? Call to mind the thief. Are you a heinous offender? Call to mind Paul the blasphemer, and after that an apostle; first a persecutor, and afterwards an evangelist; first tare, and after that, wheat; first a wolf, and afterwards a shepherd; first lead, and after that, gold," etc.[760]

Now why does God single out from among sinners, such notorious and flagitious [villainous] offenders, to bestow his sanctifying and pardoning mercies upon, but that thereby he might the more gloriously exalt the rich grace of his pardons, in those patterns of pardons, for the encouragement of all such as after should believe?[761]

---

[760] John Chrysostom Hom. 2 in Psalm 50. p. 997, 998 Tom. 3. (Paris, 1636).
[761] 1 Timothy 1:13-16

[Position 7] That God remits sin only upon and for the satisfaction made to his justice for sin by the obedience and death of Jesus Christ.

For clearing this, consider:

{1} That God (having in his Covenant of Works declared to Adam for himself and his posterity that in the day he should transgress by eating the forbidden fruit, he should die the death)[762] could not, according to the exactness and strictness of his truth and justice, pass by Adam's first sin (wherein all sinned in him)[763] without punishing it with death. If in some sense that sin had not been punished with death, how then should God have been true, that threatened it? How should God have been just, that spared it contrary to justice?

{2} That lapsed man being utterly unable to pay this debt, to undergo this death eternal without sinking under it, and being swallowed up wholly by it forever,[764] the Lord was pleased to find out a sufficient surety that should fully pay the debt, by undergoing death[765] (even a death through the infinite dignity of his person,[766] equivalent to eternal, namely: Jesus Christ, God-man).

{3} That Jesus Christ, God-man, our only Mediator and Surety, by his obedience and death, did make a proper, real and full satisfaction to God's justice for the sins of all his elect,[767] wherewith God is forever well pleased (Isaiah 53:4-6, 8, 10-12, Romans 5:8-10, 19) *I lay down my life for the sheep* (John 10:15) – *The Son of man came not to be ministered unto, but to minister, and to give his life {δουναι} a ransom for many.*[768] – *Who gave himself {δους}*

---

[762] Genesis 2:17, Romans 5:23
[763] Romans 5:12
[764] Romans 6:23
[765] Hebrews 7:22 & 9:12-15; 1 Timothy 2:5-6, Hebrews 10:5-20
[766] Acts 20:28
[767] 1 Timothy 3:16; John 1:14
[768] Matthew 20:28

i.e. precium ex adverso respondens; vel aequale redemptionis precium)[769] *a full ransom for all.*[770] That is. for all that he would have come to the knowledge of the truth, as in the former verse, namely: not absolutely all, but of all sorts some.[771] Again: *But now once in the end of the world, hath he appeared to put away sin by the sacrifice of himself.*[772] – *By his own blood he entered in once into the holy place, having obtained* {αιωνιαν λυτρωσιν} *eternal redemption for us.*[773] – *In whom we have* {απολυτρωσιν} *redemption through his blood, even the forgiveness of sins.*[774] Now how acceptable this ransom, this price of our redemption was to God, the apostle declares: partly, By comparing Christ's death to the most fragrant perfume of incense: *Christ hath loved us, and hath given himself for us, an offering and a sacrifice to God for a sweet smelling savour;*[775] partly, by declaring how God preferred this one sacrifice of Christ's dying, before all the sacrifices of the law whatsoever;[776] partly by the event and effects of Christ's offering up himself once, namely: his sitting down at God's right hand; his perfecting them forever that are sanctified;[777] his utter taking away all need of anymore expiatory sacrifice for sin. By all these passages and expressions it is very evident that Christ has, by his death and blood as an invaluable price of our redemption, made full satisfaction to God's justice for the sins of all his elect, and that God has fully accepted the same forever,[778] so that now the mercy of God may embrace the sinner without the least impeachment of wrong to his truth or justice.

{4} That Jesus Christ, having fully satisfied God's justice for the sins of all his elect, by his death and blood (the incomparable price of their redemption),

---

[769] 1 Timothy 2:5-6
[770] Sic αντι in nomine απολυτρωσιν i.e. aequilibrium, usuraptur
[771] 1 Timothy 2:4
[772] Hebrews 9:26, 28
[773] Hebrews 9:12
[774] Colossians 1:14, Ephesians 1:7
[775] Ephesians 5:2
[776] Hebrews 10:5-7
[777] Hebrews 10:12-20
[778] Acts 20:28; 1 Peter 1:18-19

has thereby meritoriously purchased and obtained for all his elect remission of sins – even their everlasting relaxation and freedom from the guilt of sin, that is: from their obligation to death; even to all punishment properly so called, temporal, spiritual and eternal. This is very plain by that expression of Paul's in two of his epistles: *in whom we have redemption through his blood, even the forgiveness of sins.*[779] Here note:

(i) A great benefit obtained for us by Christ, namely: redemption. From what? From sin (Hebrews 9:13-14; 1 Peter 1:18-19), from the wrath of God (1 Thessalonians 1:10), from the power of darkness (Colossians 1:13-14), and from the curse of the law (Galatians 3:13).

(ii) The way that Christ obtained this redemption for us, namely: through his blood, by paying his matchless price.

(iii) The interpretation of this redemption by way of apposition; namely: even remission of sins. God's justice being satisfied by the price of our redemption, Christ's blood: remission of sins is obtained for us. His redeeming us from wrath, takes off our guilt and obligation to eternal condemnation: and this is properly remission of sins. Thus though God remit our sins most freely, as touching us who cannot deserve it, but rather, the contrary; yet he remits our sins justly, as touching Christ, who has meritoriously purchased and obtained it by his death. Remission of sins cost Christ dear, though it cost us nothing. Remission of sins drops down from God to us through Christ's wounds, and swims to us in Christ's blood. Oh, kiss those wounds with the lips of faith. Oh, drink that precious blood with the mouth of faith. And then all your sins, all your guilt, all your condemnation shall flee away. I conclude this position with that of Ambrose:

"I have not whence I may glory in my own works, I have not whence I may boast myself, and therefore I will glory in Christ. I will not glory that I am righteous, but I will glory, that I am redeemed. I will glory, not because I am without sin, but because my sins are forgiven. I will not glory because I have

---

[779] Colossians 1:14, Ephesians 1:7

profited, or because any has profited me, but because Christ is an advocate with the Father for me, but because the blood of Christ is shed for me."[780]

Hence the popish doctrine of man's own satisfaction in part for his sins, is most derogatory to the plenary and complete satisfaction of Jesus Christ for all the punishment temporal, spiritual and eternal due for the sins of the elect, whereby the guilt of all their sins is universally removed. Papists say, this universal remission of sin by Christ's satisfaction has place in the first remission, which is by baptism, but not in the second remission, which is given to them that sin after baptism; in which, eternal punishment is remitted to the penitent, but not temporal punishment.[781]

And that this temporal punishment is to be endured before a man can enter into the kingdom of heaven,[782] either (a) here in this life by laborious works, patiently endured; namely: (1) punishments inflicted by God, (2) enjoined by the priest, Or (3) voluntarily undertaken, as fastings, prayers, alms, etc.; or (b) hereafter in purgatory in the life to come. But this is a wretched doctrine, robbing Christ of the glory of his full satisfaction which belongs to him, and attributing to sinful man a satisfaction which cannot belong to him, contrary to what has been said, and to the clear current of Scripture, so that I need add no more by way of refutation.[783]

---

[780] Non habeo igitur unde gloriari in operibus meis possim, non habeo unde me jactem; & ideo gloriabor in Christo. Non gloriabor quia justus sum, sed gloriabor quia redemptus sum. Gloriabor, non quia vacuus peccati sum, sed quia mihi remissa sunt peccata. Non gloriabor, quia profui, ne{que} quia profuit mihi quispiam, sed quia pro me advocatus apud Patrem Christus est, Sed quia pro me Christi sanguis effusus est. Ambros. de Iacob & vita beat. lib. 1. cap 6. pag. 290, 291. (Basil, 1567)

[781] Council of Trent, Session 14, Cap. 2 & Session 6

[782] Bellarmine, *De Poenit* L. 4. C. 10. Tom. 2. Concil. Trident. Ses. 14. cap. 13

[783] Vid. Gom. Illustr. Loc. Luc. 1. 77. p. 228, 229. Tom. 1.

[Position 8] That God actually remits sin to all truly believing and repenting sinners, and (in his ordinary dispensation) to them only.

I say *actually* because pardon of sin (though purposed and decreed of God, before all time, in which sense God may be said to remit sin decretorily;[784] and though purchased and obtained for all God's elect by the meritorious obedience and death of Christ, in fullness of time, in which sense God may be said to remit sin meritoriously;[785] yet) is not actually applied to any person in due time, but only to such as truly believe in Jesus Christ for pardon, and sincerely repent of all their sins which they desire to have pardoned, as afterwards shall be evidenced. Again I say *in his ordinary dispensation* because of elect infants, who dying in their infancy doubtless are pardoned and justified in and through Jesus Christ, applied unto them by the Spirit of God extraordinarily, according to his unsearchable wisdom and counsels, although they attain not to the actual exercise of faith and repentance. Yet Luther held that elect infants have actual faith; Calvin, Peter Martyr, Whitaker, and others of our acute Protestant writers, though they dare not go so far, yet they hold they may have faith as they have reason, *in principio et radice*, in the principle root or fountain: as the reasonable soul in them is the principle and root of reason, so the Spirit of God in them is the principle and root of faith.[786] However it be that elect infants are pardoned, justified, and saved, it must needs be confessed to be in an extraordinary, not in an ordinary way.

Now setting aside this extraordinary case, God actually remits sin unto none but such as truly believe and repent. Faith and repentance are in order of nature antecedent unto actual remission of sins, and pre-required in the

---

[784] Romans 8:29-30, Ephesians 1:4-12
[785] Colossians 1:14, Ephesians 1:7, Hebrews 9:12-15, Romans 3:24-25
[786] See William Whitaker *Praelection. de Baptism* Q.4 cap 5 & 6, pp. 282-29 (Frankfurt, 1624)

subject to be pardoned before the actual application of pardon to the soul, but differently. Faith is pre-required as an instrumental cause or means in order to receive the pardon promised from God in Christ. Repentance is pre-required as a necessary qualification of the sinner for pardon. But neither of them are pre-required for any merit or desert thereof to the procuring of pardon from God. God will not pardon without faith and without repentance, yet he does not pardon for faith and for repentance, but only for Christ. This is discreetly to be considered, and still to be remembered. Now the necessity of faith and repentance unto pardon, may thus appear.

(1) **True faith in Jesus Christ according to the promise is pre-required as a necessary instrumental means to the actual perception, reception and application of remission of sins, without which there is no actual remission of sins**, as has been explained. This is evident by many Scriptures: *To him give all the prophets witness, that through his name whosoever believeth in him, shall receive remission of sins.*[787] – *Through this man is preached unto you the forgiveness of sins. And by him all that believe are justified from all things, from which ye could not be justified by the law of Moses.*[788] That is, all believers are justified from all their sins, have remission of all their sins by Jesus Christ really and effectually, which the rites and ceremonies of the law without him could never afford, they being only types and shadows of the virtue of Christ that should afterwards be revealed, and they being often repeated, because of their insufficiency to take away sins, until Christ – the life and substance of them all – came.[789] One Christ crucified is of more avail and efficacy for remission of sins than all the sacrifices, purgations, washings, and ceremonies of the law. *To open their eyes, and to turn them from darkness to light, and from the power of Satan unto God, that they may receive forgiveness of sins, and inheritance among them which are sanctified, by faith that is in*

---

[787] Acts 10:43
[788] Acts 13:38-39
[789] Hebrews 10:1-3

me.[790] Faith (as Calvin has well noted)[791] is here to be referred to the *totum complexum*: not to the word sanctified, as if the apostle intended to show they were sanctified by faith; but rather to the word receive, faith being here declared to be the hand or instrumental mean whereby we receive both remission of sins, and inheritance among the sanctified. That of Paul's also, touching justification, is very pregnant: *being justified freely by his grace, through the redemption that is in Jesus Christ: whom God hath set forth to be a propitiation through faith in his blood, to declare his righteousness for the remission of sins that are past, through the forbearance of God* (Romans 3:24-25). And all such Scriptures as declare that we are justified by faith, (as Romans 3:28, 30, and 4:5, 9, etc., and 5:1, Galatians 2:16, with sundry others) do also imply that we have remission of sins by faith: remission being part of our justification.

(2) **Sincere repentance from all sin, and from all dead works, is also pre-required as a necessary and congruous qualification of the subject that shall receive pardon of sin.** As: *Repent and turn yourselves from all your transgressions: so iniquity shall not be your ruin.*[792] Christ said after his resurrection: *Thus it is written, and thus it behooved Christ to suffer, and to rise from the dead the third day: and that repentance and remission of sins should be preached in his name among all nations, beginning at Jerusalem.*[793] Thus Peter urged his hearers to repent in order to their remission of sins: *Repent, and be baptized everyone of you in the name of Jesus Christ, for the remission of sins.*[794] Repentance qualifies for remission of sins, and baptism

---

[790] Acts 26:18

[791] "Some do read it falsely in one text, among those who are sanctified by faith, because this word is extended unto the whole period. Therefore, the meaning thereof is, that by faith we come unto the possession of all those good things which are offered by the gospel."
John Calvin's commentary on Acts 26:18
[https://www.studylight.org/commentaries/eng/cal/acts-26.html]
<Accessed 4/5/2024>

[792] Ezekiel 18:30

[793] Luke 24:46-47

[794] Acts 2:38

sacramentally assures of that remission: *him hath God exalted with his right hand to be a prince and a savior, for to give repentance to Israel, and forgiveness of sins.*[795] But first repentance, and then forgiveness of sins: *Repent therefore of this thy wickedness, and pray God, if perhaps the thought of thine heart may be forgiven thee.*[796] So conversion, under which repentance is comprised, is made the way to the obtaining of remission of sins by faith (Acts 26:18). And penitent confession of sins has the promise of remission (1 John 1:9). To this effect said Chrysostom: "Speak your sins, that you may blot them out. – Speak of them here, that you may not speak of them there. Speak and weep. Your sins are written in a book; your tears are a sponge, weep, and they are wiped away. Weep, and the book will be found clear," etc.[797] Not that all the repentance or tears in the world, can give any satisfaction to God for sin, or any way demerit or deserve pardon from him, or make him amends, etc., as papist and pharisaical persons do fondly imagine; but that it is very congruous that such as have offended should have a true sense of their offense, bewail it, confess it, and repent of it, when they expect to be forgiven; which brokenness of heart is a spiritual sacrifice most acceptable unto God.[798]

What the nature of true faith[799] and sincere repentance[800] is, I have elsewhere already manifested. Now, forasmuch as God remits sin only to them that sincerely believe and repent, and that true faith and repentance are antecedent unto actual repentance, as the former Scriptures do clearly evince, therefore, hence these consectaries [corollaries] do plainly result, namely:

[1] Hence God's actual pardon of the sins of the elect (and so consequently their justification, whereof pardon of sin is one part), is not eternal before all time: but temporal, and in time. Why? Because actual faith and repentance, which are necessarily pre-required to the remission of

---

[795] Acts 5:31
[796] Acts 8:22
[797] John Chrysostom, Homily 2 on Psalm 50
[798] Psalm 51:17
[799] In Book 3, Chapter 3, Aphorism 5, Questions 1-3
[800] Ezekiel 18:30

sins, are only in time.[801] It is true, that from eternity God decreed, that all his elect should believe and repent, and so be pardoned and saved, but it is as true that the actual execution of this decree is only in time. To say that a man is actually pardoned and justified from eternity is to confound God's decrees with the execution of his decrees, to destroy the use of faith and repentance prescribed in Scripture, and to make a man actually pardoned before he actually was a sinner, which would be very absurd.

[2] Hence God's actual pardon of the sins of his elect is not an immanent, but a transient act because it is not eternal, before all time, but temporal, in due time. Now this is the difference between God's immanent and transient acts: {1} His immanent acts abide in God, producing no real effect out of him, as his decree, etc.; but his transient acts make a real effect without, as creation, providence, etc. {2} His immanent act, is the same with his essence, and eternal: God's decree is God decreeing, God's will is God willing, etc.; but his transient acts are the same with the effect wrought. By this, it is plain, that God's actual remission of sin is not an immanent, but rather, a transient act.

[3] Hence unto actual remission of sins, the cooperation of all the causes of remission is required. It is not enough that there is the efficient impulsive cause, God's free grace, or the meritorious cause, Christ's death, but there must also be the instrumental cause, true faith. None of these con-causes can be left out. Until they all meet together in their influence and activity, the effect of remission is not actually produced. And the instrumental cause is in its kind as necessary, as the impulsive and meritorious causes in their kind.

[4] Hence all that desire to have remission of sins actually conferred upon them, must sincerely endeavor to be partakers of actual faith and repentance. It is not enough that God freely wills the pardon of his elect, and that Christ has dearly bought it by his blood, but they must also actually

---

[801] That faith and repentance are antecedents to justification; is judiciously proved by sundry arguments, and the contrary arguments or objections resolved by my learned and godly brother Mr. Anthony Burgess, in his *True Doctrine of Justification*, Lectures 20-22

believe in this Christ and his death, and repent of their sins, if they mean that pardon shall be actually theirs.

[5] Hence, as actual faith and repentance are necessary for the first application of pardon at our first conversion; so the renewed acts of faith and repentance are alike necessary for the after applications of pardon after relapses. When David[802] and Peter[803] fell into new sins after their conversion and justification, they renewed their repentance and faith, for the obtaining of remission – and so must we. And because we sin daily, we are taught by our savior to beg pardon daily.[804] That the medicine may be as frequent, as the malady.

[6] Hence all such persons as are pardoned actually, are sanctified effectually. For none are pardoned but such as truly believe and repent, and wheresoever there is actual faith and repentance, there is effectual habitual sanctification, whence they are disposed and enabled to believe and repent.[805] Acts presuppose habits. By the truth therefore of our sanctification, we may proceed to assurance of the remission of our sins and justification. And on the contrary we may certainly conclude that such persons as are unsanctified, are – beyond all doubt – unpardoned.

---

[802] 2 Samuel 12:12-13, etc, Psalm 51
[803] Matthew 26:69 to the end
[804] Matthew 6:12
[805] Acts 26:18, Romans 8:29-30

[Position 9] That when God actually and savingly pardons sin to the believing and repenting sinner, he pardons fully and finally all his sins past and present, but not his sins to come.

This position has in it three branches very considerable. When God savingly pardons sin to any, {1} he pardons all sin past and present fully without exception, {2} he pardons all such sins finally, without revocation, and {3} he pardons no future sins by way of anticipation.

{1} **When God pardons sin savingly to the true believing and penitent person, he pardons all sin past and present – fully and absolutely without exception.** He pardons original sin, whether original sin originating, even their first sin in Adam, in whom all sinned (Romans 5:12), or original sin originated; even the corruption of nature (Psalm 51:5, John 3:6). He pardons all past and present actual sins, of omission or commission, of ignorance or against knowledge, weaknesses or wilfulnesses, against God or man, in thought, word or deed, together with all the sinful circumstances and aggravations thereof. When God savingly pardons one, he also pardons all fully – so fully, that he leaves not one sin behind unpardoned; so fully, that he takes away all the guilt of sin totally: that a man is wholly freed from all obligation to punishment properly so called, whether temporal, spiritual or eternal: so fully, that sin cannot be more fully forgiven, or better pardoned than they are pardoned. This is plain:

(i) *Partly by Scripture expressions about pardon.* God pardons iniquity, transgression, and sin.[806] He will cover; he will not impute sin.[807] He remits unrighteousnesses, sinful-errors, and unlawfulnesses.[808] He blots out their transgressions as a cloud.[809] He removes our transgressions from us, as far

---

[806] Exodus 34:7
[807] Psalm 32:1-2; 2 Corinthians 5:19
[808] Hebrews 8:12
[809] Isaiah 43:25

as the east is from the west.[810] He casts all our sins behind his back.[811] He subdues our iniquities. He casts all our sins into the depths of the sea.[812] *The blood of Jesus Christ cleanseth us from all sin.*[813] – *In those days, and in that time, saith the LORD, The iniquity of Israel shall be sought for, and there shall be none; and the sins of Judah, and they shall not be found: for I will pardon them whom I reserve.*[814] The guilt of sin shall be so fully removed, that it shall be as if it had never been. That it shall never be prosecuted with deserved punishment. O how sweet and comfortable a blessing is this to every true believing and penitent soul! None can know it but those who taste it, for from these and like expressions, it is plain that God does not pardoned sins anymore to the touch, nor does he exact punishments for them from his reconciled people. For if God punishes sin, he still imputes it. If he avenges sin, he remembers it. If he calls it into judgment, he does not cover it. If he examines it, he tastes it not behind his back. If he beholds it and looks into it, he does not blot it out as a cloud. If he ventilates and scans it, he does not cast it into the bottom of the sea.

To this effect said Augustine: "Sins are covered, are hid, are abolished. If God has covered sins, he will not advert [consider] them. If he will not advert, he will not animadvert [speak out against] them; If he will not animadvert, he will not punish, he will not acknowledge them; he had rather pardon them. Why does he say "sins covered"? That they might not be seen. For what was God's seeing sins, but his punishing sins?"[815]

So Jerome: "That which is covered is not seen, is not imputed; that which is not imputed, shall not be punished." And a little before that: {*Whose sins*

---

[810] Psalm 103:12
[811] Isaiah 38:17
[812] Micah 7:19
[813] 1 John 1:7
[814] Jeremiah 50:20
[815] Augustine on Psalm 32

are covered} – "That is, that by repentance here, sins may be veiled, lest in the judgment, they should be revealed."[816]

Hence that verse in the old glosses and canons (perhaps taken out of Prosper) which I may thus English: "God pardons all or none to each repenting one."[817]

(ii) **Partly by reason**, for: (a) The same free grace that inclined God to pardon one sin, does as much incline him to pardon all sins.[818] (b) The same merit of Christ and blood of Christ that has purchased remission for one sin, has also done it for all. (c) The same person that truly repents of one sin, repents of all: that believes in Christ for pardon of one sin, believes in him for the pardon of all.

{2} **When God pardons sin, he pardons all sin past and present finally and utterly forever, without revocation.** No after-sins shall make God revoke his former pardons. No new sins into which a justified person may fall, shall make void God's old pardons, or bring his old sins to be imputed to him again, unless he re-engages himself sinfully in his old sins again. For:

(i) Scripture is very express for this: therein God assuring his people of their final pardon. *I, even I am he that blotteth out thy transgressions for mine own sake, and will not remember thy sins.*[819] – *But if the wicked will turn from all his sins that he hath committed,* – *All his transgressions that he hath committed, they shall not be mentioned unto him;*[820] that is: not one of them all shall be mentioned or imputed to him, etc. – *I will forgive their iniquity, and*

---

[816] Jerome on Psalm 32

[817] In veteribus Canonibus & Glossis recitatur versiculus; [Larga] Dei Pietas veniam non dimidiabit, Aut nihil aut totum te [lachiymante] dabit. Desumptum hoc est ex ilio Prosperi; Ex toto veniam dabit, & non dimidiabit. Gerh. in loc. Com. de Poenitent. C. 11. Sect. 3. N. 121.

[818] Colossians 2:13; 1 John 1:7

[819] Isaiah 43:25

[820] Ezekiel 18:21-22

their sins and their unlawfulnesses will I remember no more.[821] *Their iniquities shall be sought for, but they shall not be found; there shall be none.*[822]

(ii) God's counsel and love is immutable; his gifts and calling (namely: the gifts of his effectual calling) are without repentance.[823] Therefore God will not revive the guilt of pardoned sins.

(Objection 1): But it is said, *When the righteous man turneth away from his righteousness, and commits iniquity, – All his righteousness that he hath done shall not be mentioned: in his trespass that he hath trespassed, and in his sin that he hath sinned, in them shall he die.*[824] Therefore the guilt of sin remitted may be revived.

Answer: Not so, for:

[1] This commination [threatening of divine vengeance] does not necessarily conclude that a truly righteous man shall thus fall to all the abominations of the wicked, but is a holy caution and means sanctified to him to keep him from such falling, and dying in his sins.

[2] The intent of this place is not so much to show the righteous man's infirmity (who of himself, without divine grace upholding, might quickly miscarry), as to set forth the most righteous God's equity and equality in his proceedings. If a righteous man should become wicked (which yet is not possible, upon supposition of divine grace, etc), the righteous God would deal with him as with the wicked.

[3] Nothing in this Scripture implies a revocation of the guilt of old sins formerly pardoned, but only a punishment for other new sins since committed.

---

[821] Jeremiah 31:34, Hebrews 8:12 & 10:17
[822] Isaiah 43:25
[823] Romans 11:28-29
[824] Ezekiel 18:24, 26

(Objection 2): But in the parable it is intimated, that the debt formerly remitted by God, may again be exacted, in case we forgive not one another.[825]

Answer:

[1] The direct scope of this parable is, not to show that when we commit new sins, God will charge the guilt of old sins upon us, that have been already pardoned; but to teach us, That unless we forgive one another, we cannot comfortably and groundedly believe that God does or will forgive us, we are not qualified for his pardons. This is plain from the reddition [elucidation] of the parable in verse 35.

[2] Besides the scope of parables, there is nothing in them argumentative.[826] In a sword, there is hilt, and back, and edge, but only the edge cuts; in an instrument, there is wood, and brass, and belly, and frets, and strings, but only the strings do make the melody: So there are many passages in parabolic Scriptures subservient to the main scope, which must only be understood with tendency and reference thereunto. The scope of a parable is the key of a parable.

{3} Though God pardons all sin past and present to the true believing and penitent soul, yet he pardons not any sin to come, by way of anticipation. God actually pardons no sin before it is committed, although God has declared the pardon thereof before, and Christ has purchased pardon before. God so provides for his elect already pardoned, by supplies of constant grace, that future sins shall be so repented of, and pardoned, that they shall never be condemned for them.[827] But sins are not remitted by God before they are committed by us, for:

---

[825] Matthew 18:23 to the end, especially verses 27 & 34
[826] Theologia parabolica non est argumentativa.
[827] Romans 8:1-2

(i) Scripture speaks of *pardon of sin* still in reference to sins past or present, not to sins to come, as in 2 Samuel 12:13, Jeremiah 33:8, Ezekiel 18:22; 1 John 2:1. (ii) God's actual pardon is his remembering of sin no more.[828] Properly, things past or present are remembered or not remembered; but not things to come.[829] (iii) God actually pardons no sin, but to such as actually repent of sin, as has been shown; now no man actually repents of any sin to come, but only of sin past or present. (iv) If sin to come is pardoned to the elect, as well as sin past and present, then they need not daily pray that petition as Christ has taught them: *Forgive us our debts, as we forgive our debtors*.[830] But that is false. (v) If future sin is pardoned before it is acted, then it need not be confessed nor repented of when it shall be acted, because it is already forgiven. But this is repugnant both to Scripture directions, and the practices of the saints.[831]

---

[828] Jeremiah 31:31, Hebrews 8:12
[829] Memoria non datur futurorm, sed praesentium & praeteritorum.
[830] Matthew 6:12
[831] 2 Samuel 12:1-15, Matthew 6:12, Psalm 51 throughout, Matthew 26:75

[Position 10] That God's elect, whose sins are pardoned, do daily need renewed pardons, for future and renewed sins.

This is very evident, for:

{1} The best and holiest of all God's pardoned people whilst they continue in this life, have still original corruption remaining in them;[832] whence they daily break forth into many actual offenses,[833] namely: invincible infirmities, and sometimes into grosser sins, as Noah into drunkenness, Lot into incest, David into murder and adultery, Solomon into idolatry, Peter into cursing, swearing and denying of his Master. Insomuch that David said: *Who can understand his errors? cleanse thou me from secret faults. Keep back thy servant also from presumptuous sins*, etc.[834] James said: *In many things we offend all.*[835] And John is very peremptory, saying: *If we say that we have no sin, we deceive ourselves, and the truth is not in us. – If we say that we have not sinned, we make him a liar; and his word is not in us.*[836] In the former speech he seems to intend our original; in the latter our actual sins. And surely, if we sin daily, we have need to be pardoned daily. If we daily contract defilements, we daily need cleansings from those defilements.

{2} God sees and observes the sins of his own people, and is displeased at them, yea sometimes judges them severely. Christ heard Peter denying, cursing, and swearing, and the Lord looked upon Peter.[837] God observed David's murder and adultery, was displeased at them, and did in many ways severely plague them.[838] God took notice of the Corinthians' profanations of the Lord's Supper, for which cause he so judged them, that many of them were sick and

---

[832] Romans 7:23-25, Hebrews 12:1, Psalm 51:5
[833] Romans 7:15 to the end
[834] Psalm 19:12-13
[835] James 3:2
[836] 1 John 1:8, 10; 1 John 2:1-2
[837] Matthew 26:69 to the end, Luke 22:61-62
[838] 2 Samuel 11:27 & 12:7-15

weak, and many slept.[839] If then our renewed sins after pardon are renewed offenses against God, we have need of renewed remissions from God.

{3} Christ directs us to pray daily for remission of sin.[840] Therefore we have daily maladies, and need daily remedies. Sin daily discovered by us has need to be daily covered by God.

---

[839] 1 Corinthians 11:29-32
[840] Matthew 6:12

[Position 11] That pardon of sin, though full without exception, and final without revocation, yet is not complete and consummate in this present life until the very Day of Judgment.

That this is so, is evident by the testimony of Peter: *Repent ye therefore and be converted, that your sins may be blotted out, when the times of refreshing shall come from the presence of the Lord.*[841] Though sin repented of, is now pardoned and blotted out fully and irrevocably, yet there remains some further blotting out to be accomplished when the times of refreshing shall come. What times are those? The times of the last judgment. Then all the elect shall be raised from the dead, or changed from mortality; then all their souls shall be reunited to their bodies forever; then all their sins, miseries, and enemies shall be removed forever; then they shall meet Christ in the air, be set at his right hand, receive their blissful sentence: "Go into eternal life, and be ever with the Lord." Oh, what glorious refreshments will these be! Well may those times be styled {*times of refreshing*}.

Question: But how shall our sins be blotted out at the times of refreshing, at the last judgment, so as not until then?
Answer:
{1} Then, and not until then, all the scars of our guilt shall be taken away. All our guilt, all our obligation to due and proper punishment for sin, is now in this life removed as soon as we are pardoned; but the scars of this guilt – namely: afflictions, chastisements, corporal death, grave, corruption, etc – will remain until the last judgment. But then, even all these very scars of sin and guilt shall be totally and finally wiped away.[842]

{2} Then, and not until then, all the elect of God shall be so completely assured of the pardon of their sins, as that there shall not be left in their hearts

---

[841] Acts 3:19
[842] Romans 8:23; 1 Corinthians 15:42-44, 51-56, Philippians 3:21, Revelation 21:1, 4

the least doubt, fear, scruple, or hesitancy about it, nor any shadow thereof. In this life David himself had his tremblings about his pardon, though Nathan had told him from God: *The Lord hath put away thy sin, thou shalt not die.*[843]

{3} Then, and not until then, the elect of God will all of them be beyond sinning, and consequently none of them shall ever anymore need the reiteration of pardons. In this world, iteration of sins still needs iteration of pardons.

{4} Then, and never until then, the remission and absolution of all the elect of God. shall be openly published by Jesus Christ before all the world, of men and angels, to their everlasting glory.[844]

---

[843] 2 Samuel 12:13 with Psalm 51 throughout
[844] Matthew 25:34-41

[Position 12] That in persons savingly pardoned sin may remain, yet those persons are in the account of God no longer sinners, but righteous.

Sin may remain in pardoned persons, in regard of the inbeing, in-dwelling, inherence or residence thereof[845] – yea, in regard to the stain spot pollution or deformity of it; yea, in regard to the lustings, warrings, and rebellings of it against the Spirit and his graces, etc.[846]

I say that sin may thus remain in pardoned persons, yet not reign over them,[847] nor bring condemnation to them.[848] Yet notwithstanding all this remaining of sin in pardoned persons, God accounts them not sinners, but righteous. As, righteous Abel (Hebrews 11:4), righteous Noah (Hebrews 11:7, Genesis 7:1), righteous Abraham (Romans 4:11), righteous Lot (2 Peter 2:7-8), and so on. And they are by this denomination of righteous contra-distinguished from the wicked.[849]

Yea God accounts them so righteous, as if they had never been unrighteous: so righteous, that they are called righteousness itself, yea the righteousness of God in Christ.[850] Oh what riches of free grace, mercy, and loving kindness, do flow and overflow from God in Christ to a poor sinner in this remission of his sins! Who would not believe, who would not repent, who would not be content to do anything or be anything, that he may be fitted for this blessed remission?

---

[845] Romans 7:17, 23
[846] Galatians 5:17, Romans 7:19, 21, 23-24
[847] Romans 6:12-14
[848] Romans 8:1-3
[849] Psalm 1:6; 1 Peter 4:18
[850] 2 Corinthians 5:21

[Position 13] That sometimes sin may be universally and savingly pardoned, when yet the sense of that pardon may be suspended, and the contrary sense of God's displeasure for sin may be continued.

This was David's case. Nathan had pronounced his pardon to him from the Lord,[851] and yet David's spirit wanted the sweet sense of that pardon from God, which therefore he so vehemently and frequently begs, still bleeding under the sense of God's displeasure.[852] Nathan had spoken pardon to his ear, but God had not yet spoken pardon to his heart. He had God's salvation, but he lacked the joy of God's salvation. He had God's Spirit, but he lacked the establishment of his Spirit. The Lord had put away David's sin from his eye, but David could not put away his sin from his own eyes: *my sin is ever before me*.[853] The Lord, by pardoning and acquitting David from death, had reconciled him again unto God, and so had knit again his broken bones: but yet for all that the bones which God had broken could not rejoice. Now God may for a time continue upon a pardoned soul the sense of his displeasure, and withhold from him the comfortable sense and apprehension of the pardon of sin vouchsafed; for many causes, as:

{1} To humble the soul more deeply for some notorious and scandalous sin into which he has fallen, and make him experimentally feel the wormwood and the gall of such an offense upon his heart. David's sin was great and scandalous; God therefore keeps his conscience upon the rack, and withholds his wonted smiles even after pardon, that David might thoroughly perceive the extreme sinfulness of his sins.[854] Slender cuts are soon healed up, but deep and dangerous wounds require the longer cure. And in some cases scarifying and

---

[851] 2 Samuel 12:13
[852] Psalm 51:1-2, etc.
[853] Psalm 51:3
[854] 2 Samuel 12:14

lancing, yea opening of a vein to bleed a while, are most approved for making a safe and speedy cure.

{2} To warn the offender, and others also by his example, to beware of like sins for time to come, which cost the soul so dear, before restitution. We never read that David fell into those sins again, for which his bones were so sorely broken-to-shivers.[855] Nor that Peter ever denied his Master again, after he had lamented his denial with bitter tears.[856] And what pardoned soul, considering these instances, even trembles not at the thoughts of such sins, resolving by divine grace assisting not to buy repentance at so dear a rate, nor for a few vanishing pleasures of sin to contract such deep, and painful, and lasting wounds upon the conscience.[857]

{3} To commend so much the more unto the soul the sweetness of pardon, peace, and reconciliation to God in Jesus Christ, when true apprehensions thereof shall again be recovered. Health is always pleasant, but most pleasant after some deep and dangerous sickness; The haven is always welcome, but never more welcome than after the roughest and violentest tempest; life is always sweet, but to be restored to life from the brink of the grave is a double life. So here, after deepest terrors of conscience, peace is most welcome; after the gall of sin, pardon is most sweet; after the long frowns of God, his smiles are most pleasant to the soul.

{4} To teach his people wisdom, tenderness, and compassionateness to the souls of others in like distresses. To make them of patients, experimental physicians. *Restore unto me* (said David) *the joy of thy salvation; and uphold me with thy free spirit. Then will I teach transgressors thy ways, and sinners shall be converted unto thee.*[858] Passion breeds compassion; suffering sympathizing. And oftentimes they prove the best and tenderest bone-setters, who themselves have had experience of broken bones.

---

[855] Psalm 51:8
[856] Matthew 26:75
[857] Nolo tanti emere poenitentiam
[858] Psalm 51:12-13

[Position 14] That wherever God remits sin, not imputing it to the sinner unto condemnation, there he accepts the person as righteous, imputing Christ's righteousness to him unto justification.

Not, that God's remission of sins, and acceptation of our persons as righteous, are one thing, or ought to be confounded (for they are very distinct branches of justification), but that in regard to God's actual application of them they ought not to be divided. No man's sins are remitted for Christ, but his person also is accepted by God as righteous in Christ. These are twin-blessings, and go together, for:

{1} How absurd would it be to imagine that God may have pardoned all a man's sins, and yet his person should remain abhorred by God as an unrighteous sinner?

{2} In order of nature, acceptation of our persons as righteous, for Christ's imputed righteousness, goes before the remission of our sins in Christ, and is as the cause thereof, for Christ's righteousness actually imputed to us, as the matter of our righteousness, is the foundation of our remission, namely: that robe whereby our sins are covered; that fountain whereby our sins are cleansed, that medicine whereby our sins are healed. So that he who has his sins remitted, must also be looked upon as a justified person.

Hence, from the whole that has been said touching remission of sins, It may be briefly thus described:

> **Remission of sins (namely: universal remission) is a special act of God's grace whereby he fully and finally absolves or acquits all and everyone of his elect, sincerely believing and repenting, and them only, from the offense, and guilt of all their sins, that is, from all obligation to any proper punishment for them, temporal, spiritual and eternal, for the plenary and meritorious satisfaction made for their sins to the justice of**

God by the obedience, death and blood of Jesus Christ, their only Mediator and Surety, apprehended and applied by faith unfeigned.

The confirmation and explication of this description is easily deducible from what has been said already, and therefore avoiding repetitions, I thither refer the reader for his further satisfaction.

Thus of the second question: what the nature of remission of sins is, which is here promised and covenanted in this New Covenant.

Question 3: May those who have their sins remitted, may know that they are remitted, and how may this be known?

Resolution: I shall briefly satisfy this question in these four particulars, namely:

(1) **That it is a most excellent, comfortable, and desirable-mercy to know that our sins are forgiven,** for:

[1] By knowing that our sins are forgiven, we may know that God's wrath is appeased,[859] and that the guilt of all proper punishment, curse, and condemnation for sin is forever removed from us.[860] When God pardons us, he ceases to be wrathful with us, and he removes all our guilt or obligation to deserved punishment from us. To have these removed is a great deliverance; to know they are removed is a double deliverance.

[2] By knowing that our sins are forgiven, we may know that we are brought into a blessed condition, for: *O the blessednesses of him whose transgression is forgiven, whose sin is covered! O the blessednesses of the man, unto whom the LORD imputeth not iniquity.*[861] It is a most sweet thing to be blessed, but it is a double sweetness to know that we are blessed.

[3] By knowing that our sins are forgiven, we may know, that we are effectually called and converted,[862] that we have unfeignedly repented,[863] that we have unfeignedly believed,[864] and that the blood of Jesus Christ is actually sprinkled upon our consciences by believing.[865] For none are pardoned but sincere converts, penitents, and believers that have Christ's blood sprinkled

---

[859] Micah 7:18-19
[860] 2 Samuel 12:13, Hebrews 8:12
[861] Psalm 32:1-2
[862] Acts 26:18
[863] Acts 2:38 & 5:31
[864] Acts 10:43 & 26:18
[865] Romans 3:25, Ephesians 1:7

upon their consciences. To be such, is comfortable; to know we are such, is doubly comfortable.

[4] By knowing that our sins are forgiven, we may know that we shall be eternally saved, for: *Whom he hath justified, them he hath glorified.*[866] To be saved, how glorious; to know beforehand that we shall be saved is glory upon glory.

[5] By knowing that our sins are forgiven, we evidently have peace with God, our broken bones rejoice, we have the joy of God's salvation, we joy in hope of the glory of God, and we glory in tribulation.[867] And to walk before the Lord in the sense and evidence of these most sweet enjoyments, is to have a heaven on earth, and when we die, to pass from one heaven unto another.

(2) **That as it is a most excellent privilege, so it is a very difficult attainment to know that our iniquities are forgiven**, for:

[1] Although David was told by Nathan the prophet that the Lord had put away his sin, he should not die,[868] yet even after this, he was destitute of this assurance upon his own spirit, The Lord did not presently make it known to his heart, and therefore he begs for pardon and the joy of God's salvation, etc, as fervently as if Nathan had said nothing at all to him about his pardon.[869]

[2] Although the apostles of Christ, were all of them (except Judas) washed, cleansed and pardoned, as our Savior himself tells them;[870] yet notwithstanding for the establishing, clearing and increasing of their assurance of pardon, as well as for other reasons, our Savior teaches them daily to pray: *Forgive us our debts, as we forgive our debtors.*[871] Pardon of sin must be daily begged; and if by all our praying we can come to be assured our sins are forgiven, we have obtained a very rich return to our prayers.

---

[866] Romans 8:30
[867] Romans 5:1-3, Psalm 51:8, 12
[868] 2 Samuel 12:13
[869] Psalm 51 throughout
[870] John 13:8, 10-11 & 15:3
[871] Matthew 6:12

[3] It is by faith especially that we both receive pardon from God, and also come to the knowledge and assurance of pardon received. Now it is a wonderful hard thing to believe that God will pardon us, and that we are pardoned: pardon of sin in Christ being a mere supernatural revelation of God's acts of favor without us, and Faith being a mere supernatural donation from his Spirit within us: unto either of which natural reason or abilities cannot contribute any assistance, but oftentimes rather makes resistance.[872]

[4] Finally, the multiplicity and grievousness of our sins committed before pardon, make assurance of pardon exceedingly hard to be obtained; our frequent lapses into iniquities and infirmities after pardon, render the assurance of pardon very difficult to be retained. Our former sins do so amaze and astonish our consciences, that they can hardly be persuaded of their pardon, and our following sins do so blur, soil, and dim our evidences, that our pardon of sin can hardly be discerned. Thus, it is a very hard matter to know that our sins are forgiven.

(3) That though it is difficult, yet it is possible to know that our sins are forgiven, for:

[1] *We have received the Spirit which is of God, that we might know the things that are freely given to us of God.*[873] Now the Spirit advances our assurance in many ways: as a witness,[874] as a seal,[875] as an earnest,[876] as a firstfruits,[877] etc. The Spirit of God helps us to know our pardon and all our spirituals which we have of God.

[2] It is possible to know that we are effectually called, converted, and sanctified (1 John 3:14, 24 & 2:3 & 5:13; 2 Corinthians 13:5). Consequently, it is possible to know that we are justified and pardoned, for justification and

---

[872] Ephesians 2:8
[873] 1 Corinthians 2:12
[874] Romans 8:16
[875] Ephesians 1:13
[876] Ephesians 1:14
[877] Romans 8:23

remission of sins are inseparably linked to effectual calling, conversion, and sanctification (Romans 8:29-30, Acts 26:18).

[3] It is possible for God's people now to know what God's people knew heretofore, but heretofore, God's people, many of them, knew that their sins were pardoned. As, Job: *I know that my Redeemer lives*, etc.[878] Job could not know these things, but he must also know his sins were pardoned. Hezekiah: *Thou hast cast all my sins behind thy back*.[879] Paul: *who was before a blasphemer, and a persecutor, and injurious. But I obtained mercy*, etc.[880]

(4) **That those that are pardoned come to know they are forgiven: extraordinarily or ordinarily.**

Extraordinarily, as by the testimony of a prophet. So Nathan told David: *the LORD hath put away thy sin*, etc.[881] By the immediate testimony of Jesus Christ in the days of his flesh – to his apostles: *Ye are clean*;[882] to the palsy man: *Son, thy sins be forgiven thee*;[883] and to the penitent woman: *And he said unto her, thy sins are forgiven*, etc.[884] But these extraordinaries may not be drawn into precedents; we cannot expect to have our pardon assured in such extraordinary ways.

Ordinarily: thus we may come to know and be assured that our sins are remitted by certain ordinary discoveries, signs or tokens thereof laid down in the Scriptures, and more especially, by these evidences of the remission of sins, namely:

[1] By our effectual calling and conversion from darkness to light, and from the power of Satan unto God. Effectual calling and conversion is still accompanied with forgiveness of sins and justification.[885] No unconverted man is pardoned; no converted man is unpardoned. Now we may try our

---

[878] Job 19:25-27
[879] Isaiah 38:17
[880] 1 Timothy 1:13, 16
[881] 2 Samuel 12:13
[882] John 13:8, 10-11
[883] Mark 2:5-13
[884] Luke 7:48
[885] Acts 26:18, Romans 8:29-30

conversion by the newness of heart and spirit given at conversion – of which formerly.[886]

[2] By the unfeignedness and truth of our faith. For faith is the hand, the organ, the instrumental means whereby we receive and apply pardon from God in Christ to ourselves, as has been evidenced in Position 8 Question 2. Where therefore there is unfeigned faith apprehending, there is saving pardon of sin apprehended. Now we may try our faith by the nature and acts of true justifying faith formerly described.[887]

[3] By the sincerity of repentance required, as a qualification rendering the subject fit and capable of pardon. Repentance and remission of sins still go together, as has already been manifested in Position 8 Question 2. Make sure of your sincere repentance, and your repentance makes you sure of remission. Try your repentance by the nature and characters of true repentance, which I have elsewhere unfolded.[888] Pardoned sinners do – of all others – most abandon and abhor their sins.

[4] By the integrity of true affectionate soul-melting love to Jesus Christ. Where sins are pardoned, Christ – pardoning those sins – is most dearly and entirely affected. This is most eminently observable in the penitent woman: *Her sins, which are many, are forgiven, for she loved much.*[889] {*For*} is not here to be taken causally, but illatively [inferentially]. Her love was not any antecedent cause, but a consequent fruit and effect of her pardon. She was not forgiven, because she loved much; but she loved much, because many sins were forgiven her. And that this was directly our Savior's meaning, is evident by the next words: *But to whom little is forgiven, the same loveth little*. But whom did this pardoned woman love so much? Jesus Christ who pardoned her. But how did she testify her great love to Christ? She stood at his feet behind him

---

[886] In Book 3, Chapter 6, Aphorism 2, Section 1
[887] In Book 3, Chapter 3, Aphorism 4, Question 1; in my *Communicant Instructed* p. [116]-126 (London, 1651)
[888] In Book 3, Chapter 3, Aphorism 4, Section 2; but see especially my *Communicant Instructed*, pp.127-138 (London, 1651)
[889] Luke 7:47

weeping, and began to wash his feet with tears, and did wipe them with the hairs of her head, and kissed his feet, and anointed them with ointment.[890] Oh what actions! What affections towards Christ! His pardoning mercy overcame her. She had nothing too good, nothing good enough for Christ, therefore she bestows all her highest expressions, her weeping, her washing, her wiping, her kissing, her anointing, upon his meanest and lowest part, his feet. Do you have like love and affections towards Christ? Then you have received like remission of sins from Christ. The trial of true love to Christ, I have elsewhere discovered.[891]

[5] By a hearty and sincere disposition, inclination, and propensity to pardon the injuries and offenses done against us by our brethren. He that is forgiven of God his ten thousand talents: can willingly forgive man his hundred pence.[892] None can more readily forgive than such as are forgiven. Hence Christ makes our forgiveness of one another to be a great argument and sign that we shall be, yea are forgiven ourselves of God.[893] But if we cannot forgive one another, if we retain wrath and malice, if we seek and meditate revenge, if we take one another by the throat for every trifle, for an hundred pence, and show all extremities without mercy, if we are implacable and can never forget, etc, then how can we have any encouragement or assurance at all that God has forgiven us our trespasses?[894]

Thus of the third question: whether we may know that our sins are pardoned, and how we may know it.

---

[890] Luke 7:37-38, 44-48
[891] In my *Communicant Instructed*, pp.150-164 (London, 1651)
[892] Matthew 18:23 to the end
[893] Matthew 6:12, 14-15
[894] Matthew 18:28-30

Question 4: Wherein does God's remission of sins under the New Covenant differs from and excel the remission of sins that was under the Old Covenant?

Resolution. This question is somewhat intricate, and might easily occasion a very large discourse, but the volume swells too fast under my hand. Therefore thus I in brief resolve, namely:

(1) **Concedendo: by way of concession.** I grant that, as this New Covenant differs from and far excels the Old Covenant, in the first article about the inscription of God's laws in their minds and hearts, and in the second article about the knowledge of the Lord, so in like sort it differs from, and excels the Old Covenant in this third article about remission of sins. Calvin also accounts this a third point of difference between the Old and New Covenant, wherein also the New excels the Old, saying: "Here he treats of the grace of regeneration: he treats of the gift of understanding: and with all he promises that God will be propitious unto his in another manner, and more perfectly than he had been of old."[895] Here then is a difference between these two Covenants – and that difference is diligently to be sought out.

(2) **Limitando: by way of caution and limitation.** That remission of sins under the Old Covenant – yea, and before also – did not in essence, substance and kind differ from remission under the New Covenant. Remission of sins was essentially, substantially, and specifically one and the same under the New Covenant and the Old, for:

[1] All the elect of God before and under the Old Covenant, as well as under the New, had their sins expiated and purged away, and satisfaction made to the justice of God for them, and remission of sins, by one and the same

---

[895] John Calvin's commentary on Jeremiah 31:34

Sacrifice of Jesus Christ our Mediator. Hence said Christ to the Jews: *Your father Abraham rejoiced to see my day: and he saw it, and was glad.*[896] Hence Christ is called {*the lamb slain from the foundation of the world*}.[897] He was slain in the decree and purpose of God, before the foundation of the world (1 Peter 1:19-20). He was slain in the promises of God, which fore-implied his death (Genesis 3:15 with Colossians 2:14-15, Hebrews 2:14-15).

In the ancient sacrifices, which were types of Christ's death (Genesis 3:21 with 4:3-4). In the efficacious virtue of his death, extended and reaching backward towards the foundation of the world, as well as forward towards the consummation of the world (Hebrews 11:4-6, etc). Christ's death profited to remission and salvation, before it was, when it was, and after it was; as the sun at midday illuminates not only the meridian where he is; but also the east backwards whence he came; and the west forwards, whither he is going.[898] Hereupon he is styled: *Jesus Christ the same yesterday, and today, and forever.*[899] And Peter, having reference to the fathers of old, ascribes the same salvation of Christ to them and to themselves under the New Covenant: *But we believe that through the grace of the Lord Jesus Christ, we shall be saved, even as they.*[900] They then were saved through the grace of Christ.

Yea the apostle Paul testifies plainly that it was by Jesus Christ, that they were redeemed from their transgressions and the punishment thereof under the Old Covenant: *And for this cause he is the mediator of the new testament, that by means of death, for the redemption of the transgressions that were under the first testament* (that is, of transgressors from their transgressions and the punishments thereof, for properly, as Beza notes,[901] transgressions are not said to be redeemed), *that they which are called might receive the promise of eternal*

---

[896] John 8:56
[897] Revelation 13:8
[898] Christi mors profuit antequam fuit, quum fuit, & postquam fuit
[899] Hebrews 13:8
[900] Acts 15:11
[901] Beza's Annotations on Hebrews 9:15

inheritance.[902] To like effect is that in Romans 3:25-26, where the apostle shows that by the blood of Christ, both the sins of the Jews that were past, and the sins of us now in this present time of the New Testament, were propitiated and forgiven, as Beza excellently expounds the place,[903] to whom Ludovicus de Dieu in effect subscribes.[904] Calvin also thinks that the apostle in that to the Romans had reference to the legal expiations, which were testimonies of the future satisfaction by Christ, etc: there being but one pacification for all.[905] Dr. Sclater also speaks clearly to this purpose in expounding this text – see his words in the margin.[906]

[2] The elect of God before and under the Old Covenant, as well as under the New, were justified, and so consequently had their sins remitted through faith in Christ's blood that afterwards was to be shed. Notable is that of the apostle to this effect: *For all have sinned and come short of the glory of God; being justified freely by his grace, through the redemption that is in Jesus Christ: whom God hath set forth to be a propitiation through faith in his blood, to*

---

[902] Hebrews 9:15
[903] Beza's Annotations on Romans 3:25-26
[904] Lud. De Dieu in *Animadvers. ad Rom.* 3:25-26
[905] John Calvin's commentary on Romans 3:25
[906] "{*To declare his justice*}, etc. – Now follows an amplification of the sins forgiven, by a distinction or distribution of them, according to several times of committing. Some were προγεγονοτα, that is: done or committed in time, before Christ's exhibiting in the flesh. Some after. To both which the merit of Christ's passion extends itself: προγεγονοτων αμαρτηματων. Several are the interpretations that are now specified, I judge most probable, comparing this place with that Hebrews 9:15. Consent of other interpreters, both popish and others, might be shown. Whence the collection is easy, that the virtue of Christ's passion reached unto the fathers of the Old Testament; and that the Lord give the plenary forgiveness of their sins, respecting the future humiliation of his Son. This point needed not much proof, but that our Romish adversaries, by a consequence of their doctrine, seem to deny it. For truth of it, see these Scriptures: Acts 15:11, John 8:56, Hebrews 13:8, Revelation 13:8. And what should let then to infer that they were admitted to heaven properly so called, without detainment in their Limbus, the skirt of hell, until Christ's coming thither to deliver them? Now if it is true, (1) their sins were remitted, (2) they were justified and reconciled unto God, by faith in Christ to come, (3) they were adopted for sons, how then can it be imagined that they were thus punished?"
(And so he goes on, refuting the popish Limbus Patrum, and vindicating the Scriptures abused to maintain it).
Dr. William Sclater in his exposition on Romans 3:25-26, p. 326 to 332."

declare his righteousness for remission of sins that are past (namely: before Christ's coming) *through the forbearance of God. To declare, I say, at this time* (namely: since Christ's coming) *his righteousness: that he might be just, and the justifier of him that believeth in Jesus.*[907]

Thus, by faith in Christ to come were Abel,[908] Enoch,[909] Noah,[910] Abraham,[911] and other believers of old justified: and received remission of sins.[912] And Paul – proving our remission of sins and justification by faith without works now under the New Covenant from David's description of remission of sins under the Old Covenant – plainly gives us to understand that remission of sins and justification, were for substance and kind one and the same under both Old and New Covenant (Romans 4:6-8 with Psalm 32:1-2). As they who lived in the days of Christ, when he was crucified, had remission of sins by faith in Christ then present, so they who lived before Christ was manifested, had remission of sins by faith in Christ, then future and promised; and we who live since Christ's exaltation at God's right-hand, have remission of sins in Christ now past, actually performed and glorified. But all have actual remission of sins before, at, and after Christ's coming, only by faith in him.

(3) **Explicando: by way of explanation**. Remission of sins under the New Covenant (though substantially the same, yet) accidentally differs from, and excels the remission of sins which was under the Old Testament and before, in various regards – especially in spirituality, clarity, perfection, and extensiveness.

[1] *In spirituality*. Remission of sins under the Old Covenant and before, was set forth more carnally and externally, in certain outward and carnal ordinances, as gifts and sacrifices, meats and drinks, divers washings, the

---

[907] Romans 3:23-26
[908] Hebrews 11:4
[909] Hebrews 11:5-6
[910] Hebrews 11:7
[911] Hebrews 11:8, etc, Romans 4:3-5, 9-11, 23-24, Genesis 15:6
[912] Psalm 32:1-2

blood of bulls and of goats, the ashes of an heifer sprinkling the unclean, etc.[913] All of these of themselves had only a carnal issue and effect, namely: cleansing or sanctifying to the purifying of the flesh, as the apostle plainly declares: *but none of them could make him that did the service perfect, as pertaining to the conscience.*[914] So that remission of sins was tendered and applied to them in a very carnal, outward and earthly way. But remission of sins under the New Covenant is set forth more spiritually, internally and celestially, without all those carnal ordinances, namely: in that high and heavenly sacrifice and blood of Jesus Christ himself immediately tendered to us in the word; applied to us and sprinkled upon us – not with a bunch of hyssop, but with a lively faith, prevailing even to purge the very conscience from all sinful guilt and defilements. *How much more shall the blood of Christ, who through the eternal Spirit offered himself without spot to God, purge your conscience from dead works to serve the living God.*[915]

[2] ***In clarity***. Remission of sins under the Old Covenant and before, was represented and revealed under a dark veil of figures, types, and shadows, as of the mercy seat or covering of the ark, which did hide the tables of the law, by which is the knowledge of sin;[916] pre-figuring Jesus Christ our true mercy seat and propitiation covering our sins with his righteousness; of the high priests taking of two goats, sacrificing one for a sin offering, and presenting the other alive before the Lord, laying both his hands upon his head, and confessing over him all the iniquities, transgressions and sins of Israel, putting them upon his head, and then sending him away by a fit man into the wilderness, etc,[917] shadowing forth Christ's death for our sins, and resurrection for our justification, his bearing all our sins upon his own body on the tree, and taking quite away from his people all their transgressions, never more to return to

---

[913] Hebrews 9:9-13 with Leviticus 16 throughout
[914] Hebrews 9:9
[915] Hebrews 9:9, 12, 14
[916] Exodus 25:10-23 with Romans 3:25; 1 John 2:1-2
[917] Leviticus 16:7-23 with Romans 4:25; 2 Corinthians 5:21, Isaiah 53:4-6; 1 Peter 2:24

them, or be charged upon them; of sprinkling the unclean with blood and water of purifying, etc.,[918] typifying Christ's blood, and taking away sin off the conscience, etc. Now what dark and obscure emblems were these of remission of sins! And how hard was it to spell out this blessed mystery of pardon of sin in such figures!

But now under the New Covenant, remission of sin in Christ through Faith is represented clearly, plainly, evidently with open face, all shadows being vanished away (Acts 10:43, 13:38-39 & 26:18, Romans 3:23-26). *Behold the Lamb of God, which taketh away the sins of the world* (John 1:29). *The blood of Jesus Christ our Lord cleanseth us from all sin* (1 John 1:7). *Who hath loved us, and washed us from our sins in his own blood* (Revelation 1:5). Besides, remission of sins was under the Old Covenant revealed in Christ at a great distance as only promised, but to come afterwards. Now things promised in the future and at a great distance are beheld dimly and darkly, but now it is revealed in Christ as performed, as come already, as near unto us; so that it is beheld conspicuously and with open face.

[3] *In perfection.* Under the Old Covenant, remission of sin was held forth very weakly and imperfectively. There were many sacrifices, washings, and other ordinances, because no-one was enough – and those many were often repeated year by year because they were all imperfect. They could not make the comers thereunto perfect,[919] they could not take away the guilt of sin from off the conscience, they could purify the flesh, but not the spirit – *the law made nothing perfect* – yea in all those sacrifices there was a remembrance made again of sin every year, and they were thereby still as it were accused, arraigned, convicted, and condemned afresh as guilty of death before God for their sins. Therefore there was no safety for the people to rest in any or all those legal expiations; they must look further to Christ himself, and there was a necessity of disannulling that administration, because of the weakness and

---

[918] Hebrews 9:13-14
[919] Hebrews 10:1-4 & 9:9-10 & 7:18-19

imperfection thereof: it was but the ABC of pardon, etc.[920] But now Jesus Christ by one sacrifice of himself for sins once forever hath perfected forever them that are sanctified, has expiated all sin from their consciences forever, so that they shall never need anymore expiatory sacrifice for sins forever, than that one sacrifice once offered. *Through this man is preached unto you forgiveness of sins. And by him all that believe are justified from all things, from which ye could not be justified by the law of Moses.*[921] Yea, all the elect of God which obtained pardon and remission of sins from the beginning of the world until the incarnation of Christ, had that remission, not from any rites, ceremonies, sacrifices, washings, or any such like things, but only from Jesus Christ and the virtue of his death apprehended and applied by faith (Romans 3:23-26 with Hebrews 9:15).[922] So that this New Covenant remission of sins is the perfection, the life, and soul of all remission.

[4] *In extensiveness*. Remission of sins under the Old Covenant was extended to one nation of the Jews, and some few Gentile proselytes laying hold of God's Covenant with that nation: and before God's Old Covenant, only to a few select families in covenant with God, as Adam's, Enoch's, Noah's, Abraham's, etc. Pardon of sin, and all saving blessings until Christ came were under a great restraint, and very sparingly vouchsafed. But now since Christ, under the New Covenant, which is extended to all nations,[923] remission of sins and all other New Covenant blessings are likewise universally extended to all nations of the world without exception (Hebrews 8:8-12, Romans 3:23-26, Acts 2:38-39, 13:38-39 & 26:18). This Christ himself testified to his apostles after his resurrection, saying: *Thus it is written, and thus it behooved Christ to*

---

[920] Hebrews 7:18-19
[921] Acts 13:38-39, Romans 8:3-4
[922] "Now, if anyone asks, whether sins under the law were remitted to the fathers, we must bear in mind the solution already stated, – that they were remitted, but remitted through Christ. Then notwithstanding their external expiations, they were always held guilty." John Calvin's commentary on Hebrews 9:15
[https://www.studylight.org/commentaries/eng/cal/hebrews-9.html]
<Accessed 4/5/2024>
[923] Matthew 28:19-20, Mark 16:15

suffer, and to rise from the dead the third day: and that repentance and remission of sins should be preached in his name among all nation, beginning at Jerusalem.[924] Now in this extensiveness of remission of sins to all nations, the New Covenant far excels the Old, under which remission was so limited and restrained.

Hitherto of the first proposition in this third article; namely: that under the New Covenant, the Lord God, in and through Jesus Christ will freely, fully and utterly remit all his true federates' sins whatsoever.[925] Herein the body of this article has been unfolded.

---

[924] Luke 24:46-47
[925] Hebrews 8:12, Jeremiah 31:34

Proposition 2

That God will therefore bestow upon his sincere federates all other the promised benefits of the New Covenant, because he will so freely, fully and utterly remit all their sins in and for the satisfaction of Jesus Christ.

This proposition flows from the causal particle {*for*} expressed both by Jeremiah and Paul: *for I will forgive their iniquity*, etc;[926] *for I will be merciful to their unrighteousnesses*, etc.[927] Wherein the Lord gives a reason why he will do all the former things to them, why he will write his law in their minds and hearts, why he will be their God, and they shall be his people, why all shall know him from the least to the greatest of them, namely: because he will remit all their sins freely, fully and utterly: *for I will be merciful to their unrighteousnesses, and their sinful errors and their unlawfulnesses will I remember no more*. This is here laid down as a reason, ground or foundation of all the former promised favors.

That of Calvin's here, I highly approve: "There is no doubt," he says, "but that the prophet here shows the foundation of this benefit, because God will be favorable to his people, not imputing their sins. If therefore we seek the original of the New Testament, it is the gratuitous remission of sins. Because God reconciles himself to his people. And hence we collect that we are not to imagine any other cause why God has appeared in his only Son, and has used so much liberality: because here the prophet brings all the glory of flesh into nothing, and throws down all merits, when he says that God will be so liberal towards his people, because he will be propitious, he will forgive their sins, and he will not remember their iniquities."[928] So he.

---

[926] Jeremiah 31:34
[927] Hebrews 8:12
[928] John Calvin's commentary on Jeremiah 31:34

Now God's covenanted remission of all his sincere federates' sins freely, fully and finally, in and for the satisfaction of Jesus Christ, may well be given in here as a reason why God will do and perform to them all the fore promised blessings of this New Covenant, for:

(1) **God – freely giving Jesus Christ for the effecting of remission of sins for us – will, with Christ thus given, freely give us all things.** Remission of sins is here promised with reference and respect to Jesus Christ and his plenary satisfaction by his obedience, sufferings, and death to the justice of God for our sins, in that phrase {ιλεως εσομαι ταις αδικιαις αυτων} in Hebrews 8:12: *I will be pacifiedly favorable to their unrighteousnesses*; as I have already shown in this chapter, and therefore shall not now need to insist any further upon it.[929]

God decreed, devised and contrived this way of redemption of sinners and remission of sins, from eternity (Ephesians 1:3-12; 1 Peter 1:18-20). God accordingly sent his Son in fullness of time in the similitude of sinful flesh (yet without sin) and for sin, to condemn sin in the flesh, to obtain remission of sins for his elect, by offering up himself a sacrifice to God's justice for their sins, and shedding his blood to expiate, purge and wash them away forever, without shedding of blood, there being no remission, because otherwise no proper and due satisfaction for our sins to the justice of God (Galatians 4:4-5, Romans 8:3, Ephesians 1:7, Colossians 1:14, Hebrews 9:14-15, 22 to the end, & 10:10-22).

Hence Christ is said to be an offering, a sacrifice for sins forever (Hebrews 10:12), to be offered to bear the sins of many (Hebrews 9:28), to bear our sins upon his own body on the tree (1 Peter 2:24), to redeem us from the curse, being made a curse for us (Galatians 3:13-14), to be made sin for us, who knew no sin, that we might become the righteousness of God in him (2 Corinthians 5:21), to love us, and wash us from our sins in his own blood (Revelation 1:5,

---

[929] In this 5th Chapter, Sections 1 & 2, Question 3, Expression 3 about Pardon, & Position 7

with many like expressions). Now God, giving Christ thus for effecting of our redemption and remission; what blessing in the world will he stick at? *He that spared not his own Son, but hath delivered him up for us all; how shall he not with him also freely give us all things?*[930] It is an argument from the greater to the less. Has God not spared, not withheld a son, his Son, his own Son; but delivered him up to humiliation, to reproach, to contradiction of sinners, to sorrows, to temptations, to betraying, to false accusing, to shame and spitting, to buffeting, to unjust condemnation, to death, to death on the cross in Golgotha between two thieves, to desertion for a time, and to burial in the grave; and this for us all, for us sinners, for us enemies to God, for us dead in sins and trespasses, for us worthless, loveless wretches, abominable, disobedient, and to every good work reprobate, etc. How shall he not with him freely give us all things! How shall not he call us effectually, justify us freely, sanctify us thoroughly, glorify us eternally, and make all things work together for good to us universally! How shall not he write his law in our minds and hearts, make us all know the Lord from the least to the greatest, and perform all other New Covenant blessings unto us! For:

[1] Christ is nearer and dearer to God than all things else in this or the world to come, temporals, spirituals, or eternals (John 3:16, Matthew 3:17, Colossians 1:13, Hebrews 1:3). [2] Christ is better in himself than all things, being *over all, God blessed forever, Amen*; and the gift of God; and the mercy of mercies (Romans 9:5, Hebrews 1:3, John 4:10, Luke 1:72; 1 Peter 2:10). [3] Christ brings all other blessings with him: all temporals (Matthew 6:33), and all spirituals and eternals (1 Timothy 4:8; 2 Corinthians 1:20; 2 Peter 1:3-4).

[2] Remission of sins finds us most incapable, and leaves us most capable of all saving blessings of the New Covenant. Before God pardons us, what are

---

[930] Romans 8:32

we? Sinners,[931] ungodly,[932] unholy,[933] unrighteous,[934] enemies to God,[935] at enmity to his law, etc,[936] bound over by guilt to eternal death, etc. And what is there in the world so abominable to God as sin, so obstructive to all his mercies as sin, so destructive to us as sin, so separating between God and us as sin? Sin is as a cloud, and a thick cloud between us; sin is the great partition wall between us; sin is as mountains and hills between us, etc. Therefore sin makes us most incapable of all blessings. But when God has pardoned sin once, then the enmity is removed, the thick cloud is dispelled, the partition wall is demolished, the mountains and hills are leveled; now a facile, plain, and easy way is made, a smooth and large channel is prepared for the streams of all divine blessings to flow in upon us. That of the apostle is very pregnant to this purpose: *But God commendeth his love towards us, in that while we were yet sinners, Christ died for us. Much more then, being now justified by his blood, we shall be saved from wrath through him. For if when we were enemies we were reconciled to God by the death of his Son, much more being reconciled, we shall be saved by his life.*[937] If God will remit sins unto sinners. What mercies can God deny unto them who by remission are made righteous?

[3] Remission of sins is interlinked and interwoven with all saving blessings of the New Covenant in Christ: that where remission of sins is bestowed, all other blessings are bestowed likewise. This is part of that golden chain of salvation, from which no link can be taken away: *whom he hath predestinated, them he hath called; whom he hath called, them he hath justified* (there is remission of sins), *and whom he hath justified, them he hath glorified.*[938] All other spirituals are inseparably knit unto this remission of sins, either as causes or effects; as antecedents, concomitants, or consequences in

---

[931] Romans 5:8
[932] Romans 4:5
[933] Titus 1:15; 2 Timothy 3:2
[934] 1 Corinthians 6:9-11
[935] Colossians 1:21
[936] Romans 8:7
[937] Romans 5:8-10
[938] Romans 8:29-30

one regard or another, so that our actual interest in this does most sweetly and effectually interest us in all spiritual blessings in heavenly things in Christ (Ephesians 1:3-12, Romans 4:6-8, etc., 5:1-5 & 8:29-30, Hebrews 9:12-15 & 10:10-22, Revelation 1:5). And therefore, God promises here in the New Covenant this great blessing of remission of sins – not only as an excellent distinct and most desirable mercy, but also as a radical fundamental mercy assuring his federates of all other covenant mercies.

Thus of the explanation of remission of sins.

Inferences from the whole thus explained and confirmed

In these inferences, I shall but briefly point out particulars, having already handled this precious subject so largely. Will the Lord in this his New Covenant be thus pacifiedly favorable to their unrighteousnesses, and will he remember their sinful-errors and unlawfulnesses no more? Then,

(1) **Hence remission of sins is a covenant blessing.**

There is such a thing as remission of sins. It is not a fancy, figment or mere imagination: but a real blessing and mercy which God has in store for his people, and it is a covenant blessing: for, this passage in the New Covenant: *and their sins and iniquities will I remember no more*,[939] the apostle interprets of remission of sins, expressly. Now every covenant blessing, especially every New Covenant blessing has a reality, an excellency, yea a certainty in it. God's federates may depend upon it.

(2) **Hence remission of sins promised under the New Covenant, not only differs from, but far excels the remission revealed under and before the Old Covenant.**

This point of remission of sins is here brought in as one particular article wherein the New Covenant should not be according to the covenant made with the fathers when they were brought out of Egypt.[940] Now how far this New Covenant remission agrees with, differs from, or excels that under the Old Covenant, has been already manifested – there see.[941] All remission salvific is from Christ's blood of the New Covenant. Hither all look, hither all must come for remission, and hence all that have it do receive it: whether living

---

[939] Hebrews 8:12 & 10:16-18
[940] Jeremiah 31:31-34, Hebrews 8:8-12
[941] In this 5th Chapter, Section 3, Proposition 3, Question 4

before, at, or after Christ's coming. Christ and his blood of the New Covenant, is the only center, root and fountain of all remission (Romans 3:23-26, Hebrews 9:15, Acts 13:38-39).

(3) Hence the Lord God himself alone remits and forgives sin.

Pardon of sin is God's peculiar royal prerogative (Exodus 34:7, Isaiah 43:25, Micah 7:18-19, Mark 2:5-13). His glorious name is {*the God of pardons*}.[942] But of this enough formerly. Therefore, do you have remission? Let God alone in Christ have all the glory of it. Do you lack forgiveness? Repair to God alone in Christ for it. *I will forgive – I will remember no more*.[943]

(4) Hence the Lord forgives sins to all his sincere federates.

To all such he extends this mercy – and to such alone he limits it. *I will forgive – I will remember their unrighteousnesses*, etc, *no more*.[944] Whose sins? The sins of his true federates, of his sincere covenant people, of the house of Israel and Judah. In whose hearts and minds he has written his laws, and who savingly know the Lord, and of them only. They that have obtained no effectual federation with God, hitherto have received no remission of sins from God. None out of covenant may presume of it: none in covenant need despair of it.

(5) Hence, the Lord God forgives sins to all his sincere federates, most freely, most fully, and finally.

Freely, without, yea contrary to all their desert; fully, without exception of any one sin of theirs; and finally, without all revocation or annulling of pardon once vouchsafed. Freely: *I will be pacified – I will remember no more*;[945] fully:

---

[942] Nehemiah 9:17
[943] Jeremiah 31:34, Hebrews 8:12
[944] Hebrews 8:8-11
[945] Hebrews 8:12

their unrighteousnesses, sinful-errors, and unlawfulnesses; what comprehensive expressions are these? And finally: *I will remember no more*; I will obliterate them, and forget them, so as not to punish them forever. But of these also formerly.[946]

(6) Hence whatsoever sins God forgives to his federates, he remits them all in Christ, and for his meritorious satisfaction to God's justice for them.

ιλεως εσομαι, etc. *I will be pacified*, or *pacifiedly-propitious to their unrighteousnesses*.[947] This has direct reference to Christ's expiation of our sins by his blood, whereby God's justice is satisfied and appeased – as I have formerly proven.[948] Then: [1] Christless persons are unpardoned persons. The guilt of sin still remains upon the conscience, if the blood of Christ has not besprinkled the conscience. [2] They that lack pardon must by faith come to Christ for it. They must come and wash in this fountain opened for sin and for uncleanness.[949] The Old Covenant had a laver and other vessels of water for sprinkling and washing the unclean, but they had not the fountain opened, that was in a sort shut up and sealed under types and figures, etc. But this New Covenant has this fountain opened, now no veil or shadow hides it from us, now every cover of this fountain is rolled away, come all that will, come freely; drink and live; wash, and be clean. If your sins are as an issue still running; if as a well, still springing up: yet be not dismayed: here is a fountain against a fountain; here is Christ's fountain ever springing, against your issue and fountain ever running. Though your sin and uncleanness spring still, yet Christ's purging pardons and remissions spring still also. Therefore, wash and cleanse yourself daily in this fountain. Here is cleansing enough, and Christ's

---

[946] In this 5th Chapter, Section 3, Proposition 1, Positions 6 & 9
[947] Hebrews 8:12
[948] In this 5th Chapter, Section 3, Proposition 1, Positions 7
[949] Zechariah 13:1

fountain will run longest, it will run and overflow for you until your fountain is quite dried up in you.

(7) Hence the Lord thus remitting all sins in Christ freely, fully, and finally, there remains no need of any more expiatory sacrifice for sin.[950]

Christ is already offered up for sins once for all, having by that one sacrifice forever perfected them that are sanctified, having obtained eternal redemption and remission for us.[951] He has fully satisfied God's justice, God expects no more expiatory sacrifice, no more blood, no more satisfaction, Christ has done enough, he has done all. Then: [1] Farewell all legal sacrifices, blood, expiations, and washings, forever. Christ has done that which they could never do: he has fully forever purged the consciences of his elect from sins. And in so doing, he has annulled and abrogated them all. [2] Away with all papal-masses, as proper, propitiatory, bloody, unbloody sacrifices for quick and dead.[952] They are a bundle of blasphemous idolatries against Jesus Christ, and the al-sufficiency of his sacrifice: and so, most abominably antiChristian, treading underfoot the Son of God, and counting his blood of the New Covenant an unholy, imperfect and insufficient thing. But those who desire it, may see this absurd and abominable popish dotage about the mass sufficiently refuted by these learned authors here alleged in the margin.[953]

(8) Hence those who would have sin pardoned to them, must embrace this promise and accept Jesus Christ by unfeigned faith.

For in Christ and through his satisfaction alone it is that sin is pardoned, according to the tenor of the New Covenant, and the promises thereof. Actual remission comes only by actual application of Christ by believing. O therefore,

---

[950] Hebrews 10:17-18
[951] Hebrews 10:10-20 & 9:12, 14-15, Ephesians 1:7, Colossians 1:14
[952] Council of Trent Ses 22. cap. 2. & cap. 9. can. 1, 2, 3, 4.
[953] John Calvin, *Institutes of the Christian Religion*, Book 4, Cap. 18; Dr. Joan Prideaux in Lection XVI, Anton. Walaeus in Operi. Pag. 510-512, Tom. 1 & Andrew Willett in his *Synopsis Papismi*, 13th General Controversy, Question 2

you who long for pardon, come to Christ, believe in him, make haste to him, actually apply his blood, and despair not of pardon. Think of the great sinners that he has pardoned: the penitent woman, that was a manifold sinner;[954] Peter, that was a frequent denier of Christ;[955] the thief, that was a reviler and railer against Christ;[956] Saul, that was a persecutor of Christ;[957] yea the Jews, that were bloody murderers of Christ, even they were pricked in their hearts, they had remission of sins tendered and given to them in the same blood which was wickedly shed by them, repent and be baptized everyone of you for remission of sins, etc.[958] Whereupon said Augustine sweetly: "Who would despair of his sin's[959] pardon, when the crime of killing Christ was pardoned to the guilty?"[960]

(9) Hence those who have not sin pardoned are as yet none of God's sincere New Covenant people.

They may possibly be within the external administration of the New Covenant, by a visible profession, but they are not within the internal and effectual salvation of the Covenant, by this invisible power of grace. Yea, perhaps they may be within the decree of God's election to eternal life: and yet they are without the actual execution of that decree upon them in a saving covenant state. And being without covenant, they are without Christ, without the law of God in their minds and hearts, without the true and saving knowledge of the Lord, yea and without God himself: for all these have a mutual and inseparable connection one to another.[961] Therefore, as we desire to be, and to know that we are God's New Covenant people: so we should strive to be, and to know that we are God's pardoned people. Now we may

---

[954] Luke 7:37, 47
[955] Matthew 26:70 to the end with John 21:15-17
[956] Luke 23:42-43; Matthew 27:44
[957] 1 Timothy 1:13, 15-17
[958] Acts 2:35-36, 38-39
[959] Or: *sins'* – it is unclear in Roberts which is meant.
[960] Augustine, *De Tempore*, Sermon 74
[961] Hebrews 8:8-13, Jeremiah 31:31-34

know whether we are God's pardoned people or not, by what has been spoken already, touching the expressions of pardon, the nature of pardon, and the evidences of pardon more at large.[962]

(10) Hence finally, all God's sincere New Covenant people are in a most happy, sweet, and comfortable state.

Why? Because, their unrighteousnesses, sinful-errors, and unlawfulnesses, are freely, fully and finally pardoned to them by God in Jesus Christ.[963] O what tongue of man can tell, or what heart can think sufficiently of the privilege and comfort of this remission? For they that are thus pardoned:

[1] Are acquitted from all their sins, as if they had never been. God will never impute them more, will never remember them more unto them.[964]

[2] Are utterly absolved from all guilt of punishment and condemnation. They may undergo many fatherly chastisements and tribulations, but shall never come into condemnation.[965]

[3] Are redeemed and reconciled to God by the blood of Jesus Christ, wiping out all their sins and transgressions.[966]

[4] Are quickened together with Christ, by supernatural principles of life: that they should no longer remain dead in trespasses and sins.[967]

[5] Are justified by God through Jesus Christ; remission of sin being a branch of justification, so that henceforth God looks upon them no longer as sinners, but as righteous; and not only as righteous men and women, but as the righteousness of God in Christ.[968]

[6] Are at peace with God, and with their own consciences.[969] So that neither the wrath of God above them, nor the horror, terror and anguish of

---

[962] In this 5th Chapter, Section 3, Proposition 1, Questions 2 & 3
[963] Hebrews 8:12 & 10:16-18
[964] Psalm 32:2, Hebrews 8:12; 2 Corinthians 5:19
[965] Romans 8:1
[966] Ephesians 1:7, Colossians 1:14, Romans 5:9-10
[967] Colossians 2:13
[968] Romans 4:6-8; 2 Corinthians 5:21
[969] Romans 5:1-5

conscience within them, nor the troubles of the creature round about them, shall ever be able to overthrow their peace: but contrariwise, they joy in hope of the glory of God, and glory even in tribulations also.

[7] Are happy now even unto admiration. *O the happiness of him whose transgression is forgiven, and whose sin is covered! O the happiness of the man unto whom the Lord imputeth not iniquity!* (Psalm 32:1-2, Romans 4:6-8). All the distresses in this world shall never be able to overthrow this impregnable happiness. God is theirs, Christ is theirs, all theirs; they must needs be ineffably and invincibly happy.

[8] Finally, those who have their sins forgiven in this life, shall certainly be glorified in the life to come: *whom he hath justified, them he hath glorified.*[970] Their glory is as sure, as if they were glorified already, as if they were in heaven already. Here is honey out of the rock, here is sweetness out of strength, here is a well of salvation indeed. Oh, you pardoned souls, come lick this honey, come taste this sweetness, come draw water out of this well with joy. Oh, comfort yourselves with these words, with these considerations. Oh, everyone of you take up David's words with David's spirit: *Bless the LORD, O my soul: and all that is within me bless his holy name. Bless the LORD, O my soul: and forget not all his benefits, who forgiveth all thine iniquities: who healeth all thy diseases: who redeemeth thy life from destruction: who crowneth thee with lovingkindness and tender mercies.*[971]

Thus of the third article of the New Covenant: God's free, full, and final pardoning of all his true federates' sins in Jesus Christ forevermore.

---

[970] Romans 8:29-30
[971] Psalm 103:1-4

Article 4

Of the grand New Covenant relation, interest, and communion, mutually, between God and his sincere federates.

Now we are come to the fourth, and last, and greatest article of all, in this sweet New Covenant: namely: the mutual New Covenant-relation, interest, and communion between God and his sincere federates: *and I will be to them a God, and they shall be to me a people.*[972] Oh, what manner of mercy is here promised, when God himself is promised! And what manner of duty is required and restipulated, when federates themselves are restipulated! Here is mutual relation of God and his federates, to one another; here is their mutual interest in one another; here is their mutual communion, with one another.

What does not God promise to us, when he says: {*I will be to them a God*}? What do not his federates re-promise to him, when they say, they will be to him a people? Nay rather, what does not God promise and undertake, when himself alone promises and undertakes the performance of both these: not only, that he will be to them a God; but also, that they shall be to him a people? That the Lord will be our God, is a ravishing and satisfying mercy; who can sufficiently fathom it? That we should be his people, is an amazing and astonishing duty; who can exactly fulfill it? But that the Lord undertakes both these, that he will, and we shall, is a most comfortable and heart-reviving privilege; who can choose but exult in it, triumph in it, and be overcome with it?

All the former articles and promises of this covenant, yea and in the whole sacred volume, are but as inferior limbs in the body; this is the head of all. They are as pearls and precious stones; but this is the jewel. They are as drops, but this is the fountain. They are as springs or streams, but this is the ocean.

---

[972] Hebrews 8:10, Jeremiah 31:33

They are as the glittering stars, but this is as the glorious sun himself. If the tongues of men and angels were ever desirable for describing and magnifying any promise in all the Bible, this certainly is the promise in reference to the displaying of which they are most desirable.

Well said that judicious Calvin: "This is the fruit of the Covenant; that God takes us for his people, and asserts himself president of our salvation."[973] And elsewhere: "Generally here, God comprehends **the sum of his Covenant**. For whereunto did the law tend, but that his people might invocate him, and he again would take the care of his people? For as oft as God pronounces himself to be our God, he also offers his Fatherly favor, and declares his care to be for our salvation, he gives us free entrance unto prayers, he commands us to rely upon his grace, and to conclude, **this promise contains under it all the parts of our salvation.** – Thence the latter depends: {*they shall be to me a people*}, for the one cannot be severed from the other. Therefore by these words the prophet briefly signifies, **the sum of the Covenant** to tend hither, that he may be to us a Father, from whom we may ask and expect salvation; and we again may be his people."[974]

Upon this transcendent theme, my very spirit has vehement desire to expatiate, it is such a delicious bed of spices, flowers and roses, of most sublime spiritual delights. But I must compendiously contract: partly, because the volume swells too fast; partly, because I have already at large explained this promise of promises in various places of this treatise. And therefore: (1) by way of explanation, I shall superadd no more, but only indigitate the particulars already explained, and where they may be readily found; (2) by way of application, I shall somewhat enlarge myself; because I have formerly been more brief therein, reserving the enlargement of some inferences from this grand premise, purposely for this article of the New Covenant. Thus this

---

[973] John Calvin's commentary on Hebrews 8:10
[974] John Calvin's commentary on Jeremiah 31:33

glorious promise shall not be passed over, without its due and deserved consideration.

(1) **First, by way of explanation**, I have already unfolded this promise: [1] more generally, and [2] more particularly in both branches of it.

[1] *More generally*, I have shown these three things, namely:

{1} That this promise is much insisted upon in most of the eminent covenant expressures.[975] As, in the Covenants of Promise with Abraham, with Israel, with David, and with the captives in Babylon, and in this New Covenant – this being the very sum, abstract, quintessence and soul of all God's Covenants.

{2} That of all federal clauses, articles or promises laid down in the book of God, this promise is: (i) the highest, (ii) the fullest, (iii) the surest, and (iv) the sweetest.[976] No wonder then that Augustine – reciting this promise {*I will be to them a God, and they shall be to me a people*} – presently adds: "What is better than this goodness! What is happier than this happiness!"[977]

{3} That this promise is most excellent.[978] And the excellency of it is attested by the high eulogies of many eminent learned men, as is evident in some of their expressions particularly recited.

[2] *More particularly*, for clearing:

{1} **The first branch of this promise** {*I will be to them a God*}, I have explained these particulars especially, namely:

(i) To whom the Lord will be a God.[979]

(ii) What the Lord promises, when he promises to be a God to his people, namely: (a) whatsoever he is as God: (1) in essential properties and (2) in

---

[975] Book 2, Chapter 2, Aphorism 2, Section 3
[976] Book 2, Chapter 2, Aphorism 2, Section 3
[977] "Ero, [itquit], illis in Deum: & ipsi erunt mihi Populus. Quid hoc bono melius: Quid hac faelicitate faelicius!" etc. August. *Lib. de Spiritu & Litera ad Marcellin*. cap. 22. pag. 823. A. Tom. 3. (Basil, 1569).
[978] Book 3, Chapter 3, Aphorism 3, Section 1
[979] Book 3, Chapter 3, Aphorism 3, Section 1

personal subsistences (Book 3 Chapter 3 Aphorism 3 Section 1)]; (b) whatsoever he has as God; there see; and (c) whatsoever he can do, or is wont to do for his people as God – and this is laid down at large in thirteen particular acts of his favor to his people; there see.

(iii) How the Lord will be a God to his people, namely: (i) by covenant, (ii) by covenant of his own establishing, and (iii) by an everlasting covenant.[980]

(iv) How the Lord is our Covenant God only in and through Jesus Christ. (Book 3 Chapter 4 Aphorism 4 Section 1).

(v) Why the Lord was pleased to be a Covenant God to Israel, and so proportionably to us.[981]

Thus in these particulars, I have already explained the first branch of this promise.

{2} **For opening also of the second branch of this promise {*And they shall be to me a people*},** I have explained these particulars, namely:

(i) That this is the greatest of all duties imposed upon God's people – they therein promising and restipulating to God,[982] (a) all they are, (b) all they have, (c) all they can do, and (d) all they can endure: to be for him, and at his command or appointment.

(ii) That God required and Israel restipulated this, namely: that they would be God's covenant people.[983]

(iii) What it implies to be God's covenant people. These things especially, namely: (a) to be God's people only – not sin's, not the world's, not Satan's nor their own, but God's by peculiar appropriation;[984] (b) to be his by federal profession and denomination;[985] (c) to be his covenant people in Christ;[986] (d) to be his covenant people in all relations;[987] and (e) to be his covenant people

---

[980] Book 3, Chapter 3, Aphorism 3, Section 1
[981] Book 3, Chapter 4, Aphorism 4, Section 1
[982] Book 2, Chapter 2, Aphorism 2, Section 3
[983] Book 3, Chapter 4, Aphorism 4, Section 2
[984] Book 3, Chapter 4, Aphorism 4, Section 2
[985] Book 3, Chapter 4, Aphorism 4, Section 2
[986] Book 3, Chapter 4, Aphorism 4, Section 2
[987] Book 3, Chapter 4, Aphorism 4, Section 2

wholly and entirely,[988] namely: (1) in all they are, (2) in all they have, (3) in all they can do or procure, and (4) in all they can undergo or endure, according to his will. These four particulars, formerly insisted upon more generally and briefly, are here again handled more particularly and fully.

(iv) Why Israel (and so proportionably we) must be such a covenant people to God, manifested by six causes hereof.[989]

Thus in all these particulars, I have already explained the second branch of this promise.

By all this, the judicious reader will easily see, especially if he consult the places here quoted, This admirable promise so far explained already, that I may now wholly desist from any further explications thereof, desiring him for his satisfaction in all or any of these particulars, to cast his eye (as he has occasion) upon these fore-cited explications.

(2) Secondly, by way of application, I offer these inferences:

Will the Lord be to them a God, and shall they be to him a people, that are his New Covenant-federates? Does he by his New Covenant establish and assure them of such a covenant relation, interest, and communion between himself and them? Has God thus undertaken for both parties, both for himself, that he will be theirs: and for them, that they shall be his? Then, what excellent matter is here: [1] for information, [2] for probation, [3] for exhortation, and [4] for consolation.

---

[988] Book 3, Chapter 4, Aphorism 4, Section 2
[989] Book 3, Chapter 4, Aphorism 4, Section 2

[Matter 1]: *Information*

[1] *Here is excellent and manifold matter for information*: that the Lord will be to his federates a God, and they shall be to him a people. For, this may inform our understandings of these things especially, namely:

{1} **Of the fullness of the New Covenant.** The three former articles evince, that this New Covenant is very rich and full, in regard of effectual grace, saving knowledge of the Lord, and remission of sins;[990] but this fourth article demonstrates that this New Covenant is most rich and full in all regards. It has in it God's all and our all. (i) God's all, for what is there in the whole world, present or to come, of temporals, spirituals or eternals, which comes not within the verge and limits of this vast comprehensive promise: {*I will be their God*}?[991] What fullness is there not in God! Glory, majesty, life, love, grace, mercy, goodness, sweetness, beauty, blessedness, purity, holiness, righteousness, peace, yea all desirableness, and all infinite. God made all things; God has all things; God is all things in all and to all his covenant people. And therefore, when this New Covenant promises that the Lord will be our God, it promises God's all. What fullness can we desire more? (ii) Our all, for all we are, all we have, all we can do, all we can endure, comes within the extent of this promise: {*and they shall be my people*}. What fullness can we retribute more? Oh the plenitude and riches of this New Covenant, in this grand promise.

{2} **Of the goodness and bountifulness of God to his federates.** Oh how matchless, how infinite! God promises for himself what he will be, and God promises for them what they shall be – God undertakes all for both

---

[990] Hebrews 8:10-12, Jeremiah 31:33-34
[991] Hebrews 8:10

parties, and what he undertakes must needs be. Behold, admire, and adore this boundless bounty and goodness of God.

(i) What does God promise for himself? That he will be to them a God.[992] And, what could God promise more than God? What can God give more than God? What can his federates want, desire, or enjoy more than God? God is above all goodness that can be desired, promised, performed or possessed. What does God not promise in this promise of himself to us? If God had promised: "I will be their refuge, and strength and present help in trouble;[993] I will be their rock, fortress, deliverer, buckler, horn of their salvation, and their high tower;[994] I will be their shield about them, their glory, and the lifter up of their head;[995] I will be their sun, their shield, and their exceeding great reward; I will be their Lord, their king, their father, their husband,"[996] etc. – if I say God had promised these things, he would have promised very great and precious blessings; but when he promises {*I will be to them a God*}, now he promises most of all. Beyond this promise, what can be promised? Or what is there that is promisable?

(ii) What does God promise for his federates? That they shall be to him a people. And what can they perform more to God than themselves! Nay, because they cannot perform themselves to God, he undertakes for them, he will see this shall be done. There shall be no impediment of unwillingness in him, he will be theirs; there shall be no impediment of weakness in them, they shall be his. Here is bounty upon bounty; here is goodness upon goodness.

{3} **Of the happiness of all God's sincere federates**. Wherein? In this especially and principally; that the Lord is their covenant God, and they his covenant people. When the psalmist had reckoned up many outward blessings, and thereupon concluded {*O the happinesses of that people that is in such a*

---

[992] Hebrews 8:10, Jeremiah 31:33
[993] Psalm 46:1
[994] Psalm 18:2
[995] Psalm 3:3
[996] Psalm 84:11, Genesis 15:1

case},[997] by way of correction, he presently adds to the happinesses of that people of whom the Lord is their God, this is, of all others, *the* happiness – no happiness in the world like this happiness, for: (i) Herein God's federates are (as has formerly been shown)[998] a privileged people above all people of the world. (ii) Herein their dignity is very high, and their advantage manifold, as has been in six particulars formerly manifested.[999] (iii) Hence they may be abundantly assured, that they shall want neither promises nor mercies: having this promise of promises, this mercy of mercies, theirs, as has been evidenced.[1000] (iv) Hereby, God's federates are established in the sweetest relation to God, in the richest interest in God, in the nearest and dearest communion with God. Oh, what familiarity is there, in that relation! What sufficiency, in that interest! What felicity, in that communion! This familiarity is most delighting, this sufficiency is most satisfying, this felicity is most ravishing to all the sincere federates of God.

{4} **Of the fewness of God's true and sincere federates even under this New Covenant.** There are many formal and nominal, but few real federates with God. There are many federates by outward profession, but few, oh how few, federates by inward constitution. Why? Because they are few, very few, that have the Lord for their covenant God, or that have resigned up themselves again unto God to be his covenant people. How few are they that are God's people only? His in Christ; his in all relations; his wholly and entirely, in all they are, in all they have, in all they can do, in all they can endure? Now none are God's sincere New Covenant federates indeed, but those alone who have the Lord for their God, and are themselves his people.

{5} **Finally, of the wretchedness of all non-federates whatsoever,** for: (i) the Lord is not their God in covenant, nor are they God's covenant people – they have as yet no saving covenant relation to God, interest in him, or

---

[997] Psalm 144:12-15
[998] In Book 3, Chapter 3, Aphorism 3, Section 1
[999] In Book 3, Chapter 3, Aphorism 3, Section 1
[1000] In Book 3, Chapter 3, Aphorism 3, Section 1

communion with him. (ii) In despising and neglecting God's Covenant, they neglect and despise God, Jesus Christ, and all true happiness.[1001] And this is wretchedness unspeakable (Ephesians 2:12).

[1001] In Book 3, Chapter 3, Aphorism 3, Section 1

[Matter 2]: *Probation & Examination*

Here is notable matter for probation and examination of our true New Covenant condition. Let us diligently examine ourselves, accurately prove our own selves, whether we be of the house of Israel and Judah, whether we be among the number of God's sincere New Covenant federates, or no.

But how shall we discover this? In two ways: {1} if the Lord is our covenant God, and {2} if we are God's covenant people. If this glorious promise and clause of the New Covenant is effectually verified and performed to us, and fulfilled upon us, and if God is savingly ours and we sincerely his, then we are in a right New Covenant state.

{Question 1}: Has the LORD become our God in covenant?

That the Lord is our Covenant God, we may discover three ways, namely: (i) by his federal impressions and operations upon us, (ii) by our covenant relation unto him, and (iii) by our suitable deportment towards him as our God in Covenant.

(i) *First, by his federal impressions and operations upon us, as our covenant God.*

When the Lord becomes our covenant God, he imprints and works upon us certain marks and characters of his Covenant. He effectually delineates and deeply engraves upon our spirits the blessings, benefits, effects and fruits of his special favor, promised in his Covenant. Hereby he makes a great, and a very observable alteration upon us: so that they on whom these federal impressions are instamped, cannot choose but in some measure discern them. Take these instances:

(a) **He puts a new Spirit, even his own Spirit, within us: as our covenant God.**[1002] By this new Spirit, I here understand God's own Spirit, called {*God's Spirit*} in opposition to our own mere carnal spirit; and {*a new spirit*} in opposition to our old natural corrupt sinful frame of heart and spirit,[1003] as also in regard to its excellent new effects upon us: renewing, new-creating, making all things new within us, mind, conscience, will, affections, old things pass away, and all things become new (Titus 3:5; 2

[1002] Ezekiel 11:19-20 & 36:26-28, John 7:37-39, Acts 2:4, etc., 16-34
[1003] Romans 6:6, Ephesians 4:22-24

Corinthians 5:17). This is God's great covenant impression upon us: he puts his own Spirit within us, he makes him ours, and he gives us actual possession of him. Has the Lord put his own Spirit within us? Then he is our God in covenant.

Hereby we shall know if God's Spirit be within us, for then, he is become to us:

(1) *A convincing spirit* (John. 16:9-11). He convinces us: [1] of our own sinfulness and misery, especially in regard to our not believing in Jesus Christ: unbelief being the great sin of the world; [2] of the all-sufficient remedy against this sin and misery, namely: Christ's perfect mediatory righteousness, herein clearly discovered, that death and grave were not able to hold him, as they hold sinners, but he revived, rose, and ascended to his father as a righteous conqueror of sin and death. Had there been but one sin in him, or but one sin of his elect imputed to him for which he had not fully satisfied his fathers justice, he could never have got out of his grave, or have ascended to his Father; [3] of Christ's supreme lordship or sovereignty over all his and his people's enemies, in that he has subdued and judged Satan, the prince of this world, his and their grand enemy.

(2) *A converting, renewing, regenerating and sanctifying Spirit* (Titus 3:5, John 3:3, 5; 1 Corinthians 6:11). The immediate author and worker of all grace in the soul, sanctifying it throughout, so that every true grace is an evidence of the Spirit of grace in us.

(3) *An enlivening or quickening Spirit* (Romans 8:2). It makes those who were dead in sin alive to God. All acts of such life, as spiritual nourishment, growth, motion, sense, fruitfulness, etc., are discoveries of the power of Christ's spirit of life in us.

(4) *A guiding and governing Spirit* (Romans 8:14). He guides and leads all God's children in the ways of God. Are we led by this spirit?

(5) *A praying Spirit* (Romans 8:15, 26). He enables us to cry {*Abba Father*}, with servant desires and groans that cannot be uttered. It is not words

and phrases and method in praying (which art may suggest) but unutterable sighs and groans which this spirit of supplication furnishes us also.

(6) *A witnessing Spirit*. It bears witness with our spirits that we are the children of God (Romans 8:15-16). It discovers to our spirits whom the word counts God's children, with their several notes and characters. It also discovers to us that there notes and properties of God's children are in us. For the Spirit is therefore given us, that by him we might discover and know the things that are freely given us of God (1 Corinthians 2:12). And upon these two discoveries it enables our spirits or consciences to digest all into a practical syllogism, or experimental discourse, for the evincing of our good estate to us.

(7) *Finally, God's Spirit is a comforting Spirit*, still dwelling in God's people: and yielding them a continual stream (if not of sensible refreshing, yet) of secret supporting comfort. He keeps them from fainting, sinking and despairing under greatest discouragements.[1004]

(b) **He writes his law in their hearts and inwards.**[1005] He writes his law in their hearts, powerfully, universally, evidently, and indelibly [in a way that cannot be forgotten]. (1) So powerfully, that he leaves an impression, a dint, and an image of his law upon the heart, which the heart is not able to withstand or resist. (2) So universally, that there is not any branch of God's law left out. Every law, every branch of his law, is in some measure put there. He has something in his heart that answers to every particle of the law, as the counter-pain to the deed. (3) So evidently, that if others cannot read the inscription, yet themselves can spell it out in some good measure by the assistance of God's Spirit, whereby they know the things given them of God.[1006] (4) So indelibly, that the impression of God's law can never be blotted out of the heart. This is not like writing letters in the dust or water, that are presently obliterated; but like writing in marble or steel, most permanent. God's law is interwoven into the very frame and texture of the heart, that it is

---

[1004] John 14:16-17
[1005] Jeremiah 31:33, Hebrews 8:10, Psalm 40:8
[1006] Revelation 2:17, 1 Corinthians 2:12

inseparably fixed there. Thus it was written in David's heart, that he could never forget his statutes.[1007]

Question: But how may we know that God's law is written thus in our hearts?

Answer: This I have elsewhere cleared by four discoveries, namely: (1) the heart's conformity to the law, (2) the heart's newness, (3) the heart's spiritual tenderness and softness, and (4) the heart's obedientialness [obedience]; there see.[1008]

(c) **He gives them a heart to know God, that he is the Lord**: the covenant-keeping and promise-performing Lord, to know him truly, experimentally, affectively, obedientially, etc.[1009] Evidences of true covenant knowledge of the Lord have been also elsewhere hinted – consult them.[1010]

(d) **He takes away their hard and stony heart, giving them a tender, tractable, fleshy heart.**[1011] He transforms stone into flesh. This tender, soft broken spirit is God's sacrifices, which he will not despise.[1012] The truth of this tenderness and brokenness of spirit, I have formerly elsewhere discovered:[1013] (1) by the concomitants or companions attending upon a broken spirit, namely: [1] a spirit of prayer, [2] humility, [3] love to Jesus Christ, and [4] obedience; (2) by the adjuncts or properties of true tenderness of heart, namely: [1] mourning for sins of others, especially public sins; [2] clearest and saddest apprehensions of its own sinfulness; [3] greatest perplexity at sin, as against God and Jesus Christ; [4] trembling at God's Word, and at God's rod; [5] endeavoring seriously, and setting speedily upon a real reformation.

[1007] Psalm 119:20, 93, 112

[1008] In Book 3, Chapter 3, Aphorism 3, Section 1

[1009] Jeremiah 24:7; 1 John 2:20, 27

[1010] In my *Communicant Instructed*, pp.6-8

[1011] Ezekiel 11:19-20 & 36:26-28

[1012] Psalm 51:17

[1013] In my sermon before the house of peers, on Psalm 51:17, pp.24-33. See also the nature, and characters of the heart of flesh, at large. In Book 3, Chapter 6, Aphorism 2, Section 1.

(e) **He converts them entirely and effectually to himself from sin and iniquity.**[1014] He converts them both in heart and life; both in inward disposition, and outward conversation. The truth of such conversion, I have already discovered in another treatise – there see.[1015]

(f) **He sets his tabernacle amongst them, walks amongst them, dwells with them and in them,**[1016] that is: he affords them special communion with himself – fellowship with Father, Son, and Holy Spirit.[1017] The sweet presence, influence and refreshments of his Spirit, graces, and comforts, he imparts unto them. This is heaven on earth. Now of this fellowship with God and Jesus Christ, I have elsewhere laid down many evident discoveries, to which I refer the reader for his fuller satisfaction: in perusal whereof I hope he shall not lose his labor.[1018]

(g) **Finally, he makes them constant and steadfast to himself in covenant.**[1019] He so principles them, and overrules them; he so secures them, and undertakes for them, that they shall not depart away from him, that they shall be his people. These and like federal impressions the Lord works and stamps upon us, when he becomes our Covenant God. And this is one way whereby we may discern whether the Lord be our God in Covenant or not. Have we these covenant impressions and characters upon us?

(ii) *Secondly, By our covenant relation unto God, we may evidently know whether the Lord has become our Covenant God.*

In all Covenants there is established a covenant relation, a mutual reciprocal relation between the federates. So in this New Covenant most

---

[1014] Jeremiah 24:7, Acts 26:18
[1015] In my *Communicant Instructed*, pp.135-138.
[1016] Leviticus 26:11-12, Ezekiel 37:26-27; 2 Corinthians 6:16
[1017] 1 John 1:3; 2 Corinthians 13:14
[1018] In my *Believers' Evidences for Eternal Life*, Chapter 7
[1019] Jeremiah 32:38, 40, Hebrews 8:10, Jeremiah 31:33

eminently between God and us, if we are Christ's, if we are true believers: There is a mutual relation (Jeremiah 13:33, Hebrews 8:10). If the Lord become our Covenant God, then we become his covenant people. And if we become his covenant people, then he also is our Covenant-God. These relations do mutually imply one another, do reciprocally and necessarily infer and answer one another. Are we brought into this covenant relation unto God? Are we become – not only in profession and name, but in deed and in truth – God's covenant-people? Then the Lord is our Covenant God.

Question: But how may we discover that we are God's covenant people, not only in name and by visible profession, but also in deed by invisible participation of the saving benefits of the Covenant?

Answer: By these ensuing adjuncts and properties of God's covenant people, namely:

(a) God's New Covenant people are effectually called. Not only outwardly and ineffectually, but also inwardly and effectually called. The vessels of mercy fore prepared unto glory, are a called people, and so become God's people. They are called from darkness into his marvelous light:[1020] from sin to grace, from the power of Satan to God.[1021] God called Abraham effectually, when he first entered into covenant with him savingly.[1022] People uncalled by God, are as yet un-covenanted with God. They are in a contrary covenant and league with sin and Satan, inconsistent with the Covenant of God. This wretched league is broken and dissolved by effectual calling, that we may join in Covenant with God. Are we effectually called?

(b) God's New Covenant people are a holy, select, and separated people. They are selected and culled out from among all other people. They are drawn out and segregated from the common corrupt mass of the world. Holiness implies a separation from common, profane, impure state, society and use, to peculiar, spiritual, sacred state and use. *I will dwell in them, and walk in them,*

[1020] 1 Peter 2:9-10
[1021] Acts 26:18
[1022] Genesis 12:1-3 with Galatians 3:16

said God; *and I will be their God, and they shall be my people. Wherefore come out from among them, and be ye separate, saith the Lord, and touch not the unclean thing, and I will receive you,* etc.[1023] Upon this their being separated from their common and impure condition and society to God and his ways, they are styled {*a chosen generation*}, {*an holy nation*}, and {*a peculiar treasure unto God*} – above all people.[1024] Are we separated from the common, impure mass of mankind, or are we mingled with them? Have we renounced ungodliness and worldly lusts (Titus 2:11-12), or do we still live therein? When God brought Abraham to be one of his covenant people, he called and separated him from his corrupt, ungodly and idolatrous state in chaldea, unto himself, and to a godly state in him (Genesis 12:1-3, etc).

(c) God's New Covenant people are a self-denying people. This, Christ frequently calls for in his disciples.[1025] This the grace of God,[1026] that is, God's doctrine of grace (which is especially contained in the gospel and New Covenant), teaches them that are to be his people in reference to their enjoyment of God in Jesus Christ: *Hearken, O daughter, and consider, and incline thine ear: Forget also thine own people, and thy father's house. So shall the King greatly desire thy beauty: for he is thy Lord, and worship thou him.*[1027] And this they perform, that accept God's Covenant. They are content to deny not only all their self-sinfulness: but all their self-righteousness, self excellency, self-perfection, self-wisdom, self-will, self-love, self-relations, and whatsoever self-enjoyments in the world, that might stand in opposition to, or in competition with this Covenant with God. They see so much transcendent worth and excellency in God, that they can freely sell all, part with all, that they may enjoy the Lord as their Covenant God. Thus Abraham denied and forsook his native country, kindred, and father's house, for God.[1028] Thus Paul

---

[1023] 2 Corinthians 6:16-17
[1024] 1 Peter 2:9-10, Exodus 19:5-6
[1025] Matthew 10:37-39, Luke 9:23, Matthew 16:24, etc.
[1026] Titus 2:11-12
[1027] Psalm 45:10-11
[1028] Genesis 12:1-3

denied all his carnal prerogatives, counting them and all things but loss and dung for the excellency of Jesus Christ, and that he might be found in him.[1029] Can we thus deny ourselves?

(d) God's New Covenant people are a willing people. God said to Jesus Christ: *Rule thou in the midst of thine enemies. Thy people shall be willing in the day of thy power;*[1030] that is: thy peculiar people, especially thy true new covenant people and members, they shall not be as naturally they once were; enemies to God and all his ways; or compulsorily, forcedly, unwillingly willing through predominance of fear, danger, punishment, etc,[1031] as the Samaritans feared God for his lions;[1032] or half-willing, having in some good pangs or moods, certain imperfect and faint velleities and ungrounded inclinations to good, as agrippa almost persuaded to be a Christian;[1033] but they shall thoroughly and willingly subject and devote themselves to your government, to you and your ways; and they shall freely yield up themselves souls and bodies as cheerful volunteers to serve in thy wars against your enemies. Jesus Christ is their chief-captain.[1034] He now rules and will still rule in the midst of his enemies, until the world's end, when they shall all be put under his feet.[1035] His peculiar people they shall lay aside their enmity against God and Christ, they shall not remain enemies with the world as once they were, but shall be a willing people: willing to be ruled by Christ; willing to serve him, to side with him, to do anything for him; their members shall be weapons of righteousness for him, themselves shall be even sacrifices to him.[1036] They will serve him with a perfect heart and willing mind, they will run the ways of his commandments with enlarged hearts, they will delight to do his will, it shall be their meat and drink, etc. Murmuring, grumbling, irksomeness, etc, shall be far from them.

[1029] Philippians 3:5-10
[1030] Psalm 110:2-3
[1031] Romans 8:7-8, 10
[1032] 2 Kings 17:25-26, Jeremiah 2:27
[1033] Acts 26:28
[1034] Hebrews 2:10
[1035] 1 Corinthians 15:24-26
[1036] Romans 6:19 & 12:1 & 15:16

An excellent pattern of this willing-heartedness, see in the primitive Christians (Acts 2:41 to the end & 4:4, 32 to the end). Are we God's volunteers?

(e) God's New Covenant people are his temple. *Ye are the temple of the living God, as God hath said, I will dwell in them, and walk in them, and I will be their God, and they shall be my people.*[1037] What the temple at Jerusalem was of old materially and typically, that God's people now are spiritually and truly in reference unto God. (1) The temple was the special place of God's presence and habitation.[1038] He dwelt between the cherubims.[1039] There he met with his people, and communed with them.[1040] So God's people are built up a spiritual house, *for an habitation of God through the Spirit.*[1041] *Know ye not that ye are the temple of God: and the Spirit of God dwelleth in you?*[1042] God dwells in them,[1043] manifests himself to them,[1044] sups with them and they with him,[1045] affords them sweet heavenly communion with himself. (2) The temple was the place of public worship and sacrifices.[1046] So God's people are the receptacles of God's spiritual inward worship in heart and soul. (3) The temple – in regard to both God's presence and worship – was relatively holy, and not to be defiled with legal impurities.[1047] So God's people are holy, and not to be defiled with sinful impurities.[1048] Are we such temples of God? Does God dwell in us? Is his worship seated in our hearts? Do we keep ourselves holy and undefiled?

[1037] 2 Corinthians 6:16-18
[1038] Psalm 46:4
[1039] Romans 8:7-8, 10
[1040] Psalm 80:1
[1041] 1 Peter 2:5, Ephesians 2:21-22
[1042] 1 Corinthians 3:16
[1043] 2 Corinthians 6:16-17
[1044] John 14:21, 23
[1045] Revelation 3:20
[1046] Deuteronomy 12:5-7, 11-12; 1 Peter 2:5
[1047] 1 Kings 9:3, Psalm 46:4
[1048] 1 Peter 2:9; 1 Corinthians 3:17

(f) God's New Covenant people are a holy and royal priesthood.[1049] Peter styles those who are God's people, sometimes {*a holy priesthood*}, sometimes a royal priesthood. That is {*kings and priests to God*}, as elsewhere it is expressed in Scripture:[1050] {*kings*}, as having rule and dominion, in and by Christ's kingly power, over all our spiritual enemies, sin, the world, afflictions, death, and all the powers of darkness. Over all these, we are in Christ more than conquerors, even triumphers. And shall at last sit as kings with Christ to judge the world, at least by acclamation and assent to Christ's righteous judgments. After which, we shall reign with Christ in heavenly glory forever and ever.[1051] Priests to offer up spiritual sacrifices acceptable to God by Jesus Christ,[1052] as prayers, praises, thanksgivings, obedience, etc. And *to shew forth the virtues of him, who hath called us out of darkness into his marvelous light,*[1053] namely: to show forth his power, wisdom, grace, love, mercy, long-suffering, etc. Are we such kings and priests, have we such kingly and priestly abilities?

(g) God's New Covenant people are God's children, his sons and daughters; and God is a Father unto them. *And it shall come to pass, that in the place where it was said unto them, ye are not my people; there they shall be called, the children of the living God.*[1054] Had the exact opposition of the phrase been observed here, the words should have run thus: "There they shall be called the people of the living God," but he says {*the children of the living God*}, intimating that God's people are also God's children. And elsewhere having said: {*I will be their God, and they shall be my people*}, he adds {*And I will be a Father unto you, and ye shall be my sons and daughters, saith the Lord Almighty*}.[1055] Are we God's children? Then certainly we are God's New Covenant people. God's children may hereby be discerned: (1) They are born

---

[1049] 1 Peter 2:5, 9-10
[1050] Revelation 1:6, Leviticus 19:6, Revelation 3:21
[1051] 2 Timothy 2:12, Revelation 3:21 & 22:3-5
[1052] 1 Peter 2:5
[1053] 1 Peter 2:9-10
[1054] Romans 9:26
[1055] 2 Corinthians 6:16-18

again of the Spirit of God, supernaturally.[1056] (2) They have received Jesus Christ by faith, and he dwells in their hearts.[1057] (3) They have the Spirit of adoption in their hearts, crying Abba Father, with groans that cannot be uttered.[1058] (4) They are like their heavenly Father that spiritually begat them.[1059] They partake his divine nature, and have the very image of God in knowledge, righteousness, and true holiness imprinted upon them. (5) They are conformed to Jesus Christ, *the firstborn among many brethren*.[1060] (6) They are led and guided by the Spirit of God.[1061] He acts and moves in them, he steers and regulates them, and he works all in them. But contrariwise, Satan is *the spirit that worketh in the children of disobedience*.[1062] By that evil spirit, they are acted and guided. Now if we have these characters of God's children, we are his children and New Covenant people. But besides these, I have elsewhere largely opened and cleared nine other evidences of our regeneration, adoption and sonship, whereby we may know whether we are the children of God.[1063] Thither I refer the reader for fuller satisfaction – the main body of that treatise being spent about this very argument.

(h) Lastly, God's New Covenant people are Christ's. They are more Christ's than their own – yea, they are not their own but Christ's. *All things are yours, and ye are Christ's, and Christ is God's*.[1064] *And if ye be Christ's, then are ye Abraham's seed, and heirs according to the promise*.[1065] So that all who are Christ's, are Abraham's covenant seed and heirs. Now all Abraham's sincere covenant seed since Christ, are God's New Covenant people – see Romans 4:10-12, 16-17, 23-24, Galatians 3:7-8, 14 & 4:24, 26-28, 31. They

---

[1056] John 1:12-13 & 3:3, 5
[1057] John 1:11-12, Ephesians 3:17
[1058] Romans 8:15, 26, Galatians 4:6
[1059] Matthew 5:45, 48; 2 Peter 1:4, Colossians 3:12, Ephesians 4:24
[1060] Romans 8:29
[1061] Romans 8:14
[1062] Ephesians 2:2
[1063] In my *Believers' Evidences*, etc, Chapter 2 throughout, pp. 21-180.
[1064] 1 Corinthians 3:22-23
[1065] Galatians 3:29

are first Christ's, as Mediator, and then they are God's in Christ. Are we Christ's? Are we his redeemed ones, his branches, his members, his espoused ones, etc? Then we are God's covenant people. And we may know whether we be Christ's or not by five evidences of being Christ's, formerly pointed at only,[1066] but now handled at large in the sixth chapter of this fourth book, and also by other discoveries laid down elsewhere to that effect.[1067] Consult those places.

By these things, we may know whether we are God's Covenant-people; whether we have a true saving covenant relation to God, and consequently, whether the Lord be our God in covenant, which is the highest covenant mercy of all. For by this covenant relation unto God, we may discern that the Lord is our Covenant God.

(iii) *Thirdly, by our deportment and carriage towards him as our God in Covenant, we may notably discern that he is our Covenant God, and that we have so accepted him.*

Question: By what carriage of ours towards God, may this be discovered?

Answer: (a) By esteeming him as our God. (b) By loving him, as our God. (c) By trusting in him, as in our God. (d) By fearing him, as our God. (e) By serving him, as our God.

(a) *Do we esteem the Lord as our God?* None can have the Lord to be their God in covenant, who do not set him up and esteem him as their God. To esteem him as God, implies:

(1) **The truth of estimation.** When the Lord is accounted, esteemed and judged to be, as indeed he is, the only true God,[1068] and that all others are but

---

[1066] Book 2, Chapter 3, Aphorism 2, Corollary 3
[1067] In my *Believers' Evidences*, etc, Chapter 3, pp. 189-191.
[1068] 1 Corinthians 8:4-6, John 17:3

pretended, imaginary and false gods, idols, and nothing in the world. Thus the psalmist esteemed God: *I know that the LORD is great, and our Lord above all gods – the idols of the heathen are silver and gold, the work of men's hands. They have mouths but they speak not*, etc.[1069] Do we thus look upon all other deities mentioned in the world, as mere idols, fancies, lies, and vanities?

(2) **The height of estimation.** When the Lord is valued and esteemed as most excellent, absolutely supreme, and infinitely high over all beings and creatures in the world; infinitely above gold and silver, infinitely above honors, riches, and pleasures, infinitely above heaven and earth, men and angels, infinitely above all creatures and every name that is named both in this and the world to come – being *the king eternal, immortal, invisible, the only wise God; the blessed and only potentate, the king of kings, and Lord of Lords, who only hath immortality, dwelling in the light which no man can approach unto, whom no man hath seen nor can see.*[1070] When we esteem and prize him, as the only riches, the only portion, the only treasure; the only happiness, the only heaven. When we esteem and value our part and interest in him, in his love and favor in Christ, far beyond all our part and interest in any or all other created comforts and enjoyments: and upon deliberate choice, could freely part with whatsoever is dear to us, in the world, rather than with him alone. When we thus enthrone the Lord in highest esteem over all, we notably esteem him and accept him as our God. What we estimate over all, that we account and accept as our God.

(b) *Do we love him as our God?* Estimating is an act of the judgment; affecting is an act of the will and heart. Affection answers our estimation, and flows from it. If we esteem the Lord as our God, we cannot choose but desire, love and delight in the Lord as our God. That is, we shall love him wholly; we shall love him only.

[1069] Psalm 135:5, 15-18 & 115:3-9
[1070] 1 Timothy 1:17 & 6:15-16

(1) **We shall love the Lord wholly**, with all that is within us. *This is the first and great commandment; thou shalt love the Lord thy God with all thine heart, and with all thy soul, and with all thy might, and* (as our Savior adds) *with all thy mind.*[1071] When we once love the Lord as our God, we shall not reserve or divide our affections from him, but we shall turn the whole stream and united current of our affections towards him. We shall willingly let God have all, and think our all too little for him. Why? Because we esteem him as most desirable, most amiable, most delectable over all the world.[1072] Because he has loved us first – and that with an infinite love, when we were altogether loveless and loathsome.[1073] Therefore we owe him our whole love, for what is our love, to his love; or our all, to his all? Do we thus love him as our God, with an entire, perfect and whole love? Do our hearts turn wholly to him, as the needle to the pole, or loadstone? Do our affections flow wholly to him, as all the rivers flow towards the sea? This is a sign that he is our Covenant God indeed.

(2) **We shall love the Lord only**, so as to love none besides him with the like predominant and intensive love. When we truly love him as God, we in effect love nothing else but God. We love nothing else that stands in opposition against God. Not sin: *ye that love the LORD hate evil.*[1074] Not the world: *the love of this world is enmity against God*, etc.[1075] We love nothing else that comes in competition with God. We find more in our God, than in all things else. As David: *whom have I in heaven but thee? And there is none upon earth that I desire besides thee.*[1076] Our love to all inferior objects will be so small, that comparatively it may be counted as no love at all, yea as hatred to them.[1077] Do we thus love the Lord wholly and only as our God? Then the

---

[1071] Deuteronomy 6:5, Matthew 22:37-38, Luke 10:27
[1072] Psalm 73:25; 1 John 4:8, 16
[1073] 1 John 4:19
[1074] Psalm 97:10
[1075] James 4:4; 1 John 2:15
[1076] Psalm 73:25
[1077] Luke 14:26, Matthew 10:37

Lord is our God when we truly love God, we love all things in and for God, and with reference to God, namely: God in them. But contrariwise they that intensively love their belly over all, make their belly their God;[1078] love their pleasures over all, make their pleasures their God;[1079] love their gold, silver, children, anything over all, or above what is meet such creatures should be loved, make such things their God.[1080]

(c) ***Do we trust in the Lord as in our God?*** Then we trust in him, more than in all things else in the world. For, God is to be trusted in, rested and relied upon, more than all means, helps, refuges, or creatures whatsoever. None can so supply our wants, suppress our fears, remove our dangers, facilitate our difficulties, and bestead us in all deepest and desperate plunges, as God alone. He can do it with means, without means, contrary unto means. Therefore affiance, trust and confidence peculiarly belongs to God, as a special part of that homage and natural worship which is due to him by the first commandment.[1081] *Trust in the Lord with all thine heart.*[1082] *Trust in him at all times ye people,*[1083] etc. Trust and affiance in creatures, or in corruptions, or in anything besides the living God, is frequently forbidden and condemned. *Lean not to thine own understanding. – Trust not in the uncertainty of riches. – If riches increase, set not your hearts thereon. – Trust not in oppression. – It is better to trust in the Lord, than to put confidence in man: it is better to trust in the Lord, than to put confidence in princes.*[1084] Creature-confidence is a kind of idolatry; a putting creatures in God's stead. Hereupon God's faithful people have fled to their God as their only refuge and relief in straits and extremities, as having their saving interest in him only. Job said: *Though he slay me, yet will I trust in him.*[1085] Asa, being to encounter with the huge host of the

---

[1078] Philippians 3:19
[1079] 2 Timothy 3:4
[1080] Colossians 3:5
[1081] Exodus 20:3
[1082] Proverbs 3:5
[1083] Psalm 62:8
[1084] Proverbs 3:5; 1 Timothy 6:17, Psalm 62:10 & 118:9-10
[1085] Job 13:15

Ethiopians and Lubims, rested and relied only upon God.[1086] David expresses himself sweetly: *My soul, wait thou only upon God: for my expectation is from him. He only is my rock and my salvation; he is my defense, I shall not be moved. In God is my salvation and my glory: the rock of my strength, and my refuge is in God. Trust in him at all times,* etc.[1087] *What time I am afraid I will trust in thee.*[1088] And blessed Paul relating his trouble in Asia, says: *We were pressed out of measure, above strength, insomuch that we despaired even of life. But we had the sentence of death in ourselves, that we should not trust in ourselves, but in God, which raiseth the dead.*[1089] Thus God's covenant people, when they are themselves, make God their peculiar and only trust: in straits, difficulties, deep plunges and desperate extremities, to him alone they fly, and with him they, as it were, clothe themselves by faith. *The name of the LORD is a strong tower, the righteous fly unto it and are safe.*[1090] But those who are not God's true covenant people, in their exigence and extremities they trust not in God, fly not to him, but to other vanities and broken reeds. They trust in horses and chariots,[1091] in wealth and riches,[1092] in men and second causes,[1093] in oppression and perverseness,[1094] in idols and lying vanities,[1095] as the mariners in Jonah his ship in a storm, every man to his God, his paganish God, etc. Now what is our confidence and chief refuge in difficulties? Do we fly to God? Is he only our rock and salvation, etc? Then he is our God in covenant, who hath enabled us thus to carry ourselves towards him as to our God.

(d) ***Do we fear the Lord as our God?*** The Lord is his people's chief fear. The chief object of their fear. Hence he is called {*the fear of Isaac*}.[1096] And the

---

[1086] 2 Chronicles 14:11 & 16:8
[1087] Psalm 62:5-8
[1088] Psalm 56:3
[1089] 2 Corinthians 8:9-10
[1090] Proverbs 18:10
[1091] Psalm 20:7
[1092] Psalm 49:6, Proverbs 18:11, Jeremiah 49:4, Psalm 52:7
[1093] Isaiah 36:5-6
[1094] Isaiah 30:12
[1095] Isaiah 42:17, Jonah 1:5
[1096] Genesis 31:42, 53

psalmist says: *Vow and pay unto the LORD your God, let all that be round about him bring presents to **the fear**.*[1097] So the Hebrew ought to be translated. That is, to God the chief object of fear; who is the fear, the fear of fears. Such awe, dread and fear is in their hearts towards God, not slavish but childlike fear, that they fear nothing in the world like him; they are more afraid to offend him than to offend any prince, potentate, yea, or tyrant on earth. Their fear of him that can kill both body and soul, and cast them into hell, predominates over all other fears, prevails over them, eats them out, swallows them up as Moses' rod devoured the magicians' rods.[1098] Moses' parents hid him for three months so that he might not be destroyed, because fearing God they were not afraid of the king's commandment.[1099] Noah so feared God that he made an ark to save his house at God's command, not fearing what the world of the ungodly could do against him for such an undertaking.[1100] The three courageous Jews so feared God that they would not idolatrously worship Nebuchadnezzar's golden image: and in that case they feared not the kings threats, nor the burning fiery furnace into which they were cast. Daniel so feared God that he would not desist from his worshiping, calling upon, and praying to his God, as in former times; for any base fear of the king's decree, prince's malice, or cruelty of the den of lions into which he was to be cast.[1101] The apostles so feared God, that they could not but preach in the name of Jesus Christ, nor did they fear the prohibitions and threats of the elders, scribes and rulers on the contrary.[1102] This is to fear the Lord as God: when his fear is most prevalent and predominant in us over all other fear; when his fear more effectually preserves us from evil than the fear of any creature can push us upon the evil of sin; when his fear so strongly obliges us to duty, that no creature-fear can deter us from duty. Do we thus fear the Lord?

[1097] Psalm 76:11
[1098] Matthew 10:28, Isaiah 8:12-13
[1099] Hebrews 11:23
[1100] Hebrews 11:7
[1101] Daniel 3:13-19, etc.
[1102] Acts 4:17-21

(e) ***Do we serve the Lord as our God?*** The Lord's people are his servants, and they serve him.[1103] Yea they serve him, as God, as their God. This serving of the Lord as God, is very Comprehensive, and of large extent. It implies:

(1) **Their subjecting themselves to him**, to his will, dominion, laws, etc,[1104] As those that will be acted, ruled, ordered, commanded by him peculiarly: being delivered by him from subjection and thraldom to sin, Satan, etc.[1105] Such are said to serve him.

(2) **Their devoting, addicting and giving up themselves wholly to God** and his ways:[1106] not serving or addicting themselves, to sinful lusts and pleasures, to wine, to their bellies, to mammon, to the wills, placits [decrees or petitions], and humors of men in matters of religion, or to anything either in opposition against God, or in competition with God.[1107]

(3) **Their worshiping him as God** with all acts of religious worship both in public and in private, as also their pious, holy and religious conversation before God. Hence {*serving of God*} is frequently used in Scripture for worshiping God. As: *When thou hast brought forth this people out of Egypt, ye shall serve God upon this mountain.*[1108] That is: {*Ye shall worship God there*}. – *Thou shalt worship the LORD thy God, and him only shalt thou serve.*[1109] – *Anna departed not from the temple, but served the lord with fastings and prayers night and day.*[1110] {*Serving of God*} is also used for a pious and holy course of life. As: *That we being delivered out of the hands of our enemies without fear, might serve him, in holiness and righteousness before him all the days of our life.*[1111] This is called {*serving the Lord in newness of the Spirit*},[1112]

[1103] Revelation 22:3
[1104] 2 Chronicles 12:8, Psalm 2:11-12
[1105] Luke 1:74, Romans 6:6
[1106] 2 Corinthians 8:5, Matthew 6:24
[1107] Genesis 31:42, 53
[1108] Exodus 3:12 & 4:23 & 7:16 & 8:1, 20, Acts 7:7
[1109] Matthew 4:10, Luke 4:8
[1110] Luke 2:37
[1111] Luke 1:74-75
[1112] Romans 7:6; see also Romans 12:11 & 14:18; 1 Thessalonians 1:9; 2 Timothy 1:3

inasmuch as it proceedeth from the renewing Spirit. To this effect, those who fruitfully employ their talents which they receive from God, are styled {*good and faithful servants*} to their heavenly Master.[1113] Thus {*serving of God*} (not to mention anymore acceptations thereof) intimates, our subjecting ourselves unto God and his dominion; our addicting and devoting ourselves to him and his ways; our worshiping him religiously, and walking piously before him. And thus all God's people do serve their God, as Abraham,[1114] Job,[1115] David,[1116] Paul,[1117] etc. Do we thus serve the Lord, as God, as our God?

Hereby we may discover whether we serve our God aright, namely:

(1) **If we serve him reverently.** *Let us have grace, whereby we may serve God acceptably with reverence and godly fear.*[1118] – *Serve the LORD with fear.*[1119] Awful reverence and childlike fear, becomes the service of God. Yea, true serving of God and obedience to him arises from God's fear: *Only fear the LORD and serve him.*[1120] – *Fear God and keep his commandments.*[1121] Hereupon God acknowledges Job as his peculiar servant, in that he was a perfect and an upright man, one that feared God, and eschewed evil.[1122] Have we such a fear of God implanted in our hearts? Are we afraid to offend him? Have we high and reverential thoughts of him?

(2) **If we serve him obediently**, when we so serve him, as to obey him, do his will and keep his commandments: *If ye will fear the LORD, and serve him, and obey his voice, and not rebel against the mouth of the LORD,* etc.[1123] They that will not obey God, but rebel against his mouth and word, they serve not God, but Satan, sin, and their own lusts.

[1113] Matthew 25:14-15, 21, 23
[1114] Genesis 26:24
[1115] Job 1:8-9 & 2:3
[1116] Psalm 116:16
[1117] 2 Timothy 1:3
[1118] Hebrews 12:28
[1119] Psalm 2:11
[1120] 1 Samuel 12:24
[1121] Ecclesiastes 12:13
[1122] Job 1:8 & 2:3
[1123] 1 Samuel 12:14

(3) **If we serve him cheerfully, readily, and willingly**, from a principle and disposition of love which we bear to him and to his service. Thus David instructed Solomon: *And thou Solomon my son, know thou the God of thy Father, and serve him with a perfect heart, and with a willing mind.*[1124] Willingness and cheerfulness in God's service is most acceptable to him. It flows from true love to God. Whatsoever we do from love, we do cheerfully, delightfully. God first requires love, then service: *And now Israel, what doth the LORD thy God require of thee, but to fear the LORD thy God, to walk in all his ways, and to love him, and to serve the LORD thy God with all thy heart.*[1125] Are we volunteers in serving God? Are our hearts enlarged, delighted, lifted-up, like Jehoshaphat's, in the ways of God? Do we, with our blessed Savior, count it meat and drink to be doing God's will? etc.

(4) **If we serve him purely**. The Lord is infinite in purity and holiness, and requires purity and sincerity in all his servants and services.[1126] The pure in heart are blessed, and shall see God.[1127] He desires truth in the inwards.[1128] He will be worshiped in spirit and truth.[1129] There is a double purity with which we are to serve God; namely: [1] purity of heart and conscience within. When we regard not any guile, hypocrisy, or iniquity in our heart; we do not approve it, or allow it; it is not mingled or woven into the frame and constitution of our spirits: but we work it out and reject it, as lees, dregs, dross, and scum, etc.[1130] *The blood of Christ hath purged our conscience from dead works to serve the living God.*[1131] With such heart-purity, Paul served God: *I thank God, whom I serve from my forefathers with pure conscience.*[1132] [2] Purity of life and conversation without – when it is without scandal and hypocrisy; when we

---

[1124] 1 Chronicles 28:9
[1125] Deuteronomy 10:12 & 11:17
[1126] Habbakuk 1:13, Isaiah 6:3
[1127] Matthew 5:8
[1128] Psalm 51:6
[1129] John 4:24
[1130] Psalm 66:18
[1131] Hebrews 9:14
[1132] 2 Timothy 1:3

decline evil, and still approve ourselves in all our actions as in God's presence: *That we might serve him, in holiness and righteousness before him*. Hereupon God commends his servant Job, in that he was a *perfect and upright* man, *one that feared God, and eschewed evil*. He walked purely in the service of God. Do we serve the Lord with such purity of heart and life?

(5) **If we serve God only**. *Thou shalt worship the Lord thy God, and him only shalt thou serve*.[1133] How is the Lord only to be served? Thus: God only, is to be served with divine worship, and religious adoration.[1134] No idols or creatures may so be served; for that would be idolatry. God only is to be served primarily and for himself – he alone having supreme dominion and sovereignty over us, and over our consciences. Others may be served secondarily, and in subordination to God. But nothing may be served which stands either in opposition to him, or competition with him. We must so serve God, as not to serve sin, lusts, pleasures, Satan, mammon, etc.

(6) **If we serve God wholly and entirely**, with the whole stream of our united faculties and affections – and that in all acts of service which he requires from us. This is the integrity and perfection of God's service, discovering the truth of it. [1] The integrity of the object: when we serve him fully; walking in all his ways, having respect to his commandments, without indenting, reserving, or omitting.[1135] [2] The integrity of the subject: when we serve him with a perfect heart.[1136] That is, when we serve the Lord our God with all our heart, and with all our soul.[1137] When the heart is not parted and divided between God and sin, God and the world, etc. But it is united and wholly carried to God alone.

(7) **Finally, if we serve God continually**, all the days of our life.[1138] Counterfeit serving of God is but for a time, and then vanishes. The hypocrite

---

[1133] Matthew 4:10, Luke 4:8
[1134] Deuteronomy 6:13
[1135] Deuteronomy 10:12, Psalm 119:6
[1136] 1 Chronicles 28:9
[1137] Deuteronomy 10:12 & 11:13; 1 Samuel 12:24
[1138] Luke 1:75

will not always pray, not always obey, etc., but God's sincere servants are constant and persevering.[1139] Hannah *served God with fastings and prayers night and day*.[1140]

By these three sorts of evidences, we may groundedly discover whether the Lord is our Covenant God or not, according to the New Covenant, and consequently, whether we are actually and effectually brought into a good New Covenant condition.

[1139] Job 27:10
[1140] Luke 2:37

{Question 2}: Have we become God's people in covenant?

That we are God's true and sincere covenant people, we may evidence to our own hearts and consciences by these three ways, namely:

(i) *By the mystery and nature of this being God's people, formerly described.* To be a people to God in covenant, has in it five things principally. It implies they are God's people only, etc., as has been manifested.[1141] Now search and consider: (a) are we God's people only, by peculiar appropriation? Not sins: not the world's; not Satan's; not our own. (b) Are we God's people by covenant, profession and denomination? (c) Are we his in and through Jesus Christ? (d) Are we his in all relations? (e) Are we God's people wholly and entirely; in all we are, have, can do, or endure? Let us consider these things thoroughly according to the several explanations of them here alleged.

(ii) By the adjuncts or properties peculiarly belonging to God's true covenant-people. These properties, I have heretofore briefly pointed at in twelve particulars.[1142] And also, in the former branch of this present inference, have more fully explained the first eight of them. Have we these properties in ourselves? (a) Are we inwardly and effectually called? (b) Are we a holy, select, and separated people? Etc.

(iii) By our due deportment towards God as becomes his covenant-people. This due deportment or carriage of God's people towards God, as his people, has been unfolded in five particulars at large in the former branch of this present inference. (a) Do we esteem the Lord as our God? (b) Do we love him, as our God? Etc. These two last sorts of discoveries, do evidence our

---

[1141] Book 3, Chapter 4, Aphorism 4, Section 2; and Book 2, Chapter 2, Aphorism 2, Section 3

[1142] Book 3, Chapter 4, Aphorism 4, Section 2

covenant-state, in regard to both the branches of this glorious promise, namely: that the Lord is our God, and also, that we are his people.

But this may suffice for probation.

[Matter 3]: *Exhortation*

Here is singular matter for exhortation. Does the Lord promise and covenant to and with all his sincere New Covenant federates, that he will be to them a God, and they shall be to him a people? Then here is a threefold word of exhortation, namely: (i) to those in the visible church that are strangers to an inward saving New Covenant state; (ii) to all that are of the number of sincere federates with God in this New Covenant; and (iii) To the faithful ministers of the New Testament.[1143]

(i) **First, a word to all those in the visible church, that hitherto are mere strangers to an inward and saving New Covenant condition** (And such are all those: (a) who are in their unregenerate state, having no effectual inscription of God's law in their minds and hearts; (b) who are grossly ignorant of God and all the things of God; (c) whose sins through their unbelief and impenitency, have found no remission from the Lord).[1144]

All such, I earnestly exhort and beseech, sincerely and speedily to take hold of God's New Covenant, to accept and embrace it; in the life and spirit of it, as well as in the letter; in the inward power, efficacy and reality of it, as well as in the outward profession, name and formality thereof: if ever they desire savingly to have the Lord to be their God, and themselves to be his people. Oh, ponder upon this seriously, in the morning when you rise up, in the evening when you lie down to sleep; when you are in the house, and when you are in the field; commune with your own hearts, and ask your own souls, each of you, these few questions.

[1143] 2 Corinthians 3:6
[1144] Hebrews 8:10-12, Jeremiah 31:33-34

(a) O my soul, is there any true happiness or salvation actually to be enjoyed by you, until you are effectually brought into New Covenant with God? Is not this the only happiness, to have the Lord your God in covenant, and you yourself to be one of his people; and can you be thus happy? Will God be yours? Can you be his, until his laws are written effectually in your mind and heart? Until you know the Lord savingly? Until all your sins are forgiven and forgotten by God forever?

(b) O my soul, have you not thus far to this very hour contented yourself with a mere outward profession, form, name, and shadow of a New Covenant state, without all inward life and substance? And can this ever carry you beyond the condition of a hypocrite, reprobate, and castaway? Do not the greatest number by far of visible Christians deceive and undo themselves eternally, by resting in the mere visibles and externals of the New Covenant; and will you perish with them also? Will you have so much part in the New Covenant only as to leave thee without excuse, and aggravate your condemnation?

(c) O my soul, can you judge it safe to delay or put off your acceptance of a New Covenant state in the inward efficacy, power, life and spirit thereof, for another week, for another day? What if you are snatched by death out of your body before this great work is done? What if God knocks no more at the door of your heart by his Spirit and word, offers you no more softening and converting grace? Yea, what if he gives you up to final hardness in impenitence and unbelief before this work is done – are you not then quite undone to all eternity?

(d) O my soul, will not a real, inward, efficacious New Covenant condition, immediately vest you with this matchless happiness: the Lord will be to you a God, and you shall be to him one of his people?[1145] Will the Lord be to you a God? Then the Lord will be to you more sweet than all your sins and sinful pleasures, more rich than all earthly treasures and enjoyments, more

---

[1145] Hebrews 8:10-12, Jeremiah 31:33-34

honorable than all worldly dignities, more sure and faithful than all your friends and relations in the world; yea more than earth, more than heaven, more than grace, more than glory. Then, the Lord will be all, and above all unto you. Beyond him, nothing can be promised, or performed by God; nothing can be desired or enjoyed by you. Do you lack God? Nothing can make you happy. Do you have God? Nothing can make you miserable. Again, shall you be to him one of his people? Then, you shall not be your own any longer, to be misled by self-delusions; you shall not be the worlds any longer, to be cheated with perishing vanities; you shall not be Satan's any longer, to be led captive at his will by his temptations;[1146] you shall not be sin's any longer, to be enthralled under its guilt and dominion; you shall not be death's any longer, to be exposed unto curse or condemnation. You are and shall be God's for your eternal bliss and salvation. O who would not accept God's New Covenant in inward power and efficacy, wherein he shall thus accept God, and thus be accepted of God? No motives can be more moving, no reasons can be more persuading, and no arguments can be more compelling.

(ii) **Secondly, a word to all that are of the number of God's sincere federates within this New Covenant.** The Lord has brought you and placed you (as once Adam at first) in a very paradise, when he brought you into this New Covenant, for as Adam sweetly enjoyed God in paradise: so you as sweetly in Christ enjoy God in this New Covenant: *I will be to them a God*. And God enjoyed, was the supreme glory of that paradise, and of this covenant. Nay, what if I say that this New Covenant is beyond that paradise? For in that paradise, God was enjoyed but a while; in this New Covenant, God shall be enjoyed, and that forever. In that paradise Adam enjoyed God, but speedily lost him: in this New Covenant ye so enjoy him, that you shall never lose him. Here's a mystery: man has not lost his paradise, but changed it – yea, changed it for a better, that shall never be lost. This New Covenant is that

---

[1146] 2 Timothy 2:26

better paradise, wherein the federates having tasted of the tree of life, Christ Jesus, shall enjoy their good God always. O give me that paradise, wherein I may never lose my God, the glory, and crown, and paradise of paradise.

Now O all you who are savingly instated in the spiritual paradise of this New Covenant, and have the Lord your God, and are his people indeed: be persuaded: (a) to live upon this promise, (b) to live up to this promise, and (c) to bring (what lies in you) all your near and dear allies and relations within this New Covenant effectually, that they may with you partake the blessed fullness and influence of this promise.

(a) *Live upon this promise*. If there is food and matter of life for the soul by faith in any promise of the blessed Bible, it is in this glorious New Covenant promise: *I will be to them a God, and they shall be to me a people.*[1147] Should I be put to point out one promise only in all the holy Scriptures, whereupon I would repose my soul with fullest satisfaction; whereon I would daily feed with sweetest delight; wherewith I would enlarge, raise and ravish my heart with richest consolations; whereby I would steel my spirit against all spiritual maladies, fill my spirit with all complete felicities, and assure my spirit of eternal salvation – this, this alone should be that phoenix promise among all the promises.

(1) This promise has free grace in it, for the mere good-pleasure of God's will is the motive of it: *I will be their God*. (2) This promise has effectual vocation, sanctification, justification, and communion with God in it, for otherwise, how can we be God's people? (3) This promise has all mercy and consolation in it, for he that will be our God is the Father of tender mercies, and the God of all consolation.[1148] (4) This promise has Christ in it: for the Lord is savingly a God to none, nor are any sincerely a people to God, but only in Jesus Christ through faith. (5) This promise has the Spirit of God and of Christ in it, for, actually and effectually, we become God's people by the

---

[1147] Hebrews 8:10
[1148] 2 Corinthians 1:3

operation of the Spirit of God and of Christ only.[1149] (6) This promise has God in it: for herein the Lord says: {*I will be to them a God*}. (7) This promise consequently, has all temporals, all spirituals, and all eternals in it, for that Lord that freely gives his Christ, his Spirit, and himself to us to be our God, who is best of all things, *how shall he not with himself freely give us all things*? Now therefore you that art actually and effectually within this blessed promise, live upon it, feed upon it, rest upon it, dwell upon it: in your prosperity, in your adversity; in your strength, in your weakness; in your health, in your sickness; in your triumphs, in your trials and temptations; in your fullness, in your wants; in your joys, in your griefs; in your comforts, in your disconsolations; in your youth, in your age; in your life, and in your death.

(i) What distresses will not this promise allay; the Father of mercies being your God?[1150] (ii) What discomforts will not this promise remove; the God of all consolation being your God?[1151] (iii) What wants will not this promise supply; the possessor of heaven and earth being your God?[1152] (iv) What enemies will not this promise overthrow; God all-sufficient, the Lord of Hosts, being your God?[1153] (v) What sins will not this promise subdue; the God of pardons being your God?[1154] (vi) What grace and glory will not this promise assure; the God of all grace; the author of every good and perfect gift therein assuring you that he will be your God?[1155] (vii) And, what doubts, scruples or difficulties about your eternal salvation, will not this promise resolve and satisfy? Seeing this promise lets you know, (1) that the Lord will be your God: and what cannot God do for you?[1156] (2) That you shall be one of his people;

[1149] 2 Corinthians 6:16-18 with Ephesians 2:21-22, Romans 8:2, 14, 16; 1 John 3:24
[1150] 2 Corinthians 1:3
[1151] 2 Corinthians 1:3
[1152] Genesis 14:22
[1153] Genesis 17:1, Psalm 46:7, 11
[1154] Nehemiah 9:17
[1155] 1 Peter 5:10, James 1:17
[1156] Genesis 18:14

and what can creatures do against you?[1157] (3) That both these God freely promises, because he will: and then no unworthiness of yours shall hinder the inchoation of your happiness. (4) That both these God will faithfully perform, because he hath freely promised and undertaken both for himself and his federates: and then no infirmity, impotency or weakness of your shall ever hinder the consummation of your happiness. Therefore live, O live still upon this lively promise; that you mayst live evermore. Let your mind live upon it, by contemplation: let your conscience live upon it, by pacification: let your will live upon it, by contentation [being content]; let your heart and affections live upon it, by exhilaration.

(b) *Live up unto this promise*. This promise is most sweet, full, high, holy, comfortable, etc; let thy life and conversation be answerable.

The Lord is your covenant God. Oh, live as one possessing such a God. Live not carnally, but spiritually. Live not earthly, but heavenly.[1158] Live not so much below, as above.[1159] Live not scandalously, but inoffensively towards God and man.[1160] Live not sordidly, but generously. Live not murmuringly, distrustfully, and disconsolately; but contentedly, believingly and comfortably.[1161] Live not as swine, on husks below; but as angels, on this manna which is above. Live not like those who are without covenant, without Christ, without hope, and without God in this world; but as those that are effectually in covenant, full of Christ, full of hope, and full of God.[1162] So live, you who have the Lord to be your God, that it may appear that God lives in you, and that you are primarily acted, guided, enabled, over-powered, upheld, and comforted by the Lord your God.

You are one of his covenant people; O live as one possessed by such a God. And therefore: (1) disclaim sin, the world, and Satan; (2) know God more

---

[1157] Romans 8:31, 33-34, Hebrews 13:5-6
[1158] Philippians 3:20
[1159] Colossians 3:1
[1160] Acts 24:16
[1161] Hebrews 13:5, Galatians 2:20, Acts 9:31
[1162] Ephesians 2:12

clearly and experimentally; (3) endear your heart to God sincerely and intensively; (4) fear, serve, and obey God uprightly, universally and continually; (5) walk with God in holy communion; (6) stand for God, and take his part against all opposition; (7) and advance God's glory over all for his admirable virtues expressed in your effectual vocation, for these are proper and peculiar duties of God's covenant people, as I have heretofore more at large demonstrated.[1163]

(c) *Labor (what lies within you) to interest and engage all your near allies and dear relations in this New Covenant effectually*, that they with you may partake of the unparalleled influence of this promise abundantly. Has the Lord become savingly your God in covenant, and do you not desire that he may also become the Covenant-God of your husband, wife, parents, children, and (if it were possible) of all your endeared relations? Have you found such a blissful advantage, by becoming one of God's covenant people. and do you not heartily wish that all your allies were altogether herein as you are, except your infirmities? Oh then, commend this New Covenant unto them frequently, magnify the treasures of it highly, display the glory and fullness of this chief promise pathetically, urge them to press after an inward New Covenant condition sincerely, etc, that the Lord may be their God, and they his people eternally.

(iii) **Thirdly and lastly, here is a word of quickening to the faithful ministers of the New Testament.** Your office is to be ministers of the New Covenant, or New Testament;[1164] O strive to be ministers of the Spirit, not of the letter. It is your singular honor and privilege to be preachers of God's New Covenant, which excels all former covenants; oh, lay out your chief skill, strength and diligence, in disclosing the glory and perfections of this New Covenant, and especially of this paramount promise of the New Covenant to

---

[1163] In Book 3, Chapter 3, Aphorism 3, Section 1
[1164] 2 Corinthians 3:6

all the flock; in persuading them to embrace unfeignedly the inward spirit of this Covenant. Then they know indeed, when they understand the New Covenant solidly; then they believe indeed, when they embrace the New Covenant unfeignedly; then they live indeed, when they live upon, and live up unto the New Covenant experimentally; then they are Christians indeed, and happy indeed, when the Lord is their Covenant God, and they his covenant people reciprocally and effectually.

But hitherto of exhortation.

[Matter 4]: *Consolation*

Lastly, here is wonderful matter for consolation. Here is manna from heaven here's honey indeed out of the bowels of the lion. Here is a golden mine, a living spring, a spacious sea of consolation, to all God's true covenant-people, that the Lord is their God, and they his people, according to this New Covenant in Jesus Christ! And this against all the grounds of discomfort which principally are wont to afflict and sadden their hearts, namely: {1} relics of inherent corruption, {2} fears and dangers of apostasy, {3} outward or inward wants, {4} strong and violent temptations, {5} sad and dismaying desertions, {6} sharp afflictions and persecutions, and {7} the very terrors and pangs of death itself! The comfort of this grand promise against all these seven disconsolations comes now to be enlarged, as formerly I promised.[1165]

{1} **What an impregnable comfort may this be to each of God's true covenant people, against all relics of inherent sin and corruption remaining in them: that the Lord is their Covenant God.**

Though they are sanctified throughout in soul, spirit and body; in all the faculties and affections of the soul, and in all the senses and members of the body: yet in all these they are but sanctified in part.[1166] As in every of them there is some spirit, so there remains some flesh (Galatians 5:17). As there is a spiritual law in their mind, so there is a carnal law in their members: and this ofttimes captivates them to the law of sin.[1167] So that, the good they would do, that they do not: and the evil they would not, that they do. Yet not they, as sanctified: but sin that dwells in them, so far as unsanctified.[1168] Hence, how

---
[1165] Book 3, Chapter 3, Aphorism 3, Section 1
[1166] 1 Thessalonians 5:23
[1167] Romans 7:23
[1168] Romans 7:18-19

often do they suspect their spiritual condition, that all is unsound, all is hypocrisy, their condition worse than the condition of any; none of God's people so hard-hearted, unbelieving, impenitent, hypocritical, and every way so wretched as themselves. Hereupon, how do they break their hearts with sighs and groans! How do their eyes pour out tears to God! How do they cry out and lament: "Oh when shall all these cursed Canaanites be cast out and subdued? When shall all these iniquities be cast into the bottom of the sea? When shall this old leaven be purged out; when shall this body of sin and death, and this old man be destroyed? When shall neither spot nor wrinkle, nor any such thing remain in us; when shall we sin no more; o wretches that we are, who shall deliver us from the body of this death?[1169] Oh! When shall we be secured of a good spiritual estate?!"

Yet against all these remains of sin and corruption, every true believer may comfort himself by this New Covenant, assuring him in Christ's blood that the Lord is his Covenant God forever, and this, principally three ways:

(i) The Lord is their New Covenant God, and they his people, therefore in Christ, he has blotted out all their iniquities, and will remember them no more.[1170] He will not upbraid them with them, nor impute them to them: because he is their God in covenant. This is clear by the tenor of the New Covenant. Satan, wicked men, and their own mis-deeming hearts may impute them to them, and cast them in their face: but God himself will not impute them to them, nor remember them anymore. Christ says: *Thou art all fair, my love, there is no spot in thee.*[1171] How sweet is their comfort! *Who shall lay anything to the charge of God's elect? It is God that justifieth, who is he that condemneth? It is Christ that died, yea rather that is risen again, who is even at the right hand of God, who also maketh intercession for us.*[1172]

[1169] Romans 7:24
[1170] Jeremiah 31:34, Hebrews 8:12 & 10:16-18
[1171] Song of Solomon 4:7, Hebrews 8:12
[1172] Romans 8:33-34

(ii) The Lord is their Covenant God, and they his people, therefore in Christ, by his Spirit, he is daily writing his laws in their minds and hearts; daily sanctifying and cleansing them: *that he may present them to himself glorious at last, not having spot or wrinkle, or any such thing, but that they should be holy and without blemish*.[1173] So that though many relics of sin remain in them, yet they are daily wasting, weakening, consuming, decaying, dying, like the house of Saul, which waxed weaker and weaker, until it was totally abolished. At death, all the inherent and actual sins of the righteous totally cease;[1174] their spirits being then made perfect,[1175] and eternally freed from all corruptions and imperfections.[1176] Pharaoh and his host were strong and terrible, to frighten and trouble Israel; but Israel's God was stronger to drown them all in the bottom of the Red Sea. The remains of sin are strong and dismaying to perplex and grieve the saints, but their Covenant God is stronger, to subdue their iniquities, *and thou wilt cast all their sins into the depths of the sea. Thou wilt perform the truth to Jacob, and the mercy to Abraham, which thou hast sworn unto our fathers from the days of old*.[1177] What a comfort is this that our God will utterly extirpate every sin, and completely obliterate every spot, wrinkle and shadow of corruption?

(iii) The Lord is their Covenant God, and they his people notwithstanding all the remains of corruption. Relics of sin cannot destroy or disturb their covenant-relation to God, nor their covenant communion with God. What sweet fellowship had Noah, Abraham, Isaac, Jacob, Moses, David, etc. with God in covenant, notwithstanding all their inherent sins and infirmities? Their sins shall not separate them from their Covenant God: their Covenant God will separate them from all their sins.

[1173] Song of Solomon 4:7, Hebrews 8:12
[1174] Romans 6:7
[1175] Hebrews 12:23
[1176] 1 Corinthians 13:10
[1177] Micah 7:19-20

{2} What a comfort is this to all Abraham's true seed against all fears or dangers of apostasy!

Their graces infused are but weak, their corruptions remaining are strong, their temptations fierce and violent, their difficulties which they wrestle withal in the way to heaven are not a few, The gate to life is exceeding strait, many miss it, few enter; hereupon they are apt to faint and be discouraged; they shall not holdout, they shall fall away, they shall not persevere faithful to the death.[1178]

But oh, you of little faith, and much fear, are you in covenant with God, and do you question your perseverance? Consider well:

(i) The Lord is your Covenant God, and you are one of his true covenant people. Did the Lord ever cast off, or suffer to fall away any one of his true covenant people? And will he now begin with you? With him is no variableness nor shadow of turning.[1179] His gifts of effectual calling are without repentance.[1180] He may suffer you to fall, to fall frequently, to fall foully, to fall from some sense of comfort, from some degrees of grace, for your further caution, confirmation and spiritual advantage, but totally and finally, he will never suffer you to fall away or perish, because he is your God in covenant. For then his Covenant should fail forevermore.

(ii) The Lord's New Covenant is a covenant of his own establishment in Christ's blood;[1181] and what God has established in Christ's blood, who or what shall overthrow?

(iii) God's New Covenant is an everlasting covenant.[1182] And an everlasting covenant has no end: from an everlasting covenant there can be no apostasy or total backsliding.

[1178] Luke 13:23
[1179] James 1:17
[1180] Romans 11:29
[1181] Jeremiah 31:31-34, Hebrews 8:8-13, Luke 22:20
[1182] Hebrews 13:20

(iv) The Lord God in his New Covenant with his people undertakes for both parties; and their reciprocal constancy in covenant one to another, as once he did for his captives.[1183] *And I will make an everlasting covenant with them, that I will not turn away from them, to do them good; but I will put my fear in their hearts, that they shall not depart from me.* So in this New Covenant, God says: *I will be to them a God, and they shall be to me a people.* He undertakes for himself, and for us. In other covenants and contracts, the several parties undertake only for themselves severally: in the marriage covenant the husband undertakes not both for himself and his wife, nor the wife for herself and her husband; but the husband undertakes only for himself, and the wife only for herself, to be constantly faithful. But God in his New Covenant with his people is pleased to be an extraordinary undertaker altogether. He undertakes for both sides, both for himself and for his people: for himself, that he will be theirs; for his people, that they shall be his. So that the faithful God himself, who cannot possibly lie; the all-powerful God, who is fully able to perform what he promises; he has engaged himself strongly for his people's constancy and perseverance towards him, so that in this regard there is no place left for utter apostasy, no possibility of total and final falling away from him and his grace, because he is their Covenant God.

{3} What a comfort is this to all Abraham's true seed against all outward or inward wants, and consequently, against all discontents and perplexities thence arising!

Has the Lord become your God by this everlasting New Covenant?

How may this comfort and quiet your spirit against all outward wants? Do you lack food or raiment, credit or wealth, strength or health? Do you lack liberty, lands, livings, house, harbor, friends, kindred, children, or any other near and dear relations? Yea, perhaps you lack these things, while your

---

[1183] Jeremiah 32:40 with Jeremiah 31:31-34 & Hebrews 8:8-13

enemies, while the wicked of the world flow and overflow with them.[1184] Yet you have an enjoyment beyond all these wants: the Lord is your God by an everlasting New Covenant. Therefore look not down so much at your wants, as look up to your enjoyment, to your God, and comfort yourself, for:

(i) *Your God is your all.* The Lord being your God in covenant, is instead of all supplies unto you: your health in sickness, your strength in weakness, your ease in pain and torments, your honor in dishonor, your glory in reproaches, your wealth in poverty, your friend in friendlessness, your habitation in harborlessness, your enlargement in bondage, your cordial and strength of heart, when heart and strength fail;[1185] yea your very life, in the valley of the shadow of death. Solomon says: *a feast is made for laughter, and wine maketh glad the life: but money answereth all things.*[1186] Feasts and wine, meat, and drink, though in the number of externals most necessary, yet have but a peculiar and limited usefulness; but money, being an instrument and means of commerce, that has a general use, and answers to all things. Money feeds, clothes, heals, honors, befriends, sets at liberty, procures all necessary moveables, purchases houses, lands, manours, makes war, and makes peace, etc. But God's covenant people may much more fully, say, their God answers all things. Money answers all things, but respectively, restrictively, finitely, and with many limitations; but their God answers all things absolutely, unlimitedly, infinitely without all exception.

(ii) *Your God is much more to you, than anything you lack.* Why then should you repine or murmur at your wants? When Hannah was greatly distressed through her barrenness and want of children, Elkanah her husband thus comforted her: *Hannah, why weepest thou? And why eatest thou not? And why is your heart grieved? Am not I better to you than ten sons?*[1187] How much more may every true New Covenant federate comfort himself against all his

---

[1184] Job 21;7, etc, Psalm 73:2-3, etc
[1185] Psalm 73:25-26
[1186] Ecclesiastes 10:19
[1187] 1 Samuel 1:5-8

wants, saying: O my soul, why are you cast down? Why are you so disquieted within me? Why do I weep, and grieve, and take on for want of these externals? Is not the Lord, my God? And is not my God more to me than ten Elkanahs; than ten thousand earthly enjoyments? What Augustine said of Job, may be said of every true believer that has the Lord for his God, against all his wants and losses: "A righteous man shipwrecked escapes rich and naked."[1188] Holy Job was full of these riches. Nothing remained in his house, all those things perished at one blow by which he was thought to be rich a little before; suddenly he sits down as a beggar upon the dunghill, abounding with worms from head to feet. What more miserable than this misery? What more happy than his inward happiness? He had lost all those things which God had given him: but he had him, who gave all things, God himself.

Consider well, O Christian: if you had all those earthly treasures, which you lack, or which this whole world can afford: yet your God in covenant is infinitely more to you than them all, for:

(a) Your God is more desirable, amiable and delightful to you than them all. He is the supreme good; the only essential and primitive good.[1189] These things are scarce drops and shadows of his goodness; infinitely inferior to him. He therefore is infinitely desirable before them.

(b) Your God is more influential and comfortable to you, than they all. All the influence, comfort and benefit that these things afford you, it is merely from God and his blessing. Without him, it is not in food to nourish, in physic

---

[1188] "Iustus enim naufragus evadit dives et nudus. His divitiis plenus erat Sanctus Iob. Nihil in domo remanserat, omnia uno ictu perlerunt, quibus opulentus paulo ante videbatur; subito mendicus in stercore sedet; a capite us{que} ad pedes vermibus scatens. Quid ista miseria miserius? Quid interiore felicitate felicius? Perdiderat omnia illa quae dederit Deus; Sed habebat ipsum qui omnia dederat Deum." August. *De Tempore*, Serm. 105. (Basil, 1569)
Also: [https://www.augustinus.it/latino/discorsi/discorso_498_testo.htm] <Accessed 4/13/2024> &
[http://www.monumenta.ch/latein/text.php?tabelle=Augustinus&rumpfid=Augustinus,%20Sermones,%2011,%20%20%2034&level=4&domain=&lang=0&links=&inframe=1&hide_apparatus=] <Accessed 4/15/2024>
[1189] Matthew 19:17

to heal, in clothes to warm, in beds to refresh, in houses and gardens to delight, in friends to comfort, in strongholds or armies to defend, etc. And with him anything shall serve turn. Gideon and Israel shall be defended against the Midianites with lamps and earthen pitchers;[1190] Daniel and his companions shall be best liking with coarsest pulse;[1191] the blind man shall recover sight by clay and spittle put upon his eyes,[1192] etc.

(c) Your God is more satisfying and contenting to you than they all. They all have a vanity and an emptiness in them, and cannot fill you; they have a disproportion to your soul, and cannot satisfy you. You may have much of them; but never enough, though you had them all. But your God is all-sufficient.[1193] He can fill all your desires to the full, and make them overflow. Having him, you shall have enough – yea, you have all.

(d) Your God is more constant and continuing to you than they all. They vanish and crumble away, and then all your small comforts and contentments in them vanish also. But your God continues to you forever; and therefore he is the most constant and lasting consolation.

(iii) *Your God can and will, so far as is good for you, supply all your wants, in the fittest season, because he is your God.* He can *do all things.*[1194] He is able to do for us *exceeding abundantly above all that we can ask or think.*[1195] And he has promised, that, *they that fear the Lord shall not want any good thing;*[1196] *The LORD will give grace and glory: and no good thing will he withhold from them that walk uprightly.*[1197] Why then should you be troubled at your wants? Say with David: *the LORD is my shepherd, I shall not want*[1198] – yea, say rather: "The Lord is my Covenant God, I shall not want." He can

---

[1190] Judges 7
[1191] Daniel 1:12, 15
[1192] John 9:67
[1193] Genesis 17:1
[1194] Job 42:1-2
[1195] Ephesians 3:20
[1196] Psalm 34:9-10
[1197] Psalm 84:11
[1198] Psalm 23:1

and will give you every good thing. He has given himself to you; how shall he then deny you anything? If you lack anything, either it is because he sees it not good for you, or because it is not yet good for you. God's time is the best time for receiving mercies.

(iv) *Your God can so sanctify and bless your want of outward blessings, that your want of them shall be a far greater advantage to you than your enjoyment of them*. Outward wants:

(a) Sometimes become occasions of inward wealth. *Hearken my beloved brethren, hath not God chosen the poor of this world rich in faith, and heirs of the kingdom, which he has promised to them that love him?*[1199]

(b) Sometimes they draw forth the faith and graces of the saints to more lively exercise and activity. Abraham's long want of a son by Sarah, greatly improved his faith and expectation on God, so that his faith thereupon became so famous throughout the world, that he is counted the father of the faithful. Had Abraham not been exercised so long with the want of a son, his faith in God's promise would never have been so renowned.

(c) Sometimes they minister occasion to God's extraordinary provisions and providence for his people. When Israel was in many wants in the wilderness, then was God's time to furnish them extraordinarily. The heavens rained them bread;[1200] the rock of flint ran water for them;[1201] their garments waxed not old;[1202] their feet did not swell for forty years together.[1203] When Elijah in the famine wanted ordinary food, God appointed the very ravens to seed him with bread and flesh morning and evening.[1204]

(d) Sometimes outward wants are God's opportunities of drawing nearer to his people by secret supports, sensible comforts, sweet refreshments, and reviving experiences of his peculiar presence, assistance and light of his

---

[1199] James 2:5
[1200] Psalm 105:40, Exodus 16
[1201] Exodus 17:6, Numbers 20:11, Psalm 105:41, Deuteronomy 8:3, 15, Psalm 114:8
[1202] Deuteronomy 8:4
[1203] Deuteronomy 8:4
[1204] 1 Kings 17:4, 6

countenance. Hence John Bradford – lacking his liberty, and being in prison – said: "God does thus punish me, nay, rather in punishing, blesses me."[1205] And indeed I thank him more of this prison, than of any parlor – yea, than of any pleasure that ever I had, for in it I find God my most sweet, good God always." Thus, if the Lord be your God in covenant, this may be your universal comfort against all outward wants.

How comfortable may this be also against all your inward wants? As Israel of old in the wilderness, so the Israel of God in the wilderness of this world are in an imperfect, unsettled and wanting state. Nor have they only outward, but also inward wants, to exercise and afflict them. They want [lack] degrees of graces, assurance, and evidence of their good spiritual state; the light of God's countenance, peace of conscience, comforts of the Holy Spirit, strength in the inward man against corruptions and temptations, and for all spiritual undertakings, etc. And because of these defects, they are ofttimes much discouraged, and drive on very heavily towards heaven. Now if the Lord be your God in covenant, this may abundantly comfort you against all these inward wants, for:

(1) Your Covenant God is fully able to supply all these your inward wants. He is the God of all grace: and can bestow all grace for kind and degree upon you.[1206] He that gave such faith to Abraham,[1207] such meekness to Moses,[1208] such patience to Job,[1209] such zeal and uprightness to David,[1210] such wisdom to Daniel,[1211] such love to John,[1212] such courage and self-denial to Paul,[1213] etc., is fully able to do as much for you. He gives his own Spirit to us, *that we*

[1205] John Foxe, *Acts and Monuments*, Volume 3, Epistle to his Mother
[1206] 1 Peter 3:10
[1207] Romans 4:16, etc.
[1208] Numbers 12:3
[1209] James 5:11
[1210] Psalm 84:1-2, etc & 18:22
[1211] Daniel 5:11-12
[1212] John 21:20
[1213] Acts 20:24 & 21:13, Philippians 3

might know the things which are freely given to us of God.[1214] Even *his Spirit of adoption, which witnesseth with our spirits that we are the children of God; which sealeth us, and is the earnest of our inheritance.*[1215] He is *the God of peace,*[1216] whose *peace passeth all understanding*, whereby he can keep our hearts in the knowledge and love of God.[1217] And if he gives peace, who can give trouble?[1218] He is the God of all consolation,[1219] and can give more comforts than we can have discomforts. He can fill with joy and peace in believing.[1220] Yea, he can send the comforter himself into our hearts to abide with us forever.[1221] Finally, he by his divine power can give us all things pertaining to life and godliness;[1222] can grant us according to the riches of his glory to be strengthened with might by his spirit in the inward man;[1223] and can bless us with all spiritual blessings in heavenly things in Christ.[1224] He is God: therefore he can easily do all these things, and so supply all our wants.

(2) Your Covenant God will daily supply these wants, and at last set you in a state of perfection above them all. For: [1] he has in this life prepared such spiritual supplies and blessings for them that love him, as are utterly beyond all carnal men's capacity of apprehension.[1225] [2] He has promised to give grace and glory, and to withhold no good thing from them that walk uprightly.[1226] And in the tenor of his Covenant, he has promised explicitly to furnish his covenant people with knowledge, repentance, renovation, the fear of the Lord, the spirit of the Lord, perseverance, etc., implicitly to furnish them with all

---

[1214] 1 Corinthians 12:2
[1215] Romans 8:15-16
[1216] Hebrews 13:20
[1217] Philippians 4:7
[1218] Job 34:27
[1219] 2 Corinthians 13
[1220] Romans 15:13
[1221] John 14:16-17
[1222] 2 Peter 1:3
[1223] Ephesians 3:14-16
[1224] Ephesians 1:3
[1225] 1 Corinthians 2:9
[1226] Psalm 84:11

things that pertain to godliness, in that he promises to be their God.[1227] [3] He has ordained and given *apostles, prophets, evangelists, pastors and teachers for the perfecting of the saints, for the work of the ministry, for the edifying of the body of Christ: until we all come in the unity of the faith, and of the knowledge of the Son of God, unto a perfect man, unto the measure of the stature of the fullness of Christ.*[1228] [4] He has built us *upon the foundation of the apostles and prophets, Jesus Christ himself being the chief cornerstone: in whom all the building fitly framed together, groweth unto an holy temple in the Lord. And though now we do but know in part*, etc.[1229] *Yet when that which is perfect is come, that which is in part shall be done away.*[1230] Then all imperfection shall be swallowed up of perfection.

There is a four-fold perfection wherewith God furnishes all his covenant people, namely: {1} A perfection of integrity and uprightness instilled into them, when he first takes them into covenant with himself.[1231] This some call a perfection of parts: all the other perfections of degrees. {2} A perfection of comparative growth; according to which one believer is counted comparatively perfect in respect of another of less growth in grace. *Let us therefore, as many as be perfect, be thus minded.*[1232] {3} A perfection of incomplete vision and fruition; when the souls of believers loosed from their bodies, are conveyed instantly into heaven, and there being perfected in grace, do see and enjoy God immediately face to face: but incompletely, inasmuch as not the body but only the soul, doth thus see and enjoy God. *But ye are come, – to God the judge of all, and the spirits of just men made perfect.*[1233] {4} A perfection of complete vision and fruition; when believers, not only in soul, but also in body reunited, shall see and enjoy God as he is, fully, immediately and eternally.[1234] Our God

---

[1227] Jeremiah 31:34, Ezekiel 36:31, 26, Jeremiah 32:38-40, Ezekiel 36:27
[1228] Ephesians 4:11-13
[1229] Ephesians 2:19-21
[1230] 1 Corinthians 13:9-10
[1231] Psalm 119:1, Genesis 17:1
[1232] Philippians 3:15
[1233] Hebrews 12:23
[1234] 1 John 3:2

is carrying us on daily from perfection to perfection, from the very lowest to the highest degree of these perfections: and consequently he is daily supplying all our wants more and more, until in the supreme perfection every want vanish and be done away.

{4} What a comfort is this against all strong and violent temptations of the flesh, the world, or the devil!

With temptations of these three grand spiritual enemies none are more evidently exercised than God's own covenant people, for:

(i) Carnal men are under their full dominion, like prisoners in dungeons and irons, the jailer is sure of them, troubles not himself much about them: therefore they are seldom buffeted by their temptations.[1235] But believers are brought out of prison, rescued from the power of sin, Satan, etc. Therefore Satan raises all his force and fury of temptations upon them to re-enslave them, as the jailer raises all the country with hue and cry after prisoners escaped when they have broken out of prison.[1236]

(ii) Carnal men need not many temptations to carry them down the stream: their whole nature is only prone to evil, and therefore is carried away with every bare suggestion, with every slight proffer of a temptation.[1237] They are like tinder; they catch fire at every spark of temptation. Yea they ofttimes tempt Satan, to tempt them. But God's people having sanctification as well as corruption, grace as well as sin, they resist and repel temptations, and often get the victory.[1238] Hereupon Satan, etc, reassaults them more fiercely, with all his malice, stratagems, and violence.

(iii) God's people are not only the most eminent of all people, but the greatest enemies to Satan, etc.[1239] If these cedars and oaks fall, many lesser

---

[1235] Acts 8:23; 2 Timothy 2:25
[1236] Luke 4:18, Acts 26:18, Romans 6:12-14
[1237] Psalm 51:5, John 3:6, Romans 7:18, Genesis 6:5
[1238] Galatians 5:17
[1239] Psalm 16:3

shrubs will be brought down with them, and Satan's kingdom more advanced by foiling one of these than a hundred others. Therefore above all, Satan desires to have them, to sift them as wheat.[1240] Them he will buffet; on them he runs like a roaring lion with open mouth to devour them.[1241] Against them he uses all his depths,[1242] all his devices;[1243] he deals with them, sometimes as an angel of light,[1244] sometimes as a black devil indeed, but always as an old serpent, the devil, and Satan.[1245] Hereupon what fears, straits, tears, prayers, plunges and discomforts are God's dear people put upon? Yea, sometimes they are hereby so buffeted, weather-beaten, tossed and tired, that they begin to despond and faint, and are even weary of their lives.

But against all possible temptations, no people in the world have greater ground of encouragement and comfort than God's people. And what greater comfort against temptations than this, that the Lord is their Covenant God? For:

(a) Their God is stronger than all their tempters or temptations. Our best friend is above our worst foe. Our Covenant God is with us; the flesh, world and Satan are against us; there are more with us, than against us: *Ye are of God, little children, and have overcome them: because greater is he that is in you, than he that is in the world.*[1246] And Christ says in reference to his sheep: *My father that gave me them, is greater than all; and no man is able to pluck them out of my Father's hand.*[1247]

(b) Their God is wiser than all their tempters. Satan is an old crafty serpent, an old deceiver, having his depths and devices, etc., but the Lord is *God only wise*; unsearchable in counsel; *his understanding is infinite.*[1248] He

---

[1240] Luke 22:31
[1241] 1 Peter 5:8
[1242] Revelation 2:24
[1243] 2 Corinthians 2:11
[1244] 2 Corinthians 11:14; 1 Peter 5:8
[1245] Revelation 12:9
[1246] 1 John 4:4
[1247] John 10:29
[1248] 1 Timothy 1:17, Romans 11:33, Psalm 145:7

has caught Satan in his own craftiness, both in his tempting of the first, and last Adam. And *the Lord knoweth how to deliver the godly out of temptations.*[1249] He hath depths beyond Satan's depths, and devices beyond Satan's devices. He has more wisdom to bring us out of temptation, then Satan has subtlety to bring us into temptation.

(c) Their God is more tender over his people than the devil is cruel against them. The devil is cruel against them to the uttermost of his ability: *Your adversary the devil, as a roaring lion walketh about, seeking whom he may devour.*[1250] – *Woe to the inhabitants of the earth, and of the sea: for the devil is come down unto you, having great wrath, because he knoweth that he hath but a short time.*[1251] Yet as the devil himself, so all his cruelty is finite and limited. But God's tenderness over his people is infinite and boundless. No father can be so tender over his children,[1252] no mother so tender over her sucking babe,[1253] no man so tender over the apple of his eye,[1254] as God is over his peculiar people. How sweet this comfort! Their God loves them, more than their enemy the devil can hate them. They may triumph in his divine compassion, over all diabolical cruelty.

(d) No temptation can befall God's people, but by the wise permission of their God. Satan cannot tempt them but as their God permits. *God is faithful, who will not suffer you to be tempted above that ye are able.*[1255] Temptations then befall God's children, not when and as their tempters please, but when and as their God permits.

(e) Their God limits both tempters and temptations. The devil himself, the grand tempter, is in God's chain, and cannot go one link beyond his leave. He could not touch Job's goods, or children, or his body, but only according to

---

[1249] 2 Peter 2:9
[1250] 1 Peter 5:8
[1251] Revelation 12:12
[1252] Psalm 103:3
[1253] Isaiah 49:14-15
[1254] Zechariah 2:8
[1255] 1 Corinthians 10:13

God's permission and limitation.[1256] Yea he was not able to touch the herd of swine until Christ gave leave.[1257] That passage is very observable: *Behold the devil shall cast some of you into prison, that ye may be tried, and ye shall have tribulation ten days*, etc.[1258] Here are four limitations upon the devil's temptations by persecuting the church: the persons, their punishment, the event of it, and the duration of it are all limited and confined. The persons tempted: {*some of you*}, not all. The punishment inflicted: {*they shall cast you into prison*}, not into merciless waters, not into devouring flames, not into the grave, not into hell. The event of it: {*that ye may be tried*}, not that ye may be ruined and destroyed. The time of duration: {*for ten days*}, not for twenty days, not during their pleasure, not for your whole lives, not forever. All is under restraint. He that bounds the unruly waves of the sea, saying, "Thus far shall you go, and no further," he bounds the more unruly rage of Satan, that he cannot pass or tempt beyond his bounds.

(f) Their God will not permit them to be tempted above their ability. He knows their strength to the uttermost, and he is so faithful, he will not suffer them to be tempted above what they are able; but *will with the temptation also make a way to escape, that ye may be able to bear it*.[1259] The apostle chiefly here intends temptations by afflictions and sufferings. Against these, he comforts them from the faithfulness of their God three ways, namely: (1) in that he will not permit them to be tempted above their ability. That is, he will so allay, qualify and moderate the temptation, that it shall not be above their ability which they have from God. Otherwise, God's people are sometimes *pressed out of measure, above strength*:[1260] as Paul in Asia, above his own mere human strength. (2) In that *he will with the temptation, make a way to escape*; if that is best, just as he made way for David often to escape from Saul,[1261] for Peter out

---

[1256] Job 1:12 & 2:6
[1257] Mark 5:12-13
[1258] Revelation 2:10
[1259] 1 Corinthians 10:13
[1260] 2 Corinthians 1:8
[1261] Psalm 18 Title

of prison to escape Herod,[1262] etc. (3) In that they shall be able to bear the temptation, if they escape not. He let Peter escape out of prison, but not James, yet he enabled James to bear it.[1263] This is very comfortable against all temptations of the world or Satan: our God is so faithful, that he will either decrease and bring down the temptation to our strength, or deliver from it, or increase and bring up our strength proportionally to the temptation.

(g) Their God furnishes them with complete armor against all temptations: that they *may be able to withstand in the evil day, and having done all, to stand*. This is called {the panoply} or {the whole armor of God}.[1264] The apostle excellently describes it. He makes every saint a soldier, and arms him spiritually from top to toe, but appoints no armor for the back, because there should be no turning the back; no running away in time of temptations from Satan.

(h) The grace of their God is sufficient for them against all their temptations. He that was caught up into the third heavens, which is paradise, had afterwards a thorn in the flesh, the messenger of Satan buffeting him.[1265] For this he prayed thrice that it might depart from him. The Lord would not remove the temptation, but encourages the tempted, with this: *My grace is sufficient for thee*. Satan desired to have the apostles, that he might sift them as wheat, and Christ – foreknowing that Peter would be peculiarly endangered by that sifting – did especially pray for him that his faith might not fail.[1266] And his faith did not totally and finally fail, though he foully fell, for he speedily repented, and his dis-located faith was set in joint again.

(i) Their God shall give them complete victory over Satan and his temptations. Christ *has* conquered him in his own person, as our head,[1267] *is*

[1262] Acts 12:6-12
[1263] Acts 12:2
[1264] Ephesians 6:10-19
[1265] 2 Corinthians 12:4, 7-9
[1266] Luke 22:31-32 compared with Matthew 26:75 & John 21:15-20
[1267] Matthew 4:3-12

daily conquering him by his graces in his members,[1268] and *will* at last day both for himself and his members completely tread him underfoot: *The God of peace shall bruise Satan under your feet shortly.*[1269] Jerome says: "{*Swiftly*}: some say {*shortly*}, that is, opportunely, seasonably, when he is in the height of his temptations and insolence against them."[1270] Some refer this to the day of judgment, which hastens apace, and will come shortly, when Satan shall be utterly crushed under our feet forevermore, and shall never be able to tempt or trouble us anymore.[1271]

(j) Finally, their God turns their temptations to great advantage. He that brought light out of darkness at first, is wont to extract medicines out of these poisons, and good to his people out of these evils of Satan's temptations, for: (1) hereby they are made conform to Jesus Christ their head. He was forty days together most subtly and dangerously tempted of the devil.[1272] Yea, *he was in all points tempted like as we are, yet without sin.*[1273] (2) Hereby they are frequently necessitated to improve the complete armor of God – especially the shield of faith, and sword of the Spirit.[1274] This spiritual warfare keeps their heavenly armor from rusting, and experimentally evidences it to be armor of proof. (3) Hereby they are singularly experienced and instructed in this spiritual warfare. Exercise makes them expert soldiers of Jesus Christ, so that their hands are taught to war, and their fingers to fight, against all the enemies of their salvation. (4) Hereby they are forced to fly to God by prayer, and obtain at least this sweet answer, as a return of prayer particularly: *My grace is sufficient for thee.*[1275] (5) Hereby they are driven to cling closer to Jesus Christ, that they be not overthrown. The more the tops of well-rooted trees are shaken with the winds: the more deeply their roots are fixed in the earth.

[1268] James 4:7; 1 Peter 5:8-9, Galatians 5:24
[1269] Romans 16:20
[1270] Velociter. Jerome on Romans 16, Tom. 9
[1271] David Pareus in his commentary on Romans 16:20
[1272] Luke 4:1-14, Matthew 4:1, etc.
[1273] Hebrews 4:15
[1274] Ephesians 6:10-19
[1275] 2 Corinthians 12:7-9

When the wind blows hardest, the traveler girds his cloak to him the closest. When temptations are most violent and impetuous, we cling fastest to Christ lest we fall, and Christ clasps us fastest because we shall not fall. (6) hereby Christ gives them frequent occasions of triumphant victories. No conflict; no conquest. No temptation: no triumph. Christ himself in his own person was pleased to be tempted, that thereby he might take occasion to triumph over the tempter. And he sometimes leads us into temptation, that we may conquer by his conquests, and triumph by his triumphs, over temptation. (7) Finally, hereby they are taught to compassionate and succor others in temptations, themselves having had a feeling of temptations. Passion breeds compassion. Yea, and if God's people sometimes be foiled by temptations, yet hereby they are provoked to more watchfulness for future, in regard of themselves; and are enabled to more helpfulness towards others. As Christ said to Peter: *When thou art converted, strengthen thy brethren.*[1276] And as David promised after his recovery: *then shall I teach transgressors thy ways, and sinners shall be converted to thee.*[1277] Of patients, they become physicians. And by having their own bones out of joint, they become skillful bone-setters unto others.

{5} **What a comfort is this against deep and dismaying desertions, wherewith the Lord sometimes exercises his own people!** Here consider briefly: (i) the nature of these desertions, (ii) the comfort which God's people may have against desertions, from this: that the Lord is their God by his everlasting New Covenant.

(i) *The nature and mystery of divine desertions (to omit all other sorts of desertions) seems in general to consist in God's forsaking, or with-drawing from his creature*, namely: not in God's withdrawing his essence from his creature, which is immense, infinite and omnipresent, and cannot be excluded from any creature: but in God's withholding or

---

[1276] Luke 22:32
[1277] Psalm 51:13

withdrawing in some sort his Spirit, grace, favor, comforts, assistance, etc., from his creature. According to this latter sense, God's desertions or forsakings of his creatures are either: (a) absolute or (b) limited. That, as of a supreme Lord and righteous judge; this, as of a faithful and loving Father.

(a) **God's absolute desertion extends itself to all the vessels of wrath, whether reprobate angels or men.** Them he forsakes, from them he totally and finally withholds all saving grace (which he is no way bound to give them) as a supreme Lord and righteous judge of all the world, suffering them to perish, as:

(1) He deserted all the reprobate angels so that they left their first estate and habitation (which was mutable) by sinning,[1278] and God left them in their sin and misery without providing any savior for them.[1279] Though he deserted mankind so as to leave them to fall into sin and misery;[1280] yet he provided a savior for recovery of all his elect among mankind.[1281]

(2) He deserts all reprobate men, denying them the pure, sanctified and right use of outward benefits, which is the chief excellency or all such outward enjoyments;[1282] and yet he heaps many temporal benefits upon them, as honors, pleasures, riches, friends, peace, liberty, etc.[1283]

(3) He deserts great part of mankind, in vouchsafing them no tender of Jesus Christ or the gospel at all, so that he wholly leaves them to perish in their sins, without offering them any remedy, or vouchsafing them so much as an external call to Christ.[1284]

(4) He deserts multitudes of people in the visible church that have the outward means of salvation, by withholding the effectual and saving

---

[1278] Jude 6
[1279] Hebrews 2:16
[1280] Genesis 3, Romans 5:12
[1281] Luke 2:30-32; 1 Timothy 1:15, John 17:2
[1282] Titus 1:15
[1283] Psalm 17:14, Matthew 5:45, Psalm 73:4-5
[1284] Psalm [145:19-20], Acts 14:16, Ephesians 2:12

cooperation of his Spirit by those means.[1285] They have Word, sacraments, etc, but not saving benefit by these.

(5) He deserts many that seem to partake of his Spirit, of faith, repentance, obedience, etc, denying them the saving truth and perfection of these, so that they content themselves with shows, shadows and imperfect degrees of them, the common endowments of the Spirit.[1286] But here is no comfort against this absolute desertion, whereby God forsakes all reprobates, and none but reprobates.

(b) **God's limited desertion is peculiar to his elect.**

Them he deserts sometimes as a faithful and loving Father: not absolutely, but only in some respects; not totally, but only in some degrees; not finally and forever, but only for some little time. Against this limited desertion the present consolation is intended. Now thus the Lord deserts and leaves his own people, in temptation, in sin and infirmity, in trouble and distress.

(1) *In temptation*. Herein God deserts his people in different ways, namely: [1] sometimes, by leaving them to be grievously exercised with them: even as wheat is tossed and sifted with a sieve,[1287] or as a man is beaten and buffeted about his head and face.[1288] Thus he left Paul to be buffeted with the messenger of Satan: not delivering him from those buffetings, no not upon his many prayers.[1289] Thus probably, Christ left his disciples to be sifted as wheat by Satan, about the time of his passion.[1290] This is to be left to the trouble and vexation of temptation. [2] Sometimes, by leaving them to be overborne and foiled for a season by the temptation, as David,[1291] Peter,[1292] and others.

(2) *In sin and infirmity*: thus God deserted king Hezekiah, and left him to the pride of his heart expressed in his vainglorious ostentation before the

---

[1285] Isaiah 6:9-10; 2 Corinthians 4:3, Acts 28:26
[1286] Matthew 13:19-23, Luke 8:12-14, Matthew 25:3, 11-12, Hebrews 6:4-6; 2 Peter 2:20-22
[1287] Luke 22:31
[1288] 2 Corinthians 12:7
[1289] 2 Corinthians 12:7, etc.
[1290] Luke 22:31-32
[1291] 2 Samuel 11 throughout
[1292] Matthew 26:70, 72, 74

king of Babylon's ambassadors: *Hezekiah prospered in all his works. Howbeit, in the business of the ambassadors of the princes of Babylon, who sent unto him to inquire of the wonder that was done in the land, God left him to try him, so that he might know all that was in his heart.*[1293] In sin, God deserts his people variously, namely:

[1] He leaves them in some measure during this present life under original sin, the corruption of their natures.[1294] He at their effectual calling sanctifies them in every part, but not throughout in any part. There are relics and powerful remains of sin indwelling in them, together with habits and principles of grace: as Canaanites among the Israelites.[1295] These relics of sin are the flesh contrary to the Spirit;[1296] the old man, opposite to the new man;[1297] a body of death,[1298] and law of sin and death,[1299] repugnant to the law of the Spirit of life; a law in their members rebelling against the law of their mind, and leading them into captivity to the law of sin, as Paul notably evidences.[1300] And this proves matter of great affliction to God's people. Hence Paul sadly sighs and laments: *O wretched man that I am! Who shall deliver me from the body of this death?*[1301] These relics of sin maintain such a continual conflict with the gracious part in God's people that they are hereby often filled with discomfort – yea, and sometimes make question of the truth of their grace.

[2] He leaves them ordinarily during this mortality to various invincible infirmities,[1302] namely: involuntary weaknesses, both in omitting good, and committing evil, against their wills.[1303] As doubts, staggerings, fears, spiritual

---

[1293] 2 Chronicles 32:30-31, Isaiah 39:1 to the end
[1294] Galatians 5:17, Romans 7:24
[1295] Romans 7:15 to the end
[1296] Galatians 5:17
[1297] Ephesians 4:22-23
[1298] Romans 7:24
[1299] Romans 8:2
[1300] Romans 7:23
[1301] Romans 7:24
[1302] Romans 8:26
[1303] Romans 7:19-20

dullness, sluggishness, listlessness in the ways of God, wandering and distracted thoughts in duties, etc. By which their hearts are oftentimes much saddened and dejected; they think it is not with any of God's people as with them herein. Thus the Lord Christ left his spouse in her spiritual sluggishness, slumber and security, once and again: *By night on my bed I sought him whom my soul loveth: I sought him, but I found him not. I will rise now, and go about the city in the streets, and in the broad ways I will seek him whom my soul loveth: I sought him, but I found him not. The watchmen that go about the city found me: to whom I said, saw ye him whom my soul loveth? It was but a little that I passed from them, but I found him whom my soul loveth, etc.*[1304] And afterwards: *I sleep, but mine heart waketh. It is the voice of my beloved that knocketh, saying, open to me, my sister, my love, my dove, my undefiled; for my head is filled with dew, and my locks with the drops of the night. I have put off my coat, how shall I put it on? I have washed my feet, how shall I defile them? – I opened to my beloved, but my beloved had withdrawn himself, and was gone: my soul failed, when he spake; I sought him, but I could not find him; I called him, but he gave me no answer.*[1305]

[3] He sometimes leaves them for a time to fall into gross and scandalous sins, as Noah into drunkenness,[1306] Lot into incest with his two daughters,[1307] David into murder and adultery,[1308] Peter into his triple denial of his Lord and Master Jesus Christ,[1309] and every time worse than others, etc. And these falls cost them many bitter tears, when they come to themselves again: yea hereby their very bones are broken, their joy of God's salvation is lost, their assurance of God's love and evidences for eternal life so blurred and defaced, that they

---

[1304] Song of Solomon 3:1-5
[1305] Song of Solomon 5:2-8
[1306] Genesis 9:20-21
[1307] Genesis 19:32, etc.
[1308] 2 Samuel 11:2, etc.
[1309] Matthew 26:70, 72, 74

call all into question.[1310] And of all God's deserting his people in sin, this is most dangerous, and most to be lamented.

(3) *In trouble and distress.* Herein God deserts his people in many ways, as:

[1] By leaving them to be exercised under affliction, especially after great experience of God's mercies. Hence Gideon complained to the angel: *O my Lord, if the LORD be with us, why then is all this befallen us? And where be all his miracles which our fathers told us of, saying: Did not the LORD bring us up from Egypt? But now the LORD hath forsaken us, and delivered us into the hands of the Midianites.*[1311] God in a sort forsakes his people, while he afflicts his people.

[2] By leaving them to unusual and extraordinary extremities of affliction. Thus God left Job in the hands of satan to be miserably afflicted and distressed in his goods, in his children, and in his own body;[1312] so that at last, Job curses his birth, wisheth for death, utters many passionate and distempered speeches, his friends think him to be a wicked hypocrite, and his wife estranged herself from him.[1313] And how hard a thing is it for God's people not to faint in the day of extreme affliction, because their strength is but small!

[3] By leaving them under affliction a long time, the Lord delaying his help. O this is a sad aggravation of their distress, when the Lord deserts them for a long time together! Hence David complains: *How long wilt thou forget me O LORD, forever? How long wilt thou hide thy face from me? How long shall I take counsel in my soul, having sorrow in mine heart daily; how long shall mine enemy be exalted over me?* [1314] And Asaph most sadly expostulates: *Will the Lord cast off forever? And will he be favorable no more? Is his mercy*

[1310] Matthew 26:65, Psalm 51:8, 12
[1311] Judges 6:12-13
[1312] Job 1:12 & 2:6
[1313] Job 3:1, etc & 6 & 7
[1314] Psalm 13:1-2; see especially Psalm 89:38-47

clean gone forever? Doth his promise fail for evermore? Hath God forgotten to be gracious? Hath he in anger shut up his tender mercies? Selah.[1315]

[4] By withholding from his afflicted people the wonted [habitual] sense and sweet experience of his comforts, favor and loving-kindness in their afflictions. When God hides his countenance, withdraws himself from them, seems not to lay to heart or consider their trouble. This was David's case, the type; and Christ's condition upon the cross, the antitype: *My God, my God, why hast thou forsaken me?*[1316] Etc.

This was the lot of Mr. Robert Glover,[1317] in prison at Coventry after he was condemned to be burned for the truth, two or three days before his death, his heart was dull, heavy, and lumpish; desolate of all spiritual consolation in reference to the bitter cross of martyrdom. So that he feared the Lord had withdrawn his wonted favor from him; and made his moan to Augustine Bernher, a minister, his familiar friend, signifying how earnestly he had prayed night and day unto the Lord, and yet could receive no motion nor sense of any comfort from him.

Augustine wished him to wait patiently the Lord's pleasure, and however his present feeling was, yet seeing his cause was just and true, constantly to stick to the same, and play the man, not doubting but the Lord in his good time would satisfy him with plenty of consolation, desiring him to show some signification thereof when his heart began to be touched with them.

The next day, as he was going to the place of martyrdom, and was now come to the sight of the stake (although all the night before praying for strength and courage he could feel none suddenly he was so mightily replenished with God's holy comfort and heavenly joys, that he cried out, clapping his hands to Augustine, and saying in these words: "Augustine, he is come, he is come," etc. And that with such joy and alacrity, as one seeming

---

[1315] Psalm 77:7-9
[1316] Psalm 22:1-2, Matthew 27:46, Mark 15:34
[1317] John Foxe, *Acts and Monuments*, Volume 3, p.427 (London, 1641)

rather to be risen from some deadly danger to liberty of life, than as one passing out of this world by any pains of death.

Mr. Peacock,[1318] a learned and godly minister, in his last sickness, was so far deserted of God, that he concluded that the Lord had cursed him, that he was a foolish vainglorious hypocrite; it was against the course of God's proceedings to save him, he has otherwise decreed, he cannot; that he desired no more to believe than a post, than a horseshoe, had no more sense of grace than those curtains, than a goose, than that block.

To his friends who were saying: "Suffer us to pray for you," he replied: "Take not the name of God in vain, in praying for a reprobate."[1319]

Mr. Dod asked him how he did.[1320]

He answered: "lamentably, wretchedly, miserably. No stamp of grace in me."

"Do you desire to be eased?"

"Infinitely. Oh if God would give me but a drop!"

Another time, he broke out into this sudden expression: "O God, reconcile me unto thee, that I may taste one dram of grace, by which my miserable soul may receive comfort."[1321]

But after many sad agonies he received much comfort before his death, as I shall after intimate.[1322]

[5] Finally, by setting himself, his wrath and terrors against his people in their distresses. It is exceedingly sad when in afflictions, God withholds his consolations from his people, but it is double grievous and intolerable when himself heaps positive disconsolations upon his people. Who may stand before him when once he is angry? This was Job's case: *Oh that my grief were thoroughly weighed, and my calamity laid in the balances together! For now it*

[1318] See *A Narration of the Grievous Visitation and Dreadful Desertion of Mr. Peacock*, p.24, etc (London, 1641)
[1319] p.28
[1320] p.57
[1321] p.77
[1322] pp.86, 92, 97-103

would be heavier than the sand of the sea, therefore my words are swallowed up. For the arrows of the Almighty are within me, the poison thereof drinketh up my spirit: the terrors of God do set themselves in array against me.[1323] This was heman's condition, who in his desertion thus complains to God: *Thou hast laid me in the lowest pit, in darkness, in the deeps. Thy wrath lieth hard upon me: and thou hast afflicted me with all thy waves. Selah.*[1324] – *LORD, why castest thou off my soul? Why hidest thou thy face from me? I am afflicted and ready to die, from my youth up: while I suffer thy terrors I am distracted. Thy fierce wrath goeth over me: thy terrors have cut me off. They came round about me daily like water: they compassed me about together.*[1325] These are the sad desertions wherewith the Lord sometimes exercises his dearest people. I have touched at the nature and sorts of them the more largely, that I may lay their foundations of comfort against them more solidly, and you discern the necessity and commodity of such comforts more fully.

(b) **The comfort which God's people may have against all these divine desertions, from this, that the Lord is their God by this everlasting New Covenant; is manifold, and singularly reviving.** For:

(1) First, the Lord remains still a Covenant God unto his people, in and under their saddest desertions; as well as before, or after such desertions. Jesus Christ forsaken by his Father when he was dying upon his cross, did yet in this extremity of desertion cry out: *My God, my God, why hast thou forsaken me?*[1326] Though he had deserted him, yet still he was his God; and still he apprehended him as his God. David – deserted by his God – could yet plead his covenant interest in him, and relation to him, as his God. *My God, my God, why hast thou forsaken me? Why art thou so far from helping me, and from the words of my roaring? O my God, I cry in the daytime, but thou hearest*

[1323] Job 6:2-4 & 7:12-15
[1324] Psalm 88:6-7
[1325] Psalm 88:14-17
[1326] Matthew 27:46, Mark 15:34

not, etc.[1327] Heman in his most doleful desertion yet was able to say: *O Lord God of my salvation, I have cried day and night before thee*, etc.[1328] Yea the Lord in desertions still remains their Covenant God, though they should not be able so to apprehend him, as the sun still shines, although we cannot always see it shine, by reason of clouds interposing, etc; or as a sick man has still a true title to, and interest in all his lands and goods, though for present he has neither apprehension of it, nor consolation in it. And the Lord must needs remain their Covenant God in desertion, as well as out; because he is their God by an everlasting covenant.[1329] Now temporary desertions cannot overthrow an everlasting covenant.

What then, though you are under a divine desertion? Yet the main is safe, the substance of your happiness is sure: the Lord still remains your God in covenant. Oh what a heart-reviving cordial! The Lord has not taken away his grace, but suspended it. He has not deprived you of the support of his comforts, but only of the sense and experimental feeling of his comforts. He has not so much left you, as concealed himself from you; he is present with you as your God, but has hidden himself a little. It is with you, as once with Hagar:[1330] the well is close by you, and you lament for water, because you do not know it; or as once with the two disciples going to Emmaus: they went lamenting Christ's death, when Christ himself risen from the dead walked and talked with them, but *their eyes were held fast that they knew him not*.[1331] Let this refresh your deserted spirit: the Lord has in some sense left you, yet still remains a Covenant God unto you.

(2) Secondly, God's sincere Covenant people may be long and deeply deserted, but shall never be totally, finally or utterly forsaken, for: [1] God's New Covenant with them in Christ's blood is sure and everlasting, and can

---

[1327] Psalm 22:1-2, 10, 19
[1328] Psalm 88:1, etc.
[1329] Hebrews 8:10 & 13:20
[1330] Genesis 21:14-20
[1331] Luke 24:13-33

never be reversed or destroyed – no more than Christ can die a second time.[1332] [2] The mediator of this Covenant, Jesus Christ, has not only died, to ratify God's New Covenant unalterably: but also is risen again, forever to trample upon all the sins and enemies of his true New Covenant people triumphantly. *What then shall separate us from the love of God which is in Christ? Shall tribulation*, etc.[1333] Jesus Christ may as soon be plucked down from God's right-hand to suffer a second time, as his New Covenant people be separated from God, and utterly cast away. [3] The promises annexed to this everlasting Covenant of God, do peculiarly secure all God's true Covenant people against his final and total forsaking. Take a taste of these few. God – promising to make a New Covenant with the house of Israel and Judah – tells them it should not be according to the former Covenant which their fathers broke, whereby he implies that this New Covenant should be of such a nature and constitution that it should not be broken.[1334] God would undertake for both sides, etc. Christ said: *All that the Father giveth me, shall come unto me: and him that cometh to me, I will in no wise cast out.*[1335] – *My sheep hear my voice, and I know them, and they follow me. And I give unto them eternal life, and they shall never perish; neither shall any man pluck them out of my hand.*[1336] And God has said: *I will never leave thee, nor forsake thee* – namely: totally, finally, utterly.[1337] The Greek has five negatives in this promise, intimating most emphatically, that it is a resolute and peremptory promise. It may be thus rendered to the original: *I will not not leave thee, nor will I not not forsake thee.*

(3) Thirdly, God keeps his covenant people from sinking, fainting and despairing under desertions. Because he will be their Covenant God and they shall be his people;[1338] he will not turn from them, nor shall they depart from

---

[1332] Hebrews 8:8-13, Luke 22:20, Hebrews 13:20
[1333] Romans 8:35 to the end
[1334] Jeremiah 31:31-35, Hebrews 8:8-13
[1335] John 6:37
[1336] John 10:27-29
[1337] Hebrews 13:5
[1338] Jeremiah 31:33, Hebrews 8:10

him: namely: not totally, finally, utterly.[1339] And consequently when their God gradually and for a time deserts them, yet under those desertions he secretly supports them from utter despondency and despair, because he is, and will be their God. Hence, David deserted, could pray to God as his God upon many grounds of confidence.[1340] Yea he could say: *O my God, I cry in the daytime, etc.*[1341] – *Thou art my God from my mother's belly. Be not far from me, for trouble is near, for there is none to help.*[1342] – *Be not far from me, O LORD; O my strength haste thee to help me.*[1343] Thus he was secretly supported to plead his covenant interest in his God, though deserted by his God. Asaph deserted, was yet so far supported as to pray to God prevailingly: and at last to raise up his spirit upon the former experiences of his people. *And I said, this is my infirmity: but I will remember the years of the right hand of the Most High.*[1344] Heman – deserted – could pray: *O LORD God of my salvation, I have cried day and night before thee.*[1345] The church deserted of Christ, was yet so far supported by Christ, as to seek him whom her soul loved.[1346] She still loved him dearly, and sought him earnestly. Yea Jesus Christ himself was deserted by his Father upon the cross, yet was so far kept from despondency under his desertion, as to cry: *My God, my God, why hast thou forsaken me?*[1347] Though then such desertions are sad and lamentable, yet such support under them against fainting is comfortable. And the Lord as our God thus supports us herein, when we could not support ourselves, nor could any other relieve or help us. As David intimates in his desertion: *Be not far from me, for trouble is*

[1339] Jeremiah 32:40
[1340] Psalm 22 throughout
[1341] Psalm 22:2
[1342] Psalm 22:9-10
[1343] Psalm 22:19
[1344] Psalm 77:1, etc, 10-12, etc.
[1345] Psalm 88:1, etc.
[1346] Song of Solomon 3:1-4 & 5:5-8
[1347] Matthew 27:46

near, for there is no helper.[1348] This comfort God's people have under desertions, in having the Lord to be their God in covenant.

(4) Fourthly, God seasonably recovers his people out of desertions, in his own season – and his season is the best season. Because he is their Covenant-God, he will not turn away from them, utterly. And if he turns not away from them utterly, he must needs return again to them seasonably. Though he deserts them a long time, it shall not be overlong. Christ deserted his church; she sought him, enquiring of the watchmen for him: *It was but a little* (she says) *that I passed from them, but I found him whom my soul loveth.*[1349] David and Asaph in the beginning of their prayers complain of God's forsaking them; before the end thereof, they intimate God's return unto them.[1350] Christ himself was deserted by his Father upon the cross, but the same day received by his Father into paradise.[1351]

Mr. Robert Glover,[1352] martyr, was deserted by God, and deprived of all sweet sense of his comforts for about three days together after his condemnation, though he prayed to God night and day for divine refreshments. But when he was going to the place of execution, and was now come within sight of the stake, the Spirit of God returned to him, with such singular comfort, that he triumphantly cried out to his dear friend: "Augustine, he is come, he is come."

Mr. Peacock was sadly deserted of God in his last sickness: but about two hours or more before his death, the Lord did so graciously return to him with the light of his countenance gladdening his soul, that he broke forth into these passages: "Do you expect to hear from me, what I believe concerning my eternal salvation? Truly God does forever so endearedly tender, and is so inconceivably merciful to all those whom he has once loved, that he never

---

[1348] Psalm 22:9-10
[1349] Song of Solomon 3:1-4
[1350] Psalm 22:1, etc; Psalm 77:1, etc.
[1351] Matthew 27:46 with Luke 23:43
[1352] John Foxe, *Acts and Monuments*, Volume 3 (London, 1651)

finally does forsake them; and therefore I am most assuredly confident, that I shall depart from hence into heaven. Happy! Thrice happy be these cords of affliction in which my most gracious God has tied and bound me!"[1353]

One telling him, "You have fought a good fight;" he said: "It behooves, it behooves me to strive for heaven. Lift me up, lift me up, rid me hence that I may come to heaven."[1354]

Being remembered of God's goodness to him, in filling his soul with such comfort, after so great temptation, he said: "I do (God be praised) feel such comfort from that – what shall I call it?"

"Agony," said one that stood by.

"Nay, that's too little; that if I had five thousand worlds, I could not make satisfaction for such an issue.[1355] – What great cause have I to magnify the goodness of God, that has humbled, nay, rather, that has exalted such a wretched miscreant, and of so base condition, to an estate so glorious and stately? The Lord has honored me with his goodness; I am sure he has provided a glorious kingdom for me. The joy that I feel in my soul is incredible!"[1356]

Now, O deserted Christian, stay your heart with this: the Lord who sadly deserts you will seasonably return unto you. And when he returns, he will come with healing and joy. If he comes again to you but two or three hours before your death, or as you are going to the stake, it will be so sweet, that all the bitterness of former affliction and desertion will be forgotten.

(5) Fifthly, God overpowers and orders his people's desertions for their singular benefit. He brings light out of this darkness; he turns this poison into a medicine, for: [1] Hereby, God's people are mightily put upon prayer. God seems to fly from them, by withdrawing himself. They fly after him by strong cries and prayers until they overtake him. And when did they ever pray more

---

[1353] *Mr. Peacock's Grievous Visitation and Desertion*, pp.96-98
[1354] p.99
[1355] pp.99-100
[1356] p.101

fervently to God than when they were deserted most sadly by God? Witness David,[1357] Asaph,[1358] Heman,[1359] Paul,[1360] the church,[1361] and Jesus Christ himself.[1362] [2] Hereby, God's people are proved and tried, that God may see what is in their hearts; yea, rather that God may let themselves see, what is in their own hearts. Thus, in the business of the ambassadors of the princes of Babylon, God left Hezekiah to the pride, vanity, and vain-glory of his own spirit, to try him, that he might know all that was in his heart.[1363] God knew it fully before this desertion, but Hezekiah knew it not. Hezekiah therefore had need to know it, so that he might be sincerely and penitentially humbled for it.

(c) **Hereby, the Lord provides a singular remedy and antidote against his people's sins, past, present and future.** For by withdrawing from them and deserting them:

(1) He corrects their sins past. As in Job, who in his distress thus complains to God: *Wherefore hidest thou they face, and holdest me for thine enemy? Wilt thou break a leaf driven to and fro? And wilt thou pursue the dry stubble? For thou writest bitter things against me, and makest me to possess the iniquities of my youths.*[1364] That is: "You make my sins stick as fast to me in their punishments as a possession to a purchaser; you bring all my youth's sins afresh to my memory, and they are as an heavy load upon my conscience, as if I had never repented of them, and you had never pardoned them."

(2) He curbs and restrains their sins present. As in the church, Christ knocks and waits that he might spiritually enter into her by nearer communion; he invites her to open to him by all sweet alluring words.[1365] She was in a slumber on her bed of sluggishness and carnal security. She had put

---

[1357] Psalm 22:1, etc.
[1358] Psalm 77:1, etc.
[1359] Psalm 88:1, etc.
[1360] 2 Corinthians 12:7-9
[1361] Song of Solomon 5:6
[1362] Matthew 27:46
[1363] 2 Chronicles 32:31
[1364] Job 13:24-26
[1365] Song of Solomon 5:2-9

off her coat, how should she put it on? She had washed her feet, how should she defile them? Hereupon, Christ leaves some memorials of his love and sweetness behind him, and withdraws himself from her, lest she should be lulled asleep in deeper security. Seeing his presence did not persuade her against it; his absence should rouse her out of it. And now that Christ had left her, she was awakened to the purpose, and restlessly seeks him, and calls after him.

(3) He prevents their sins to come. As in Paul after he had been caught up into the third heavens, he left him a while to be buffeted with temptations, to preserve him from spiritual pride through his revelations.[1366] *And lest I should be exalted above measure through the abundance of the revelations, there was given to me a thorn in the flesh, the messenger of Satan to buffet me, lest I should be exalted above measure.*[1367] He speaks it twice over, because this was a special advantage which God intended him by his buffeting temptations. Now then, if desertions are thus gainfully improved to God's people as to correct their sins past, curb their sins present, and prevent their sins to come, what a comfort may this be against them!

(4) Hereby, the faith of God's people is awakened and exercised. When God leaves them, then they are put upon search and inquiry into their own and others' former old experiences for their support, as Asaph in his desertion – complaining: *Will the LORD cast off forever? And will he be favorable no more?* Etc. – at last recollected himself, and propped up his faith by former experiences: *And I said, this is my infirmity, but I will remember the years of the right hand of the Most High. I will remember the works of the LORD; surely I will remember thy wonders of old*, etc.[1368]

(5) Hereby, their love and desires are exceedingly inflamed after God and Jesus Christ, that they cannot rest till they recover some tastes of wonted love

---

[1366] 2 Corinthians 12:2-11
[1367] 2 Corinthians 12:7
[1368] Psalm 77:5 to the end

and favor. Thus, the drowsy and sleepy affections of the church are notably awakened to Christ, by his withdrawing.[1369]

(6) Hereby, God's return, and renewed discovery of his grace, favor, and love, are more eminently commended to God's people, as double, sweet and acceptable. When the church recovered Christ after desertion, then she entertains him with complacency of affection: {*I am my beloved's, and my beloved is mine: he feedeth among the lilies*}, namely: he feeds his eye and heart, greatly delighting himself with his people, and his own graces in them.[1370] How welcome was the Lord to Mr. Robert Glover, martyr, when he met him with his long looked-for comforts, as he was now going to the stake! His heart and spirit were transported, and his tongue cries out: "He is come, he is come." How welcome were the renewed beams of God's favor to Mr. Peacock about two or three hours before his dissolution, when he burst out into that rapture: "The Lord has honored me with his goodness; I am sure he has provided a glorious kingdom for me. The joy that I feel in my soul is incredible."

(7) Hereby, finally, God's people are experimentally instructed to retain the Lord more steadfastly and carefully, when they do recover him. His absence was bitter as death; his presence is life. Therefore they cling faster to him than formerly, they grow into nearer communion with him, they charge all about them to take heed of disturbing or offending him in the least degree. How emphatically is this declared in the carriage of the church! *It was but a little that I passed from them, but I found him whom my soul loveth: I held him, and would not let him go, until I had brought him into my mother's house, and into the chamber of her that conceived me. I charge you, O ye daughters of Jerusalem, by the roes, and by the hinds of the field, that ye stir not up, nor awake my love till he please.*[1371]

[1369] Song of Solomon 3:1-3 & 5:2 to the end
[1370] Song of Solomon 5 throughout & 6:1-3
[1371] Song of Solomon 3:1-6

{6} **What a comfort is this to all God's true federates, against all the sharpest afflictions and persecutions possible, that the LORD is their God by his own everlasting New Covenant!**

God's covenant people are ordinarily an afflicted and persecuted people above all other people in the world. *In this world ye shall have tribulation.*[1372] *– Moses chose rather to suffer affliction with the people of God than to enjoy the pleasures of sin for a season.*[1373] *– Yea and all that will live godly in Christ Jesus shall suffer persecution.*[1374] *Many are the troubles of the righteous.*[1375] *Through much tribulation we must enter into the kingdom of God.*[1376] Christ said: *If any man will come after me, let him deny himself, and take up his cross daily, and follow me.*[1377] Christ himself bare his cross. "Deus unicum filium habuit sine peccato: nullum sine flagello;" that is: God had one only Son without sin, not one without the scourge. And Christians must be *crucians*, that is, *cross-bearers*, as well as their Lord and Master,[1378] as Luther notably expresses it. "He has not learned," says holy Bradford, "his ABC in Christianity; that has not learned the lesson of the cross."[1379] Ignatius then counted himself a scholar of Christ, when he began to be a sufferer for Christ, as he himself testifies in his epistle written to the Romans.[1380] Righteous Abel in the beginning of the world was bathed in his own blood by the cruel hands of his wicked brother Cain.[1381] Isaac was mocked and persecuted by Ishmael.[1382] David was hunted up and down as a partridge by King Saul.[1383] Isaiah is reported to be sawn

---

[1372] John 16:33
[1373] Hebrews 11:25
[1374] 2 Timothy 3:12
[1375] Psalm 34:19
[1376] Acts 14:22
[1377] Luke 9:23
[1378] "Christianus, Crucianus. Qui non est Crucianus, non est Christianus." Luther on Genesis 29.
[1379] John Foxe, *Acts & Monuments*, in his letter to the town of Walden, pp.315-316, Volume 3 (London, 1641).
[1380] Ignat. *Ep. ad Roman.* p. 86 (Oxon, 1644).
[1381] Genesis 4:3-9; 1 John 3:12
[1382] Genesis 21:9, Galatians 4:29
[1383] 1 Samuel 24:11

asunder with a wooden saw.[1384] Jeremiah was put into a miry dungeon, and (as some say) sunk up to the shoulders in the mire;[1385] and was afterwards stoned to death in Egypt.[1386] Ezekiel was slain in Babylon.[1387] Daniel was cast into the hungry lions' den.[1388] Michaiah was clapped in prison, and there fed with bread and water of affliction.[1389] Amos was brained with a club. Micah was thrown headlong down a steep place, so that his neck broke, etc.

Yea, Stephen tells the Jews: *Which of the prophets have not your fathers persecuted? And they have slain them which shown before of the coming of the Just One, of whom ye have been now the betrayers and the murderers.*[1390] In the days of the Maccabees, God's people endured many horrid cruelties: they were tortured, cruelly mocked, scourged, bound, imprisoned, *stoned, sawn asunder, tempted, slain with the sword, wandered about in sheep-skins and gaot-skins, being destitute, afflicted, tormented. Of whom the world was not worthy: they wandered in deserts, and in mountains, and in dens, and caves of the earth.*[1391] In the times of the New Testament, what bloody storms of affliction and persecution fell upon the church of God! How cruelly was Stephen – the protomartyr after Christ – stoned to death?[1392] And Dorotheus relates of two thousand other believers who suffered death the same day.

All the apostles except John were violently put to death for Christ and his gospel, and John himself was cast into burning oil (thinks Tertullian)[1393] at Rome, (think others) at Ephesus,[1394] and it is thought by Nero, and suffered no harm thereby; but he was afterwards banished by Domitian into the Isle of

---

[1384] See my *Key of the Bible* on Isaiah, Section 1.
[1385] Jeremiah 38:6
[1386] Ioan Gal. Proem. In Jer.
[1387] *Key of the Bible* on Ezekiel, Section 1.
[1388] Daniel 6:16
[1389] 1 Kings 22:27
[1390] Acts 7:52
[1391] Hebrews 11:35-39
[1392] Acts 7:57-60
[1393] Tertullian, *The Prescription Against Heresies*, l c. 36. p. 211 (Frankfurt, 1597)
[1394] *The Magdeburg Centuries*, 1. Cent. l.2 c.10

Patmos, (Revelation 1:9). James was slain by the sword of Herod Agrippa.[1395] Ecclesiastical writers[1396] tell us that Peter was crucified with his heels upwards, counting himself unworthy to be crucified like Christ; Andrew was crucified by Egeas King of Edessa; Philip was crucified, and stoned to death at Hieropolis in Phrygia; Bartholomew was beaten down with staves as he was preaching in Armenia, and crucified, his skin afterwards being flayed off, and he beheaded; Thomas was slain with a dart at Caelamina in India; Matthew was run through with a sword, or as some think he was fastened with nails or spears to the earth, the other James (thinks Jerome) was cast headlong from the temple; Lebbeus was slain by Agbarus King of Edessa; Simon the Canaanite was crucified in Egypt, or as others think, he and Jude were slain in a popular tumult; Matthias was stoned, and afterwards beheaded; Paul was frequently and grievously persecuted, imprisoned at Rome, and at last beheaded by Nero.

Time would fail to mention the sad and cruel sufferings of the seventy disciples; Of the primitive Christians under the ten first persecutions, of the church in successive ages, in many countries, especially in Germany, France, and here in England, until the bloody Marian days. So that we may still see the church and people of God in all ages, as a bush in the midst of flames;[1397] and may say with him:

"Sanguine fundata est Ecclesia;
Sanguine crevit;
Sanguine successit;
Sanguine finis erit."

Namely:

[1395] Acts 12:1-2
[1396] *The Magdeburg Centuries*, 1. Cent. l.2 c.10; De vitis Doc. orum. Jerome in Catal. Scriptor. Ecclesiastic. Tom. 1. p. 262, etc. (Basil. 1553).
[1397] Exodus 3:2

"In blood the church was founded;
In blood it doth increase;
With blood 'tis still surrounded;
And so in blood will cease."

Now against all their afflictions and persecutions, all God's sincere federates may much comfort themselves in this: that the Lord is their God by this everlasting New Covenant. And hence ariseth a seven-fold comfort to God's afflicted people, for:

(i) ***First***, their God in covenant will not forget, nor forsake, nor withdraw his love from his afflicted people in any of their sufferings or extremities. God's people indeed under strong and long afflictions, may sometimes think, and fear, and complain, that the Lord has forgotten, and forsaken them, and cast them out of his love and favor, as the Jews in Babylon's captivity: *but Zion said, the LORD hath forsaken me, and my Lord hath forgotten me.*[1398] And when God's people are under a thick and black cloud of distress, how hard a thing is it for them oftentimes to behold any beam or brightness of God's countenance through that cloud?

Yet notwithstanding all their sad apprehensions, God will never forget, nor forsake, nor alienate his love from them in affliction: no not when he seems most to do it. For, hear what God says: *when the poor and needy seek water, and there is none, and their tongue faileth for thirst; I the God of Israel will not forsake them;*[1399] that is: "Though my people in Babylon, or elsewhere in their way thence, be in as great wants and distresses, as once of old when they came from Egypt in their dry and parching wilderness; yet I their God will not forsake them."

[1398] Isaiah 49:14
[1399] Isaiah 41:17

Again, when Zion (in Babylon's long captivity) said {*the LORD hath forsaken me, and my Lord hath forgotten me*}, what says the answer of the Lord? *Can a woman forget her sucking child, that she should not have compassion on the son of her womb? Yea, they may forget, yet will I not forget thee. Behold, I have graven thee upon the palms of my hands: thy walls are continually before me.*[1400] A tender mother may be so unmotherly as to forget her child, her sucking child, the son of her womb – yea, the pitiful women did so in Jerusalem's siege, when they boiled and eat their own children.[1401] But God will not forget his afflicted people, for a constant memorial of them, he has graven or portrayed them upon the palms of his hands; their walls – either their ruined walls are continually before him, still before his pitying eye; or their intended walls, in the idea or model of them, are continually before him, still in his thoughts and determinations how they shall be raised, and upon the same ground of God's tender love and faithfulness to his afflicted – these promises are applicable to God's afflicted under the New Covenant. And therefore, against all divorce of God's people from his love by affliction, or otherwise, how does the apostle triumph? *Who shall separate us from the love of Christ? Shall tribulation, or distress, or persecution, or famine, or nakedness, or peril, or sword? – Nay, in all these things we are more than conquerors through him that loved us. For I am persuaded that neither death, nor life, nor angels, nor principalities, nor powers, nor things present, nor things to come, nor height, nor depth, nor any other creature, shall be able to separate us from the love of God which is in Christ Jesus our Lord.*[1402] How should this hold up head and heart in deepest afflictions and persecutions, whoever forget us, or forsake us, or with-draw affection from us in distresses: our God will never do any of these unto us: and then in the worst of sufferings, the main is safe.

(ii) **Secondly**, God is most infinitely tender and compassionate over his people in all their sufferings. In tenderest compassions he at first made them

---

[1400] Isaiah 49:14-16
[1401] Lamentations 4:10
[1402] Romans 8:35 to the end

his covenant people. His federal tenderness, he still continues to them, and in afflictions is wont to express it most tenderly towards them. *The LORD's portion is his people; Jacob the lot of his inheritance. He found him in a desert land, and in the waste howling wilderness* (compassed about with many and sore distresses) *he led him about* (Hebrew: *he compassed him about, as it were embraced him, and clasped his arms about him*), *he instructed him, he kept him as the apple of his eye. As an eagle stirreth up her nest, fluttereth over her young, spreadeth abroad her wings, taketh them, beareth them on her wings: So the LORD alone did lead him,* etc.[1403] Oh, what yearning tenderness did God show to his afflicted Israel! Those who touch his people, touch the apple of his eye, his tenderest part.[1404] Their afflictions are his afflictions; their sufferings are Christ's sufferings. He takes all their wrongs as done to himself, and accordingly rewards them. *In all their affliction he was afflicted.*[1405] He so pities his suffering people, that he smarts in their pains, he bleeds in their wounds, he is persecuted in their persecutions. That expression is observable: {*God hath comforted his people, and will have mercy upon his afflicted*}. Such care and tenderness, God shows to his people in affliction, that they are styled by a peculiar appropriation {*his afflicted*}.[1406] No tender father can pity his sick child as God, the Father of fathers, commiserates his afflicted children.[1407] Now as to be unpitied in misery is a great aggravation of misery; so to be tendered, pitied, and commiserated in distress, is a great alleviation and lessening of distress. And above all compassions, the compassions of our God are most compassionate. The most tender human commiserations are but mere cruelties to divine compassions. O you covenant people of God, comfort yourselves against all your sufferings, in that you are not unpitied in your sufferings. You have a friend that lays to heart all your afflictions. Your God

---

[1403] Deuteronomy 32:9-11
[1404] Zechariah 2:8
[1405] Isaiah 63:9
[1406] Isaiah 49:13
[1407] Psalm 103:13

pities you, and his bowels yearn over you. He washes your stripes, he wipes off your tears, he binds up your bruises, he kisseth your wounds; your tears he puts into his bottle;[1408] every drop of your blood you shed, is registered in his book. *The very hairs of your head are all numbered* (Matthew 10:30). Not a hair falls from your head to your prejudice; your God tells them all. To him you may make your moan, and pour out all your complaint, for he tenders you infinitely.

(iii) **Thirdly**, God will hear the cries, and prayers, and groans of his people in their distresses. This he has promised to his covenant people, that struck covenant with him by sacrifice, whose God he was: *Call upon me in the day of trouble; I will deliver thee, and thou shalt glorify me.*[1409] And elsewhere he says: *When the poor and needy seek water and there is none, and their tongue faileth for thirst: I the LORD will hear them, I the God of Jacob will not forsake them*;[1410] because he is Jehovah, and the God of Jacob: that is, because he is their Covenant God, giving being to his Covenant and promises, therefore he will hear them, etc. When the Lord appeared to Moses in the burning bush, he proclaimed himself before Moses to be the Covenant God of Israel, saying: *I am the God of thy father, the God of Abraham, the God of Isaac, and the God of Jacob*. And what inferred he thence, for the comfort of Moses and Israel? *In seeing I have seen the affliction of my people which are in Egypt, and have heard their cry by reason of their task-masters; for I know their sorrows*. Hereby then, God's people may comfort themselves, that when they in their troubles pour out their complaints before the Lord: he will not turn a deaf ear, nor put away their prayers from him, but attend unto them, because he is their God. *He will regard the prayer of the destitute, and not despise their prayer. This shall be written for the generation to come. – yea, he looks down from heaven, to hear the groaning of the prisoner, and to loose the children of death*. If these were

---

[1408] Psalm 56:8
[1409] Psalm 50:5, 7, 15
[1410] Isaiah 41:17

comforts to God's afflicted people under former Covenants, then much more under this New Covenant.

(iv) **Fourthly**, God allies and qualifies the afflictions of his people. He will not suffer them to be extreme and unmeasurable upon them, because he is their God, and they his people in covenant. Yea *though their heart was not right with him, neither were they steadfast in his covenant, yet he, being full of compassion, forgave their iniquity, and destroyed them not; yea many a time turned he his anger away, and did not stir up all his wrath.*[1411] He puts a great difference in this regard between his people and others. He adds a great allay [relief] to their troubles, either in regard of manner, measure, kind, continuance or other circumstances: that they are able to bear them. *Hath he smitten him, as he smote those that smote him? Or is he slain, according to the slaughter of them that are slain by him? In measure when it shooteth forth thou wilt debate with it: he stayeth his rough wind in the day of his east wind.*[1412] All his chastisements upon his people are stinted by measure and favorable proportion – and when he fans them, he blows not all away, but stays, or keeps in, his rough wind, that it should not blow too fiercely and furiously.

(v) **Fifthly**, God will supply his people's most extreme wants in afflictions, with all necessary provisions – and this because he is their God. Wants of necessaries in an afflicted condition, greatly aggravates affliction – yea, are themselves a very great affliction. But the LORD will work extraordinarily, rather than they shall not seasonably be supplied. How sweet are those promises! *When the poor and needy seek water, and there is none; and their tongue faileth for thirst; I the LORD will hear them, I the God of Israel will not forsake them. I will open rivers in high-places, and fountains in midst of the valleys: I will make the wilderness a pool of water, and the dry land springs of water. I will plant in the wilderness the cedar, the shittah-tree, and the myrtle, and the oil-tree: I will set in the desert the fir-tree, the pine, and the box-tree*

[1411] Psalm 78:1, 37-38
[1412] Isaiah 27:7-8

together: that they may see and know, and consider, and understand together, that the hand of the LORD hath done this, and the holy one of Israel hath created it.[1413] This seems to have reference, immediately, to the extreme misery of God's people under the Babylonian captivity, and the difficulty of their return thence: mediately, to the spiritual bondage of his elect under sin, etc., typified and shadowed out under Egypt's bondage, and Babylon's captivity; and so it is most comfortably applicable, even to all God's afflicted and distressed ones under the New Covenant. The extremity of the Jews sufferings in Babylon, or in the way thence to Zion, are set forth under the metaphor of extreme thirst. Hunger and thirst are intolerable and deadly if not satisfied. But thirst is the far more intolerable of the two. Against such distress the Lord comforts them: more generally, in that he will hear them and not forsake them.

More particularly, in that he will extraordinarily and beyond the course of nature provide liberally for their necessities, namely: water against their thirst, even rivers in high places, fountains in valleys, pools in the wilderness, and springs in the dry land; shade and shelter against the parching heat of the sun, by replenishing the wilderness with great variety of pleasant, bushy, shady trees, so that the long, dry, barren and parching wilderness, which they were to pass through from Babylon to Zion, should not hinder or discourage them. Also under these waters and shady trees, are metaphorically implied the spiritual refreshments and comforts which God affords his called ones in their way to heaven.

(vi) **Sixthly**, God is graciously present with his covenant people in midst of their greatest sufferings and afflictions – and that because he is their God in covenant. Upon this consideration, the Lord comforts his Israel against his afflictions and enemies; *Fear thou not, for I am with thee; be not dismayed, for*

[1413] Isaiah 41:17-20

I am thy God.[1414] Being his God, he was with him: being with him, he need not fear nor be dismayed by reason of any evils or enemies.

To like effect was that wonder which Moses saw: *the Angel of the LORD appeared unto him in a flame of fire out of the midst of a bush; and he looked, and behold the bush burned with fire, and the bush was not consumed. - and God called unto him out of the midst of the bush, and said, Moses, Moses. - draw not nigh hither; put off thy shoes from off thy feet, for the place whereon thou standest is holy ground. - I am the God of thy father, the God of Abraham, the God of Isaac, and the God of Jacob,* etc.[1415] This was the marvel, but what was the mystery and meaning of it? This bush was the church: the {Israel of God}. This fire wherewith the bush burned, was the fire of afflictions wherewith Israel the church of God had been already exercised in Egypt, and should be yet further exercised in the wilderness and in other places. This burning of the bush without consuming, was the churches singular and admirable preservation from ruin and destruction under afflictions: she lived, like the three noble Jews, without hurt in midst of flames;[1416] or as Paul, *troubled on every side, yet not distressed; perplexed, but not in despair: persecuted, but not forsaken: cast-down, but not destroyed*; under afflictions, but not swallowed up of afflictions: in fiery trials, but not devoured by fiery trials; in the furnace and fining pot, but still unconsumed gold in the fining pot.[1417] And the angel of the Lord in the flame of fire in the midst of the bush, was the Lord God himself, the Covenant God of Abraham, Isaac and Jacob, who was graciously and powerfully present with his church in her sharpest afflictions, preserving her from destruction by those afflictions. Being their Covenant God, he was present with his people in midst of their sufferings.

Oh, what an admirable comfort is this to all the Lord's true federates! We may be a bush burning with flames of afflictions, but the God of Abraham,

---

[1414] Isaiah 41:10
[1415] Exodus 3:2-6
[1416] Daniel 3:24-25
[1417] 2 Corinthians 4:8-9

Isaac, and Jacob, our Covenant God, is present with us in the midst of those flames. We may be sharply afflicted: but our God will be with us in those afflictions. With us by his special providence, by his mighty power, by his singular wisdom, by his peculiar graces and comforts. So with us, as none in the world besides him could be with us. With us in the fire, in the water, in prisons, in dungeons, in the wilderness, in the shadow of death. God was with Joseph in prison; with Israel in Egypt, and in the wilderness; with Elisha endangered by the Syrians; with Paul in the terrible tempest at sea, when they suffered shipwreck; with Jonah in the bottom of the sea in the belly of the whale; with Daniel in the lions' den; with the three valiant and noble-spirited Jews in the burning fiery furnace; and with his martyrs at the stakes. Whoever starts [moves away] from us, our God will never start from us, but be near unto us in perplexities.[1418] And God's presence with his afflicted people, is a manifold comfort to his afflicted people. For, hence it is that: (a) he exactly observes and lays to heart their sorrows, (b) he animates them against their fears, (c) he preserves them from destruction, (d) he enables them to endure, (e) he transforms the very nature of their sufferings, (f) he avenges them of their adversaries, and (g) he seasonably delivers them out of all.

(a) Hence he exactly observes and lays to heart their sorrows and sufferings. He is present with them, therefore he cannot choose but know and pity their afflicted condition. He was in the midst of the bush burning with fire: therefore he perfectly knew the force, fury and sharpness of that fire, and how the bush smarted in it.[1419] Hence he spoke so sympathisingly: *I have surely seen the affliction of my people which are in Egypt, and have heard their cry by reason of their taskmasters: for I know their sorrows: and I am come down to deliver them out of the hand of the Egyptians*. He knows their sorrows, and pities them; he pities them, and delivers them. He observes and lays to heart, every stripe they bear, every groan they sigh out, every tear they let fall, every

---

[1418] 2 Timothy 4:16-17
[1419] Exodus 3:2-7

drop of blood they shed, etc. not one of all these shall be neglected or forgotten of their God.

(b) Hence he animates them against their fears. Afflictions, dangers, and troubles are apt to fill them with fears. David before Achish King of Gath was full of fears: *I sought the LORD, and he heard me, and delivered me from all my fears.*[1420] And says Paul: *We were troubled on every side; without were fightings, within were fears.*[1421] Now God's presence with his people in their most dangerous afflicted state, is a singular antidote against all their fears. Thus God propounds it: *Fear thou not, for I am with thee: be not dismayed, for I am thy God.*[1422] And again: *Thus saith the LORD, that created thee, O Jacob, and he that formed thee, O Israel, Fear not: for I have redeemed thee, I have called thee by thy name, thou art mine. When thou passest through the waters, I will be with thee, etc.*[1423] And thus God's people have proven it – especially when they have apprehended God's presence with them in their distresses. With what courage and resolution have they trampled upon their fears and dangers? *Though I walk through the valley of the shadow of death, I will fear no evil: for thou art with me, thy rod and thy staff they comfort me.*[1424] We fear evils because we apprehend they will be too hard for us, and over-match us; but God's presence apprehended, dissipates these fears, because we know that God can over-match all our dangers and distresses.

(c) Hence he preserves them from destruction. God's presence with his afflicted people, is their all-sufficient preservative. It was God's presence in the burning bush that kept the burning bush from being consumed.[1425] It was God's presence with the three Jews in the fiery furnace that preserved them from being burnt to death by the merciless flames – yea, from the smell of fire

---

[1420] Psalm 34 title & verse 4
[1421] 2 Corinthians 7:5
[1422] Isaiah 41:10
[1423] Isaiah 43:1-2
[1424] Psalm 23:4
[1425] Exodus 3:2

on their garments.[1426] It was God's presence with Daniel in the den of hungry lions that shut their mouths, that they did not break and tear him to pieces.[1427] When God is with us, safety is with us.

(d) Hence he enables them to endure and undergo the worst of sufferings. God's presence is an assisting and an enabling presence. When God is with us in trouble, he enables us to do and endure beyond ourselves. *Fear thou not, for I am with thee: be not dismayed, for I am thy God: I will strengthen thee, yea I will help thee; yea I will uphold thee with the right hand of my righteousness. – For I the LORD thy God will hold thy right hand, saying unto thee, Fear not, I will help thee.*[1428] If God's presence helps us, how easily shall we bear the heaviest burdens? How courageously shall we oppose the greatest dangers? How constantly shall we endure the greatest extremities? How wonderfully did God's presence uphold Job in all his unparalleled troubles from sinking and despairing! Without God's helpful presence, those troubles wou;d have broken his back. Though of ourselves in such cases we can do nothing, yet through our God assisting, we shall be able to do all things.

(e) Hence he transforms the very nature of their sufferings, that they become as no sufferings or afflictions, but rather advantages to God's people. His presence with Daniel in the lions' den, changes the tearing lions as it were into harmless lambs, and the dismal den into a safe receptacle.[1429] The lions were intended for his executioners, and the den for his grave: but the den became his chamber of safe rest, and the lions his quiet companions. God's presence with the three Jews in the fiery furnace, suspends the fury of the fire, that it burnt them no more than the temperate air. It burnt their bonds, but set them at liberty to walk therein without hurt.[1430] To this effect God, promised first his presence to his afflicted Jacob, and then from his presence,

---

[1426] Daniel 3:24-25
[1427] Daniel 6:21-22
[1428] Isaiah 41:10, 13-14
[1429] Daniel 6:21-22
[1430] Daniel 3:24-25

the transforming of their afflictions into an un-afflicting disposition: *When thou passest through the water, I will be with thee* (there is his presence in affliction), *and through the rivers, they shall not overflow thee. When thou walkest through the fire, thou shalt not be burnt; neither shall the flame kindle upon thee. For I am the LORD thy God; the Holy One of Israel, thy saviour.*[1431] God's presence turned holy Bradford's prison as into a pleasant parlor. God's presence made Laurence Sanders, martyr, say: "I was in prison, until I got into prison."[1432] And at another time: "My dear Lord Jesus Christ hath begun to me of a more bitter cup than mine shall be, and shall I not pledge my most sweet savior?" Afterwards, he took the stake, to which he should be chained, in his arms, and kissed it, saying: "Welcome the cross of Christ, welcome everlasting life." God's presence enabled James Baynham (as he was at the stake in the midst of the flaming fire, which fire had half consumed his arms and his legs) to speak these words: "O ye papists, behold! Ye look for miracles, and here now you may see a miracle: for in this fire I feel no more pain than if I were in a bed of down; but it is to me as a bed of roses."[1433] By the influence and comfort of God's presence, their sufferings are so changed and altered, that they are as no sufferings, shadows of sufferings rather than realities. As it were reproaches, and yet glory and honor; as it were imprisonment, and yet enlargement; as it were pains, and yet ease; as it were torments, and yet contentments; as it were poverty, and yet plenty; as it were miseries, and yet mercies; as it were troubles, and yet triumphs, etc. To this effect, Paul elegantly declares his own and other ministers' experiences, saying: *as deceivers, and yet true; as unknown, and yet well known; as dying, and behold we live: as chastened, and not killed; as sorrowful, yet always rejoicing; as poor, yet making many rich; as having nothing, and yet possessing all things.*[1434] Thus the presence of God in his people's troubles, brings light out of darkness, digests

---

[1431] Isaiah 43:2-3
[1432] John Foxe, *Acts & Monuments*, Volume 3, p.139 (London, 1641)
[1433] John Foxe, *Acts & Monuments*, Volume 2, p.301 (London, 1641)
[1434] 2 Corinthians 6:8-10

the viper into a treacle, turns all things (beyond the philosopher's stone) into gold.

(f) Hence he avenges his afflicted people of their adversaries instrumentally, to inflict or aggravate their afflictions. The Lord – assuring his people of his presence in their afflictions – thereupon promises to crush their afflicting adversaries.[1435] God's presence with the three Jews preserved them from being devoured by the flames; whilst they were being burnt to death by the same flames that cast them into the furnace.[1436] God's presence saves Israel in the bowels of the sea, and drowns Israel's enemies, the Egyptians, in the bottom of the sea.[1437]

(g) Hence finally, he seasonably delivers his afflicted people out of all their afflictions. God's presence is his afflicted people's deliverance. When God had declared his presence in the burning bush, in the afflicted church, and had expressed himself to be the God of Abraham, Isaac and Jacob, that is, their covenant God; he presently added: *I have surely seen the affliction of my people which are in Egypt, – and I am come down to deliver them out of the hand of the Egyptians*, etc.[1438] He was present with the three Jews in the fiery furnace, to deliver them out of the furnace and the fire. He was with Daniel in the lions' den, to deliver him both from the horrid den and from the cruel lions.[1439] He was with Joseph in the prison and in irons, to deliver him from the prison, and make him ruler of the land of Egypt.[1440] He was present with Paul at his first answer before Nero; when no man stood with him, but all men forsook him; notwithstanding the Lord stood with him, and strengthened him, that by him the preaching might be fully known, and that all the Gentiles might believe; and he was delivered out of the mouth of the lion.[1441] And thus

---

[1435] Isaiah 41:10-17
[1436] Daniel 3:22, 24-25
[1437] Exodus 14 throughout
[1438] Exodus 3:2, 6-8
[1439] Daniel 6:21-22
[1440] Genesis 41:14 to the end
[1441] 2 Timothy 4:16-18

God's promise runs to every true believer that makes the Almighty his refuge, his fortress, his God: *I will be with him in trouble, I will deliver him, and honor him.*[1442] If God is with us in trouble, we need not fear our deliverance out of trouble. If Christ is in the ship, in the storm, the disciples need not doubt their weathering out of it, and their safe arrival on the shore. These are the comforts which flow from God's presence with his covenant people in their afflictions. And he will be thus present with them therein, because he is their Covenant God.

(vii) Seventhly and lastly, the Lord God will do much good to all his covenant people by all their afflictions and persecutions. He is their God and father, and they his children: therefore all his chastisements upon them, are for their benefit. *He for our profit, that we might be partakers of his holiness.*[1443] He actually becomes their God, by calling them effectually according to his purpose. *And* (says Paul) *we know that all things* (and he especially intends afflictions and persecutions) *work together for good to them that love God, that are the called according to his purpose.*[1444] Their God so loves them, and holds them so dear unto him, that he would not suffer any evil of affliction and persecution to befall them, but out of which he will extract a greater good, yea a manifold good, for:

(a) Hereby he more clearly convinces them of their sins, and of the sinfulness thereof. As blots appear broadest in wet paper. *And if they be-bound in fetters, and be holden in cords of affliction: then he showeth them their work, and their transgressions that they have exceeded.*[1445] Joseph's brethren, being brought into some straits and distress in Egypt, call to mind afresh their cruel dealing with their brother Joseph many years ago.[1446]

[1442] Psalm 91:1-2, 15
[1443] Hebrews 12:6-11
[1444] Romans 8:28
[1445] Job 36:8-10
[1446] Genesis 42:[2-4], 21-22

(b) Hereby he more kindly melts and humbles them for their iniquities. The fire of tribulation softens their hearts like wax to take any impression, and melts them like mettle fit to run into any mold. Hezekiah, after his recovery, had *his heart lifted up: therefore there was wrath upon him, and upon Judah and Jerusalem.* Notwithstanding, Hezekiah humbled himself for the lifting up of his heart – both he and the inhabitants of Jerusalem.[1447] Yea, when that precious king Josiah discerned but God's rod shaken against the land in the threatenings of the book of the law, he rent his clothes, and humbled himself, and his heart was tender, and he wept before the Lord.[1448]

(c) Hereby he purges and purifies them from their iniquities. *Then he openeth their ear to discipline, and commandeth that they return from iniquity.*[1449] *He stayeth his rough wind, in the day of his east wind. By this therefore shall the iniquity of Jacob be purged, and this is all the fruit to take away his sin.*[1450] David himself could say: *Before I was afflicted, I went astray; but now have I kept thy word.*[1451] Afflictions hunt us again into God's park, when we have leapt out. They are God's furnace to burn up our dross, God's files to rub off our rust, God's soap and fuller's earth to fetch out our stains and spots, God's fan to blow away our chaff, and God's purgatives [laxatives] to evacuate our corrupt and peccant humors. Distresses and persecutions are much like the fiery furnace to the three Jews, which hurt not their bodies, but only burnt their bonds in sunder: they consume not us, but our bonds and cords of sin, to set us at more spiritual liberty.[1452]

(d) Hereby they are conformed to Christ, the firstborn among many brethren, who took up his cross, and was a man of sorrows, even perfected and

---

[1447] 2 Chronicles 32:24-26
[1448] 2 Chronicles 34:26-27
[1449] Job 36:8-10
[1450] Isaiah 27:8-9
[1451] Psalm 119:67
[1452] Daniel 3:23-25

consecrated through sufferings.[1453] Now it is the honor and perfection of the members to be conform to their head.[1454]

(e) Hereby their graces are proved and tried, whether they are true or counterfeit. The heat of persecution made the fruit of the stony-ground hearers to wither away, when the fruit of the good-ground hearers persevered to perfection.[1455] The storm tries the building, and discovers which is built upon a rock, which upon the sands.[1456] *The devil shall cast some of you into prison that you may be tried.*[1457] – *Think it not strange concerning the fiery trial, which is to try you.*[1458] – *That the trial of your faith being much more precious than of gold that perisheth, though it be tried with fire, might be found unto praise and honor and glory.*[1459] The storm tries the pilot. The touchstone tries the metal, whether it is gold or copper. The furnace tries the gold, whether it is pure or drossy. So afflictions and persecutions try the Christian. Paint will rub off with washing, but true beauty by washing will appear more beautiful.

(f) Hereby their graces are improved and advanced to greater perfection. *Tribulation worketh patience; and patience experience; and experience hope; and hope makes not ashamed.*[1460] As Israel, the more they were afflicted, the more they grew;[1461] or, as the palm-tree the more it is pressed downward, the more it contends upward; so their faith, patience, etc, are improved and excited by sufferings and opposition. The sun shows biggest face in lowest state, the nail shines the brighter by wearing, the pomander smells the sweeter by rubbing, the camomile grows better by treading upon it – so sufferings

---

[1453] Romans 8:28-29
[1454] Isaiah 53:2-4, Hebrews 2:9-10
[1455] Matthew 13:20-21, 23
[1456] Matthew 7:24 to the end
[1457] Revelation 2:10
[1458] 1 Peter 4:12
[1459] 1 Peter 1:6-7
[1460] Romans 5:3-5
[1461] Exodus 1:12

draw forth the activity, beauty and fragrance of graces. But for sufferings, Job's patience had never been so renowned.[1462]

(g) Hereby their saint-like duties and devotions are notably incited and revived. Their meditations, prayer, obedience, etc., are then put upon the wheels. David said: *It is good for me that I have been afflicted: that I might learn thy statutes.*[1463] David never prayed more pathetically and fervently than when under God's rod. We read not of David's scandalous miscarriages while he was under Saul's persecutions, but then he frequently poured forth his purest devotions. As the strings of an instrument make no melody until they are struck, or as the birds in the spring sing most sweetly when it rains most sadly.

(h) Hereby their son-like relation to God is notably cleared.[1464] He chastises them as a Father, while they are enabled to endure his chastisements as children. God will not spend his rods upon bastards and strangers; but upon his own children, because he loves them. Such afflictions, though bad things, yet are good signs.

(i) Hereby, their future condemnation is prevented: when you are judged, you are chastened of the Lord, that you should not be condemned in the world.[1465]

(j) Hereby, finally, God prepares his people for their eternal glory in the world to come. The cross is the way to the crown; martyrdom to the kingdom. Christ was first humbled, and then exalted; first he descended into the lower parts of the earth, and after ascended far above all heavens.[1466] And his members must go to heaven the same way. *Through much tribulation we must enter into the kingdom of God.*[1467] *If we suffer, we shall also reign with him.*[1468]

[1462] James 5:11
[1463] Psalm 119:71
[1464] Hebrews 12:6-10, Amos 3:2; 1 Peter 4:17-18
[1465] 1 Corinthians 11:32
[1466] Ephesians 4:9-10, Luke 24:26
[1467] Acts 14:22
[1468] 2 Timothy 2:12, Romans 8:17

Our light affliction which is but for a moment; worketh for us a far more exceeding and eternal weight of glory.[1469] The harbor is more grateful to the mariner after a tempestuous voyage; rest is more sweet to the laborer after a weary day; health is more gladdening to the patient after sharp and tedious sickness; liberty is more delightful to the captive after long and rigorous imprisonment: and doubtless heaven itself will be more ravishing, even a double heaven to God's people, after all their earthly sufferings and persecutions. These things being so, write upon all your losses, crosses, pains, diseases, poverty, reproaches, bonds, imprisonments, chains, prison doors, and upon the forehead of all your sufferings, this universal and most cordial consolation: **yet the Lord is my God by his own everlasting Covenant.**

{7} **Finally, what a singular comfort is this against all the terrors and pangs even of death itself: that the Lord is our God by an everlasting New Covenant!**

Death is the privation of life, and separation of soul from the body. Life is most precious. *Skin for skin, and all that a man hath will he give for his life.*[1470] Death is *the wages of sin*; and has *passed upon all men, for that all have sinned.*[1471] Death is the king of terrors – מֶלֶךְ בַּלָּהוֹת – the most terrible of terribles.[1472] Death is a dangerous enemy, and the last enemy that shall be destroyed by Christ.[1473] Naturally, until Christ delivers them, men are through fear of death all their lifetime subject to bondage.[1474] What slavish fears, terrors, tremblings, agonies, etc. enthrall men in regard to death? Yea, Jesus Christ himself, when his death approached, prayed earnestly thrice: *Father, if it be possible, let this cup pass from me,* etc.[1475] No wonder then that the serious

---

[1469] 2 Corinthians 4:7
[1470] Job 2:4
[1471] Romans 6:23 & 5:12
[1472] Job 18:24
[1473] 1 Corinthians 15:24
[1474] Hebrews 2:15
[1475] Matthew 26:38-39, 42, 44

apprehensions of death approaching, sometimes perplex the children of God, fill them with fears, sadness, and discomfort. They had need therefore to store up choicest cordials against that hour.

Now against death, what cordial can more comfort and revive God's people than this: that the Lord is their God by his everlasting New Covenant? For, this affords a fivefold comfort against death.

(i) *First*, the Lord is still the God of his covenant people in death as well as in life, and in death they all live unto him. He is their God by an everlasting Covenant, therefore he is their God forever: their God in life, their God in death, and their God to all eternity.[1476] Death cannot disannul an everlasting Covenant, though it should destroy a temporary covenant. After Abraham, Isaac, and Jacob – God's covenant people – had been dead and buried long ago, God told Moses out of the burning bush: *I am the God of Abraham, and the God of Isaac, and the God of Jacob*.[1477] God's Covenant with them lived still, though they were dead, and they were still his covenant people, and he their God. Even death dissolved not this covenant union and relation between them. Hence Christ infers the resurrection of the dead, saying: {*he is not the God of the dead, but the God of the living*};[1478] namely: according to his everlasting covenant. His covenant people, though deceased, yet are not absolutely dead, but all alive to him, that is: their souls are actually alive with him; their bodies are virtually and potentially alive to him, in that he can, and will at last raise them from the dead; and their whole persons are federally alive to him, as being still his in covenant, which cannot be destroyed by death. Their living souls, their dead bodies, their dead dust are his: death may divide the soul from the body – and both from the land of the living, from earthly friends, and all worldly enjoyments, but can divide neither soul nor body from God and his Covenant. The Lord is still theirs, and they are his. *For none of us liveth to himself, and no man dieth to himself. For whether we live, we live unto*

[1476] Hebrews 8:10 & 13:20
[1477] Exodus 3:6
[1478] Matthew 22:31-32, Mark 12:26-27, Luke 20:37-38

the Lord: and whether we die, we die unto the Lord: whether we live therefore or die, we are the Lord's.[1479]

What a comfort is this! The Lord will continue your God in death, as well as life; in the grave, as well as in the land of the living. He will look down from heaven into your grave; there he will own your dead bones and ashes, which your dearest friends abhor to look upon; there he will take care of your dead dust, which others trample underfoot: there he will keep it as a dear and precious treasure until the morning of the resurrection. You do not lose your God, when you die and are laid in grave; no more than when you liest down in bed to sleep. He is your God still in death itself: and you are his.

(ii) **Secondly**, death cannot separate God's covenant people from the bosom of God's love. This flows from the former, for if death cannot separate them from God, it cannot separate them from his love: if in death he continues their God still, in death he continues his love still unto them. Hence Paul triumphs: *I am persuaded, that neither death, nor life, etc. Nor height, nor depth, nor any other creature, shall be able to separate us from the love of God which is in Christ Jesus our Lord.*[1480] Death may separate you from the love of friends, acquaintance, kindred, family, children, parents, wife, husband, and of all in this world: but can never separate you from the love of your God. They may love you till death: but God will love you in death. God will love you, when none in this world besides will love you: when your strength is weakness, when your beauty is paleness and ghastliness, when your honor is in the dust, when you are a deformed lump of dead cold clay, when you are surrounded with worms and rottenness, when thou art returned into ashes, etc. Even then will God continue his dear love unto you. And God's love infinitely transcends all love of creatures in all the world.

(iii) **Thirdly**, the Lord is with them in the shadow of death. For, if the Lord remain their God still, and love them still, even in death: consequently he

---

[1479] Romans 14:7-9
[1480] Romans 8:38-39

must needs be graciously with them in death itself. *Fear thou not, for I am with thee: be not dismayed, for I am thy God*, etc.[1481] Hence David encourages himself: *The Lord is my shepherd; I shall not want. – Yea though I walk through the valley of the shadow of death, I will fear no evil: for thou art with me, thy rod and thy staff they comfort me.*[1482] That is, "your shepherd's staff and crook, your special providence, protection and guidance they comfort me: you will keep me safe in greatest danger, you wilt order and overrule all things for best for me, therefore I fear not." He that will be their refuge in straits, a very present help in trouble;[1483] will he not be with his people in the greatest strait, and shock of death, when they have most need? Yea, he will then be with them peculiarly – and that in three ways, namely:

(a) With them by his special providence, to protect and preserve them from deadly danger, until their appointed time come, as with David,[1484] with Paul,[1485] etc., and to order their death and all the circumstances of it for their best, when their time is come. Herein they are much comforted.

(b) With them by his Spirit and grace; assisting, strengthening and supporting them against all faintings of spirit, slavish fears, sad apprehensions of death, and temptations which may then arise: enabling them constantly to persevere notwithstanding all.

Thus he was with Job, when he said: *though he slay me, yet will I trust in him.*[1486] *– I know that my redeemer liveth, and that he shall stand at the latter day upon the earth. And though after my skin, worms destroy this body, yet in my flesh shall I see God: whom I shall see for myself, and mine eyes shall behold, and not another, though my reins be consumed within me.*[1487]

[1481] Isaiah 41:10
[1482] Psalm 23:1, 4
[1483] Psalm 46:1-2
[1484] Psalm 23:4
[1485] 2 Timothy 4:16-18
[1486] Job 13:15
[1487] Job 2:4

Thus he was with David, saying: *Whom have I in heaven but thee? And there is none upon earth that I desire besides thee. My flesh and my heart faileth: but God is the strength of my heart, and my portion forever.*[1488]

Thus he was with Stephen immediately before he was stoned to death; for, *he being full of the Holy Ghost, looked up steadfastly into heaven, and saw the glory of God and Jesus standing on the right hand of God; and said, behold I see the heavens opened, and the Son of man standing on the right hand of God.*[1489] And hereby he was so supported against that mortal and murdering shower of stones; that he not only commended his spirit sweetly unto the Lord, calling upon God, and saying: {*Lord Jesus receive my spirit*}; but also *he kneeled down and prayed with a loud voice for his bloody persecutors, Lord lay not this sin to their charge.*[1490]

Thus he was with Thomas Hawks the martyr, who, "when his speech was taken away by the violence of the flame, his skin drawn together, and his fingers consumed with the fire, so that all men thought certainly he had been gone, suddenly and contrary to all expectation, he reached up his hands burning on a light fire over his head, triumphantly clapping them three times together."[1491]

Thus he was with James Baynham martyr in the flames, who when his legs and arms were half consumed with fire, said; "O ye papists, behold, ye look for miracles, and here now you may see a miracle, for in this fire I feel no more pain than if I were in a bed of down, but it is to me as a bed of roses."[1492]

Thus the Lord – being with his people by his Spirit and grace – is their strength in weakness, their courage in fears, their cordial in faintings, their ease in pain, their triumph in troubles, their liberty in bondage, their life in death.

[1488] Job 19:25-27
[1489] Acts 7:55-56, etc.
[1490] Acts 7:59-60
[1491] John Foxe, *Acts & Monuments*, Volume 3, p.266 (London, 1641)
[1492] John Foxe, *Acts & Monuments*, Volume 2, p.301 (London, 1641)

(c) With them by the ministry of angels sent forth to minister for them who shall be heirs of salvation.[1493] These angels, sometimes miraculously keep them from death, in deadly danger, as the three Jews in the fiery furnace,[1494] Daniel in the lions' den,[1495] Paul in his shipwreck at sea,[1496] etc, sometimes comfort, strengthen, and encourage them against death, as when Christ himself was in his agony a little before his death, *there appeared an angel unto him from heaven strengthening him.*[1497] And always, they immediately, upon dissolution of soul and body, conduct the souls of God's people into Abraham's bosom, into heaven. Lazarus the beggar died and was carried by the angels into Abraham's bosom.[1498] Yea the angels like a chariot and horses of fire carried up Elijah both soul and body by a whirlwind into heaven.[1499] Oh then, why should God's people be so appalled at death? Their God is with them in the valley of the shadow of death.[1500] Why should they be afraid? There is more with them than against them.

(iv) **Fourthly**, the Lord has pardoned all the sins of his New Covenant people, and will remember them no more.[1501] This the tenor of his New Covenant with them. Now all their sins being pardoned, death is utterly disarmed, the sting of death is plucked out, for *the sting of death is sin.*[1502] The sting of death being plucked out, death is become but a drone, a name, a noise to God's people. Who fears a hornet, or a snake, or a scorpion, etc., when he knows they have lost their stings? Then they may handle them, put them into their bosoms without harm. In this regard God's people may triumph over death: *O death where is thy sting? O grave where is thy victory?*[1503] Our God has

---

[1493] Hebrews 1:14
[1494] Daniel 3:24-25
[1495] Daniel 6:22
[1496] Acts 27:23-24
[1497] Luke 22:43-44
[1498] Luke 16:22
[1499] 2 Kings 2:1
[1500] Psalm 23:4
[1501] Hebrews 8:10-12
[1502] 1 Corinthians 15:56
[1503] 1 Corinthians 15:55

destroyed all your venom, poison, curse, mischief; he has plucked out your sting, he has pardoned our sins – now Death, do your worst.

(v) *Fifthly*, the Lord God has given unto his covenant people Jesus Christ the mediator of his Covenant, as their absolute conquest and triumph over death, and antidote against death. If they tremble, when they look down at death: they may triumph, when they look up to Christ. Christ is their true Joshua: by him they are called forth to set their feet upon the very neck of this conquered enemy, as sometimes Israel upon the necks of the five conquered kings,[1504] for:

(a) Christ by dying has conquered death, and has buried the grave by being buried in the grave, and rising again. He died and was buried for our sins, who himself knew no sin;[1505] and so receiving in himself the sting of sin, has plucked out that sting for us, as the bee – striking his sting upon a dead body – retains his sting still; but striking it into a living body he loses his sting, and becomes a drone; so death – striking his sting into Christ's living body wherein was no spiritual deadliness – has lost his sting as to Christ's members forevermore. Actually he has subdued death in his own person, and virtually he hath subdued it for his members. His rising from the dead proclaimed his victory;[1506] his ascending into heaven was his triumph, for then he led captivity captive.[1507]

(b) Christ – having conquered death – has also by death subdued *him that had the power of death, that is, the devil*.[1508] The devil has the power of death, not authoritatively, that is God's prerogative; but executively, as the hangman has power over the gallows: him Christ has destroyed by dying. He has given him his mortal heart-stab, that by death he shall not have such cursed and full dominion over his elect, as once he had.

[1504] Joshua 10:24
[1505] Romans 4:25; 1 Corinthians 15:3-4; 2 Corinthians 5:21
[1506] Acts 2:24, Romans 1:4
[1507] Ephesians 4:8, etc.
[1508] Hebrews 2:14, Colossians 2:14-15

(c) Christ – having conquered death, and him that had the power of death, the devil – now has the keys of hell and death.[1509] It is an allusion to stewards in kings houses that have the rule of the house committed to them, and the keys thereof delivered to them as a badge of their authority. So here, Christ has the keys of hell and death, that is, the power and rule over hell and death. He opens and none shuts, he shuts and none opens. He lets in, and he keeps out of, death, grave and hell, whom, when and how he pleases. Death and grave shall not touch any of his members, till he please; nor further then he orders or permits. The time, place, manner and all circumstances of their death, are all appointed and determined by him.

O Christian, fear not to enter into the house of death, when your time is come, for Christ's time is the best time. He has the keys of death, he lets you in, and he will let you out again. What a comfort is this! Not the devil, nor any of your enemies have the keys of death but only Jesus Christ your Savior. Whilst you shall continue in state of the dead, you shall be only under Christ's lock and key. When death or grave fright you, remember this. Christ hath the keys of death: shake Christ's keys at hell and death, and triumph over them. Jesus Christ reigns over death: therefore death shall not reign over you.

(d) Jesus Christ died and rose again, not only to *destroy him that had the power of death, that is, the devil*, but also to *deliver* his people *who through fear of death were all their lifetime subject to bondage*.[1510] Fear of death has a bondage and slavery in it; Christ delivers his people from this servile fear by dying for them. For, hereby he purged away their sins, and so plucked out the sting of death.[1511] Hereby he destroyed the power of death.[1512] Hereby he took occasion to rise again from the dead victoriously, and to ascend triumphantly.[1513] Like Samson bearing away the bars and gates of the city

---

[1509] Revelation 1:18
[1510] Hebrews 7:14-15
[1511] Hebrews 1:3; 1 Corinthians 15:56
[1512] Hosea 13:14; 1 Corinthians 15:54
[1513] 1 Corinthians 15:3-4, Ephesians 4:8-10

wherein he was encompassed, Christ carried away the bars and gates of death wherein he was held.[1514] Fear not therefore this king of fears, death. Christ purposely died to deliver you from these fears. If you give way to them, if you suffer them to have dominion over you, how do you cross and frustrate one eminent end of his death? When Christ came into the world, God sent him, in performance of the mercy promised to our fathers, and in remembrance of his holy covenant; *the oath which he sware to our father Abraham, that he would grant unto us, that we being delivered out of the hands of our enemies without fear,* (death being one of these enemies), *might serve him in holiness and righteousness before him all the days of our life.*[1515]

(e) In and through Jesus Christ the malignity, venom, poison, and mischief of death is removed – yea, turned into great advantage unto God's covenant people. Not only the world, and life, but death also, with things present and to come, even all things are theirs, and they are Christ's, and Christ is God's.[1516] Death is theirs for good as well as life, or any other thing here instanced in.

What? Death is theirs? Would it not be better for them if death were not theirs?

No. Death is their friend, not their foe: their advantage, not their prejudice. Of carnal men, it may be said, they are death's; they are death's slaves, death's captives, etc; but of Christians it may be said "death is theirs:" theirs to serve them, to befriend them, to do them good, namely: (1) death is their dissolution, separating soul and body for a while: not their desolation or destruction.[1517] (2) Death is their rest from their labors in sin and sorrow, wherewith they have been so woefully toiled and tired.[1518] They rest in their beds of their graves, sweetened and perfumed by Christ's own burial for

---

[1514] Judges 16:2-3
[1515] Luke 1:72-75 with Genesis 22:16
[1516] 1 Corinthians 3:21-23
[1517] Philippians 1:23, Luke 2:29
[1518] Revelation 14:13

them.[1519] What wearied bones or body are afraid to go to rest? (3) Death is their sleep in Jesus.[1520] They sleep as in the arms and bosom of Jesus under his peculiar custody: for he hath the keys of death. If they sleep, they shall do well; they shall awake again in the morning of the resurrection: and then they shall awake mightily refreshed with heavenly qualifications.[1521] (4) Death is their unclothing, or putting off of their earthly tabernacle, that they may be clothed upon with their house which is from heaven: that mortality may be swallowed up by life.[1522] Their changing of earthly rags, for heavenly robes; of perishing clay tabernacles, for eternal mansions in the heavens. (5) Death is their departure, or [loosening] from the earthly shore, that they may presently land in the desired haven and harbor of heaven itself.[1523] (6) Death is their absenting from the body, that they *may be present with the Lord Christ, which is far best of all*.[1524] (7) Death is their endless gain of immortality, of perfect grace, of glory, of paradise, of glorified saints, of glorious angels, and of the most glorious God in Jesus Christ face to face, the glory of glory.[1525]

(f) Jesus Christ will at last completely swallow up death in victory. *For, he must reign, till he hath put all enemies under his feet. The last enemy that shall be destroyed is death.*[1526] Christ has destroyed death already fully in his own person: he has destroyed death also incompletely in his members, removing the sting and curse of death: and he will destroy death completely for all his members when they shall be wholly freed from the very state of death and all corruptibility forever at the general resurrection, for: *then shall be brought to pass the saying that is written, death is swallowed up in victory. O death, where is thy sting? O grave, where is thy victory? The sting of death is sin: and the strength of sin is the law. But thanks be to God, which giveth us the victory*

[1519] Isaiah 57:2
[1520] 1 Thessalonians 4:14
[1521] 1 Corinthians 15:42-44
[1522] 2 Corinthians 5:1-4
[1523] Luke 2:29
[1524] 2 Corinthians 5:8, Philippians 1:23
[1525] Philippians 1:21
[1526] 1 Corinthians 15:25-26

through our Lord Jesus Christ.[1527] So that death shall fully be destroyed, though the last enemy that shall be destroyed. Yea then, *death and hell shall be cast into the lake of fire; this is the second death.*[1528] Thus Jesus Christ the mediator of the Covenant, is our victory and triumph over death, and effectual antidote against death. The Lord as our God in covenant, has thus comforted us against death in Jesus Christ.

In this regard, let us triumph against death with that blessed Jerome: "O cruel and hard-hearted death that divides brothers, and partest lovers! The Lord has brought up from the wilderness a burning wind, which has dried up your veins, and desolated your fountain. You have devoured (the true) Jonah, but in your belly he was alive. You carried him away as dead, that the tempest of the world might cease: and our nineveh be saved by his preaching. He, he has conquered you; he has stabbed you. Even the flying prophet, who left his house, forsook his inheritance, and gave his dear life into their hands that sought him. Who by Hosea of old rigidly threatened you: *O death I will be thy death: O grave, I will be your plague.* By his death, you are dead; by his death, we are made alive. You have devoured and you are devoured. And whilst you are solicited with the enticement of his assumed body, and with greedy jaws take him for a prey: he has eaten through your inward bowels. O Christ our savior, we your creature give you thanks, that our so potent adversary you have slain, whilst you were slain."[1529]

[1527] 1 Corinthians 15:54-57
[1528] Revelation 20:14
[1529] "O death that divides brothers knit together in love, how cruel, how ruthless you are so to sunder them! The Lord has fetched a burning wind that comes up from the wilderness: which has dried your veins and has made your well spring desolate. You swallowed up our Jonah, but even in your belly He still lived. You carried him as one dead, that the world's storm might be stilled and our Nineveh saved by his preaching. He, yes he, conquered you, He slew you, that fugitive prophet who left his home, gave up his inheritance and surrendered his dear life into the hands of those who sought it. He it was who of old threatened you in Hosea: *O death, I will be your plagues; O grave, I will be your destruction.* (Hosea 13:14). By his death you are dead; by his death we live. You have swallowed up and you are swallowed up. Whilst you are smitten with a longing for the body assumed by him, and while your greedy jaws fancy it a prey, your inward parts are wounded with hooked

Thus comfort yourselves, O you true New Covenant federates with God against Death, the King of Terrors, in that the Lord is your Covenant God, who is the King of Heaven. Upon your dying bed, upon your coffin, upon your hearse, upon your tomb and tombstone, write this triumphant sentence in capital characters:

THE LORD IS MY GOD
BY AN EVERLASTING NEW COVENANT.

Therefore death is mine – and all is mine.

Hitherto of the matter of the New Covenant, on the part of God, consisting in many excellent blessings, explicitly promised unto his federates. Next: of the matter of it, on the part of his federate people.

---

fangs. To you, O Saviour Christ, do we your creatures offer thanks that, when you were slain, you slew our mighty adversary."
Jerome's Letter 60, to Heliodorus [https://www.newadvent.org/fathers/3001060.htm] <Accessed 4/15/2024>

Aphorism 2

The matter of this New Covenant, on the part of God's New Covenant federates, consists in certain New Covenant duties, implicitly here required from, and restipulated by his New Covenant people.

[These duties are] namely: (1) knowledge, (2) faith, (3) repentance, (4) conformity to God's law in heart and life, and (5) entire, self-denying, self-resignation unto God.

The body of this New Covenant explicitly contains only promised mercies: but implicitly it also intends required and restipulated duties.[1530] Having already opened the mercies expressed: come we now to unfold the duties implied. And because all these five duties are implied in the blessings promised, which have been largely explained, it will be sufficient very briefly to indigitate and delineate these duties re-promised.

(1) **Knowledge**.

When in this New Covenant, God explicitly promises to his federates, a more excellent and universal knowledge of himself, and so of all the things of God, than ever was promised to his federates of the Old Covenant,[1531] as I have already manifested in opening the second article of the New Covenant; then God in this promise implicitly requires that all his New Covenant people be diligent and careful to abound and excel in the knowledge of God and his ways. I say, to excel in knowledge those of old under the Old Covenant; and God's federates do by consequent implicitly repromise and restipulate, through his grace, thus to know God. God's promise of such knowledge

---

[1530] Hebrews 8:10-12, Jeremiah 31:33-34
[1531] Hebrews 8:11, Jeremiah 31:34

obliges his federates to all possible endeavors after such knowledge, and to all due exercise of such knowledge.[1532]

For further clearing of this, it is to be diligently noted:

[1] That God in his New Testament calls for a more ripe, abounding, and increasing knowledge. *Brethren, be not children in understanding: howbeit, in malice be ye children, but in understanding be men;*[1533] τελειοι γινεσθε {*be ye perfect*}, or {*be ye of ripe age*}. And besides this: *giving all diligence, add to your faith, virtue; and to virtue, knowledge,* etc. *For if these things be in you and abound, they make you that you shall neither be barren, nor unfruitful in the knowledge of our Lord Jesus Christ.*[1534] And again: *but grow in grace, and in the knowledge of our Lord and savior Jesus Christ.*[1535] – *For the time ye ought to be teachers.*[1536] Under the Old Covenant, they knew as children under elements or rudiments: but under the New Covenant we should know as sons come to ripeness of age.[1537]

[2] That God under his New Covenant has given his federates a more plentiful measure of his Spirit, as a holy unction upon them, to make them know God and all things; more than ever was given under the Old Covenant.[1538]

[3] That under the New Covenant, God has purposely given all his New Covenant ministry – both extraordinary and ordinary – *for the perfecting of the saints, for the work of the ministry, for the edifying of the body of Christ; till we all come in the unity of the faith, and of the knowledge of the Son of God, unto a perfect man, unto the measure of the stature of the fullness of Christ: that we henceforth* (that is, from the time of the New Covenant dispensation) *be no more children, tossed to and fro, and carried about with every wind of*

[1532] 1 Corinthians 14:14-21
[1533] 1 Corinthians 14:20
[1534] 2 Peter 1:5-9
[1535] 2 Peter 3:18
[1536] Hebrews 5:12
[1537] Galatians 4:1-8
[1538] John 7:37-39; 1 John 2:20-21, 27

doctrine.[1539] The church's childlike knowledge should be over, and her man-like knowledge succeed, now under the New Covenant.

[4] That Jesus Christ makes so great reckoning of the knowledge of God under the New Testament, that he by his prophet ascribes justification to the knowledge of Christ: *By his knowledge shall my righteous servant justify many*;[1540] and by his own personal doctrine, places eternal life fundamentally in the knowledge of God and of Jesus Christ: *This is life eternal, to know thee the only true God, and Jesus Christ whom thou hast sent.*[1541]

[5] That gross ignorance of God and of his gospel, is so dangerous a sin now under the New Covenant in the midst of the glorious sunshine of the gospel, that it is a great evidence of such persons' lost condition, that Satan the god of this world has blinded them, through the just judgment of God;[1542] and that when the Lord Jesus shall be revealed from heaven with his mighty angels, he shall in flaming fire take vengeance on them that know not God, and obey not the gospel of our Lord Jesus Christ.[1543] By all this laid together, it is evident that now under the New Covenant, God requires from his federates, and they implicitly restipulate, to endeavor after a more excellent knowledge of God than was in ordinary under the Old Covenant.

What manner of knowledge of God this is, which is now under the New Covenant required and expected from us; and How we may know whether we have such a knowledge; hath been already manifested.[1544]

(2) Faith.

This New Covenant is laid down wholly in promises, and therefore God implicitly requires and expects faith from his federates to accept, embrace, and

---

[1539] Ephesians 4:11-14, to which purpose, the apostle notably prays for the knowledge of God in the Ephesians (Ephesians 1:16-19) and in the Philippians (Philippians 1:9-10).
[1540] Isaiah 53:11
[1541] John 17:3
[1542] 2 Corinthians 4:3-4
[1543] 2 Thessalonians 1:7-8
[1544] In opening the 2nd Article of this New Covenant in this 5th Chapter, Aphorism 1

apply those promises: God's promises and our faith are relatives. When God promises, he intends we should believe, otherwise how shall his promises, or promised mercies be appropriated to us as our own, without faith? But more particularly, when God promises here remission of sins, and so consequently justification in Christ, and for his satisfaction, as has been shown in opening the third article of this New Covenant;[1545] he also implicitly requires and expects from all his federates, and they implicitly restipulate (through his grace) true saving and justifying faith in Jesus Christ already revealed and exhibited, for as has been shown, remission of sins is promised only in Christ through faith; and by faith only is to be received.[1546] And we are justified by faith without the deeds of the law.[1547]

True faith in Christ to come afterwards, was required of the federates under the Old Covenant; they being by the law (not shut out from the faith, but) *shut up unto the faith, that after should be more clearly and fully revealed. The law being our school-master to bring us to Christ, that we might be justified by faith* (Galatians 3:22-24). But true faith in Christ, come already, humbled and exalted for us already, etc, is now much more called for and required of the federates under the New Covenant, for:

[1] Now the doctrine of justification by faith is come, being now more clearly and fully revealed than ever under the Old Covenant: *But after that faith is come, we are no longer under a school-master: for ye are all the children of God by faith in Christ Jesus.*[1548] Now under the New Covenant he says: {*faith is come*}; not, that it was not come at all under the Old Covenant (for even then, it was revealed more imperfectly, darkly and sparingly: Genesis 15:6 with Romans 4:3-5, Deuteronomy 30:11-15 with Romans 10:6-11, Psalm 32:1-2 with Romans 4:6-8) but, that it is now so clearly and fully revealed since Christ, that all are to be justified by faith in Christ, that comparatively

---

[1545] Hebrews 8:12 & 10:16-18, Romans 4:6-9
[1546] Acts 10:43 & 13:38-39 & 26:18, Romans 3:24-25
[1547] Romans 3:28, 30 & 4:5, 9, etc. & 5:1 & 10:4-16, Galatians 2:16, and often
[1548] Galatians 3:25-27

faith is not said to come till now. Faith came before, but very darkly, obscurely, imperfectly, sparingly, etc. But faith is come now very clearly, evidently, perfectly, plentifully. That coming of faith, was comparatively as no coming, in respect of this coming. Read those two accurate and admirable epistles of Paul to the Romans and Galatians, and therein you shall easily see, that this blessed doctrine of justification and salvation by faith in Jesus Christ, is more plainly and fully stated than in all the books of the Old Testament.

[2] Now under the New Covenant, God – more positively and peremptorily than ever under the Old – commands believing in Christ for life and righteousness, as the great work that he expects and accepts: *This is his commandment, that we should believe on the name of his Son Jesus Christ.*[1549] – *Jesus answered and said unto them, this is the work of God, that ye believe on him whom he hath sent.*[1550] How earnestly does our savior Christ in his doctrine call for believing? As Mark 1:14-15, John 12:36 & 14:1, 11, 29. And how did his apostles press believing upon such as desired Jesus Christ and salvation by him? As Acts 8:36-37 and 16:30-31.

[3] Now under the New Covenant the promises of righteousness, pardon, life and salvation are more clearly and plentifully annexed to faith in Christ, than ever formerly under the Old Covenant. *By him all that believe are justified from all things,* etc.[1551] – *Through his name whosoever believeth in him shall receive remission of sins.*[1552] *That whosoever believeth in him should not perish, but have eternal life.*[1553] – *Whosoever believeth on him, shall not be confounded.*[1554] – *Whosoever shall call upon the name of the Lord shall be saved: how then shall they call on him in whom they have not believed?*[1555] – *He that comes to me shall never hunger, and he that believes in me shall never*

[1549] 1 John 3:23
[1550] John 6:28-29
[1551] Acts 3:38-39
[1552] Acts 10:43 & 26:18
[1553] John 3:15-16, 36
[1554] Romans 9:3 & 10:11
[1555] Romans 10:13-14

thirst.[1556] – *Him that cometh to me, I will in no wise cast out.*[1557] – *He that believes, shall be saved;*[1558] with many promises of like nature.

[4] Now under the New Covenant, unbelief in Jesus Christ is more condemned as the grand sin of sins, and more threatened with damnation than ever under the Old Covenant. Though unbelief in Christ to come was very sinful and damnable then, yet unbelief in Christ already come is doubly sinful and damnable now: *And when he* (namely: the Holy Spirit) *is come, he will convincingly-reprove the world of sin, of righteousness, and of judgment. Of sin, because they believe not on me.*[1559] Among pardonable sins, no sin is comparable to this not believing in Christ, therefore this is the only sin mentioned to be reproved: *he that believeth not is condemned already: because he hath not believed on the name of the only begotten Son of God.*[1560] – *He that believeth not the Son, shall not see life; but the wrath of God abideth on him.*[1561] From all these particulars, it is very clear that God much more expects and requires faith under the New Covenant than under the Old. Under the Old Covenant, faith was in its infancy, minority, obscurity, etc. But under the New Covenant, faith should be in its maturity, high excellency and glory.

What true faith in Christ is, how it acts, and how we may discover it to be in ourselves, has been already unfolded,[1562] as also, how we are to walk before God in true faith,[1563] and how we are to live by faith in general,[1564] and in the particular case of tribulations and distresses[1565] – see all of these, for your satisfaction, pointed at in the margin.

[1556] John 6:35
[1557] John 6:37
[1558] Mark 16:16
[1559] John 16:8-9
[1560] John 3:18
[1561] John 3:36
[1562] Book 3, Chapter 3, Aphorism 4, Question 1; and in my *Communicant Instructed*, pp.110-126 (London, 1651).
[1563] Book 3, Chapter 3, Aphorism 3, Section 2
[1564] Book 3, Chapter 3, Aphorism 3, Section 2
[1565] Book 3, Chapter 6, Aphorism 2, Section 2

(3) **Repentance**.

God in this New Covenant – promising to write his laws in the minds and hearts of his federates – promises in and under that blessing to give them renovation, repentance, sanctification, etc., as has been manifested in opening of that article. And promising remission of sins, in not remembering them anymore, he implicitly requires them to exercise repentance. And when they close with this promise, they also implicitly re-promise to repent.[1566] This is evident, for:

[1] Under this New Covenant, God commands and calls for true and unfeigned repentance, more fully and universally than under the Old Covenant. Of old, God commanded only the Jews to repent, they only being taken into covenant with God;[1567] *but now God commandeth* (not only the Jews,[1568] but) *all men everywhere to repent* – in all nations, having extended his New Covenant to all nations.[1569] And Christ plainly instructs his apostles in this point after his resurrection, saying: *Thus it is written, and thus it behooved Christ to suffer, and to rise from the dead the third day. And that repentance and remission of sins should be preached in his name among all nations, beginning at Jerusalem.*[1570] Thus also the apostles managed their preaching: first calling the Jews,[1571] then the Gentiles,[1572] to repentance. And this was Paul's course, according to his commission, showing *first unto them of Damascus, and at Jerusalem, and throughout all the coasts of Judea, and then to the Gentiles, that they should repent, and turn to God, and do works meet for repentance.*[1573]

[1566] Hebrews 8:12 & 10:16-18
[1567] As Ezekiel 18:30-32
[1568] Mark 1:15
[1569] Acts 17:30-31
[1570] Luke 24:46-47
[1571] Acts 2:38 & 3:29 & 8:22
[1572] Acts 11:7, 18
[1573] Acts 26:17-20 & 10:21

[2] Remission of sins is under the New Covenant preached and promised more clearly and fully upon repentance and turning unto God than it was under the Old.[1574]

[3] The apostolic practice under this New Covenant was to admit men as federates to the New Covenant, and baptize them upon testification and profession of their faith and repentance.[1575]

[4] When any church members had been cast out of church society for their scandalous and contagious deportment, the primitive churches did not receive them again into wonted [habitual] fellowship till they had given very good demonstration of their sincere repentance.[1576]

By all this, it is plain that under this New Covenant, God requires, and his federates restipulate and perform (through his grace) repentance from dead works.

What true repentance is, and how we may know whether we have attained it or not, has been elsewhere manifested.[1577]

(4) Conformity to God's laws in heart and life, in inward constitution, and outward conversation.

In this New Covenant, God promises this great blessing, whilst he covenants to give his laws into the minds, and to write them in the hearts of his federates.[1578] For what is this his giving of his laws into their minds and hearts, but his new framing and new principling their minds and hearts so with his Spirit, image, and grace, that they shall be sweetly conform and answerable in all points to his laws? And also a harmonious answerableness of life and practice, resulting from those principles, is consequently promised. Now, the Lord – promising explicitly such inscription of his laws in their

---

[1574] Luke 24:40, 47, Acts 2:38 & 5:31 & 8:22 & 26:18
[1575] Acts 8:37-38 & 2:38-39, etc.
[1576] 2 Corinthians 2:6-11
[1577] Book 3, Chapter 4, Aphorism 4, Section 2; and in my *Communicant Instructed* (London, 1651).
[1578] Hebrews 8:10 & 10:16-17, Jeremiah 31:33

mind and heart, to bring their mind, heart and life into a sweet conformity to his laws – implicitly expects and requires from his federates a universal conformity and agreeableness of heart and life to his laws. This is plain, for:

[1] The Lord, in this his New Covenant, therefore promises a new inscription of his laws in the minds and hearts of his people, that both their hearts and lives may be conformed to his laws, and may keep the same. When God, in the Old Covenant administration, wrote his laws only upon tables of stone, without the people, that writing did not at all prevail to make either their hearts or lives conform and answerable to God's laws, but they contrariwise did violate and break the same.[1579] God therefore purposely contrives a New Covenant and new tables for his laws, the fleshly tables of mind and heart;[1580] and a new inscription of his laws in these new tables, by his spirit: that their minds and hearts might be conform and agreeable to his laws, that they might have a law within them answerable to the law without them, that so God's law and New Covenant might not be broken as his Old Covenant was. This is a principal thing which God aimed at in the constitution of his New Covenant that the hearts of his people, as fleshy, flexible and compliant tables, might in all things so answer his laws, that in their lives and practices they might sincerely keep them.

[2] *The grace of God*, the doctrine and gospel of God's grace in Christ now under the New Covenant, *appearing to all men*, to all sorts of men, Jews and Gentiles, *teacheth us to live soberly towards ourselves, righteously towards man, and godly towards God, in this present world.*[1581] This comprises in it a universal and complete conformity of life to the whole law of God. For what duties of the first or second table do not those three words, those three great adverbs {*soberly*}, {*righteously*}, and {*godly*} comprehend – as I have already evidenced.[1582] And to like effect, in the books of the New Testament, there are

---

[1579] Deuteronomy 4:13 with Jeremiah 31:31-34, Hebrews 8:8-12
[1580] 2 Corinthians 3:3, etc.
[1581] Titus 2:11-12
[1582] Book 3, Chapter 3, Aphorism 3, Section 2

many exhortations, directions and commands of walking answerably to the law of God.[1583]

[3] Christians now under the New Covenant are *God's workmanship created in Christ Jesus unto good works, which God hath before ordained that we should walk in them.*[1584] Therefore in the New Covenant God intended that our walk, way and course of life should be conformed to the law of God, especially considering that the inward frame of the divine nature and image of God wherein they are newly created in Christ, consists in knowledge, righteousness, and true holiness.[1585] This implies a plenary answerableness of their hearts (whence their actions flow) to the law of God.

[4] The doctrine of the New Covenant much commends and urges love, as the sweetest principle enabling and inclining to keep the law of God sincerely, cheerfully, delightfully. *If you love me* (said Christ) *keep my commandments.*[1586] – *For this is the love of God, that we keep his commandments, and his commandments are not grievous.*[1587] Love makes everything light and easy. Yea love is highly magnified as the very fulfilling of the law;[1588] as the substance and soul of the law and of all obedience.[1589]

[5] Sincere observance of God's commandments from a principle of love, is encouraged by various great and precious promises in the doctrine of the New Covenant.[1590]

[6] The sins and abominations against the law of God are in the books of the New Testament threatened with severest judgments and eternal

---

[1583] James 2:8-13, Romans 13:8-10, Matthew 22:37-40
[1584] Ephesians 2:10
[1585] Colossians 3:10, Ephesians 4:24; 2 Peter 1:4
[1586] John 14:15
[1587] 1 John 5:3
[1588] Romans 13:8-10
[1589] Matthew 22:37-40
[1590] John 14:15-17, 21, 23

condemnation.[1591] And therefore by all this, it is clear that God expects an universal conformity of his federates' hearts and lives to his holy laws.

Wherein this conformity stands, see in the opening of the first article of the New Covenant, and elsewhere in unfolding walking before God in obedience.[1592]

(5) **Entire self-denying, self-resignation unto God.** When God promises in his New Covenant, this blessing: {*and they shall be my people*}, he implicitly requires from them, and they tacitly re-promise unto him, in accepting of his Covenant, that they will be his people; that they will yield up themselves souls and bodies in an entire self-denying, self-resignation unto God. As God promises: {*they shall be my people*}, so they sweetly echo again to God, "We will be your people," that is, "We are well contented, to be yours only in Christ – not our own, not sin's, not the world's, not Satan's – and yours wholly in Christ: in all we are, have, can, do, or endure for your glory." This is a very comprehensive duty. It has in it especially two grand branches, plainly implied in this New Covenant, and expressly required in the books of the New Testament again and again, namely: [1] self-denial, or self-abnegation, for God in Christ; and [2] self-resignation to God in Christ.

[1] Self-denial, or self-abnegation, for God in Christ. This is one of the first and fundamental lessons in Christ's school: *If any man* (says Christ) *will come after me, let him deny himself.*[1593] That is, whatsoever belongs to himself, that stands in opposition against God, or comes into competition with God, as: {1} all self-sinfulness, ungodliness, and worldly lusts (Titus 2:11-12); {2} all self-righteousness, as did Paul (Philippians 3:4-12); {3} all self-wisdom (1 Corinthians 3:18-20): *Let him become a fool, that he may be wise*; {4} all self-willedness: *Thy will be done in earth, as in heaven* (Matthew 6:10, Luke 11:2); {5} all self-relations to dearest natural allies, as father, mother, wife,

---

[1591] Romans 2:8-9, 12; 1 Corinthians 6:9-10, Galatians 5:19-21; 2 Thessalonians 1:6, 8-9, Revelation 21:8 & 22:15
[1592] Book 3, Chapter 3, Aphorism 3, Section 2
[1593] Luke 9:23-24

children, sister, brother, etc. (Matthew 10:37-38, Luke 14:26, etc); {6} all self-possessions and worldly enjoyments (Luke 14:28-34; 1 John 2:15); {7} all self-love. He must deny not only his liberty, but even his very life for God in Christ (Matthew 10:38-39, Luke 14:26, Acts 20:24 & 21:13). All must be denied; that God in Christ, better than all, may be enjoyed.

[2] Self-resignation of all we are, have, can do, or endure unto God: *Present your bodies a living sacrifice, holy, acceptable unto God, which is your service according to the Word.*[1594] – *Ye are not your own. For ye are bought with a price: Therefore glorify God in your body, and in your spirit, which are God's.*[1595]

Inferences

(1) **Hence as God's New Covenant mercies expressly promised, so our New Covenant duties implicitly restipulated are very comprehensive.**

What mercy is not comprised in those mercies! What duty is not comprehended in those duties!

(2) **Hence the New Covenant duties are so required from us, as is most consistent with God's free grace unto us.**

For he first expressly promises ability, and then implicitly requires answerable duty. First he enables us to do what he will require, then requires us to do what we are able. We must know him, but first he will teach us: we must believe and repent, and be conformed to his laws in heart and life, but first he will write his law in our minds and hearts; we must be his people, but

---

[1594] Romans 12:1
[1595] 1 Corinthians 6:19-20

first he will make us his people. Well said Augustine: "Lord give me to do what you command, and then command what you please."[1596]

(3) **Hence as we would receive the New Covenant blessings from God, so we should return the New Covenant duties to God.**

Thus far of the matter of the New Covenant.

[1596] "Domine da quod jubes, & jube quod vis." Augustine, *Confessions*. l. 10. cap. 29.

Chapter 6

Of the blessed Messiah, our Lord Jesus Christ God-man; the only Mediator, Testator, and Surety of the New Covenant between God and man.

Having thus unfolded the matter of the New Covenant, consisting, partly in precious blessings promised on God's part to his federates; partly in spiritual duties required from and actually restipulated by his federates to God, when they come actually to close with God in this Covenant; in the next place, take we into serious consideration. The Mediator,[1597] Testator,[1598] and Surety[1599] of the New Covenant, Jesus Christ; in and by whom, this New Covenant is dedicated or established, and all the New Covenant mercies and blessings are obtained for us, promised to us, applied and effectually conferred upon us. And touching the Mediator of this New Covenant, I shall principally endeavor to set forth: (1) the necessity of a Mediator between God and man; (2) the person of the Mediator: who and what manner of person he is, and ought to be; (3) the office of this Mediator, wherein it consists, and how he executes it; (4) the dedication and application of this New Covenant, by virtue of that his Mediatory office. These four heads will easily comprise what is here necessary to be spoken touching the Mediator of the New Covenant: **Jesus Christ**.

And now, being come to **Jesus** the Mediator of the **New Covenant**, and to the blood of sprinkling that speaks better things than the blood of Abel,[1600] we are come to look into that profound, supernatural mystery, which our Savior himself says: *flesh and blood hath not revealed, but his Father which is in heaven*.[1601] And Paul intimates that the preaching of Christ is *according to the*

[1597] Hebrews 9:15 & 8:6
[1598] Hebrews 9:16-17
[1599] Hebrews 7:22
[1600] Hebrews 12:24
[1601] Matthew 16:17

revelation of the mystery, which was kept secret since the world began, but now is made manifest – and made known to all nations for the obedience of faith.[1602] Jerome said: "We know Christ to be wisdom. This treasure is bred in the field of the Scriptures: this gem is bought with many pearls. – Christ is sanctification, without which none shall see the face of God. Christ is redemption, the Redeemer, and the price. Christ is all, so that he who has left all for Christ, may find one for all."[1603] And elsewhere he styles Christ: "the head of all the Scriptures. The head and beginning of the whole body, and of them that believe, and of all spiritual understanding."[1604]

Sweetly and elegantly said Ambrose: "We have all things in Christ. Let every soul come to him, whether it be sick of corporal sins, or wounded with some nails of worldly desire, or as yet imperfect, but profiting by intentive [attentive] meditation, or already perfect with many virtues: each one is in the Lord's power, and Christ is all unto us. If you desirest to have your wound cured, he is the physician; if you burn with fevers, he is a fountain; if you are laden with iniquity, he is righteousness; if you need help, he is strength; if you fear death, he is life; if you desire heaven, he is the way; if you decline darkness, he is light; if you seek food, he is your nourishment. O taste and see, how sweet the Lord is; happy is the man that hopes in him!"[1605]

[1602] Romans 16:25-26

[1603] "We know that Christ is wisdom. He is the treasure which in the Scriptures a man finds in his field (Matthew 13:44). He is the peerless gem which is bought by selling many pearls. [...] Christ is that sanctification without which no man shall see the face of God. Christ is our redemption, for He is at once our Redeemer and our Ransom. Christ is all, that he who has left all for Christ may find One in place of all."
Jerome, Letter to Pammachius
[https://www.newadvent.org/fathers/3001066.htm]
<Accessed 4/15/2024>

[1604] "Et non tenens Caput omnium Scripturarum, illud de quo Scriptum est; Caput viri Christus est. Caput autem ac principium totius corporis eorumque qui credunt, & omnis intelligentiae spiritualis."
Hieronym. Algasiae. Quaest. 10. p. 169. B. Tom. 3. Basil. 1553

[1605] "Omnia igitur habemus in Christo. Omnis anima accedat ad eum, sive corporalibus aegra peccatis, sive clavis quibusdam saecularis cupiditatis infixa, sive imperfecta adhuc quidem, sed intenta tamen meditatione proficiens, sive multis aliqua sit jam perfecta virtutibus: omnis in Domini potestate est, et omnia Christus est nobis. Si vulnus curare

Now therefore we are come, to the marrow of all the Scriptures,[1606] to the kernel of the New Covenant and of all the Covenants of Promise,[1607] to the center of all God's promises,[1608] to the mystery of Christianity;[1609] to the head, hope, and life of the church and all true Christians,[1610] and to the only foundation of all true peace, happiness and consolation[1611] – even to Jesus Christ God-man,[1612] Mediator between God and man,[1613] whose: (1) necessity; (2) person and office, more generally; (3) execution of his office, more particularly; and (4) New Covenant establishment and application thereby, I shall for clearness' sake, represent in four distinct aphorisms ensuing.

---

desideras, medicus est: si febribus aestuas, fons est: si gravaris iniquitate, justitia est: si auxilio indiges, virtus est: si mortem times, vita est: si coelum desideras, via est: si tenebras fugis, lux est: si cibum quaeris, alimentum est. Gustate igitur, et videte quoniam suavis est Dominus: beatus vir qui sperat in eo (Psal. XXXIII, 9) ."
Ambrose, *De Virginibus* lib 3. Pag. 100. Tom. 1. Basil. 1567
Also:
[1606] John 8:39, Acts 10:43, John 1:45
[1607] Hebrews 12:24, Luke 12:20
[1608] 2 Corinthians 1:20; 2 Peter 1:4; 1 Timothy 4:8
[1609] 1 Timothy 3:16, Romans 16:25-26
[1610] Ephesians 5:23; 1 Timothy 1:1, Colossians 3:4
[1611] Isaiah 9:6, Genesis 22:18, John 14:16-17, etc.
[1612] John 1:14; 1 Timothy 3:16
[1613] 1 Timothy 2:5, Hebrews 12:24

Aphorism 1

Of the necessity of a Mediator between God and man, in general.

That, a true, fit, and sufficient Mediator of the New Covenant was most necessary between God and man.

For evincing of this, I shall show: (1) how, and in what sense a mediator was necessary. (2) Why, and in what respects such a mediator was so necessary between God and man.

(1) **How, and in what sense a mediator may be said to be necessary between God and man.** For resolving this, note:

[1] *There is (as the Schoolmen well observe)*[1614] *a threefold necessity, namely:*

{1} **A most perfect and absolute necessity**, when a thing is so, that it cannot not be, by the power of any agent whatsoever. This necessity belongs only to the divine nature which is most perfect, and cannot by any agent whatsoever be brought not to be, or to be other, or otherwise than he is, (James 1:17; 1 Timothy 1:17).

{2} **A natural necessity** whereby anything so is, that by virtue of a natural agent, it cannot be or behave itself otherwise. So, the heavens are necessarily moved about, and no natural thing can hinder their motion. So, fire is necessarily hot, and tends upwards: no creature can take these properties from fire. Thus, man necessarily flees misery, desires happiness, true or false, etc.

{3} **A hypothetical necessity**, which is also called a necessity of consequence when anything is necessary (*aliquo supposito*) upon supposition of some other thing. And this is not a necessity absolute, in the things

---

[1614] Thomas Aquinas, *Summa*, 1st Part, Q. 19. Article 3; Guillaume Estius *Comment. in Sent.* lib. 1. Dist. 38. §. 7.

themselves, but respective and upon connection of one thing with another. Thus, supposing that the sun enlightens all the world, it must necessarily have light in itself. Supposing God's Covenant, truth and justice, man sinning must necessarily die, if satisfaction be not made to God's justice;[1615] supposing God's decree, those who shall be glorified must necessarily be called and justified.[1616] And in this last sense, a mediator between God and man was necessary: that is, his *suppositis*, these and such like things being supposed, namely:

(i) That God has decreed to create mankind and to glorify his mercy, and justice in mankind peculiarly, preparing some as vessels of mercy unto glory, and passing by others as vessels of wrath fitted to destruction (Romans 9:22-23).

(ii) That those of mankind whom God intended as vessels of mercy for glory, he elected in Jesus Christ (Ephesians 1:4-5).

(iii) That God purposed to create man upright under a Covenant of Works upon pain of death, but to leave man to himself, so as to suffer him to fall, that thereby he might take occasion to express the riches of his free grace and mercy in saving his elect by Jesus Christ: and that God did this accordingly (Genesis 1:26-28, Ecclesiastes 7:29 & Genesis 2:16-17 & chapter 3 throughout, Romans 5:12) – God working *all things according to the counsel of his own will* (Ephesians 1:11).

(iv) That man – being upright, but mutable, being left to himself – fell from God through the enticement of Satan, and so in Adam all mankind became guilty of eternal death, and at utter enmity with God (Genesis 3 throughout, Romans 5:12 & 6:23. & 8:7-8).

(v) That God having threatened death to Adam in case of sin (Genesis 2:16-17), and Adam sinning – and in him all mankind, the elect, as well as others (Genesis 3 throughout. Romans 5:12) – the elect could not be restored and saved according to God's decree, without impeachment to his truth and

---

[1615] Genesis 2:16-17 with Romans 6:23, Deuteronomy 32:4
[1616] Romans 8:29-30

justice (Genesis 2:16-17, Romans 2:5-6, 11, Deuteronomy 32:4), unless God's truth should be verified, and his justice satisfied, by man offending, or by a sufficient Mediator or Surety for man, which should fully pay man's debt by undergoing death for man (Hebrews 9:22 to the end & 10:7-20 & 7:22; 1 Peter 2:23-24), so reconciling God and man (2 Corinthians 5:18-21, Romans 5:8-11).

(vi) That the elect according to God's decree must be eternally saved (Romans 8:29-30). Upon presupposition of these, and such like things, a mediator between God and man was necessary. That is, a mediator was necessary by a hypothetical necessity.

[2] *Again, I say: a true, fit, and sufficient Mediator was necessary under the New Covenant.*

True, that is: more than typical; *fit*, that is: equally middle between God and man; *sufficient*, that is: being every way able to reconcile God and man. Moses under the Old Covenant was a mediator, but neither true, fit, nor sufficient.[1617] Not true, but typical: being herein a dark type and figure of Christ. Not fit, but very unfit: being no equally middle person, but a mere man, nearer to man than to God. Not sufficient, but very insufficient: being utterly unable to reconcile God and the people, yea himself needing reconciliation to God by a higher Mediator.[1618] Such a typical, unfit, insufficient mediator was Moses. But the New Covenant being ordained purposely for reformation of the imperfections of the Old Covenant, the mediator of the New Covenant must be true, fit and sufficient fully to bring God and man into unity and peace: he must every way transcend Moses.[1619]

(2) **Why, and in what respects a Mediator of the New Covenant – yea, such a true, fit and sufficient Mediator, was necessary between God and man.**

[1617] Galatians 3:19 with Deuteronomy 5:23
[1618] Psalm 106:32-33, Numbers 20:12-13, 23-24, Deuteronomy 32:49-52
[1619] Hebrews 9:10 & 7:18-19

Resolution: a true, fit and sufficient Mediator of the New Covenant between God and man was hypothetically most necessary in several regards, for:

[1] *Without a Mediator, and that such a Mediator, God's eternal decree touching man's true, spiritual and everlasting happiness should never have been brought unto actual execution*, for as all man's spiritual and eternal happiness is eternally decreed;[1620] so it is all decreed to man in and through a Mediator.[1621] Man's redemption is decreed in, and through a Mediator (1 Peter 1:18-20). His adoption into God's family is decreed, in and through a Mediator (Ephesians 1:5). His holiness and unblameableness in love is decreed, but in and through a Mediator (Ephesians 1:4). His obedience is decreed, but in and through a Mediator (1 Peter 1:2). His eternal happiness of both soul and body (comprised under adoption, Romans 8:23) is decreed, but in a Mediator (Ephesians 1:4-5). His vocation, justification and glorification are decreed, but in a Mediator (Romans 8:28-30). Therefore without a Mediator, God's decrees touching man's spiritual and eternal happiness cannot have their full execution and accomplishment. Thus a Mediator between God and man was most necessary for the execution of God's decrees.

[2] *Without a Mediator, and that such a Mediator, the prophecies, promises, and types laid down in holy Scripture could never actually have been fulfilled and accomplished*, for: {1} Moses and the prophets have foretold the mystery of a Mediator, and how all spiritual and eternal blessings are procured for, and applied unto the elect of God, by a Mediator.[1622] {2} The promises of all saving blessings to mankind: as, of the seed of the woman to bruise the serpent's head,[1623] of the seed of Abraham in whom all the families of the earth should be blessed,[1624] of a prophet like Moses to be heard in all

---

[1620] Ephesians 1:12-13
[1621] Ephesians 1:3-5
[1622] John 1:45, Acts 10:43 & 26:22-23
[1623] Genesis 3:15, Colossians 2:14-15
[1624] Genesis 22:18 & 12:3, Galatians 3:8

things,[1625] of a priest after the order of Melchizedek,[1626] of the seed of David that should sit upon his throne to rule the house of Jacob forever,[1627] of redemption and deliverance from all our spiritual enemies,[1628] of blessing all nations in their effectual calling and conversion from their iniquities,[1629] of remission of sins and justification,[1630] of the Holy Spirit and sanctification,[1631] of eternal life and salvation[1632] – I say, all these, and all other promises in the book of God, are either promises of a Mediator, or promises in and through a Mediator: *in whom all the promises of God are yea, and amen* (2 Corinthians 1:20). {3} The types and shadows of old did all intend a Mediator, and center in a Mediator, representing something or other of a Mediator, namely: either his person, that he should be God-man, shadowed out in the pillar of fire and cloud (Exodus 13:21-22. & 14:19-20), as formerly I have shown in opening the Sinai Covenant; or his offices of prophet, priest, and king – shadowed out by those three famous offices among his people, of his being sacrificed to expiate our sins, shadowed out by all the Levitical sacrifices, etc. (Hebrews 10:1, etc. & 9:-12, Colossians 2:16-17), all the ceremonials were purposely ordained to adumbrate a Mediator one way or another, as heretofore I have abundantly evidenced in explaining the Sinai Covenant.[1633] Now that all such prophecies, promises and types (so notably foretelling, fore-assuring, and prefiguring a Mediator) might at last have their due and intended accomplishment, it was necessary there should be a Mediator between God and man, without whom they would have proved false, and vain, and null, and void.

[3] ***Without a true, fit and sufficient Mediator, the New Covenant would have been as weak and imperfect as the Old.*** The Old Covenant was

---

[1625] Deuteronomy 18:15-16, 18-19, Acts 3:22 & 7:37
[1626] Psalm 10:4, Hebrews 5:5-7 & 7 throughout
[1627] Psalm 132:11-12, Acts 2:30, Luke 1:31-33, 69-70
[1628] Genesis 22:16, Luke 1:68-76
[1629] Genesis 22:18, Acts 3:25-26
[1630] Isaiah 53:11, Acts 10:43
[1631] Ezekiel 36:26-27, Galatians 3:13-14
[1632] Ezekiel 36:24, 29, Matthew 1:21, Luke 1:71
[1633] In Book 3, Chapter 4, Aphorism 7, Corollary 7 throughout

very imperfect, weak, ineffectual, unprofitable. Why? Especially and principally because it lacked the true, fit and sufficient Mediator, having only some dark types and shadows of a Mediator, in Moses, in the priesthood, in the sacrifices, etc, as the apostle shows.[1634] But the New Covenant was to be, and is a better Covenant, reforming all the defects and imperfections of the former Covenant by *a better priesthood, a better sacrifice, a better and more perfect tabernacle,* etc.[1635] That is, by the true, fit and sufficient Mediator of the New Covenant, by whom the Covenant and all things under the Covenant are made better. Take away this Mediator from the New Covenant, and it is as weak, unprofitable, imperfect and ineffectual as the Old.

[4] *Without a true, fit and sufficient Mediator, the extreme enmity by reason of sin between God and lapsed mankind could never have been removed, nor God and man reconciled.* For, consider deliberately:

{1} God on the one hand (who made man upright in his own image)[1636] is: (i) infinitely pure and holy, so that he cannot endure sin in his creature; but forbids it upon pain of death (Isaiah 6:3, Habbakuk 1:13, Exodus 34:7, Genesis 2:16-17). (ii) Infinitely just. So that he cannot but take vengeance of sin acted by his creature, and punish it to the uttermost, unless full satisfaction be made by man, or for man (Deuteronomy 32:4, Romans 3:5-6. & 6:23). (iii) Infinitely true and faithful. So that his threatening of death for sin, must be accomplished and verified (Deuteronomy 32:4, Genesis 2:16-17, Romans 6:23).

{2} Man on the other hand, being made in God's image upright:[1637] (i) was most justly obliged, by the law of nature and creation, to be exactly obedient and subject to the just and equal law of his Maker; (ii) was as justly exposed to the curse and malediction of God's law, in case he transgressed it, and therefore as soon as man had offended God by transgressing his law, he became presently

---

[1634] Hebrews 7:11-12, 18 to the end & chapters 9 & 10
[1635] Hebrews 7:22, 19 & 8:6 & 9:9-12, etc. See Hebrews chapters 7-10 throughout.
[1636] Ecclesiastes 7:29, Genesis 1:26-28
[1637] Genesis 1:26-28, Ecclesiastes 7:29

guilty of death and condemnation;[1638] (iii) lapsed man could no way satisfy the infinite justice of the offended God, nor could he of himself do or endure anything that could prevail to make reconciliation between God and him, being but a mere finite creature – yea, a wretched sinner without strength, still treasuring up unto himself wrath, by increasing sin continually.[1639]

{3} Hence, from all this it follows: (i) that there is an utter enmity between God and lapsed man, which neither man nor any mere creature in the world can possibly remove;[1640] (ii) that of necessity, the holy, righteous and faithful God must inflict the penalty of his broken law, death, upon all mankind lapsed, according to his truth and justice; and then, either mankind should forever lose all happiness in fruition of God, and God should lose all the voluntary service and subjection of mankind unto himself; or God must not punish lapsed man for his sin, which would be utterly against his truth and justice; or some middle way must be devised, to devolve, translate and put man's sins and punishment upon some fit and sufficient person fully able to bear them, and make complete satisfaction for them to God: as also to interest lapsed man in that sufficient person's righteousness for his acceptance with God.[1641] And this middle way is by way of Mediator. Thus, man lapsed must forever perish, or God must be unfaithful and unjust, or there must be a Mediator interposing to satisfy God's justice and fulfill his truth, that the sinner may be saved.

[5] *Without a true, fit and sufficient Mediator, lapsed man could never have been redeemed*. This is evident especially in two ways, for:

{1} The bondage and thraldom into which lapsed man is implunged, is such and so great, that none but such a Mediator can rescue and redeem him from it,[1642] namely: a bondage: (i) under the power and dominion of sin and

---

[1638] Genesis 2:16-17 & 3 throughout, Romans 5:12
[1639] Romans 5:6, 8, Genesis 6:5, Romans 2:5
[1640] Romans 8:7-8
[1641] 2 Corinthians 5:21
[1642] Luke 1:74

iniquity, (Romans 6:6, 12-14 & 8:8, Acts 8:23, Ephesians 2:1); (ii) under the guilt of eternal death and condemnation for sin (Romans 3:19, 1:32 & 6:23, Ephesians 2:3); (iii) under the irritation, rigor, and curse of the law (Romans 7:8-14, Galatians 3:10); (iv) under the fear and terror of death (Hebrews 2:15); (v) under the merciless tyranny and cruelty of Satan and the powers of darkness (Hebrews 2:14; 2 Timothy 2:25, Colossians 1:13).

{2} The way of lapsed man's redemption and deliverance from all this thralldom, from the hand and power of all those enemies, is such, namely: by right, price and power, that none in the world but such a Mediator can possibly effect or accomplish the same. The right of redemption belongs, not to a stranger, but to a near kinsman, by the law.[1643] None but a near kinsman is a fit Redeemer. The price of redemption must be beyond all corruptibles that mere creatures can perform, that it may be fully satisfactory to God's infinite justice (1 Peter 1:18-19, Acts 20:28). And the power of the Redeemer must transcend the power of all our spiritual enemies that enthrall us (Matthew 12:29).

[6] *Without a true, fit and sufficient Mediator, lapsed man could never have been effectually called, sanctified, justified, and saved.* For it is by the bounty, fulness, virtue, power and efficacy of such a Mediator, that lapsed man is converted from his sins and iniquities (Acts 3:25-26), sanctified through the Spirit (1 Peter 1:2; 1 Corinthians 1:30 & 6:11), justified in the sight of God by imputed righteousness covering all sin (Acts 13:38-39; 1 Corinthians 1:30), and saved from eternal wrath and condemnation (Romans 5:9-10).

By all this we may plainly see, in the general, the great necessity of a true, fit and sufficient Mediator between God and man.

[1643] Hebrews 2:11-15, Leviticus 25:23-35, 47 to the end

Aphorism 2

Of the person of Christ; and of his mediatory office, more generally.

That Jesus the only Son of God, is also the son of the virgin Mary, God and man in one person, the Christ and promised Messiah, is, as God-man, the only true, fit and sufficient Mediator, Testator and Surety of the New Covenant between God and man.

In this aphorism is set forth:

(1) **The person of the Mediator**: who and what he is. And this: [1] by his proper denomination: {*Jesus*};[1644] [2] by his descent and filiation; which is twofold, namely: {1} eternal, before all time. And so he is the only Son of God;[1645] (2) temporal, in fullness of time (Galatians 4:4); so he is also the son of the virgin Mary;[1646] [3] by his two natures, divine and human, personally united: God and man in one person.[1647] God incarnate, the word made flesh; God manifest in the flesh, {*Immanuel*}, that is: {*God-with-us*}.

(2) **The office of this Mediator**. And this in three ways: [1] by his designation and unction for it: **the Christ** and promised **Messiah**.[1648] The Greek word {*Christ*}; and the Hebrew word {*Messiah*} do both of them signify {*anointed*}; [2] by the nature of his office, and the peculiar appropriation of it to him alone; the only true, fit, and sufficient Mediator, Testator, and Surety of the New Covenant between God and man;[1649] [3] by the capacity in which he became Mediator, Testator, and Surety, namely: not

---

[1644] Luke 1:31 & 2:21, Matthew 1:25
[1645] John 1:14, 18 & 3:10, 16-17; 1 John 4:19
[1646] Matthew 1:18 to the end, Luke 1:27-39 & 2:5-22
[1647] John 1:14, Galatians 4:4; 1 Timothy 3:16, Matthew 1:23, Romans 1:3-4
[1648] John 4:25-26, Matthew 16:16-17, Acts 9:20, 22 & 18:28, John 1:[45]
[1649] Hebrews 12:24 & 9:15-17 & 7:22; 1 Timothy 2:15, Hebrews 2:14 to the end & 7:25, 10:10-19

as God alone, nor as man alone; but, as God-man.[1650] All these particulars touching the person and office of the Mediator, are couched closely together in this short aphorism, and are evident by these Scriptures annexed in the margin.

But, these being fundamental principles of faith, and of very high consequence to salvation (yet several of them very intricate and hard to be understood), they need to be more largely explicated and evidenced. And therefore for greater clarity herein, I shall resolve the aphorism into these four distinct positions, also explaining and confirming them, namely: (1) that Jesus the only Son of God, and the son of the virgin Mary, is God and man in one person; (2) that Jesus, God-man, is the Christ the promised Messiah, and he alone; (3) that Jesus Christ – God and man – is the only true, fit, and sufficient Mediator, Testator, and Surety of the New Covenant between God and man; (4) that Jesus Christ is Mediator, Testator, and Surety of the New Covenant between God and man, as he is God-man. All the former particulars will easily be reduced to these four positions.

[1650] Romans [3]:25 with 1:3-4

Position 1

That Jesus, the only Son of God, and the son of the virgin Mary, is God and man in one person.

Here note: (1) what this name Jesus imports, (2) that this Jesus is the only Son of God, (3) that this Jesus also is the son of the virgin Mary, and (4) That this Jesus, Son of God and of the virgin Mary, is God and man in one person.

(1) **What this name Jesus imports**. This name ιησους in the Greek most frequently given to our Savior in the New Testament,[1651] which in Latin and English is {*Jesus*}, is originally a Hebrew name, namely: יֵשׁוּעַ *Yeshua*, or יְהוֹשֻׁעַ *Yehoshua*: a Savior. From יָשַׁע *yasha*, which in hiphil is הוֹשִׁיעַ *hoshia*, to save, to preserve, to help. This Hebrew name was first given to Hoshea the son of Nun, whom Moses called {*Yehoshua*} (Numbers 13:10), and the apostle calls {*Jesus*} (Hebrews 4:8). He saved Israel from their enemies, the Canaanites, etc. And brought them into the promised land of rest; therein being a type of our true Jesus, that saves all the elect Israel of God from all their spiritual enemies, and brings them into heavens everlasting rest (Hebrews 4:8 to the end). Sundry witty allusions or allusive etymologies are given of this name Jesus, to show the signification and reason thereof;[1652] but waving those curiosities, we are to acquiesce in the angel's reason, why our Mediator should be called Jesus, as

---

[1651] Matthew 1:21, 25, Luke 1:31 & 2:21 & often elsewhere

[1652] Quod Andreas osiander. vir doctissimus in Harmonia sua Evangelica statuat, Illud nomen IESU esse ipsum nomen Dei IEHOVAH, quod cum fuerit [ανεκφονητιν] seu ineffabile, dicit insertione literae שׁ (ex voce שִׁילֹה Gen. 49. 10.) factum fuisse effabile, ut ita hoc nomine significatur. (1) Christum esse verum Deum, ob nomen IEHOVAH, & verum hominem ob literam שׁ ex Schilo, quae [humanitatem] ejus notet; & quod sunt unitae illae duae Naturae in unam Personam, sicut ex divinae & humanae Naturae nominibus factum est unum Nomen. (2) Incomprehensibilem Deum, assumpto homine, coepisse nobis esse cognoscibilem Scribi igitur, inquit, proprie suis Literis יהושוה & per Contractionem ישׁי. Solomon Glasius in ονοματολογια *Mesiae Prophetica*. p. 167. ad p. 178. Ienae 1624. Vid. etiam Io. Gerhard in *Loc. Commun.* Loc 4 cap. 1. Tom. 1.

most authentic and unexceptionable. – *and thou shalt call his name Jesus, for he shall save his people from their sins* (Matthew 1:21).[1653]

Our blessed Mediator is called {*Jesus*}, that is, {*a savior*}: [1] because he saves his people from their sins. This is the angel's reason, and it is the grand reason, whereupon other reasons do depend. [2] Because he saves them from the wrath of God – God's wrath being only for sin.[1654] [3] Because he saves and redeems from the accusation, malediction, rigor and terror of the law of God – God's law accusing, cursing and terrifying only for sin.[1655] [4] Because he saves from death, judgment, and eternal condemnation – those being the proper and peculiar wages of sin.[1656] [5] Because, he saves and delivers us from Satan and all the powers of darkness – yea from all our spiritual enemies, who have got advantage against us only by sin.[1657]

Now our blessed Jesus so saves that: [1] he is the only Savior: *Neither is there salvation in any other: for there is none other name under heaven given among men whereby we must be saved.*[1658] [2] He saves universally all the elect people of God that are lost in the first Adam, whether Jews or Gentiles, of whatever nation in the whole world.[1659] [3] He saves variously, with all manner of necessary salvation, namely: meritoriously, by himself and his own mediation with God for us;[1660] efficaciously, by his Spirit and his effectual operation in us;[1661] instrumentally, on his part, by his Word[1662] and ministers;[1663] on our part, by faith embracing Christ for salvation.[1664] [4]. He saves most sufficiently, and forever, all that come unto God by him. *He is able*

[1653] Matthew 1:21, 25
[1654] Romans 5:8-9 & 1:18
[1655] Galatians 4:4-5 & 3:10, 13-14
[1656] Matthew 1:21, 25, Luke 1:31 & 2:21 & often elsewhere
[1657] Hebrews 2:15, Romans 8:1 & 6:23
[1658] Acts 4:12
[1659] Matthew 1:21, John 10:15-16 & 11:51-52; 1 John 2:1-2
[1660] Hebrews 1:3 & 9:12 & 10:14, Romans 5:8-11, 15 to the end
[1661] Titus 3:5
[1662] James 1:21; 1 Corinthians 1:21
[1663] 1 Timothy 4:16; 1 Corinthians 9:22
[1664] Hebrews 10:39, Mark 16:16

to save to the uttermost (παντελες: to all end) *all that come unto God*, etc.[1665] Hence he is called not only *Savior*, but *salvation* itself, {σωτηρίαν} (Genesis 49:18), and {σωτήριον} Luke 2:30. He is his people's only, manifold, perfect and all-sufficient salvation: from sin, wrath, curse, death, condemnation, and all the powers of darkness. All these are comprised in this one word *{Jesus}*.

"The whole gospel is hidden in this name *{Jesus}*."[1666] [1] When we are first initiated into the church, we are baptized into the name of Jesus (Acts 2:38 & 19:5). [2] When we are converted to God, we put on the Lord Jesus (Romans 13:14). [3] When we act anything, whatsoever we do in word or deed, we should do all in the name of the Lord Jesus (Colossians 3:17). [4] And when we are dissolved, and lay aside these earthly tabernacles; we sleep in Jesus (1 Thessalonians 4:14). The saints' dead dust is under the key and custody of this Jesus. O sweetest, and most delicious name! For what can be sweeter to a sinner than a Savior; to a lost soul than a Jesus? The name *{Jesus}* is the music of the gospel, the comfort of repenters, the triumph of believers, the terror of the devil and of all the powers of darkness. The name *{Jesus}* is light and life, meat and medicine, health and hope unto the soul.[1667] This sweet name Jesus, is honey in the mouth, melody in the ear, and a very jubilee in the heart.

(2) That this Jesus is the only Son of God.

[1] ***How?*** {1} Not by creation; so the angels and all mankind are sons of God (Job 1:6, Hebrews 12:9, Numbers 16:22 & 27:16). {2} Not by adoption; so all the elect of God actually called, are the sons and daughters of God (Galatians 4:4-6; 2 Corinthians 7:17-18, Romans 8:15-16, John 1:11). {3} But by generation. Even by eternal, ineffable, and unconceivable generation of the father before all world's, according to his deity. He is also called *{the Son of*

[1665] Hebrews 7:25
[1666] "In nomine *{Iesu}* totum latet Evangelium." Sol. Glassius quo supra, p. 176
[1667] "Nomen *{Iesu}* est lux cibus & Medicina animae nostrae Nomen *{Iesu}*esu, in ore Mel, in aure Melos in corde Iubilus. Sol. Glassius ibid p. 176

God} according to his humanity, in regard to his miraculous conception in the virgin's womb, without man, by the Holy Ghost (Luke 1:35). But that comes not under this present consideration.

[2] ***Whence may it appear that this Jesus is in this sense, according to his Godhead, the only Son of God?*** In several ways, namely:

{1} **From clear testimonies of Scripture**, wherein he is styled {*the Son of God*}, yea the only begotten Son of God: μονογενης. Peter confessed: *Thou art Christ, that son of the living God.*[1668] Here is a demonstrative particle, ο υιος, {*that Son*}: denoting Christ to be Son of the living God so peculiarly, as neither Elijah, nor Jeremiah, nor John the Baptist, nor any of the prophets were the sons of God. *And the word was made flesh, and dwelt amongst us, and we beheld his glory, the glory as of the only begotten of the Father.*[1669] – *The only begotten Son, which is in the bosom of the Father, he hath declared him.*[1670] – *God so loved the world, that he gave his only begotten Son, etc.*[1671] – *because he hath not believed in the name of the only begotten Son of God.*[1672] – *God sent his only begotten Son into the world, that we might live through him.*[1673]

{2} **From the glorious and exact resemblance of this Son begotten, to the Father begetting.** *God hath in these last days spoken to us by his Son, – who being the brightness of his glory, and the express image* (or *character*) *of his person, etc.*[1674] None but Jesus Christ is the brightness of God's glory, and the express image of his person, this is here ascribed to him alone by peculiar appropriation. Therefore he alone is God's natural and eternal Son.

{3} **From the sufficient enumeration of the persons of the blessed Trinity.** Those persons or distinct divine subsistences are only three in one essence. *There are three that bear record in heaven, the Father, the Word*

[1668] Matthew 16:15-16
[1669] John 1:14
[1670] John 1:18
[1671] John 3:16
[1672] John 3:18
[1673] 1: John 4:9
[1674] Hebrews 1:1-3

(elsewhere called, *the Son*), *and the Holy Ghost: and these three are one*.[1675] Among these three, there is but one son, the Word; as there is but one Father: and this Son, this Word, was made flesh (John 1:14). This is that Jesus, the only eternal Son of God.

{1} Hence in holy Scripture, the (i) names, (ii) attributes, (iii) works, and (iv) worship, which properly and peculiarly belong to God, are ascribed to Jesus, this Son of God.

(i) *The names of God are given to Jesus the Son of God*, as:

(a) {*God*}. *The word was God* (John 1:1) – *The flock of God, which he hath purchased with his own blood*.[1676] – *God manifest in the flesh*,[1677] *the great God* (Titus 2:13), *the true God* (1 John 5:20), *over all God blessed forever, amen* (Romans 9:5).

(b) {*The Lord*}, κυριος – by this word, the Septuagint is wont to render the Hebrew יְהוָה Jehovah, which is God's most proper essential name. And the apostles so render it also:[1678] *my Lord and my God* (John 20:28); *one Lord Jesus Christ* (1 Corinthians 8:6); *the only Lord God, and our Lord Jesus Christ* (Jude 4); *he is Lord of all* (Acts 10:36); *the Lord from heaven* (1 Corinthians 15:48), *the Lord of glory* (1 Corinthians 2:8); *Lord of Lords, and king of kings* (Revelation 19:16).

(c) {*The Most High*} (Luke 1:76, etc).

(ii) The essential attributes and properties of God are ascribed or given to this Jesus, as: (a) Equality to, and unity with the Father (Philippians 2:6. John 5:18. & 16:6. & 17:10; 1 John 5:7. Colossians 2:9); (b) omniscience: that he knows all things; *searcheth hearts and reins* (John 2:25, 16:30 & 21:17, Revelation 2:23); (c) omnipotence: *the mighty God* (Isaiah 9:6), *Almighty* (Revelation 1:8 & 11:17); his mighty power whereby he can subdue all things. (Philippians 3:21); (d) immortality: *hath life in himself* (John 5:26), prince of

---

[1675] 1 John 5:7, Matthew 28:19
[1676] Acts 20:28
[1677] 1 Timothy 3:16
[1678] Compare Jeremiah 31:31-35 with Hebrews 8:8-13 & Hebrews 1:10 with Psalm 102:25

life (Acts 3:15), life (John 14:6); (e) immutability: *still the same* (Hebrews 1:11 & 13:8); (f) Infiniteness and omnipresence. He is boundless, and everywhere present (John. 3:13, etc., Revelation 1:13, John 1:18); (g) eternity (Isaiah 9:6, John 1:1, Hebrews 7:13 & 13:8). I need not mention anymore.

(iii) The works proper and peculiar to God, are ascribed to this Jesus (John 5:17, 19-21 & 14:13). As in particular: (a) creation (John 1:1, 3, Hebrews 1:11, Colossians 1:16); (b) conservation of all things created (Hebrews 1:3; 1 Corinthians 8:6, Colossians 1:16); (c) redemption of sinners (Luke 1:68, Matthew 20:28, Hebrews 9:12-14, Acts 20:28); (d) donation of his Spirit (John 14:16, etc, 15:26 & 14:26); (e) raising himself from the dead (John 2:19. & 10:18, Romans 1:3-4); (f) institution of ordinances and officers in his church (Matthew 28:18-20; 1 Corinthians 11:23, Ephesians 4:8-10, etc); and (g) judging the world at last (John 5:22, Matthew 25:31 to the end, Acts 17:31).

(iv) The worship proper and due only unto God, is given also to Jesus Christ (John 5:23), as (a) believing in him (John. 14:1); (b) hoping or trusting in him (Isaiah 11:10, Psalm 2:12); (c) being baptized in his name (Acts 2:38-39, Matthew 28:19); (d) living to him, etc. (Romans 14:9) – by all which, and many such like particulars, the Godhead of Jesus, the only begotten Son of God, is abundantly manifested.

(3) That this Jesus, the only begotten Son of God, was also the son of the virgin Mary.

For the more clear evincing of this, these particulars are to be evidenced, namely: [1] whence the virgin Mary herself descended; [2] that Jesus was the son of the virgin Mary; [3] how Jesus was the son of the virgin Mary; [4] what denominations are given to him in Scripture hereupon. These things need to be rightly understood for the due knowledge of Jesus our Mediator.

[1] *Whence the virgin Mary herself descended?*

Answer: The virgin Mary naturally descended from David, and was of his house in the tribe of Judah, for:

{1} Our Lord Jesus, son of the virgin Mary, sprang of the tribe of Judah, out of the house of David: *For it is evident that our Lord sprang out of Judah.*[1679] – *concerning his Son Jesus Christ our Lord, which was made of the seed of David according to the flesh.*[1680]

{2} It is said: *the angel Gabriel – was sent, to a virgin, espoused to a man whose name was Joseph, of the house of David*, ἐξ οἴκου δαβιδ, *whose name was Mary*, etc (the intent of the angel's message was to assure her that Jesus should be conceived and brought forth from her).[1681] Here those words {*of the house of David*} may refer, according to the Greek, to Mary as well as to Joseph.

{3} The genealogy described by Luke, puts the matter quite out of question, that the virgin Mary descended from David naturally, and not only legally.[1682] For it is evident beyond doubt that (according to the genealogy by Matthew) Joseph the husband of Mary was the natural son of Jacob, because it is said: *and Jacob begat Joseph the husband of Mary*, etc.[1683] So that Eli – mentioned in Luke to be Joseph's father – was only his legal or civil father, but Mary's natural father. Husband and wife becoming one flesh, the father of one is father of both (Genesis 37:35), as Petrus Galatinus has well observed. The genealogy therefore described by Luke, plainly describes the natural descent of the virgin Mary from the house of David.[1684]

Objection: But why then does Luke carry his genealogy upwards from Joseph and not from Mary, she being not mentioned in his genealogy.

[1679] Hebrews 6:14
[1680] Romans 1:3
[1681] Luke 1:27, etc.
[1682] Luke 3:23 to the end
[1683] Matthew 1:16
[1684] Petrus Galatinus, lib. 7, cap. 12

Resolution: Because (as Galatinus has noted)[1685] it is not the manner of Scripture to make up genealogies by women, therefore Luke in the genealogy of the glorious virgin, did put Joseph himself instead of the virgin, calling him the son of Eli, that is, of Jehoiakim. Thus the genealogies of Matthew and Luke are clearly reconciled, as touching the father of Joseph and of Mary: Jacob was Joseph's natural father, but Eli was Joseph's civil, and Mary's natural father. Or, they may thus be easily reconciled without forcing anything in the text, by placing the parenthesis in that of Luke, not as it is in our translation: *being* (as was supposed) *the son of Joseph*, etc., but thus: *and Jesus himself began to be about thirty years of age, being* (as was supposed, the son of Joseph) *the son of Eli*, etc. That is, the grandchild of Eli, by his daughter Mary. And this resolution greatly satisfies that learned Spanheim.[1686] And he very well answers Calvin's objection against drawing the line of Mary and of Christ, from David by Nathan, and not by Solomon.[1687] The learned reader may consult him for his further satisfaction.

[2] *That Jesus was the son of the virgin Mary*. This is very plain, for:

{1} This was fore-prophesied by the prophet Isaiah, behold a virgin shall conceive, etc. Isaiah 7:14. Matthew 1:22, 23

{2} This was fore-promised by the angel Gabriel to the virgin Mary herself, that she should conceive and bring forth a son, and call him Jesus, etc (Luke 1:28-39).

{3} This was actually fulfilled, for when the days were accomplished, she brought forth her firstborn son in the city of David, which is Bethlehem, and on the eighth day when he was circumcised, his name was called Jesus, who was so named of the angel before he was conceived in the womb (Luke 2:4-7, etc. 21, etc., Matthew 1:18 to the end & 2:1, etc).

[1685] "Quod mos non esset Scripturarum per mulieres gene logius te xere, idel: co Lucam in genealogia gloriose virginis ipsam Ioseph posuisse eumque filium [Eli[, hoc est, Iehojakim nuncupasse."
Petrus Galatinus, lib. 7, cap. 12
[1686] Frederick Spanheim in *Dub. Evangel. Dub.* 20-22, Section 30, p.124 (Geneva, 1624)
[1687] Ibid. p.127 (Geneva, 1624)

[3] *How was Jesus the son of the virgin Mary?*

Answer: Jesus became the son of the virgin Mary:

{1} **Extraordinarily**, in a way altogether extraordinary and miraculous. Partly, in that he was conceived, not by ordinary human generation, but by the Holy Spirit's extraordinary and miraculous operation, who wonderfully formed the human nature of Christ from the substance of the virgin Mary, perfectly sanctifying it in the first moment of conception. *Then said Mary unto the angel, how shall this be, seeing I know not a man? And the angel answered and said unto her, the Holy Ghost shall come upon thee, and the power of the highest shall overshadow thee: therefore also that holy thing which shall be born of thee, shall be called the Son of God.*[1688] Partly, in that he was conceived and born of a virgin: she still remaining a virgin until after his nativity.[1689] For a virgin to conceive is ordinary, but for a virgin to conceive and bring forth, remaining a virgin – this is extraordinary and miraculous. Partly, in that he was conceived most purely, in the womb of a sinner, without sin;[1690] for the virgin was a sinner, and needed a Savior, and was liable to death.[1691]

{2} **Truly and really**: Jesus partaking of the true human nature of the virgin (Luke 1:31, 35 & 2:6-7, 21-22). And not only a phantasm [illusory], imaginary, or seeming nature only, as the Marcionites, Manicheans, and other heretics falsely pretended. He had the true properties, affections and actions of man; he was conceived, born, circumcised, did hunger, thirst, was weary, was clothed, did eat, drink, sleep, hear, see, touch, speak, sigh, weep, grow in wisdom and stature, etc., as the four evangelists do abundantly testify.

{3} **Completely and perfectly.** He took to himself the whole human nature, in both the essential parts of man: soul and body – a true human and reasonable soul;[1692] a true real human body also (Mark 14:8, John 2:21,

---

[1688] Luke 1:34-35
[1689] Isaiah 7:14, Luke 1:34-35, Matthew 1:23-25
[1690] Luke 1:35, Hebrews 4:15 & 7:26, Isaiah 53:9
[1691] Luke 1:46-47
[1692] Matthew 20:28 & 26:35, Luke 23:46, John 10:15, Isaiah 7:15, Luke 2:46, John 5:21

Colossians 2:22, Luke 24:39, Matthew 26:26). There is often mention of his flesh, blood and bones, etc. (Romans 1:3, Luke 24:39, John 19:33, Acts 20:28, John 6:54). Hence said Augustine: "Therefore he took the whole man without sin, that he might heal the whole, of which man consists, of the plague of sin."[1693] And Fulgentius to like purpose: "As the devil smote by deceiving the whole man, so God saves by assuming the whole man."[1694] Yea, he so took the human nature of the virgin, that he took our infirmities, wants and weaknesses (but without sin) together with our nature.[1695] Not man's personal infirmities, which from some particular causes befall this or that person, such as leprosy, blindness, dumbness, palsy, epilepsy, etc. – I do not say he took any such infirmities. But man's natural infirmities, which belong to all mankind since the fall, such as hunger, thirst, wearisomeness, sorrowfulness, sweating, bleeding, wounds, death, burial, etc., as the evangelists abundantly testify.

[4] ***Denominations given unto Jesus in Scripture hereupon are many, setting forth further unto us the verity and reality of his human nature***. Hence, Jesus is called {*the son of the virgin*} in Isaiah 7:14, {*her firstborn son*} in Luke 2:7, {the branch} in Zechariah 3:8 & 6:12, {*the branch of righteousness growing up to David*} in Jeremiah 33:15. & 23:5, {*a rod out of the stem of Jesse, and a branch out of his roots*} in Isaiah 11:1, {*the fruit of David's loins*} in Psalm 80:36 & 132:11 and Acts 2:30, {*of the seed of David according to the flesh*} in Romans 1:3 & 2 Samuel 7:2, {*the son of David*} in Matthew 1:1, {*David*} – Jesus being the true David – in (Hosea 3:5, Ezekiel 24:23 & 37:24-25), {*the lion of the tribe of Judah*} in Revelation 5:5, {*the seed of Jacob*} in Genesis 28:14, {*the seed of Isaac*} in Genesis 26:4, {*the seed and son of Abraham*} in Genesis 22:18 & Matthew 1:1, {*the seed of the woman*} in Genesis 3:15, {*a son born to us, a child given to us*} in Isaiah 9:6, {*the Son of man*} in Matthew 8:20, 16:13 & Revelation 1:13, {*God's Son made of a*

[1693] Augustine, *City of God*, Book 10 C. 27
[1694] "Sicut totum hominem Diabolus decipiendo percussit; ita Ceus totum suscipiendo salvavit." Fulgent. Ad Traesymund. lib. 1. p. 251.
[1695] Hebrews 2:10-11, 14, 16-18 & 5:2, 7 & 4:15

woman} in Galatians 4:4, {*man*} in 1 Timothy 2:5 & Luke 23:47, and {*flesh*} in John 1:14.

(4) That this Jesus – Son of God and of the virgin Mary – is God and man in one person.

That he is God, and that he is man, have been sufficiently proved. Now we are to consider that Jesus our Mediator is not two persons, but only one individual person, consisting of two natures really and essentially distinct one from another, namely: the divine and human, whereupon he is God-man. He is one and the same begotten of the Father without time, the Son of God without mother; and born of the virgin in time, the son of man without father – the natural and consubstantial son of both. *This without controversy is the great mystery of godliness, God manifest in the flesh.*[1696] Here note touching this mystery: [1] the fitness of the Son, the second person, to become man; [2] the nature of the union between his divinity and humanity; [3] the unity or oneness of his person, though consisting of these two natures; [4] similitudes illustrating this union; and [5] the effects or consequences resulting from this union.

[1] *The fitness of the Son of God, to become the son of man, the son of the virgin*. It was more fit the Son should be incarnate for the office of Mediatorship than either the Father or Holy Spirit, for:

{1} The Son is the middle person between the Father and the Holy Spirit, and therefore fittest to be a middle officer between God and man.

{2} By the Son all things were at the beginning created;[1697] therefore by the Son, most fitly, all things were to be re-created, newly created.[1698] Hence

---

[1696] 1 Timothy 3:6
[1697] John 1:14, Hebrews 1:2
[1698] 1 Timothy 3:6

said Augustine: "It would be an injury to him, if the work formed by him should be reformed by another."[1699]

{3} Having lost the image of God by sin, in which image we were at first fashioned by the Son, the substantial image of God and express character of his person (Genesis 1:27, Colossians 3:10, Ephesians 4:24 & Hebrews 1:3), who was so fit to restore the image of God to us, as the substantial image of God the Son, who at first did fashion it in us?

{4} Mankind by sin being at enmity with God (Colossians 1:21, Romans 8:7), who was fitter to reconcile us unto God again, and make us accepted of God, than the Son of his love in whom he was well pleased (Romans 5:10, Ephesians 1:6, Colossians 1:13 & Matthew 3:17)? For a double mission was necessary: one for redeeming and reconciling of enemies; the other to confer gifts upon the reconciled. Hence, the Father, being of none, sent his Son to redeem and reconcile sinners (John 3:16-17; 2 Corinthians 5:19), and both Father and Son send the Holy Spirit, to seal them that are redeemed and reconciled (John 14:26 & 15:26, Ephesians 1:13-14).

{5} The Son – being the only begotten Son of God by nature[1700] – was fittest to make us the adopted sons of God by grace,[1701] who *were by nature the children of wrath.*[1702]

{6} The Son – being the word of life (1 John 1:1) in whom is life, and that life the light of men at first (John 1:4) was fittest to repair life in us, who were estranged from the life of God, and dead in trespasses and sins (Ephesians 4:18 & 2:1, etc, John 5:26).

{7} The Son of God was fittest to be the Son of man, that so both God and man in the unity of person might be one Son of God.[1703]

[1699] "Id ini uriam ejus pertineret, si opus per eum factum, per alium reformaretur. Aug. Quest. ex utro{que}" Test. Quest. 113. p. 826. C. Tom 4.
[1700] John 1:14, 18 & 3:16, 18; 1 John 4:9
[1701] Ephesians 1:5
[1702] Ephesians 2:3
[1703] "Non Pater carnem assumpsit, ne{que} Spiritus Sanctus, sed filius tantum; ut qui erat in Divinitate Dei patris filius, ipse fieret in homine hominis matris filius: ne filii nomen ad

[2] ***The nature of the union between the God-head and manhood of Jesus Christ is***: {1} personal, {2} indivisible., and {3} of natures remaining still distinct from one another.

{1} **Personal and intimate.** It is not a natural, but a personal conjunction of two natures, not of two persons, in Christ; not such as is of superiors with inferiors, of accidents with substances, or of the part with the whole; but whereby two natures mediately are united in one person, and the human nature is immediately united to the divine person in a secret and most strict manner (1 Timothy 3:16, Galatians 4:4, Colossians 2:9).

{2} **Indivisible.** This conjunction is made indivisibly and inseparably forever, so that the Son of God will never lay aside the assumed manhood, and cease to be man, nor shall the human nature be severed from his person, from the first moment of his conception. Yea, when his soul and body were divided by death, yet even then, the human nature remained united to the divine. For should the human nature of Christ ever subsist without the divine; then, Christ must needs have two persons; which is repugnant to Scripture (1 Timothy 2:5; 1 Corinthians 8:6, Ephesians 4:5).

{3} **Of natures preserved and remaining still distinct one from another.** Though this union of divine and human nature in Christ be personal, intimate, and indivisible, yet these two natures in Christ are preserved from confusion and commutation. From confusion: so that of these two natures is not made one; from commutation: so that the one is not changed into the other. But they remain distinct, and their properties distinct: the human nature being created, finite, visible, etc; the divine: uncreated, infinite, invisible, etc.

[3] ***The unity or oneness of his person, though consisting of two distinct natures.*** Though Jesus Christ be God and man, yet is he only one

---

alterum transiret, qui non esset aeterna nativitate filius, &c."
Aug. lib. de Ecclesiast. dogmat. Cap. 2. Tom. 3.

person God-man. Several things evince this oneness or unity of his person consisting of two natures, as:

{1} **Scripture testimonies.** For, Jesus Christ is: *Immanuel, that is: God with us.*[1704] – *The Son of God; which should be born of the virgin Mary.*[1705] – *The Word made flesh.*[1706] – *God's Son made of a woman.*[1707] – *God manifested in the flesh.*[1708] — *of the fathers according to the flesh, who is over all, God blessed forever, Amen.*[1709] Scripture expressly says: *There is one Lord, and one Mediator* (Ephesians 4:5; 1 Corinthians 8:6; 1 Timothy 2:5). But if Christ had two persons, we should have two lords, and two mediators.

{2} **The properties and actions of each nature**, divine and human, attributed to one and the same Christ, who as God and man, is, eternal, yet born in time: infinite, and finite; a creator, and a creature: invisible, and visible: was dead, and yet immortal, etc, namely: eternal as God, born in time as man, etc.

{3} **The end, scope, or intent of Christ's incarnation** – namely: that Jesus Christ might be a true, fit, and sufficient Mediator between God and man – evinces that it was requisite, God and man should become one in person: not by communication of grace, but by truth of nature: not by confusion of substance, but by unity of person, for:

(i) He must be man, our near kinsman, that he might have the right of redemption,[1710] be a merciful and faithful high priest, being in all things like his brethren;[1711] and he must be God, that he might be fully able to redeem us, to destroy death, and him that had the power of death, the devil, deliver us

---

[1704] Isaiah 7:14
[1705] Luke 1:35
[1706] John 1:14
[1707] Galatians 4:4
[1708] 1 Timothy 3:16
[1709] Romans 9:5
[1710] Leviticus 25:23-35, but especially verse 47 to the end
[1711] Hebrews 2:14-18

from the guilt of sin, and curse of the law, and preserve us safe to his heavenly kingdom.[1712]

(ii) He must be man, that he might as our Surety suffer for us, shed his blood and die for our offenses,[1713] become a curse and sin for us, it being most congruous that he should have some communion with us, who suffers for our faults;[1714] this he could not do as God: he must be God, that he might undergo the wrath of God without sinking, satisfy God's justice to the full by his suffering; obtain eternal redemption for us, reconcile us to God by his death, put away our sin by the sacrifice of himself, purge our conscience from dead works, redeem us from the curse and wrath of God, that the blessing of Abraham might come upon us, etc.[1715] This he could not do as mere man.

(iii) He must be man, one with us in participation of our human nature, passions, infirmities, temptations, etc, that he might be experimentally touched with the feeling of our infirmities, might sympathetically and compassionately succor them that are tempted and might the more readily suffer for us, having in so many things suffered with us.[1716] He must be God, one with God in his divine nature, that he might purge away our sins by his death, justify us by his resurrection, be king and head of his church, crush all our enemies, and captivate our very captivity, appear in the presence of God for us as our continual intercessor and advocate; send forth his Spirit into us, sanctify our natures in us, perfume all our spiritual services and sacrifices by his merit, raise up our bodies at the last day, and present us to himself a glorious church, not having spot or wrinkle, or any such thing.[1717]

[1712] Hebrews 2:14-15

[1713] Hebrews 7:22 & 9:22, Romans 4:25

[1714] Galatians 3:13; 2 Corinthians 5:21

[1715] Acts 2:24, John 10:17-18, Hebrews 10:12-14, Ephesians 5:2, Hebrews 9:12, 14, Romans 5:10, Hebrews 9:26, Galatians 3:13-14

[1716] Hebrews 2:14, 16-18 & 4:15

[1717] Hebrews 1:3, Romans 4:25, Ephesians 1:20-22, Revelation 19:16, Hebrews 2:14-15, Ephesians 4:8, Hebrews 9:24 & 7:25; 1 John 2:1-2, Acts 2:33; 1 Corinthians 6:11; 1 Peter 2:5, Revelation 8:3, John 6:54, Ephesians 5:25-27

(iv) He must be man, that he might be humbled deeply, and so discharge all the acts and parts of his Mediatorship which were to be executed in his humiliation: he must be God, that after his humiliation he might be highly exalted, and so accomplish the rest of his mediation in all such acts as are to be fulfilled in his exaltation.

(v) He must be God and man in one person, a middle person between God and man, having perfect interest in both God and man: that he might be a fit middle officer, a fit and prevalent Mediator between God and man, to bring God and man into one covenant.

{4} **The similitudes used, by both ancient and modern writers**, to illustrate this mysterious union of God and man in one person of Jesus our Mediator: are various, and very useful. These are more observable:

(i) Of the soul and body making but one man.[1718] The soul and body are different natures; the soul immortal, the body mortal; the soul reasons, the body accordingly executes. Yet soul and body united make but one individual man; so there is Godhead and manhood in Christ. They are two different and distinct natures: the Godhead immortal, the manhood mortal; the Godhead wrought miracles, the manhood was crucified, etc, yet both make one Christ. But this similitude comes short,[1719] in that: (a) soul and body are imperfect natures, and make up but one perfect nature of man, but Christ's Godhead and manhood are perfect distinct natures. (b) Soul and body have no perfect subsistence, but in the whole: but Christ's Godhead perfectly subsists of itself without the manhood, and assumed unto it, and sustains in it the manhood which never had subsistence of itself, but in union with the Godhead.

(ii) Of the primordial light at first created (Genesis 1:3-4), and of the body of the sun in which that light was afterward seated (Genesis 1:14, etc) – both making one luminary.[1720] The light and solar body are two distinct natures,

---

[1718] Justin Martyr in Exposit. Fidei de recta Consessio. p. 300. An. 1593. He shews the parity and disparity of this Similitude. Athanas. in Symbolo.
[1719] As is noted by Rich. Field *Of The Church*, Book 5. Chap. 12.
[1720] Justin Martyr *quo supr.* pp.301-302

which make one sun: so the two natures, the divine which subsisted first, eternally, and the human which was created in subsistence with the divine, make one Christ. But this similitude comes short, in that: (a) neither light nor solar body did ever perfectly subsist alone. Not the solar body: for in the creation, light was seated in it. Not the light, for that subsisted all abroad in the air, before it was seated in the sun.[1721] (b) Neither light nor solar body are drawn into the unity of the subsistence of one another.

(iii) Of a sword fired and inflamed.[1722] The subsistence of a sword and fire are so conjoined, that their operations notably concur, and there is as it were a communication of properties from the one to the other. For, this fired sword in cutting burns, and in burning cuts. And we may say; that this fiery thing is a cutting sword, and this cutting sword is a fiery thing. But in this it comes short, namely: in that the nature of fire is not drawn into the unity of subsistence with the sword, nor the sword of fire, so that we cannot say: "This sword is fire," or "this fire is a sword."[1723]

(iv) Of one man having two accidental forms, or qualities, as skill in divinity and in physic.[1724] For, here are two qualities or natures different, meeting in one and the same person. And that one person may be denominated from either, and does the works of both, and there is a communication of properties hence resulting. So that we may say: "this divine is a physician," and "this physician is a divine" – this divine is happy in curing diseases, and this physician is happy in converting of souls.

(v) Of a scion or branch grafted into a tree.[1725] This similitude Dr. Field (*Of The Church*, Book 5 Chapter 12) prefers before all the former for setting forth the personal union of the two natures of Christ. And says: "It fails but in two things, namely: (a) in that the branch has a distinct and separate

---

[1721] As Justin Martyr, Ibid. p.301
[1722] Basil. in Orat. in Sanct. Nativ. & Damascen. de Orthod. Fide. Lib. 3. cap. 11.
[1723] D. Rich. Field, *Of The Church*, Book 5 Chapter 12.
[1724] D. Rich. Field. Ibid.
[1725] Alex. de Hales *Sum. Theol.* part. 3. Q. 7. Memb. 1. Artic. 1.

subsistence of itself, and then loosing [disconnecting] it, is drawn into the unity of subsistence with the tree or stock into which it is grafted. (b) In that the branch lacks a root, and so it lacks an integral part of the nature of a tree. But if the branch of one tree should by divine power be created in the stock of another tree, then this similitude would fail only in one point, namely: in the want of the root, whereas Christ's human nature wanted neither essential nor integral part."

(vi) Finally, therefore to supply these defects, I will add my similitude also to illustrate this profound mystery in Christ, namely: of the mistletoe in the oak, or in the apple tree. In this similitude those two defects [do not exist], but an excellent and manifold resemblance, for: (a) the apple tree and the mistletoe are two perfect and different natures in one tree, the mistletoe wanting no integral part that belongs unto mistletoe; so the Godhead and manhood are two perfect and different natures in one person, in one Christ. (b) The mistletoe never had a separate and distinct subsistence of its own; but only subsists in union with the apple tree, which sustains and maintains it; so the human nature of Christ never had any distinct and separate subsistence of its own, but from the first conception subsisted in union with the divine subsistence. (c) The apple tree and the mistletoe are so one tree, that their two different natures are neither confounded together, nor changed one into another, to make up a third nature, but are so individually united, that retaining their different natures, they are but one tree: so the two natures of Christ are without confusion or commutation united in one person, and yet still retain their real differences. (d) The apple tree and mistletoe, though one tree, yet having different natures, bear different fruits, namely: apples and berries: so the Godhead and manhood of Christ, though but one person, yet being different natures, perform distinct and different actions peculiar to each of them. (e) As we may truly say, by reason of this union, this apple tree is a mistletoe, and this mistletoe is an apple tree, and consequently this mistletoe bears apples, and this apple tree bears berries; so we may truly say, by reason of the personal union of God and man in Christ, this son of Mary is the Son of God, and this Son of God is the son of Mary; the Son of God was crucified, and the son of Mary created heaven and earth.

{5} **The effects or consequences resulting from this personal union of the human nature into the person of the Son of God.** These are of three sorts: (i) the communication of properties.[1726] When the properties of either nature are attributed, and truly agree to the whole person, whether they have their denomination from either nature, or from his office, in the concrete. And this communication of properties is of various sorts. (ii) Endowments. The human nature, by reason of its union with the divine, being adorned and fitted to the utmost with most excellent and admirable gifts (John 3:34, Colossians 2:9-10 & 1:19). (iii) Operations accomplished. The person of our Mediator, by reason of this personal union, performs his mediatory acts according to both natures, of which more hereafter. This personal union is the base and foundation of all these three.

But thus of Position 1: that Jesus, the only Son of God, and the son of the virgin Mary, is God and man in one person.

[1726] Of this, see at large in Field *Of The Church*, Book 5, Chapters 13-15, and in Frid. Wendelini *Christian. Theolog.* lib. 1. cap. 16.

Position 2

That this Jesus, God-man, is the Christ, the promised Messiah; and he alone.

To err about the person of Jesus Christ the Mediator, accounting the true Christ to be false, and a false Christ to be true, is a most dangerous and desperate error: forasmuch as there is no salvation to be had under heaven, but only in the true Christ.[1727] The Jews rejected the true Messiah of God's providing, when he came, and expecting another messiah of their own devising, to come they know not when, have miserably dashed themselves upon this stumbling stone, now for 1600 years together, to their own destruction and eternal ruin.[1728] This therefore is a high and necessary point, wherein we should be fully resolved and established. To this end I shall (1) explain and (2) confirm this position.

(1) **For explanation, there are only two words – namely: {*Messiah*} and {*Christ*} – that are to be expounded.**

They are two eminent names given to the true Mediator between God and man, and true Savior of sinners: that, in the Old Testament; this in the New – both of them signifying one and the same thing, namely: {*anointed*}. Messiah מָשִׁיחַ *mashiach*, *anointed*, from מָשַׁח *mashach*, *to anoint*. This name is often given to the true Mediator in the books of the Old Testament, as: – *and exalt the horn of his Messiah.*[1729] – *The rulers take counsel together against the LORD, and against his Messiah.*[1730] This prophecy is interpreted of, and applied to Christ by the apostles in the New Testament. But especially in

---

[1727] Acts 4:12
[1728] John 1:11 & 5:43
[1729] 1 Samuel 2:10
[1730] Psalm 2:2 with Acts 4:25-28

Daniel: *From the going forth of the commandment, to restore and to build Jerusalem, unto the Messiah the prince, shall be seven weeks – And after threescore and two weeks shall Messiah be cut off, but not for himself.*[1731] The Greek word also Χριστός, *Christos*, *Christ*, signifies: *anointed*. From χρίω: to anoint. It answers to the Hebrew word {*Messiah*}, as not only the Septuagint, but also the New Testament renders it.[1732] The New Testament gives and appropriates this name to Jesus God-man very often, as in Luke 2:26. John 4:25. Matthew 1:1, 16, 18 & 16:16, 20, etc.

Now these two names are attributed to Jesus, God-man, our Mediator, in reference to his Mediatory office, which as prophet, priest and king he was to execute, and did actually execute for us: and they denote his qualification and designation to his office for under the Old Testament, God ordained a holy anointing oil, and gave the composition of it, wherewithal three sorts of officers were anointed, namely: prophets (1 Kings 19:16), priests (Exodus 40:12, etc.), and kings (1 Samuel 10:1 & 16:13; 1 Kings 19:16) – the anointing oil being poured upon their heads, ran down to the skirts of their garments (Psalm 133:2-3).[1733] This was a sign and means of their qualification for, and designation unto those offices, for as as that sacred oil did outwardly warm, refresh and make agile the bodily members to employment, so the endowments of God's Spirit did inwardly fit the soul with prudence, wisdom, joy, cheerfulness, zeal, courage, fortitude, magnanimity, etc, for managing those offices.

Thus Jesus (of whom prophets, priests, and kings were but types) was anointed by God, not with material oil but with the Holy Spirit and with power for his mediatory office.[1734] And having the fullness of the Godhead in him; and all fullness;[1735] and receiving the Spirit not by measure, but above

---

[1731] Daniel 9:25-26
[1732] Acts 4:26 from Psalm 2:2
[1733] Exodus 30:22, etc.
[1734] Acts 10:38
[1735] Colossians 2:9-10 & 1:9

measure;[1736] he is said to be anointed with the oil of gladness above his fellows – the Holy Spirit being called {*oil of gladness*} from the effect thereof upon us, by Christ's office.[1737] And with this oil, Christ was anointed more abundantly than all his fellows, namely: above all his members, and above all prophets, priests and kings before him. Or (as Illyricus has observed)[1738] the particle מִ prefixed in the word מֵחֲבֵרֶךָ *mechabareka* {*above thy fellows*}, may be rendered: {*for thy fellows*} – Christ being thus anointed, that out of this fullness they might receive, and grace for grace, and so be complete in him.[1739] Now Jesus being thus anointed, is thereby fully qualified for, and constituted in his Mediatory office; as prophet, like Moses (Deuteronomy 18:15, etc, Acts 7:37, Isaiah 61:1-2, etc), a priest after the order of Melchizedek (Psalm 110:4, Hebrews 7 throughout), a king in Zion, to rule over the house of Jacob forever (Psalm 2:2, 6, Luke 1:32-33). Hence, from **Christ**, his disciples are called **Christians** (it being usual to denominate disciples from their master),[1740] and deservedly, because they partake of Christ's anointing, being anointed in their measure with the Holy Spirit, teaching them all things as prophets, and making them kings and priests unto God (2 Corinthians 1:21-22; 1 John 2:20, 27, Revelation 1:5-6).

(2) **For confirmation of this necessary position** – that this Jesus, God-man in one person, is the promised Messiah, is the only true Christ, the anointed, qualified and constituted of God Mediator between God and man, and none but he alone – take these few demonstrations, namely:

[1] *From God's eternal decree before the foundation of the world*. This Jesus, God-man, and he alone, is that very person whom God has eternally foreordained before the world began to be our Mediator and

---

[1736] John 3:34
[1737] Psalm 45:7
[1738] Illyricus on Psalm 45:7
[1739] John 1:14, 16, Colossians 2:9-10
[1740] Acts 11:26

Redeemer, and that by means of his death: *ye were not redeemed with corruptible things*, etc, *but with the precious blood of Christ, as of a lamb without blemish and without spot. Who verily was fore-ordained before the foundation of the world, but was manifest in these last times for you.*[1741] Hence Christ is said, to be *delivered by the determinate counsel and foreknowledge of God*, etc.[1742] And that Herod and Pontius Pilate with the Gentiles and people were gathered together against this holy child Jesus, for to do whatsoever God's hand and his counsel determined before to be done.[1743] To this effect, all that are predestinated and elected to adoption, life, and salvation, are elected thereunto in this Jesus Christ, and predestinated to be conformed unto him.[1744]

[2] ***From God's promises and prophetic predictions which have been since the world began.*** For, this Jesus and he alone is the person which in all the promises and prophecies in former ages was intended by God for a restorer, Redeemer and Savior of lapsed mankind, and a Mediator between God and man. As may appear more generally and more particularly:

{1} **More generally: that the law and prophets intended him**, as is very observable in various testimonies as:

(i) Of Jesus Christ himself. *Search the Scriptures, – they are they which testify of me. – Moses wrote of me.*[1745] To the two disciples going to Emmaus: *O fools and slow of heart to believe all that the prophets have spoken! Ought not Christ to have suffered these things, and to enter into his glory? And beginning at Moses and all the prophets, he expounded unto them in all the Scriptures the things concerning himself.*[1746] To the apostles a little before his ascension: *These are the words which I spake unto you, while I was yet with you, that all things*

[1741] 1 Peter 1:18-20
[1742] Acts 2:23
[1743] Acts 4:27-28
[1744] Ephesians 1:3-5; 1 Peter 1:2, Romans 8:29-30
[1745] John 5:39, 46
[1746] Luke 24:25-27

must be fulfilled which were written in the law of Moses, and in the prophets, and in the psalms, concerning me.[1747]

(ii) Of Peter, who, preaching Christ to Cornelius, said: *to him give all the prophets witness, that through his name, whosoever believeth in him, shall receive remission of sins.*[1748] And before that, he told the Jews that killed the prince of life: *I wot that through ignorance ye did it, as did also your rulers. But those things which God before had shown by the mouth of all his prophets, that Christ should suffer, he hath so fulfilled.*[1749]

(iii) Of Stephen the proto-martyr (Acts 7:52).

(iv) Of Paul: – *saying none other things than these things which the prophets and Moses did say should come: that Christ should suffer, and that he should be the first that should rise from the dead, and should show light unto the people and to the Gentiles.*[1750]

{2} **Note particularly that it is not difficult to show from promise to promise, and from prophecy to prophecy, throughout all ages before Christ, how they did all intend, and had their accomplishment in this Jesus.** To mention some noted instances:

(i) This Jesus is that seed of the woman that should bruise the serpent's head (Genesis 3:15 with Galatians 4:4, Colossians 2:15, Hebrews 2:14-15).

(ii) This Jesus is that seed of Abraham, in whom all the nations of the earth should be blessed (Genesis 12:3. & 22:18 with Acts 3:25-26, Galatians 3:8, 13-14, Hebrews 2:16, Matthew 1:1, etc).

(iii) This Jesus is that great prophet like unto Moses, which God would raise up to Israel, from among themselves (Deuteronomy 18:15-20 with Acts 3:20-23, & 7:37).

[1747] Luke 24:44
[1748] Acts 10:43
[1749] Acts 3:13-19
[1750] Acts 26:22-23 & 13:26-27, 29

(iv) This Jesus is that priest forever after the order of Melchizedek, consecrated by God's own sacred oath, of which he will not repent (Psalm 110:4 with Hebrews 7 throughout).

(v) This Jesus is that seed of David which God would raise up to sit upon his throne to reign over the house of Jacob forever (Psalm 89:3-4, 19-38 & 132:11-12 with Acts 2:22-37, Matthew 1:1, etc. Luke 1:32-33).

(vi) This Jesus is the sure mercies of David, raised from the dead, and not suffered to see corruption (Isaiah 55:3, Psalm 16:10, etc., with Acts 13:28-38)

(vii) This Jesus is that anointed of the Lord, against whom the heathen raged, and the people imagined a vain thing, the kings of the earth stood up, and the rulers took counsel together (Psalm 2:1-3, etc., with Acts 4:25-29). Thus Jesus is the scope and mark at which the promises and prophecies of old do peculiarly aim, and therefore he alone is the very Christ.

[3] *From the lineal descent of Christ, according to the flesh.* For this Jesus, and he alone, did lineally and naturally descend according to his humanity, of Abraham, and David, by a virgin, according to the Scriptures; as is evident in the genealogy of this Jesus described by Luke (Luke 3:23 to the end) – this being the natural line of Christ, as has been formerly noted, though the name of the virgin Mary his mother be not expressed, but her husbands instead of hers, according to the custom of the Jews, who draw down genealogies by men and not by women, as is observed by Petrus Galatinus and others.[1751]

[4] *From the complete and exact accomplishment of the Scriptures of the Old Testament.* They are most admirably fulfilled and accomplished in all particulars touching the Messiah, in this Jesus Christ as is most evident in all the four evangelists' histories, and the Acts – this being one principal intent of the four evangelists histories of Jesus Christ: to prove that this Jesus is the Christ: *These are written that ye might believe that **Jesus is the Christ** the Son*

[1751] Peter Galatinus l.7 c.12

of God, and that believing ye might have life through his name.[1752] Hereupon Piscator has very appositely digested into a syllogism the predictions touching Christ in the Old Testament, and the accomplishments there of in this Jesus according to the history of those four evangelists – those in the major, these in the minor of a syllogism – thence concluding that this Jesus is the very Christ. Let the learned consult him diligently.[1753]

[5] ***From Jacob's prophecy, and the accomplishment thereof.*** The prophecy: *The scepter shall not depart from Judah, nor a law giver from between his feet, until Shiloh come, and unto him shall the gathering of the people be.*[1754] By {*Judah*}, we are here to understand not the person of Judah, one of Jacob's sons, but the tribe of Judah so denominated from him.[1755] By {*scepter*}, we are generally to understand the political rule, regiment, or government of the commonwealth. It cannot be restrained to kingly rule, for that was taken away by Nebuchadnezzar from Zedekiah, as was foretold in Ezekiel 21:26-27; nor to princely government, by princes and governors, who governed after the captivity, for that is confessed by learned men to be injuriously translated by the Hasmoneans (or Maccabees), Levites, and priests to the tribe of Levi, and so propagated in that tribe; but to be extended also to such magistrates and judges, as the Greek calls συνέδριον: the council, which the Jews corruptly styled {*Sanhedrin*}: a grand council at Jerusalem, governing the commonwealth. After Judah became a distinct kingdom, it was not destitute of civil government, either by kings, or by princely governors, or by the council, until Shiloh came, although this grand council was extremely weakened, and divided into lesser councils, by the Romans, as Josephus confesses;[1756] yet it was not wholly taken away and demolished until Shiloh came, for then the Jewish commonwealth would have been wholly dissolved.

[1752] John 20:30-31
[1753] Piscat. ante [partic.] Histor. 4. Evangelist
[1754] Genesis 49:10
[1755] See this prophecy most learnedly explicated and vindicated by that accurate Franciscus Gomarus in *Operum*, Tom. 1. p. 235. ad 243.
[1756] Josephus, *Jewish Antiquities*, 14.8 & 14.10

By {*Shiloh*}, it is generally agreed that Christ is intended, though the proper signification of the Hebrew word שִׁילֹה *Shiloh* is much controverted. So then, until Jesus Christ came, the government in one kind or another remained in Judah; but after he was come, the scepter quickly departed, and that Jewish commonwealth was utterly dissolved to this day; and therefore this Jesus must needs be the Shiloh: the true Christ here intended.

[6] **From Daniel's weeks.** Daniel positively determines the time *when the Messiah should be cut off, but not for himself, to finish transgression, make an end of sins, and bring in everlasting righteousness*; namely: seventy weeks of years.[1757] There is some small difference among learned men about the beginning and end of these seventy years, by reason of several commands that went forth to restore and build Jerusalem. Hence, some place the Messiah's death in the year of the world 3960,[1758] some in the year 3952,[1759] and Helvicus in the year 3983.[1760] As the late large English Annotations note, there was a fourfold commandment, decree, or precept went out for the rebuilding of Jerusalem, mentioned in Ezra and Nehemiah, to some of which, the beginning of these seventy weeks must be referred, and to the ending of which the cutting off of Jesus Christ the Messiah exactly agrees.[1761] Not to enter now into that intricate dispute, which of them it was, it is plain on all hands against the Jews, that the promised Messiah is already come and cut off, and that Daniel's weeks had their particular accomplishment in this **Jesus Christ**.

[7] ***From the general agreement of all the types to this Jesus, as the body and center of them*** all (Colossians 2:16-17, Hebrews 10:1, John 1:17). There were many types and shadows,[1762] personal and real, ordinary and extraordinary, etc., but this Jesus, God-man, is the truth and substance of them all. He is the true Adam that justifies and quickens all his supernatural

---

[1757] Daniel 9:24-27
[1758] H. Broughton in his *Consent of Scripture*
[1759] Roger Drake in his *Sacred Chronology*
[1760] Helvicus, *Chronol.* p.22
[1761] Large English Annotations on Daniel 9:24
[1762] See D. T. Taylor's *Treatises of the Types of our Savior*

seed, as the first Adam condemned and killed all his natural seed.[1763] He is the true Melchizedek, first king of righteousness, and then king of Salem, that is, king of peace: without father according to his manhood, without mother according to his Godhead, without beginning of days, or end of life.[1764] He is the true passover that is sacrificed for us.[1765] He is the true bread of life, that true manna that came down from heaven, whereof a man may eat and not die.[1766] He is the true rock that affords living water indeed to his church in the wilderness of this world.[1767] *That rock that followed them was Christ*. And that manna and water are called spiritual meat and drink, because they were types and sacraments representing Christ unto them. He is the true serpent lifted up in the wilderness to heal the mortal stings of the old serpent the devil, that whosoever believeth in him, looks up to him by the eye of faith, may not perish but have eternal life.[1768] He is the true prophet, like Moses, to be hearkened to in all things, etc.[1769] He is the true Joshua that brings his Israel, all true believers, into the eternal rest.[1770] He is the true seed of David, that reigns over the house of Jacob forevermore.[1771] And what shall I say, he is the mystery and substance of all the Levitical ceremonies, they all intended him, shadowed out him, as I have already manifested at large in opening the Sinai Covenant.[1772] Now he that is the body and substance of the types of old, must needs be the Messiah, the very Christ, for those figures and types were God's way of revealing Christ unto his people, until he was exhibited.

[8] *From the testimony of John the Baptist*. John the Baptist was the Elijah that was to come, in the power and spirit of Elijah, as the harbinger of

---

[1763] Romans 5:12 to the end; 1 Corinthians 15:21-22
[1764] Hebrews 7:1
[1765] 1 Corinthians 5:7-8
[1766] John 6:31-59
[1767] 1 Corinthians 10:1-3
[1768] John 3:15-16
[1769] Acts 3:20-23
[1770] Hebrews 4 throughout
[1771] Luke 1:31-33
[1772] Book 3, Chapter 4, Aphorism 7, Corollary 7

Christ, to prepare his way before him. And he began to preach a little before Christ began his public ministry.[1773] Now he pointed out Christ as with the finger. *Behold the lamb of God that taketh away the sins of the world.*[1774] And John the Baptist confesses: *I knew him not, but he that sent me to baptize with water, the same said unto me, upon whom thou shalt see the Spirit descending and remaining on him, the same is he that baptizeth with the Holy Ghost. And I saw and bare record, that this is the Son of God.*[1775] And after he tells the Jews plainly: *I am not the Christ, but sent before him* – not the bridegroom that has the bride the church, but the bridegroom's friend, rejoicing to hear the bridegroom's voice. *He must increase: but I must decrease*, etc.[1776]

[9] **From God's authorizing, constituting, ordaining and establishing this Jesus to be the Christ.** None can be the Messiah, or Christ, but whom God calls, anoints, seals, and appoints thereunto. Now God has constituted and ordained this Jesus, God-man, and him alone to be the Christ, the Mediator and Savior, the judge of quick and dead, etc. *God sent his Son into the world, – that the world through him might be saved.*[1777] – *God sent his Son, made of a woman, made under the law, to redeem them that were under the law.*[1778] – *Labour for the meat which endureth to everlasting life, which the Son of man will give unto you: for him hath God the Father sealed.*[1779] – *Christ glorified not himself to be made a high priest: but he that said unto him, thou art my son, this day have I begotten thee,* etc.[1780] – *God anointed **Jesus** of Nazareth with the Holy Ghost and with power*, etc. – *and he commanded us to preach unto the people, and to testify, that it is he, which was ordained of God to be the Judge of quick and the dead.*[1781] Hence God furnished him with all

---

[1773] Matthew 3 & 4
[1774] John 1:29
[1775] John 1:30-34
[1776] John 3:28 to the end
[1777] John 3:17
[1778] Galatians 4:4-5
[1779] John 6:27
[1780] Hebrews 5:4-6
[1781] Acts 10:38-44 & 17:31

authority, power and ability for his mediatory office (Matthew 28:18-20, John 5:21-23 & 3:34-35, Colossians 1:19 & 2:9-10).

[10] *From the testimony of Father, Son, and Holy Spirit.* He must needs be the Mediator, Messiah and Christ, whom Father, Son, and Holy Spirit testify and declare to be such. Now this Jesus has the testimony of Father, Son, and Holy Spirit:

{1} **The Father testified twice by voice from heaven:** *This is my beloved son, in whom I am well pleased.*[1782] Hence God the Father is said to have sealed him.[1783] And Christ hereupon said: *The Father himself which hath sent me, hath born witness of me.*[1784] And the Father's testimony of him has special respect to his mediatory person and office. The Father bore record to Christ, sealing and approving him, at his baptism, and at his transfiguration:

(i) At his baptism – and that in three ways,[1785] namely: (a) by opening the heavens unto him; (b) by sending down his Spirit in likeness of a dove upon him; and (c) by voice from heaven: *This is my well-beloved Son, in whom I am well-pleased.*

(ii) At his transfiguration also, and that in three ways,[1786] namely: (a) by the heavenly glory put upon Christ, to encourage him against his passion approaching; (b) by the appearance of Moses and Elijah, talking with him about his decease, which he should accomplish at Jerusalem, according to the law and prophets, which meet in Christ and bear witness to him; and (c) by his voice from heaven: *This is my beloved Son, in whom I am well-pleased, hear him.*

{2} **The Son himself testified by his works and miracles that he was the Christ, sent of God.** *The works which the Father hath given me to finish, the same works that I do bear witness of me that the Father hath sent me.*[1787]

[1782] Matthew 3:17 & 17:5
[1783] John 6:27
[1784] John 5:37
[1785] Matthew 3:16-17
[1786] Luke 9:29, etc, Matthew 17:2, etc, Mark 9:2, etc
[1787] John 5:36

And therefore when John in prison heard of the works of Christ, and sent to him, saying: *Art thou he that should come, or do we look for another? Jesus answered and said unto them. Go and show John again the things which ye do hear and see: the blind receive their sight, and the lame walk, the lepers are cleansed, and the deaf hear, the dead are raised up, and the poor have the gospel preached to them. And blessed is he whosoever shall not be offended in me* – as if he had said: "My works, my miracles are an evident demonstration that I am the Christ."[1788]

{3} **The Holy Spirit testified that this Jesus is the Christ**: partly, by his descending and resting upon him in a visible shape of a dove, when Jesus was baptized, and began solemnly to enter upon the public execution of his mediatory office;[1789] partly, by his plentiful and miraculous falling upon the apostles (Acts 2:-4, 32-33, 36) and primitive Christians (Acts 10:43-46, etc.); and partly, by his effectual attestation to our hearts and consciences (1 John 5:6-12). Who can experimentally discern and feel the efficacy of the Spirit of Jesus upon his heart, enlightening, converting, sanctifying, comforting, attesting, sealing, etc., and not conclude that this Jesus who gives such a Spirit into us must needs be the Christ?

These, among many other arguments, may suffice to convince any sober mind; that this Jesus, God-man, and he alone is the promised Messiah, the Christ. And that *there is no other name under heaven given among men whereby we may be saved.*[1790]

[1788] Matthew 11:2-7, Acts 2:22, etc.
[1789] Matthew 3:16-17
[1790] Acts 4:12

Position 3

That Jesus Christ, God and man, is the only true, fit and sufficient Mediator, Testator, and Surety of the New Covenant between God and man.

This I shall evidence in two branches, namely:

(1) That Jesus Christ is the Mediator, Testator, and Surety of the New Covenant.

This is clear in all these three branches:

[1] *Jesus Christ is the Mediator of the New Covenant. For there is one God, and one Mediator between God and men, the man Christ Jesus.*[1791] – He is the Mediator of a better covenant, which was established upon better promises.[1792] – And for this cause he is the mediator of the new testament, etc.[1793] – But ye are come unto Mount Sion, – and to Jesus the mediator of the new covenant.[1794] The Greek word μεσίτης in all these places, most properly signifies {*a mediator*} or {*a middler*} (that I may so express it) because he is both a middle person, and a middle officer between God and man, to reconcile and reunite God and man. This, of all others, is the most proper and genuine signification of this name {μεσίτης}.

Jesus Christ is the middle, that is, the second person in the Trinity, between the Father and the Holy Spirit.[1795] He is the only middle person between God and man, being in one person God-man.[1796] And he is the middle officer, intervening, or interposing, or coming between God and man

---

[1791] 1 Timothy 2:5
[1792] Hebrews 8:6-8
[1793] Hebrews 9:14-15
[1794] Hebrews 12:22-24
[1795] Matthew 28:19; 1 John 5:7
[1796] 1 Timothy 3:16

by office, satisfying God's justice to the full for man's sins by his obedience to the death, and continually interceding for his elect, to whom he reveals and effectually applies this his satisfaction, intercession, redemption, etc., for their actual reconciliation unto God.[1797]

Hence (as one observes), "Jesus Christ as a true Mediator, is still found, *in medio*, in the middle. He was born, as some think from Wisdom 18:14, about the middle of the night; he suffered in the middle of the world, that is, at Jerusalem, seated in the middle of the earth; he was crucified in the midst between the two thieves; he died in the air on the cross, in the midst between heaven and earth; he stood after his resurrection in the midst of his disciples (John 20:19). He promises that where two or three are gathered together, to be in the midst of them (Matthew 18:20). He walks in the midst of the golden candlesticks, the churches (Revelation 1:13). And he, as the heart in the midst, distributes spirit and virtue to all the parts of his mystical body."[1798] So he. Thus Jesus Christ is the Mediator between God and man; middle in person, and middle in office.

Yea, Jesus Christ is Mediator of the New Covenant, and that κατ' ἐξοχήν[1799] more peculiarly and eminently than of any other covenant. Moses was a typical Mediator under the Old Covenant: he went between God and Israel, he typed out Christ the only true Mediator (1 Timothy 2:6, Hebrews 13:8, Galatians 3:19, etc).[1800] But Christ is the true Mediator of the New Covenant, the better covenant most eminently and singularly, for: {1} he dedicated and established the New Covenant in his own blood.[1801] The best blood that ever was shed, for covenant sanction, in the world. {2} He ratified and confirmed this New Covenant with the sacramental tokens of his blood, baptism and the Lord's supper.[1802] {3} He obtains for us all New Covenant

---

[1797] 1 Timothy 2:5-6, Hebrews 9:14-16 & 7:25; 2 Corinthians 5:19-21
[1798] Io. Gerhard. In *Loc. Com.* loc. 4 *De Person. et Offic. Christi*, c.3 §26.
[1799] This Greek phrase means *par excellence*
[1800] Exodus 20:18-22, Deuteronomy 5:22 to the end
[1801] Hebrews 9:14-16
[1802] Matthew 28:19-20, Luke 22:19-20

blessings from God, by his merit fully satisfying God's justice for all our sins and debts: and enables us to all New Covenant duties to God by his Spirit.[1803] {4} He brings God and man into this blessed New Covenant, as confederates in him: to which end he manages all the mysteries and affairs of this New Covenant, as prophet, priest, and king most advantageously and effectually.

[2] *Jesus Christ is the Testator of this New Testament*. As this New Covenant is a federal testament, or a testamental covenant, so Jesus Christ – Mediator of this New Covenant – is a Mediatory Testator, or a Testatory Mediator. Hence in the same context Christ is styled, μεσιτης: {*a mediator*}, and διαθεμενος: a {*disposer*} or {*testator*}. *And for this cause he is the mediator of the new testament, that by means of death, etc., they which are called might receive the promise of the eternal inheritance. For where a testament is, there must also of necessity be the death of the testator.*[1804] How fitly is Jesus Christ counted the Testator of this New Testament, of this his last will and testament, for: {1} Jesus Christ confirmed and made of force this his New Testament by his blood and death as Testator.[1805] {2} All the blessings promised in this New Testament, are as so many bequests and legacies of Christ the Testator, that was dead, and is alive, to his church and members in this his last will. {3} The Scripture, the written Word of Christ,[1806] is the instrument,[1807] or evidence. {4} The prophets, apostles, and holy penmen of Scripture, were the notaries or scribes that wrote his will. {5} The sacraments are the seals annexed to this New Testament.[1808] {6} The witnesses are *three that bear record in heaven: the Father, the Word, and the Holy Ghost*: and *three that bear witness on earth: the Spirit, and the water, and the blood*.[1809] {7} The executor of Christ's last will and testament is Jesus Christ himself by his Spirit,

---

[1803] 1 Timothy 2:6-7, Hebrews 9:14-16 & 7:22
[1804] Hebrews 9:15-16
[1805] Hebrews 9:15-16
[1806] Colossians 3:16
[1807] Jeremiah 31:31, etc, Hebrews 8:8-12
[1808] Matthew 28:19 & 26:26-31
[1809] 1 John 5:6-10

effectually applying it and the benefits of it to all his members. And to this end though he dIed to ratify his testament, yet he revived and rose again to execute it, and behold he is alive for evermore. But of these things I have already spoken heretofore.[1810]

[3] Jesus Christ is Surety of this New Covenant. *By so much was Jesus made surety* (εγγυος) *of a better covenant.*[1811] Our English translation has it: {*of a better testament*}, but not so fitly, because properly a testament neither tends to have, nor needs to have a surety as a covenant does. Beza therefore justly blameth both Erasmus and the Vulgar translation for rendering it {*testament*}, for that a surety is not added in testaments, and should he be added, how can the same be both a testator and as surety?[1812] So that this word {*surety*} has reference properly to a covenant, and not to a testament. The Greek [εγγυος]: sponsor, fidejussor, praes; a surety, a pledger, etc. is very significative, being derived, as some think, from γυῖον a hand, as it were [εο] γυῖοις in hands, because the security, or pledge is given in hand.[1813] Or as Soudas and others, from γυῆ or γυια: the earth, because the earth is the most firm and stable of all the elements.

A surety is properly one that willingly promises and undertakes to pay and discharge the debt, if the debtor fails and is not able to make satisfaction himself. Thus Paul willingly and spontaneously, from the love that he had to his converted Onesimus, promised and undertook to make satisfaction to Philemon for any wrong that Onesimus had done to him: *If he hath wronged thee, or oweth thee ought, put that on mine account. I, Paul, have written it with mine own hand, I will repay it.*[1814] Hence Jesus Christ being called *mediator of a better covenant* (Hebrews 8:6) and *surety of a better covenant* (Hebrews

---

[1810] In Book 4, Chapter 2, Aphorism 1, etc.

[1811] Hebrews 7:22

[1812] "Vulgata & Erasmus, Testamenti; quod non convenit huic loco. Ne{que} enim in Testamentis adhibitur fidejussor. Deinde etiamsi adhiberetur, quomodo idem esset Testator, & fidejussor?" Bez. Annot. in Hebr. 7 22.

[1813] Scapul. in Lexic.

[1814] Philemon 18-19

7:22), namely: so a mediator as a surety, and so a surety as a Mediator – this may clearly let us see what manner of Mediator Christ is. For, one of these words is to be explained by the other, namely {*mediator*} by {*surety*}. So that Jesus Christ is not only such a mediator as is a legate ambassador, or messenger, only between God and men, as that dangerous heretic Socinus pretends; but properly an intercessor, a pacifier, an atoner, a satisfier, because Christ the Mediator is Surety of the New Covenant, that is, our satisfier, our pacifier, our appeaser, our intercessor, etc, with God.[1815]

How? It is expressed in 1 Timothy 2:5-6 by: *giving himself* – αντιλυτρον – *a ransom for us*, and in Hebrews 1:3 by: *purging our sins by himself*, and in Hebrews 2:17 by: *making reconciliation for the sins of the people as a merciful and faithful high priest*, and in Hebrews 7:27 & 9:12, 14 by *offering up himself once for the sins of the people to God the father, by the eternal Spirit, having obtained eternal redemption for them*, and in 2 Corinthians 5:21; 1 Peter 2:24, and Hebrews 10:10, 12 by *being made sin for us, bearing our sins* (that is, the punishment and curse of our sins) *upon his own body on the tree, even by offering one sacrifice for sins forever, the body of Jesus Christ once for all*. Thus Christ, as our Mediator was our Surety, and as our Surety, fully paid all our debt, setting us perfectly free forever.

Thus, Jesus Christ is Mediator, Testator and Surety of the New Covenant.

(2) That Jesus Christ is the only true, fit and sufficient Mediator, etc. Of the New Covenant between God and man. Christ is the sole and whole Mediator: not the blessed virgin, not any saint, not any or all the prophets, apostles, martyrs, or glorious angels, as the papists fondly do imagine. Here consider: [1] the state of this position and [2] the confirmation of it.

[1] *For the state of this position*, note that there is a twofold mediation, namely: of redemption and of intercession.

[1815] Socin. de Servator. lib. 1. cap. 2.

{1} Of redemption and reconciliation, whereby a full price or ransom is paid for us, by enduring death for our sins to the satisfying of divine justice. And in this sense Christ alone is Mediator: he alone redeeming us by his death, and reconciling us to God by his blood.[1816]

{2} Of intercession, and this again is twofold, namely: (i) *meritoria*, meritorious: by way of merit or desert. And so Christ only is our advocate with the Father, and continual intercessor, appearing in the presence of God for us, presenting his death and merits before God, and so making intercession for us. (ii) *Petitoria*, petitory: by way of petition or supplication; whereby, the saints on earth more generally, or this or that saint more particularly, pray one for another in this world according to Christ's command, having in general or in particular a knowledge and fellow-feeling of one another's wants, miseries, temptations, etc.[1817] Thus Paul prayed earnestly for the churches, as in Hebrews 13:20, 21. Philemon 4; 1 Thessalonians 1:4, Philippians 1:4, and desired most earnestly their prayers again for himself, as in Ephesians 6:18-19, Hebrews 13:18-19; 1 Thessalonians 5:25, and Romans 15:30-32. This state of the position duly improved, will easily cut asunder all the popish arguments made to the contrary.

For the confirmation of this position, thus stated, briefly consider:

(i) That the Scripture mentions only one Mediator and Surety of the New Covenant;[1818] only one Testator of the New Testament, between God and man;[1819] only one Advocate and Intercessor with the Father;[1820] and only one Savior, namely: Jesus Christ the righteous, God and man.[1821] And therefore Jesus Christ and he alone, is Mediator, Surety, Testator, and Savior. The Scripture reveals no other: and we ought to receive no other. Christ was the true Mediator, even of the Old Covenant (Galatians 3:19-20, Hebrews 13:8),

---

[1816] 1 Timothy 2:5-6, Hebrews 9:12-16 & 7:22, Romans 5:8-10; 1 Peter 2:24
[1817] Matthew 6:9, etc, Luke 11:2, etc, James 5:16
[1818] 1 Timothy 2:5-6, Hebrews 8:6 & 9:15 & 7:22
[1819] Hebrews 9:15-16
[1820] 1 John 2:1-2, Hebrews 7:25, Romans 8:34
[1821] Acts 4:12

but more darkly and more imperfectly revealed – and that under the type of Moses that stood between God and the people (Exodus 20, Deuteronomy 5), and under the shadows of typical sacrifices and blood of innocent beasts (Hebrews 9 & 10). But he is Mediator of the New Covenant most eminently, clearly, perfectly, by his own death and blood, etc.

(ii) That Jesus Christ – and he alone – was a fit and sufficient person, for the office of a Mediator of the New Covenant between God and man. This his fitness and sufficiency – (a) as the second person in Trinity, the Son of God; (b) as God-man, an exact middle person between God and man, equally near to, and interested in both God and man – has been already declared.[1822]

(iii) That Jesus God-man – and he alone – is the Messiah, the Christ, anointed with the Holy Ghost and with power, for the mediatory office, sealed, commissionated, and called by the father to this office, accepted and approved in this office, as has been abundantly manifested;[1823] and therefore Jesus Christ alone must needs be the only fit and sufficient Mediator of the New Covenant, *able to save to the uttermost all that come unto God by him* (Hebrews 7:25).

Thus, Jesus Christ is the only Mediator, Surety, and Testator of the New Covenant and Testament between God and man.

[1822] In this 6th Chapter, Aphorism 1, Position 1, Section 4
[1823] In this 6th Chapter, Aphorism 2, Position 2

Position 4

That Jesus Christ is Mediator, Testator and Surety of the New Covenant between God and man, as he is God-man.

He is Mediator, etc, not as God only, nor as man only, but as God-man in one person. Here consider: (1) the sense and (2) the grounds of this position.

(1) **For the sense of this position**, note:

[1] There is a conjunction and union of two natures divine and human in one and the same individual person of the Mediator. This is by some styled {*substantial mediation*}. And this is so necessary to the office of Mediatorship; that without this (as is confessed on all hands) Christ could not have been a fit Mediator.

[2] There is a cooperation and concurrence of these two natures in the person of the Mediator, unto the acts or works of mediation, according to the peculiar propriety of each nature: which acts he performs, divine as God, human as man, one and undivided as Mediator; the real difference of the two natures being still preserved distinct and entire.

Papists do grant the former, namely: the conjunction of the divine and human natures in the person of the Mediator: but they deny the latter, namely: the cooperation of both those natures in the acts of mediation, for they hold that Christ performs the acts of Mediatorship, not as God, but only as man: from his humanity, not from his deity.[1824]

[1824] "Christ was head of the Church, and our chief Bishop and Priest according to his Manhood, etc Rhemist Annotation on N. Testam. on Mat. 9 §. 6. & 8. – "Christ is the chief Minister, according to his man hood, of all our reconciliation to God" – Rhemist Annotation on 2 Corinthians 5:18. And elsewhere: "Beware of the wicked heresy of the Arians and Calvinists,—that stick not to say, that Christ was a priest, or did sacrifice, according to his Godhead, which is to make Christ, God the Father priest, and not his Son, and to do sacrifice and homage to him as his Lord, and not as his equal in dignity and nature." Rhemist Annotations on Heb. 5. §. 6. Bellarmine also insists much upon this, as

Bellarmine speaks plainly, thus distinguishing; the principium quod, the principle or beginning which did the works of Mediatorship, was not God alone, nor man alone, but both together – namely: God-man – but the *principium quo*, the principle or beginning whereby these works were done of the Mediator, was his human nature, not his divine.

But the orthodox resolve better, that Jesus Christ acts as Mediator from both his natures, his humanity doing what is properly human, his divinity what is properly divine, both of them concurring unto one work of Mediatorship. The worker is one person, the work is one mediation, but the formal principles or beginnings of this work are the two distinct natures in that one person of the Mediator. As the divine and human nature concur to make one person of Christ the Mediator, so the distinct acts of these two natures in Christ concur to make up one and the same complete work of mediation. Christ did his *opera authoritatis* or *magisterii*, his works of authority from his Godhead, but his *opera ministerii*, his works of ministry, from his manhood; but as his natures are united in one person, so his acts and operations from his two principles, are conjoined in one mediation.

(2) **The grounds of this position, thus stated and explained, are several**, for:

[1] *The holy Scriptures do frequently ascribe the acts of Christ's mediation to his divine, as well as to his human nature*. And the holy Scriptures are our best guides in this mystery, which is not of natural cognizance; but only of mere supernatural revelation, as:

---

the Common Opinion of the Catholics: "Est au[t]em sententia Communis Catholicorum, ipsum quidem Mediatorem, sive (ut Theologi loquuntur) Principium quod operabatur opera Mediatoris, non fuisse Deum solum, vel hominem solum, sed utrum{que} simul, id est, verbum incarnatum, sive Deum Humanatum. Principium tamen quo illa opera à Mediatore fiebant, fuisse Naturam humanam, non divinam. Tametsi enim Deus inearnatus erat, qui Orabat, patiebatur, obediebat, sat faciebat, tamen haec omnia faciebat secundum formam servi, non secundum formam Dei." Bellar, de Christo, lib. 5. c. 1. &c. 2. Tom. 1.

{1} God was in Christ reconciling the world to himself, not imputing their trespasses unto them (2 Corinthians 5:19). Therefore God in Christ, as well as man in Christ, acted to the reconciliation of the world, and to their justification; consequently, to the works of mediation.

{2} The law (that Covenant of God at Mount Sinai)[1825] was *ordained by angels in the hand of a mediator* (Galatians 3:19-20).[1826] Of what Mediator? Not of Moses, who was only an intervening messenger between God and Israel, in the solemn transactions of that Sinai Covenant, or at most but a typical mediator; but of Christ the promised Messiah, that angel[1827] (namely: *the Angel of the Covenant*)[1828] who spoke to Moses in Mount Sinai, and with our fathers, of whom Moses was but a dark type or shadow. This promised Messiah did then act as Mediator of the covenant and that according to his God-head, for at that time he had not assumed the manhood.

{3} *To feed the church of God, which he hath purchased with his own blood* (Acts 20:28). Therefore, Jesus Christ as God has purchased his church with his own blood as man. The purchase, is the church; the price whereby this purchase was made, was the blood of God, namely: the human blood of Christ, the God-man; but the purchaser was Christ as God – his Godhead making his human blood a price sufficient. His Godhead therefore did cooperate with his manhood in this work of redemption.

{4} *How much more shall the blood of Christ, who through the eternal Spirit, offered himself without spot to God, purge your conscience from dead works to serve the living God? And for this cause he is the mediator of the new testament*, etc. (Hebrews 9:14-15). Here touching Christ our Mediator, note that Christ as priest, offered himself without spot as man, through the eternal spirit, namely: by the power and virtue of his own Godhead. As God-man, he

---

[1825] Deuteronomy 5:2-3, Jeremiah 31:31-32, Hebrews 8:8-9
[1826] See Andre Rivet in *Cathol. Orthodox*, Tract. 2, Question 49 §. 4. Tom. 1.
[1827] Acts 7:37-38
[1828] Malachi 3:1

was priest: as man, he was sacrifice; as God, he made his sacrifice sufficient and prevalent for our redemption.

{5} *The Lord swore and will not repent, thou art a priest forever after the order of Melchizedek. – The word of the oath maketh the son* (high priest) *who is consecrated for evermore* (Hebrews 7:21, 28). If Christ is high-priest as he is the Son, then as he is God, for as he is the Son when God swore, he is God.[1829] Again, if he is an eternal priest after the order of Melchizedek, then he must be priest as God and man: for Melchizedek is set forth, without father, without mother, without pedigree, having neither beginning of days, nor end of life.[1830] And all, that he might be a fit type of Christ: who is without father according to his manhood, without mother according to his Godhead, without beginning of days according to his divine nature, and without end of life according to his mediatory person. And if Christ must needs be priest as God and man; consequently, he must needs act in his priestly office, as both God and man.

{6} *There is one God, and one mediator between God and men, the man Christ Jesus: who gave himself a ransom for all, to be testified in due time* (1 Timothy 2:5-6). Here Jesus Christ is declared, that one Mediator between God and men: and his Mediatorship is described by one eminent act thereof, his redemption; who gave himself a ransom for all. The ransom-given, is himself, namely: as man: the ransom-giver, is himself also, namely: as God, his man-hood also consenting. Therefore as God he acted in his mediation, as well as man.

Objection: But it is said "*The man Christ Jesus*}; why does he add {*the man*}, but to express according to which nature Christ is Mediator?"[1831]

Answer: (i) He expresses the nature according to which he is Mediator, not according to which only. (ii) The word {*man*} here may be taken

---

[1829] Psalm 110:4
[1830] Hebrews 7:3
[1831] Cur quaeso addidit, Homo; nisi ad [experimentum] naturam, secundum quam Christus est Mediator? Bellarmine, *De Christo Mediator*. lib. 5. cap. 3. Tom. 1.

personally, to denote the person of Christ, who is man as well as God, rather than naturally to designout his human nature only – it being usual with Scripture to denominate the whole person from either nature. So Christ is called {*the Lord of glory*},[1832] when his person is understood. Thus here, the man Christ Jesus; to show that in him there was the human, as well as the divine nature in one person,[1833] and that consequently he was a fit middle person, or Mediator between God and man. And we have the more cause to understand this word {*man*} here, not naturally, but personally; because it is not barely said the man, but the man Christ Jesus – Christ Jesus denoting that person, who is God and man. (iii) This phrase, the man Christ Jesus, seems also to be added; partly, for our greater consolation and encouragement, that we may the more confidently draw near to him and to God in him, who is our elder brother, partaker of flesh and blood with us, that he might be a merciful and faithful high-priest for us in things pertaining unto God partly, to admonish us not to despair of the salvation of any sort of men: Christ taking unto him the common nature of man.[1834]

[2] *The scope, end or intent of the personal union of the divine and human natures in one Christ, was that he might act and execute his mediatory office completely according to both those natures.*[1835] Agents do act or work, according to their essence and form. If Christ does not act according to both his natures, as forms and beginnings of his mediatory actions, to what end was his person constituted of those two natures, when one would have sufficed? Are there not some mediatory actions so proper and peculiar to one nature, that they cannot belong properly to the other? Do not various necessary and essential acts of Christ's mediatory office, flow from his Godhead, as the immediate, proper and formal beginning thereof?

[1832] 1 Corinthians 2:8
[1833] Iun. Animadvers. in *Bellarm. Co[n]tr.* lib. 5. cap. 3. Not. 11, 12
[1834] Ames. Bellarm. *Enervat. de Christ. Mediat.* l. 5. p. 117. (Amsterdam, 1630).
[1835] Operari, sequitur esse.

{1} His incarnation was from his Godhead, assuming his manhood, for the manhood, not being, could not assume itself. {2} His manifestation of God in the flesh was efficiently and primarily from his Godhead; instrumentally in and by his manhood.[1836] {3} His delivering and offering himself up to God by death for us, was actively from his Godhead: *through the eternal Spirit he offered up himself*,[1837] – *I have power to lay it down*,[1838] etc, but passively from his manhood. Christ's dying was an act of power, and an act of weakness, that power belonged to his Godhead, this weakness to his manhood. {4} His resurrection from the dead was by the power of his Godhead.[1839] His human flesh was that which did rise: but his divine power was that whereby he did rise. {5} His ascension into heaven was in his humanity, but the virtue or power whereby he ascended, was from his deity. {6} His captivating captivity was in his human nature ascending; but from his divine nature, conquering. {7} His sitting on the right hand of God and coming again to judge the world belong to his manhood, but from his Godhead, etc. These and like acts, which primarily and necessarily appertain to his mediatory office, have their proper rise and origin from Christ's divine nature. And therefore he was God and man in one person, that he might act as God and man in one office.

[3] *The nature of the mediatory office is such that it could not be completely executed and fulfilled if Christ God-man should not act therein both as God and man.* This may be easily evinced in all the primary parts or functions of his Mediatorship, by induction of particulars, as:

{1} **In his prophecy**: Jesus Christ as God, knows his Father's will fully, reveals it completely,[1840] and opens our understandings to receive it effectually;[1841] as man he teaches us familiarly and according to our capacity.[1842]

[1836] 1 Timothy 3:16
[1837] Hebrews 9:14
[1838] John 10:18
[1839] Romans 1:4; 1 Timothy 3:16 {*justified in the Spirit*}
[1840] Matthew 11:27, John 1:18
[1841] Luke 24:45
[1842] Deuteronomy 18:15-20

{2} **In his priesthood**, in many ways, for: (i) Jesus Christ, as man, suffered; as God, supported himself under his sufferings. (ii) As man, was sacrificed for us; as God, did offer up himself for a sacrifice (Hebrews 9:14-15). (iii) As man, died and was buried; as God, overcame death, and rose again from the dead.[1843] (iv) As man, was in his body and blood the price of our redemption, and a ransom for us;[1844] as God, he made that price and ransom of infinite worth, dignity, value, efficacy, acceptableness, etc.[1845] (v) As man, he did bear our sins upon his body on the tree, and the wrath of God for them; as God he sustained his man-hood from sinking, and being utterly swallowed up under the wrath of God, which no mere creature in the world could ever have undergone without being utterly overwhelmed.[1846] (vi) As man, he prayed with strong cries and tears, and intercedes for us (Hebrews 5:6-7 & 9:24; 1 John 2:1-2, Romans 8:34); as God, he makes his intercession of infinite acceptance with his heavenly Father forever (Hebrews 7:21, 25).

{3} **In his kingship**, for: (i) as man, he did conflict with his and our spiritual enemies, sin, Satan, death, etc.; but as God he conquered them, by being in his humanity in some sort conquered by them (Romans 8:3, Colossians 2:14, Hebrews 2:14-15). (ii) As man, he did triumph over them in his going up into heaven, and shall finally doom and judge them in his coming again from heaven; but as God he has the power and authority of this victory, triumph and judgment (Acts 10:42 & 17:31, Romans 2:16, John 5:22). And what shall I say? As all his acts of ministry and meanness in his mediation, have their primary and proper rise from his manhood; as, to be conceived, born, circumcised, afflicted, scourged, crucified, slain, buried, etc.; so all his acts of magistery and authority have their proper and primary rise from his Godhead, as: to know the heart, to work miracles, to rise from the dead, ascend into

---

[1843] 1 Peter 3:18
[1844] 1 Peter 1:18, etc; 1 Timothy 2:6
[1845] Hebrews 9:14, Acts 20:28
[1846] 1 Peter 2:24

heaven, sit down at God's right hand, shed forth his Spirit, gather and preserve his elect, subdue their enemies, and judge the world, etc.

[4] *I conclude this position with that excellent passage of Augustine*: "*I (saith the Lord) will be to them a God, and my servant David a prince in the midst of them*. Why in the midst of them? Because the word was made flesh, and dwelt amongst us. A prince in the midst of them: thence he is Mediator both of God and man, because he is God with the father, and man with men. Not a Mediator as man besides the deity: not a Mediator as God besides the humanity. Behold the Mediator. The divinity is not Mediator without the humanity, the humanity is not Mediator without the divinity: but between divinity alone, and humanity alone, Christ's human divinity, and divine humanity is Mediator."[1847]

To this, I will only add the notable testimony of Claudius Espensus, a Sorbon doctor among the papists, who at large defends Christ's mediation according to both his natures, and has this passage: "And this is altogether a saving and enlivening mediation, and the action, execution, efficacy, efficiency, and (as the Greeks speak) the energy thereof as such, is neither divine only, being not of mere God, but of Godman, or made man: nor human only, being not of mere man, but of man deified: but theandrical, namely: of God and man existing together."[1848]

[1847] "Ego, inquit Dominus, ero illis in Deum, & servus meus David princeps in medio eorum. Quare in medio eorum? Quia verbum caro factum est, & habitavit in nobls. Princeps in medio eorum: inde & Mediator Dei & hominum, quia Deus cum Patre, quia homo cum hominibus. Non Mediator homo praeter Deltatem: Non Mediator Deus praeter Humanitatem. Ecce Mediator. Divinitas sine humanitate non est mediatrix: Humanitas sine Divinitate non est Mediatrix; Sed inter Divinitatem solam, & humanitatem solam, Mediatrix est humana Divinitas, & Divina Humanitas Christi."
August. in *Lib. de Ovibus* cap. 12. Tom. 9.

[1848] "Et Omnino salutaris haec, & vivisica Mediatio, ejus{que} QUATENUS TALIS, actio, executio, efficacia, efficientia, & ut Graeci loquuntur ἐνέργειαι, ne{que} divina tantum est, cum non sit Dei nudi, sed Humanati, seu Hominis facti: Ne{que} Humana tantum, cum nihilo magis sit hominis nudi, sed Deificati: Sed [θεανδρικαὶ] Deivira, seu Deivirilis, nimirum ut Dei simul existentis & hominis, ut ample deducit."
Damascenus de Orth. Fide lib. 3. cap. 19. Sic Claud. Espensaeus in Tract. de Mediator. cap. 5. in fine Digression. in 1 ad Timoth. 2.

Let the learned reader for his further satisfaction about Christ's mediation according to both natures, consult that learned and judicious Andre Rivet in his *Catholicus Orthodoxus*, Tract. 2. Quest. 50. Tom. 1.

Hitherto, of the person of Christ: as also of his Mediatory office, more generally.

Aphorism 3

Of Christ's execution of his mediatory office, more particularly.

That, Jesus Christ, God-man, executes his mediatory office in a prophetic,[1849] priestly,[1850] and kingly[1851] way, or, as prophet, priest and king: both in his state of humiliation[1852] and exaltation.[1853]

For the better clearing of this aphorism, three things are to be explained especially, namely: (1) whence it may be evinced that Christ executes his Mediatory office in these three ways, (2) wherein the nature of Christ's prophecy, priesthood, and kingship consists, and (3) what are those two states of Christ's humiliation and exaltation, wherein he thus executes his mediation between God and man. I shall unfold these in three distinct sections.

[1849] Deuteronomy 18:15-20, John 1:45, Acts 3:22 & 7:37, Luke 24:19
[1850] Psalm 110:4, Hebrews 7 throughout; see also chapters 2, 5, 8 & 9
[1851] Psalm 2:6, Ezekiel 37:24-25, Hosea 3:5, Isaiah 9:6, Luke 1:32-33, Revelation 19:16
[1852] Philippians 2:6-8, Isaiah 53 throughout, Galatians 4:4, etc.
[1853] Acts 2:33-36, Hebrews 2:9-10, Philippians 2:9-11, Ephesians 1:20-23

Section 1

Whence it may be evinced, that Christ executes his Mediatory office, in a prophetical, priestly and kingly way.

These three, some call the *species* or *kinds* of his mediatory office; some, the *parts* or *branches* thereof. It does not much matter which notion we make use of, seeing as for substance they come both to one. Now, that Jesus Christ executes his mediatory office in this threefold capacity, as prophet, priest. and king, may be evinced in these six ways especially, namely: (1) from the condition of lapsed man, without Christ; and his necessity of restoration by Christ, (2) from the personal types of old prefiguring these functions in Christ, (3) from the order of conferring salvation upon us, (4) from the reality of Christ's unction hereunto, (5) from the sufficient enumeration of Christ's benefits, and his way of procuring them, and (6) from Christ's many denominations given to him in Scriptures, and notably reducible to these three functions.

(1) **From the condition of lapsed man, without Christ; and his necessity of restoration by Christ.** Lapsed man by reason of sin is miserably involved in a threefold disease; namely: [1] gross ignorance of God and of all the mysteries of salvation[1854] – yea, and of his own poor, blind, naked, wretched and undone condition;[1855] [2] utter alienation and estrangement from God and all happiness – yea extreme hostility and enmity to God, his laws, and all his ways;[1856] and [3] total impotency and inability of returning again to God from sin and Satan, for recovering of his favor, happiness and salvation.[1857] Now lapsed man had need to have such a Mediator, as has an

---

[1854] Ephesians 4:17-18; 1 Corinthians 2:8-9, 14
[1855] Revelation 3:17
[1856] Ephesians 2:12, Colossians 1:21, Romans 8:7
[1857] Romans 5:6, Acts 8:23, Ephesians 2:1-3, Philippians 2:13, Jeremiah 31:18

office and ability sufficient for healing of all these grand evils and diseases: otherwise he cannot be restored and saved. The remedy must fully answer the malady. Behold therefore how richly and fully God has provided for lapsed man's recovery in Christ, for his ignorance is cured by Christ's prophecy; his alienation from, and enmity against God, is healed by Christ's priest-hood; his impotency and inability, is remedied by his kingship – all of which will evidently appear in the particular opening of these functions.

(2) **From the personal types of old, prefiguring these three functions in Christ.** Christ under and before the Old Testament was revealed to his church more darkly and imperfectly under types and figures, representing some excellency or other that should be in the person office or benefits of the promised Messiah. Those types and shadows were either persons or things: persons represented Christ in many regards – amongst others, in the eminent offices which they did bear and discharge for the good of God's people, namely: of prophets, priests, and kings, by which three offices God usually conveyed all his choice blessings to his people of old, as I have formerly shown.[1858] Thus: [1] Moses the great prophet, was a special type of Jesus Christ, God's greatest prophet of all: that prophet of prophets.[1859] [2] The Levitical priests – especially the high priest, and Melchizedek the priest of the Most High God, of another and more excellent order, were special types of our great high priest Jesus Christ.[1860] [3] The excellent kings also, as Melchizedek, king of Salem, David and Solomon, kings of Israel, etc,[1861] were singular types of Jesus Christ our true King of Righteousness, Prince of Peace, and King of Kings, to whom the Lord God gave the throne of his father David, that he might reign over the house of Jacob forever, of whose kingdom there shall be

---

[1858] In Book 4, Chapter 5, Section 2, General 4
[1859] Deuteronomy 18:15-20, John 1:45, Acts 3:22 & 7:37
[1860] Hebrews 2:17 & 5:4-6 & 7:2 to the end
[1861] Hebrews 7:2, Jeremiah 23:6-7, Ezekiel 37:24-25, Luke 1:32-33, Revelation 19:16

no end.[1862] Now how Moses, Melchizedek, the priests, David, and Solomon did typify Christ in these three functions, I have already manifested.[1863]

(3) **From the order of conferring salvation upon us. Which is especially threefold**, namely: [1] it must be revealed in the mystery of it, to us that are ignorant; [2] it must be acquired and procured, for us that are aliens and enemies; [3] it must be applied effectually, to us that are without strength and impotent. If it is only revealed, and not acquired, it is only as a remedy in the theory or contemplation. If it is only revealed and procured, but not applied, it is only as a remedy in readiness or in composition. But if it is revealed, acquired, and applied, then it is as a remedy in actual and effectual operation to the cure. Now Jesus Christ reveals the whole way and mystery of salvation; as a prophet: acquires and purchases salvation revealed; as a priest: applies, efficaciously salvation revealed and purchased as a king.

(4) **From the reality of Christ's unction hereunto**. For, as in former times men were anointed with material oil, with the holy anointing oil,[1864] denoting their designation and vocation to, their endowments and qualifications for, those three eminent offices of prophet,[1865] priest,[1866] and king;[1867] so Jesus Christ was anointed with the true spiritual immaterial oil, *with the oil of gladness above his fellows*, namely: *with the Holy Ghost and with power* most plentifully and abundantly, whereby he was most plenarily and transcendently qualified for, and most authentically called unto his triple office of prophet, priest, and king to his church, and became the true Christ, Messiah and anointed of the living God.[1868]

[1862] Luke 1:32-33

[1863] Moses in his prophecy (Book 3, Chapter 4, Aphorism 2, Inference 2); the Levites, priests and high priest, as also Melchizedek in his priesthood (Book 3, Chapter 4, Aphorism 7, Corollary; as also in Book 3, Chapter 3, Aphorism 4); Melchizedek, David, and Solomon, in his kingship (Book 3, Chapter 3, Aphorism 4, and Book 3 Chapter 5), where also is shown, that in some sense David was both prophet, priest, and king.

[1864] Exodus 30:23-24, etc.

[1865] 1 Kings 19:16

[1866] Exodus 28:41 & 30:30

[1867] 1 Samuel 16:12-13

[1868] Psalm 45:7, Acts 10:38, John 3:34, Colossians 1:19 & 2:19, Hebrews 5:5-6, etc.

(5) From the sufficient enumeration of Christ's benefits, and his way of procuring them for us:

[1] *Christ's benefits towards us are chiefly of three sorts*, namely:

{1} He makes known unto us the whole counsel and will of God touching sinners' salvation in his Word, enlightening our minds by his Spirit to understand the same.[1869] This he does as a prophet.

{2} He suffers and satisfies for the sins of his elect;[1870] he redeems, them from spiritual thralldom by the invaluable price of his own blood;[1871] he reconciles them to God by his own death;[1872] he obtains remission of their sins, removing their guilt, and covering all their iniquities, that they may become the righteousness of God in him, who was made sin for them;[1873] *he ever lives to make intercession for them*, and thereby to impetrate all saving blessings upon them.[1874] All these and such like blessings he works for us, as a priest.

{3} He effectually applies to us all the benefits and purchases of his mediation: he subdues, calls and governs us by the spiritual scepter of his word and Spirit (Psalm 110:2-3, Acts 26:17-18, Romans 10:14-15, etc. & 8:14). He restrains and conquers all our enemies (Psalm 110:1; 1 Corinthians 15:26. Hebrews 2:14-15, Colossians 2:14-15), and he will come again at last to judge the world, to take us home unto himself, that we may be where he is, to behold his glory (Acts 17:31, Matthew 25:31 to the end, John 14:2-4 & 17:24). Now all these and such like benefits he vouchsafes to us, as a king.

[2] *Christ's order and way of working and procuring such benefits for us is answerable*, for: {1} he first teaches as a prophet, {2} then he offers himself as a priest, and {3} at last enters into his kingdom most powerfully and gloriously administering the same, as a king.

[1869] John 1:18 & 4:25, Matthew 11:25, John 17:6-8; 1 John 2:20, 27
[1870] Isaiah 53:4-6, Romans 4:25; 1 Timothy 2:6
[1871] Hebrews 9:12; 1 Peter 1:18-19
[1872] Romans 5:10
[1873] Acts 13:38-39; 2 Corinthians 5:21
[1874] Hebrews 7:25

(6) **Finally, from Christ's many denominations given to him in Scriptures, which are eminently reducible to these three functions,** for:

[1] Christ is styled *{a counselor}* in Isaiah 9:6, *{a teacher come from God}* in John 3:2, *{a master}* in Matthew 23:10, *{the apostle of our profession}* in Hebrews 3:1, *{a shepherd}* in Ezekiel 34:23 & 37:29, *{that good shepherd}* in John 10:11, *{the great shepherd of the sheep}* in Hebrews 13:20, *{the chief shepherd}* in 1 Peter 5:4, *{a prophet like Moses}* in Deuteronomy 18:15-20, *{that great prophet}* in Luke 17:19 & 24:19, and *{our lawgiver}* in Isaiah 35:22. These and such like point out his prophetic office.

[2] Christ is styled *{our peace}* in Ephesians 2:14, *{our propitiatory}* in Romans 3:25, *{the propitiation for our sins}* in 1 John 2:1-2, *{a ransom for many}* in Matthew 20:28 and 1 Timothy 2:5-6,[1875] *{the lamb of God}* – alluding to the lamb daily sacrificed in John 1:19 c.f. Exodus 29:38-39, *{the lamb slain from the foundation of the world}* in Revelation 13:8, *{our passover which is sacrificed for us}* in 1 Corinthians 5:7, *{a sacrifice for sin}* in Romans 8:3 and Hebrews 10:12, *{our advocate with the Father, ever living to make intercession for us}* in 1 John 2:1-2 and Hebrews 7:25, *{the minister of the sanctuary and true tabernacle which God hath pitched, and not man}* in Hebrews 8:2, *{a priest forever after the order of Melchizedeck}* in Psalm 110:4, *{our high priest}* in Hebrews 3: *{a high priest of good things to come}* in Hebrews 9:11, *{a high priest over the house of God}* in Hebrews 10:21, and *{a merciful and faithful high priest in things pertaining to God, to make reconciliation for the sins of the people}* in Hebrews 2:17. These and such like appellations have special reference to Christ's priestly office.

[3] Christ is styled *{the head of the church}* in Ephesians 5:23, *{head over all things to the church}* in Ephesians 1:22, *{a governor that shall rule God's people Israel}* in Matthew 2:6, *{he that is to be ruler in Israel}* in Micah 5:2, *{the archduke of our salvation}* in Hebrews 2:10,[1876] *{the prince of peace}* upon

---

[1875] Λυτρον & αντιλυτρον
[1876] αρχηγον

whose shoulder is the government in Isaiah 9:6-7, {*the prince of life*} in Acts 3:15, {*the Lord of glory*} in 1 Corinthians 2:8, {the Lord of Lords} in Revelation 19:16, {*a leader and commander to the people*} in Isaiah 55:4, {*our judge, our lawgiver or statute-maker, our king*} in Isaiah 33:22, {*David their king and prince forever*} in Hosea 3:5 and Ezekiel 37:24-25, {*God's king*} set on his holy hill of Zion in Psalm 2:6, {*the Son of the Highest, having the throne of his father David, reigning over the house of Jacob forever*} in Luke 1:32-33, {*King of Kings*} in Revelation 19:16, and {*ordained of God to be Judge of quick and dead*} in Acts 10:42. These and such like glorious and majestic titles, do eminently denote his kingly office.

From all these it is evident that Christ executes his mediatorship as prophet, priest, and king.

Section 2

Wherein the nature of Christ's prophecy, priesthood, and kingship consists.

This may best be resolved, by considering them particularly.

(1) **Christ's prophetic office is that branch of his mediatorship, whereby he fully reveals to, and in his elect, his church, both before, and under the New Covenant, the whole counsel and will of God touching their restoration and salvation.**

The nature of his prophetic office, consists in his primary and plenary teaching of his church: namely: [1] by revelation or promulgation of his doctrine, and [2] by illumination of his people's minds to receive the same.

[1] *Christ reveals and promulgates his doctrine, in his word; called therefore* {the word of Christ}.[1877] And he reveals his doctrine in his word, immediately, and mediately:

{1} **More immediately, by himself:**

(i) Under, and before the Old Covenant. Thus Jesus Christ according to his divine nature, made known the doctrine and will of God touching sinners restitution and salvation, to the patriarchs, prophets and holy men of God,[1878] by visions, dreams, urim and thummim, inspirations, vocal oracles, etc,[1879] until at last by the inspiration of his Spirit, they had written all the books of the Old Testament, comprising fully and perfectly the whole counsel of God, sufficient for their salvation who lived before Christ's incarnation. Christ's revelations of his doctrine were still from age to age more and more clear,

---

[1877] Colossians 3:16
[1878] Hebrews 13:8; 1 Peter 1:10-11
[1879] Genesis 46:2 & 15:1 & 31:11, Daniel 7:1; 1 Samuel 28:6, 15, Numbers 27:21; 2 Peter 1:20-21; 2 Samuel 16:23, Acts 7:38, Romans 3:2

though always far short of those now under his New Covenant; yet sufficient for his elect's instruction to salvation in every age respectively.

(ii) Under the New Covenant. Thus Jesus Christ, according to both his natures, as God and man, *in whom are hid all the treasures of wisdom and knowledge*,[1880] has finally, clearly, and completely revealed the last, fullest and most perfect counsel and will of God touching sinners life and salvation. This is that *manifold wisdom of God*:[1881] that so great salvation which at first began to be spoken by the Lord,[1882] the neglect whereof is much more dangerous than the neglect of the Old Covenant, which yet was severely punished. This is *the wisdom of God in a mystery, the hidden wisdom which God ordained before the world unto our glory, which none of the princes of this world knew*, etc, touching such things as carnal man's *eye hath not seen, nor ear heard neither have entered into the heart of man*[1883] – things that the very *angels desire to look into*,[1884] and disdain not to learn from and by the church of God.[1885]

This plenary and final revelation of saving doctrine, Jesus Christ – our teacher come from God[1886] – has most gloriously vouchsafed under the New Covenant (John 1:18 & Matthew 11:27). For he himself testifies: *All things that I have heard of my Father I have made known unto you.*[1887] And again in his prayer to his Father: *I have given them the words which thou gavest me, and they have received them*, etc.[1888] Now Jesus Christ God-man has under this New Covenant, immediately revealed or promulgated this so great salvation, principally two ways, namely:

[1880] Colossians 2:3
[1881] Ephesians 3:10
[1882] Hebrews 2:1-3
[1883] 1 Corinthians 2:7-10
[1884] 1 Peter 1:12
[1885] Ephesians 3:10
[1886] John 3:2
[1887] John 15:15
[1888] John 17:8

(a) By his own personal ministration in the church of God, according as was formerly prophesied of him.[1889] He, after his baptism, beginning to be about thirty years of age, did in the days of his flesh, for the space of about three years and a half, or four years, preach the gospel of the kingdom; expound the law of God, vindicating it from the corrupt glosses and mis-interpretations of the pharisees; erect and appoint New Covenant ordinances and officers, and indefatigably discharge all the then necessary parts of his prophecy. And this in Judea, Samaria, and Galilee, throughout the holy land: and that not in private, but publicly in the temple, synagogues, or other places where the multitude resorted to him. And in regard to his personal coming into, and teaching in Zerubbabel's temple, the glory of that later house was greater than the glory of the former.[1890] And the church in these last days, is dignified and privileged far more than in all former ages; in that, *God, who at sundry times, and in divers manners, spake in time past to the fathers by the prophets, hath in these last days spoken unto us by his Son, – who is the brightness of his glory, and the express character of his person.*[1891]

(b) By his instruction and information of his apostles about the mysteries of the kingdom: opening their understandings,[1892] and giving them commandments,[1893] not only before, but also and especially after his resurrection, about his preaching of the doctrine of salvation. *Go disciple all nations, – teaching them to observe all things whatsoever I have commanded you*, etc.[1894] Yea, Christ did by his Spirit so infallibly inspire his apostles and other holy men, leading them into all truth, taking of Christ's, and showing it unto them; and bringing all things unto their remembrance:[1895] that they penned the whole Scriptures of the New Testament completely, the revelation

---

[1889] Deuteronomy 18:15-20, Psalm 40:7-10, Isaiah 49:1-7 & 61:1-2
[1890] Haggai 2:7-9
[1891] Hebrews 1:1-3
[1892] Luke 24:45
[1893] Acts 1:2-3
[1894] Matthew 28:19-20
[1895] John 16:13-14 & 14:26

(setting forth the affairs of the church until the end of the world) closing up the canon of holy Scripture so perfectly, that nothing may be added thereto, or taken thencefrom, but under the most severe penalties.[1896] And thus Jesus Christ as our great prophet, revealed his doctrine of salvation immediately by himself, both under and before the Old Covenant, and under the New Covenant.

{2} **More mediately, Christ our prophet revealed his doctrine for sinners' life and salvation, to his church and people:**

(i) Under the Old Covenant and before, Christ teaching his church the mysteries and ways of salvation: (a) sometimes extraordinarily, by the ministry of fathers, patriarchs, and prophets. To which effect it is said that *Christ* by his Spirit (that is, by his Godhead assisting Noah, *a preacher of righteousness*, 2 Peter 2:5) *went and preached to the spirits in prison* (that is, to men then on earth, but dying impenitent, now spirits in the prison of hell, when Peter wrote this epistle) *which sometimes were disobedient, when once the longsuffering of God waited in the days of Noah while the ark was preparing.*[1897] Christ by his Godhead preached to the world in the days of Noah, but it was mediately by the ministry of Noah, who preached repentance and righteousness to the wicked world both by his doctrine and life; and especially by his making the ark for 120 years together – every knock upon the ark being a warning to the wicked world. (b) Sometimes ordinarily, by the standing ministry of the priests and Levites. The *priest's lips should keep knowledge; and they should seek the law at his mouth: for he is the messenger of the LORD of hosts.*[1898]

(ii) Under the New Covenant, Christ teaching his church: (a) at first plantation, by officers and ministers extraordinary; as, apostles, prophets, evangelists, given by Christ for that end.[1899] (b) Afterwards by ministers

---

[1896] Revelation 22:18-19
[1897] 1 Peter 3:28-30
[1898] Malachi 2:7
[1899] Ephesians 4:11-13, Matthew 28:20-21; 2 Corinthians 4:6-7

ordinary, namely: pastors and teachers, which are to be a settled, standing ministry to his church[1900] – all being ambassadors for Christ, praying men in Christ's stead to be reconciled unto God (2 Corinthians 5:19-20). And thus Jesus Christ, as a prophet reveals his doctrine of salvation.

[2] ***Christ illuminates the minds, and inclines the wills of his elect efficaciously, to understand and receive his doctrine revealed.*** The former was outward; this is inward teaching. That was Christ's revealing his doctrine to them; this, his revealing his doctrine in them. This is that chief perfective-effect of Christ's prophetic office. One of the eminent blessings promised in the New Covenant: and performed both to Christ's ministers, and members. Christ opened his apostles' understandings to understand the Scriptures.[1901] He gave them the words, which the Father gave to him, and they received them.[1902] And Christ's members, *have an anointing from the holy one, and know all things.*[1903] Yea they are so taught of God, as to come to Christ.[1904] Under the Old Testament, God's people were under a veil;[1905] but under the New, the veil is done away in Christ. *And, we all with open face beholding as in a glass the glory of the Lord, are changed into the same image, from glory to glory, even as by the Spirit of the Lord.*[1906]

Thus of Christ's prophetic office.

(2) Christ's priestly office, is that branch of his Mediatorship, whereby he is our great high priest, completely fulfilled the law of God and suffered death for his elect, so making a proper and plenary satisfaction to God's justice for them, and also presenting himself and his

---

[1900] Ephesians 4:11-13
[1901] Luke 24:45
[1902] John 17:8
[1903] 1 John 2:20, 27
[1904] John 6:45
[1905] 2 Corinthians 3:12-14
[1906] 2 Corinthians 3:18

merit before God, he undertakes for them, and makes continual intercession for them.

This priestly office of Christ was notably shadowed out under the Old Covenant, under the type of the high priest,[1907] and of Melchizedek,[1908] of whose order Christ is said to be, both for the dignity of his person, and manner of his calling. Now the high priest typed out the priesthood of Jesus Christ our great high priest (Hebrews 4:14) in many ways, as I have already manifested,[1909] to which now I further add: the high priest typed out Christ's priesthood in the acts of his office chiefly three ways, namely:

[1] *By his keeping and fulfilling the law of God.* The high priest was singularly to fulfill the law. And therefore to his peculiar care the keeping of the two tables of the law in the ark of the covenant was singularly committed, and none but he was to enter into the holy of holies. Thus Jesus Christ most exactly fulfilled the law of God, for: {1} his person was holy, harmless, undefiled, separate from sinners (Hebrews 7:26). The law of God was in his heart fully, as the law was in the ark (Psalm 40:7-8). His mind and will being perfectly conform thereunto. {2} His life and actions were also exactly agreeable in every point to the law of God, without sin in the least degree.[1910] And Christ fulfilled the law exactly both in person and conversation for our sakes. As he became Θεάνθρωπος: God-man for our sakes; so whatsoever he had, or did, as man, was for us. Hence it is said: *by the obedience of one shall many be made righteous.*[1911] – *Christ is the end of the law for righteousness to everyone that believeth.*[1912]

[2] *By his offering unto God, expiatory and propitiatory sacrifices of innocent beasts, to purge away sin and make reconciliation with God for the people.* This he did:

[1907] Hebrews 2:17 & 4:14 & 5:5 & 7:26 and often
[1908] Psalm 110:4, Hebrews 7 throughout & 5:9-10
[1909] In Book 3, Chapter 4, Aphorism 7, Corollary 7
[1910] Galatians 4:4, Matthew 3:15, John 17:4, 19, Isaiah 53:9, John 8:46, Luke 23:41
[1911] Romans 5:19
[1912] Romans 10:4 & 8:3-4

{1} By the burnt-offering, slain, and wholly burnt to ashes (Leviticus 1:23, etc). This was: (i) ordinary and perpetual, either for every day, morning and evening, two-lambs (Exodus 29:38-43), or for the sabbath days, the offering was to be doubled (Numbers 28:9-10), or monthly in the new-moons (Numbers 28:12, etc), or yearly, as on several set feasts (Numbers 29 throughout); (2) extraordinary and incidental, either for the whole people, as in 1 Samuel 7:9-10, or for particular persons, as for David, as in 2 Samuel 24:25.

{2} By the sin offering, whereby some certain sins were expiated and purged away, as (i) sins done ignorantly, as in Leviticus 4; (ii) sins done knowingly and willingly as in Leviticus 5 and 6 – and both these at the feasts of new moons, passover, and pentecost (Leviticus 23:19, etc., Numbers 28:11 to the end). Thus Jesus Christ the antitype offered one sacrifice for sins forever,[1913] when through the eternal Spirit he offered himself without spot to God, to purge our conscience from dead works.[1914] *And by this one offering he hath perfected forever them that are sanctified*, so that there needs no more expiatory sacrifice for sin.[1915] In this offering of himself Christ was priest, sacrifice and altar: *priest*, as God and man (Hebrews 5:6); *sacrifice*, as man (Hebrews 12:13; 1 Peter 2:13, Colossians 1:22), though the virtue, force, and excellency of this sacrifice depended chiefly upon the Godhead to which it was personally united – his whole man, soul, and body suffering so that thereby our whole man, soul, and body might be saved; *altar* as God (Hebrews 9:14 & 13:10): the altar, sanctifying the gift, being greater than the gift (Matthew 23:19).

{3} By his intercession. The high priest presented himself daily before the Lord, offering incense upon the golden altar morning and evening for an odor

---

[1913] Hebrews 10:12
[1914] Hebrews 9:12-15
[1915] Hebrews 10:13-14, 18

of a sweet smell,[1916] praying for, and blessing the people.[1917] Thus Jesus Christ: (i) appears in the presence of God for us as our advocate,[1918] (ii) presents the sweetest odors of his own merits,[1919] and (iii) makes continual intercession for us.[1920]

Thus the priesthood of Christ is executed by him chiefly two ways, namely: [1] in his making satisfaction to God by his sufferings and death for the sins of his people, and [2] in his continual intercession for them with the father.

This priesthood of Christ is a most excellent foundation of hope, and fountain of consolation to poor sinners; and therefore Satan has extremely bestirred himself against it by dangerous and heretical opinions sown in the minds of many (Socinians on the one hand denying Christ's satisfaction; papists on the other hand extending his death to all, and destroying Christ's intercession by setting up saint-intercessors), so that by this means he might eclipse the glory of Christ's priesthood, and so dash the hopes and comforts of poor sinners.

And were not this volume swelled too big already, I should here very much have enlarged myself against these intolerable errors. But I must – full sore against my will – forbear.

Only let me a little more fully explain these two sweet points and parts of Christ's priesthood, namely: his satisfaction and his intercession, wherein I shall positively assert the truth against those errors, by some brief Scripture grounds for the support and benefit of Christ's purchased people.

[1916] Leviticus 24:2-3, Exodus 32:7-8
[1917] Numbers 6:23
[1918] Hebrews 9:24
[1919] Ephesians 5:2, Revelation 8:3 & 5:8; 1 Peter 2:5
[1920] Hebrews 7:25; 1 John 2:1-2, Romans 8:38

[Part 1 of Christ's priesthood]: Of Christ's satisfaction.

Here I shall show: {1} that Jesus Christ by his obedience and death has made satisfaction to God for his people's sins, {2} what are the parts of this his satisfaction, {3} what are the fruits or effects of his satisfaction, and {4} for whom Christ made such his satisfaction.

{1} *First, that Jesus Christ by his obedience and death has made a true, real, proper and full satisfaction to God for his people's sins.*

The word {*satisfaction*}, I grant, is not syllabically and literally expressed in the Scriptures, but the thing is expressed abundantly therein, and that is enough. As the words, trinity, sacrament, etc. Are not expressly named; yet the things which we intend by them are sufficiently set forth in Scripture. Now that Christ hath by his obedience and death made a true, real, proper and full satisfaction to God for his people's sins, is evident many ways. For,

(i) **Christ is εγγυος: the Surety of the better Covenant,**[1921] **the New Covenant — of the sense of which word formerly.**[1922]

A surety confirms the agreement, promises to pay the debt, and actually does pay it, if the principal fails, as in Philemon verses 18 and 19. Thus Christ is not only Mediator and Testator, but also Surety of the New Covenant. God is as the creditor, we as debtors; our sins the debts, Christ the Surety; his obedience and death the satisfaction, the New Covenant the deed according to which Christ has made voluntary satisfaction to God. If Christ's satisfaction is denied, his suretyship is destroyed. Now that Christ suffered punishment and

---

[1921] Hebrews 7:22
[1922] In this 6th Chapter, Aphorism 2, Position 3

death for us and our sins; not only for our good, as one man may suffer for the good of another, as Paul in Colossians 1:24. And martyrs suffered for the good of the church, but also as our Surety substituted, and voluntarily substituting himself, in our room and stead, is evident many ways, as:

(a) *By Christ's dying and suffering for us.* The Scriptures often testify that Christ suffered and died for us, or words to that effect: *in due time Christ died for the ungodly. – When we were yet sinners Christ died for us.*[1923] *– He that spared not his own son, but delivered him up for us all.*[1924] *– He gave himself a ransom for all*, etc.[1925] *– to give his life a ransom for many.*[1926] *– I lay down my life for the sheep – no man taketh it from me, but I lay it down of myself.*[1927] The Scripture abounds with like expressions, as in Mark 10:45, John 11:50, Hebrews 2:9; 2 Corinthians 4:14 and 5:21, and Galatians 3:13. *Christ hath once suffered, – the just for the unjust, being put to death in the flesh* (1 Peter 3:18, etc). Therefore if Christ has suffered death for us, he suffered as our Surety substituted in our stead – and not as Socinus falsely pretends, only for our good, to confirm his doctrine, and make way for his glory and intercession, etc, for:

(1) The apostle Paul suffered for the church in this sense, that is, for her good, Colossians 1:24. Who yet counts it a heinous thing to say, that any other than Christ was crucified for us. *Is Christ divided? Was Paul crucified* υπερ υμων *for you?*[1928]

(2) Though the words υπερ for, and περί for, are sometimes used to denote, for any good or utility: yet the word αντι for, which Scripture often uses in this matter, does always signify a substitution of one for another, in another's stead and place, a compensation, as: *not rendering* {κακον αντι

[1923] Romans 5:6, 8
[1924] Romans 8:32
[1925] 1 Timothy 2:6
[1926] Matthew 20:28
[1927] John 10:15, 17-18
[1928] 1 Corinthians 1:13

κακου} *evil for evil.*[1929] – {οφθαλμον αντι οφθαλμου και οδοντα αντι οδοντος} *an eye for an eye, tooth for a tooth*[1930] – so Luke 11:11, Romans 12:17; 1 Corinthians 11:15, and Hebrews 12:16. Nor can there be given an instance in the New Testament of any other sense of this word. And thus it is used in the present case: *that he might give his life a ransom* αντι λύτρον: *for many,* instead of *many.* [1931]And so the compound word αντιλυτρον (a ransom) used in 1 Timothy 2:6 properly signifies (as learned Gomarus has well noted)[1932] an equal price of redemption; an answerable price, even as one scale answers another exactly.

(3) In some passages this substitution of Christ for us, and this compensation, is manifestly noted: *It is expedient for us, that one man should die for the people* {υπερ} *and that the whole nation perish not* (John 11:50-51). So – *in due time Christ died for the ungodly. For scarcely for a righteous man will one die,* Romans 5 6, 7, 8. And: *if one died for all; then were all dead* (2 Corinthians 4:14) – here there would be no consequence in this inference, unless that phrase *{one died for all}* does signify that he died in their room and stead as their substituted Surety. So: *Christ hath once suffered, the just for the unjust, being put to death in the flesh* (1 Peter 3:18). That is, Jesus Christ being in himself most just and innocent, suffered as Surety substituted for us unjust. The Scripture is much in such expressions.

(b) *By Christ's bearing our sins upon himself, suffering and dying for our sins, being made sin and a curse for us.* By these and such like expressions, Christ's suretyship, subrogation, substitution, compensation, satisfaction, etc, for us and for our sins is very significantly denoted in the Scriptures.

[1929] 1 Peter 3:9
[1930] Matthew 5:38
[1931] Matthew 20:28, Mark 10:45
[1932] αντιλυτρον id est, ex adverso respondens, seu [aequate] redemptionis praecium. 1. Tim. 2. 5. quo modo, vox αντι, in nomine αντιλυτρον id est, aequilibrium, usurpatur. Franciscus Gomarus. Illustrat. loci Luc. 1. 77. p. 228. Tom. 1. αντιλυτρον, vicissim redimo, caput capite redimo, Aristot. Eth. 9. cap. 2.

(1) Christ bore our sins upon himself, namely: our sins were imputed to him charged upon him, and he bore the punishment of them. As: *who his own self bare our sins in his own body on the tree.*[1933] – *For he shall bear their iniquities.*[1934] – *The LORD hath laid (or, made to meet) on him the iniquity of us all. He was oppressed and he was afflicted.*[1935] That is, he bare our sins, by bearing the affliction of them. Our sins and their punishment were devolved and translated upon Christ. And this phrase of {*bearing sin*} in Scripture use, denotes frequently bearing the punishment of sin.[1936] Christ then bearing the punishment of our sins, stood as our Surety, in our stead, to satisfy our debt.

(2) To these also may be referred those phrases: {*he knew no sin*}, {*was made sin for us*};[1937] *Christ hath redeemed us from the curse of the law, being made a curse for us,*[1938] etc.

(3) Besides Christ is said to suffer and die for our sins, offenses, etc: *That Christ died* {υπερ} *for our sins according to the Scriptures* (1 Corinthians 15:3), *giving himself* {υπερ} *for our sins* (Galatians 1:4); *but this man having offered one sacrifice* {υπερ} *for sins* (Hebrews 10:12; see also Romans 5:6 and 1 Corinthians 5:21. *Because even Christ once suffered* {περι} *for sins*, 1 Peter 3:18. Who was delivered {παραπτωματα ημων} for our offenses (Romans 4:25).

In these passages, those Greek particles, υπερ, περι, and δια translated {*for*}, being applied to Christ's sufferings, do note to us the meritorious, deserving, procuring cause of those his sufferings, namely: our sins. Applied to other things they may sometimes denote the final cause, but being applied to sufferings, they point out only the meritorious cause.

(c) **By God's delivering of Christ up to death for our sins, and that an ignominious, violent cursed, judicial death, having the sense of God's**

[1933] 1 Peter 2:23-24
[1934] Isaiah 53:11
[1935] Isaiah 53:6-7
[1936] Leviticus 19:8 & 20:17 & 24:15, Numbers 14:23 & 30:16, Lamentations 5:7, Ezekiel 18:20
[1937] 2 Corinthians 5:20
[1938] Galatians 3:13

wrath annexed.[1939] Death is so the proper wages of sin (Romans 6:23 & 5:12) that divine justice neither does nor can inflict it upon anyone; but rather, either upon the sinner, or the sinner's surety. Death could not be inflicted upon Christ as a sinner, for he was absolutely without all sin, therefore it was inflicted on him only as the sinner's Surety;[1940] making true, proper and real satisfaction for sinners to offended justice and the law of God.

(ii) Christ is said often in Scripture to redeem us, to buy us, or purchase us with a price, to give himself a ransom or price of redemption, etc., for us: therefore as in all redeeming, purchasing, etc. So in this of Christ's there is given a price, a compensation, a satisfaction for that which is bought, purchased or redeemed.

The former is evident abundantly. As, *the son of man came – to give his soul* {λυτρον} *a ransom for many*. The Greek word properly signifies: a price of redemption for which we are set at liberty.[1941] *There is one mediator between God and man, the man Christ Jesus, who gave himself* {αντιλυτρον} *an equal ransom* (or, *a fully answerable ransom*) *for all*, etc.[1942] – *In whom we have* {απολυτρωσιν} *redemption by his blood*: eternal redemption, etc.[1943] – *Ye are bought with a price* {ηγορασθητε γαρ τιμης} (1 Corinthians 6:20) – *Thou wast slain* {ηγορασας τω θεω ημας} *and hast bought us to God by thy blood*.[1944] That's the price. *Christ* {εξηγορασεν}, *has thoroughly bought us* (or, *bought us out*) *from the curse of the law, being made a curse for us*;[1945] – *made under the law, that* {εξαγοραση} *he might buy out them that are under the law*.[1946] Now buying us, and redeeming us with a price, even the price of Christ's invaluable

---

[1939] Romans 8:32, Galatians 3:13; 2 Corinthians 5:21, Luke 22:42-44, Matthew 27:46

[1940] 2 Corinthians 5:21, Isaiah 53:9, Hebrews 4:15 & 7:26

[1941] Matthew 20:28, Mark 10:45

[1942] 1 Timothy 2:5-6

[1943] Ephesians 1:7, Colossians 1:14; the same word is also used in Romans 3:24, Hebrews 9:12, Titus 2:14; 1 Peter 1:18

[1944] Revelation 5:9

[1945] Galatians 3:13

[1946] Galatians 4:4

blood, plainly imports the substitution of Christ, and his compensation or satisfaction made for us by his death, to God (Ephesians 5:2, Hebrews 9:14, Revelation 5:9).

(iii) **The sins of those that lived and died before Christ was revealed, were expiated, purged and pardoned only by the death and blood of Jesus Christ.**

The legal sacrifices did expiate typically as pertaining to the flesh: but only Christ and his blood typified by them did purge as pertaining to the conscience.[1947] *And for this cause he is the mediator of the new testament, that by means of death, for the redemption of the transgressions that were under the first testament, they which are called might receive the promise of the eternal inheritance.*[1948] *– whom God hath set forth to be a propitiation through faith in his blood, to declare his righteousness for remission of sins that are past.*[1949] Hence, this is one reason why Christ is called {*the lamb slain from the foundation of the world*} because the virtue of his death profited and saved his elect, even from the foundation of the world.[1950] To this effect, it was only once that Christ appeared in the end of the world to put away sin by the sacrifice of himself,[1951] the virtue and merit of his sacrifice extending itself backward to the foundation of the world, otherwise Christ should have suffered often from the foundation of the world, as the high priest every year entered into the holy place with the blood of others. Now if Christ's death and blood did redeem them from their transgressions that were under the first Covenant, his death could be no other than a meritorious moving cause of their redemption, by way of satisfaction for them. For Christ's death, being then not distinctly

---

[1947] Hebrews 9:9-10 & 10:1-4 & 9:23
[1948] Hebrews 9:23
[1949] Romans 3:25
[1950] Revelation 13:8
[1951] Hebrews 9:25-26

understood by them of the Old Covenant, it could not possibly profit them as an example or confirmation of Christ's doctrine, but as a real satisfaction only.

(iv) Christ is said to reconcile us unto God, and to be our propitiation with God by his blood and death.

If when we were enemies we were reconciled to God by the death of his Son: much more being reconciled, we shall be saved by his life.[1952] – *God was in Christ reconciling the world unto himself*, etc. *For he hath made him to be sin for us,* etc. *All things are of God, who hath reconciled us to himself by Jesus Christ, and hath given to us the ministry of reconciliation.*[1953] – *And that he might reconcile both* (namely: Jews and Gentiles) *unto God in one body by the cross, having slain the enmity thereby.*[1954] — *and (having made peace through the blood of his cross) by him to reconcile all things unto himself,*[1955] etc. In that to the Corinthians the apostle hints to us a double reconciliation:

(a) The one virtual and meritorious, by the death of Christ, in our redemption, when the enmity between God and us is by Christ's satisfaction taken away, and we that were children of wrath are restored to favor – in which respect Christ is called {*the propitiation for our sins*}[1956] and {*a propitiatory through faith in his blood*}.[1957]

(b) The other actual and efficacious, by the Spirit and ministry of the gospel, in our conversion: when we who hated God before, do now actually love him, and set our hearts upon him. This latter is the fruit of the former. But here we are chiefly to understand the former, even that reconciliation of God and sinners by Christ's blood; so that in Christ, God becomes propitiously favorable to them. Now in what way, or in what sense can Christ

---

[1952] Romans 5:10
[1953] 2 Corinthians 5:18-21
[1954] Ephesians 2:16
[1955] Colossians 1:20-22
[1956] 1 John 2:2 & 4:10
[1957] Romans 3:25

be said to reconcile us to God by his death, but by satisfying his offended justice and violated law?

(v) **Christ is Mediator between God, and man, not only by teaching as a prophet, and by ruling and efficacious applying the means of salvation as a king, but also by sacrificing and interceding for us as a priest.**

Christ sacrificed himself for us as our great high-priest once for all here on earth to expiate our sins forever, which implies his satisfaction made to God for our sins forever.[1958] And Christ intercedes for us in heaven, appearing there in the presence of God, and still representing before God his merit and satisfaction.[1959] Otherwise, if Christ by his death had only confirmed his doctrine, and not made satisfaction for our sins, he had not died as our priest, whose office it is to offer sacrifice, and make atonement thereby.

(vi) **As there were many expiatory sacrifices, both burnt offerings and sin-offerings forementioned for purging away of sin typically under the law: so Christ, the truth of all those types, the substance of all those shadows, did truly and really expiate all his people's sins by the sacrifice of himself, and therefore made satisfaction to God for them.**

Here note:

(a) That the sacrifices under the law were in the nature of them expiatory sacrifices, to purge away sin, and make atonement for the sinner, that his sin should not be imputed to him, nor the punishment thereof inflicted upon him. As, the burnt-offerings; and he shall put his hand upon the head of the burnt-offering, and it shall be accepted for him to make atonement (or, expiate, or, purge away sin by covering it, as the Hebrew לְכַפֵּר *le-cappar*

[1958] Hebrews 7:26-27 & 9:12, 14, 26 & 10:10-19, Ephesians 5:2
[1959] Hebrews 7:25 & 9:24

properly signifies) for him (Leviticus 1:4).[1960] The sin-offerings also were expiatory, with them the priest made atonement for sin, and the sin was forgiven – see Leviticus 16:11, 24, 27, 33-34. & 4:20, 26, 31, 35. The goat of the sin-offering made atonement for the priest, and his house, and all the congregation of Israel: after which, on the live-goat, the scapegoat, Aaron laid both his hands, and confessed over him all the iniquities of the children of Israel, putting them upon the head of the goat, and sent him away by the hand of a fit man into the wilderness, that he might bear upon him all their iniquities, into a land not inhabited (Leviticus 16:15-23). And in a word, the blood of all the sacrifices was expiatory, and therefore it was not to be eaten: *for the life of the flesh is in the blood, and I have given it to you upon the altar, to make an atonement for your souls; for it is the blood that maketh atonement for the soul.*[1961] Thus the typical sacrifices were expiatory.

(b) That Christ and his sacrifice of himself, the truth of all these types, was also truly expiatory, and satisfactory – [yea], much more so:

(1) Those sacrifices were shadows of good things to come, but the body and truth of them all was Christ.[1962] Hence Christ is called {*one offering*} in Hebrews 10:14., and {*one sacrifice for sins forever*} in Hebrews 10:12, {*the lamb of God taking away the sins of the world*} in John 1:29, alluding to the daily lamb for a burnt-offering in Exodus 29:34-43, and {*Christ our passover*} sacrificed for us in 1 Corinthians 5:7. He is our scapegoat, on whom God laid the iniquities of us all, that he might bear them away from us forever (Isaiah 53:4-6).

(2) And Christ the true sacrifice of sacrifices did much more sanctify to the purging of the conscience than those typical sacrifices sanctified to the purifying of the flesh. *Christ being come a high priest of good things to come, by*

[1960] "*Caphar*, est Bituminare, tegere, oblinire, &c. in Piel. Expiare, Emundare, Perpurgare, quod est immunditiem aut erratum abscondere; iram vel offensum amovere, ne ultra appareat, vel imputetur." Mercer. in Pagn. Thesaur ad verb.
[1961] Leviticus 17:10-12
[1962] Hebrews 10:1, Colossians 2:17, John 1:17, Hebrews 10:5-10

a greater and more perfect tabernacle, not made with hands, that is to say, not of this building: neither by the blood of goats and calves, but by his own blood he entered in once into the holy place, having obtained eternal redemption for us. For if the blood of bulls, and of goats, and the ashes of a heifer sprinkling the unclean, sanctifieth to the purifying of the flesh: how much more shall the blood of Christ, who through the eternal spirit offered himself without spot to God, purge your conscience from dead works to serve the living God?[1963] And afterwards: *and almost all things are by the law purged with blood; and without shedding of blood is no remission. It was therefore necessary that the patterns of things in the heavens should be purified with these; but the heavenly things themselves with better sacrifices than these.*[1964] And again: *Every priest standeth daily ministering and offering often-times the same sacrifices which can never take away sins: but this man, after he had offered one sacrifice for sins forever, sat down on the right hand of God, from henceforth expecting until his enemies be made his footstool.*[1965] These things declare Christ's satisfaction for, and expiation of, his people's sins by his own death and blood, by his true, real, proper and expiatory sacrifice of himself, beyond contradiction.

(vii) **Finally, the perfection, fullness and completeness of Christ's satisfaction for sin and expiation of sin by his obedience, death and blood,** (and not by a fiction in law, or divine acceptilation,[1966] as they diminutively phrase it) **is evident in many ways** (it being still presupposed, that God gave a law, promised life upon perfect and perpetual personal obedience, but threatening death in case of failing, etc),[1967] as:

[1963] Hebrews 9:11-14
[1964] Hebrews 9:22-23
[1965] Hebrews 10:11-12
[1966] {Medieval Latin *acceptilation-, acceptilatio*, from Latin} in the theology of Duns Scotus : the act of God by which the merit of Jesus Christ was accepted as sufficient for the salvation of humankind.
[https://www.merriam-webster.com/dictionary/acceptilation]
<Accessed 3/26/2024>
[1967] Genesis 2:16-17

(1) By the extremity of Christ's death and sufferings. His sufferings were various and grievous throughout his whole life, but especially towards his dissolution, as:

[1] His agony in the garden: {1} saddening and wounding his soul most deeply even unto sore amazement (Matthew 26:37-38, Mark 14:33-34, John 12:26); {2} making him pray more earnestly, with strong cries and tears, that that cup might pass from him – and this thrice over (Matthew 26:39, etc., Luke 22:44, Hebrews 5:7); {3} causing, in a cold night, a bloody sweat, in so great abundance, that it went through his apparel, and fell in great drops to the ground, wherewith he was so spent and weakened, that at present, an angel from heaven was seen to comfort him, and the next day he was not able to bear his cross (Luke 22:43-44. & 23:26).

[2] His desertion upon the cross by his heavenly Father for a time, so that he cried out: {*My God, my God, why hast thou forsaken me?*}[1968]

[3] His cursed and bitter death itself upon the cross (Philippians 2:8, Galatians 3:13): the wages of sin (Romans 6:23). Now why did God exact such sufferings, such an agony, such a desertion, such a bloody and cursed death of his Son Jesus Christ, if it [would have] pleased him to acquiesce in any slight satisfaction for our sins? These sufferings of Christ were necessary to make full satisfaction, because it is impossible that the blood of bulls and goats should take away sins (Hebrews 10:4-5, etc). This argument does not conclude, if Christ satisfied only imperfectly, and the Father accepted his imperfection as if it had been perfect satisfaction.

(2) By Christ's mediation and sufferings as our Surety, to whom it properly belongs to pay and satisfy fully for the whole debt (Hebrews 7:22) – of which formerly.

(3) By the expressions of Christ's purchasing, buying and redeeming us, at a proper and plenary price, according to the exactness of commutative justice and arithmetical proportion. Of which before.

[1968] Matthew 27:46, Mark 15:34

(4) By the infinite valor and boundless worth of his obedience, blood and death, being his that was God as well as man. The infinite dignity of his person infinitely dignified his passion. So that his sufferings for a time were equipollent to our deserved sufferings forever. Hence, blood is called: {*the precious blood of Christ*};[1969] {*the blood of Jesus Christ his Son*};[1970] {*the blood of God*}.[1971] He is called: {*the bread that came down from heaven*}.[1972] And it is said of him: *The blood of Christ, who through the eternal Spirit offered himself without spot to God.*[1973]

(5) By the witness of the New Covenant itself, dedicated, and established in this blood of Christ, wherein God says: *and their sins and iniquities will I remember no more. Now, where remission of these is, there is no more offering for sin. For by one offering he hath perfected forever them that are sanctified*, as the Holy Spirit – by these words of the Covenant – witnesses.[1974]

(6) By the effects and fruits of Christ's obedience, sufferings and death, as: his purging our sins by himself, and then sitting down on the right hand of the majesty on high;[1975] his obtaining eternal redemption for us;[1976] his perfecting forever, by one sacrifice, them that are sanctified;[1977] his giving himself for us, that he might redeem us from all iniquity;[1978] the blood of Jesus Christ our Lord cleansing us from all sin;[1979] reconciling us to God by his death;[1980] his condemning sin in the flesh, that the righteousness of the law may be fulfilled in us, which walk not after the flesh, but after the Spirit.[1981] And Christ's

---

[1969] 1 Peter 1:19
[1970] 1 John 1:7
[1971] Acts 20:28
[1972] John 6:35
[1973] Hebrews 9:14
[1974] Hebrews 10:14-18
[1975] Hebrews 1:3 & 10:12-13
[1976] Hebrews 9:12
[1977] Hebrews 10:14
[1978] Titus 2:14
[1979] 1 John 1:7
[1980] Romans 5:10
[1981] Romans 8:3-4

death was so fully satisfactory and pleasing to God for us, that it is said: *Christ hath loved us, and hath given himself for us, an offering, and a sacrifice to God for a sweet smelling savour.*[1982]

By all this, it is evident that Jesus Christ by his obedience, sufferings, blood and death, has properly, really, truly, perfectly, and plenarily satisfied God justice and law for the sins of all his people, and has by that perfect sacrifice of himself expiated and purged them away forever.

{2} *Secondly, what are the branches, or chief parts of Christ's satisfaction.*

The parts of Christ's satisfaction are chiefly two, namely:

(i) **His exact, perfect, and constant fulfilling of the law for us: for our redemption, justification, and salvation.**

This is called his active obedience. This is that, whereby in part, we are redeemed and justified, etc: *God sent his Son, made of a woman, made under the law* (that is, under the obedience of the law, as well as under the penalty and curse thereof for our disobedience) *to redeem them that were under the law, that we might receive the adoption of sons.*[1983] – *By the obedience of one shall many be made righteous.*[1984] – *Christ is the end of the law for righteousness to everyone that believeth.*[1985] And Christ said: *Thus it becometh us to fulfill all righteousness.*[1986] And again: *Think not that I am come to destroy the law or the prophets: I am not come to destroy, but to fulfill.*[1987] This therefore is one branch of his satisfaction.

[1982] Ephesians 5:2
[1983] Galatians 4:4-5
[1984] Romans 5:19
[1985] Romans 10:4
[1986] Matthew 3:15
[1987] Matthew 5:17

(ii) **His undergoing or voluntarily suffering the punishment, penalty or curse of the law, even unto death itself, the death upon the cross, as our Surety, for our transgressions,** as Philippians 2:8, Galatians 4:4-5 & 3:13-14, Isaiah 53:5-6, and Romans 8:3-4.

This is styled his passive obedience. Both were necessary for our righteousness and salvation: this against our iniquity and sin whereby we had broken God's law already for time past; that, against our impotency and inability, whereby we are wholly insufficient to keep the law for time to come.

Now both Christ's active and passive obedience, in order to satisfaction, must be (i) perfect, (ii) meritorious, and (iii) for us.

(i) **Perfect.** Not only in regard to parts, but also of degrees (Matthew 3:15, Hebrews 10:14). And this perfection must be, [and is] acknowledged in Christ. Partly, in regard to the sanctity of his person, which was altogether holy, pure and spotless, without sin (Hebrews 7:26 & 4:15, Isaiah 53:9, John 8:47, Hebrews 9:14-15; 1 Peter 3:18, 22); partly, in regard to the infinite dignity of his person (1 Corinthians 2:8, Luke 1:31-33, Hebrews 1:2-3, Hebrews 9:14, Zechariah 12:10, etc., Acts 20:28).

(ii) **Meritorious:** able to impetrate, obtain and deserve redemption and life for sinners (as Hebrews 9:12, 14, 15; 1 Corinthians 6:20; 1 Peter 1:18, etc. 1 John 2:1-2. & 1:7).

(iii) **For us, and for his elect people.** That all his obedience was performed, not for himself, but for us and in our stead, by Christ as our Surety, is plain in many Scriptures (Hebrews 7:22): his active obedience (Galatians 4:4-5, Romans 5:19; 1 Corinthians 1:30), and his passive obedience also (Isaiah 53:4-7, John 1:29; 1 Peter 2:24, Galatians 3:13-14; 2 Corinthians 5:21). Jesus Christ suffered and satisfied for us, who had no need at all to suffer for himself.[1988]

[1988] Pro me doluit, qui non habuit quod pro se [doleret].

{3} Thirdly, what are the fruits or effects of Christ's death and satisfaction.

The fruits and effects of Christ death and satisfaction thereby, are many and most comfortable, as:

(i) Sanction, dedication, and establishment of the New Covenant and all the promises thereof (Matthew 26:28, Hebrews 9:15-16).

(ii) Pacification, or appeasing of God: Christ is our peace (Ephesians 2:14), our propitiation (1 John 2:1-2), and our propitiatory (Romans 3:25).

(iii) Reconciliation to God; the enmity being taken away and destroyed by the cross of Christ: (a) more generally (Colossians 1:20), and (b) more especially (Ephesians 2:20, Romans 5:10; 2 Corinthians 5:18-21).

(iv) Redemption, purchasing and buying of his elect unto God and to himself, from all manner of thralldom and bondage whatsoever (Revelation 14:4; 1 Corinthians 6:19, 20. Titus 2:14). More particularly, Christ by his death and satisfaction has redeemed us: (a) from all our sins, original and actual (Titus 2:14, Hebrews 1:3; 1 John 3:8; 1 Peter 1:18); (b) from the wrath to come (1 Thessalonians 1:10); (c) from the curse of the law (Galatians 3:13-14); (d) from the wages of sin, death (Hebrews 2:14-15); (e) from Satan, and all our spiritual enemies (Hebrews 2:14-15, Luke 1:74); (f) from this present evil world (Galatians 1:4); and (g) from the earth, and from among men (Revelation 14:3, 5).

(v) Donation of the Spirit promised, the great comprehensive blessing of Abraham (Galatians 3:13-14).

(vi) Adoption unto God's own family (Galatians 4:4-6).

(vii) Remission of sins and justification (Ephesians 1:7, Colossians 1:14, Romans 5:19; 2 Corinthians 5:20-21, Revelation 1:5, Romans 5:9, Hebrews 10:16-18).

(viii) Sanctification (1 Corinthians 6:11 & 1:30, Titus 2:14).

(ix) Free liberty of entrance by faith now, and fruition hereafter, into the holiest of all, heaven itself, *by the blood of Jesus, by a new and living way, which he hath consecrated for us, through the veil, that is to say, his flesh* (Hebrews 10:19-20).

{4} Fourthly, for whom Christ made this his proper and plenary satisfaction by his obedience and death.

In general it may thus be resolved; Jesus Christ did properly and fully satisfy for them, for whom he peculiarly, purposely, intentionally, and savingly died. In particular, Jesus Christ did not by an universal grace and favor suffer and die intentionally and savingly for all and singular, as well reprobates that are damned, as the elect that are saved; but by special grace and favor, Christ did peculiarly, intentionally, savingly die for the elect of God, and in their stead, who shall be eternally saved. For the Scripture peculiarly limits and appropriates Christ's death to his elect only; declaring that Christ suffered, died, etc., for his church, his sheep, his people, his brethren, his children, the people and children of God, and for those that are given to him of the Father.

(i) **For his church**: Christ is the head of the church, and he is the Savior of the body. – *Christ loved the church, and gave himself for it*, etc.[1989] *Take heed to yourselves, and to all the flock, over which the Holy Ghost hath made you overseers, to feed the church of God, which he hath purchased with his own blood.*[1990] Hence the church confesses to Christ: *Thou art worthy to take the book, and open the seals thereof: for thou wast slain, and hast redeemed us to God by thy blood, out of every kindred, and tongue, and people, and nation.*[1991]

[1989] Ephesians 5:23, 25-27
[1990] Acts 20:28
[1991] Revelation 5:9

– *unto him that loved us, and washed us from our sins in his own blood*[1992] – *who gave himself for us, that he might redeem us from all iniquity, and purify unto himself a peculiar people, zealous of good works.*[1993]

(ii) **For his sheep**: *As the Father knoweth me, even so know I the Father, and I lay down my life for the sheep. – I am the good shepherd, the good shepherd giveth his life for the sheep.*[1994] Hence Christ is styled: {*the great shepherd of the sheep, through the blood of the everlasting covenant*}.[1995] But as for the goats, opposed to Christ's sheep, Christ will shed and divide them from his sheep, fully and finally at last day; setting his sheep at his right hand, the goats on the left, judging these to eternal punishment, but those to life eternal (Matthew 25:32 to the end).

(iii) **For his people**: *Thou shalt call his name Jesus; for he shall save his people from their sins.*[1996]

(iv) **For his brethren**: *For both he that sanctifieth, and they who are sanctified, are all of one: for which cause he is not ashamed to call them brethren*, etc. *Wherefore in all things it behooved him to be made like unto his brethren, that he might be a merciful and faithful high priest, in things pertaining to God, to make reconciliation for the sins of the people.*[1997]

(v) **For his children – sons and seed**: *Behold I, and the children which God hath given me. For as much then as children are partakers of flesh and blood, he also himself likewise took part of the same, that through death he might destroy him that had the power of death, that is the devil*, etc.[1998] – *That he by the grace of God should taste death for every man* (namely: for every sort of men, Gentiles as well as Jews, which after is limited to sons, brethren and children of Christ in verses 10-14) *for it became him, for whom are all things,*

[1992] Revelation 1:5
[1993] Titus 2:13-14
[1994] John 10:15, 11
[1995] Hebrews 13:20
[1996] Matthew 1:21, Titus 2:14
[1997] Hebrews 2:11 to the end of the chapter
[1998] Hebrews 2:13-15

and by whom are all things, in bringing many sons unto glory, to make the captain of their salvation perfect through sufferings.[1999] – *When thou shalt make his soul an offering for sin, he shall see his seed.*[2000] These spiritual children and seed of Christ, are Christ's all, and Christ's many, which shall be justified: as the natural children and seed of the first Adam are his all, his many that are condemned (Romans 5:15 to the end). And that's the true intent of that parallel between the two Adams.

(vi) **For the people and children of God**: *and this spake he not of himself; but being high priest that year, he prophesied, that Jesus should die for that nation: and not for that nation only, but that also he should gather together in one, the children of God that were scattered abroad.*[2001]

(vii) Finally, for those that are given to Christ by the Father: *As thou hast given him power over all flesh, that he should give eternal life to as many as thou hast given him.*[2002] And Christ gives eternal life to them, by dying for them, and applying his death to them by faith here, and full fruition hereafter (John 6:50-51, 53-54 & 17:24). And Christ would not die for all, or give eternal life to all: for he would not pray for all: *I pray for them, I pray not for the world, but for them which thou hast given me, for they are thine.*[2003] Thus the Scripture declares for whom Christ peculiarly, intentionally and savingly died, and for whom he satisfied God's justice and law by dying. And though Christ's death in some expressions of Scripture seem to be extended to all, to every man, to the world, to the whole world, etc., yet in all such places, those large and universal expressions are restrained, limited and appropriated to the elect in some or other of those aforementioned notions, as the intentive [attentive] and intelligent reader may observe, if the context is heedfully considered.

[1999] Hebrews 2:9-10
[2000] Isaiah 53:10, Psalm 22:30
[2001] John 11:50-52
[2002] John 17:2
[2003] John 17:9

If any learned reader desire to see further into the state of this question; and what further arguments may be drawn from Scripture for asserting of this truth, and how the contrary arguments from pretended Scriptures may be refelled, and the Scriptures cleared, I must for brevity sake, refer him to others, who have learnedly and judiciously handled this question at large, because I may not now expatiate, nor is it my intent (further than needs must) to be polemical in this treatise.[2004]

But thus far, of Christ's satisfaction: the first part of his priesthood.

[2004] Especially consult. Mr. John Ball in his *Treatise of the New Covenant* Chapter 2, and that learned Franciscus Gomarus in *Explicat. Epist. ad Galat.* cap. 1. p. 90. ad [p.] 111, Tom. 2, who most solidly asserts the truth by many Scripture arguments, and most excellently (and sometimes singularly, and by unusual, yet well-grounded interpretations), vindicates the Scriptures that are alleged by the patrons of universal redemption. He is worthy to be read diligently. Vid. etiam Fran. Gomar. Disp. 18. *De Morte Christi*. Tom. 3.

[Part 2 of Christ's priesthood]: Of Christ's intercession.

This is the second part of Christ's priesthood. Touching the intercession of Christ, consider: {1} that Christ is our intercessor, {2} the nature of his intercession, and {3} the difference of it from his satisfaction, and from his Spirit's intercession. In the fruits and benefits of it in reference to his people.

{1} *That Jesus Christ is our intercessor, interceding with God for his people*, is evident in two ways, namely:

(i) **By the title of {*advocate*} given to him.** *And if any man sin, we have an advocate {παρακλητον} with the Father, Jesus Christ the righteous: and he is the propitiation for our sins.*[2005] Christ's person is righteous: his priestly office is, to be our propitiation, by way of satisfaction; and our advocate, by way of intercession. παρακλητον: *advocate*, signifies also a comforter, and so it is translated when ascribed to the Holy Spirit.[2006] But learned men are of the opinion that it most properly and primarily signifies {*an advocate*}.[2007] *Advocates* in common acceptance were friends of guilty persons called in to entreat for them, and differed from the patron or orator that managed their cause, as Beza notes.[2008] More strictly it imports an officer at law, an advocate, attorney, etc., that appears and answers in court for a man that is there accused, and pleads his cause. Thus Jesus Christ is our advocate by office, appointed of God, to appear for us, answer for us, plead and intercede for us: when the justice or law of God shall object anything against us for our sins; or when Satan, who is ο αντιδικος, properly) our court-adversary (1 Peter 5:8 with Matthew 5:25),[2009] the old accuser of the brethren (Revelation 12:10).

[2005] 1 John 2:1-2
[2006] John 14:16-17, 26 & 16:7
[2007] See Fra. Gomar. *Illustr. Verb. Christi in Ioan* 14:16-17, p.483, Tom. 1
[2008] Beza's Annotations on John 14:16-17
[2009] Vox αντιδικος pro prie notat Adversarium in in causa forensi. Fran. Gomar. ibid.

(ii) **By the acts of intercession ascribed to him.** He prayed on earth for them that did believe, or should believe (John 17:9, 20). He now appears in the presence of God for us (Hebrews 9:24). He ever lives to make intercession for us (Hebrews 7:25). He is *at the right hand of God, who also maketh intercession for us* (Romans 8:34). The Greek word εντυγχανει, {*maketh intercession*}, properly signifies one that attains the mark intended by darts or other weapons cast, etc.[2010] And thence metaphorically it denotes to impetrate, to obtain what we desire, etc. Thus Christ attains exactly, impetrates, and obtains fully for us from the Father whatsoever he desires.

{2} **The nature of Christ's intercession, consists in Christ's gracious will,**[2011] **fervently, immovably, and continually desiring, that, for the plenary merit and satisfaction of his obedience and death,**[2012] **the persons and spiritual sacrifices**[2013] **of all and each one of his elect members**[2014] **might be forever acceptable with the Father, whereunto the Father fully and continually assents.**[2015]

Here note: (i) the execution, and (ii) The perfections of Christ's intercession.

(i) *The execution of Christ's intercession*. Christ executes his priestly intercession:

(a) **Inchoatively**, on earth, in his state of humiliation, by prayers for all and singular his elect people, with strong cries and tears: and in such posture or gesture, lifting up his eyes, kneeling down, prostrating himself or falling to the ground, etc, as was suitable to his humiliation (John 17:9, 20. Luke 22:31-32, Hebrews 5:7, John 17:2, etc, Luke 22:41, etc, Matthew 26:39, etc, Mark 14:35, John 11:42, Matthew 3:17 & 17:5. & 26:53).

[2010] Scap Lex. in verb.
[2011] John 17:24, Hebrews 9:24, Romans 8:34
[2012] Hebrews 9:24; 1 John 2:1-2
[2013] Hebrews 7:25, Revelation 8:3; 1 Peter 2:5, Romans 8:34
[2014] John 17:9, 20, Luke 22:31-32
[2015] Matthew 17:5, John 11:42

(b) **Perfectively** and **consummatively** in heaven, in his state of highest exaltation. And this he does:

(1) By his appearing or presenting of his person, God-man, as our Mediator and Surety, in the presence of God for us, Hebrews 9:24 with Hebrews 8:6. & 7:22), as Judah both mediated and engaged as surety for Benjamin,[2016] or as Paul mediated and became surety for Onesimus.[2017] Christ appears as a public officer in our stead, as the high priest of old did appear in the holiest of all with the names of the twelve tribes of Israel upon his breast, and upon his two shoulders, for a memorial, before the Lord, so that Israel might never be forgotten (Exodus 28:9-12, 17-22), to which the church alludes: *Set me as a seal upon thine heart, as a seal upon thine arm.*[2018] That, denoting Christ's love; this, the manifestation of his love. Jesus Christ still appears before God, for an everlasting memorial of his elect, so that they may never be forgotten any of them before God.

(2) By his presenting his obedience and death, together with the infinite satisfaction and merit thereof, before his Father in heaven, desiring continually that for the same all his elect in their persons and sacrifices may be fully and eternally accepted of God (1 John 2:1-2, Romans 8:34, Hebrews 7:25). This was notably typified in the action of the high priest of old: he killed the sin-offerings, and then brought the blood of them within the veil into the holiest of all, and sprinkled it upon the mercy-seat, and before the mercy seat.[2019] This was one continued action of the high priest: his act was not complete, until the blood was represented within the veil, before the mercy seat.

Thus Christ first shed his blood, and offered himself by dying, and then entered as our intercessor within the veil, into heaven itself, there to present his blood before God, to sprinkle it as it were on and before the mercy-seat,

---

[2016] Genesis 43:8-9
[2017] Philemon 9-10
[2018] Song of Solomon 8:6
[2019] Leviticus 16:11, 14-16

and to present his satisfaction and merit perpetually there for us. Otherwise, if *Christ were still on earth, he should not be a priest* (that is, not a complete priest) *seeing that there are priests that offer gifts according to the law*, that is, until Christ, by consummating his sacrifice, in presenting it before the mercy-seat in heaven, did abrogate the Levitical priests.[2020] The inchoation of Christ's priesthood did not abolish the Levitical priesthood on earth, but the consummation thereof in heaven by his intercession did.

Now Christ in his appearing, presenting his satisfaction and merit, and interceding for us in heaven, does not fall down, kneel, prostrate himself or pray to his Father as he did on earth, for such acts are inconsistent with the majesty of his glory and exaltation – but all this must be understood to be performed suitably to his present and most excellent glory.

(ii) *The perfections and excellencies of Christ's intercession are many and matchless*, for:

(a) It is grounded and bottomed upon his satisfaction and meritorious propitiation, which was, by reason of the dignity of his person God-man, of infinite value.[2021] He first pacified God for us, then intercedes with him on our behalf.

(b) Hence it is not caritative, as our intercessions are for others when we pray for mercies of free grace for them, which nor we nor they can any way deserve; but authoritative, when Christ so intercedes for blessings for his members, as that he has merited them, and has also a joint right and authority of bestowing them.[2022]

(c) Hence it is universally prevalent with God.[2023] The Father infinitely accepts him and delights in him: and hears him always in all his suits. This master of requests is never denied. His one intercession, the voice of his blood of sprinkling, is more prevailing and effectual than the prayers and

---

[2020] Hebrews 8:1-4
[2021] 1 John 2:1-2, Romans 8:34, Hebrews 9:12 to the end
[2022] John 17:2, Matthew 28:18, John 5:21-22, 26-27
[2023] John 11:42, Colossians 1:13, Matthew 3:17 & 17:5, Hebrews 12:24, John 14:16 & 16:17

intercessions of all the saints in the world. Whilst Christ appears and intercedes, no accusations of God's justice, law, our sins, or Satan's malice shall be heard against his members: the voice of his blood silences all.[2024]

(d) It is glorious, namely: his intercession now in heaven for it is at God's right hand.[2025]

(e) It is general and universal: for all and singular his elect that are or shall be his members.[2026]

(f) It is fully salvific to all that come unto God by him.[2027]

(g) It is perpetual and eternal. *He ever liveth to make intercession for us.*[2028] Oh! No intercession is like Christ's intercession. When we know not what to pray for as we ought (Romans 8:26-27), Christ intercedes, and speeds for us. Our names are always upon the heart and shoulders of this our great high priest before God.

(iii) *The difference of Christ's intercession from his satisfaction, and from his Spirit's intercession is observable.* Christ's intercession and satisfaction are joint acts of Christ's priesthood that may not be severed, yet must be distinguished, for: (a) his satisfaction was properly expiatory by his death and sufferings;[2029] his intercession is especially presentatory, presenting himself and his merits for us in heaven.[2030] (b) His satisfaction was chiefly accomplished on earth, in his humiliation, when he suffered without the gate.[2031] No sin, nor punishment for sin, can come within the holy place; his intercession is chiefly accomplished and completed in heaven, in his exaltation, at God's right hand.[2032] (c) His satisfaction was by offering himself up for a

---

[2024] Romans 8:34
[2025] Romans 8:34
[2026] John 17:9, 20, Hebrews 9:24; 1 John 2:1
[2027] Hebrews 7:25
[2028] Hebrews 7:25
[2029] Hebrews 1:3 & 9:14
[2030] Hebrews 9:24
[2031] Hebrews 13:12
[2032] Romans 8:34, Hebrews 9:24

sacrifice; his intercession is by commemoration of that sacrifice. (d) His satisfaction was by suffering; his intercession is now without suffering. (e) His satisfaction was made but once by once dying, though the virtue of his death be everlasting;[2033] his intercession is continual and unceasing forevermore.[2034] (f) His satisfaction, obtained our redemption, reconciliation, etc.; his intercession tends especially to apply those benefits obtained to us.

Christ and the Spirit, are both of them called our παρακλητον: *advocate* – compare 1 John 2:1 with John 14:16, 17, 26. & 16:7. And both of them are said to make intercession for us – compare Romans 8:34 and Hebrews 7:25 with Romans 8:26-27. But there is a great deal of difference between their intercession, for: (a) Christ intercedes without us, with the Father;[2035] but the Spirit intercedes within us, to the Father.[2036] (b) Christ intercedes for us, as our high-priest and advocate by office, by presentation of his death, satisfaction and merit, and undertaking our cause with the Father against all contrary charge, or accusation of any adversary whatsoever.[2037] But the Spirit intercedes, not as our high priest, but as an assistant to us by his energy and operation, who by Christ are made kings and priests to God to offer up spiritual sacrifices acceptable to God by him.[2038] The Spirit instructs, counsels, inspires, acts, moves, suggests, assists us, and so makes intercession for us, by enabling us to intercede for ourselves, and plead our own cause with God in Christ. (c) Christ intercedes for us, by the voice of his own blood speaking better things than the blood of Abel, by the merit whereof he covers our infirmities and iniquities;[2039] but the Spirit intercedes for us, by raising up in our hearts groans unutterable, by his virtue and efficacy helping our infirmities.[2040]

[2033] Hebrews 9:25-26 & 10:10, 12, 14
[2034] Hebrews 7:25
[2035] 1 John 2:1, Romans 8:34
[2036] Romans 8:15, 36, 27
[2037] Hebrews 7:25; 1 John 2:1, Hebrews 9:24, Romans 8:34
[2038] Romans 8:26-27, Revelation 1:5-6; 1 Peter 2:4-5
[2039] Hebrews 12:24
[2040] Romans 8:26-27

(iv) *The fruits, effects, or benefits of Christ's intercession are manifold and very precious*, as is evident by these particularly, namely:

(a) Hereby, all the infirmities, sins and iniquities, which the people of God, the elect members of Christ may possibly fall into, are remedied, and the full pardon of them assured. *If any man sin, we have an advocate with the Father, Jesus Christ the righteous: and he is the propitiation for our sins: and not for ours only, but also for the sins of the whole world.*[2041]

(b) Hereby, the persons, performances, and all the upright spiritual sacrifices of God's people, are presented to God as acceptable, and remain as a sweet memorial in his presence continually through Jesus Christ (Exodus 28:9-12, 17-22, Hebrews 7:24, Revelation 8:3; 1 Peter 2:4-5), notwithstanding all their frailties.

(c) Hereby, all God's elect in Christ are sweetly secured against all the oppositions, temptations, charges, accusations, etc, that any spiritual enemies whatsoever, world, flesh or Satan can possibly lay against them. *I pray not that thou shouldst take them out of the world, but that shouldst keep them from the evil.*[2042] They may – and you must – be tempted, but shall be delivered from the mischief of the temptation. Christ would not intercede for Peter, that he might not be sifted, but that his faith might not fail. *Who shall lay anything to the charge of God's elect? It is God that justifieth: who is he that condemneth? It is Christ that died, yea rather that is risen again, who is even at the right hand of God, who also maketh intercession for us.*[2043]

(d) Hereby, God's people become more plentifully partakers of the Holy Spirit the comforter to lead them into all truth, and dwell in them forever: *If I go not away the Comforter will not come unto you, but if I depart I will send him unto you.*[2044] – *I will pray the Father, and he shall give you another Comforter* (or, *Advocate*), *that he may abide with you forever, even the Spirit of*

[2041] 1 John 2:1
[2042] John 17:15
[2043] Romans 8:33-34
[2044] John 16:7 with 7:38-39

truth, etc.[2045] Christ our advocate, will intercede for the Spirit another advocate: that so we may have an advocate in earth, as well as an advocate in heaven; an advocate within us, as well as an advocate above us with the Father. Oh, where this comforter comes and dwells, there a confluence of all grace, truth, peace, consolation, joy and spiritual blessings comes and dwells also. The Comforter brings all fruits and effects of the Spirit with him.

(e) Hereby, we have great encouragement to hold fast our profession, against all our infirmities within, and temptations without, for our great high priest is in heaven, who was in all points tempted as we are, yet without sin, and therefore he has a feeling of our infirmities.[2046]

(f) Hereby, the faithful have sweet and free access to the throne of grace for all manner of blessings in time of need. *Let us therefore come boldly unto the throne of grace, that we may obtain mercy, and find grace to help in time of need.*[2047] We have a friend in the high court of heaven, the great master of requests, that will succeed and speed our petitions. *Whatsoever ye shall ask in my name; that will I do, that the Father may be glorified in the Son. If ye shall ask anything in my name, I will do it.*[2048] Ask, and have; oh, what an encouragement unto prayer! Christ offers up much incense with the prayers of all saints.[2049] If the incense of Christ's intercession be offered up with our prayers, they must needs be most fragrant, acceptable, and prevalent.

(g) Hereby, the faithful are assured of that sweetest oneness, union, and communion with the Father and Jesus Christ. This is that one only thing on earth which Christ begs for the faithful in his solemn prayer (John 17:21-23). They that gain this, gain all spiritual blessings with it, and in it.

(h) Hereby, the saints obtain perseverance and stability in grace, and inseparableness from the love of God in Christ Jesus our Lord against all

---

[2045] John 14:16-17
[2046] Hebrews 4:14-15 & 10:19-21, 23
[2047] Hebrews 4:14-16 & 10:19-22
[2048] John 14:13-14
[2049] Revelation 8:3

adversaries and possible oppositions (Luke 22:32, Romans 8:34-39). *It is Christ – who is even at the right hand of God, who also maketh intercession for us, who shall separate us from the love of Christ?* Etc.

(i) Hereby, all the faithful that come unto God by Christ are assured of eternal salvation. *Wherefore he is able to save to the utmost* (Greek: to all end) *all that come unto God by him, seeing he ever liveth to make intercession for them.*[2050] He intercedes eternally, therefore they shall be saved eternally.

(j) Finally, hereby, Christ takes care that all his elect may live with him in heaven, to behold his glory beatifically for their glory. *Father I will that they also whom thou hast given me, may be with me where I am, that they may behold my glory which thou hast given me.*[2051] What a ravishing, beatifical, transforming, ineffable vision will that be! "The Lord Jesus," (said Augustine upon these words) "lifts up his unto great hopes, then which there cannot be greater. – Hear, believe, hope, desire what he says: Father I will, etc."[2052]

Thus of Christ's priestly office.

[2050] Hebrews 7:25 εις το παντελες
[2051] John 17:24
[2052] "In magnam spem Dominus Iesus suos erigit, qua major omnio esse non possit.—Audite, Credite, Sperate, desiderate quod dicit; Pater," &c.
August in Evangel. Ioan. c. 17. Tract. 111. Tom. 9.

[Part 3 of Christ's priesthood]: Of Christ's kingly office.

Christ's kingly office, is that branch of his Mediatorship,[2053] whereby Jesus Christ our Mediator, God-man, anointed with the Holy Ghost and with power,[2054] and most highly exalted at God's right hand to be head over all things to the church,[2055] powerfully calls,[2056] governs,[2057] defends,[2058] and rewards[2059] all that are given him for subjects by the Father;[2060] sufficiently restraining,[2061] and at last utterly conquering all his and their enemies,[2062] for his people's exceeding benefit[2063] and his own eternal glory.[2064]

For the unfolding of this regal office of Christ more particularly, I shall very briefly show: {1} that Jesus Christ our Mediator is king, {2} the nature of his kingdom, {3} his regalities appertaining to him as king, {4} his actual administration or execution of his kingly office, {5} the benefits of his kingship, and {6} the continuance of this royal office.

{1} *That Jesus Christ our Mediator is king: is evident in several ways*, as:

(i) By the prophecies that went of him, which are true and must needs have their due accomplishment in him, as that the scepter of Judah should terminate in him (Genesis 49:10); that he should be God's king in Zion, etc. (Psalm 2 throughout with Acts 4:25-28); that he should be full of glory and

---

[2053] Acts 2:30-37, Ephesians 1:20 to the end, Hebrews 7:1, etc.
[2054] Acts 10:38, 42, Psalm 45:6-7
[2055] Acts 3:33, Philippians 2:9-11, Ephesians 1:20-23
[2056] Psalm 110:2-3, Isaiah 55:4-5, Acts 15:14-16 & 26:17-18, Genesis 49:10
[2057] Isaiah 9:6 & 55:4, Hebrews 2:10, Matthew 18:17-18; 1 Corinthians 5:4-5, Matthew 28:18-20, Ephesians 4:8-13
[2058] Isaiah 32:1-2
[2059] Revelation 22:12 & 2:10, Matthew 25:34, etc.
[2060] Psalm 2:8-9, John 17:2
[2061] Revelation 2:10, Acts 18:9-10, Revelation 20:1-3
[2062] 1 Corinthians 15:25, Psalm 110:1, etc., & 2:9
[2063] Ephesians 1:22-23, Romans 8:28
[2064] Romans 14:9-11

majesty, etc. (Psalm 45 throughout); that he should succeed David and sit upon his throne (Psalm 132:11-12 with Luke 1:31-33, Acts 2:30, see also Isaiah 11:1-3, etc., Hosea 3:5, Ezekiel 34:23-24 & 37:24-25); that he should be a prince of peace, having the government upon his shoulder, of the increase of whose government and peace there shall be no end, upon the throne of David, and upon his kingdom, to order it, and to establish it, with judgment and with justice, from henceforth and forever (Isaiah 9:6-7); that he should be the Messiah the Prince (Daniel 9:25), who should break in pieces all other kingdoms, but of his kingdom there shall be no end (Daniel 2:44 & 7:14, 27).

(ii) By the types and shadows prefiguring Christ as king. As, of Melchizedek, first king of righteousness, then king of peace: a singular type of Christ our king, who first justifies and then pacifies.[2065] Of David, and Solomon: both, royal types of Jesus Christ the true David, and Solomon, as I have already manifested in many particulars.[2066]

(iii) By the many regal and princely titles attributed to Christ in holy Scripture, which I have in this chapter already mentioned.[2067]

(iv) By Christ's own acknowledgement before Pilate, that he was a king, that his kingdom was not of this world, and that for this end he was born, and for this cause he came into the world, to bear witness to the truth, namely: especially to the truth touching his kingly office.[2068] For this cause especially, he was condemned and put to death, having this title written upon his cross in Latin, Greek, and Hebrew: *Jesus of Nazareth the king of the Jews*[2069] – the truth of whose spiritual kingship the convert thief had revealed unto him upon the cross, whereupon he prayed: *Lord remember me when thou comest into thy kingdom.*[2070]

[2065] See Hebrews 7 throughout, Romans 5:1.
[2066] In Book 3, Chapter 5, Aphorism 7, Inference 2
[2067] In Aphorism 3, Section 1
[2068] John 18:33-38
[2069] John 19:12-23
[2070] Luke 23:42-43

{2} *The nature of Christ's kingdom*.

It is not a carnal, earthly, temporal kingdom, but a spiritual, heavenly and eternal kingdom. *My kingdom is not of this world – but now is my kingdom not from hence.*[2071] *He shall reign over the house of Jacob* (that is, the church) *forever, and of his kingdom there shall be no end.*[2072] The kingdom of the Son of God, is twofold: (i) essential and (ii) personal.

(i) Essential, which belongs to him in regard to his divine essence and nature, as well as to the Father and Holy Spirit. God– who is Father, Son, and Holy Spirit, creator of the whole world – is absolutely Lord and king of the whole world. This essential or natural kingdom belongs, as to the Father and Holy Ghost, so to the Son, as God the Creator. But of this essential kingdom, I am not now to speak.

(ii) Personal, which by the Father's voluntary dispensation, properly and peculiarly belongs to the person of Jesus Christ, God-man, as our Mediator.[2073] This his personal kingdom is hereupon by some styled, his {*mediatory kingdom*}, because it properly appertains to him, and is administered by him as Mediator; by others his economical, or dispensatory kingdom, because it is delegated, committed and dispensed to him as Mediator from the Father.[2074] This personal and mediatory kingdom of Christ, God-man, dispensed to him from the father, is again twofold: (a) general and (b) special.

(a) General and universal over all the world for his church's good, and his own glory. Jesus Christ God-man, as our Mediator is constituted and ordained of God, head, Lord, king and judge over all creatures in heaven and earth, to the church. – *according to the working of his mighty power which he wrought in Christ when he raised him from the dead, and set him at his own right hand in the heavenly places, far above all principality and power, and might, and dominion, and every name that is named, not only in this world, but also in*

[2071] John 18:36
[2072] Luke 1:31-33
[2073] Psalm 2:6, John 18:36, Ephesians 1:20-22, Luke 1:31-33
[2074] Matthew 28:18, John 5:21-22, 26-27, Ephesians 1:20, etc, Philippians 2:8-9

that which is to come: and hath put all things under his feet, and gave him to be the **head over all things** *to the church, which is his body, the fullness of him that filleth all in all.*[2075] To the like effect are these ensuing testimonies, and such like: Matthew 28:18. John 5:22. & 17:2. Philippians 2:9, 10:11. Acts 2:36. & 17:31. Revelation 1:8. & 2:23; 1 Peter 3:22. And therefore all persons, kingdoms, creatures, and revolutions of affairs, times and seasons in the whole world are ordered and overpowered by our Mediator Jesus Christ. Nothing comes to pass in the world, but what he wills; and all one way or another shall at last be turned about in a sweet subserviency and co-operation, to his people's good.[2076]

The parts of this universal kingdom of Christ are two, namely: (1) the government of it, ruling over all creatures with supreme and greatest power, (Psalm 110:1-3, Matthew 28:18; 1 Peter 3:22). (2) The bringing of all creatures, according to God's appointment, into a certain and plenary subjection at last to himself, and putting all things under his feet (Psalm 110:1, Hebrews 1:6, Philippians 2:9-11; 1 Corinthians 15:27). And although all things are not as yet in act and perfectly put under him, Hebrews 2:8. Yet in right and inchoatively all things are put in subjection under his feet (Hebrews 2:8. Ephesians 1:22; 1 Corinthians 15:27). And this subjection of all things to him shall at last be universally completed.

The manner how these things are done and shall be done, is diverse, according to his two distinct natures, namely: according to his divine nature, by manifestation and approbation of that power which the Son of God, made man, has by his own right forever over all creatures as their omnipotent creator, for as he in a sort emptied himself of the glory of his kingdom for the time of his humiliation; not by any privation of his dominion; but by veiling of it under mean flesh and in a servile afflicted form (Philippians 2:7); so contrariwise he is said to have received a kingdom, after the glorification of his

---

[2075] Ephesians 1:19-23
[2076] Hebrews 1:3, Daniel 2:32-46, Romans 8:28-30

flesh; not by accession of new power, which he formerly wanted, but by a famous revelation and confirmation of his ancient kingdom which he always had; whereby he, though clothed with flesh, may be by all acknowledged, to be Lord (Psalm 110:1-2, Philippians 2:9-11).[2077] And according to his human, by having all finite power, far above and over all creatures attributed to him (Matthew 28:18. Ephesians 1:21). And this is the nature of his personal Mediatory-kingdom, which is general and universal.

(b) Special and particular over his church and people peculiarly. This special Mediatory kingdom of Christ, is that his supreme and glorious power and authority for calling, governing, defending, and saving, or rewarding his church gathered out of all nations (Luke 19:12, 15, Psalm 2:8, Matthew 28:18-20, Ephesians 1:22-23). And this is done, (1) partly, in this present world (Matthew 28:19-20, Acts 1:8. & 13:47 & 26:17-18; (2) partly, at the end of this world (Matthew 25:31 to the end; 1 Thessalonians 4:14 to the end; 1 Corinthians 15:24 to the end, Revelation 20:11 to the end, Luke 19:27 & Ephesians 5:27); and (3) partly in the world to come (Matthew 25:46 & 5:8; 1 John 3:2). And this is the nature of Christ's personal mediatory kingdom, which is special or particular. Now from all this, it is evident who are the subjects of this king, namely: more generally, all the creatures in the world; more especially and peculiarly, the church and people of God.

{3} *The regalities appertaining to Jesus Christ as king, are many and very majestical*, as: (i) his unction, (ii) his inauguration, (iii) his throne, (iv) his crown, (v) his scepter, (vi) his laws, and (vii) his prerogatives.

(i) **His unction.** Kings in former times were anointed with the holy oil before their actual investiture and coronation, as David was anointed, long before he was crowned.[2078] This unction did import their qualification for and designation to the royal office (1 Samuel 16:12-13). Thus Christ was *anointed*

[2077] Sic. Clariss. Fran. Gomarus *De Sessione Christi*, &c. [Disp 22] Tom. 3.
[2078] 1 Samuel 16:12-13; 2 Samuel 2:4

with the oil of gladness above his fellows, namely: *with the Holy Ghost and with power*; and God gave not the Spirit to him by measure, as to others of his members.[2079] Christ had all fullness dwelling in him, for his mediatory offices: extensively, all kinds of fullness; intensively, all degrees of fullness. And all for us, see Colossians 1:19 and John 1:14, 16. By this unction, he was fitted for his kingship.[2080]

(ii) **His inauguration**. Christ was designed to be king, by God's decree (Psalm 2:6-8). He was fore-promised, and fore-typified to be king, in the Old Testament, as has been shown; he was proclaimed to be Lord and king before and at his birth (Luke 1:31-33, Matthew 2:2, 11, Luke 2:10-11). He was acknowledged to be king at his death (John. 18:33-38 & 19:12-23, Luke 23:42-43). But his solemn investiture, installment or inauguration was when he ascended into heaven and sat down on the right hand of God. *Who is gone into heaven, and is on the right hand of God, angels, and authorities, and powers being made subject unto him.*[2081] – *He hath set him on his own right hand in the heavenly places, far above all principality, and power, and might, and dominion, and every name that is named, not only in this world, but also in that which is to come: and hath put all things under his feet, and gave him to be the head over all things to the church.*[2082] *He is set down at the right hand of the throne of God.*[2083] – *He is set on the right hand of the throne of the majesty in the heavens.*[2084] This is Christ's advancement far above angels. *For, to which of the angels said he at any time, sit on my right hand, until I make thine enemies thy footstool?*[2085]

This phrase of {*sitting at God's right hand*}, the apostle expounds of reigning there: *for he must reign, till he hath put all enemies under his feet.*

[2079] Psalm 45:6-7 with Acts 10:38, John 3:34, Colossians 1:19
[2080] Isaiah 11:1-2, etc.
[2081] 1 Peter 3:22
[2082] Ephesians 1:20-22; see also Philippians 2:9-11
[2083] Hebrews 12:2
[2084] Hebrews 8:1
[2085] 1 Corinthians 15:25

Jesus Christ is said to be at the right hand of God (Romans 8:34; 1 Peter 3:22), to stand at the right hand of God (Acts 7:56), most usually to sit at the right hand of God, etc (Psalm 110:1, Hebrews 1:13, Mark 16:19, Luke 22:69, Hebrews 1:3, 8:1. & 12:2) – all of which are metaphorical expressions, borrowed from men. Man's right-hand, is the hand of honor (1 Kings 2:19), the hand of might and power (Psalm 26:10. & 144:8, 11), and the hand of skill and cunning (Psalm 137:5). Answerably, the right hand ascribed to God denotes his majesty, glory, honor, authority, power, strength, aid, assistance, counsel, fidelity, etc., as is evident by many phrases in Scripture.[2086]

To stand at the right hand, implies in Scripture phrase: (a) to oppose, resist, withstand or hinder the acts or endeavors of any one, as Zechariah 3:1 and Psalm 109:6; (b) to aid, assist, protect, defend against enemies, evils or dangers, as Psalm 16:8 & 109:31; and (c) to have the next place and degree of honor to them at whose right hand they stand, as Psalm 45:9. Thus Christ standing at God's right hand, is next to God in honor, majesty and power; protects and defends his church against all evils; and opposes and withstands all their adversaries. To sit at the right hand, imports special honor, dignity, majesty, rule, power, authority, love and favor, manifested or conferred upon them that are so set (1 Kings 2:19, Matthew 10:21, 23).

Thus, Christ sitting at God's right hand, denotes the supreme exaltation of Jesus Christ God-man, after his death and sufferings, far above all created beings; to be immediate and next unto God in majesty, glory, honor, power, authority, etc., over all things, for his church (1 Peter 3:22, Ephesians 1:20-23, Hebrews 2:7-9, Philippians 2:8-11). I say the supreme exaltation of Jesus Christ God-man, for, though properly the Godhead of Christ is not capable of any intrinsical and essential exaltation or humiliation, as his manhood was, yet the majesty, glory, etc,[2087] of his Godhead, veiled, and shadowed a while under his manhood in his humiliation, by manifestation is magnified at God's right

---

[2086] Hebrews 1:3, Luke 22:69, Psalm 16:8 & 89:13 & 20:6 & 21:8 & 17:7 & 48:10 & 139:10 & 44:3 & 77:10, Habbakuk 2:16
[2087] John 17:5

hand. And so in some sense Christ's whole person may be said to be exalted (Acts 2:33, 36. Ephesians 1:20, etc. Philippians 2:9, 10, 11. Act. 5:31. & 10:42. Hebrews 2:7-8).

More particularly, Christ's sitting down on the right hand of God, implies these things, namely:

(a) The Father's most supreme, highest and compleatest manifestation of his infinite love, favor, delight, and acquiescence to, and in Jesus Christ God-man our Mediator, for his sufferings and death for his elect. Upon this account, God testified his love to him often: but most completely and gloriously in setting him at his right hand, next to himself forevermore (Ephesians 1:20-23, Philippians 3:8-11 with John 10:17).[2088]

(b) The matchless and incomparable replenishing of Christ's human nature to the uttermost capacity with all fullness of the Spirit in knowledge, wisdom, grace, life, power, authority, etc., beyond all creatures, for the plenary, powerful and most effectual administration of his Mediatorship.[2089] The Spirit was not given to him by measure (John. 3:34) as to Stephen and other saints, said to be *full of the Holy Ghost*,[2090] namely: according to their measure, as a bottle or glass is full of water, or as a star, or torch is full of light, but beyond measure – not infinitely, but comparatively, in regard to all creatures; Christ being full extensively with all kinds, intensively with all degrees of fullness, as the sun is full of light, or as a fountain, or the ocean is full of water. For his fullness is to be diffused and communicated to his church: he is full, that he might fill all things (Ephesians 1:22 & 4:10, John 1:14, 16).

(c) Christ's preeminence and prerogative, not only as God-man, but also as man; above all creatures in heaven and earth, men or angels. In him, the human nature is advanced next to God himself (Ephesians 1:19-21). *He is the*

[2088] Isaiah 42:1-4, Matthew 3:17 & 17:5, Ephesians 1:6, Colossians 1:13, John 10:17, Ephesians 5:2
[2089] Colossians 1:19, Psalm 45:7, John 1:14-15
[2090] Acts 7:55 & 6:3, Luke 1:15

beginning, the firstborn from the dead, that in all things he might have the preeminence.[2091]

(d) Not only Christ's dignity above, but his power and supreme authority as God-man over all things in the world for the good of his church, having all things (de jure and inchoative) of right, and by inchoation, put under him. *And he hath put all things under his feet, and gave him to be the head over all things to the church.*[2092] Here he is also called {*the head of all principality and power*} (Colossians 2:10).

(e) Christ's glorious headship more peculiarly over the church. Christ is head over all things to the church, more generally: but he is head only of the church peculiarly; to animate, guide, direct, inform, actuate, and replenish the church with all saving influences. *And he is the head of the body, the church*[2093] – *Christ is the head of the church, and he is the Savior of the body.*[2094] And as supreme and sole head of the church, he has all power and authority in heaven and earth given to him as Mediator, for her constitution, conservation and salvation (Matthew 28:18-20).

(f) The due of divine adoration and worship from all men and angels. *The Father hath committed all judgment to the Son: that all men should honor the Son, even as they honor the Father.*[2095] – *And let all the angels of God worship him.*[2096] The Scriptures frequently ascribe divine worship to him, and require it to be performed – see Philippians 2:9-11, Psalm 2:12, John 14:1, Isaiah 45:23, Romans 14:11, and Acts 7:59-60. The apostles in the salutations of their epistles desire grace and peace from God the Father and our Lord Jesus Christ (2 John 3, Revelation 1:4-5, Romans 1:7; 1 Corinthians 1:3; 2 Corinthians 1:2, Galatians 1:3, Ephesians 1:2; 2 Timothy 1:1). And in like sort in their valedictions of their epistles, they beg for the grace of our Lord Jesus

---

[2091] Colossians 1:18
[2092] Ephesians 1:22, Hebrews 2:7-8, Revelation 19:16
[2093] Colossians 1:18
[2094] Ephesians 5:23
[2095] John 5:23
[2096] Hebrews 1:6

Christ, unto the churches, 1 Corinthians 15:23. Galatians 6:18; 2 Corinthians 13:13. Philippians 4:23; 1 Thessalonians 5:28; 2 Thessalonians 3:18. Philemon 25; 2 Timothy 4:22; 7. Finally, Christ's sitting down at God's right hand, implies Christ's admission, installment or inauguration into all divine, royal, celestial fullness of glory and blessedness, fixedly, settledly, and eternally to enjoy the same, without all eclipse or shadow of the least cessation, interruption, diminution, or alteration (John. 17:5, Acts 13:34, Revelation 1:18).

(iii) **His throne**. A throne is a majestical seat of royalty, peculiar to kings and princes when they would appear in all their glory and majesty.[2097] Christ has his throne as God, the same throne with his Father; as God-man, the next throne unto his Father, which he sat down upon after he overcame all his and our enemies. *To him that overcometh will I grant to sit with me on my throne: even as I also overcame, and am set down with my Father in his throne.*[2098] The further sense of these words I have laid down elsewhere.[2099] Now this throne of Christ is in the highest heavens, according to his humanity. *He is set on the right hand of the throne of the majesty in the heavens.*[2100] There Christ is (Ephesians 1:20, Hebrews 1:3, Colossians 3:1). There Christ intercedes for us (Hebrews 9:24 & 8:4). There he must be received, until the times of restitution of all things (Acts 3:21). Thence at last we expect him, and he shall be revealed (Philippians 3:20-21; 2 Thessalonians 1:9-10). Christ according to his humanity, is only in heaven; according to his Godhead, he is everywhere – and so with his ministers and churches to the world's end (Matthew 28:20). Now this throne of Christ is glorious, and everlasting: Thy *throne O God is forever and ever.*[2101]

[2097] 1 Chronicles 29:23; 2 Chronicles 9:17-19
[2098] Revelation 3:21
[2099] In my *Key of the Bible* on Revelation 3:22
[2100] Hebrews 10:1
[2101] Hebrews 1:8, Psalm 45:6-7

(iv) **His crown.** Kings have crowns of gold put upon their heads: eminent ensigns of royalty;[2102] so Jesus Christ, after his cross, came to his crown: and that not a fading crown of corruptible gold, etc, but an unfading crown of incorruptible glory: *but we see Jesus, who was made a little lower than the angels, for the suffering of death, crowned with glory and honour.*[2103] His crown of thorns on earth, could not keep him from his crown of glory in heaven. And his members, that are contented here to be crowned with Christ's thorns, shall hereafter be crowned with Christ's glory.[2104]

(v) **His scepter.** Kings have scepters to sway: signal rods of royal majesty, rule, and dominion: scepters of gold.[2105] Jesus Christ also has his scepter: *Thy throne O God is forever and ever, a sceptre of righteousness* (Greek: *rightness*, or *straightness*) *is the sceptre of thy kingdom.*[2106] Now Christ has a double scepter ascribed to him in Scripture:

(a) The one, as it were, a scepter of gold, wherewith he rules and governs his subjects (Psalm 45:6, Hebrews 1:8): *The LORD shall send the rod of thy strength out of Zion: rule thou*, etc. (Psalm 110:2). This rod of his strength out of Zion, is Christ's ruling rod, or scepter. Now there were two things sent out of Zion (as is by some well observed),[2107] namely: (1) the word or gospel of the Lord: *The law shall proceed out of Zion, and the word of the LORD from Jerusalem* (Micah 4:2). (2) The Spirit of the Lord, which was first sent unto Zion, upon the apostles at Jerusalem (Acts 1:4 & 2:4, etc). And from thence was shed abroad upon all flesh (Acts 2:17). Both of these are the power or strength of Christ. His word, a gospel of power, the power of God to salvation; and his Spirit, a Spirit of power, which is therefore called *the finger and arm of the Lord* (Luke 11:20, Matthew 12:28, Isaiah 53:1).[2108] Thus Christ's rod, or

---

[2102] Psalm 21:3, Esther 6:8
[2103] Hebrews 2:9
[2104] Romans 8:17; 1 Peter 1:4; 2 Corinthians 4:17
[2105] Esther 5:2
[2106] Hebrews 1:8, Psalm 45:6
[2107] Dr. Edward Reynolds on Psalm 110:2
[2108] 1 Corinthians 2:4; 2 Timothy 1:7

scepter of his kingdom is his Word and Spirit. By these, he powerfully rules and guides his kingdom and all his subjects.

(b) The other scepter is his rod of iron, wherewith he breaks and dashes in pieces all his enemies, as a potter's vessel.[2109]

(vi) **His laws.** Kings rule according to certain known laws; tyrants rule arbitrarily, their will and pleasure is their law. But Jesus Christ rules by laws, known laws, holy, just and good;[2110] the best laws in the world. The whole of Scripture – styled {*the Word of Christ*}[2111] – is his great pandect, or statute-book: an excellent abridgement whereof we have in the ten commandments. Christ's laws are holy, without the least corruption or sinfulness; righteous, without the least injustice or oppressiveness; good, without the least incommodiousness; perfect, without the least defectiveness; true, without the least error or deceivableness; pure, without the least drossiness; wise, without all shadow of foolishness, etc. See how David extols and admires them.[2112] And lest they should be, as men's laws are, a mere weak, ineffectual dead letter without us, Christ puts his laws into our minds, and writes them in our hearts, that they be most powerful and efficacious within us. Not only outward rules of duty, but also inward principles of ability.[2113]

(vii) **His prerogatives.** Kings have many prerogatives royal, and they insist much upon them, that they should not in the least be infringed or diminished, as:

(a) Tributes and customs (Romans 13:6-7); so Christ has a spiritual tribute of worship due unto him (Psalm 96:8).

(b) Magazines for military provisions for defense of his kingdom. So Christ has his armory for our defense against our spiritual enemies, armor of

---

[2109] Psalm 2:9, Revelation 2:27
[2110] Romans 7:12
[2111] Colossians 3:16
[2112] Psalm 19:7, etc & 119 throughout
[2113] Hebrews 8:10

light, etc, the panoply of God (Ephesians 6:11-19, Romans 13:12-14; 1 Thessalonians 5:8).

(c) Highways are called {*the king's ways*}, wherein men go under the king's protection. So Christ has his royal ways of faith, repentance, and new obedience, called {*the law of Christ*} (Galatians 6:2), and {*the royal law of liberty*} (James 2:8). They who walk herein are under Christ's protection.[2114]

(d) Ambassadors (2 Chronicles 32:31) – so Christ has his ambassadors, beseeching men in his stead to be reconciled unto God (2 Corinthians 5:20, 21.

(e) Goods of an uncertain lord, concealed lands, not challengeable by any particular owner, etc, belong unto kings as supreme within their dominions. So those persons belong to Christ in the world, who belong not to Satan, sin, or other lords.[2115]

(f) The laws and values of coin that shall be currency in their dominions. So it appertains to Christ only to coin and institute what ordinances he will in the church.[2116]

(g) Power of judgment is in kings, as fountains of human equity to their inferior officers and subjects. So Christ has all judgment committed to him from the Father (John 5:22), to which may be referred the power of princes to reprieve and pardon malefactors and condemned persons. Herein Christ excels, he remits sins, he redeems from the curse of the law, and delivers from death, poor condemned sinners.[2117]

{4} ***Christ's execution or actual administration of his kingly office.*** This has a twofold consideration, namely: (i) according to his general mediatory kingdom over all things for his church, and (ii) according to his special mediatory kingdom over his church.

[2114] James 1:25, Psalm 91:11, Proverbs 10:29
[2115] Isaiah 26:13
[2116] Matthew 28:18-19, Ephesians 4:8, 11-12
[2117] Mark 2:5, 9-11, Hebrews 10:16-17, Galatians 3:13, Hebrews 2:14-15

(i) **His general mediatory kingdom over all things for his church** (Ephesians 1:22). Christ manages and administers, especially by these and like royal acts, namely:

(a) *Sustentando*: by sustaining and upholding all things by the word of his power, continuing the world, etc., until all his elect be gathered and perfected.[2118]

(b) *Permittendo*: by permitting Satan and his instruments, wicked men in the world, to hate, oppose, afflict and persecute most cruelly the church and people of God, for wise ends, according to the counsel of his will (Revelation 2:10 & 12:2, 4, 17 & 13:6-7 & 19:19 & 20:7-9).

(c) *Coercendo*: by restraining, limiting, chaining up, girding in, both Satan, wicked men, and all their malicious rage against the church and members of Christ, that they cannot do what they list, but what, and when, and how Christ will let them or suffer them (Revelation 2:10). He lays hold of the dragon, that old serpent the devil and Satan, and binds him a thousand years with a great chain;[2119] how much more does he chain up devilish and wicked men.

(d) *Protegendo*: by protecting, preserving and defending his church and people from ruin and destruction by Satan and his instruments (Revelation 2:10). Michael and his angels fought against the dragon and his angels, who would have destroyed the man-child, Christ mystical, as soon as he should have been born, in primitive times: the child being caught up unto God.[2120] And the woman, the church, persecuted by the dragon, had wings given her to fly into the wilderness for her preservation, the earth helping her, and swallowing up the flood of persecution which the dragon cast out after her.[2121] And in the most corrupt times, Christ preserved a pure virgin company of sincere

---

[2118] Hebrews 1:3, Colossians 1:17, Ephesians 1:[23] & 4:11-13, Matthew 28:19-20
[2119] Revelation 20:1-3
[2120] Revelation 12:2-13
[2121] Revelation 12:13-16

worshippers, namely: 144,000, following the lamb whithersoever he goes, having his Father's name written in their foreheads.[2122]

(e) *Ordinando*. By ordering, disposing, directing, and over-pouring all things in the world, yea their worst afflictions and persecutions, one way or other for the good of his church, people, gospel and kingdom at last (Romans 8:28; 2 Corinthians 4:17, Philippians 1:12-14). The persecution about Stephen, is made an occasion of spreading the gospel and increasing the church.[2123] Saul is powerfully made a Paul, Christ from heaven converting him miraculously from a persecutor to be a preacher, from a destroyer to be a builder of the church, from a wolf to be a shepherd, etc.[2124] The antichristian cruelties against Christ's pure worshipers do but provide for them a first resurrection, a thousand years before the rest of the dead revive, and a reigning with Christ.[2125] Yea, all things are so wheeled about by Christ, that they are made subservient to his people's happiness in this and the world to come.

(f) *Vindicando*: by avenging his church and people of all their enemies to the full at last, utterly destroying all opposite kingdoms and empires in the world, the great whore of Babylon, the beast and false prophet, the dragon, Gog and Magog, death and hell, casting them into the lake of fire.[2126]

(g) *Liberando*: by full and final delivering, freeing and setting his church and people at complete liberty from all evils and enemies forever.[2127]

(ii) **His special mediatory kingdom over his church and people**, Christ administers and executes principally by these and such like kingly actions, namely:

(a) *In this present world*:

(1) By pouring forth his Spirit more plentifully and efficaciously upon all flesh than ever formerly, for the actual and effectual application of all the

---

[2122] Revelation 14:1-6
[2123] Acts 8:1, 3-5, etc
[2124] Acts 9 throughout
[2125] Revelation 20:4-6
[2126] Luke 18:7-9, Daniel 2:31-46, Revelation 17-20; 1 Corinthians 15:25
[2127] Revelation 21:1-4

merits and benefits of Christ to his elect (John 7:38-39, Act. 2:2-4, 33, John 16:7-16).

(2) By giving gifts to men, namely: by sending, illuminating, qualifying, and conserving a New Covenant ministry to his church both extraordinary and ordinary: extraordinary, as apostles, prophets, evangelists, for a time for the laying of the foundation of the New Testament church; ordinary, as pastors and teachers until the end of the world for the further edification and perfecting of the church until Christ's second coming (Ephesians 4:8-13, Matthew 28:19-20, Mark 16:15, Acts 1:2-3, 8), to which may be referred *elders*, who are to assist in church-governing (1 Timothy 5:17; 1 Corinthians 12:28), and deacons, who are to take care of the church's public goods, and minister to the the necessities of the sick and poor members of the church, called {*helps*} (Acts 6:1-9; 1 Corinthians 12:28, Philippians 1:1).

(3) By instituting his New Covenant ordinances which are to be managed and administered by these his officers, as preaching the gospel to all nations, for making them disciples (Mark 16:15, Matthew 28:18-20); dispensing of baptism and the Lord's supper (Matthew 28:18-19, Mark 16:16, Matthew 26:26-31; 1 Corinthians 11:23, etc.); public prayers for all sorts (1 Timothy 2:1-3, Acts 6:4); public praises and singing of psalms, etc. (James 5:13, Colossians 3:16, Hebrews 13:15, Ephesians 5:18-20); censures (Matthew 18:15-22; 1 Corinthians 5 throughout; 2 Corinthians 2:6-12); and sanctification of the Lord's day, etc., the first day of the week (Matthew 28:1, 2-7, Revelation 1:10, Acts 20:7; 1 Corinthians 16:1-2).

(4) By gathering and constituting his New Testament church out of all nations of the world, by the ministry of the word and sacraments (Matthew 28:18-19, Mark 16:15, Acts 26:17-18, Acts 2:38-41).

(5) By building up, confirming and perfecting of the church gathered, and of the saints called, and all his ordinances and officers *till they all come to be one complete man in Christ, to the measure of the stature of the fullness of Christ* (Ephesians 4:10-13, Acts 14:22).

(b) *At the end of this world*:

(1) By descending most gloriously from heaven with a shout, with the voice of the arch-angel and trumpet of God, in his own, and his Father's glory, with all his holy angels attending him.[2128]

(2) By raising the dead, and changing of the living, in a moment, in the twinkling of an eye, at the sound of the last trumpet.[2129]

(3) By catching up all the elect to meet the Lord in the air (1 Thessalonians 4:16-18).

(4) By gathering together all nations, raised and changed, before Christ, by his angels, from all the four winds: and setting them before his tribunal: the sheep on his right hand; the goats on his left.[2130]

(5) By pronouncing his last and final sentence of salvation upon the sheep, and damnation upon the goats forevermore.[2131]

(6) By purifying the whole creation, heaven and earth with fire: that there may be a new heaven and new earth wherein dwells righteousness. *Behold I make all things new; said he that sat upon the throne.*[2132]

(c) *In the world to come*:

(1) By distributing everlasting rewards to all according to their works (Romans 2:6-17, Jude 6), taking his elect unto himself, that they may be ever with the Lord, to behold his glory, and enjoy him fully and immediately face to face, as their supreme happiness to all eternity;[2133] but casting all reprobates from his presence, into the lake of fire and brimstone, which is the second death, there to be punished and tormented forever and ever.[2134]

(2) By reigning immediately, as God-man, head and king of his elect, in and over his church triumphant in glory forever and ever, they also reigning

---

[2128] 1 Thessalonians 4:16; 1 Corinthians 15:52, Matthew 24:30 & 25:31, Mark 8:38

[2129] 1 Thessalonians 4:16-17; 1 Corinthians 15:51, etc.

[2130] Matthew 24:31 & 25:31-33

[2131] Matthew 25:34-46

[2132] 2 Peter 3:10-13, Revelation 21:1, 5

[2133] John 14:3; 1 Thessalonians 4:17, John 17:24; 1 John 3:1-2, Philippians 3:20-21

[2134] Matthew 25:30, 41, etc, 46, Revelation 20:10, 14-15

with him forever and ever (Luke 1:32-33, Hebrews 7:1, 21, 25, Matthew 25:34, 46, Revelation 22:5, Romans 8:17; 2 Timothy 2:12). For, although Jesus Christ shall give up his mediatory kingdom to the Father at last when he shall have put down all rule, and all authority, and power (1 Corinthians 15:24-29), yet this is to be understood, only in regard to the accidents or manner of his mediatory kingdom's administration – he shall not rule them anymore by his Word preached, sacraments dispensed, donation of his spirit, etc as he does now (1 Corinthians 13:8), but in regard to the substance and essence of his kingdom, that shall still remain; he shall be head and king of his church forever and ever, even then when God shall be all in all (Hebrews 1:8-9).

{5} *The benefits of Christ's kingdom are many and excellent.*
But these are in effect laid down in what has been already spoken, especially touching his actual execution or administration of his kingdom there see.

{6} *The continuance of Christ's royal office.*
Christ's essential or natural kingdom which belongs to him as God equally with Father and Holy Spirit, is absolutely eternal, without beginning or end. Christ's mediatory kingdom, for the essence and substance of it, shall never end, but continue forever and ever;[2135] otherwise the church would be deprived at last of her head, and Christ would cease to be Mediator, etc., which things cannot stand with the church's eternal happiness. But for the manner of his royal government, and administration of his kingly office, so it shall cease;[2136] he shall rule his church no more, after the last judgment, by his Word, sacraments, censures, and such ordinances as he rules her now by; but more immediately, gloriously, triumphantly, ineffably.

[2135] Luke 1:32-33, Hebrews 1:8-9, Psalm 45:6-7
[2136] 1 Corinthians 15:24-29

By all this that has been said, the nature of Christ's prophecy, priest-hood and kingship, wherein he actually exercises his mediatorship is in some measure represented.

Section 3

What are those two states of Christ's humiliation and exaltation, wherein he, as prophet, priest and king, thus executes his mediation between God and man?

This will best be discovered, by unfolding the several steps or degrees of Christ's humiliation and exaltation severally.

(1) **Christ's state of humiliation, was that his exceeding abased condition, wherein, for his elect, he for a time emptied himself of his glory, taking upon him the form of a servant** (Philippians 2:6-8).

This he did especially in his conception, birth, life, death, burial, and continuance in the state of the dead under the dominion of death for three days.

[1] *In his conception*, Christ deeply humbled himself. Forasmuch as: {1} being the eternal Son of God, he assumed the true human nature perfectly, into personal union with his divine nature in fullness of time. Oh what self-abasure! The maker of all things, was made man, made of a woman, etc.[2137] God was manifest in the flesh, and so veiled in that manifestation. {2} He was conceived by a virgin, of David's race, but of a very low, mean, poor and despicable condition for the outward man.[2138]

[2] *In his birth*, Christ deeply abased himself, for: {1} he that from eternity to eternity was the living God, was in fullness of time born of a woman.[2139] He that gives life and breath to all his living and breathing creatures, took life and breath of a woman.[2140] {2} His birth was attended with

---

[2137] Galatians 4:4, John 1:14; 1 Timothy 3:16
[2138] Luke 1:48, Matthew 13:55, Mark 6:3
[2139] Psalm 90:2, Matthew 1:25
[2140] Acts 17:25

many abasing circumstances. As, he was born, not at his mother's home, but in her absence from home (Luke 2:4-6); not in a palace, but in a common inn; not in the guest-chamber, but in the very stable, there being no room for such poor guests as they in the inn (Luke 2:6-7). He that is clothed with bright glory and majesty, is wrapped in swaddling clothes;[2141] he that laid the foundations of heaven and earth, is laid in a manger (Luke 2:6-7).[2142] Oh, how extremely was he debased below the ordinary sort of men! Oh, how highly is human nature advanced, even above the angels! Oh why should sinful dust and ashes, disdain or be ashamed of mean birth and parentage, when the undefiled Savior of sinners, became thus mean in his conception and nativity!

[3] *In his life*, Christ greatly humbled himself, for: {1} he was made under the law, to fulfill it, and he did exactly fulfill it, though himself was the lawgiver;[2143] {2} he was exposed to the violent, and subtle temptations of Satan, who holds Satan in his chains of darkness to the judgment of the great day;[2144] {3} he was exercised with much course entertainment, and many vile indignities of the world. What hatred, opposition, contempt, reproach, contradiction of sinners, conspiracies, treacheries, and persecutions did he undergo (John 15:18, Matthew 13:55, Mark 6:3, Psalm 22:6, Hebrews 12:2-3, Mark 3:21, Matthew 12:10, 24 & 22:15. & 26:14-15, 16:4). He had much experimental sense of human infirmities, and afflictions:[2145] both common to human nature, as hunger, thirst, weakness, faintness, etc,[2146] and peculiar to his own low estate wherein he had debased himself.[2147] Yea, his whole life, as it were from his manger to his cross, was a continued passion. Oh! Why should sinners think they should live without afflictions in the world, when Jesus

---

[2141] Psalm 104:1-2
[2142] Psalm 104:3, 5
[2143] Galatians 4:4, Matthew 5:17, Galatians 3:19, Isaiah 33:22
[2144] Matthew 4:1-12, Luke 4:1-14, Jude 6
[2145] Hebrews 2:17-18 & 4:15
[2146] Matthew 4:2, John 4:6-7, Luke 23:43-44
[2147] Isaiah 53:2, etc.

Christ, God's only Son, without sin, could not pass through the world, without many sorrows?

[4] *In his death*, Christ yet humbled himself more deeply, for: {1} he was villainously betrayed by one of his twelve apostles, Judas.[2148] {2} He was sadly deserted by all his disciples, when he was apprehended.[2149] {3} He was thrice most shamefully denied by Peter, who a little before professed he would die rather than he would deny him.[2150] {4} He was most odiously abused by false witnesses, by spitting in his face, blindfolding, mocking, buffeting, etc.[2151] {5} He was most causelessly, and unjustly condemned by Pilate.[2152] {6} He was disgracefully handled after he was condemned, by the barbarous soldiers.[2153] {7} He was ignominiously crucified, between two notorious thieves, and in that filthy stinking place, without the gate of the city, called Golgotha, to fix the deeper infamy upon him.[2154] {8} As before his condemnation in the garden of Gethsemane he was in so deep an agony, that he was sorrowful to the death, and sweat great drops of blood falling down to the ground;[2155] so whilst he was hanging on the cross, the wrath of God was so heavy upon him for our sins, that he cried out: *My God my God, why hast thou forsaken me?*[2156] {9} Whilst he hanged upon the cross he was reviled, reproached and mocked most blasphemously by the bystanders, yea by the very thieves that were crucified with him. {10} He yielded up his life an offering for our sins, by enduring a painful, shameful, cruel, and cursed death upon the cross; being made a curse, to redeem us from the curse.[2157] Thus, the light of the world was extinguished, the health of the world was wounded, the life of the world was put to death

---

[2148] Matthew 26:14-16 & 27:4
[2149] Matthew 26:56
[2150] Matthew 26:69, etc.
[2151] Matthew 26:59-69
[2152] Matthew 27:11-27
[2153] Matthew 27:27-35
[2154] John 19:17-18, Matthew 27:33
[2155] Luke 22:41-45, Matthew 26:38
[2156] Matthew 27:46
[2157] Isaiah 53:10, Hebrews 9:14, Philippians 2:8, Hebrews 12:2, Galatians 3:13-14

and murdered, and the Savior of the world, who knew no sin, was made sin, for sinners.

[5] *In his burial*, Christ was yet further abased: {1} In that, he who has the keys of hell and death, of grave and death, was laid dead in the grave;[2158] he who should see no corruption, was buried in the pit of corruption, as the grave is styled (Isaiah 38:17).[2159] {2} In that, he was buried meanly and obscurely without funeral, pomp or solemnity. Not by his own kindred, but by two strangers, yet disciples of Christ: Joseph of Arimathea and Nicodemus.[2160] Not with heralds, escutcheons, hearse or coffin; but in a winding sheet of linen with spices, as the Jews' manner is to bury.[2161] Not in any burial-place of his ancestors: but in the new sepulcher of Joseph of Arimathea which he had in his garden, near the place of his execution.[2162] As he had not where to lay his head, while he was alive, so had he not where to lay his body, when he was dead;[2163] although he was Lord of all, and heir of all things.[2164] Oh, why should sinners stand so much upon pompous funerals, when Jesus Christ the sinner's Savior was so obscurely interred!

[6] *In his continuance in the state of the dead, and under the dominion of death for three days current [running]*.[2165] Christ was also yet further abased, for: {1} So long Christ remained as a bondman and prisoner of death for our sins, as if he himself had been a sinner; so long the power, pains, or cords of death did hold him fast.[2166] {2} So long he was a companion of the dead, in the land of darkness and forgetfulness. {3} So long, Satan, sin, death, and the world, seemed to have gotten the victory of him, and to have insulted

---

[2158] Revelation 1:18; 1 Corinthians 15:14, Acts 13:29
[2159] Psalm 16:8, etc, Acts 2:25-29
[2160] John 19:38-40
[2161] John 19:39-40
[2162] John 19:40-41, Matthew 27:57-62
[2163] Luke 9:58
[2164] Acts 10:36, Hebrews 1:2
[2165] Matthew 12:40
[2166] Acts 2:24-27, 31 with Psalm 16:10, Romans 6:9

over him.[2167] This now was his last and lowest degree of abasement, which some think is expressed in the apostles' creed, by those words {*he descended into hell*} which, being so understood, do set forth very clearly, and orderly, the series and degree of Christ's humiliation, beyond any other interpretation given thereof.[2168]

[2167] Hebrews 2:14, Romans 6:23, 9, Matthew 27:62 to the end

[2168] This article {*He descended into hell*} is not anciently found in the Apostles' Creed. For several of the ancient writers in their recitals, and expositions of this creed, do presently pass from the burial, to the resurrection of Christ, not once mentioning his descending into hell, as:
(1) Irenaeus. *Against Heresies*, lib. 1. cap. 2. p. 50, 51, 52. Col. 1596;
(2) Tertullian. *De Virginibus Velandis*, lib. cap. p. 188. Franck. 1597. & lib. *Adversus Praxean, De Trinitat*. cap. 2. p. 494.
(3) Origen. Libr. Περὶ Ἀρχῶν [*On The First Principles*], ad initium.
(4) Augustine, he expounds the Apostles' Creed often: As, [1] In lib. *De Fide & Symbole*, pp. 139-151. Tom. 3. Basil. 1569. [2] In lib. 4. *De Symbolo ad Catechumenos*. p. 1094. ad 1139. Tom. 9. [3] *De Tempore*, Serm. 123. pag. 869, &c. Tom. 10. And [4] Serm. 125. pag. 872, &c. ibid. In all these places Augustine – expounding the Apostles' Creed – mentions not the article of Christ's descent into hell at all. (So that Bellarmine takes it for granted that Augustine mentions not this part of the creed at all, though he expound the creed five times. Bellarmine *De Christi Anima* lib. 4. cap. 6. Tom. 13. But Bellarmine is much mistaken, for though Augustine in those forecited places does not mentions it, yet in three other places he expresseth it plainly, namely: [1] De Tempore, Serm. 115. De traditione Symboli, p. 849. Tom. 10. He – showing what every apostle contributed to the making up of the Creed – says: "Thomas ait Descendit ad inferna, tertio die Resurrexit a mortuis." [2] *De Expositione Symboli ad Cempetentes*. Sermon 131. *De Tempore* p. 887, 888. Tom. 10. Reciting the whole Creed, he says, "Descendit ad inferna," etc. [3] *De expositione Symboli*. Sermon *De Temp*. 181. pag. 989. Expressing that article {Descendit ad inferna} he expounds it, but very unsoundly. Had Ballarmine observed his words, he would greatly have triumphed in them.)
(5) Ruffinus Aquileiensis, presbyter, expounding the Apostles' Creed, mentions and expounds this article, but adds: "That it is not in the creed of the Roman church, nor of the eastern churches." Apud Cyprian. Tom. 3. p. 570. Sect. 20. Preux 1593. & apud Hieronim. Tom. 4. pag. 101. ad 116. Basil 1553.
(6) This article is not in the Nicene Creed.
But this article of Christ's descent into hell is very generally received in after times, and found in the recitals and expositions of the Apostles' Creed, both with Protestants and papists. Yet there is very much discord among writers about the sense of this clause, {*He descended into hell*}.
[1] Some thus: {*He descended into hell*}, namely: "He descended into the grave." And (as Beza, in his annotation on Acts 2:27, notes): to descend into hell, properly signifies to be buried; translatitiously [metaphorically], to be so oppressed with extreme dolours of soul or body, as to be nigh unto utter destruction, as Genesis 37:35 & 42:38; 1 Samuel 2:6, Psalm 18:6 & 49:15, and elsewhere frequently. But this interpretation is rejected: {1} Partly,

because it brings in a needless tautology into the compendious creed. {2} Partly, because this darker expression is made exegetical or explanatory to the former (and buried) which is far clearer, and that is absurd.

[2] Some thus, {*He descended into hell*}, namely: his soul descended into the place of the damned, to deliver the fathers from the skirts of hell, Limbo Patrum. So the papists. Yet herein they differ among themselves: {1} Some of them holding that his soul descended thither not in its substance, but in certain effects wrought there by it. So Durandus in 3. D. 22. Q. 3. whom Bellarmine refutes, lib. 4. *De Christi Anim.* cap. 15. Tom. 1. {2} Some that Christ's soul in substance went really and locally into hell. So Bellarmine, de Christ. Anima. lib. 4. cap. 10-16. Tom. 1. But this Popish interpretation is unsound: (i) Partly, because that Limbus Patrum, and Christs fetching them thence, is a mear fable, without any solid ground of Scripture. As John Calvin in *The Institutes of the Christian Religion* 2.12.9. (ii) Partly, because Christ dying, and satisfying for our sins, his soul went that day into Paradise: as Adam sinning; was that day cast out of paradise, (Luke 23:43, Genesis 3:23-24). Perkins *on the Creed*, p. 232. vol. 1 (London, 1626). And his soul could not be in two places at once: Though Bellarmine be forced to grant this absurdity, saying: "Nec enim Deo impossibile er at efficere, ut Christi Anima simul, esset in duobus locis." Bellarmine *De Christi Anim.* lib. 4. cap. 15. sub fin. Tom. 1. (iii) Partly, Because this descent of Christ's soul was altogether needless, and to no end. What need was there of it, or to what end? Not to suffer in hell: For that was finished on the cross (John 18:30), not to redeem or rescue the fathers out of hell: For, the elect were never there; and redemption from hell was wrought by Christ's death (Hebrews 9:12; 1 Thessalonians 1:10), not to triumph there over the devils, etc. For Christ triumphed over them, on his cross (Hebrews 2:14-15, Colossians 2:14-15, and by his ascension: Ephesians 4:8-11).

[3] Some thus, {*He descended into hell*}, namely: he endured hellish torments of loss, and sense in his soul. As in his agony, and especially on the cross. And these sufferings of his soul, are in this phrase of descending into hell, set after all his bodily sufferings, for the more distinctness of order. This interpretation is embraced by many learned and godly writers: as Calvin in Institut. lib. 2. cap. 16. Sect. 10, 11, 12. Ursinus & Paraeus, in Vrsin. Catechet. Explicat. Quest. 44. Kekerm. in System. Theolog. lib. 3. cap. 4. With many others. And extreme sorrows or sufferings are in Scripture phrase sometimes styled, sorrows of hell, etc. Psal. 18. 5. and 116. 3. 1 Sam. 2. 6. and this exposition is pious. But yet seems not so suitable here: 1. Partly, because those hellish sufferings in Christ's soul were implied in the former expressions, suffered under Pontius Pilate, was crucified, dead and buried. For they were not any ordinary sufferings and death which Christ endured, but cursed and extreme, and having deepest impressions of God's wrath upon them, to his soul for our sins (Galatians 3:13). Therefore here to mention these soul-sufferings of Christ again, would bring in a kind of tautology. 2. Partly, because the phrase of his descending into hell seems to point out some degree of his humiliation between his burial and resurrection, neither expressed nor implied before, namely: his bondage under death's power and dominion for a time.

[4] Some thus, {*He descended into hell*}, namely: when he was dead and buried, he was held captive in the grave, and lay in bondage under death for the space of three days. Thus Mr. William Perkins, in his *Exposition of the Creed*, pag. 233. vol. 1. (London, 1626). And the Assembly of Divines in their larger Catechism, as also in the lesser Catechism and Confession of Faith. This interpretation I prefer before the rest: {1} Partly, because it sets forth a degree of Christ's humiliation after his burial, and before his resurrection, which is nowhere else expressed, or necessarily implied in the Creed: and this degree is also pointed

(2) **Christ's state of exaltation**, is that his highly exalted condition after his abasement, wherein he has obtained a name above every name, in heaven, earth, and under the earth;[2169] being set at God's right hand, in a heavenly place, far above all principality, and power, and might, and dominion, and every name that is named, not only in this world, but also in that which is to come; God having put all things under his feet, and given him to be the head over all things to the church.[2170] This his exaltation more peculiarly consists in his reviving, resurrection from the dead, ascension into heaven, sitting down at God's right hand, and his coming again to judge the world at the last day.

[1] *In his reviving*, Christ was exalted very much, for: {1} he was restored from death to life; never to die more, but to be alive forevermore.[2171] {2} He revived, and quickened himself by the Spirit, namely: by the power of his own God-head: before he should see corruption.[2172] {3} He so quickened himself, as really to unite his soul to his own numerical body that was crucified and buried, retaining all the essential properties thereof, yet the mortality, and all other infirmities thereof being utterly removed forever (John 20:27, Romans

---

out in Acts 2:24, namely: his bondage under death, and grave three days. {2} Partly, because this most excellently agrees with the series and order of the creed, setting last in order this his last and lowest degree of humiliation as it befell Jesus Christ. These things may a little clear that dark, but useful clause in that excellent and very ancient creed, called the Apostles' Creed, (i) More conjecturally, by some of the ancients, who say that it is a tradition of the elders, that after Christ's ascension, when the Holy Ghost fell upon the apostles, enabling them to speak all manner of languages, that they might preach the gospel to all nations, before they departed to this work, one from another, they jointly agreed upon a rule of faith or sum of true doctrine, which they would preach, and so being altogether, and full of the Holy Ghost, they composed this rule of faith, to be given to believers. See Augustine. Serm. 181. *De Tempore*. Tom. 10. & *Exposit. Symbol*. per Ruffinum apud Cyprian. Tom. 3. p. 564, &c. (ii) More certainly, by some modern writers: who count it an Apostolic Creed, only because it is very consonant to the apostolic doctrine recorded by them in the New Testament.

[2169] Philippians 2:9-11
[2170] Ephesians 1:20-22
[2171] Romans 6:9, Revelation 1:18
[2172] 1 Peter 3:18, Psalm 16:10, Acts 13:37

6:9, Acts 13:34, Revelation 1:18). Christ that quickened his own dead body, can easily quicken our dead souls and bodies.

[2] *In his resurrection from the dead*, Christ was exalted more, for:

{1} Christ rose from the dead the third day, by the power of his own God-head, never more to return to the pit of corruption.[2173]

{2} Christ by rising thus from the dead, mightily and convincingly declared himself: (i) to be the Son of God (Romans 1:4); (ii) to have satisfied divine justice to the uttermost, for the sins of all his elect (Romans 8:34); (iii) to have purged away their sins forever, by his death and blood, once offered (Hebrews 10:10-15); (iv) to have conquered death and grave fully, and him that had the power of death, the devil (Acts 2:24, Hebrews 2:14-15) – and much more, to have defeated the malicious Jews that sealed and watched his sepulcher (Matthew 27:62 to the end & 28:1-3, etc.); (v) to be Lord of quick and dead (Romans 14:8-9).

{3} Christ rose from the dead, not in a private, but in a public capacity; as a second Adam, as the first fruits of them that slept (1 Corinthians 15:20-23, 45-50), as the head of the church (Ephesians 1:20, 22-23, Colossians 1:18), and therefore every way for our benefit, namely: (i) for our spiritual quickening by grace and sanctification, who were naturally dead in trespasses and sins, Ephesians 2:1, 5, 6. Colossians 2:12; (ii) For our justification (Romans 4:25). (iii) For the effecting and assuring us of our corporal resurrection at last (1 Corinthians 15:12-24).[2174] (iv) For consolatory demonstration to us of Christ's full and final subduing of all his and our enemies (1 Corinthians 15:20-29, Ephesians 1:20-23). (v) For certifying or assuring us that Christ shall be judge of quick and dead (Acts 17:30-31).

{4} Christ risen from the dead:

(i) Did manifest himself for forty days to his disciples, and to many witnesses, evidencing by many infallible proofs that he was alive after his

---

[2173] 1 Corinthians 15:4, Luke 24:21, etc, Matthew 28:1-7, John 10:18, Acts 13:34

[2174] "Fiducia Christianorum, Resurrectio mortuorum." Tertull. *De Resur. Carnis*. lib. c. 1.

passion,[2175] as (a) to Mary Magdalene, at the sepulcher, out of whom he had cast seven devil (Mark 16:9-11, John 20:14-19); (b) to two of the disciples (whereof Simon was one) as they went into the country the same day towards Emmaus, (Mark 16:12-13, Luke 24:13-36; 1 Corinthians 15:5); (c) to the eleven the same day at even, Thomas not being with the (John 20:19-26, Mark 16:14, etc); (d) after that he was seen of above five hundred brethren at once (1 Corinthians 15:6); (e) after that to James (1 Corinthians 15:7); (f) then of all the apostles (1 Corinthians 15:7), Thomas being with them (John 20:26-30); (g) after these things to the disciples at the sea of Tiberius (John 21:1-25); (h) to his apostles immediately before his ascension, showing them his hands and feet, bidding them to handle him, and eating with them a piece of a broiled fish, and of a honeycomb, etc. (Luke 24:36 to the end, Acts 1:2-12); (i) to the apostle Paul last of all (1 Corinthians 15:8).

(ii) Did give commandments to the apostles, speaking of the things pertaining to the kingdom of God (Acts 1:2-3).

(iii) Opened the Scriptures, and their understandings (Luke 24:44-49).

(iv) Gave them commission to preach the gospel, and dispense the sacraments to all nations, annexing many encouraging promises (Mark 16:14-19).

(v) Directed them to tarry at Jerusalem until the promised spirit was shed forth upon them (Luke 24:49, Acts 1:4-9).

(vi) Lifted up his hands and blessed them, and as he blessed them, he was taken up into heaven (Luke 24:50-52, Acts 1:9-11). Thus he was exceedingly exalted by his resurrection from the dead.

[3] *In his ascending visibly up on high into heaven*, yea far above all heavens, forty days after his resurrection,[2176] Christ was yet further exalted, for:

[2175] Acts 1:3; 1 Corinthians 15:4-9
[2176] Luke 24:50-52, Acts 1:3, 9-11, Ephesians 4:10

(i) Christ ascended into heaven in a public capacity, for us, as our head and forerunner, and great high priest entering within the veil (Hebrews 6:19-20).

(ii) Christ ascending, did triumphantly lead captivity captive; as it were chained all his and our conquered enemies to his triumphant chariot, (Ephesians 4:8, Psalm 68:18).

(iii) Christ ascended into heaven for high and excellent ends, as: (a) that he might be both Lord and Christ (Acts 2:34-36); (b) to receive gifts for men, and to give them, (Ephesians 4:8, 11, etc); (c) to prepare a place in heaven for us (John 14:3); (d) to allure and draw up our hearts and earnest affections after him into heaven (Colossians 3:1-2, Philippians 3:20); (e) to fill all things (Ephesians 4:8); (f) to sit down at God's right hand, enthroned in highest majesty and glory (Hebrews 1:3 & 8:1).

(iv) In his session at God's right-hand, Christ was most gloriously exalted. But of this formerly.[2177]

(v) Finally, in his coming at last to judge the whole world, Christ shall be most visibly and openly exalted before men and angels. But of this also heretofore.[2178]

These are the two states of Christ: his humiliation, and exaltation, wherein he most mysteriously executes his prophetical, priestly, and kingly mediation for his church.

Thus of the third aphorism.

[2177] In Section 2, *Of His Kingly Office*, 2: His Inauguration.
[2178] In Section 3.2, at the latter end.

Aphorism 4

Of Christ's establishment of his New Covenant, and application of it to God's elect: that Jesus Christ, by virtue of this his prophetical, priestly and kingly mediation, Surety-ship and Testator-ship, has established his New Covenant forever; and is continually bringing all those whom the father hath given him into this New Covenant with God, to partake all the mercies, and perform all the duties thereof.

In this aphorism are two things especially considerable, namely: (1) Christ's establishment of his New Covenant, and (2) Christ's bringing of persons into this Covenant with himself. *That* is his dedication of it, to make it of force in itself; *this* is his application of it, to make it of force and efficacy unto us. Without *that*, there would have been no New Covenant; without *this*, we have no benefit by the New Covenant.

(1) **Jesus Christ, as Mediator, Surety and Testator, has established his New Covenant forever.**

[1] *As Mediator.* By virtue of his mediation, Christ has established the New Covenant in various ways, namely:

{1} By his prophecy, revealing it, and founding it upon better promises than those of the Old Covenant: *he is mediator of a better covenant, which was established upon better promises.*[2179]

{2} By his priesthood: (i) dedicating, and by solemn sanction confirming it at first by sacrifice and blood, by the best blood that ever was shed,[2180] even his

---

[2179] Hebrews 8:6
[2180] Hebrews 9:14-15, Matthew 26:28

own most precious blood, the blood of God;[2181] and by the best sacrifice that ever was offered up to God, even the sacrifice of himself, by the eternal Spirit.[2182] The Old Covenant was dedicated with blood and sacrifices, but alas those were but shadows: no blood is like Christ's blood, no sacrifice like Christ's sacrifice, whereby he dedicated his New Covenant forever.[2183] This is *the blood of the everlasting covenant*.[2184] The virtue of this blood shall last forever, and so the vigor of this New Covenant shall last ever. Christ can never die any more, nor shall the New Covenant in his blood ever die, for the substance of it; nor shall any other covenant succeed it, for the administration of it, so long as the world shall continue. (ii) Ratifying it ever since his ascension into heaven, by his continual appearing there in the presence of God for us, representing the merits of his obedience and blood, so making continual intercession for us: that all the New Covenant benefits may be eternally ours.[2185]

{3} By his kingship and supreme authority over all in heaven and earth;[2186] authoritatively annexing (i) federal tokens to this his New Covenant: baptism and the Lord's supper;[2187] (ii) authoritatively requiring the publication of this New Covenant to all nations;[2188] (iii) and powerfully bestowing the great blessing of the New Covenant – the Holy Spirit and his influences – both upon his ministers and on other believers (Acts 2:1-2, etc. & 10:44, etc), as a pregnant seal both of the New Covenants authority and efficacy.

[2] *As Surety*. By virtue of his Surety-ship, Christ has established his New Covenant: *and in as much as not without an oath, he was made priest (for those priests were made without an oath: but this with an oath, by him that said unto him, the Lord sware and will not repent, thou art a priest forever after the*

[2181] Hebrews 9:14, Acts 20:28
[2182] Hebrews 9:14 & 10:10, 14
[2183] Exodus 24 with Hebrews 9:18-19, etc.
[2184] Hebrews 13:20
[2185] Hebrews 9:23-24, Romans 8:34; 1 John 2:1-2, Hebrews 7:25-27
[2186] Matthew 28:19
[2187] Matthew 26:26, etc.
[2188] Matthew 28:18-20

order of Melchizedek), by so much was Jesus made a surety of a better covenant.[2189] Hence:

{1} Christ is priest after the order of Melchizedek forever.

{2} Christ is made priest by God's oath which cannot be changed, of which God will not repent.

{3} Therefore the New Covenant, wherein he exercises this his Melchizedekian and unchangeable priesthood, is a better Covenant than the Old (the word διαθηκης should be here translated *covenant* rather than *testament*, because properly a Surety has no place in testaments).

{4} And of this better New Covenant Christ is so priest and Mediator, that he is Surety, to confirm establish and make good the covenant. The term εγγυος, {*surety*}, I have already explained in this chapter. Jesus Christ, as Surety establishes this New Covenant especially three ways, namely:

(i) *Solvendo*: by paying our debt, enduring a cursed death upon the cross under the wrath of God for our sins, against God's law, and in our stead,[2190] as has been manifested.[2191] Christ hath redeemed us from the curse, being made a curse for us. When the Surety has discharged the debt, the principal is set at liberty from it, it can, in justice, be exacted no more of him: Christ having satisfied for our sins, God requires no more satisfaction from us, if we will accept and apply Christ's satisfaction to ourselves.

(ii) *Servando*: by keeping and fulfilling God's law and Covenant of Works most exactly for us, who in ourselves are utterly unable to keep it.[2192] By whose obedience, as well as by his satisfaction, we are made righteous (Romans 5:9, 19).

[2189] Hebrews 7:20-22, Psalm 110:4
[2190] Isaiah 53:4-6, etc; 2 Corinthians 5:21; 1 Peter 2:24, Galatians 3:13-14
[2191] In this Chapter, Aphorism 3, *Of His Priesthood*
[2192] Galatians 4:4, Matthew 5:17-18, Romans 5:19

(iii) *Spondendo*: By promising and undertaking for us, as our sponsor and fidejussor,[2193] that we shall in uprightness keep the law of God.[2194] Now, Jesus Christ having as our Surety fully satisfied God's justice for our breach of the law, fulfilled the law perfectly for us who could not keep the law, and enabled us by his spirit and grace to keep it in uprightness, the law and justice of God have now nothing against us, that may hinder our acceptance with God in Christ, according to this New Covenant. So Christ, as our Surety establishes this New Covenant, for us, and to us.

[3] *As Testator*. By virtue of his Testator-ship, Christ establishes also this New Covenant, as his last will and testament by his death.[2195] Whilst a testator lives, he has power and liberty of altering his testament as often as he pleases, hence no man's testament is of force while the testator lives, but after he is dead; then none may add thereto, or take thence from, or alter therein. Thus Christ is Testator: his New Covenant is his New Testament, confirmed by his death, beyond all revocation, addition, detraction, or alteration forever.[2196] It can no more be disannulled, than Christ can be brought down again from the right hand of God to die a second time.

Thus Christ as Mediator, Surety and Testator has established his New Covenant.

(2) Jesus Christ our Mediator, Surety, and Testator – having established his New Covenant forever, especially by his blood of the everlasting Covenant[2197] – in the next place he proceeds to apply this New Covenant, and to bring men into this Covenant with God in Christ, by vocation or calling them thereinto.

[2193] One under Roman and civil law who enters into or authorizes a fidejussion, a guarantor, or surety.
[https://www.merriam-webster.com/dictionary/fidejussor]
<Accessed 3/27/2024>
[2194] Romans 8:34, Ephesians 3:10
[2195] Hebrews 9:14-17, etc.
[2196] Matthew 26:28, Mark 14:14, Luke 22:20; 1 Corinthians 11:25
[2197] Hebrews 13:20

Here consider: [1] that Christ brings men into this New Covenant, and applies it to them, by vocation, or calling them; [2] Wherein the nature of his vocation consists.

[1] *That Jesus Christ's our Mediator, Surety, and Testator, brings men into this New Covenant with God, by calling them*, is evident:

{1} **By Scripture testimony**, for:

(i) Peter's hearers are exhorted to repent and be baptized (baptism being the New Covenant token) because the promise (namely: the famous promise made to Abraham, Isaac, and Jacob of blessing all nations in their seed, Christ) belonged not only to the Jews and their seed, but also to all the Gentiles afar off, who should be called by God, and to their seed – but the Gentiles must be first called, and then partake of the promise: *Repent and be baptized – for the promise is unto you, and to your children, and to all that are afar off, even as many as the Lord our God shall call.*[2198] So, though the New Covenant be extended to all nations, yet they must be brought into it, and have it actually applied to them by calling.

(ii) Paul tells the Hebrews that Christ, by his death, redeemed not only us under the New, but the fathers also under the Old Testament, from transgression: but the benefit of this redemption, and the Covenant, are applied unto the called only. *And for this cause he is the mediator of the new covenant, that by means of death, for the redemption of the transgressions which were under the first testament, they which are called might receive the promise of eternal inheritance.*[2199]

{2} **By Christ's mission of, and commission to his apostles**, for preaching the gospel and New Covenant doctrine to all nations in the world, that they might be brought into this New Covenant, upon embracing whereof they were to be marked with baptism the first New Covenant token (Matthew 28:18-20, Mark 16:15-16, etc., Acts 26:17, 18), which the apostles did execute

---

[2198] Acts 2:38-39
[2199] Hebrews 9:15

accordingly, beginning at Jerusalem (Luke 24:46-47, Acts 2:14-37, 41, etc. & 10:34 to the end & 13:46, etc).

{3} **By the constant order of Christ's proceedings**, in making people partakers of his New Covenant blessings, which is:

(i) First, by making them partakers of Christ, the fountain of all those blessings, by union to him (1 Peter 2:3-5, 9-10, Ephesians 4:12). *God is faithful, by whom ye are called into the fellowship of his Son Jesus Christ our Lord* (1 Corinthians 1:9). Hence they are said to be *in Christ* (Philippians 3:9; 1 John 3:24; 2 Corinthians 5:17; 1 Thessalonians 1:1 & 2 Thessalonians 1:1). Yea we are called {*Christ*} (1 Corinthians 12:12). The union between him and us is so close and intimate (Ephesians 5:30).

(ii) Secondly, by making them in Christ partakers of all the covenanted benefits and blessings of Christ: as all communion, so this with Christ, is founded upon, and results from union. *Who hath blessed us with all spiritual blessings in heavenly things in Christ.*[2200] – *All things are yours, whether Paul, or Apollo, or Cephas, or the world, or life, or death, or things present, or things to come, all are yours, and ye are Christ's.*[2201] And usually the covenant blessings of Christ, are said to be ours, in reference to our union to Christ, or being in Christ, as redemption (Ephesians 1:7-9), reconciliation (2 Corinthians 5:19), adoption (John 1:11-12, justification (Philippians 3:9), sanctification (1 Corinthians 1:2), inheritance (Acts 26:18, Ephesians 1:11), and all things (Romans 8:32, etc.) Thus all our communion with Christ in his redemption, reconciliation, Son-ship, righteousness, etc., flows from our union to Christ, and our union to Christ is effected by our vocation or calling to him (1 Corinthians 1:9).

Now, when by calling we are united to Christ, and by union to Christ have communion with him in all his New Covenant benefits promised, by this

---

[2200] Ephesians 1:3
[2201] 1 Corinthians 3:21-23

calling we are actually brought into this New Covenant with God, and instated therein.

[2] *Wherein the nature of this vocation or calling consists, by which Jesus Christ brings men into his New Covenant with God, to partake the benefits, and perform the duties thereof.* Thus I shall open it very briefly, by considering: the author, instrumental means, matter, terms, form, and end thereof.

{1} **The author or efficient cause of calling**, is God – Father, Son, and Holy Ghost, namely: the Father by the Son, through the Holy Spirit: *According to the power of God, who hath saved us, and called us with a holy calling.*[2202] *God is faithful, by whom ye were called unto the fellowship of his son Jesus Christ our Lord.*[2203] See also 1 Corinthians 1:26-28; 2 Thessalonians 2:13-14, Romans 8:28, 30. *But the God of all grace who hath called us into his eternal glory by Christ Jesus,*[2204] – *renewing of the Holy Ghost.*[2205]

God calls:

(i) According to his eternal decree and purpose, and not otherwise (2 Timothy 1:9, Romans 8:28, 30).

(ii) Therefore, of his own mere grace, whom, when, whereby, and how he pleaseth: not according to any works or worth in man (2 Timothy 1:9, Romans 9:15-16, 18, Titus 1:5, James 1:18; 1 Corinthians 1:26-28).

{2} **The instrumental means of calling**, under God, is ordinarily, the New Covenant gospel preached. *God hath from the beginning chosen you to salvation, through sanctification of the Spirit and belief of the truth, whereunto he called you by our gospel, to the obtaining of the glory of our Lord Jesus Christ*[2206] – sometimes by reading the Scriptures, and Scripture doctrine in good books, as also by conference even with private Christians, men may

---

[2202] 2 Timothy 1:8-9
[2203] 1 Corinthians 1:9
[2204] 1 Peter 5:10
[2205] Titus 3:5, John 3:5
[2206] 2 Thessalonians 2:13-14

instrumentally be called; but ordinarily this is wrought by the public preaching of the New Covenant doctrine. This only is that doctrine which extends the gospel, and offers Christ to all nations (Mark 16:15-16, Matthew 28:18-20, Hebrews 8:8-9, etc., Acts 9:15). The law is herein of use to detect sin, convince and humble the sinner, and so to prepare him for Christ (Romans 3:20 & 7:7, 9-10). But herein the law is to be used with subservience to the New Covenant, and in order thereunto. Hence the ministers of the New Testament are sent forth to preach this New Covenant doctrine to all nations, thereby calling, inviting, persuading men to come in, believe in Christ, and be converted (Matthew 28:19-20, Mark 16:15-16, Acts 9:15 & 26:17-18). And therefore, they are said to call men (Galatians 1:6).[2207] They are the servants that call to the marriage of the king's son (Matthew 22:2-15). They are planters, waterers, co-workers with God, ministers by whom men believe, etc. (1 Corinthians 3:5-11), but all the efficacy is of God.

{3} **The subject-matter of this calling**, or parties called, are wretched, lost, undone sinners of all nations, Jewish or Gentile, of all sexes, ages, conditions, even of all sorts of sinners some, without respect of persons, Matthew 22:2-15; 1 Corinthians 1:26, 27, 28. Acts 10:34, 35, etc. & 26:17-18 & 9:15, Luke 24:46-47).

{4} **The terms, points, or states from which, and to which they are called**, are: from sin, Satan and the world: to Jesus Christ, to his grace, fellowship, glory, etc., and in him, unto God. To *show forth the virtues of him that hath called you, out of darkness into his marvelous light: which in time past were not a people, but now are the people of God*, etc.[2208] – *Delivering thee from the people, and from the Gentiles, unto whom now I send thee, to open their eyes, and to turn them from darkness to light, and from the power of Satan unto God, that they may receive forgiveness of sins, and inheritance among them that are sanctified, by faith that is in me.*[2209] – *From him that*

[2207] See Mr. Perkins on Galatians 1:6
[2208] 1 Peter 2:9-10
[2209] Acts 26:17-18

called you into the grace of Christ.[2210] – *By whom ye were called unto the fellowship of his son Jesus Christ our Lord.*[2211] – *Who by him do believe in God.*[2212]

{5} **The form or manner of this calling**, is chiefly: (i) in the tender or offering of Christ, and of all saving happiness in him, unto sinners; (ii) in sinners accepting, embracing or closing with this tender.

(i) Christ, and all saving happiness in him, is offered or tendered unto sinners, on God's part, etc (Acts 4:12, Hebrews 7:25; 1 Corinthians 1:23-24; 2 Corinthians 5:19-21, Matthew 22:2-15, 11:28-30). This tender or offer of Christ to sinners is twofold, namely: (a) ineffectual, and (b) effectual.

(a) Ineffectual, which becomes not fully efficacious to conversion and salvation. And this again is either, outward only, when Christ and his benefits are only outwardly tendered in his gospel, New Covenant promises, etc., preached and propounded (Acts 2:38-39 & 9:15 & 13:38-39), as when the preaching of the gospel is tendered to them, that refuse to hear it, but put it from them, stop their ears against it, contradict, etc (Acts 7:57 & 13:45-46), Or if they do hear it, yet do not understand it, (much less assent to it) as the hearer compared to the ground by the wayside (Matthew 13:4, 19). Inward also, when the word is not only offered and propounded to the outward ear, but also to the inward heart: so that they not only hear it, but understand it, (Matthew 21:45-46). Yea sometimes not only understand it, but also by a temporary faith for a time assent to it and receive it with joy (Matthew 13:5-6, 20-21, Luke 8:6, 13). All of these degrees of calling, outward and inward, are ineffectual, and insufficient to salvation; yet are they of great use, consequence, and advantage to the interesting of persons in the visible church, to the partaking of all the ordinances and means of grace, whereby much sin may be prevented, and perhaps true grace may be conveyed.

[2210] Galatians 1:6
[2211] 1 Corinthians 1:9
[2212] 1 Peter 1:21

(b) Effectual, when Christ and his benefits are so tendered to the mind and heart in the New Covenant doctrine, that the mind is savingly illuminated to understand, and the heart effectually opened to assent to the tender, and fiducially to apply it (Luke 8:15, Ephesians 1:17, John 6:45, Acts 16:14 & 8:35-37). From this different tender of Christ ineffectual and effectual, arises that distinction of ineffectual calling: {*many are called and few chosen*},[2213] and effectual calling, namely: according to God's purpose of election.[2214] *That* may befall hypocrites and reprobates; *this* is peculiar only to the elect. Thus Christ and all saving happiness in him is propounded and tendered to sinners.

(ii) This offer and tender of Christ and of all saving happiness in him; is accepted, entertained and embraced by sinners: so that Christ becomes theirs, and they Christ's (John 6:56; 1 Corinthians 3:23), his house (Hebrews 3:6), Christ dwelling in their hearts by faith (Ephesians 3:17), his branches (John 15:1, 5), his members (1 Corinthians 12:12), members of his body, of his flesh, and of his bones (Ephesians 5:30) – yea, the very name Christ is given them, in a collective sense (1 Corinthians 12:12). As this tender of Christ, is properly styled {*vocation*} wherein the Father draws the sinner to Christ;[2215] so this acceptance or reception of Christ tendered, is called {*regeneration*}[2216] and {*renovation*}[2217] as it is a beginning of new life, and {*conversion*} in as much as they that obey the divine call are turned from darkness to light, and from the power of Satan unto God.[2218] This reception of Christ tendered is twofold; namely: (a) passive and (b) active.

(a) Passive: when God apprehends the sinner, infusing into his soul, habits, principles, seeds of faith, repentance, grace, etc, whereby the dark mind is enlightened, the dead heart is quickened, the unwilling will is made willing, etc. (Philippians 3:11, Ephesians 1:17; 2 Corinthians 4:6, John 6:44, Ephesians

---

[2213] Matthew 22:14 & 20:26
[2214] Romans 8:28, 30
[2215] John 6:44
[2216] Romans 8:28, 30
[2217] Titus 3:5
[2218] Acts 26:17-18; 1 Peter 2:8-9

2:1, 5, Philippians 2:13). This is properly regeneration, renovation, new-creation, habitual sanctification (Titus 3:5; 2 Corinthians 5:17; 1 Corinthians 6:11; 1 Peter 1:2, Ephesians 2:10). This mighty work of grace upon the heart and will of the sinner, is not upon the will or heart, either as a free agent, or as a natural patient, but in regard to that obediential disposition wherein it stands to God's almighty power, which it cannot but obey, and yield unto, coming to anything whereunto he will bring it, powerfully and efficaciously (Philippians 2:13, John 6:44, Ephesians 2:8).

(b) Active, when the mind, will and heart of a sinner thus apprehended, qualified and principled by God, through his assistant and co-operating grace, accepts Jesus Christ by faith, fiducially resting and relying upon Christ alone, and upon God in him, for life and salvation (John 6:37, 44 & 3:15-16; 1 Peter 1:21). And as the soul by faith turns to Christ as his chief good, so by repentance it also turns from sin as the chief evil, inconsistent with that good. Hence, faith and repentance are linked together in Scripture, as two inseparable twin graces (Mark 1:15, Acts 19:4), and as faith, so true repentance, is the mere gift of God (Acts 11:18; 2 Timothy 2:25). But of the nature both of faith[2219] and repentance,[2220] I have spoken heretofore – there see. And thus the sinner is savingly brought by Christ into his New Covenant.

{6} **The end of vocation of sinners to Christ is:** (i) more immediate and subordinate: the spiritual and eternal happiness of the called (1 Corinthians 1:9, Galatians 1:6, Acts 26:17-18; 1 Peter 5:10, Romans 8:28-30); (ii) more mediate and ultimate; the glory of God calling and converting them (1 Peter 2:8-9).

Thus Jesus Christ our Mediator applies his New Covenant, bringing all into it that are by election given him of the Father (John 6:37 & 17:2).

[2219] In Book 3, Chapter 3, Aphorism 5, Questions 1-7
[2220] In Book 3, Chapter 4, Aphorism 4, Section 2, etc; and in my *Communicant Instructed*, p.127, etc.

Inferences from the whole, touching Jesus Christ the Mediator of this New Covenant.

(1) Hence behold and admire the infinite severity and goodness of God, in giving so necessary and sufficient a Mediator between God and man, as Jesus Christ, God-man.

His severity against sin: his goodness to the sinner. His severity against sin was such, that he would not pass it by without full satisfaction by sinners or their Surety; the violation of his law must be duly punished with death, the truth of his threatening must be fulfilled, his offended justice must be appeased: otherwise no pardon or peace with God could be obtained.[2221] The sinner could not do it; the Surety must: that the creature might not lose his happiness, nor the creator his glory. His goodness therefore was boundless towards sinners, that rather than they should die and perish eternally as they had deserved, Jesus Christ, God-man, the spotless Son of God (Hebrews 7:25) shall suffer and die for them (John 3:16, Romans 5:6-10 & 8:32; 1 Peter 2:24 & 3:18; 2 Corinthians 5:21, Galatians 3:13-14).

Here is love, mercy, bowels, goodness, even to astonishment; that God should give a Son, his own Son, his righteous son, his only Son, his Son who was God; for whom? For us, us wretches, us sinners, us rebellious enemies.

"Oh who can estimate this love sufficiently?" (says Salvian)[2222] "God loves us more than a father his son, for he spared not his own Son, but delivered him up for us all (Romans 8:32)." To this point, Augustine speaks sweetly and

---

[2221] Genesis 2:16-17

[2222] "Plus nos amat Deus, quam filium pater. Evidens quippe res est[,] quod supra affectum filiorum nos Deus diligit, qui propter nos filio non pepercit. Et quid plus addo? & hoc filio justo, & hoc filio unigenito, & hoc filio Deo. Et quid dici amplius potest? & hoc pro nobis, id est, pro malis, pro impiissimis, pro iniquis. Quis aestimare hunc erga nos Dei amorem queat, nisi quod justitia Dei tanta est, ut in eum aliquid injustum cadere non possit?" &c. Salvian, *De Gubernatione Dei*, lib. 4. p. 121, &c.

pathetically: "Oh, admirable condition of the censure; oh ineffable disposition of the mystery! The unjust sins, and the just is punished; the guilty transgresses, and the innocent is scourged; the impious offends, and the pious is condemned. The good suffers what the bad has deserved; the Lord pays what the servant has perpetrated; God undergoes, what man has committed," etc.[2223]

(2) Hence Jesus the Son of God, and of the virgin Mary, the Mediator, Surety and Testator, of the New Testament, is the only true *Christ* and promised *Messiah*.

This has already been demonstrated.[2224] And therefore everyone pretending to be Christ (besides that Jesus), to whom this person and office does not, nor can agree, or belong, is a false Christ, and an antichrist. This is a most high, and necessary fundamental of Christian religion, to believe that Jesus is the Christ, to pitch our faith upon this one only true Christ: all other Christ's being but mere human fictions, vanities and lies. Consider:

[1] The whole Scriptures of Old and New Testament do singularly intend to show, that this Jesus is the Christ, and are for this end specially written, that we might believe that Jesus is the Christ the Son of God, and that believing, we might have life through his name.[2225]

[2223] "O wonderful process! Mystery of justice! That the wicked should offend, and the righteous be punished for it! that the guilt and the condemnation should thus be separated! That the servant should contract a debt, and the Lord to whom it was due, make satisfaction! that man should provoke the divine vengeance, and God should feel the smart of it! How low, O Son of God, did your humility stoop! How fervent was your love! How boundless your compassion!" Augustine, *Meditations*. cap. 7. Tom. 9.
[https://www.monergism.com/thethreshold/sdg/augustine/MeditationsAugustine.pdf] <Accessed 4/15/2024>
[2224] In this 6th Chapter, Aphorism 2.
[2225] Acts 4:11-12

[2] This is that grand truth which the ministers of the gospel should prove and clear from the Scriptures, that this Jesus is the Christ;[2226] as they diligently did in the primitive times almost in every sermon.[2227]

[3] This is that saving truth beyond the ability of flesh and blood to reveal, which makes such as truly receive it by faith, really and presently blessed.[2228]

[4] This is that rock upon which Christ builds his church so firm and sure, that the gates of hell, all the policy and power of Satan, shall not prevail against it.[2229]

[5] This truth, rightly believed, is a notable evidence of regeneration. *Whosoever believeth that Jesus is the **Christ**, is born of God*.[2230] "But then in the visible church, all will be regenerate!" Not so: it is right believing this, that discovers regeneration. So to believe this, as to come to Christ, to accept Christ, to love Christ, to obey Christ, to live to Christ, and upon Christ, to be wholly Christ's. Notably Augustine: "Who does not believe that Jesus is the Christ? He that does not so live, as is commanded by Christ."[2231] Many say, "I believe," but faith without works does not save.

[6] The denying of this point makes a man a liar, and an antichrist, a lying antichrist, and an antichristian liar. *Who is a liar, but he that denieth that Jesus is the Christ? He is antichrist, that denieth the Father and the Son* (1 John 2:22).

[7] The believing of this truth is of such necessity to salvation, that the not believing it will inevitably bring damnation. *If ye believe not* (said Christ) *that I am he, ye shall die in your sins* (John 8:24). Oh this is a blessed and

---

[2226] John 5:39, Luke 24:27, Acts 10:43 with John 20:31
[2227] Acts 2:36 & 3:13 to the end & 9:29 & 18:28
[2228] Matthew 16:16-17
[2229] Acts 4:11-12
[2230] 1 John 5:1
[2231] "Who is he that believes not that Jesus is the Christ? He that does not so live as Christ commanded. For many say, I believe: but faith without works saves not." Augustine, *Homily 10* on 1 John
[https://www.newadvent.org/fathers/170210.htm]
<Accessed 4/15/2024>

glorious truth! Believe it; not only with a bare dogmatical assenting faith, but also with a fiducial and practical faith (Galatians 5:6).

(3) **Hence Jesus Christ is indeed the wonderful**[2232] **and the great**[2233] **mystery of godliness, both in his person and office.**

[1] How wonderful, what a mystery in his person! His person consisting of God and man, of creator and creature, of Son of God, and Son of man, of omnipotent, and impotent, of infinite, and finite, of eternal, and temporal, of omnipresent, and sitting only at God's right hand, of omniscient, and yet nescient when the day and hour of the last judgment shall be, of invisible, and visible, etc.[2234] Oh wonderful and mysterious person! Who can understand, or sufficiently admire, this humanized deity, this deified humanity, this God-man Immanuel![2235]

[2] How wonderful, and what a profound mystery also is his office! He is God offended, and yet a Mediator between God, and man offending. He is both Surety and Testator of the New Testament.[2236] He is both Covenant (Isaiah 49:8 & 55:3) and Mediator of the Covenant (Hebrews 8:6 & 9:14 & 12:24). He is a prophetic and priestly king, a prophetic and royal priest, a priestly and royal prophet, being at once both prophet, priest and king. He is priest, sacrifice and altar: altar as God, sacrifice as man, priest as God-man. He died, and yet is *a priest forever, after the order of Melchizedek.*[2237] He could not sin, knew no sin, and yet was made sin for us. He could not suffer, and yet suffered death for us he is glory, yet was abased. He is innocence, yet was condemned. He is the life, and yet was murdered. He is the resurrection, and yet was buried and enthralled in the grave. He descended to deepest abasement, he ascended to highest advancement, and all for his elect, that they

---

[2232] Isaiah 9:6
[2233] 1 Timothy 3:16
[2234] Mark 13:32
[2235] Matthew 1:23, Isaiah 7:14
[2236] Hebrews 7:22 & 9:14-16
[2237] Hebrews 7:26; 2 Corinthians 5:21

might be brought to glory. Oh, how wonderful and mysterious are the effects of his offices, and his way of producing them! By Christ's offices, we slaves are redeemed, we enemies are reconciled, we aliens are adopted, we dead are quickened, we buried are raised, we cursed are blessed, and we sinners are sainted.

But how? By his bondage, by his condemnation, by his rejection, by his death, by his burial, by his curse, and by his becoming sin for us. How are we bound to God for the matter of our salvation! How bound also for the mystery of our salvation! His incarnation is our deification, his humiliation is our exaltation, his stripes are our healing, his blood is our balm, his accusation is our clearing, his condemnation is our righteousness, his curse is our blessing, his death is our life and victory over death and Satan, his temptation is our triumph, his exaltation is our glory. Here are mysteries upon mysteries, in Christ our wonderful. What paradoxes are these to flesh and blood! Blessed Lord, bring about our salvation as strangely and mysteriously as you will, so we may be eternally saved. We adore your Christ; we admire his mysteriousness.

(4) Hence, as God's Covenants are the marrow of holy Scriptures, and the New Covenant the flower and spirits of the Covenants; so Jesus Christ our Mediator, is the life and soul of the New Covenant.

The Covenant of Works before man's fall;[2238] the Covenants of Faith, since his fall, either in Christ promised, as all the Covenant of Promise;[2239] or in Christ performed, as the New Covenant,[2240] do plainly take up the whole body and series of the Scriptures. Among all these Covenants, the New Covenant excels and predominates, as the sun among the stars.[2241] But whence has this New Covenant such preeminence? Especially from Jesus Christ. He is the

---

[2238] Genesis 2:16-17
[2239] Ephesians 2:12
[2240] Hebrews 8:8, etc.
[2241] Hebrews 8:9, 6 & 7:22; 2 Corinthians 3:6 to the end

author, the chief matter, the Mediator, Surety, and Testator, the end and primary mystery of the New Covenant, more clearly and fully than of any other: he exhibited is the very life and soul of it. Before John the Baptist was God's time of promises; since (as Augustine has well noted) is his time of performances."[2242] And all God's performances of promises meet in Christ. O therefore wouldst thou compendiously be possessed of all covenant treasures at once! Possess yourself of this one treasure of treasures, Jesus Christ, and you have all.

(5) **Hence the New Covenant far excels the Old Covenant and all foregoing Covenants, in having Jesus Christ actually exhibited, to be Mediator, Surety and Testator thereof.**

Christ was promised darkly[2243] and typified obscurely[2244] in former Covenants; and especially under the Old Covenant, wherein he is set forth as a Mediator, the law being ordained by angels in the hand of a Mediator.[2245] By which Mediator, whether we understand the Son of God according to his Godhead, as some; or Moses as a typical Mediator shadowing out Christ, as others, and perhaps better;[2246] yet still we are to understand the Mediator only promised, not as yet performed in human flesh. But Christ actually exhibited

---

[2242] "God established an era of promises and another era for the fulfillment of his promises. The time for promises was the age of prophets down to John the Baptist. From his day, and thenceforth until the end, is the era of fulfillment. God is faithful and has put himself in our debt not because we have given him anything but because he has promised so much. Yet even promising was not enough for him. He wanted to be bound in writing as well, so he gave us a signed copy of his promises, as it were, so that once he had begun to fulfill them we could study the Scriptures and learn the sequence of their realization. Thus the era of prophecy was that in which things were promised for the future."
Augustine, *The Works of St. Augustine, v.1 Sermons on the Old Testament, 20-50* (New City Press, 2003) p.261
[https://www.google.com/books/edition/The_Works_of_Saint_Augustine_v_1_Sermons/0XvYAAAAMAAJ?hl=en&gbpv=1]
<Accessed 4/10/2024>
[2243] Genesis 3:15 & 12:3 & 22:18
[2244] Genesis 3:21 with 4:4 & 14:18, etc, with Hebrews 7, etc
[2245] Galatians 3:19
[2246] Andre Rivet in *Cathol. Orthodox Tract.* 2 Question 49.4

and incarnate is Mediator, Surety, and Testator of this New Testament, most immediately, clearly, fully, efficaciously, etc. Therefore this New Covenant must needs as far excel the Old, and all before, as the performance excels the promise.

(6) Hence, Jesus Christ – God-man, Mediator, Surety, and Testator of the New Covenant – is an all-sufficient Savior of sinners.

His person, and office demonstrate undeniably this his all-sufficiency. What can be required to sinners plenary salvation, which is not fully found in him? Is sinner's salvation, and the way of it to be revealed? Christ is our prophet, in the Father's bosom. Is it to be obtained, by satisfying God's law and justice for sin, by fulfilling the law for the sinner, and by appearing in the presence of God for the sinner forever? Christ is our great high-priest, who satisfies, by dying, who fulfills by exact obeying, who appears before God, ever living to make intercession for us. Is salvation to be effectually applied to the sinner? Christ is our king at God's right hand, who sends forth his spirit to apply all his benefits to us. Are we slaves? He redeems us. Are we enemies to God? He reconciles us. Are we carnal? He calls and converts us. Are we filthy? He sanctifies us. Are we aliens? He adopts us. Are we guilty? He justifies us. Are we inglorious? He glorifies us. Could not these things be effected for us, only on earth, or only in heaven? On earth, Christ was deeply humbled; in heaven he is highly exalted: that both in heaven and earth our salvation might be accomplished. And must our Mediator be a right middle person between God and man, having equal interest in both? Thus also Jesus Christ is true and perfect God-man, that he might be an all-sufficient Mediator. As man, he could discharge all mean acts, as God, all magisterial acts of his mediation. The infinite dignity of his person, adding infinite worth to all his mediation.

(7) Hence, Jesus Christ the New Covenant Mediator, Surety, and Testator, is the only hope, and refuge of bruised sinners; and most complete consolation of believing saints.

For:

[1] *Whither else shall bruised sinners fly hopefully for refuge against sin, guilt, wrath of God, curse of the law, malice of Satan, etc., but to Jesus Christ alone?* He, he alone is their door of hope, and tower of safety;[2247] he has *condemned sin in the flesh*.[2248] He justifies them by his blood;[2249] he delivers them from wrath to come;[2250] he redeems them from the curse of the law;[2251] he by death has destroyed death, and him that had the power of death, the devil.[2252] He is mighty to save, he is ready to save, he alone can save: whither then can the sinner fly but to such a Savior?

{1} **Mighty to save.**[2253] For, he is a mighty Mediator; he has a mighty mediation; his merit is beyond all our misery, his righteousness is above all our unrighteousness, his pardons, are more than all our debts, his life is stronger than our death, his salvation far transcends our condemnation. Why? Because we sinners are but finite men, but he the Savior is also the infinite God. When he saved Matthew the publican, Mary Magdalene, the demoniac possessed of seven devils, Saul the persecutor, and blasphemer, the thief upon the cross (that famous experiment of his cross) – yea, the betrayers and murderers of himself; who can but admire, as the grace, so the power, of his salvation?

{2} **He is ready to save.** Why else did he come into the world, but to save sinners?[2254] Why else did he preach so many heavenly sermons, work such divine miracles to confirm his doctrine, endure so much contempt, ignominy, reproach, hard usage and sufferings in the world, shed so many tears, pour out

---

[2247] Acts 4:12
[2248] Romans 8:3
[2249] Romans 5:10
[2250] 1 Thessalonians 1:10
[2251] Galatians 3:13
[2252] Hebrews 2:14-15
[2253] Hebrews 7:25
[2254] 1 Timothy 1:15, John 3:17, Galatians 4:4-5

so many strong cries and prayers, sweat so much blood, and at last expose himself willingly to such a painful, shameful and cursed death; his head, hands, feet, side and heart, streaming out his vital blood, but that he thirsted for sinners' salvation? Why else did he rise again, ascend into heaven, and sit down at God's right hand, but to allure and draw sinners after him? Why else does he invite sinners by so many sweet promises and importances[2255] to come to him, and believe in him?[2256] And why else does he denounce so many sad and severe threatenings to them that will not come to him that they might be saved? (3) he alone can save, and none other under heaven (Acts 4:12).

[2] *As for believing saints, Christ is their most complete consolation.* For, in his person their human nature is elevated above that of angels: by his office they are redeemed, reconciled to God, called, sanctified, adopted into his own family, justified, privileged, and glorified; by him the New Covenant is irrevocably established, and they instated in it;[2257] *in him all the promises of God are yea, and amen*, and all entailed upon godliness;[2258] in him they have abounding consolations in all their abounding tribulations (2 Corinthians 1:5). And in a word, having Christ, with Christ they have all things.[2259] Therefore Christ that affords believers such heaps of cordials, such a sea of comfort, must needs be their most complete consolation.[2260]

(8) **Hence, the New Covenant's dedication was most bitter to Christ; although the New Covenant application is most sweet to Christians.**

This New Covenant was dedicated by his blood, this New Testament was established and made of force by his death.[2261] And what death? A death upon the cross. Therefore, a death painful, shameful, cursed, having also the wrath

---

[2255] The original word here is "importancies," as may be meant in the sense of "importunities," that is: urgent requests.
[2256] Matthew 11:28-30, John 3:15-16 & 6:35, Mark 10:29-30
[2257] John 3:18, 36, Mark 16:16
[2258] Hebrews 9:14-17, Matthew 26:28
[2259] 2 Corinthians 1:20; 1 Timothy 4:8
[2260] Romans 8:32, Matthew 6:33; 1 Corinthians 3:21-23
[2261] Matthew 26:28, Hebrews 9:14-15 & Philippians 2:8, Galatians 3:13

of God imprinted on it. Oh, this was a bitter dedication! Consider well, his agony in the garden, his bloody sweat, his pricked head, his scourged back, his pierced hands and feet, his opened side, his wounded heart, his sad desertion and doleful cry upon the cross, and then think how bitter this New Covenant's establishment was to Christ, it cost him very dear.

But on the other hand, how sweet is the New Covenant application unto Christians! Yea therefore this Covenant was so bitter to Christ in its dedication, that it might be the sweeter to us in its application. This makes all the promises and blessings of the New Covenant ours: this makes temporals, spirituals and eternals ours: this makes Jesus Christ, and all that is Christ's ours: this makes God, and all that is God's, ours. O sweet and blissful soul enriching application! The agony was Christ's, but the victory was ours. The condemnation Christ's; the justification ours. The pain Christ's; the ease ours. The stripes Christ's; the healing by those stripes ours. The wounds Christ's; the balm flowing out of those wounds ours. The gall and vinegar Christ's; the honey ours. The curse Christ's; the blessing ours. The death Christ's; the life ours. The crown of thorns was Christ's; but the crown of glory ours. O what pleasant fruit springs from this bitter root! Oh how was Christ abased, that we might be exalted! How willing should we be to be abased for Christ, that he may be exalted! What a value should we set upon this New Covenant, which was so bitter and costly for Christ to confirm, which is so sweet and gainful to us to enjoy!

(9) Hence, let all such as long to know that they are within this New Covenant savingly, examine with all diligence whether they be brought into it by being called to Christ, and made Christ's effectually.

For Christ brings his elect into this New Covenant by effectual vocation, as has been evidenced;[2262] and whom he effectually calls, he calls unto himself, that he may be theirs, and they Christ's.[2263]

Now (having formerly promised more largely to unfold in this fourth book, the signs of being Christ's)[2264] hereby we may discover whether we are Christ's, or not; and consequently, whether we are in New Covenant with God or not.

[1] *Have we Christ's Spirit dwelling in us?*

Ye are not in the flesh, but in the Spirit, if so be the Spirit of God dwell in you. Now if any man have not the Spirit of Christ, he is none of his (Romans 8:9). The Spirit of God, and the Spirit of Christ, are here counted one and the same. And as all the members of the natural body are actuated and enlivened by one and the same human spirit from the head; so all the members of Christ's mystical body are actuated and enlivened by one and the same divine Spirit from their head Christ.

Question: Has Christ given his Spirit into our hearts? We have no saving gift from Christ until we have this gift, but whereby may we know that we have Christ's Spirit?

Answer: Hereby, Christ's Spirit is:

{1} **A convincing Spirit**: effectually convincing the sinner, both of his own sinful malady, and of Christ's saving remedy (John 16:9-11).

{2} **An enlivening Spirit**: instilling spiritual life into the dead soul, freeing it from the law, or power of sin and death (Romans 8:12).

{3} **A holy and sanctifying Spirit**: purifying and washing the persons of those that are Christ's from the stains and defilements of sin (1 Corinthians 6:11) by infusing holy habits and principles of grace into the heart, which resist corruption, and work it out daily more and more, as pure honey works out the wax and dross, and as generous wine works out the lees and dregs.

[2262] Hebrews 9:14, Acts [2:38-39]
[2263] 1 Corinthians 1:9
[2264] In Book 3, Chapter 3, Aphorism 3, Section 1

{4} **A filial, child-like Spirit**: enabling all that are Christ's to cry {*Abba Father*} (Galatians 4:6, Romans 8:15). His spirit is a spirit of supplication in their hearts: a praying spirit. He teaches them to pray with childlike confidence, familiarity and importunity, to God as their tender and compassionate Father. *Of ourselves we know not how to pray, or what to pray for as we ought, but the Spirit itself maketh intercession for us* (that is, enables us to pray for ourselves) *with groanings which cannot be uttered* (that is, with such fervent desires and groans of the heart, as the lips and tongue cannot express – Romans 8:26).

{5} **A comforting Spirit**: secretly, but strongly supporting, cherishing, encouraging, and comforting their hearts that are Christ's; against corruptions, temptations, tribulations, persecutions, and all occasions of disconsolation whatsoever, and that continually (John 14:16-17, Acts 9:31, Romans 14:17; 2 Corinthians 1:3-5). Those who are Christ's have manifold discomforts, but yet their comforts from Christ's Spirit, namely: either their sensible refreshing comforts, or at least their secret supporting comforts, are prevailing and predominant over them all.

[2] *Are we new creatures?* All that are in Christ, that are Christ's; are new creatures. *If any man be in Christ, he is a new creature: old things are past away, behold all things are become new. And all things are of God, who hath reconciled us to himself by Jesus Christ* (2 Corinthians 5:17-18). The first Adam by sinning made all things old, decaying and vanishing; he ruined and destroyed all things. The last Adam, Jesus Christ by suffering and satisfying for sin, repaired and renewed all things. More generally, he renews the whole frame of the creation: creating a new heaven and new earth, wherein dwells righteousness, according to his promise (Isaiah 65:17; 2 Peter 3:13, Revelation 21:1).

More specially, he new-creates his church, breaking down the wall of partition between Jews and Gentiles: *for to make of twain one new man, so making peace* (Ephesians 2:13-18), whereupon this time under the New

Testament wherein this is effected, is called {*the time of reformation*} (Hebrews 9:10). Yea more particularly and individually Jesus Christ calling his elect from their sinful state and condition, he new-creates their persons; makes everyone of them a new creature. He leaves them not in their old condition, in their old sins (2 Peter 1:9), in their old carnal state; but he makes old things pass away; and he brings them into a new state of grace and righteousness. Not that he abolishes the substance of soul or body, or the natural essence of the faculties, affections, senses and members thereof: but only the qualifications, qualities or dispositions of these. The old carnalness, sinfulness, etc. He makes pass away: and makes the whole man more holy and spiritual, etc. More distinctly, they become new creatures that are in Christ, in these three respects, namely: in regard to their: {1} condition, {2} constitution, and {3} conversation.

{1} **In respect to their condition, they are new creatures**: they were in the flesh, in the gall of bitterness, and bond of iniquity;[2265] they are in the Spirit, placed in a sweet and free state of righteousness by the Son of God.[2266] They were under the power of Satan; they are under the dominion of God.[2267] They were enemies to God by their sins; they are reconciled to God by Christ's sufferings.[2268] They were children of wrath even as others; they are vessels of mercy.[2269] They were not a people; but now are the people of the living God. They had not obtained mercy; but now they have obtained mercy.[2270] They were quite lost, but are found.[2271] They were dead in trespasses and sins; but are alive again with and by Jesus Christ risen from the dead.[2272] Are you brought into this new-created condition?

[2265] Romans 8:8, Acts 8:23
[2266] Romans 8:9, John 8:36
[2267] Acts 26:18
[2268] Romans 8:7 & 5:10, Colossians 1:20-21
[2269] Ephesians 2:3, Romans 9:23
[2270] 1 Peter 2:9-10
[2271] Luke 15:32
[2272] Ephesians 2:1, 5

{2} **In respect of their frame and inward constitution, they are new creatures.**

(i) Their faculties are new-created. (a) Their minds that were wholly blinded with gross darkness, ignorance, error, and inapprehensiveness of the things of God,[2273] are now opened, become light in the Lord, and savingly furnished with truth, wisdom and apprehensiveness of all the things of Christ.[2274] (b) Their consciences, that were evil, secure, senseless, feared, full of guilt, and ofttimes filled with horror;[2275] are become good, tender, pure, void of offense towards God and towards man, and filled with peace passing all understanding.[2276] (c) Their wills, that were averse to all good, froward, rebellious, and perverse in all evil, and wholly opposite to the will of God,[2277] are now made averse to all evil, fixed and resolute in all good, holy, righteous and universally subordinate to the will of God, in willing what he wills, being acted and carried by God's will, as the star in its proper orb, so far as it is new-created.[2278]

(ii) Their affections are new-created. Their desires, love, joy, delight, etc, were wickedly set upon sin,[2279] inordinately upon the empty perishables of this world,[2280] not at all, unless hypocritically, upon spirituals and the things of a better life,[2281] and contrariwise, their flight, hatred, grief, detestation, etc., were against God, his people, and all his ways;[2282] but now they desire, love, joy, delight in nothing more, in nothing so much as in God, Jesus Christ.[2283] The

---

[2273] Ephesians 4:18 & 5:8, Acts 26:18, James 5:20; 1 Corinthians 2:14
[2274] Acts 26:18, Ephesians 5:8; 1 Corinthians 2:10-13, 15
[2275] Hebrews 10:22, Ephesians 4:18-19; 1 Timothy 4:2, Titus 1:15, Romans 2:15, Matthew 27:3-5
[2276] Acts 23:1; 2 Chronicles 34:27; 1 Timothy 3:9, Acts 24:16, Romans 5:1, Philippians 4:7
[2277] Matthew 23:37, John 5:40, Ezekiel 33:11, Jeremiah 44:16-17
[2278] Psalm 119:104, 110:2, Philippians 2:14
[2279] Genesis 6:5, Isaiah 66:3
[2280] Luke 12:5-22
[2281] Matthew 13:20-21, Mark 6:20
[2282] Romans 1:30; 2 Timothy 3:3, John 3:20
[2283] Psalm 73:25, Philippians 3:6-10, Psalm 4:6-7, Philippians 2:9-10, Psalm 119:20 & 63:1-3 & 84 & 42 & 16:3

light of his countenance, communion with him, his Covenant, promises, ordinances, people, and in all spirituals; and they fly, hate, grieve for, abominate nothing so much, as sin, corruption, and all ungodly ways.[2284]

(iii) Their senses and bodily members are new-created. They were thorough-fares for vanity, instruments and weapons of all unrighteousness unto sin;[2285] but now are receptacles and harbingers of spirituals, and weapons of righteousness unto holiness.[2286] Are your faculties, affections, senses, and members thus new-created? Doubtless then you are in Christ.

{3} In respect of their life and conversation, they that are Christ's are new creatures. *For we are his workmanship, created in Christ Jesus unto good works, which God hath before ordained that we should walk in them.*[2287] By nature we are abominable, disobedient, and to every good work reprobate,[2288] altogether without strength to any spiritual acts or exercises.[2289] Walking *according to the course of this world, according to the prince of the power of the air, the Spirit that now worketh in the children of disobedience. Among whom also we all had our conversation in times past, in the lusts of our flesh, fulfilling the wills of the flesh, and of the mind,*[2290] and running with them to all excess of riot, etc.[2291] But by the grace of this new-creation, we are brought to walk in newness of life: *to deny ungodliness and worldly lusts, and to live soberly, righteously and godly in this present world;*[2292] to live by faith, walk in love, and abound in all well-pleasing, being fruitful in every good work;[2293] to have our conversation in heaven, and to mind the things that are above[2294] – in a word, to walk worthy

---

[2284] Psalm 119:104
[2285] 2 Peter 2:14, Romans 6:12
[2286] Psalm 101:3 & 119:148, 136, Romans 6:13
[2287] Ephesians 2:10
[2288] Titus 1:16
[2289] Romans 5:6
[2290] Ephesians 2:2-3
[2291] 1 Peter 4:3-4
[2292] Romans 6:4, Titus 2:11, Galatians 2:20, Ephesians 5:2
[2293] Colossians 1:10
[2294] Philippians 3:20, Colossians 3:1, etc.

of the Lord, and of his kingdom whereunto we are called;[2295] herein exercising ourselves to *have a conscience always void of offense, both towards God, and towards men.*[2296] Are you thus renewed and newly-created in your conversation?

[3] ***Are we one with Christ, by faith and love?*** They that are Christ's, are mystically one with him. And this oneness is most near and intimate. As stones are one with the foundation;[2297] as vine-branches are one with the root;[2298] as members are one with the head;[2299] as the wife is one with her husband, *for we are members of his body, of his flesh, and of his bones.*[2300] Yea, *he that is joined to the Lord, is one spirit,*[2301] insomuch that both head and members thus united, are, and are styled {*one **Christ***}.[2302] Are we thus united, incorporated, consolidated with Jesus Christ? This union is wrought, partly by Christ's Spirit apprehending us, that we may be Christ's.[2303] Do we have Christ's Spirit, according to former evidences of it? Partly, by our faith and love re-apprehending Christ Jesus.

By faith, we come to Christ,[2304] we receive him,[2305] we put him on,[2306] we eat his flesh, and drink his blood,[2307] we have Christ living in us[2308] – yea, by faith we have Christ dwelling in our hearts.[2309]

By love, we are sweetly linked and endeared to Christ, and Christ to us reciprocally. So that from this spirit of sincere love to him: {1} we bear a most

---

[2295] 1 Thessalonians 2:12
[2296] Acts 23:1 & 24:16
[2297] 1 Peter 2:4-5
[2298] John 15:1
[2299] 1 Corinthians 12:12, etc.
[2300] Ephesians 5:30-32
[2301] 1 Corinthians 6:17
[2302] 1 Corinthians 12:12, Galatians 3:16
[2303] John 3:5, Philippians 3:12
[2304] John 6:35
[2305] John 1:11-12
[2306] Romans 13:14
[2307] John 6:47, 54
[2308] Galatians 2:20
[2309] Ephesians 3:17

benevolent affection towards him, wishing him all good, all glory, etc;[2310] {2} we have strong desires and longings after more complete union to him: *Make haste O my beloved, and be as the hinds or the roes upon the mountains of spices.*[2311] {3} And so far as we are united to Christ, we have delightful complacency and heart-satisfying acquiescence in him, glorying herein with the church: *My beloved is mine, and I am his.*[2312]

[4] ***Have we crucified and mortified our corruptions?***

They that are Christ's, have crucified the flesh, with the affections (Greek: *passions*) *and lusts.*[2313] Christ our head was crucified for the sins of his members, therefore all that are Christ's true members must be conformed to their head, by being crucified and dead to their own sins. By {*the flesh with the passions and lusts*}, understand the original corruption of nature, together with actual sins thence flowing, whether elicit or imperate, inward or outward. As Calvin, well: "Flesh and its lusts, are put for the root and fruits, for the flesh is the vitiosity [defect] of corrupt nature, whence all evils proceed."[2314] These are the malefactors to be crucified.

By {*crucifying*} (which is a metaphorical allusion to Christ's crucifixion), understand the mortifying, deadening, destroying of sin: original and actual – and that by exemplary imitation of Christ's death, and by efficacious virtue from Christ's death. Not that sin in this life can be completely crucified all at once, for sin will be in the best of saints, while this natural life continues;[2315] but when we first become Christ's, sin receives its death-wound, the reign and dominion of it is destroyed: and it is daily a-wounding, bleeding, weakening, decaying, gasping and dying. By that phrase, {*they that are Christ's*}, understand all that are Christ's. Being an indefinite expression, it is equivalent

---

[2310] John 3:28-32; 2 Corinthians 12:9
[2311] Song of Solomon 8:14
[2312] Song of Solomon 2:16
[2313] Galatians 5:24 συν τοις παθημασιν και ταις επιθυμιαις
[2314] "Caro & Concupiscentiae ejus, pro radice & fructibus: caro enim ipsa est naturae corruptae vitiositas, unde mala omnia prodeunt" John Calvin on Galatians 5:24
[2315] Romans 7:24 & 6:7, Galatians 5:17

to a universal. All that are Christ's, one as well as another, have in some good degree (though not equally), crucified the flesh with the passions and lusts.

More particularly, they that are Christ's do crucify the flesh with the passions and lusts, by their conformity to, and communion with Jesus Christ and him crucified, namely:

{1} Christ was discovered; so they detect and discover their sins convincingly, the Spirit convinces them of their sin, spreading all open before them, that they see the extreme sinfulness thereof[2316] – as David,[2317] Paul,[2318] and Peter's hearers.[2319] True sight of sin is the first step to repentance.

{2} Christ discovered was apprehended and attached; so they apprehend and lay hold of their sins, and bring them into the presence of God, and before his tribunal.

{3} Christ was arraigned, indicted and accused before Pilate's judgment-seat; so they that are Christ's, arraign, indite and accuse their sins, and themselves for their sins, with all the aggravations they can, before God's bar, as David.[2320]

{4} Christ was judged and condemned; so they that are Christ's, judge and condemn their sins, and themselves for their sins, that they may not be condemned. They judge themselves worthy of shame, confusion, condemnation and death.[2321]

{5} Christ after he was condemned was executed; so they that are Christ's, having judged and doomed themselves for their sins, proceed to execution of them, and actual crucifying and deadening them in various ways, namely: (i) Partly, by applying to themselves Christ's death and cross for their sins by faith. Hereby they fetch virtue from Christ crucified, to crucify their flesh. Thus they reason; Christ dying bare our sins, represented our persons.

[2316] John 16:9-10
[2317] Psalm 51:3-5
[2318] Romans 7:7, 9
[2319] Acts 2:36-37
[2320] Psalm 51:1-4, etc.
[2321] Daniel 9:7-8

Therefore Christ being crucified, we were crucified: Christ dying, we died. If then we are one with Christ, we may no longer serve sin. (ii) Partly by making Christ's crucifying an exemplary cause, pattern or motive, to the crucifying of the flesh. In this sort did Christ endure such sorrows, such shame, such bruises, such wounds, such pain, such a cruel and cursed death for our sins; and shall we love, or live in those sins, shall we love those sins for which Christ was hated, or excuse those sins, for which Christ was accused, or justify those sins, for which Christ was condemned: or cleave to those sins, for which Christ was deserted of God: or spare those sins, for which Christ was pierced, or live in those sins, for which Christ was crucified and murdered? Oh, hate, abhor, destroy the flesh with the affections and lusts; as the Judas that betrayed him, as the Pilate that condemned him, as the nails and spear that pierced him. How shall we be destroyed for our own sins: if they are not destroyed by Christ's death? Thus let our old man be crucified with Christ, *that the body of sin may be destroyed, that henceforth we should not serve sin.*[2322] (iii) Partly, by daily stabbing, wounding, and hewing in pieces this body of sin by the sword of the Spirit, the word of God, as Samuel hewed Agag in pieces.[2323] Opposing the flesh and the lusts thereof by God's commands, prohibitions, threats and judgments, recorded in his word. (iv) Partly, by ceasing to make provision for the flesh, to fulfill the lusts thereof,[2324] and so starving sin out. (v) Partly, by cutting off, and shunning all the occasions, inlets, inducements, temptations, and beginnings of sin.[2325]

[5] ***Do we walk after the Spirit, not after the flesh?***

They that are in Christ, walk not after the flesh, but after the Spirit.[2326] They do not habitually follow the lusts, motions, guidance, instigations, etc., of the flesh, as sometimes they did; but the motions, stirrings, actings and

---

[2322] Romans 6:6
[2323] Psalm 119:9, Ephesians 6:16
[2324] Romans 13:14
[2325] Genesis 39:8-10
[2326] Acts 2:36-37

guidance of God's Spirit,[2327] being led by him according to the Word.[2328] They may sometimes step awry after the flesh, but that is not their walk, their course which they delight in, but their error and infirmity which they strive against.[2329]

By these things we may know whether we are Christ's. And they that thus are Christ's effectually, are within his New Covenant actually and savingly.

(10) Hence, finally, let all who are convinced they are Christless and covenantless persons,[2330] and yet thirst after a New Covenant state, sincerely accept Christ tendered;[2331] and let all that find they are in New Covenant with God, through Christ, walk worthy of Christ accepted.[2332]

[1] *Let all that thirst after a New Covenant state, sincerely accept Christ tendered.*

For those who accept Christ aright, accept his New Covenant also. Christ is the jewel; the New Covenant is the casket or cabinet that contains this jewel. Sell all that you have to purchase this pearl of greatest price.[2333] Count all things loss and dung, deny all self-sinfulness, all self-righteousness, all self-fullness suffer willingly, the loss of all things, that you may win Christ, and be found in him.[2334] Christ is wrapped up in the promises: embrace them, and Christ therein.[2335] Christ is tendered in all the gospel ordinances, especially in the Word[2336] and sacraments,[2337] and this pathetically [pitifully],

---

[2327] Romans 8:1
[2328] Romans 8:14
[2329] Romans 7:15-16, 19-23, Galatians 5:17
[2330] Ephesians 2:12
[2331] John 1:11-12
[2332] 1 John 2:2-6, Colossians 2:6-7
[2333] Matthew 13:45-46
[2334] Philippians 3:7-8
[2335] 2 Corinthians 1:20
[2336] John 5:39, Ephesians 3:8, Acts 10:43
[2337] 1 Corinthians 10:1-2, Colossians 2:10-12, Romans 6:3-6; 1 Corinthians 5:7-8, 11:23, etc.

importunately, and frequently.[2338] Accept the tender of Christ, neglect not so great salvation. Christ stands at the door of your heart and knocks.[2339] He stands patiently, he knocks importunately; he waits and knocks. He knocks by his Word; he knocks by his rod; he knocks by his Spirit's convictions, motions, impulses, strivings, instigations, etc. He knocks restlessly, audibly; how fain [gladly] would he enter!

Oh, shut not Christ still out of your soul. Set open the everlasting doors, and this King of Glory shall come in.[2340] Christ is the best guest, the most blessed inmate that can possibly be entertained in your soul. Oh, lodge him in the inmost cabinet of your heart. That day, that hour that Christ comes into your soul, salvation comes into your soul, heaven comes into your soul – yea, God blessed forever comes into your soul. Deeply lay to heart, and seriously ponder upon these ensuing considerations. They may be as so many steps or degrees towards Christ, and as so many urgent motives to thee to press and strive after him.

{1} **By nature since man's fall in Adam, all the people in the world are utterly without Jesus Christ.**

Naturally all people are Christless, having no saving right at all to him, or interest in him. This is true of the Gentiles. *Remember that ye being in time passed Gentiles in the flesh, – that at that time ye were without Christ.*[2341] And it is also true of the Jews, while in their carnal and unregenerate state, as Peter, writing to the dispersed Jews, notably testifies: they came not to Christ the living stone by faith indeed, so as to taste that the Lord is gracious, until they were newborn babes. Until then, they were not a people, had not obtained mercy, namely: saving mercy in Christ the mercy of mercies.[2342] And of both

---

[2338] Hebrews 2:3
[2339] Revelation 3:20
[2340] Psalm 24:7-10
[2341] Ephesians 2:11-12
[2342] 1 Peter 1:1 with 2:1-11

Jews and Gentiles, the apostle Paul has proven that they are all under sin, and consequently, that all the world has become guilty before God.[2343] Now to be under sin – namely: under the state, dominion, and curse of sin – is to be without Christ. For, they that are in Christ, are freed from the state, power and curse of sin, though not from the in-being of the relics of sin.[2344]

{2} **All persons whilst Christless are most wretched and miserable**, for:

(i) Whose are they, whilst they are not Christ's? They are the world's: men of the world,[2345] children of this world,[2346] the world's own,[2347] etc. They are sin's: they are sin's vassals, drudges, slaves;[2348] they serve sin,[2349] they are in sin,[2350] in the flesh,[2351] in the bond of iniquity,[2352] etc. They are wholly involved, engulfed, overwhelmed therein. They are death's: spiritual death has actual dominion over them, they are dead in sins and trespasses,[2353] and the curse of death corporal with the adequate wages of eternal death do wait upon them.[2354] Yea, they are the devil's: Cain *was of that wicked one, and slew his brother*;[2355] *ye are of your father the devil* (said Christ to the wicked Jews) *and the works of your father ye will do*;[2356] Judas was a very devil.[2357] Not to be Christ's; but the world's, and sins, and the devils, how sad and woeful is it!

(ii) Christless persons are *aliens from the commonwealth of Israel, strangers from the covenants of promise, having no hope, and without God in*

[2343] Romans 3:9, 19
[2344] Romans 8:1-2, 10
[2345] Psalm 17:14
[2346] Luke 16:8
[2347] John 15:19
[2348] Acts 8:23
[2349] Romans 6:6, Titus 3:3
[2350] 1 Corinthians 15:17
[2351] Romans 8:8
[2352] Acts 8:23
[2353] Ephesians 2:1, 5
[2354] Romans 6:23
[2355] 1 John 3:12
[2356] John 8:44
[2357] John 6:70-71

the world;[2358] that is, church-less, Covenant-less, promise-less, hopeless and God-less, forasmuch as Jesus Christ is the only head of the church, Testator and Mediator of the New Covenant, substance and accomplishment of the promises, foundation of our eternal hope, and the only way unto God.

(iii) Christless persons are actually under the rigor and curse of the broken Covenant of Works, the law: in that they have not accepted Christ, nor the Covenant of Faith in him, by way of remedy.[2359] And besides Christ, there is no remedy against that curse in the whole world.

(iv) Christless persons are enemies to God, and utterly unable to please God in anything, whilst they so remain.[2360]

(v) Christless persons are without faith: in state of unbelief.[2361] And unbelievers have the wrath of God abiding on them,[2362] so remaining cannot possibly be saved; shall certainly be damned;[2363] yea, are condemned already, because they believe not in the only begotten Son of God.[2364] Who would not strive to be Christ's, and to have Christ theirs: rather than still remain in this sea of misery?

{3} There is such necessity of Jesus Christ for saving of sinners; that without him there is no escaping of damnation, no obtaining of salvation.

They that become not Christ's, must inevitably die in their sins.[2365] *Neither is there salvation in any other: for there is no other name under heaven given among men whereby we must be saved.*[2366] And, no wonder, for:

[2358] Ephesians 2:12
[2359] Galatians 3:10-15
[2360] Romans 8:7-8, Titus 1:14-15
[2361] Galatians 3:7, 29, Ephesians 3:17
[2362] John 3:36
[2363] Mark 16:16
[2364] John 3:18
[2365] John 8:24
[2366] Acts 4:12

(i) No lapsed sinner can possibly save himself. Being darkness, how should he illuminate himself?[2367] Being without strength, how should he help himself?[2368] Being enmity against God, how should he reconcile himself to God?[2369] Being wholly lost, how should he find himself?[2370] Being utterly dead in trespasses and sins, how should he quicken himself?[2371] Etc. Nay, the sinner is so far from effecting his own salvation,[2372] that without supernatural grace he cannot will or desire his own salvation; but contrariwise is willfully set upon his own destruction.[2373]

(ii) No mere creature or created being can save sinners. Nay, all the angels in heaven are not able to save one sinner from eternal wrath, though they should give themselves to die for his sins to all eternity. For they are but finite creatures, and therefore their sufferings being finite also, can never fully satisfy God's infinite justice offended. Should all the mere creatures in the world burn forever in hell's torments for man's sin, all these sufferings could not expiate one sinful thought.

(iii) None in all the world can save sinners, but he that was eternally ordained to be a Savior of sinners.[2374] For sinners' salvation is only effected according to God's eternal decree and predestination. Now Jesus Christ alone is from eternity pre-ordained to be a Savior of sinners.

(iv) None in all the world can save sinners, but he that was since the fall of man, fore-promised, fore-typified and foreprophecied, all along under the Old Testament,[2375] before the fullness of time, to be the only Savior of sinners, and was in fullness of time accordingly exhibited. But Jesus Christ alone is he that was fore-promised, fore-typified and fore-prophesied in all ages of the Old

---

[2367] Ephesians 5:8, Acts 26:18
[2368] Romans 5:6
[2369] Romans 8:7
[2370] Luke 15:32
[2371] Ephesians 2:1, 5
[2372] Philippians 2:13
[2373] Ezekiel 18:31, Matthew 23:37, John 5:40
[2374] 1 Peter 1:20, Acts 10:42 & 17:31
[2375] Acts 10:43, John 5:39, Acts 3:21, 24

Testament, as the seed of the woman,,[2376] seed of Abraham,[2377] the prophet like Moses,[2378] our great high priest after the order of Melchizedek, the son of David,[2379] etc, and was accordingly performed under the New Testament as a Savior of sinners.

(v) None in the whole world can save sinners, but he that can fully and to the uttermost reveal God's counsels touching their salvation, satisfy and appease divine justice offended. Remove the wrath and curse of God from the sinner, conquer sin, death, hell, and all the enemies of sinners salvation, and effectually subdue the sinner to himself, applying all his sufficiencies to him for salvation. But Jesus Christ is the sole person in the whole world that can do these things.[2380]

(vi) All that is in or from sinners, without Christ, tends only and fully to their condemnation. There is nothing in them but flesh, nothing comes from them but flesh. *That which is born of the flesh, is flesh.*[2381] And in their flesh dwells no good thing.[2382] Their minds are darkness and enmity against God;[2383] the small glimmerings of light remaining in them tending only to leave them without excuse. Their consciences are defiled with manifold guilt.[2384] Their wills are perverse and obstinate in evil.[2385] Their affections are wholly distempered and disordered, set more upon sin, the world, etc, than upon God.[2386] Their corporal senses and members are wholly depraved and poisoned with sin.[2387] Every imagination of the thoughts of their hearts is only evil

---

[2376] Genesis 3:15, Galatians 4:4
[2377] Genesis 12:3, Matthew 1:1
[2378] Deuteronomy 18:15, Acts 3:22 & 7:37
[2379] Psalm 110:4, Hebrews 5:10 & 7 throughout
[2380] Colossians 2:2-3, John 1:18, Psalm 40:7-10, Hebrews 10:12-14, 18, Ephesians 5:2, Romans 5:9, Galatians 3:13-14, Romans 8:3, Colossians 2:15, Hebrews 2:14-15, Luke 1:74, Psalm 110:1-3
[2381] John 3:6
[2382] Romans 7:18
[2383] Ephesians 5:8, Romans 8:7 & 1:19-20
[2384] Titus 1:15
[2385] Jeremiah 44:16-17
[2386] Ephesians 2:3, Galatians 5:24
[2387] Romans 3:13-19

continually.[2388] Out of the abundance of their hearts their mouth vents nothing but corrupt communication.[2389] Their righteousness is but dung and filthy rags.[2390] Their duties, prayers and all their sacrifices are abominable before God.[2391] Their plowing, eating, drinking, sleeping, with all their natural actions, even their whole way, is sin[2392] – so that all that sinners are, or can do, without Christ, can only damn them, not at all save them.

(vii) Finally, all things in the world do in one sort or other help forward the condemnation of Christless sinners. By the patience and longsuffering of God abused, they are the more encouraged and resolved in evil;[2393] by the mercies and prosperity they enjoy, they embolden themselves to cast off God's fear, to forget God, to despise and oppose God;[2394] by the judgments inflicted on them, they are hardened the more in their wickedness, and trespass yet more against the Lord – yea, sometimes proceed to blaspheme the Most High;[2395] by the lewdness of the wicked, they are emboldened to run *with them to the same excess of riot*;[2396] by the godliness of the faithful, they are exasperated to hate, revile, and persecute them – yea, sometimes to the death.[2397] Yea, by the very gospel and means of grace, they are blinded, hardened and wax worse and worse.[2398] While they live, they treasure up wrath against the day of wrath;[2399] and when they die, they are actually plunged into a sea of wrath forevermore.[2400] Thus all things help Christless persons to

---

[2388] Genesis 6:5
[2389] Matthew 12:34
[2390] Philippians 3:7-8, Isaiah 64:6
[2391] Isaiah 1:13-15 & 66:3, Proverbs 15:8
[2392] Proverbs 21:4 & 4:14-20 & 15:26, 9
[2393] Ecclesiastes 8:21, Romans 2:4-5
[2394] Psalm 55:19, Proverbs 1:32, Psalm 9:17 & 10:13, Job 21:7-16
[2395] Exodus 7:22 & chapters 8-12
[2396] Psalm 50:16-19; 1 Peter 4:3-4
[2397] 1 John 3:12, Galatians 4:29
[2398] 2 Corinthians 2:15-16, Acts 28:25-27
[2399] Romans 2:5
[2400] Acts 1:25, Luke 16:22-24

perdition. Hence, without Christ there is no salvation, nothing but condemnation.

{4} Jesus Christ is fully able to save sinners, and to make them completely happy to all eternity, for mark what Scripture testifies: *He is able to save them to the uttermost* (Greek: εις το παντελες, perfectly, wholly, fully, absolutely, or for evermore) *that come unto God by him, seeing he ever liveth to make intercession for them.*[2401] All saving abilities, all perfections of a Savior, are eminently in him, whether we respect his person or his office.

The person of Jesus Christ is such that he is fully able to save sinners, for he is God-man in one person:[2402] the Son of God, the second person in Trinity, personally and individually uniting to himself the whole human nature both soul and body.

(i) This human nature of Christ, never distinctly subsisted but in union to the word; (ii) is so united to the word, as therewith to make up but one distinct individual person; (iii) and in that personal union still retains its true human nature and essence wholly distinct and differing from the divine nature and person.

As the mistletoe in the apple-tree: (i) it never distinctly subsisted but in union to the apple tree; (ii) it is so united to the apple tree, as therewith to make up but one individual tree; (iii) and yet in that union it still retains its own nature really differing from the apple tree.

Now:

(i) This Θεάνθρωπος God-man in one person, Jesus Christ, is most sufficient and suitable for saving of sinners, being *medius persona*, that he might be *mediator officio*, he is a middle person between God and man, that he might be a Mediator in office between God and man.[2403] God and man are united in Christ's person, that they might be united and reconciled by Christ's

---

[2401] Hebrews 7:25-26
[2402] John 1:14; 1 Timothy 3:16
[2403] 1 Timothy 2:5

office. Christ as man suffered and died for man's sin – without shedding of blood there being no remission;[2404] Christ as God fully satisfied God's justice by such suffering, the infinite dignity of his Godhead putting a kind of infinite and incomparable value upon the sufferings of his manhood.[2405] Had Christ been God only, he could not have suffered or died: had he been man only, he could not have satisfied by suffering or dying: but being God man, he could both suffer for man, and satisfy by such suffering.

(ii) This God-man is most grateful and acceptable to God above all other persons of men and angels in order to the saving of sinners. His beloved Son in whom he is well pleased,[2406] the Son of his love,[2407] his elect in whom his soul delights,[2408] etc. And therefore, giving himself for us, he was an offering and a sacrifice to God for a sweet-smelling savor.[2409] What this person of infinite dearness to God once did and endured for sinners, more pleased God than if all men, angels, and creatures in the world had endured the utmost extremities of hell's torments for evermore. The office of Jesus Christ God-man is such that he is fully able to save sinners, for:

(a) His office taken upon him for saving of sinners is full and complete for sinners' salvation, namely: his mediatorship, wherein he is prophet,[2410] priest,[2411] and king,[2412] as God-man. Prophet: fully to reveal the great mystery of God's counsel and will touching the saving of sinners by Christ: of which lapsed sinners were wholly ignorant.[2413] Priest: fully to effect and accomplish sinners' salvation, revealed by his perfect satisfaction to divine justice for sinners through his obedience and death, and by his continual intercession for

---

[2404] Romans 4:25, Hebrews 9:22
[2405] Ephesians 5:2, Hebrews 10:12, etc, Acts 20:28
[2406] Matthew 3:17
[2407] Colossians 1:13
[2408] Isaiah 42:1
[2409] Ephesians 5:2
[2410] Acts 3:22
[2411] Hebrews 2:17
[2412] Psalm 2:6 & 110:1
[2413] Luke 4:18-19

them in heaven.[2414] These things, lapsed sinners were never able to effect or work out for themselves. King: to conquer fully all the spiritual enemies of sinners' salvation, sin, death, grave, world, hell and all the powers of darkness; to subdue lost sinners completely to himself, and apply effectually the purchased salvation to them, as their king and head, inchoately in this life, and consummately in the life to come.[2415] This regal conquest and application of salvation purchased lapsed sinners could never have achieved by themselves. And therefore, that mediatory office of Christ whereby, he reveals salvation to sinners wholly ignorant thereof, he obtains salvation revealed for sinners wholly alienated from God, and he applies salvation revealed and obtained to sinners wholly impotent thereunto. That mediatory office must needs be fully complete and sufficient for sinners' salvation.

(b) His calling to this office was such as fully proclaimed his complete ability for sinners' salvation, for: (1) he was preordained to be the Savior of sinners before the foundation of the world was laid.[2416] (2) He was sent, sealed, and commissioned by his heavenly Father in fullness of time, to save sinners.[2417] (3) He was incomparably qualified and furnished with all mediatory fullness, perfections and endowments, that he might be able to save sinners to the uttermost.[2418] (4) He has fully executed and discharged this office whereunto he was called. For he has revealed the whole mystery of God's counsel for saving of sinners,[2419] effectually wrought that salvation revealed for all his elect,[2420] and actually applies in all ages that salvation wrought for all his chosen,[2421] so that no ability for saving of sinners, can possibly be imagined, which is not to be found in Jesus Christ our Savior. Whither therefore should

---

[2414] Hebrews 5:1 & 9:26 & 7:25
[2415] Psalm 110:1-2, Colossians 2:15; 1 Corinthians 15:28, John 10:16, Haggai 2:7, Ezekiel 34:23-24
[2416] 1 Peter 1:20, Acts 10:42 & 17:31
[2417] Galatians 4:4, John 6:27, Matthew 28:18
[2418] John 1:14, 16 & 3:34, Colossians 1:19 & 2:9
[2419] Luke 4:18-19
[2420] Hebrews 9:12
[2421] Psalm 110:1-2, John 16:9-10 & 14:6

poor lost sinners fly, but to Jesus Christ, who is fully able to save them? Jesus Christ is the last Adam.[2422] The first Adam by his disobedience damned all his natural posterity; Jesus Christ the last Adam is much more able by his obedience to save all his spiritual posterity.[2423]

{5} **Jesus Christ is as willing, as able to save sinners.**

He is infinitely able and infinitely willing to save sinners. Shall the Savior be so willing to save: and sinners be so unwilling to be saved? Behold and admire Christ's incomparable willingness to save sinners, most abundantly discovered:

(i) By his cheerful willingness to suffer and die for sinners salvation. Hence Christ is prophetically brought in by the psalmist, saying: *Lo I come, in the volume of the book it is written of me: I delight to do thy will, O my God; yea thy law is in the midst of my bowels.*[2424] This doing of God's will, the apostle expounds of Christ's sufferings, saying: *By the which will we are sanctified, through the offering of the body of Jesus Christ once for all.*[2425] So that Jesus Christ delighted even in suffering his Father's will for sinners. And he professed: *My meat is to do the will of him that sent me, and to finish his work.*[2426] He finished his Father's will, in dying; then, *it was finished.*[2427] Would Christ so humble himself, to such sufferings and such a death, and that so readily for sinners salvation: and was he not most willing to save them?

(ii) By his frequent and sweet invitations of sinners to come to him for salvation: *Ho, everyone that thirsteth, come ye to the waters, and he that hath no money; come ye, buy and eat, yea, come, buy wine and milk without money, and without price,* etc.[2428] – *If any man thirst, let him come to me and drink*[2429] –

[2422] 1 Corinthians 15:45
[2423] Romans 5:12 to the end
[2424] Psalm 40:6-8
[2425] Hebrews 10:5-11
[2426] John 4:34
[2427] John 19:30
[2428] Isaiah 55:1-3
[2429] John 7:37

come unto me all ye that labor and are heavy laden, etc.[2430] – *Let him that is athirst, come; and whosoever will, let him take of the water of life freely.*[2431]

(iii) By his precious soul-alluring promises. What variety of blessings and mercies does he promise to all that will come to him and believe in him? As plenteous enjoyment of the Spirit,[2432] rest of soul,[2433] life,[2434] living water,[2435] and salvation itself.[2436]

(iv) By his rejecting of none that truly come unto him, though never so weak, and worthless in themselves. *All that the Father giveth me, shall come to me; and him that cometh to me, I will in no wise cast out.*[2437] Christ never yet rejected any: and he will not now reject you.

(v) By his expostulating lamentations, when sinners neglect their own salvation, despise their own mercy. *Cast away from you all your transgressions, whereby ye have transgressed, and make you a new heart, and a new spirit; for why will ye die, O house of Israel?*[2438] – *O Jerusalem, Jerusalem, – how oft would I have gathered thy children together, even as a hen gathereth her chickens under her wings, and ye would not!*[2439]

(vi) By his singular joy when sinners are saved, or in the way of salvation. The converting of the Samaritan woman, and afterwards of other Samaritans upon that occasion, was his meat to eat which his disciples knew not of.[2440] Christ is so dearly and delightfully affected with the truly godly, that he says: *Whosoever shall do the will of my Father which is in heaven, the same is my brother, and sister, and mother.*[2441] To this effect the parables of the lost groat,

---

[2430] Matthew 11:28-29
[2431] Revelation 22:17
[2432] John 7:37-39
[2433] Matthew 11:28-29
[2434] Isaiah 55:1-3
[2435] John 4:10, 14 & 6:35
[2436] Mark 16:16
[2437] John 6:37
[2438] Ezekiel 18:31
[2439] Matthew 23:37
[2440] John 4:32 compared with the context before
[2441] Matthew 12:50

of the lost sheep, and of the lost son, emphatically declare the surpassing joy that there is in heaven upon the recovery of the lost sinner.[2442]

(vii) By his actual saving, even of greatest offenders, Christ shows his singular desire and willingness to save lost sinners. Palpable instances of this kind are these: Matthew[2443] and Zacchaeus,[2444] the publicans; the woman of Samaria, and other Samaritans, reputed as a refuse people;[2445] the prodigal son, adumbrating [representing] the miserable Gentiles;[2446] the penitent woman, that had many sins, and was a sinner with a witness;[2447] Mary Magdalene, that had been a very cage of unclean spirits, out of whom Christ cast seven devils;[2448] the thief upon the cross;[2449] Saul himself, that was a cruel persecutor of Christ and his church, and a blasphemer, and injurious; yet he obtained mercy, that in him first Christ Jesus might show forth all longsuffering, for a pattern to them which should hereafter believe on him to life everlasting[2450] – yea, many of them that had a hand in crucifying Jesus Christ, were saved by Jesus Christ.[2451] Oh! When Christ saves such sinners as these, who is not encouraged to believe? Oh how infinitely does Jesus Christ our Savior thirst and long after sinners salvation! And shall not lost sinners thirst after their own salvation: and cheerfully hasten to such a Savior?

{6} **None can ordinarily become Christ's, or be saved by him, but** (i) by rejecting what is inconsistent with him; (ii) by strong desires after him; and (iii) by actual accepting of him, at the gospel propounds him.

[2442] Luke 15 throughout
[2443] Matthew 9:9
[2444] Luke 19:2-11
[2445] John 4
[2446] Luke 15
[2447] Luke 7:37 to the end
[2448] Luke 8:1-3
[2449] Luke 23:40-44
[2450] 1 Timothy 1:13, 16, Acts 26:9-19 & 9:1 etc.
[2451] Acts 2:36 to the end of the chapter

(i) All that would be Christ's must reject and deny all things inconsistent with Christ, namely: they must deny themselves,[2452] their self-sinfulness,[2453] their self-righteousness,[2454] their self-wisdom,[2455] their self-will,[2456] their self love, their self-excellencies and perfections of all sorts,[2457] and all their self-interests in the creature that are any way repugnant to, or inconsistent with Christianity. Otherwise whilst a man remains self-full, he is incapable of Christ's fullness.

(ii) All that would be Christ's must have strong and fervent desires after him. True sense of the want of Christ, and of the misery of that want, fills the soul with pantings and longings after him, hungerings and thirstings for him. The more Christ is desired and thirsted after while wanted, the more he will be esteemed and delighted in when enjoyed. Christ loves nor to come to the soul, until he shall be welcome indeed. Hence, such fervent hungerings after him have the promises of satisfaction.[2458]

(iii) All that would be Christ's must actually close with him, and accept him as the gospel propounds him, namely: they must receive him by true faith,[2459] as their Jesus, their Christ, their Lord, to be saved and ruled by him, to live upon him, and every way to walk worthy of him.[2460] This is the way to become Christ's, and consequently God's New Covenant people in him.

{7} Finally, the great cause why most people in the visible church do not become Christ's, is not because they cannot, but because they will not become his.[2461]

[2452] Luke 9:23
[2453] Titus 2:11-12
[2454] Philippians 3:6-8
[2455] 1 Corinthians 3:18
[2456] Matthew 6:10 & 26:39, 42
[2457] Matthew 10:37, Luke 14:26 to the end
[2458] Isaiah 55:1-3, John 6:25 & 7:37-38, Revelation 22:17
[2459] John 1:11-12
[2460] Colossians 2:6-7
[2461] John 5:40

And at the last day the greatest part of visible professors that shall perish, shall be damned, not so much because they could not, as because they would not come unto Christ for salvation. Let us therefore so strive to be Christ's, so vigorously press after him, and salvation by him, to the uttermost of all our ability and opportunity: that we may not through willfulness neglect or reject Christ, and salvation by him, lest thereby we receive the greater damnation: let us never be found among the number of the will-nots.

I grant indeed that no mere carnal man, can completely come to Christ, accept him, and become his by any, or all his mere natural abilities, or perfections whatsoever, without divine, supernatural renewing grace, for:

(i) Holy Scriptures are full and clear for this. Jesus said: *No man can come unto me except the Father which hath sent me draw him.*[2462] – *It is God which worketh in you, both to will, and to do, of his good pleasure:*[2463] – *which were born, not of blood, nor of the will of the flesh, nor of the will of man, but of God.*[2464]

(ii) Repentance and faith, whereby we come out of ourselves to Christ, are not of ourselves, but are the mere gifts of God.[2465]

(iii) The mere carnal man has – in and of himself – no abilities sufficient to bring him unto Christ. He is without strength,[2466] without light,[2467] without life, and without hope.[2468] His mind is enmity against God and his law,[2469] his conscience is defiled,[2470] his will is rebellious against Christ,[2471] his heart and affections are hardened and estranged from God,[2472] his way is

---

[2462] John 6:44
[2463] Philippians 2:12-13
[2464] John 1:12-13
[2465] 2 Timothy 2:25, Ephesians 2:8
[2466] Romans 5:6
[2467] Ephesians 5:8
[2468] Ephesians 2:1, 12
[2469] Romans 8:7
[2470] Titus 1:15
[2471] Luke 19:14
[2472] Romans 2:4-5

abomination to God,[2473] *the poison of asps is under his tongue*[2474] – yea, *every imagination of the thoughts of his heart is only evil continually.*[2475] He is *dead in sins and trespasses;*[2476] *in the gall of bitterness and bond of iniquity;*[2477] under the power of Satan, *the prince of the air,*[2478] *led captive by him at his will;*[2479] reprobate to every good work;[2480] and remaining *in the flesh cannot please God.*[2481]

(iv) Effectual calling and conversion of a carnal man to Christ is so great a work, as that it utterly transcends, not only all carnal man's abilities, but all mere finite creatures activities: and can only be effected and completed by the infinite power of God himself. For it is no less than the renewing of them that were wholly old and corrupt,[2482] the regenerating of them that were unregenerate,[2483] the releasing of them that were wholly captivated under sin and Satan,[2484] the quickening and passing of them from death to life that were dead in sins and trespasses,[2485] and the new-creating of those who were wholly old creatures.[2486] Hence in the first and fundamental saving work of God upon the soul, the infusion of gracious habits and principles into the soul, the carnal man is merely passive, and can actively do nothing at all therein.

Notwithstanding, a mere carnal man by natural abilities and activities, helped forward by common and restraining grace, may make a great progress towards Christ, and go very far towards salvation, for:

[2473] Proverbs 15:9
[2474] Romans 3:13-14
[2475] Genesis 6:5
[2476] Ephesians 2:1
[2477] Acts 8:23
[2478] Acts 26:18, Ephesians 2:2
[2479] 2 Timothy 2:25
[2480] Titus 1:16
[2481] Romans 8:8
[2482] Titus 3:5
[2483] Titus 3:5, John 3:3
[2484] Luke 4:18-19
[2485] Ephesians 2:1; 1 John 3:14
[2486] 2 Corinthians 5:17

(i) He may disclaim and avoid many gross sins and pollutions of the world: so that he may be blameless among men.[2487]

(ii) He may do all imperate acts of piety and righteousness, namely: all outward imitable acts that a true believer can do. He may profess Christ, read and hear the word, receive the sacraments, fast, pray, confer about matters of religion, give alms, etc. Witness Herod,[2488] the three false grounds,[2489] the Pharisees,[2490] the foolish virgins, etc.[2491]

(iii) He may manifest much zeal, and affection in these performances.[2492]

(iv) He may have a great inward work upon his soul, may be enlightened, may taste of the heavenly gift, may partake of the Holy Spirit, in his common endowments, may taste of the good word of God, and powers of the world to come;[2493] and may believe for a time.[2494] Thus far a mere carnal man may go towards Christ, and yet still remain a mere carnal man, without Christ.

And yet very many (oh that I could not say *most*) in the visible church never came thus far towards Christ and salvation: not because they cannot, but because they will not. Christ said to the Jews: *Ye will not come unto me, that ye might have life.*[2495] And to Jerusalem: *O Jerusalem, Jerusalem, thou that killest the prophets, and stonest them which are sent unto thee, how often would I have gathered thy children together, even as a hen gathereth her chickens under her wings, and ye would not?*[2496] – *We will not have this man to reign over us.*[2497] As no carnal man can of himself fully come to Christ, and be his, so few carnal men will come to him, few will put forth themselves towards Christ so far as they are able, few will go so far as they may go in these four steps

---

[2487] 2 Peter 2:20
[2488] Mark 6:20
[2489] Matthew 13
[2490] Matthew 5 & 6 & 23
[2491] Matthew 25:1, etc.
[2492] Matthew 13:20-21
[2493] Hebrews 6:4-5
[2494] Luke 8:13
[2495] John 5:40
[2496] Matthew 23:37
[2497] Luke 19:14

forementioned, therefore they are willing to be without Christ, willing to perish, yea willful to their own destruction. And if men are condemned not only for weakness, but for willfulness also, how dreadful and inexcusable will that condemnation be.

Seeing then that all these things are so: (a) that naturally since the fall, all people in the world are Christless; (b) that all persons, whilst Christless, are most miserable; (c) that without Christ there is no escaping of damnation, no obtaining of salvation; (d) that Jesus Christ is fully able to save sinners to the uttermost; (e) that Jesus Christ is as willing as able to save sinners; (f) that ordinarily none can be saved by Christ, but by rejecting what is inconsistent with Christ, by strong desires after him, and actual accepting of him according to the tender of the gospel; and (g) that the great cause why most in the visible church become not Christ's, is not so much because they cannot, but because they will not – for one cannot, a thousand will-nots shall be condemned – oh how should all strive and endeavor to the utmost to accept Christ tendered, and to become Christ's, that so they may in Christ become God's New Covenant people!

[2] *Let all, that upon good grounds find they are in New Covenant with God, through Christ, walk worthy of Jesus Christ, the Lord accepted,* **unto all pleasing.**[2498]

They that have received Christ, should answerably walk in Christ: *as ye have therefore received Christ Jesus the Lord, so walk ye in him.*[2499] But how are we to walk worthy of Christ? According to these and such like Scripture directions:

{1} **Know Jesus Christ and his will, clearly and judiciously:**

[2498] Colossians 1:10
[2499] Colossians 2:6

This is life eternal, that they might know thee the only true God, and Jesus Christ whom thou hast sent.[2500] – *I know my sheep, and am known of mine.*[2501] – *and to desire, that ye might be filled with the knowledge of his will in all wisdom and spiritual understanding, that ye might walk worthy of the Lord unto all pleasing, being fruitful in every good work, and increasing in the knowledge of God.*[2502] Christ is most worthy to be known, for: *in him are hid all the treasures of wisdom and knowledge.*[2503] There is such an excellence of the knowledge of Jesus Christ our Lord, that Paul counted all things loss and dung for it, desiring to know nothing else.[2504] And he bowed his knee to God, for the Ephesians, that they *might be able to comprehend with all saints, what is the breadth, and length, and depth, and height, and to know the love of Christ, which passeth knowledge.*[2505] In comparison to this, all knowledge is but ignorance, all learning is but barbarism. Know Christ, and know all. *Si Christum nescis*, etc.

{2} **Be rooted and grounded in the faith and love of Christ more and more.**

As ye have therefore received Jesus Christ the Lord, so walk ye in him: rooted – and stablished in the faith, as ye have been taught, abounding therein with thanksgiving.[2506] – *that Christ may dwell in your hearts by faith, that ye being rooted and grounded in love*, etc.[2507] There is faith, the doctrine of Christ: be rooted in that strongly, against all errors and deceits of men. There is faith, the grace of Christ – be grounded in that sincerely and vigorously, against all corruptions and temptations. By that faith, let Christ dwell in your

---

[2500] John 17:3
[2501] John 10:14
[2502] Colossians 1:9-10
[2503] Colossians 2:2-3
[2504] Philippians 3:7-10; 1 Corinthians 2:2
[2505] Ephesians 3:14, 18-19
[2506] Colossians 2:6-7
[2507] Ephesians 3:17-18

hearts, and let Christ live in you continually.[2508] Think seriously of Christ's grounded love to you (Ephesians 3:18-19, Galatians 2:20, Revelation 1:5, John 15:9, 13-14, Romans 5:6-8), and then strive to return a cordial and grounded love to Christ – such a love to Christ, as: (i) to love him sincerely for himself (Song of Solomon 1:2-3 & 5:10 to the end); (ii) to love him intensively over all, counting no enjoyments, relations, no nor life itself dear, for his sake (Matthew 10:37, Luke 14:26, Acts 20:24 & 21:13), with love as strong as death and grave, having a vehement and unquenchable flame (Song of Solomon 8:6-7); (iii) to keep his commandments delightfully (John 14:15 & 15:10, 14; 1 John. 5:3); (iv) to abide and continue in his love constantly (John 15:9-10), loving the Lord Jesus Christ in incorruption (Ephesians 6:24); and (v) to love his members, and our Christian brethren sincerely: yea as Christ has loved us; which is his new commandment, because love is therein urged by a new pattern (John 13:34, Colossians 3:12-13).

{3} Walk as Christ walked, in all imitable acts and excellencies, taking him for an example, treading in his steps.

He that saith he abideth in him, ought himself also to walk, even as he walked.[2509]

Question: How did Christ walk?

Answer: (i) in meekness and holiness of heart (Matthew 11:28-29). (ii) Holily, righteously, soberly, unblamably, without sin or offense (Isaiah 53:9, Hebrews 7:26, John. 8:46); (iii) in all zealous obedience to his Father's will, and finishing of his work given him to do (John 4:32, 34 & 2:17); (iv) most fruitfully, walking about and doing good everywhere (Acts 10:38, Matthew 4:23. & 9:35, Mark 6:6); (v) most spiritually and heavenly, taking all occasions to raise up his disciples and hearers to spirituality (John. 4:32, 33, 34. & 15:1, etc & 4:7, 10, etc., Luke 10:21, and often); (vi) most devoutly, being much in

---

[2508] Ephesians 3:17, Galatians 2:20
[2509] 1 John 2:6

servant prayers night and day, Matthew 14:23, Luke 6:12, Mark 6:46, Matthew 26:36, John 17:1 to the end, Hebrews 5:7), teaching us to pray daily (Matthew 6, Luke 11); (vii) most compassionately towards poor sinners, (Matthew 9:36 & 14:14, Mark 1:41, Luke 7:13 & 15:20, Hebrews 5:2), both in reference to their bodies and souls; (viii) most patiently, in his afflictions, though most unjustly inflicted (1 Peter 2:21-24, Isaiah 53:7) – yea, praying for his murderers: *Father forgive them, for they know not what they do* (Luke 23:34). Thus Christ walked, and Bernard says well: "Christians, having their name from Christ; it is meet, as they are heirs of his name, so they should be imitators of his holiness."[2510]

{4} **Eschew all evil possible, and pursue all good.**

Let us cast off the works of darkness, and put on the armor of light. Let us walk honestly as in the day, not in rioting and drunkenness, not in chambering and wantonness, not in strife and envying. But put ye on the Lord Jesus Christ, and make no provision for the flesh to fulfill the lusts thereof.[2511] – *They that are Christ's, have crucified the flesh, with the passions and lusts.*[2512] Christians are *God's workmanship, created in Christ Jesus unto good works; which God hath before ordained, that we should walk in them.*[2513]

{5} **Have your hearts and conversations fixedly in heaven.**

Christ is risen and ascended; let your hearts and affections, lives and actions rise and ascend after him.[2514]

[2510] "Christiani à Christo nomen acceperunt; & operae pretium est, ut sicut sunt haeredes nominis ita sint imitatores sanctitatis" Bern *Sentent*. l. p. 496. 1. (Antwerp, 1616)
[2511] Romans 13:12-14, Titus 2:13-14
[2512] Galatians 5:24
[2513] Ephesians 2:10
[2514] Colossians 3:1-3, etc, Philippians 3:20

{6} Grow and increase daily in grace and in the knowledge of Jesus Christ our Lord.[2515]

Forgetting what is behind, and reaching forth unto those things which are before, press towards the mark for the price of the high calling of God in Christ Jesus.[2516]

{7} Maintain sweet communion with Jesus Christ, whereunto you are called.[2517]

This is light in darkness, liberty in prison, joy in sorrow, heaven in earth, life in death.

{8} Love, long for, and hasten unto the coming of our Lord Jesus Christ to judgment, that you may be taken home unto himself, and be ever with the Lord to behold his glory (2 Timothy 4:7; 2 Peter 3:11-12, Philippians 3:20-21, John 14:2, 3:24; 1 Thessalonians 4:17).

Make haste O my beloved, etc (Song of Solomon 8:14) *Even so, come Lord Jesus* (Revelation 22:20). *I desire to be dissolved and be with Christ, which is far more best* (Philippians 3:23).[2518]

{9} Strive that whether you be present with Christ, or absent from him, you may be accepted by him.[2519]

Whether you live, live to the Lord; whether you die, die to the Lord; whether you live or die, endeavor to be the Lord's – for to this end, Christ both died, and rose, and revived, *that he might be Lord both of the dead and living*.[2520] And as Christ is the door and gate of paradise, the only way to the

---

[2515] 2 Peter 3:18
[2516] Philippians 3:12-14
[2517] 1 Corinthians 1:9; 1 John 1:3
[2518] πολλω μαλλον κρεισσον Philippians 1:23
[2519] 2 Corinthians 5:6-9
[2520] Romans 14:8-9

Father and to eternal life: so let him be to you, the way, the truth, and the life.[2521]

Chrysostom says hereupon: "I am the way, because you shall come by me; the truth, because doubtless these things shall be, nor is there any lie in me; the life, because even death itself shall not hinder your coming to me. And if I be the way, you need no guide: if the truth, I speak no falsehood: if the life, though you die, yet shall you obtain what I have promised."[2522]

Augustine: "I am the way, and the truth, and the life: that is, by me they go, to me they come, in me they abide. All must begin their journey from Christ, who desire to come to the truth, and abide in eternal life."[2523] And again: "Would you walk? I am the way. Would you not be deceived? I am the truth. Would you not die? I am the life."[2524] And elsewhere: "What way will you go? I am the way. Whither will you go? I am the truth. Where will you abide? I am the life."[2525]

The interlinear gloss: "The way without error, to them that seek; the truth without falsehood, to them that find: the life without death, to them that abide."[2526]

Gerson: "He is the life, animating; the way, moving: the truth, establishing."[2527]

Hugo: "He is the way leading; the truth shining; the life unending."[2528]

But Bernard most excellently: "We your people and sheep of your pasture will follow you, by you, unto you, because you are the way, the truth, and the life: the way, in example; the truth, in the promise; the life in the reward."[2529]

[2521] John 14:6
[2522] John Chrysostom, Homily 72 in John 14, p.464 (Lutet., 1633)
[2523] Augustine, *On Christian Doctrine*, 1.34.3
[2524] Augustine, *Exposition on the Gospel of John*, Tract. 22, p.195, D. Tom. 9 (Basil, 1569)
[2525] Augustine, *De Verb. Dom.*, Serm. 54 in initio, p.207, Tom. 10
[2526] "Via sine errore, quaerentibus: veritas sine falsitate, invenientibus; vita finemorte, permanentibus;" Gloss. Inter.
[2527] Gerson in prefat. lib. *De Vit. Spirit.*
[2528] Hugo *De Prat.* Serm. 1. *De Spias Coron.*
[2529] Bernard. *De Ascensione Dom.* Serm. 2. in fine. p. 195 (Antwerp, 1626)

And elsewhere more fully: "I am the way, by which you are to go; the truth, to which you are to come; and the life, in which you are to abide. I am the way without error, the truth without falsehood, the life without death. I am the way in example, the truth in promise, the life in reward. I am the way passable, the truth irrevocable, the life interminable. I am the way, large, and spacious; the truth, mighty and copious; the life, delectable and glorious. I am the way of beginners, the truth of proficiency, the life of attainers. I am the way of light, serene; the truth living without pain; the life happy and pleasant. I am the way, on the cross, the truth in the grave; the life, enjoy of resurrection. I am the way wherein is no thorn or thistle; the truth, wherein is no sting of falsehood; the life, in which he that is dead, revives. I am the way, direct; the truth, perfect; the life, without end and measure. I am the way of reconciliation, the truth of retribution, the life of blessedness. *None cometh unto the Father but by me*; as if he had said, *none comes unto me the truth and the life but by me the way*, etc. Oh let this way, without wandering; this truth, without shadowing; this life, without ending; be always our way, truth, and life; our true way to eternal life, Amen."[2530]

Thus of the blessed, all-sufficient, and only Mediator, Surety, and Testator of the New Federal Testament or Testamental Covenant: Jesus Christ.

[2530] Bernard in *Cena Domini*, Sermon 7, pp. 1333-1334 (Antwerp, 1616).

Chapter 7

Of the form of the New Covenant.

Aphorism: The form of this New Covenant consists inwardly, in the mutual obligation between God and his New Covenant federates in Jesus Christ the Mediator thereof: outwardly, in the way and manner of this New Covenant's manifestation, confirmation and administration.

This aphorism needs very little explanation or proof, so much having been already spoken to this effect.[2531] Therefore briefly thus:

(1) **The inward, more essential, and constitutive form of the New Covenant, especially stands, in the mutual and reciprocal obligation of God and his federates in Jesus Christ one to another.**

This is the inward form of all covenants: herein they all agree. Without this, the very nature of a covenant is destroyed.

[1] The Lord God – Father, Son, and Holy Spirit – on his part expressly obliges himself to his federates, by promising most excellent New Covenant blessings (Hebrews 8:10, 11, 12. Jeremiah 31:33-34).[2532] "And faithful," (says Augustine sweetly) "is God, who has made himself our debtor: not by receiving anything of us, but by promising so great things to us. His promise was little, he would be bound by writing also, making, as it were, a hand writing of his promises to us, that when he should begin to perform the things which he has promised in the Scripture of promises, we might consider the order of performances. The time of prophecy was the time of the prediction of

---

[2531] In Book 4, Chapter 2, Aphorism 1 & Chapter 3, Aphorism 1 & Chapter 5, Section 2
[2532] See before in Chapter 3, Aphorism 1

promises; the time from John the Baptist to the end, is the time of performances."[2533]

[2] The house of Israel and Judah, even all the New Covenant federates with God in Christ in all nations, Jewish and Gentile, do on their part implicitly re-oblige themselves to God by re-promising many important New Covenant duties answerable to, and grounded upon, or flowing from those New Covenant blessings, as I have formerly noted, in Chapter 5, Section 2, General 2. These promised blessings and repromised duties of the New Covenant, have been abundantly unfolded, in Chapter 5, Section 3, Aphorisms 1 & 2.

(2) **The outward and more accidental form of the New Covenant**, is principally comprised in the way and manner of this New Covenant's [1] manifestation, [2] confirmation, and [3] administration.

---

[1] *The manifestation of this New Covenant.*

This has in it two things, namely:

{1} God's first and promissory revelation of it. God revealed his New Covenant at first, immediately to the prophet Jeremiah; mediately by him unto the people of God under Babylonian thralldom; God promising therein what manner of New Covenant he would make with his church after those days, namely: in the days of Christ's incarnation.[2534] God revealed and first manifested promissorily his New Covenant: (i) partly, in reference to the Jews his own people, to comfort them in their sad Babylonian afflictions; (ii) partly, in reference to the Old Covenant, which – being weak and unprofitable –

[2533] Augustine on Psalm 110, at the start
[2534] Jeremiah 31:31-34

needed to be reformed; (iii) partly in regard to the greatness of man's sin and misery, that could not be healed but by, the New Covenant Mediator actually revealed – all of which, I have formerly manifested.[2535]

{2} God's after and preparatory inchoation of this New Covenant. The New Covenant had its preparatory inchoation, as I have already shown:[2536] (i) by the ministry of John the Baptist, who by his doctrine and baptism made way for Christ and his New Covenant kingdom, as a middle prophet between the Old and New Covenant; (ii) by the ministry of Jesus Christ himself in person, and of his disciples, who, by New Covenant doctrine miracles confirming the same, and baptism the first New Covenant token, began to lay the foundation of the New Covenant. But touching these things I need speak no further.

[2] *The confirmation of this New Covenant*

This is surpassingly eminent, namely: {1} by the Lord's choicest promises; {2} by the inviolable oath of God; {3} by the irrevocable death and most precious blood of Jesus Christ; {4} by the best sacramental tokens: baptism and the Lord's supper.

{1} **By the choicest promises of God.** Notable is that of the apostles touching Christ: b*ut now hath he obtained a more excellent ministry, by how much also he is the mediator of a better covenant, which* νενομοθετηται: *is established upon better promises.*[2537] This better Covenant, whereof Christ is Mediator, is the New Covenant: therefore this New Covenant is established, confirmed, etc, upon better promises.[2538] The Greek word here, for {*established*} properly signifies: is-put-as-a-law, is-enacted-as-a-law, is-made-

---

[2535] In this 4th Book, Chapter 3, Aphorism 2, the occasion, etc.
[2536] In this 4th Book, Chapter 3, Aphorism 2, the occasion, etc.
[2537] Hebrews 8:6
[2538] Hebrews 9:15 & 12:24

authentic, is-confirmed, is-established. It denotes such an establishment of the New Covenant as is of authority, force, virtue, and efficacy like an established law, like a law enacted by good authority.

The promises of God (for such only are here intended) are God's gracious declarations of the good-pleasure of his will in Jesus Christ, touching any future good, temporal, spiritual or eternal, which he will perform unto his people (Titus 1:2. Ephesians 1:9; 2 Peter 1:4; 2 Corinthians 1:20; 1 Timothy 4:8). This is the nature of God's promises in the general. Now God's New Covenant promises, upon which it is established, are better promises. Note here: (i) how they are better promises, and (ii) how this New Covenant is established upon them.

(i) ***The New Covenant's promises are better promises than those of the Old Covenant***, and consequently much more than those of the fore-going Covenants, in many regards, as:

(a) **Better in regard to perspicuity and clearness.** The promises of the Old Covenant were very dark, dim and obscure. They were promises under a veil, under shadows and types, especially if we consider spirituals and eternals. Christ is promised under the types of Moses, Aaron, Melchizedek, David, etc.[2539] Redemption is promised under the types of bringing Israel out of Egypt, and Judah out of Babylon:[2540] remission of sins and justification is promised under the types of expiatory sacrifices, burnt-offerings, sin-offerings, the scapegoat, etc. Sanctification is promised under diverse ceremonial washings, cleansings, purifications: heaven and eternal rest there, is promised under the types of the land of rest, Canaan, and of the holy of holies in the tabernacle and temple, etc. Thus those promises were under a veil, very dark and obscure: and it was a hard matter for the people to discern these mysteries in those shadows. Besides, the promises of Christ, and the things of Christ, under and before the Old Covenant, were at a great distance; as to come long

---

[2539] Deuteronomy 18:15-20, Hebrews 5:4-5, Psalm 110:4, Ezekiel 37:24-25
[2540] Genesis 15:13-14, 16, etc; Isaiah 49 throughout

after; the fathers beheld them afar off (Hebrews 11:13). And what we see at a distance afar off, we behold very darkly, weakly and imperfectly. But the promises of the New Covenant are clear, plain, perspicuous, without veil, the veil being so done away in Christ come, and exhibited already in our flesh, so that we may with open face behold them (2 Corinthians 3:12, 14, 18).

(b) **Better in regard to spirituality.** The promises of the Old Covenant, and of those before, were in the current and tenor of those more carnal, literal, external, temporal, and outward blessings for the most part, as: bruising the serpent's head, preservation in the ark from the flood, possession of Canaan, prosperity, peace, and rest there, a visible and earthly sanctuary, etc. And a great part of the people did carnally rest in these externals only, not aspiring to the spirituals intended therein. But the New Covenant promises in the express tenor and strain of them are more spiritual, celestial and sublime, very few externals in comparison being insisted upon in all the New Covenant explanations. And the whole body of the New Covenant[2541] (as I have already manifested)[2542] consists only of promises, and all those promises, only of spirituals, far excelling all temporals whatsoever. Diligently consult what has been formerly said to this point.

(c) **Better in regard to divine efficacy and sufficiency**, for:

(1) The Old Covenant promises under Levitical rites and shadows did figure, propound, and promise that which themselves did not perform (as Beza notes),[2543] in that they did transmit or send the minds of believers to Christ that was to come, and to the New Covenant. *The law made nothing perfect, but the bringing in of a better hope did*, etc.[2544] But the promises of the New Covenant perform what they promise, and do not refer us to any further covenant or promises to supply their defectiveness. Those under the Old Testament, as well as those under the New, that were savingly redeemed,

---

[2541] Hebrews 8:10-12, Jeremiah 31:33-34
[2542] In this 4th Book, Chapter 5, Section 2, Generals 1-3
[2543] Beza's Annotation on Hebrews 8:6
[2544] Hebrews 7:19

pardoned, justified etc, received these blessings from the virtue of the blood of the New Testament (Hebrews 9:14).

(2) The promises of the Old Covenant assured of many blessings in case of such obedience to the law, such performances, etc (Deuteronomy [28:1-15], Exodus 19:5-6, Deuteronomy 11:13 to the end), but not furnished with ability for such obedience and performances, the Covenant being written only in hard tables of stone.[2545] But the promises of the New Covenant do not only assure of blessings from God, but also of ability to perform all our duties to God; God covenanting to write his law in our minds and hearts to that end[2546] – yea (as has been shown),[2547] this New Covenant in the body of it consisting only of promises. All our duties and abilities for them as well as God's mercies are founded on those promises, and are to be fetched from them.

(3) The promises of the Old Covenant running mostly in a low, carnal, earthly strain, did not so powerfully raise the federates, to spiritualness, heavenliness and participation of the divine nature, as those of the New Covenant do.[2548]

(4) The promises of the Old Covenant, being for the generality about outward things, did not, could not so inwardly refresh and revive the souls of wounded sinners or distressed saints. But the New Covenants promises are evidently so contrived, digested, and propounded, as may most sweetly and sufficiently remove all the principal doubts, discouragements and objections, which either a bleeding, heart-wounded sinner, or a distressed saint, may make against his own salvation, as has been already manifested in many particulars,[2549] so that of all God's promises, his New Covenant promises must needs be acknowledged most consolatory, and most exquisitely cordial to a distressed soul.

[2545] Deuteronomy 4:13
[2546] Hebrews 8:10
[2547] In this 4th Book, Chapter 5, Section 2, General 2
[2548] 2 Peter 1:3-4
[2549] In this 4th Book, Chapter 5, Section 2, General 5

(d) **Better in regard to extent.** The Old Covenant promises, and others before, were more peculiarly directed and limited to certain peculiar families, or to that one particular nation of the Jews;[2550] the nations of the Gentiles being strangers from the Covenants of Promise.[2551] But the New Covenant promises are, without restraint or limitation, extended to all nations of the world.[2552]

(e) **Better in regard to duration.** A very great part of the promises of the Old Covenant and of others foregoing, as touching deliverance from Egypt, from Babylon, bringing into Canaan, victory over Canaanites, the temple at Jerusalem, etc., having received their accomplishment, are expired. But the New Covenant promises, with the New Covenant, which is everlasting,[2553] do and shall still endure until the end of the world. And the more durable promises are, the better they are. Thus the promises of the New Covenant are far better promises than those of the old and of other fore-going covenants.

(ii) *Now, upon these better promises the New Covenant is established and firmly settled – and that in various ways*, namely:

(a) Materially: as these better promises are the very matter of the New Covenant, of which it is composed and constituted, for the New Covenant mercies promised on God's part to his federates are contained in these better promises, expressly; and the New Covenant duties restipulated are comprised in these better promises, implicitly.[2554] Now all the promises of God, and consequently these better promises in an eminent sort, have these two properties in them: (1) Infallible verity and truth: it being utterly impossible that God (who is the supreme truth, and fountain of all truth) should lie in them.[2555] *God who cannot lie hath promised.*[2556] (2) Immutability or

---

[2550] Romans 9:4
[2551] Ephesians 2:12
[2552] Mark 16:15-16, Luke 24:46, Matthew 28:18-20
[2553] Hebrews 13:20
[2554] Hebrews 8:10-12
[2555] Hebrews 6:13, 18
[2556] Titus 1:2

unchangeableness. As with God there is no variableness nor shadow of turning,[2557] so God's promises are immutable promises. Now God's New Covenant being materially molded up and composed of better promises, having these two properties – certain verity and infallibility – it must needs be notably established upon such promises.[2558]

(b) Relatively and reductively: as these better promises relate to Christ, and reductively bring this New Covenant to Christ, who is the proper base & foundation upon which it is bottomed. For these – as all other the promises of God since the fall – *are in Christ yea, and in him amen.*[2559] Christ is as the center where the lines of all the promises meet: Christ is as the glorious sun, whence all the resplendent beams of the promises flow. Christ is as the very sea or ocean, whither all the streams and rivers of the promises run. Jesus Christ is the primary and precious foundation of both promises and Covenants, the promises are as pillars of gold upon this foundation, and the Covenants as chapiters of gold upon those pillars.

{2} **By the inviolable oath of God**. Although God established not his Old Covenant by his oath, but (as I have shown)[2560] by another manner of sanction, because that Covenant was to wax old and vanish away;[2561] yet has he established this New Covenant (which is still to remain new, fresh and vigorous, 2 Corinthians 3:11, Hebrews 13:20) by his own sacred and inviolable oath, of which he will never repent, in establishing Christ's New Covenant mediation in his everlasting Melchizedekian priesthood by his oath irrevocably, unalterably. *The LORD hath sworn, and will not repent, thou art a priest forever after the order of Melchizedek.*[2562] The Old Covenant priesthood was made without an oath, but Christ's New Covenant priesthood with an oath, hence the apostle concludes the New Covenant itself to be better (Hebrews

---

[2557] James 1:17
[2558] Hebrews 6:13-19
[2559] 2 Corinthians 1:20
[2560] In Book 3, Chapter 4, Aphorism 5, Section 1, Particular 6
[2561] Hebrews 8:13
[2562] Psalm 110:4, Hebrews 7 throughout, but especially see verses 20-25

7:20-22), namely: more firm, unchangeable, lasting, etc., than the Old Covenant. So then, Christ's everlasting Melchizedekian priesthood, and his New Covenant have such a near, close, inseparable relation and connection to, and dependence upon one another, that God – confirming Christ's priesthood by his oath – he consequently confirms this New Covenant by his oath. Now God established his New Covenant by oath:

(i) To declare hereby the immutability of his counsel in his New Covenant. Though God's bare saying may sometimes implicitly leave a liberty for revoking or altering (Jeremiah 18:7-8), as in the case of the Old Covenant; yet God's swearing puts things sworn past reversing. See Hebrews 6:17, Psalm 89:34-35, and Isaiah 54:9-10. For God, by his oath, pawns his own being, life, power, truth, holiness, etc, to make good what he has so ratified.

(ii) To exalt and magnify by his oath the excellency of the New Covenant so sworn, above the Old (Hebrews 6:20-22; 2 Corinthians 3:11). Every covenant or thing, the more firm and permanent it is, the more excellent it is.

(iii) To fill and furnish the hearts of his true federate people with strong consolation, assurance and encouragement in his New Covenant, who have fled for refuge to lay hold upon the hope set before us (Hebrews 6:17-20). An oath is the strongest and most inviolable bond amongst men, *an oath for confirmation is an end of all strife*;[2563] how much more strong and securing is God's oath. Who shall doubt, when God swears; who cannot possibly deny himself, or forswear himself? Oh, let us comfort ourselves in the New Covenant, and in Christ's New Covenant mediation, in this: that God has confirmed them by his oath, and he will never repent, they shall stand forever.

{3} By the irrevocable death and blood of Jesus Christ our Mediator, Surety, and Testator. The Old Covenant or testament had a solemn typical sanction by slaying of sacrifices, and blood sprinkled;[2564] but the New Covenant or testament had the most solemn, antitypical, and substantial

---

[2563] Hebrews 6:16
[2564] Exodus 24 throughout with Hebrews 9:18-20, etc.

sanction, by the death, blood and sacrifice of Jesus Christ himself, *who is over all God blessed forever, amen.*[2565] By Christ's own death, blood and sacrifice of himself, this New Covenant was dedicated and established (Hebrews 9:12, 14-17, 23, etc, Matthew 26:27-28, Mark 14:23-24, Luke 22:20; 1 Corinthians 11:25). Now Christ's death (and consequently his dedication and sanction of his New Covenant thereby), was with greatest solemnity, as I have already manifested in several particulars.[2566] And as Christ's death, bloodshed, and sacrificing of himself, was with greatest solemnity; so it was of greatest force and efficacy for the establishment of this his New Covenant forever, for:

(i) Christ Jesus died, shed his blood, and offered up himself without spot to God by the eternal Spirit, as Mediator, Surety, and Testator of the New Covenant.[2567] He died not in a private, but in this public capacity: to seal up his New Covenant, and his elect's salvation according to it, with his own blood.

(a) As Jesus Christ is Mediator, he established his New Covenant by his death, blood, and sacrifice. In that hereby, he has fully pacified God towards his elect, as their propitiation (Hebrews 8:12; 1 John 2:1-2, Romans 3:25). And reconciled his elect meritoriously unto God (Romans 5:10). So that now God and they are in Christ's blood brought unto terms of sweetest unity, peace and favor (Ephesians 2:13-19).

(b) As Jesus Christ is Surety, he has by his blood established the New Covenant. In that he has thereby completely discharged our debt which we had contracted by the violation of God's laws, having therein satisfied God's justice and laws to the uttermost for all his elect, Hebrews 7:22. & 9:12, 13, 14. & 10:10. To 19. Ephesians 5:2;

(c) As Jesus Christ is Testator, he has by his death confirmed, made authentical, and consummated this his last will and testament, inasmuch as *a testament is of force after men are dead, otherwise it is of no strength at all*

[2565] Romans 9:5
[2566] In Book 4, Chapter 1, Aphorisms 1 & 2
[2567] Hebrews 9:14-17, 23, etc, & 7:22

while the testator liveth.[2568] The testator while he lives has power of revoking his testament, and of making a later as often as he will, and as the first deed, so the last will stands in force; but when the testator has once ratified his testament by his death, there can be no more revocation or alteration thereof. Therefore Christ the Testator being dead, his New Testament is irrevocably confirmed: nothing can be added thereto, taken thence from, or changed therein, until the world's end.

(ii) Jesus Christ dying as Mediator, Surety and Testator, established this New Covenant by his death, blood and sacrifice of himself, virtually and consequentially. And this in several ways:

(a) *Adimplendo*: by fulfilling and abrogating the Old Covenant. By his death he fulfilled and vacated all the sacrifices of the Old Covenant: and the body being come, he drew a curtain over all those pictures and shadows thereof. This was one thing intended in Christ's speech on the cross: *It is finished.*[2569] This Old Covenant and sacrifices thereof were taken away, that the New Covenant, in Christ's blood might be established. *He taketh away the first, that he may establish the second.*[2570] Both could not be in full force at once. The Old therefore is abolished, that the New may be established.

(b) *Vincendo*: by conquering sin, Satan, death and curse, those spiritual enemies that stand in the way of our enjoyment of the blessings of the New Covenant.[2571] And he conquered them by his death and cross.

(c) *Merendo*: by meriting for his elect by his death all the blessings of the New Covenant, as redemption, reconciliation to God, vocation, sanctification, adoption, justification, etc. These are the purchases of his blood and death (Hebrews 9:12, Romans 5:9-10, Hebrews 9:14, Galatians 4:4-5, Romans 3:25, Hebrews 10:19-20).[2572] Now Christ – meriting and obtaining for us by his

---

[2568] Hebrews 9:14-17
[2569] John 19:30
[2570] Hebrews 10:8-10, etc.
[2571] Romans 8:3, Hebrews 2:14-15, Colossians 2:14-15, Galatians 3:13
[2572] See Book 4, Chapter 1, Aphorism 2

death all the New Covenant benefits from God – has thereby established most notably the New Covenant itself. Thus, the death of Jesus Christ, was the life of the New Covenant; his sacrifice of himself was the establishment of the New Covenant. The New Covenant can no more fail than Christ can die again or shed his blood again.

{4} **Finally, the New Covenant is confirmed and established by the best sacramental tokens, baptism, and the Lord's supper.** Ever since God's promises were in Scripture called {*covenants*}, they have been confirmed by visible and sensible tokens, as: the Covenant with Noah, by the token of the rainbow; the Covenant with Abraham and Israel at Sinai, by the ordinary tokens: circumcision and the passover, and for a time in the wilderness by the four extraordinary tokens, the cloudy fiery pillar, sea, manna, and water out of the rock: the Covenant with David and with the captives, by circumcision and the passover. Thus this last and most excellent Covenant is confirmed by two sacramental tokens excelling all that went before, namely: baptism and the Lord's supper; which are, in signification, clearer; in virtue, greater; in utility, better; in act, easier; in number, fewer, etc, as I have formerly noted out of Augustine.[2573] Those sacraments were bloody; these not bloody. Those signified darkly Christ to come afterwards; these signify clearly Christ come already. Those were painful and costly; these without pain, and cheap. Those did wax old and vanish away with the Old Covenant; these are still to continue in force until the world's end with the New Covenant. Now both in those Old and these New Covenant tokens:

(i) Some were first, for the initiating of persons visibly into the mystical body of Christ the church, etc, as circumcision, ordinarily; the cloudy fiery-pillar and the sea, extraordinarily – to all which, baptism under the New Testament most fully answers, and plainly succeeds them (Colossians 2:10-13, etc; 1 Corinthians 10:1-2, etc).

[2573] In Book 4, Chapter 2, Aphorism 2

(ii) Some were second, for continuing and nourishing up persons initiated in the church by Christ the spiritual meat and drink of the soul, as the passover, ordinarily; manna from heaven, and water out of the rock, extraordinarily: to all which the Lord's supper under the New Testament most fully answers, and evidently comes in the room of them (1 Corinthians 5:7 & 10:3-4, 16-17. & 11:23-30).

Now as I have formerly opened the nature of the covenant tokens or sacraments of Old, showing how they did confirm those covenants whereunto they were annexed, respectively;[2574] so I shall – touching baptism and the Lord's supper, those two tokens of the New Covenant – briefly show: (i) that baptism and the Lord's supper do confirm and establish the New Covenant. (ii) Wherein the nature of baptism and the Lord's supper consists. (iii) How these two tokens do confirm this New Covenant.

(i) *That baptism and the Lord's supper do confirm the New Covenant*, is evident.

(a) **Baptism confirms the New Covenant.** This is plain:

(1) From Christ's commission: as Christ gave commission to his apostles, to disciple all nations, by preaching to them the New Covenant doctrine;[2575] so he appointed them to baptize all them that should be so discipled, professing their faith. To what end should they be so baptized, and at that time: but to initiate them into, and establish them in the New Covenant.

(2) From the apostolic practice: who – when (upon their preaching the New Covenant doctrine) any did believe and profess the same – did forthwith confirm, establish, and seal them in that their New Covenant faith and doctrine, by baptizing them.[2576]

(3) From the New Covenant blessings confirmed by baptism: it confirms to us regeneration (John 3:3, 5, Titus 3:5), remission of sins and justification

---

[2574] See Book 3, Chapter 2, Aphorism 3 & Chapter 3, Aphorism 4
[2575] Matthew 28:19-20, Mark 16:15-16
[2576] Acts 2:39-41 & 10:44, 47-48 & 16:14-15, 31-33

(Romans 8:38), sanctification, by dying unto sin and living unto righteousness (Romans 6:3-12, Colossians 2:11-12, etc.), adoption into God's family, and communion with Christ (Galatians 3:26-27). Now these are New Covenant blessings.[2577] Therefore baptism – confirming the New Covenant blessings to us – consequently confirms the New Covenant itself.

[4] From the analogy between circumcision and baptism. Circumcision was a sacramental token confirming the Old Covenant; consequently, baptism – succeeding in the room of circumcision (Colossians 2:10-13) – is a sacramental token confirming the New Covenant.

(b) **The Lord's supper also confirms and establishes the New Covenant.** This is clear:

(1) From the words of the institution. Christ says of the cup in this ordinance: {*This cup is the New Testament in my blood*};[2578] that is: "This wine in the cup is a token, sign, seal and instrumental conveyance of the New Testament in my blood." The New Testament is confirmed by this cup sacramentally and symbolically; by the blood of Christ. fundamentally.

(2) From the end and use of the Lord's supper; which is, to confirm communion with Christ and his members, remission of sins and such like New Covenant benefits (Hebrews 8:10-12), and consequently, to confirm and establish the New Covenant itself.[2579]

(ii) *Wherein the nature of baptism and the Lord's supper consists.*

More generally, touching all sacraments, as also touching both these sacraments of the New Covenant, note:

(a) That as God has been pleased in all ages to deal with his church by way of Covenants, as I have already shown;[2580] so in all ages to those his Covenants, he has annexed sacraments, proportionably.

[2577] Hebrews 8:10-12
[2578] 1 Corinthians 11:25
[2579] 1 Corinthians 10:16-17, Matthew 26:28
[2580] In Book 1, Chapter 1, Aphorisms 1 & 2

(b) That sacraments are part, not of God's natural, but only of his instituted worship, and therefore both in their nature and use, they wholly depend upon God's institutions.

(c) That all sacraments instituted by God since Adam's fall, were tokens, pledges, etc, of the gratuitous Covenant of Faith.

(d) That all sacraments or tokens of the Covenant of Faith in all ages, did principally represent Jesus Christ, and him as suffering death for his elect.

(e) That these sacramental tokens were of several sorts, namely: some representing Christ as to suffer afterwards – and those both ordinary and extraordinary, as all before Christ; some representing Christ as having suffered already, as these of the New Covenant since Christ.

(f) That in all sacraments, there are two parts, namely: outward signs, representing; and inward mysteries, thereby represented, as also a sacramental union, or relation between those two parts. Of all these, I have elsewhere spoken; let the reader consult the particulars.[2581]

(g) That as touching these two sacraments or tokens of the New Covenant: baptism and the Lord's supper, the rise of them seems to be from some rites or customs in use among the Jews before these sacraments were instituted. Christ did not appoint new and unusual matters unknown to the Jews; but ancient, usual and well-known matters, rites and actions, but to new ends and purposes. He set a new stamp or superscription (as some observe) on the old metal.[2582] And hereby the Jews reception of his institutions was exceedingly facilitated: their own familiar rites, customs, and usages being improved by him to further and more excellent uses, ends and advantages under the New Covenant. Thus:

(1) Touching baptism, the initiating sacrament of the New Covenant, it seems (as learned men have observed),[2583] to have had its rise, from the Jewish custom of entering themselves into covenant with God, and of admitting

---

[2581] In my *Communicant Instructed*, pp.90-96 (London, 1653)
[2582] Mr. Richard Vines in his *Treatise of the Lord's Supper*, Chapter 6, Section 4, p.77
[2583] Hugo Grotius in his Annotations on Matthew 3:6 & 28:19

heathens thereinto after the same manner, namely: by circumcision and baptism, and sacrifice.[2584]

(2) Touching the Lord's supper – the nourishing sacrament of the New Covenant – it seems also to have had its rise from the Jewish customs in celebrating the paschal supper, and in their after supper, or second course at the same time. They are described by Ainsworth in his annotation on Exodus 12:8, and by that learned Buxtorf, well acquainted with the Jewish customs, see his *Jewish Synagogue*, chapter 13. Let the diligent reader peruse them thoroughly, and as Ainsworth there observes:

"These observations of the Jews [...] may give light to some particulars in the passover that Christ kept, such as: why they lay down, one leaning on another's bosom (John 13:23 – a sign of rest and security) and stood not, as at the first passover, neither sat on high, as we use [tend to do]; why Christ arose from supper, and washed, and sat down again (John 13:4, 5, 12); why he blessed, or gave thanks for the bread apart, and for the cup, or wine, apart (Mark 14:22, 23); and why it is said that *he took the cup after supper* (Luke

---

[2584] "By three things (say the Hebrew doctors) did Israel enter into the covenant: by circumcision, and baptism, and sacrifice. Circumcision was in Egypt, as it is written: {*No uncircumcised shall eat thereof*} (Exodus 12:48). Baptism was in the wilderness before the giving of the law; as it is written: {*Sanctify them today and tomorrow, and let them wash their clothes*} (Exodus 19:10). And sacrifice, as it is said: {*And he sent young men of the sons of Israel which offered burnt-offerings*}, etc (Exodus 24:5). And so in all ages, when an ethnic [a Jew] is willing to enter into the covenant, and gather himself under the wings of the majesty of God, and take upon him the yolk of the law; he must be circumcised, and baptized, and bring a sacrifice. And if it be a woman, she must be baptized, and bring a sacrifice; as it is written in Numbers 15:15: {*As ye are, so shall the stranger lie*}. How are ye? By circumcision, and baptism, and bringing of a sacrifice; so likewise the stranger throughout all generations; by circumcision, and baptism, and bringing of a sacrifice. And what is the stranger's sacrifice, a burnt-offering of a beast, or two turtle doves, or two young pigeons, both of them for a burnt-offering. And at this time when there is no sacrificing; they must be circumcised and baptized, and when the temple shall be builded, they are to bring the sacrifice. "A stranger that is circumcised, and not baptized; or baptized, and not circumcised; he is not a proselyte, until he be both circumcised and baptized," etc.
Maimonides, *Mishneh Torah, Issurei Biah*, Chapter 13, Sections 1-6, 11, 14, 15.
"Hereupon," (says Ainsworth), "baptism was nothing strange unto the Jews, when John the baptist began his ministry (Matthew 3:5-6). They make question of his person that did it, but not of the thing itself (John 1:25)."
Henry Ainsworth's Annotation on Genesis 17:12

22:20), also concerning the hymn which they sung at the end (Matthew 26:30); and why Paul calls it the showing forth of the Lord's death (1 Corinthians 11:26), as the Jews usually called their passover {*haggadah*}, that is, *a showing* or *declaration*. But especially we may observe, how the bread which was of old a remembrance of their deliverance out of Egypt, was sanctified by the Son of God, to be a remembrance of his death, and of our redemption thereby from Satan (1 Corinthians 11:24-26), for which we have much more cause to praise, honor and magnify the Lord, than the Hebrews had for their temporary salvation." So he.

More particularly, touching these two New Covenant sacraments, baptism and the Lord's supper, thus their nature may in brief be represented, namely:

(a) ***Baptism, and the nature thereof***, may clearly be discovered to us by the: (1) author, (2) matter, (3) form, and (4) end thereof.

(1) **The author of baptism**, as a New Covenant token, is God by Jesus Christ: and that by a double commission, namely:

[1] By a commission given to John the Baptist, for baptizing only of that one nation of the Jews. This was done in the preparations for, and inchoations of the New Covenant, that Jesus Christ might be made manifest unto Israel.[2585] And (John says): *I knew him not; but he that sent me to baptize with water, the same said unto me, upon whom thou shalt see the Spirit descending and remaining on him, the same is he which baptizeth with the Holy Ghost.* This was the first institution of baptism, but this commission was very much limited and restrained.

[2] By a commission given to the apostles after Christ's resurrection, and by Christ risen, for baptizing not only of the Jews, but also of all nations throughout the whole world.[2586] This was done after the solemn sanction of the New Covenant by the death and blood of Jesus Christ. This was for substance the same commission, but exceedingly enlarged.

[2585] John 1:31-33 with Matthew 3:5-6, 11, 13 to the end
[2586] Matthew 28:18-20, Mark 16:15-16, etc.

(2) **The matter of baptism** is twofold, namely:

[1] The matter constituent, whereof baptism is made up and constituted. And this is, {1} partly, outward, namely: the element signifying water (John 1:31, 33, Acts 8:36-37), and the action of applying this water, baptizing, or washing (Matthew 28:19, John 1:31, 33, Acts 8:36 & 16:33). This washing may be done by sprinkling, or effusion, or dipping. {2} Partly, inward, namely: the spiritual mysteries signified by this element and action, which is twofold, namely: the blood of Christ, sprinkled upon the soul and heart through faith, washing away the guilt of sin, unto remission of sins and justification (Romans 6:3, Ephesians 5:25-26 with 1 John 1:7, Hebrews 9:12, 14, Acts 3:38-39). And the Spirit of Christ poured upon the soul through grace, washing away the filth, stain, and power of sin, by regeneration, vocation, sanctification in dying to sin, and living to righteousness, etc. (John 3:3, 5-6, Titus 3:5, Romans 6:4-7, Colossians 2:11-13; 1 Peter 3:21).

[2] The matter recipient, or subjects capable of baptism are of two sorts, namely: {1} professed believers of all nations, Jews or Gentiles (Matthew 28:19, Mark 16:15-16, Acts 2:38-39 & 8:37-38. & 16:14-15, 33-34) – yea, even if their professions of faith are not sound and sincere, but hypocritical, (Acts 8:13, 23); and {2} all the children, even the infant-children of such professed believers, Jews or Gentiles (Acts 2:38-39). But this I have already demonstrated at large, proving both, that all such infants are together with their parents federates in this New Covenant,[2587] and that all such infants may and ought to be baptized, as well as their parents.[2588] There see.

(3) **The form of baptism is twofold**, namely:

[1] Inward and essential, constituting baptism, namely: that sacramental union or relation, which (by virtue of Christ's institution) is established between the sign and things signified; which relation or union consists in: {1} signifying fitly the mysteries represented; {2} sealing strongly the benefits

---

[2587] In Book 4, Chapter 4, Aphorism 1, Position 3
[2588] In Book 4, Chapter 4, Aphorism 2, Inference 5

signified; {3} exhibiting truly and really the blessings signified and sealed, to the believing soul. And this, not *ex opere operato*: from the bare work done; which does not work physically, like a medicine, nor *ex opere operantis*: from the work of the worker, or any worthiness of the minister dispensing it; for though none, no not in any pretended case of necessity, can warrantably dispense the sacrament of baptism, but a true minister of Christ lawfully called, yet the most perfect minister and his actions are full of frailties and imperfections.[2589]

[2] Outward and accidental, namely: the form or manner of administering baptism: *in the name of Father, Son, and Holy Ghost*.[2590] That is: {1} by authority and warrant from Father, Son, and Holy Spirit; {2} into professed covenant and communion with Father, Son, and Holy Spirit, to partake from all three, all the benefits, blessings and privileges of the New Covenant, which are also signified and confirmed by this sacrament; as also on our parts to perform to all three all restipulated and conditioned New Covenant duties sincerely.

(4) **The end of baptism:**

[1] Negatively considered, is: {1} not an utter obliteration of all sin and punishment (Acts 8:13, 23); {2} nor a collation of grace from the mere work done, or from the dignity of the minister dispensing it; {3} nor any impression of an indelible character; {4} nor an absolute allegation or tying, either of the thing signified to the signs, or of persons to the sacrament, as if no New Covenant grace could be conferred without this sacrament. For God can confer grace when and how he will, ordinarily or extraordinarily, with means or without means, when himself denies the means. God ties us, but not himself, to the use of means. Nor is it the simple privation, but the neglect, and contempt, and profanation of baptism that is sinful and dangerous.

[2589] Matthew 28:19-20, John 1:31, 33, Hebrews 5:4
[2590] Matthew 28:19

[2] Affirmatively considered, the end of baptism is chiefly twofold, namely:

{1} Firstly, the primary and antecedent end, having peculiar respect to faith in God and Christ; and so baptism is intended to signify, seal and exhibit, (i) our implantation or incision into Christ, union to him, and communion with him, hence those phrases of being baptized into Christ, putting on Christ,[2591] being baptized into the name of the Son,[2592] being buried with Christ by baptism, being baptized into his death and resurrection,[2593] etc; (ii) our remission of sins and justification by the blood of Jesus Christ; (iii) our regeneration and renovation by his Spirit (Titus 3:5, Ephesians 5:25-27; 1 Peter 3:21); (iv) our adoption as sons and daughters into the family and household of God;[2594] (v) our sanctification, by dying unto sin, and walking in newness of life;[2595] (vi) our resurrection from the dead at the last day (Romans 6:5; 1 Corinthians 15:29); and (vii) our eternal salvation in God's kingdom (Mark 16:15-16; 1 Peter 3:21, John 3:3, 5).

{2} Secondly, the secondary and consequent end of baptism has singular reference to our confession of faith before men. And thus baptism is intended to signify, seal and perform sacramentally these things, namely: (i) our open and professed engagement to be solely and wholly the Lord's;[2596] (ii) our incorporation into the mystical body of Christ, the church, to walk in union and holy communion with the members thereof;[2597] and (iii) an actual discrimination and difference of baptized church members from all unbaptized heathens. Thus of the nature of baptism.

(b) *The Lord's supper, and the nature thereof* may also in like manner be plainly delineated, by consideration of the (1) author, (2) matter, (3) form,

---

[2591] Galatians 3:27
[2592] Matthew 28:19
[2593] Romans 6:3-4, etc.
[2594] Galatians 3:26-27
[2595] Romans 6:3-4, etc, Colossians 2:11-13
[2596] Romans 6:4, John 4:1, Acts 2:41
[2597] 1 Corinthians 12:13

and (4) end thereof. But having elsewhere already explained all these particulars, I refer the reader thither, for the sake of brevity.[2598]

(iii) *How these two sacramental tokens, baptism and the Lord's supper do confirm the New Covenant.*

This may in great measure be resolved by what hath been already said. But I add more generally, baptism and the Lord's supper confirm the New Covenant; not physically or naturally by any natural quality, property, virtue or operation thereof; but sacramentally and spiritually, as sacramental signs or tokens, seals and instrumental means for conveying Jesus Christ and the benefits of the New Covenant to God's federates – and all this by virtue of Christ's institution of these ordinances to this end. More particularly:

(a) **Baptism confirms the New Covenant:**

(1) *As a token or sign of the New Covenant.*

That baptism is a token or sign of the New Covenant, is plain, for: [1] it succeeds in the room and stead of circumcision, and to all such federal uses and purposes (Colossians 2:10-12, etc). Now circumcision in the nature and use of it according to the first institution thereof, was a token of the Covenant.[2599] Therefore consequently, so is baptism. [2] In Christ's commission, baptism is annexed to the doctrine of the New Covenant.[2600] [3] In apostolic practice, baptism was still administered to all that embraced the New Covenant and the doctrine thereof, whereby as federates they were initiated and implanted into Christ, into his mystical body, etc.[2601]

Now baptism, as a token or sign, confirms the New Covenant, in several ways, namely:

[1] As a commemorative token, being a notable memorial of the actual incarnation and exhibition of Jesus Christ to Israel. For John the Baptist

---

[2598] In my *Communicant Instructed*, pp.96-98 (London, 1653).
[2599] Genesis 17:11
[2600] Matthew 28:18-20, Mark 16:15-16
[2601] Acts 2:41, 38-39 & 8:37-38 & 10:47-48 & 16:14-15, 33-34

therefore came baptizing with water, that he might *be made manifest to Israel*.[2602] For, John *knew him not, but he that sent him to baptize with water, the same said unto him, upon whom thou shalt see the Spirit descending and remaining on him, the same is he that baptizeth with the Holy Ghost*.[2603] And accordingly, when Jesus came to John to be baptized of him, he saw the heavens opened, and the Spirit of God *descending like a dove and resting upon him, and lo, a voice from heaven, saying, this is my beloved Son in whom I am well pleased*.[2604] Now Jesus Christ, actually incarnate, being thus manifest by baptism to John, John *bare record that this is the Son of God*;[2605] and pointed him out as with the finger: *Behold the lamb of God that taketh away the sins of the world*.[2606] Baptism therefore is a notable memorial of Christ's actual incarnation and manifestation to Israel in our flesh in fullness of time; for establishment of his New Covenant.

[2] As a significative token; baptism signifying and assuring of those seven excellent aforementioned New Covenant benefits, implantation into, and union with Christ, remission of sins, etc.

[3] As a distinctive token; baptism distinguishing baptized Christians from all unbaptized pagans, Jews, etc.

[4] As an instructing sign; discovering to us: {1} the natural guilt, stain, foulness, and filthiness of sin, in us all, which stands need of washing, cleansing, purifying, etc; {2} the spiritual and supernatural healing, cleansing, purging away of all this guilt and filthiness by the blood and spirit of Christ (Colossians 2:11-13; 1 Peter 3:21, Titus 3:5), which is a New Covenant benefit (Hebrews 8:12).

[2602] John 1:31
[2603] John 1:33
[2604] Matthew 3:13-17
[2605] John 1:33-34
[2606] John 1:29, 36

[5] As an obligatory token or sign; obliging the baptized, to put off the body of the sins of the flesh, and die unto sin: but to live unto God, and walk in newness of life (Colossians 2:11-13, Romans 6:3-6).

(2) *As a seal of the New Covenant.* Circumcision was a seal of the covenant blessing, the righteousness of faith, to Abraham;[2607] consequently baptism, succeeding circumcision, is a seal of New Covenant blessings.[2608] Baptism seals what it signifies.

(3) As an instrumental means for conveying of New Covenant benefits signified and sealed (Galatians 3:26-27, Romans 6:3-6).

(b) **The Lord's supper confirms the New Covenant also:**

(1) *As a sign and token of the New Covenant in Christ's blood*; or as a sign of Christ's blood of the New Covenant, confirming and individually applying the New Testament, with all the promises, benefits, privileges and comfort thereof to right receivers, Luke 22:20; 1 Corinthians 11:25. Matthew 26:28. Mark 14:24. Now the Lord's supper, as a token or sign confirms the New Covenant several ways, namely:

[1] As a commemorative sign, lively remembering, and bringing fresh into mind the Lord Jesus Christ, his passion, death, etc., for his elect, his infinite love, etc., in so dying. *Do this in remembrance of me. – As oft as you eat this bread and drink this cup, ye show forth the Lord's death till he come*;[2609] this is a monumental memorial of Christ crucified to the world's end. And by Christ's death the New Covenant was established (Hebrews 9:14-17).

[2] As a significative sign or token, the Lord's supper signifying: (1) Christ's body broken for us, and Christ's blood of the New Covenant shed for us;[2610] (2) our communion with Christ crucified in all the benefits of his cross and death;[2611] (3) remission of sins in his blood, shed for that end (Matthew

---

[2607] Romans 4:11
[2608] Colossians 2:10-13
[2609] 1 Corinthians 11:24-26
[2610] 1 Corinthians 11:23-24
[2611] 1 Corinthians 10:16

26:28); (4) spiritual nourishment of faith in Christ, and all grace by this Lord's supper;[2612] and (5) sweet union and communion of the saints one with another.[2613]

[3] As an instructive sign. The Lord's supper instructs us in many things, as: {1} that Christ Jesus is already actually betrayed, and put to death for our sins (1 Corinthians 11:23-25); {2} that the Old Covenant and the sacraments thereof are already abrogated, and the New Covenant actually established by his death (1 Corinthians 11:25, Matthew 26:28); {3} that Jesus Christ already crucified is complete New Covenant nourishment for us (1 Corinthians 11:20, 24-25); {4} that the contempt and abuse of the Lord's supper is a high contempt of Jesus Christ himself, of his death, and of his New Covenant, and punished by God accordingly (1 Corinthians 11:24-27, 29-30); {5} that therefore, to come to the Lord's supper ignorantly, unbelievingly, impenitently, uncharitably, or any way unworthily, is a most dangerous sin (1 Corinthians 11:27-29), and to come to it in knowledge, faith, repentance, etc., is a most necessary duty; {6} that the Lord's supper is no propitiatory sacrifice, but a remembrance of Christ's propitiatory sacrifice (1 Corinthians 11:24-26); {7} that the Lord's supper is to continue until Christ come (1 Corinthians 11:26), and consequently, the New Covenant is so long to continue also, and that in the present form of administration (Matthew 28:19-20, Hebrews 13:20).

[4] As a distinctive token, distinguishing New Covenant federates, from all aliens to the New Covenant.

[5] As an obligatory sign, binding and obliging all communicants according to the tenor of the New Covenant, fitly to prepare for it, duly to use it, and afterwards to walk suitably and answerably to it.

[2612] 1 Corinthians 11:20, John 6:5-6
[2613] 1 Corinthians 10:17

(2) *As a seal of the New Covenant in Christ's blood*, sealing all the former matters and mysteries signified. Why shall one sacrament be a seal, and not every sacrament?[2614]

(3) *As an instrumental means of conveyance.* In the right use, according to Christ's institution, it so effectually conveys Christ and New Covenant benefits to believers, by virtue of sacramental union and divine benediction, that it is said: *This is my body, this is my blood, this is the new testament in my blood.*[2615]

But thus of the New Covenant's confirmation.

---

[3] *The administration or actual execution of the New Covenant*

The administration or actual execution of the New Covenant is singularly eminent, namely:

{1} **With universal reference to all nations of the world Jewish and Gentile, and to the ecumenical or general church to be gathered out of them all**; but in the first place to the Jews, and then unto the Gentiles (Matthew 28:18-19, Mark 16:15-16; 1 Corinthians 12:12-13, etc., 28, Luke 24:46-47, Acts 13:46-47 & 26:19, 20).

{2} **By the preaching of the New Covenant doctrine, the gospel of Jesus Christ exhibited, most clearly, fully and efficaciously, by catechetical instruction in principles and otherwise, for the discipling of all nations, for bringing people of all nations in the world to be Christ's disciples** (Matthew 28:18-20, Mark 16:15-16, Luke 24:47).[2616] To whom, by whom, and how, the New Covenant doctrine is to be preached, has elsewhere been further manifested.[2617] And this course of preaching, the apostles diligently observed

---

[2614] Romans 4:11
[2615] 1 Corinthians 11:23-26
[2616] Hebrews 5:12 & 6:1-2; 1 Corinthians 3:1-2, Galatians 6:6
[2617] In *The Divine Right of Church Government*, Chapter 7

(Acts 10 throughout & 15:6-7, etc., & 13:46-47 & 26:20). Their doctrine did principally run upon Christ now already performed, and actually exhibited, according to God's promises of old, whose birth, life, sufferings, death, burial, resurrection, ascension, sitting down at God's right hand, effusions of his Spirit, giving gifts to men, etc., for the collection, edification and consummate salvation of his church – even of all his elect throughout the whole world, through faith and repentance for remission of sins etc. – is the principal subject matter of their doctrine. See Acts 2:22-37 & 3:13 to the end, 5:29-32 & 9:20, 22, & 10:34-44 & 13:16-42 & 17:22-32 & 22:3-22. & 26:2-30, Ephesians 4:7-14.

This New Covenant doctrine in Christ, since Christ's establishment of his New Testament by his death, is preached:[2618]

(i) Most clearly, plainly and with open face, the veil of all dark types, figures and shadows being done away in Christ (2 Corinthians 3:12 to the end; 2 Corinthians 4:6-7).

(ii) Most fully and completely, the mystery of Christ touching the Gentiles incorporation into the church of God with the Jews being now more fully revealed by the Spirit to the apostles and prophets, than ever in any former ages (Ephesians 3:3-6), as also: the mysteries of all future affairs and conditions of the church until the end of the world (Revelation 4 to the end of the book), the mysteries of the Jews' calling again, after the Gentiles' fullness (Romans 11), of the resurrection of the dead, change of the living, final judgment of all, etc. (1 Corinthians 15; 1 Thessalonians 4, Matthew 25). These and many other mysteries of Christians were never so fully and completely discovered as now by and under the New Covenant.

(iii) Most efficaciously to the conversion of many, both (a) among the Jews (Acts 2:41, 44 & 5:14 & 6:7 & 9:31 & 12:24 & 21:20), and (b) among the Gentiles; as, at Antioch (Acts 11:21, 24-26), at Ephesus (Acts 19:8, 10, 17-20; 1 Corinthians 16:8-9), at Corinth (Acts 18:1, 7-11), and at Rome (Romans

---

[2618] Hebrews 9:14-17, Matthew 26:28

1:7-8 & 16:19).[2619] Paul with great success preached the gospel of Christ from Jerusalem and round about unto Illyricum (Romans 15:18-19), which is in a direct line (says Pareus)[2620] 350 German miles, that is, 1050 English miles, so that the Gentiles became obedient both in word and deed, round about far and near. And if the conversion of the Gentiles throughout the world is duly considered, it is evident there was never such efficacy of any covenant doctrine since the foundation of the world, as of this New Covenant doctrine.

{3} **By sundry other ordinances of public New Covenant worship for all nations**, as: (i) by the two solemn federal tokens of the New Covenant to be continued until the world's end: baptism and the Lord's supper (Matthew 28:18-20; 1 Corinthians 11:23-30; (ii) by public prayer and thanksgiving (1 Timothy 2:1-2 with 3:14-15; 1 Corinthians 14:14-16, Acts 6:4, Matthew 18:19-20); (iii) by public singing of psalms (Ephesians 5:18-19, Colossians 3:16; 1 Corinthians 14:15-16); and (iv) by due sanctification of the Lord's days. Sabbaths on the first day of every week, in works of piety, necessity, and mercy (Acts 20:7, Revelation 1:10; 1 Corinthians 16:2) – the seventh day sabbath in memorial of the work of creation (Genesis 2:2-3, Exodus 20:8-11) being virtually changed by Christ's resurrection to the first day of the week in memorial of the greater work of the world's redemption.

{4} **By a New Covenant government of the church of God in several acts and ordinances appointed to that effect**, as: (i) by authoritative discerning and judging of doctrine, according to the rule and standard of the word (Acts 15:15, 24, 28 & 16:4); (ii) by public admonishing, warning and rebuking of sinners (Matthew 18:15-17; 1 Thessalonians 5:14, Titus 3:10; 1 Timothy 5:20, Titus 3:13; 2 Corinthians 2:6); (iii) by rejecting, purging out or putting away from church communion, scandalously wicked and incorrigible persons (Matthew 18:17-18 with 16:19, John 20:21, 23, Titus 3:10; 1 Corinthians 5 throughout); (iv) by seasonable-remitting, comforting,

---

[2619] See *The Divine Right of Church Government*, Chapter 13
[2620] David Pareus' commentary on Romans 15:19

confirming, and receiving again into the communion of the church, such as are penitent (Matthew 16:19 & 18:18, John 20:23; 2 Corinthians 2:6-9); and (v) by ordination of presbyters, after prayer and fasting, with imposition of the hands of the presbytery (1 Timothy 4:14. & 5:22, Titus 5, Acts 14:21, 23).

{5} **By a visible and successive New Covenant ministry**: extraordinary and ordinary, and by other New Covenant officers.

(i) By a New Covenant ministry, to which Christ has promised his presence to the end of the world (Matthew 28:18-20). This ministry is: (a) extraordinary, unlimited to any particular place, employed chiefly in the first planting of the New Covenant church, by laying the foundation of the New Covenant doctrine,[2621] as: (1) apostles, (2) prophets, (3) evangelists (Ephesians 4:8, 11-13) – this extraordinary work ceasing, these extraordinary officers also ceased; the ordinary succeeding them. (b) Ordinary, limited to particular places, building upon the foundation laid: as (1) pastors, (2) teachers (Ephesians 4:8, 11-12, etc). These pastors and teachers are to continue until the world's end (Matthew 28:19-20), and by them, all the former ordinances appertaining to doctrine, worship and discipline are to be managed.

(ii) Other New Testament officers are: (a) elders, whose work is to assist the pastors and teachers in matters of government and discipline (1 Timothy 5:17, Romans 12:8; 1 Corinthians 12:28); and (b) deacons, who out of the church's allowance are to take care of her poor and distressed members (Acts 6:1-7), showing mercy (Romans 12:8); helps to the helpless (1 Corinthians 12:28).

{6} **With more plenary, palpable and visible effusions of the Spirit**, both in extraordinary and ordinary endowments, than ever was under any foregoing covenant administration (Acts 2:1-3, etc., to the end; 1 Corinthians 12:4-12, Acts 10:44-46; 1 Corinthians 1:5-7, John 7:37-39). Before Christ's ascension, the Spirit was sparingly given in drops, etc; but since, as it were, in streams and rivers.

[2621] 1 Corinthians 3:10-12, etc.

{7} **With more perfect filial Christian liberty,** both from fear and bondage under sin, Satan, curse, death, and all our spiritual enemies (Luke 1:74-75, Titus 2:14, Galatians 3:13-14, Hebrews 2:14-15), and also from all the servitude of the mosaical pedagogy, the church being now past her minority, and come to maturity (Colossians 2:14, Galatians 4:4-6). Hagar the bondwoman and her children are cast out, and *we are children not of the bondwoman, but of the free.*[2622] Not of the servile Old Covenant from mount sinai: but of the free New Covenant from Mount Zion. *If the Son shall make you free, ye shall be free indeed.*[2623]

{8} **Finally, this New Covenant is managed and administered with far more glory than the Old, or any that went before it.** The Old Covenant was glorious, as appears by the glory and shining of Moses' countenance, but *that which was made glorious, had no glory in this respect, by reason of the glory that excelleth.* Herein the New Covenant glory excels: (i) It is a spiritual, not a carnal glory (2 Corinthians 3:7-8), (ii) it is a comfortable and saving, not a dismaying and condemning glory (2 Corinthians 3:7-8), (iii) it is a clear, open, and unveiled, not a veiled glory (2 Corinthians 3:12 to the end), (iv) it is an effectual, transforming, not an ineffectual glory (2 Corinthians 3:14-15, 18), and (v) it is a permanent and remaining, not a transient and vanishing glory (2 Corinthians 3:7, 11).

Inferences

(1) **Hence, the New Covenant is, of all others, most comfortable.** For it was at first manifested and revealed to the captives by Jeremiah, as a ground of stronger comfort to the captives than the Covenant with the captives, or Old

---

[2622] Galatians 4:21 to the end & 5:1, etc.
[2623] John 8:36

Covenant – as has been already observed.[2624] Now the comfortableness of the New Covenant against: [1] sin, [2] apostasy, [3] wants, inward or outward, [4] temptations, [5] desertions, [6] afflictions and persecutions, and [7] death itself, has been already at large unfolded in this book – there see.[2625] This New Covenant is a blessed cabinet of sweetest soul-reviving cordials.

(2) **Hence, the New Covenant is, of all other Covenants, most sufficient**, for it was first revealed and discovered for redress of the Old Covenant's weakness, unprofitableness and insufficiency (Hebrews 7:18-19, & 8:6-9, etc. & 9:10-14). And all saving blessings, obscurely pointed out in former Covenants, are most clearly revealed and accomplished under this New Covenant (Acts 13:38-39, Romans 3:25, Hebrews 9:15). All former Covenants lead and tend to this New Covenant, as the center, perfection, and accomplishment of them all.

(3) **Hence, the grace of the New Covenant is most complete**, and this: [1] extensively, in that it takes in all nations of the world (Luke 24:47, Matthew 28:18-19, Mark 16:15-16), and [2] intensively, in that it more efficaciously converts the abundance of both Jews and Gentiles, than any covenant expressure ever did before, and in that it more fully affords the effusions of the Spirit.

(4) **Hence, the New Covenant is most sure**, for it is most strongly established by, and founded upon: [1] the Lord's better promises, [2] his sacred oath, of which he will not repent, [3] the death and blood of Jesus Christ once for all, never to be repealed, [4] the best and surest sacraments, which shall not wear away while the world shall continue (Matthew 28:19-20; 1 Corinthians 11:26).

(5) **Hence, the New Covenant is utterly irrevocable.** It can no more be revoked, repealed, called in, or made void, than God can belie himself, or

---

[2624] In this 4th Book, Chapter 3, Aphorism 2.1
[2625] Book 4, Chapter 3, Aphorism 2; but especially see Chapter 5, Section 3, Aphorism 1.

forswear himself, or then Christ can be brought down again from God's right-hand to be barbarously crucified between two thieves

(6) Hence, the New Covenant must needs be everlasting:[2626] everlasting *absolutely* in the substance of it, as that which shall so continue with us in heaven; everlasting *respectively* for the circumstance and administration of it, as that which shall so continue until the world's end. The promises of the New Covenant are of everlasting truth, the oath of the New Covenant is of everlasting stability, the blood of the New Covenant is of everlasting virtue,[2627] and the tokens of the New Covenant are of everlasting appointment until the end of the world.[2628]

(7) Hence, in all these respects the New Covenant is most excelling. But of the excellency and preeminence of the New Covenant hereafter.

Thus of the form of the New Covenant.

[2626] Hebrews 13:20
[2627] Hebrews 9:12 & 10:14
[2628] Matthew 28:18-20; 1 Corinthians 11:26

Chapter 8

Of the intended scope, or end of the New Covenant.

Having viewed at large, the efficient, matter, and form of the New Covenant, we now come to take special notice of God's intended scope or end therein.

The intended scope or end of God and Jesus Christ our Mediator in this New Testamental Covenant, is:

(1) More immediately, to represent and describe to Israel and to all nations of the world most fully and ultimately: [1] the person of Jesus Christ actually, in fullness of time exhibited, [2] his office of mediation between God and man already executed both in his state of humiliation and exaltation, as also [3] the fruits and benefits of his mediation; and (2) more mediately: [1] to extend his church universally to all the nations of the whole world, [2] to advance the condition and enioyments of his New Covenant church to a higher perfection than ever before, in order to eternal salvation, and [3] by all to exalt the glory of his own holy name most transcendently and gloriously.

As the New Covenant, so the end thereof, is most excellent and transcendent: as laid down in this aphorism, which thus in brief I explicate:

(1) **The more immediate end intended by God in this New Covenant, is, the most full and ultimate representation of the person, office, and benefits of Jesus Christ actually exhibited, to Israel and to all nations.**

All God's Covenants of Faith intend more immediately the discovery and description of Jesus Christ. But this New Covenant intends this more than they all. Here note: [1] what this New Covenant intends immediately to represent and describe, [2] how, and [3] to whom.

[1] *What this New Covenant intends more immediately to represent and describe, namely: Jesus Christ as actually exhibited*. All former Covenants of Faith intend to set forth Christ, as promised, and to be afterwards in fullness of time performed: but this New Covenant intends to set forth, and represents Christ, as actually performed and exhibited already, according to all the promises of God's former Covenants.[2629] And this principally: {1} in his person, {2} in his office, and {3} in the fruits, effects and benefits of his office.

{1} **Jesus Christ in his person** is most excellently and clearly described in this New Covenant, and the explications thereof in the books of the New Testament, as:

That he is the only Son of God, the true God, essentially one with, and co-equal to the Father, Creator, and Preserver of all things in heaven and earth, (John 1:14, 18 & 3:16 & 6:69, Matthew 16:16-18; 1 John 5:20, 7; 1 John 1:1, Philippians 2:6, John 1:1-5, 9-10, Hebrews 1:2-3, Colossians 1:15-17).

That he is true and perfect man, descending from the woman, of Abraham, Isaac, and Jacob, and of David, by the virgin Mary according to the flesh (1 Timothy 2:5 with John 20:25-30 & Luke 24:37-40 & 1 John 1:1-3, Genesis 3:15 with Luke 3:38, Genesis 12:3 & 22:18 & 26:4 & 28:14 with Luke 3:34, Psalm 132:11 with Luke 1:31-33 & 3:31, Matthew 1:16, 18 to the end, & Luke 1:26-39 & 2:1-41 with Isaiah 7:14).

That he is God-man in one person (John. 1:14, Galatians 4:4; 1 Timothy 3:16).

That this Jesus God and man is the very **Christ**,[2630] promised in all ages of the church from the beginning of the world (John 20:31, Acts 2:36 & 10:43 & 3:22 to the end & 9:22 & 18:28). This is one special intent of the books of the New Testament, by showing how all the promises of old touching the Messiah

---

[2629] Galatians 4:4, etc, John 1:14, etc, Matthew 1 throughout, Luke 1-3 throughout
[2630] Vid John Piscator, *Praefat. in Evang. secund. Mat. Mar. Luc. & Iohan. Et Argument. Evangel. Mat. & Mark*.

have their plenary accomplishment in this Jesus, to demonstrate that this Jesus is the Christ.

His state or condition of humiliation (Philippians 2:6-8)[2631] is most lively and accurately described in all the degrees thereof, by the four evangelists especially, namely: his conception, nativity, life, acts, passions or sufferings, death and burial; together with the circumstances of time, place, manner, etc. Attending thereupon respectively.

His state or condition of glory and exaltation also is excellently delineated, especially by the four evangelists, and by Luke in the Acts of the Apostles, namely: his reviving, resurrection the third day, ascension into heaven, sitting down on God's right hand, and his coming again to judge the world at the last day: together with the circumstances attending thereupon.

{2} **Jesus Christ, in his office of mediation between God and man**, is also most notably and particularly represented, in the New Covenant and the explanations thereof, as that he alone is Mediator; that he is a fit and sufficient Mediator; that he is Mediator as God man; that he executes his mediation actually in his prophecy, priesthood, and kingship, both in his states of humiliation, and exaltation – and that by sundry acts of those three branches of his mediation. All this I have already evidenced heretofore out of the New Testament particularly.[2632]

{3} **Jesus Christ, in regard to the benefits, fruits and effects of all his offices**, is likewise set forth most excellently in the New Covenant, and the explanations thereof throughout the books of the New Testament – as I have already manifested abundantly.[2633]

[2] *How the New Covenant represents and describes Jesus Christ, exhibited already, in his person, offices and fruits of his offices*. The New Covenant represents and sets forth Jesus Christ actually exhibited, fully and ultimately:

[2631] Of Christ's humiliation and exaltation, see in Book 4, Chapter 6.
[2632] In this 4th Book, Chapter 6
[2633] In Book 4, Chapter 5, Section 2, General 4 & Chapter 6

{1} **Fully.** So that now the whole and entire mystery of Christ is clearly and completely revealed in the New Testament, in all the essential, integral and gradual perfections thereof, for the happiness and salvation of the New Covenant church, so as it was never formerly made known in any foregoing covenant expressure.[2634] Christ made known to his apostles all things that he had heard from his Father, commanding them to teach all things whatsoever he had commanded them, to the world.[2635] And his apostles accordingly kept back nothing that was profitable, not shunning to declare to the churches the whole counsel of God;[2636] which is so complete and perfect, that nothing is to be added thereto, or taken thence from.[2637]

{2} **Ultimately.** So that after this New Covenant, no further revelation of the mystery of Christ, in regard to his person, offices, or benefits, for his elect's salvation, is to be expected or hearkened unto until the end of this world, for this is Christ's New and everlasting Covenant, that shall still remain new, and never wax old until the end of this world. This is Christ's last will and testament, confirmed, and consummated by his death, from which nothing can be detracted, to which nothing can be added, in which nothing can be altered. Christ's New Covenant priesthood is everlasting, confirmed by the irrevocable oath of God, whereof he never will repent. The New Covenant tokens, baptism and the Lord's supper are to continue until the end of the world, until Christ comes. The New Covenant discoveries of the future state and condition of the church in this world, are extended to occurrences in all ages from the primitive times until the end of the world.[2638] And the New Covenant ministry is to continue, and shall have Christ's presence, blessing and assistance until the end of the world.[2639]

[2634] Hebrews 8:6 to the end; 2 Corinthians 3:16 to the end, Ephesians 3:4-13
[2635] John 15:15, Matthew 28:18-20
[2636] Acts 20:20, 26-27
[2637] Revelation 22:18-19
[2638] Revelation chapter 4 to the end of the book.
[2639] Matthew 28:18-20, Ephesians 4:8, 11-13

[3] *To whom this New Covenant more immediately intends thus fully and ultimately to discover and represent Jesus Christ in his person, offices and benefits*, namely: to the whole Israel of God, both of Jews and Gentiles, (Hebrews 8:8, 10) but first to the Jews, and then to the Gentiles (Luke 24:46-47, Acts 2:38-39. & 13:46, etc. & 26:20).

(2) **The more mediate end of the New Covenant, is twofold, namely: [1] subordinate and [2] ultimate.**

[1] *Subordinate* – and that also is twofold:

{1} To extend, spread, propagate, and plant the church of God far and near among all the nations of the world, which before the New Covenant was confined to certain particular families or tribes, or to that one select nation of the Jews.[2640] This extent and enlargement of the church under the New Covenant, was frequently foretold by the prophets, and sometimes most emphatically. See Isaiah 49:6-14 & 54 throughout & 60 throughout & 65:1 & 66:12 to the end. Christ was born to be a light to lighten the Gentiles, as well as to be the glory of his people Israel.[2641] And the amplitude of the church of God, by the access of the Gentiles and their incorporation thereinto is most abundantly revealed and fulfilled in these New Covenant days.[2642]

{2} To advance the condition and enjoyments of God's enlarged New Covenant church to a far higher perfection, in order to salvation, than ever heretofore, as (i) to more ripeness and maturity (Matthew 4:1-8); (ii) to Christian freedom and liberty from the Old Covenant yoke of bondage (Galatians 4:9-10, 21 to the end & 5:1-4, etc); (iii) to better promises of a better Covenant (Hebrews 8:6 & 7:22); (iv) to higher and more perfect federal blessings, better inscription of God's laws, better knowledge of the Lord, and better remission of transgressions (Hebrews 8:10-12); (v) to more sweet,

---

[2640] Matthew 18:18-20, Mark 16:15-16, Luke 24:46-47, Acts 13:36, etc, John 11:52
[2641] Luke 2:30-32
[2642] Ephesians chapters 2 & 3 throughout

perfect and comfortable fellowship (Hebrews 12:18-25); (vi) to more clear and spiritual ordinances (2 Corinthians 3 throughout; and (vii) to more plenary and powerful effusions of his Spirit (John 7:38-39 with Acts 2 throughout, etc). The condition of the New Covenant church comes nearest to that of *the spirits of just men made perfect*, and therefore should be – now more than ever heretofore – advanced to a sublime excellency of graciousness, spiritualness, and heavenliness.

[2] ***Ultimate***: to exalt the glory of God transcendently in all. The glory of God's infinite grace, goodness, mercy, loving-kindness, wisdom, justice, holiness, and powerfulness shines forth in this New Covenant's contrivance, manifestation, dedication, publication, and application of it to poor sinners – even to admiration.[2643] This New Covenant is fullest of God, of Christ, of the Spirit; and therefore most glorious unto God. This New Covenant has in it the marrow and extract of all foregoing covenants, and many other superadded privileges approaching nearest to celestial perfection: and therefore thereby God's glory is rendered exceeding glorious.

Inferences

(1) **Hence, this New Covenant in its intended scope and end far excels all former Covenants.** Their end was to reveal Christ, as promised, and to come afterwards: the New Covenant is to represent Christ as performed, and come already. They intended the happiness of the church in particular families or tribes, or one select nation; this intends the happiness of the church in all nations of the world. They intended to reveal blessings agreeable to the

---

[2643] This is evident in all the former particulars opened about the New Covenant – especially in the author, occasion, impulsives, federates, matter and form thereof.

church's minority; this intends and reveals blessings suitable to the church's maturity.

(2) **Hence, of all God's covenant expressures, the New Covenant should be most precious, dear and delightful to us.** Why? Because, hereby the church is most enlarged; hereby the churches condition & enjoyments are most happily improved; hereby Jesus Christ in his person, office and benefits is most plenarily and ultimately revealed; and hereby God's glory is most gloriously advanced – all of which ought to be very dear, delightful and precious to us.

(3) **Hence, those who would be acquainted with Jesus Christ most fully, should study and exercise themselves in the New Covenant most frequently.** Some Covenants represent Christ much; some more; but this New Covenant most of all. There you have Christ promised; here Christ actually performed and exhibited. Oh, peruse the New Testament diligently, there you have Christ displayed most clearly, completely and transcendently. The New Covenant is the rock, Christ the water that flows from it; the New Covenant is the cloud, Christ the manna that rained from it; the New Covenant is the honeycomb, Christ is the honey that drops from it; the New Covenant is the cabinet, Christ is the jewel thats locked up in it.

(4) **Hence, those who deny Jesus Christ to be actually exhibited and already come in the flesh, do utterly evacuate and make void a primary end of the New Covenant.** For the New Covenant eminently intends to represent Christ as actually performed according to all the promises of old. Oh, how sadly have the Jews hitherto denied Christ's coming in the flesh, and despised the New Covenant's great salvation![2644] Such spirits are not of God, but the very spirit of Antichrist.[2645]

(5) **Hence, the Gentiles' conversion and church's dilatation are peculiarly to be ascribed to the New Covenant.** The Old Covenant

---

[2644] Luke 2:30-32
[2645] 1 John 4:2-3

dispensation hindered it; this New Covenant dispensation promotes and effects it.[2646]

(6) Hence, God's New Covenant people should not content themselves with less than a New Covenant condition and enjoyments. They should aspire to a more perfect condition and enjoyments than any other Covenant affords, else they fall short of the New Covenant's intention. They that under the New Covenant content themselves, without heart-conformity to God's laws, without clear knowledge of the Lord, without remission of sins, without covenant relation to God, without Christian maturity and filial liberty, etc.[2647] They put away the New Covenant from them, counting themselves unworthy of its blessed intendments, and of eternal life.

(7) Hence, they that are truly partakers of God's New Covenant, should highly extol him for his New Covenant. Oh how has he therein displayed the riches of his grace, mercy, love, wisdom, etc., for poor sinners, for lost Gentiles! Herein he greatly intended the glory of his own great name: oh let us hereupon most triumphantly declare and spread abroad his glory.

Thus of the end or intended scope of the New Covenant.

[2646] Ephesians 2:15-18, etc.
[2647] Hebrews 8:10-12

Chapter 9

Of certain General Inferences resulting from the whole of this New Covenant.

Having thus (through the help of my most gracious God in Jesus Christ) in some measure set forth and represented: (1) the terms, or limits of continuance; (2) the denominations, and general nature; (3) the efficient cause or author, together with the occasions, and impulsives, moving thereunto; (4) the federates with God; (5) the matter, on God's part, and on theirs; (6) the Lord Jesus Christ, as Mediator, Surety and Testator; (7) the form, inward and outward; (8) and also the intended scope or end,of this highest, sweetest and most excellent federal expressure, the New Testamental Covenant, or the New Federal Testament, which is the glory of all Covenants, I shall now close up this whole discourse about the New Covenant, and also my whole treatise about the Covenants of God (as I formerly propounded),[2648] with certain general inferences from the whole of this New Covenant, which I summarily offer in this ensuing aphorism, namely:

From the whole mystery of the New Covenant thus disclosed, these things are evident: (1) that the New Covenant is the Covenant of Covenants; (2) what the properties and perfections of the New Covenant are; (3) what agreement and difference there is between this New Covenant and the Old, and consequently all other Covenants; (4) what the New Covenants preeminences and excellencies are above the Old, and all former Covenants; (5) how great are the privileges of God's New Covenant people; (6) how we may discover that we are God's New Covenant people; (7) how much it concerns all, especially us Gentiles, to

---

[2648] In Book 4, Chapter 1

esteem, embrace, rest upon, conform to, and triumph in, this blessed New Covenant; (8) that God's New Covenant people should approve themselves, answerably to this new, better and more illustrious covenant, a new, better, and more excellent people in their hearts and conversations; (9) that all distressed and disconsolate souls should chiefly have recourse to this New Covenant for their sweetest and fullest consolations; and (10) that this New Testamental Covenant approaches nearest, as in contiguity of time, so in excellency of nature, to the celestial glory.

These consectaries or inferences are so fluent from the premises, that it shall suffice very briefly to explain them, especially several of them.

(1) Hence, the New Covenant is the Covenant of Covenants.

As God's Covenants surpass all other covenants, so this New Covenant is the last and best of all God's Covenants, for:

[1] No former Covenant since the foundation of the world had such a sanction and dedication, as this New Covenant, by the death and blood of Jesus Christ.[2649]

[2] No foregoing Covenant had such a constitution, wholly of promises, and those mere spiritual promises, as this New Covenant: as has been already observed.[2650]

[3] No former Covenant had so successful a promulgation or first publication, as this New Covenant to the conversion of three thousand (Acts 2 throughout).

[4] No former Covenant was universally extended to all the nations of the world, but only this New Covenant (Hebrews 8:8, 10 with Matthew 28:18-19, Mark 16:15-16, Luke 24:46-47).

[2649] Hebrews 9:14-17, etc, Matthew 26:28; 1 Corinthians 11:26, Hebrews 13:20, Acts 20:28
[2650] Hebrews 8:10-12; see Book 4, Chapter 5, Section 2

[5] All former Covenants were but as preludes and introductions to this New Covenant, the perfection of them all;[2651] the end and accomplishment of them all.[2652]

[6] All former Covenants, like rivers run into this sea, like lines meet in this center, like beams meet in this sun of the New Covenant, being all their fullness, wealth and glory into it. The treasures which are found dispersed and scattered in and among other Covenants, are all collected and united in this New Covenant: the seed of the woman, the true Noah, the seed of Abraham, Isaac and Jacob, the priest like Melchizedek, the prophet like Moses, the king like David, etc. All of these discoveries of many several covenants in several ages meet together in this one New Covenant, etc., are at once most richly and fully represented in Jesus Christ the Son of God, and of the virgin Mary, actually exhibited to be Mediator, Surety, and Testator of the New Testament.

[7] No former covenants afford such admirable events and occurrents in their respective periods or revolutions, as this New Covenant.[2653]

[8] Finally, this New Covenant succeeds and swallows up all other Covenants, but none shall succeed this, which is to remain of force so long as this world shall continue.[2654] Upon these and sundry like considerations, it is clear that this New Covenant is a peerless and matchless Covenant – God still proceeding in his covenant expressures from the less to the more perfect, until at last he came from the first and least, to this last and greatest covenant of all.

(2) **Hence, we may easily perceive what the properties and perfections of the New Covenant are,** namely: especially these – the New Covenant is: [1] most divine, [2] gratuitous, [3] evangelical, [4] wise, [5] holy, [6] promissory, [7] spiritual, [8] testamental, [9] clear and glorious, [10] full, [11]

[2651] Hebrews 7:18-19, etc, 22, Galatians 3:21-24
[2652] Hebrews 9:15, Romans 3:25
[2653] See Book 4, Chapter 1, Aphorism 2
[2654] Hebrews 13:20, Matthew 28:19-20; 1 Corinthians 11:26

free, [12] efficacious, [13] sure and faithful, [14] consolatory, [15] extensive, and [16] continuing.

[1] ***Most divine.*** For, this New Covenant has much of God, and of his divine authority, excellency and efficacy engraven upon it. {1} God – Father, Son and Holy Spirit – is the sole author of it. {2} The Father of old time revealed it, the Son in fullness of time established it, and the Holy Spirit in due time applies it. {3} The Father, Son, and Holy Spirit do jointly undertake (but according to their order of subsisting) to confer all the New Covenant blessings upon his federates, which blessings are more peculiarly referred to the several persons, according to their peculiar order and manner of working. All these things have been already cleared.[2655]

[2] ***Gratuitous.*** Of the mere grace and good-pleasure of God's will, in Jesus Christ. These were the impulsive or moving causes inclining God to reveal, establish and apply this New Covenant, not any worth, dignity or excellency at all in Jews or Gentiles.[2656]

[3] ***Evangelical.*** All God's Covenants of Faith were evangelical, as I have shown: but God's New Covenant is of all other most purely evangelical. See the general nature and description of the New Covenant.[2657] Former Covenants were gospel in minority; this New Covenant is gospel in maturity. Former Covenants were gospel veiled; this New Covenant is gospel unveiled. Former Covenants were gospel (that is, glad tidings of sinners' salvation by faith) in Christ promised and to come afterwards; this New Covenant is gospel in Christ performed, and come in the flesh already. Former Covenants were gospel inchoate; this New Covenant is gospel consummate. In this New Covenant especially, *mercy and truth are met together, righteousness and peace have kissed each other*, etc.[2658] In this Covenant, the goodness and mercy of God has most eminently shone forth to the sinner, the severity and justice of

---

[2655] In Book 4, Chapter 3, Aphorism 1
[2656] See Book 4, Chapter 3, Aphorism 2
[2657] In Book 4, Chapter 2, Aphorism 2
[2658] Psalm 85:10-11

God has most notably been expressed upon Jesus Christ the sinner's Surety, and this mystery of mercy and justice in the sinner's salvation upon God's pacification is excellently evangelical. By way of eminence and singularity, this New Covenant is called *the grace of God bringing salvation*;[2659] the gospel through which Christ *hath brought life and immortality to light*;[2660] the coming of faith for remission of sins past, and justification of the elect under former Covenants.[2661] The grace of God, the gospel, and doctrine of faith were before, but comparatively they were not until the times of the New Covenant.

[4] *Wise*. The New Covenant is eminently wise, for: {1} it is contrived by the only wise God – Father, Son, and Holy Spirit. {2} It is stored and filled with all accomplishments of wisdom for sinners' happiness – as has been already manifested in many particulars.[2662]

[5] *Holy*. This New Covenant is very holy, in several regards: {1} the author of it is God, most holy (Hebrews 8:8, 10 with Isaiah 6:3); {2} the federates in it are the house of Israel and Judah, the Israel of God, the whole universal church of Jews and Gentiles, which are a holy nation, a holy temple of God, etc. (Hebrews 8:8, 10 with 1 Peter 2:9; 1 Corinthians 3:16-17, Ephesians 2:21-22); {3} the matter of it is: holy blessings promised on God's part, expressly (Hebrews 8:10-12), and holy duties of faith, etc., re-promised on their part, implicitly (Jude 20; 1 Peter 1:15-16); {4} the Mediator of it is holy, Jesus Christ, *the Holy One of God*;[2663] *holy, harmless, undefiled, separate from sinners*;[2664] {5} the form of it holy, consisting in a holy manifestation, confirmation and administration; as has been evidenced. It is "*foedus sanctum, quasi sancitum*," as Augustine: a holy Covenant, because a firmly settled and established Covenant; and {6} the end of it holy.

[2659] Titus 2:10-11
[2660] 2 Timothy 1:10-11
[2661] Galatians 3:22-25, Romans 3:25-26, Hebrews 9:15, etc.
[2662] In Book 4, Chapter 3, Aphorism 2
[2663] Luke 4:34
[2664] Hebrews 7:26 & 7:22 & 12:24

[6] ***Promissory***. The Old Covenant was chiefly mandatory and minatory, but this New Covenant if we look at the body of it,[2665] is (as has been manifest already):[2666] {1} altogether promissory, {2} the promises thereof whereupon it is established being better promises, and {3} all those promises being merely (as to the express terms thereof) only of spirituals. Oh how sweet is this dispensation, wherein we may fetch not only God's mercies, but also our duties and abilities for them from God's promises.

[7] ***Spiritual***. Of all Covenants, this New Covenant is most sublime, heavenly and purely spiritual. Former Covenants were more carnal, external, literal administrations; but this New more spiritual,[2667] called therefore {*the ministration of the Spirit*}.[2668] In former Covenants, spirituals were darkly couched under carnals and externals, as: under the seed of the woman, bruising the serpent's head, Christ incarnate subduing Satan;[2669] under Noah's saving of his house in the ark by water, Christ's saving his elect remnant in his church by his blood;[2670] under the promised seed of Abraham, Isaac, and Jacob; Christ's blessing of all the nations of the world;[2671] under all the ceremonial types and shadows, Christ the truth and body intended, the better hope perfecting us as pertaining to the conscience and bringing us near unto God (John 1:14, 17, Colossians 2:17, Hebrews 7:18-19 & 9:14 & 10:1-19) under David's seed, promised to sit upon his throne forever;[2672] and Christ his primary seed that should rule the house of Jacob the church forevermore; under the redemption of the captives out of Babylon, Christ's redemption of his elect from their spiritual thralldom was represented;[2673] so that though

---

[2665] Hebrews 8:10-12
[2666] See Book 4, Chapter 3, Aphorism 2, Generals 2 & 3, & Chapter 1, Aphorism 2, Particular 5
[2667] See Book 4, Chapter 2, Aphorism 1
[2668] 2 Corinthians 3:6-8
[2669] Genesis 3:15, Hebrews 2:14-15
[2670] Genesis 6 & 7, Hebrews 11:7; 1 Peter 3:21
[2671] Genesis 12:3, Acts 3:26, Galatians 3:13-14
[2672] Psalm 132:11, Luke 1:31-33
[2673] Compare Ezekiel 37 with [Isaiah] 49

they had many spirituals represented in them, yet all was under a cloud or veil of carnals. Thereby, the spirituals of former Covenants were much darkened and carnalized, but in this New Covenant, spirituals are set forth most openly, immediately and expressly in clear view, and as with open face, the veil being done away in Christ;[2674] and carnals being comprised in, and annexed to spirituals, the carnals of this New Covenant are therein spiritualized.[2675] And as under former Covenants, the federates of God remained more carnal; so under this New Covenant they become more spiritual, to worship the Lord in spirit and truth: a spiritual house, and holy priesthood to offer up spiritual sacrifices acceptable to God by Jesus Christ.[2676]

[8] *Testamental.* The New Covenant, is so a covenant, in respect of God,[2677] that it is also a testament, in respect of Jesus Christ the Testator.[2678] It is a Federal Testament, or a Testamental Covenant, as I have already shown at large in this fourth book, Chapter 2, Aphorism 1 – there see. The Old Covenant was Christ's First Will and Testament, established by typical blood and sacrifices;[2679] but this New Covenant is Christ's New, Second, or Last Will and Testament, revoking his Old Testament, being finally and irrevocably confirmed by the blood, death and sacrifice of Jesus Christ himself the Testator.[2680] In what regards it is a testament, and a New Testament, has been there unfolded.

[9] *Clear and glorious.* Under this New Covenant, the dark shadows and veil, both upon the mysteries of the Covenant, and upon the federates covenanting, are done away in Christ;[2681] so that now we may behold as in a glass clearly and transformingly the glory of the Lord in the face of Jesus Christ, having a more clear and excellent knowledge of God, and giving of his

---

[2674] 2 Corinthians 3:14, 18
[2675] Hebrews 8:10-12; 1 Timothy 4:8, Matthew 6:33
[2676] 1 Peter 2:5 with John 4:23
[2677] Hebrews 8:8, 10
[2678] Hebrews 7:22, Matthew 26:28
[2679] Hebrews 9:18-19, 30, etc, Exodus 24
[2680] Hebrews 7:22 & 9:15-17 & 8:6-8
[2681] 2 Corinthians 3:14, 18 & 4:6-7

laws in our minds,[2682] promised than ever formerly. Now the Covenant of God shines out in its perfect day. Now the sun of righteousness hath appeared in his perfect glory. Now the church of God has attained to her maturity, etc. See what has been formerly spoken to this effect at large.[2683]

[10] **Full**. Never covenant since the fall of man was so rich, full and complete as this New Covenant. They that went before were but as springs and rivers; this is as a very sea. And no wonder, for:

{1} This is the only Covenant established in fullness of time, by the fullest sanction and dedication, in the blood of Jesus Christ, full of grace and truth for us, in whom all fullness extensive and intensive dwells – yea, the fullness of the Godhead personally.[2684]

{2} This is the only Covenant in and under which the Spirit of God and all saving blessings are revealed, obtained, and applied to the elect of God most fully.[2685] So that under this Covenant, God's people are complete in Christ now in all essential and integral perfections pertaining to salvation (Colossians 2:9), and shall be at last consummate in all graduals (Ephesians 4:11-14) – Jesus Christ having *ascended up far above all heavens, that he might fill all things;*[2686] and his body the church becoming *the fullness of him that filleth all and in all*.[2687]

{3} This is the only Covenant, unto which all former Covenants collime,[2688] scope, tend and refer; into which they jointly and universally empty themselves as the rivers into the sea; and from which they derive and

---

[2682] Hebrews 8:10-11
[2683] In Book 4, Chapter [5], Section 3, Aphorisms 1 & 2
[2684] Galatians 4:4-6, Hebrews 9:15, etc, Matthew 26:28, John 1:14, 17, Colossians 1:19 & 2:9-10
[2685] John 7:37-39, Acts 2 throughout, John 1:14, 16-17, Hebrews 8:10-12
[2686] Ephesians 4:10
[2687] Ephesians 1:23
[2688] "Collimate: 1. To make parallel; line up. 2. To adjust the line of sight of (an optical device)." [https://www.ahdictionary.com/word/search.html?q=collimate] <Accessed 4/11/2024> "The only known use of the verb collime is in the late 1600s. OED's only evidence for *collime* is from 1677, in the writing of Theophilus Gale, ejected minister and theologian." [https://www.oed.com/dictionary/collime_v?tl=true] <Accessed 4/11/2024>

extract all salvifical virtue for the elect under former Covenants (Hebrews 9:15-17, Romans 3:25).

{4} This is the only Covenant that shall continue to the world's end, having no need of any more additional perfections, or any other federal administrations, to be annexed thereto, or to succeed in room thereof.

[11] *Free.* Much servitude and bondage did predominate in former covenants; witness the many gravaminous rites and observances of sacrifices, circumcision, purifications, and other carnal ordinances (imposed until the time of reformation),[2689] which were a yoke that neither they nor their fathers were able to bear.[2690] But in this New Covenant, God has so abundantly provided for the spiritual redemption, release, liberty and freedom of his church and people more than ever heretofore, that this peculiar time of Christ, this whole New Covenant time is as the churches last, greatest and continued jubilee.[2691] Especially this is most observable in the Old and New Covenant, compared by the apostle to Abraham's two wives, namely: Hagar the bondwoman, which brought forth Ishmael her bond-son, who with her son was cast out of Abraham's house, representing the Old Covenant from mount Sinai, begetting children unto bondage, which covenant with her children is cast out and laid aside; and Sarah the free-woman, which brought forth Isaac her free son, the son of the promise, the heir of Abraham, representing this New Covenant from mount Zion, gendering children unto liberty, who are heirs according to promise. Now this New Covenant is in a peculiar and eminent sort, above all that went before, a covenant of true liberty and freedom:

{1} Because under this New Covenant, all the spiritual, salvifical and eternal redemption, liberty or freedom of God's elect, which have been, are or shall be from the beginning to the end of the world, from sin, death, Satan, and all spiritual enemies, hath been meritoriously purchased, procured, and

---

[2689] Genesis 4:4, etc, & 8:20-21 & 15:9-10 & 17:10-15, Hebrews 9:1-11
[2690] Acts 15:10, Galatians 5:1
[2691] Isaiah 61:1-3 with Luke 4:18-19, 21

wrought by the merit of Jesus Christ our only Lord and Mediator.[2692] The virtue of Christ's redemption reached to all ages by-past, even to the beginning of the world; but the transaction and accomplishment of it was only under his New Covenant, inchoate or complete.

{2} Because under this New Covenant, all the bondage, servitude and slavery of foregoing covenant administrations is utterly abolished and done away: especially that of the Old Covenant, restraining to days, months and years, to external rites in worship, to places, to meats and drinks, etc (Ephesians 2:14-15, Colossians 2:14, Galatians 4 throughout & 5:1-5, etc, Hebrews 7:18-19 & 8:7-9 & 10:8-10, etc), and the contrary liberty and freedom is established by Christ (Galatians 5:1). The church while underage was in a servile condition, under tutors and governors, though heir of all; but when come to maturity, she was redeemed by Christ from all that servitude, to receive the adoption of sons.[2693] *Ye have not received the Spirit of bondage again, to fear: but the Spirit of adoption, whereby we cry Abba Father.*[2694] Christ gives ability, as well as requires duty, therefore Christ's yoke is easy and his burden is light.

{3} Because under this New Covenant, all restraint of the church, gospel, ordinances and means of salvation to the particular nation of the Jews is quite taken off: these blessings being without exception or limitation extended to all the nations of the world (Matthew 28:18-20, Mark 16:15-16, Luke 24:46, 47).

[12] **Efficacious**, for: {1} This New Covenant is a ministration of the Spirit, not of the letter; a ministration of life, not of death.[2695] Now spirit and life are full of efficacy. {2} The New Covenant is most effectually given and graven, namely: in mind and heart, not in dead tables of stone.[2696] {3} The Spirit is most powerfully and efficaciously given under the New Covenant: the

---

[2692] Luke 1:68-76, Titus 2:14, Hebrews 9:15, Romans 3:25, Hebrews 9:12 & 2:14-15; 1 Thessalonians 1:10, Galatians 3:13-14
[2693] Galatians 4:1-5
[2694] Romans 8:15
[2695] 2 Corinthians 3:6-8
[2696] Hebrews 8:10; 2 Corinthians 3:7, Deuteronomy 4:13

more Spirit, the more efficacy.[2697] {4} In this New Covenant, the fullness of Christ is most magnificently displayed, more than in all former covenants (John 1:14, 16, Colossians 1:19. & 2:9-10, Ephesians 3:8, etc). And Christ's fullness is most efficacious. {5} The conversion of the Jews by thousands;[2698] and of the Gentiles as it were by floods and seas to God, under the New Covenant, demonstrate the transcendent efficacy thereof before all the world, etc.[2699] But of this New Covenant's efficaciousness, I have spoken already in several particulars – there see.[2700]

[13] *Sure and faithful*. How can this New Covenant choose but be most sure, faithful and infallible? For:

{1} The author of it is most faithful, Jehovah (Hebrews 8:8, 10) – that gives being and subsistence to all his Covenants and promises (as that his most essential name imports, Exodus 6:3). This name of his {*Jehovah*} is mentioned four several times in this New Covenant, for the greater assurance of this Covenant's fidelity.[2701]

{2} The impulsive, or moving causes of it were merely God's most rich and free grace in Jesus Christ without any respect at all had to anything in Jews or Gentiles.[2702] It was not founded in man's worthiness, nor shall be confounded by man's unworthiness.

{3} The matter of it is so laid down in the body of the covenant, that God himself in effect undertakes both for himself and for his federates.[2703] He will be theirs, and they shall be his. Their restipulated duties, are all implicitly comprised in his expressly promised mercies. He first promises ability to them, before he calls for duty from them.

[2697] John 7:37-39
[2698] Acts 2:41 & 4:4
[2699] Isaiah 60:3-6, etc.
[2700] In Book 4, Chapter 5, Section 3, Aphorism 1
[2701] Jeremiah 31:31-34
[2702] Book 4, Chapter 3, Aphorism 2
[2703] Book 4, Chapter 5, Section 3, Generals 2 & 3

{4} The form of it is partly with such establishment and confirmation as can never be shaken or removed. It is confirmed (as has been evidenced abundantly):[2704] (i) by the choicest and best promises of God, (ii) by the sacred and inviolable oath of God, (iii) by the irrevocable death and precious blood of Jesus Christ; as also, (iv) by the best federal tokens, baptism and the Lord's supper. Now, God that promised cannot possibly lie; God that has sworn cannot repent or forswear himself; Christ that died, *dieth no more*, etc. – therefore this New Covenant can never be overthrown.

{5} The Mediator of this New Covenant is all-sufficient:[2705] both to enrich us with covenant mercies from God, and to enable us unto covenant duties to God, that as there can be no failure on God's part, so there shall be none on ours. Oh with what affiance and consolation may we lean upon this sure, faithful and immutable New Covenant in all exigence and extremities!

[14] ***Consolatory***. No covenant is consolatory like the New Covenant, for no covenant is dignified with such promises,[2706] such a Mediator,[2707] such a Comforter[2708] – and these are the very springs of consolation. But of this consolating property which abounds in the New Covenant, I have spoken so much already, that I need not to add further, having shown:

{1} That the matter of this New Covenant is so contrived, as may most sweetly and sufficiently remove all the principal doubts, discouragements and objections, which either a bleeding heart wounded sinner, or a distressed saint, may make against his own salvation. This is evinced in seven chief particulars.[2709]

[2704] In Book 4, Chapter 7
[2705] See Book 4, Chapter 6
[2706] Hebrews 8:6
[2707] Hebrews 9:15 & 12:26
[2708] John 14:14-17
[2709] In Book 4, Chapter 5, Section 2, General 5

{2} That this New Covenant is an excellent antidote against the greatest adversities and afflictions of God's covenant people. This is manifested in five particulars.[2710]

{3} That here is wonderful matter of consolation in that clause of this New Covenant: *I will be to them a God*, etc. (Hebrews 8:10). And this, against: (i) remains of sin, (ii) fears and dangers of apostasy, (iii) outward or inward wants, (iv) strong and violent temptations, (v) sad and dismaying desertions, (vi) sharp afflictions and persecutions, and (vii) the very terrors and pangs of death itself – against all and every of which, many sweet consolations are extracted from that great and glorious promise. Consult all of these diligently if you desire to taste and suck the delicious sweetness of the New Covenant's consolations.[2711]

[15] ***Extensive***. This New Covenant is beyond all other most extensive. It spreads forth its arms even to all nations of the world, Jewish and Gentile, accepting all profest believers Jews and Gentiles, and their children, into visible federation with God, and all true sincere believers into federation invisible.[2712] This is already handled at large in three distinct positions. Consider them heedfully.[2713]

[16] ***Continuing and everlasting***. It continues still new when the former Covenant waxes old and wears away.[2714] How long does it continue, has been already explained, namely: from Christ's death until the end of the world.[2715] As also in what sense it is everlasting, namely: absolutely, in regard to its substantials; respectively, only in regard to its circumstantials.[2716]

[2710] In Book 4, Chapter 3, Aphorism 2
[2711] In Book 4, Chapter 5, Section 3, Aphorism 1
[2712] Matthew 28:18-20, Mark 16:15-16, Luke 24:46-47
[2713] In Book 4, Chapter 4, Aphorisms 1 & 2
[2714] Hebrews 8:8, 13
[2715] In Book 4, Chapter 1, Aphorism 1
[2716] In Book 4, Chapter 2, Aphorism 1

(3) Hence, we may judiciously discern what agreement and difference there is between this New Covenant and the Old, and consequently between it and all other Covenants.

The agreement and difference between the Old Covenant and the three foregoing Covenants has been stated already,[2717] therefore if now we can come to a clear and true state of the agreement and difference between this New and that Old Covenant, we shall consequently most easily discern the agreement and difference between this New Covenant and all other fore-going Covenants of Faith.

The New Covenant's agreement with, or disagreement from the Old Covenant, I have referred to this, as to its most fit and proper place: according as I have heretofore propounded.[2718] The due discovery of this agreement and disagreement between them is of much consequence, for:

[1] Hereby the nature of the New Covenant will be the more distinctly discerned. [2] Hereby, the excellency of it above the Old will be discovered. [3] Hereby, several errors of men in misstating the agreement and difference between the Old and New Covenant, purposely devised for their own sinister ends and advantages, will be detected and defeated. [4] Hereby, that singular art of right distinguishing between the law and gospel, shall in some measure be exerted, which Luther so much extols: "He that well knows to discern the gospel from the law, let him give God thanks, and know himself to be a divine."[2719] For, the law given at Mount Sinai is that Old Covenant, and the gospel strictly taken is this New Covenant. [5] Hereby, several Scriptures which put sundry differences between the Old and New Covenant, shall be better understood, as Hebrews 8:8-10 & 12:18-25; 2 Corinthians 3:6 to the end, and Galatians 4:21 to the end.

[2717] In Book 3, Chapter 3, Aphorism 7, Corollary 5
[2718] In Book 4, Chapter 2, Aphorism 7, Corollary 5
[2719] Luth. in fol. 40. 6. Tom. 4. Latin.

Here therefore I shall lay down: [1] the agreement, and [2] the difference between the New Covenant and Old, which to me seems most consonant to the Scriptures – and this with all possible brevity and perspicuity.

[1] *The agreement between the Old Covenant given at Mount Sinai*[2720] *and this New Covenant from Mount Zion*[2721] (that I may use the apostle's terms) stands especially in these particulars, and such like, namely:

{1} **Both of them are Covenants of the same sort and nature, more generally**. (i) Both of them are Covenants of God with man (Galatians 4:24, Hebrews 8:8-9). (ii) Both of them are God's Covenants with man since the fall (Hebrews 8:8-9, Jeremiah 31:31-33) (iii) Both of them are Covenants, not of Works, but of Faith, and through Jesus Christ revealing righteousness, life, and salvation to lapsed sinners in and by Jesus Christ through faith. That the law was given at Mount Sinai as a Covenant, and that as a Covenant of Faith in Jesus Christ, not at all as a Covenant of Works; I have proven heretofore by many arguments, as also answered the contrary objections which are of any moment or consequence.[2722] That this New Covenant is a Covenant of Faith most eminently, needs no more proof than what has been already laid down in this fourth book.[2723] (iv) Both of them are Testamental Covenants, or Federal Testaments.[2724]

{2} **Both of them have the same author or efficient cause**, the Lord God. God as Jehovah has instituted and authorized them both (Deuteronomy 5:2-6 with Jeremiah 31:31-34, Hebrews 8:8-13). How God covenanted as Jehovah has been explained.[2725]

{3} **Both of them have the same impulsive or moving causes**, namely: the riches of God's mere grace, in and through the merit of Jesus Christ alone

---

[2720] Galatians 4:24-25, Hebrews 12:18-22
[2721] Hebrews 12:22-25, Galatians 4:26-27, etc.
[2722] In Book 3, Chapter 4, Aphorism 2, especially Opinion 4
[2723] See Book 4, Chapter 2, Aphorisms 1 & 2
[2724] Hebrews 9:15-23
[2725] In Book 3, Chapter 4, Aphorism 3

– see Exodus 19:3-6 & 20:2, Deuteronomy 5:2-6. & 7:6-9, Hebrews 8:8-13; see also Book 4, Chapter 3, Aphorism 2.

{4} **Both of them expressed in general the same bounty and benevolent affection to their federates,** accepting into Covenant with God, not only parents, but also their seed and posterity together with the parents. The Old Covenant took in the whole body of Israel, men, women, little ones, etc (Exodus 19:10-11 & 20:18, etc, Deuteronomy 5:2-6, etc, 22, compared with Deuteronomy 29:10-15, etc).[2726] All Israel of old, both parents and children were federates with God, and circumcised, until the days of Christ (Genesis 17:9, 11-12, Exodus 12:48, Luke 1:59 & 2:21, Philippians 3:5). And the New Covenant takes in as federates all profest believing parents, Jewish and Gentile, and their seed, or children, who are therefore to be baptized – as I have proven at large by many arguments.[2727]

{5} **Both of them contain for substance, the same subject matters or articles of agreement between God and his federates, in many things**, as:

(i) God on his part promises in both: (a) to be a God to his federates, (b) to give Christ to them, (c) to bestow his Spirit upon them, and (d) To furnish them with many spirituals, as: acceptance of them as his people; sanctification; justification by faith in Christ, freely remitting all their sins; supernatural ability to keep his Covenants, etc.

(i) God's federates on their part re-promising expressly or implicitly (as God requires from them): (a) to be God's people; (b) to keep God's Covenant by true faith; by sincere constant obedience in Christ; (c) to repent in case of failings and miscarriages; and (d) to take God's law (the same law of God which is written for God's federates, under Old and New Covenant – Deuteronomy 4:13 with Hebrews 8:10) as their rule for their faith and obedience. All these things are very clear by what has been already manifested

---

[2726] See Book 3, Chapter 4, Aphorism 3
[2727] In Book 4, Chapter 4, Aphorism 1 throughout

and proved touching the matters of these two Covenants, as the diligent reader may easily observe.[2728]

{6} **Both of them have for substance one and the same Mediator, Jesus Christ**, though typically represented in the mediation of Moses, in the Old Covenant;[2729] truly, in his own person actually exhibited in human flesh, in the New.[2730] See Book 4 Chapter 6.

{7} **Both of them have the same general way of sanction, dedication, or fundamental establishment** – namely: by blood, and death of sacrifices (Exodus 24:3-9, Matthew 26:28, Hebrews 9:15-23), though a most different blood and sacrifice.

{8} **Both of them had the like general season of publication** – namely: about fifty days after the sacrificing of the passover, namely: the old, fifty days after the typical passover was offered up in Egypt (Exodus 12:6, 7, 18 with Exodus 19:1, etc). The New Covenant was published on the feast of Pentecost, fifty days after Christ our true passover was offered up for us at Jerusalem (Acts 2:1-2, etc; 1 Corinthians 5:7), as Augustine also has elegantly observed this congruency.[2731]

{9} **Both of them were further confirmed and established in the same way**, for the general, namely: (i) by promises, both were established upon God's promises (Hebrews 8:6), and (ii) by visible tokens of the Covenants. See Luke 1:59 & 2:21 & 22:7-19 with Matthew 28:18-20, Acts 2:38-39, and Luke 22:19-20.

[2728] Compare Book 3, Chapter 4, Aphorism 4 throughout with Book 4, Chapter 5, Section 3, Aphorisms 1 & 2
[2729] Deuteronomy 5:2-5, Galatians 3:19-20
[2730] Hebrews 9:15 & 12:24
[2731] "i. Dies en[i]m quinquaginta computantur a celebratione Paschae, quae occisione figuratae Ovis per Moysen fieri praecepta est, in significationem uti{que} suturae Dominicae Passionis, us{que} ad diem quo Moyses legem accepit in Tabulis digito Dei conscriptis: Similiter ab occisione & Resurrectione illius qui sicut ovis ad immolandum ductus est, quinquaginta diebus completis, congregatos in Unum fideles, digitus Dei, hoc est, Spiritus Sanctus implevit, &c."
Aug. in *Lib. De Spir. & Litera*. cap. 16. p. 819. b. Tom. 3.

[10] **Both of them effect, produce, and constitute one and the same church of Christ essentially and substantially.** The Old Covenant church and New Covenant church are in essence and essential unity one and the same, having, one and the same covenant God: **Jehovah**;[2732] one and the same Mediator, Redeemer, and Savior: **Jesus Christ**;[2733] one and the same Holy Spirit for their sanctification and consolation;[2734] one and the same everlasting gospel for substance, revealing Christ and salvation to both; one and the same way of justification, both of the circumcision and uncircumcision, namely: by, or through faith (Romans 3:29-30 & 10:6-14, Galatians 2:15-16); one and the same kingdom of God, wherein men from east, west, etc, shall sit down with Abraham, Isaac and Jacob[2735] – yea, one and the same hope of resurrection and eternal life (Acts 26:6-7). This essential oneness and sameness of the church of Old and New Testament is notably demonstrated in these times of the New Covenant, by their union, incorporation, and consolidation into one body, through the death of Jesus Christ, which mystery of their oneness, the apostle most highly and emphatically magnifies.[2736]

[11] **Finally, both Old and New Covenant agree in the same common end**, namely: more immediately, the revealing of Jesus Christ for sinners' happiness; more mediately, the happiness and salvation of God's federates by Christ; and the glory of their Covenant God in all, as has been more at large explained touching both.[2737]

Herein especially, and in particulars of like nature reducible hereunto, the Old and New Covenant do most sweetly and harmoniously agree.

The disagreement or difference between the Old and this New Covenant is manifold; as several Scriptures – yea, the very body of this New Covenant expressly intimates (Hebrews 8:8-12. & 12:18-25, Galatians 4:21 to the end; 2

[2732] Romans 3:29
[2733] Hebrews 13:8 & 9:15
[2734] Deuteronomy 30:6, Ezekiel 36:25-26, John 7:37-39, Acts 2, John 14:15-16, etc.
[2735] Matthew 8:11
[2736] Ephesians 2:13 to the end & 3:1-13
[2737] Compare Book 3, Chapter 4, Aphorism 6 with Book 4, Chapter 8

Corinthians 3:6 to the end). But the difference is not so easily assigned as the agreement between these two Covenants, because sundry false differences, either corruptly devised or inconsiderately embraced, are pretended and obtruded, and some of them for sinister and unsound interests.

Here therefore, I shall propound the disagreements between the Old and New Covenant: {1} negatively, what they are not – so I shall discover the chief, false and pretended differences; {2} affirmatively, what they are – so I shall propound the true differences. We have need to judge and distinguish here exactly, for error here is dangerous.

{1} *Negatively*: the disagreement and difference between the Old and New Covenant, does **not** stand in these particulars following, namely:

(i) **Not** in this: that the Old Covenant is a Covenant of Works, holding forth righteousness, life, and salvation, only upon terms of perfect and perpetual personal doing; but the New Covenant is a Covenant of Grace, holding forth righteousness, life, and salvation upon terms of believing in Christ, for it has been already proved by many arguments: (a) that this Old Covenant was not given on Mount Sinai as a Covenant of Works,[2738] and (b) that this Old Covenant was given at Mount Sinai as a Covenant of Faith.[2739] And the contrary arguments are repelled, etc.

(ii) **Not** in this: that the Old Covenant is a mere carnal earthy covenant, containing mere carnal, external and earthly blessings, as Canaan, honor, riches, etc; but the New Covenant is a spiritual and celestial covenant, containing also spiritual and eternal blessings. This is the difference assigned by Bellarmine[2740] and other papists, and after them, by the Socinians (who muddy and poison the fountain truths of God by their carnal subtleties, as the papists do by their heresies and superstitions),[2741] who hold that the Spirit of

---

[2738] In Book 3, Chapter 4, Aphorism 2, Opinion 1
[2739] In Book 3, Chapter 4, Aphorism 2, Opinion 4
[2740] Bellarmine, *De Sacr. Baptism.* lib. 1. chap. 4. p. 62. F. Tom. 3 Colon. 1628 and *De Effectu Sacrament.* lib. 2. cap. 17. [passi]. Tom. 3. p. 44, 45.
[2741] Racovian Catechism, De Prophet. Christi munere, Q 10. Refutat. apud Henry Alsted in *Theolog. Polem.* Part 3. p. 322, &c. And A Iosua Stegman in *Photinianismo*, Disp.[20]

God and eternal life, were not promised under the Old Covenant. And this device serves the Socinian excellently, for his better debasing and decrying of the Scripture. This device is also taken up by some of the anabaptistical party,[2742] thereby the more colourably to defeat infants of their baptism; and to withstand that shrewd argument for paedobaptism drawn from circumcision.

Doubtless this is a very carnal and earthly opinion. But the falsehood and folly of this pretended difference may sufficiently appear: (a) partly, by considering the matters or blessings promised in the Old Covenant, namely: the Spirit of God, many spirituals and eternals; in Book 3, Chapter 4, Aphorism 4, Section 1, and Chapter 6, Aphorism 2, Section 1, etc; (b) partly, by perusing what my learned, judicious, and godly friend Mr. Thomas Blake (whose dexterity of judgment in matters of religion has been of high account with me ever since my first acquaintance with him) has said in refutation thereof, in his *Vindiciae Foederis* in Chapter 25 throughout.

(iii) **Not** in this: that the Old Covenant is a mixed covenant, partly legal, partly evangelical; mixed of two different covenants, the Covenant of Works and the Covenant of Grace (as one, who otherwise was very pious and learned, expressed himself; but not so soundly and wisely, as were to be desired)[2743] but the New Covenant is a pure evangelical Covenant. He seems to have run into this mistake, partly by considering the moral law too abstractedly, abstracting it from Moses' dispensation; partly by not observing heedfully the mysterious and singular way of God's revealing this Sinai Covenant. But against this error, be pleased diligently to consider: (a) that this Covenant at Mount Sinai, was given as a pure unmixed evangelical Covenant of Faith: as is already proved by many arguments, etc;[2744] (b) that God's way of revealing and establishing this Old Covenant was very singular, profound and mysterious: as has been manifested in the form of this Old Covenant.[2745] These two things heedfully

---

[2742] Blackwood in his *Storm*, etc. pp.31-32, etc.
[2743] Mr. George Walker in his *Treatise of the Old and New Covenant*, Chapter 16
[2744] Book 3, Chapter 4, Aphorism 2, Opinion 4
[2745] In Book 3, Chapter 4, Aphorism 5, Section 1 throughout

perused will, I hope, satisfy any unbiased judgment, that this Sinai Covenant was not in this sense a mixed covenant.

(iv) **Not** in this: that the Old Covenant (in a far other sense) is mixed, namely: not a pure gospel covenant, but mixed: having promises mixed, some evangelical, belonging to those to whom the gospel belongs; some domestic or civil, specially respecting the house of Abraham, and policy of Israel;[2746] but that the New Covenant is purely evangelical; this notion, I doubt is mixed and made up of [that which would all the better][2747] seclude infants of believers from baptism. But Mr. Blake has sufficiently laid open the weakness of it – to whom, for the sake of brevity, the reader is referred.[2748]

(v) **Not** in this: that God's Covenant is threefold: of nature, of grace, and subservient to the Covenant of Grace. The New Covenant is this covenant of grace: the Old Covenant, is this subservient covenant. This difference is given by that learned Cameron. How dissatisfactory this his notion is, I have declared already; there see diligently.[2749]

(vi) **Not** in this: that the Old Covenant admitted and accepted, as federates with God, all the natural seed of Abraham, Isaac, Jacob, etc., though only professing faith., etc., but the New Covenant accepts none as federates, but elect and regenerate persons. Against this pretended but groundless difference between Old and New Covenant, and against that unwarrantable restraining of New Covenant federates only to elect and regenerate persons, much might have been said, and not without great need, considering how this false difference is improved for sinister purposes both by papists, anabaptists and other separatists; but my worthily honored friend Mr. Thomas Blake has done this to my hand so fully and satisfactorily, that I need say nothing, but only request the reader diligently to peruse what he has said.[2750]

[2746] Mr. John Tombes in his *Exercitat.*, p.2

[2747] This sentence appears fragmented; my suggestion in parentheses is my best attempt at reconciling the whole sentence. – Ed.

[2748] Mr. Thomas Blake in his *Vindiciae Foederis*, Chapter 26

[2749] In Book 3, Chapter 4, Aphorism 2, Opinion 3

[2750] Mr. Thomas Blake in his *Vindiciae Foederis*, Chapters 27-34

(vii) Finally, the true difference between Old and New Covenant stands **not** in this: that the Old Covenant comprised in it as federates with God all persons professing true faith and obedience to God, and all their seed; but the New Covenant is made so personally with them that actually make such profession, that it terminates in their persons, not taking in their seed as federates with them. This difference is plainly leveled against infant-baptism. But, that professed believers, Jews and Gentiles and their seed, are taken in as federates with God in his New Covenant, I have abundantly proven already – there see.[2751] Mr. Blake has also exceedingly, and to very good purpose, enlarged himself upon this particular, in his *Vindiciae Foederis* chapters 34-43 – consult him diligently.

These especially are those unsound and unjustifiable differences between the Old and New Covenant, some whereof are unadvisedly expressed by men of sounder judgment; others are most corruptly contrived for the abetting of error by men of corrupt minds. Let all the sincere lovers of the truth with vigilant circumspection decline them all.

{2} *Affirmatively*. The true difference and disagreement between the Old and New Covenant (as is evident from the natures of them both, already unfolded) consists especially in these particulars, namely:

(i) **In the distinct peculiarity of their natures.** For though both of them are God's Covenants of Faith, yet they are two distinct individual expressures of the Covenant of Faith: the Old Covenant being one of the Covenants of Promise,[2752] in Christ promised, and to come afterwards; the New Covenant being that eminent Covenant of Performance, in Christ actually performed and exhibited, and come in human flesh already, as I have formerly distinguished them, and cleared the distinction by Scripture,[2753] so that they are rather distinct individuals of the same species, than distinct species or

---

[2751] In Book 4, Chapter 4, Aphorism 1
[2752] Ephesians 2:12
[2753] In Book 1, Chapter 2, Aphorism 3, etc, in Book 2, Chapter 2, Aphorism 3

kinds of the same genus: in as much as they differ not essentially, but only accidentally.

(ii) **In the peculiar notion and consideration of the author.** God was author of the Old Covenant, as the Lord, Israel's Covenant God, Israel's Redeemer, Lawgiver, and endeared husband, as has been formerly explained;[2754] but God was author of the New Covenant, as the Lord. Hence in laying down of this New Covenant, this his great and glorious essential name **Jehovah** is so often mentioned.[2755] Besides, this being a Testamental Covenant, Jesus Christ as Testator is author of it, confirming and establishing this his last will and testament by his death and blood, beyond revocation or alteration.[2756]

(iii) **In the peculiarity of occasion which God took of making these two Covenants.** God established his Old Covenant with Israel at Mount Sinai upon occasion of that great and eminent redemption of them out of Egypt, that he might carry them into the possession of the promised Canaan, as has been already evidenced in many particulars.[2757] But the occasion which he took of establishing his New Covenant, was, the disconsolate condition of his captives in Babylon, the weakness and unprofitableness of the Old Covenant, and the extreme sinful and miserable condition of mankind, no man to be cured but by the provisions of the New Covenant in Jesus Christ exhibited.[2758]

(iv) **In the diversity of agents, officers, and instrumental causes which God made use of for manifestation and administration of these two Covenants.** The Old Covenant was first given by the ministration of Moses a servant in God's house, as an intervening person or typical Mediator; *was ordained by angels in the hand of a mediator*;[2759] and was afterwards administered and managed, ordinarily by priests,[2760] extraordinarily by

---

[2754] In Book 3, Chapter 4, Aphorism 3
[2755] Jeremiah 31:31-34
[2756] Hebrews 9:15-17, Galatians 3:15
[2757] In Book 3, Chapter 3, Aphorism 1, Question 4
[2758] Book 5, Chapter 3, Aphorism 2
[2759] John 1:17, Hebrews 3:3-5, Deuteronomy 5:2-6, Galatians 3:19-20, Acts 7:53
[2760] Hebrews 5:1, 4

prophets.[2761] But this New Covenant (fore-promised of God by the prophet Jeremiah, in chapter 31 verse 31, etc) was in fullness of time that great salvation, that great doctrine of salvation, which *began to be spoken by Jesus Christ, as a son over his own house, and was confirmed unto us by them that heard him, God also bearing them witness both with signs and wonders, and with divers miracles and gifts of the Holy Ghost, according to his own will.*[2762] And Jesus Christ has committed the after-administration of this New Covenant, and of all the ordinances thereof, partly to his apostles, prophets and evangelists, officers extraordinary, for a time until the New Covenant church was planted throughout the world; partly, to pastors and teachers, etc. – ordinary officers – until the end of the world, that the church be edified, and the saints perfected.[2763]

(v) **In their extensiveness towards God's federates.** The Old Covenant was of less and more limited extent, only to the nation of the Jews, the natural seed of Abraham, Isaac, and Jacob, and their children,[2764] and to some few Gentile proselytes embracing the Jewish religion.[2765] These only were God's covenant people, others no people; these near unto God, others far off; these having obtained mercy, others not having obtained mercy; these of the household of God, others strangers; these God's children, others dogs, etc.[2766] But this New Covenant is enlarged and extended to all nations of the world, and accepts as federates with God all professed believers Jewish or Gentile, and their seed without exception, as has been abundantly manifested (Matthew 28:18-20, Mark 16:15-16, Luke 24:46-47, Acts 13:46-47 & 26:20, Ephesians 2:13 to the end & 3:1-13).[2767]

[2761] 1 Samuel 28:6, Hebrews 1:1
[2762] Hebrews 2:3-4 & 3:6
[2763] Matthew 28:18-20, Mark 16:15-16, Ephesians 4:11-13
[2764] Romans 9:4, Ephesians 2:12
[2765] Genesis 17:10-15, Exodus 12:48-49
[2766] Ephesians 2:12-13, 19; 1 Peter 2:8-10
[2767] In Book 4, Chapter 4, Aphorisms 1 & 2 throughout

(vi) **In the gradual perfections and excellencies of promised blessings and restipulated duties.** As to the substance of these, both these covenants agree: but as to the excellent degree and perfection thereof they differ:

(a) Promised mercies under the New Covenant are, as extensively, so gradually, full, larger and higher (Hebrews 8:8-12):[2768] (1) The law of God is given into, and engraven in, the minds and hearts of his federates more fully and efficaciously. (2) The Spirit of the Lord is poured forth more abundantly (John 7:37-40, Acts 2 throughout). (3) The knowledge of the Lord is vouchsafed more excellently and universally. (4) Remission of sins is vouchsafed more singularly, etc.

(b) Re-promised duties and abilities for them, are in the New Covenant more sweetly provided for them under the Old, that they may be performed, not so carnally, but much more spiritually; not so servilely and slavishly, but much more freely and lovingly; not so erroneously as to seek justification by working, but regularly so as to seek justification by believing, and to express the truth of justification and sanctification by working, etc.[2769]

(vii) **In their different representation of the Mediator.** Jesus Christ was Mediator in both, but in the Old Covenant he was represented darkly, under the type of Moses, and as future, to come afterwards; in the New Covenant he is set forth clearly, as the Mediator, Surety and Testator thereof actually exhibited already in human flesh, yea dead, risen, ascended and set down already on the right hand of God (Hebrews 9:15-17, etc. & 7:22 & 12:24, Galatians 4:4, etc).[2770]

(viii) **In their outward form or manner of manifestation, confirmation, administration.** Much of these two covenants difference lies in their outward form, as:

(a) In their outward form of manifestation, for: (1) the Old Covenant was manifested with great terror, out of the midst of the devouring fire; the New

---

[2768] See at large this cleared in Book 4, Chapter 5, Section 3, Aphorism 1 throughout.

[2769] Romans 9:31-32 & 10:3, etc.

[2770] Deuteronomy 5:2-5, Galatians 3:19-20

without terror, with as much sweetness.[2771] (2) The Old Covenant was written literally in two tables of stone;[2772] the New is written spiritually in the fleshly tables of mind and heart.[2773] (3) The Old filled the federates with a spirit of bondage to fear; the New fills with a Spirit of adoption and liberty to love, etc. (Romans 8:15, Galatians 4:4-6 compared with Hebrews 12:18-25). Notable is that of Augustine's: "This is the shortest and plainest difference of the two testaments: fear and love," etc.[2774] (4) The Old, hence, is called a ministration of death and condemnation; the New a ministration of life and righteousness (2 Corinthians 3:7-9). (5) The Old was glorious, but veiled; the New much more glorious, and unveiled (2 Corinthians 3:9 to the end, etc).

(b) In their outward form of confirmation, for: (1) the Old Covenant was confirmed and dedicated by typical blood and death of innocent sacrifices, (Exodus 24:3-9 with Hebrews 9:18-20), etc., but the New Covenant was dedicated with far better blood and sacrifice, namely: with the true blood and death of Jesus Christ the lamb of God without spot, taking away the sins of the world (Hebrews 9:15-17, Matthew 26:28). (2) The Old Covenant was without an oath; the New with the oath of God, of which he will never repent (Hebrews 7:19-22). (3) The Old Covenant was established upon God's good promises, but the New upon God's better promises (Hebrews 8:6). (4) The Old was confirmed by more dark, difficult, chargeable tokens, circumcision and the passover, signifying Christ to come; the New is confirmed by more clear, easy and cheap tokens, baptism and the Lord's supper, signifying Jesus Christ already come (Matthew 28:19-20, Matthew 26:28; 1 Corinthians 11:25-26).

(c) In their outward administration, for:

(1) The Old Covenant had a worldly sanctuary, whereunto the public ministrations were principally affixed (Hebrews 9:1-11). The New Covenant

---

[2771] Hebrews 12:18-15
[2772] Deuteronomy 4:13
[2773] Hebrews 8:10; 2 Corinthians 3:3-4, etc.
[2774] Augustine, *Answer to Adimantum, a Disciple of Mani*

has a better and more perfect tabernacle,[2775] that of Christ's humanity wherein our great high priest officiated, performing more perfect sacrifices, and releasing his church from restraint places, to worship him in any place (John 4:21, 23; 1 Timothy 2:8).

(2) The Old Covenant had many dark carnal ordinances, rites, ceremonies, and appointments of divine service *imposed on them until the time of reformation*, which could not make the comers thereunto perfect as pertaining to the conscience, they being only *shadows of good things to come, but the body is of Christ* (Hebrews 10:1, etc, Colossians 2:17).[2776] But the New Covenant – being established by the death, blood and sacrifice of Christ himself – raises the people of God from more carnal to more clear, spiritual sacrifices and services of divine worship, as preaching, praying, baptism, breaking of bread, thanksgiving, etc, acceptable unto God by Jesus Christ (1 Peter 2:5, Hebrews 13:15, Romans 12:1; 1 Timothy 2:1-2, Acts 6:4. & 2:42, Matthew 28:18-20; 1 Corinthians 11:23-27), as also to more spiritual acts of church government, admonition of offenders (Matthew 18:15-18), casting out of the obstinate and incorrigible (1 Corinthians 5 throughout), and restoring again of the penitent (2 Corinthians 2:6-8, 10).

(3) The ordinances of the Old Covenant were managed: extraordinarily by prophets and ordinarily by priests and Levites in the Old Covenant ministry;[2777] the ordinances of the New Covenant are managed extraordinarily by apostles, prophets, evangelists, and ordinarily, by pastors, teachers, elders and deacons (Ephesians 4:11-13; 1 Corinthians 12:28; 1 Timothy 5:17, Romans 12:4-9).

(4) The Old Covenant had many solemn set times of public worship, and a seventh-day sabbath; the New Covenant has only one solemn set time for public worship, namely: on every first-day of the week, which is the Lord's day sabbath (Revelation 1:10, Acts. 20:7; 1 Corinthians 16:1-2).

[2775] Hebrews 9:11, etc.
[2776] Hebrews 9:1, etc, 9-10 & 10:1-3, etc.
[2777] Hebrews 9:6-7, Malachi 2:7

(ix) **In certain accidentals appertaining to the condition of the church of Christ, which was essentially one under both Old and New Covenant:** as the new moon and the old is one essentially, differing only accidentally, for: (a) the church under the Old Covenant was as a heir in minority, but the church under the New Covenant is as a heir come to maturity of age.[2778] (b) The church under the Old Covenant was in a more servile condition, under tutors and governors; but the church under the New Covenant is in a more free condition, stated in son-like, and heir-like liberty.[2779] (c) The church under the Old Covenant was under a veil: but under the New Covenant, the veil is done away in Christ.[2780] (d) The church under the Old Covenant was very small and of narrow extent, confined to that one little nation of the Jews; but the church under the New Covenant is of most large extent, enlarged to all nations of the world (Matthew 28:18-20, Mark 16:15-16, Luke 24:46-47).

(x) **In duration.** The Old Covenant endured only from the giving of the law at Mount Sinai, until the death of Jesus Christ, as has been manifested;[2781] but the New Covenant – abolishing the Old, as to what was vanishing in it – continues still new from Christ's death until the end of the world, as has been evidenced (Matthew 28:19-20; 1 Corinthians 11:26, Ephesians 4:11-13).[2782] The Old Covenant is antiquated by the New; the New shall be antiquated by none.

(xi) **In regard to memorable occurrences,** falling out under these two federal expressures, which were most various; yet these of the New Covenant far transcending, compare Book 3, Chapter 4, Introduction, with Book 4, Chapter 1, Aphorism 2.

(xii) **Finally, in particularity of ends**, for: (a) the Old Covenant intended a fuller revealing of Christ than formerly as the promised Savior; the New

---

[2778] Galatians 4:1-3
[2779] Galatians 4:1-7, 22 to the end & 5:1, etc, John 8:36
[2780] 2 Corinthians 3:12 to the end
[2781] In Book 3, Chapter 4, Introduction
[2782] In Book 4, Chapter 1, Aphorism 1

Covenant intends the fullest revealing of Jesus Christ, as the exhibited and performed Savior.[2783] (b) The Old Covenant intended the particular happiness of Israel, one nation in the world; the New Covenant intends the general happiness of all the nations of the world.

(4) Hence, we may evidently discover what the additional excellencies and preeminences of the New Covenant are beyond those of the old, and of all other foregoing Covenants. The New Covenant excels them all, and particularly the Old.

[1] *In clearness.* God's Covenants with Adam and Noah, were as the day-dawning, of saving light and grace to poor sinners; his Covenant with Abraham, was as the sunrise; his Old Covenant, comprising those with David and the captives, was as the morning light growing clearer and clearer until the perfect day; but his New Covenant, is as the brightest noontide, the perfect day, the midday of clearest light, wherein the sun of righteousness shines forth in his strength most gloriously. Now, God's mysteries are most clearly unveiled; God's ordinances are most clearly laid down,[2784] the *veil is done away in Christ*;[2785] God's promises are most clearly propounded;[2786] Jesus Christ is most clearly revealed, and all spirituals in him;[2787] the way into the holiest of all, heaven itself is most clearly opened and made manifest by the blood of Jesus;[2788] and the minds of God's federates are most clearly illuminated for understanding of all *the deep things of God.*[2789]

[2] *In spirituality.* In the Old Covenant administration, there was much outwardness, earthiness, and carnality in ordinances, times, places, instruments, officers and performers of divine worship, and these outward

---

[2783] See Book 3, Chapter 4, Aphorism 6, and Book 4, Chapter 8
[2784] Ephesians 3:4-5
[2785] 2 Corinthians 3:12-18
[2786] Hebrews 8:6; 1 Timothy 4:8
[2787] 2 Corinthians 3:18
[2788] Hebrews 10:19-20
[2789] Hebrews 8:11; 1 Corinthians 2:9-10, etc; 1 John 2:20, 27

services could reach only the flesh, the outward man, they could not purify the conscience; so there was much earthiness in the promises, and in the hopes of the people, looking at an earthly Canaan, and earthly happiness there, etc. But under this New Covenant, the promises are mostly spiritual,[2790] the ordinances and whole worship of God very spiritual [2791] – yea, the hearts and lives of God's true federates are very much spiritualized.[2792] See Inference 2, Property 7.

[3] *In spiritual liberty, and holy freedom from all sorts of spiritual thralldom.* This New Covenant time is to the church of God the greatest jubilee, the greatest year of redemption and release, that ever was or shall be in this world. See Isaiah 61:1-2, etc, and Luke 4:18-19, 21. But of this formerly.[2793]

[4] *In fulness and completeness.* Of this also formerly.[2794]

[5] *In extensiveness.* The Old Covenant was extended to the Israel according to the flesh, in one nation (Romans 9:4, Ephesians 2:12). But this New Covenant is extended to the Israel according to the Spirit, in all the nations of the world (Matthew 28:18-20, Mark 16:15-16, Luke 24:46-47). But of this see more above.[2795]

[6] *In efficaciousness*: as formerly, in General Inference 2, Property 12.

[7] *In comfortableness*: as has been already manifested most abundantly in many cases of saddest disconsolation.[2796]

[8] *In durableness.*[2797] The Old Covenant vanishes away; this New still remains. It is as heart of oak – yea, it is an everlasting Covenant (Hebrews 9:13 & 13:20).

[9] *In gloriousness.* This New Covenant outshines the Old, as far as the sun outshines the moon. Yea as the moon derives and borrows all her clear

---

[2790] Hebrews 8:10-12, Ephesians 1:3
[2791] John 4:23
[2792] Colossians 3:1-3, Philippians 3:10
[2793] In General Inference 2, Property 11
[2794] In General Inference 2, Property 10
[2795] In General Inference 2, Property 15
[2796] In General Inference 2, Property 14
[2797] In General Inference 2, Property 16

light from the sun, having nothing but a dim blackish darkness of her own; so the Old Covenant (having only a darkish, blackish body of itself) derived and borrowed as it were all her clearest light from Christ, and the mysteries of the New Covenant. There was a gloriousness in the Old Covenant; but a far greater glory in the New. *For even that which was made glorious, had no glory in this respect, by reason of the glory that excelleth.*[2798] And no wonder, for: {1} the glory of the Old Covenant, was only a veiled glory, glory under a veil, Moses put a veil upon his shining face, but the glory of the New Covenant is unveiled; the veil is done away in Christ.[2799] {2} The glory of the Old Covenant was but the glory of the letter; the glory of the New Covenant is the glory of the Spirit.[2800] {3} The glory of the Old Covenant was but the glory of the ministration of death and condemnation, but the glory of the New Covenant is the glory of the ministration of life and righteousness.[2801] {4} The glory of the Old Covenant, was but a servile glory of bondage, like shining golden fetters; but the glory of the New Covenant is a glory of sweet filial liberty.[2802] {5} The glory of the Old Covenant was an affrighting and dazzling glory; but the glory of the New Covenant is an alluring and transforming glory.[2803] {6} Finally, the glory of the Old Covenant was vanishing: but the glory of the New Covenant is abiding.[2804] In all these regards, the glory of the New Covenant is a glory far transcending and excelling.

(5) **Hence, how great are the privileges of God's New Covenant people!** To be in a covenantless condition, is most wretched: such are Christ-less, church-less, hopeless and God-less in the world.[2805] To be in covenant with God, not only by outward, but also by inward federation, is most advantageous: such are safe in the ark, when the rest of the world is

---

[2798] 2 Corinthians 3:10
[2799] 2 Corinthians 3:12-14, etc.
[2800] 2 Corinthians 3:6-8
[2801] 2 Corinthians 3:6-10
[2802] 2 Corinthians 3:17
[2803] 2 Corinthians 3:7, 18
[2804] 2 Corinthians 3:11
[2805] Ephesians 2:12

drowned; such are blessed with Abraham, when all the rest of the world are cursed; such are God's peculiar treasure and special people with Israel, when all the rest of the world are not his people, etc. But to be God's sincere New Covenant people, in power as well as form, in truth as well as name, is most glorious; as the New Covenants pre-eminences are above those of all other Covenants. So the New Covenant people's privileges are above all other federates' privileges. God has done much for all his covenant people in all ages; but he has done most for his New Covenant people in this last age. They had many and great privileges, but ours are more and greater. Cast a discreet eye upon the New Covenant, as already here set forth, and then extol and admire the privileges of God's New Covenant people, even our privileges, for:

[1] We are federates in a Covenant that has removed all the darkness, weakness, imperfections, unprofitableness, bondage, and gravaminousness of all former Covenants – and that completely, so that now we have a Covenant divested of all inconveniences.[2806]

[2] We are federates in such a Covenant as is the common cistern, receptacle and treasury of all the light, strength, profitableness, perfections, benefits, liberties, sweetness, and comfortableness of all foregoing Covenants, touching temporals, spirituals, and eternals.[2807] Oh what a privilege! God in this New Covenant has given us his honey without sting, his roses without prickles, his wine without water, his burden without weight, his yolk without trouble.[2808]

[3] We are federates in such a Covenant as far transcends and surpasses the Old Covenant, and all former Covenants in multiplicity of excellencies: answerable whereunto are our enjoyments, and our privileges therein.

Being God's New Covenant people:

[2806] 2 Corinthians 3:6 to the end, Hebrews 7:18-19, 22 & 8:6 to the end & 12:18-25 & 10:5-19, Galatians 4:22 to the end & 5:1, etc.
[2807] 1 Timothy 4:8, Hebrews 8:10-12, Ephesians 1:3, Hebrews 9:12 & 10:19-20
[2808] Matthew 11:29-30

We have God's best and richest mercies wherewith his New Covenant is furnished (Hebrews 8:10-12).

We have God's best and choicest promises, whereupon his New Covenant is established (Hebrews 8:6, 10-12).

We have the sweetest way of restipulated duties. All our duties being comprised in God's promised mercies, wherein God assures us of ability from himself, for all the duty which he expects from us – yea, in effect the Lord himself undertakes for our ability, and for our duty.[2809]

We have the last and best discoveries of Jesus Christ, the only Mediator between God and man, in this New Covenant. Here we may see this seed of the woman bruising the serpent's head (Colossians 2:14-15 with Genesis 3:15); This true Noah saving his elect remnant by water (1 Peter 3:21 with Genesis 6 & 7); this blessed seed of Abraham, blessing all nations (Acts 3:25-26, Galatians 3:13-14 with Genesis 12:3); this true prophet like Moses raised up from among the people Israel (Acts 2:22-23 & 7:37 with Deuteronomy 18:15-20); this seed and son of David, sitting upon his throne, and ruling the house of Jacob forever (Luke 1:31-33 with Psalm 132:11). Here we may see, the desire of all nations already come into his temple, the Messiah already incarnate and cut off, not for himself, but for our sins; the sinner's only Savior, suffering, dying, buried, revived, raised from the dead, ascending into heaven, and sat down on God's right hand in highest glory. Never Covenant set forth Christ so fully and gloriously as this New Covenant. Many kings and prophets desired to see these things which we see, and have not seen them; to hear these things which we hear, and have not heard them.[2810]

We have the most complete effusions of the Spirit under this New Covenant.[2811]

We have a Covenant most excellently manifested, most admirably established, and most spiritually administered. Christ himself has revealed it,

---

[2809] Hebrews 8:10-12; see Book 4, Chapter 5, Section 2, Generals 2 & 3.
[2810] Luke 10:24
[2811] John 7:37-40, Acts 1

Christ's own blood and the oath of God has confirmed it, and by most spiritual ordinances, seals and censures it is administered.[2812]

We have attained a better state and condition than was ever attainable under any foregoing Covenant. All former Covenants advanced the federates no higher than to a servile state of minority; this New Covenant brings us to a free son-like state of maturity.[2813]

We are by this New Covenant instated in the most complete church that ever was on earth, namely: the ecumenical or general church of God extended to all the nations of the world.[2814]

We are federates in such a Covenant, as has, does, and will represent during its continuance, the most rare, desirable and wonderful occurrence, that were ever discovered to the world.[2815]

Yea finally, we have such a Covenant as abides and remains when others are removed, and will continue so long as the world shall continue; until it hath gathered all the elect, perfected all the saints, edified the church to the top-stone, and made all things ready for the blessed return of Jesus Christ to judgment.[2816]

(6) Hence, we may, by this New Covenant, very sweetly assure ourselves that we are God's New Covenant people.

And I need not superadd any further discoveries, or notes of trial, of our true, inward, saving New Covenant state, but only point at such as have been already laid down in several places of this fourth book.

We may be solidly and comfortably assured that we are truly and savingly God's New Covenant people:

[2812] See Book 4, Chapter 7 throughout
[2813] Galatians 4:1-7
[2814] Matthew 28:19-20, Mark 16:15-16
[2815] Book 4, Chapter 1, Aphorism 2
[2816] Matthew 28:19-20; 1 Corinthians 11:20, Ephesians 4:11-13, etc.

[1] By God's writing of his laws in our minds and hearts. Many notes whereof, see in Book 4, Chapter 5, Section 3, Aphorism 1.

[2] By our being furnished with true New Covenant knowledge of God, and of the things of God. Many evidences hereof, see in Book 4, Chapter 5, Section 3, Aphorism 1.

[3] By God's actual remission of our sins. All of us who have our sins actually remitted, are God's sincere New Covenant people. Now those that have their sins pardoned, may know that their sins are pardoned, and that by many discoveries: laid down in Book 4, Chapter 5, Section 3, Aphorism 1.

[4] By our being brought into this New Covenant by being called to Christ, and made Christ's effectually. Now whether we are truly and effectually Christ's or not, may be discovered by many evidences thereof, unfolded in Book 4, Chapter 6, Inference 9.

[5] By the Lord's being our Covenant God. For if he is savingly our Covenant God, we must needs be his covenant people. These are relatives. Now we may notably discern whether the Lord is savingly our Covenant God: {1} By his federal impressions and operations upon us, as our Covenant God. Here seven are laid down in Book 4, Chapter 5, Section 3, Aphorism 1. {2} By our covenant relation unto God, evidenced in eight particulars, there [following]. {3} By our deportment and carriage towards him, as towards our God in covenant, which is set forth at large in five particulars, there [following].

These evidences of our true and salvifical New Covenant state – dispersed in several parts of this fourth book – are here summarily collected together, and represented in one view unto our eyes. Do we desire to know that we are God's New Covenant people indeed, and that savingly? Then, let us all these topics of evidences diligently. Let us weigh ourselves in these sanctuary scales heedfully; let us try ourselves at these sacred touch-stones impartially.

(7) **Hence, how much does it concern all, especially us Gentiles to esteem, embrace, rest upon, conform to, and triumph in this blessed New Covenant**, for:

[1] Of all covenants which since the foundation of the world God revealed to man, this New Covenant is: {1} every way most excellent; and therefore to be esteemed by all; {2} every way most desirable, amiable, and delectable; and therefore to be embraced by all; {3} every way most firm, sure, faithful, immutable and irrevocable: and therefore to be believed, assented to, acquiesced in, and rested upon by all; {4} every way most holy, just, and good; most equal, upright, spiritual, and heavenly; and therefore to be complied with, and conformed unto by all; {5} and it is every way sufficient for our miseries; suitable to our necessities; satisfactory against our scruples, doubts and objections; confirmatory against our spiritual enemies and their temptations, and consolatory against all out imaginable disconsolations: and therefore it is to be triumphed in by all.

[2]. Of all the people in the world, we Gentiles have far the greatest cause, thus to esteem, embrace, rest-upon, conform to, and triumph in, this blessed New Covenant, for:

{1} From what extremities of misery did God restore us Gentiles when he brought us first into this New Covenant! We were no people, we had not obtained mercy, we *were without Christ, being aliens from the commonwealth of Israel, and strangers from the covenants of promise, having no hope, and without God in the world.*[2817] Could there be a more wretched people in the world than such Gentiles?

{2} To what high eminences of privileges did God at the very first advance us Gentiles, when he accepted us at first federates with himself in this New Covenant! His own peculiar people the Jews must wait many ages for this covenant, and pass many gradual preparatories, especially under the Old Covenant, before they could be fitted for, and capable of this Covenant; and

---

[2817] Ephesians 2:12-13; 1 Peter 2:8-10

yet we strangers, aliens, enemies to God, were at once exalted from our deepest paganish misery, to this highest New Covenant felicity.

{3} The Gentiles are so taken into covenant, that they are fellow heirs, and of the same body with the Jews. This is a great mystery (Ephesians 3:4-12). And what more?

{4} The Gentiles are so generally and universally taken in as federates with God in this New Covenant, even all professed believing Gentiles in all nations and their seed, that their glory far outshines the glory of the very Jews.[2818] *Sing O barren, thou that didst not bear, break forth into singing and cry aloud thou that didst not travel with child: for more are the children of the desolate, than the children of the married wife, saith the LORD.*[2819] The abundant access of the Gentiles to the church, is the great glory of the church (Isaiah 60:1 to the end). And what further?

{5} The Gentiles are entertained and retained as federates with God in this New Covenant, when God's ancient covenant people the Jews are rejected: Jews are broken off, and Gentiles are grafted in.[2820] God's only people become no people, and they that were not a people become the people of the living God. Behold here the goodness and severity of God! And what may be further added?

{6} When the Jews shall again be converted unto God, and grafted in, they shall obtain mercy through the Gentiles mercy, as the Gentiles obtained mercy through the Jews unbelief (Romans 11:25, 26-32). Let all this be duly considered, and then all we Gentiles may cry out with the great doctor of the Gentiles: {*O the depth*}, etc.[2821] How can we look upon this New Covenant, and not be ravished with it!

[2818] Matthew 28:18-19, Mark 16:15-16, Luke 24:46-67
[2819] Isaiah 54:1, etc.
[2820] Romans 11:11 to the end
[2821] Romans 11:33, etc.

(8) **Hence, God's New Covenant people (answerably to this New, better, and more illustrious Covenant)**[2822] **should approve themselves as a new, better and more excellent people both in their persons and conversations.** Our hearts and lives, our inward constitutions, and outward conversations should bear a harmonious agreement and correspondence with divine dispensations under which we live.

Thus, *Christ our passover is sacrificed for us: therefore we should keep the feast, not with old leaven, neither with the leaven of malice and wickedness, but with the unleavened bread of sincerity and truth.*[2823] All this New Covenant time since the death of Christ until the world's end, is our great passover feast, therefore it is to be kept without all spiritual leaven. Again: *Ye were sometimes darkness, but now are light in the Lord: walk as children of light,* etc.[2824] And elsewhere: *and that, knowing the time, that now it is high time to awake out of sleep: for now is our salvation nearer than when we believed* (that is, then when we first believed). *The night* (namely: of paganism) *is far spent, the day* (namely: of Christianity) *is at hand: let us therefore cast off the works of darkness, and let us put on the armor of light. Let us walk honestly, as in the day*, etc.[2825] God's merciful dispensations to us, should be strong obligations upon us.

The like we are to judge here touching the New Covenant dispensation under which we live: we should be conform to this New Covenant in heart and life.

[1] The Covenant is new; so should we be new: new creatures, having new minds by illumination, new consciences by purification, new wills by renovation, new affections by sanctification, and new lives and actions by reformation.[2826] What a shameful incongruity would it be for us to persist still

---

[2822] Hebrews 8:6, 8 & 7:22
[2823] 1 Corinthians 5:7-8
[2824] Ephesians 5:8-11
[2825] Romans 13:11-14
[2826] Hebrews 8:8 & 9:15

in our old carnality, in our old ignorance and unbelief, in our old sins and wicked courses, under this New Covenant, especially professing ourselves to be God's New Covenant people?

[2] This New Covenant is better than ever the Old Covenant was; so should we that are professed federates therein, be a better people than those under the Old. We New Covenant Christians, should be better than the Old Covenant Jews.[2827] Better in our minds and judgments: not having a veil of blindness and error upon them, wandering from God's truth and will; resting in the law, seeking for righteousness by the deeds of the law, stumbling at that stumbling stone (Romans 9:31-33). Better in our consciences: not corrupt, secure, erroneous, counting it duty and doing God service to betray and murder the prince of life Jesus Christ, and to kill his apostles, etc. Better in our wills and hearts: not being perverse, froward, crooked, stubborn, rebellious, hard-hearted, impenitent, earthly, carnal, etc. Better in all our principles: abounding much more with love, out of a pure heart, good conscience, and faith unfeigned (1 Timothy 1:5). Better in all our practices, being therein: not superstitious, but truly religious; not scandalous, but inoffensive; not rebellious, but obsequious unto God; not carnal and literal, but spiritual; not earthly, but heavenly (Philippians 3:20); not hypocritical, but sincere; not apostatizing from God and his fear through unbelief, drawing back unto perdition, but steadfastly persevering with God in well-doing, through faith, to the saving of the soul (Hebrews 10:38, 39).

[3] This New Covenant is more illustrious and excellent than the old, or any that went before: proportionably so should we, and all that are God's New Covenant federates, illustriously excel the federates of Old. We should excel them, in maturity of apprehensions of God and all divine mysteries; in vivacity of faith, living by the faith of the Son of God;[2828] in activity of love, to God and Jesus Christ over all; in fervency of zeal to the glory of God's most

---

[2827] Hebrews 8:6 & 7:22
[2828] Galatians 2:20

excellent name; in heroic perfections of all the graces of sanctification; in dearest soul-ravishing communion with Father, Son, and Holy Spirit; in integrity of obedience to God's whole revealed will, with true delight; in uncessant growth in knowledge, grace and all the perfections of the inner man;[2829] in unmovable steadfastness and constant abounding in all the work of the Lord;[2830] in diligent pressing towards the mark for the price of the high-calling of God in Jesus Christ;[2831] in loving, longing for, and hastening unto the appearing of our Lord Jesus Christ,[2832] who said, {*surely I come quickly*}, to whom our fervent spirits should echo out: {*Amen. Even so, come Lord Jesus*}.[2833]

(9) **Hence, all bruised, distressed and disconsolate souls should in an especial manner have recourse to this blessed New Covenant for their sweetest and fullest consolations.**

Much consolation is to be had from former covenants and their promises; but most of all from this New Covenant and its promises.[2834] They abound: but this superabounds. They flow, but this overflows (like the land of Canaan) with milk and honey of most delicious consolations.

What is it that wounds your heart, saddens your spirit, or makes your perplexed soul droop within you, which this New Covenant will not remove? [1] Is it guilt of sin? [2] Is it the wrath of God? [3] Is it the gross darkness of your mind? [4] Is it the hardness, deceitfulness, and vileness of your heart? [5] Is it the want of spiritual excellencies and abilities? [6] Is it the greatness of the distance between God, Christ, and you? [7] Is it the great difficulty or seeming impossibility of ever obtaining assurance of salvation? [8] It is the relics of corruption? [9] Is it the fears and dangers of backsliding? [10] Is it any inward

---

[2829] 2 Peter 3:18
[2830] 1 Corinthians 15:5, 8
[2831] Philippians 3:13-14
[2832] 2 Peter 3:12
[2833] Revelation 22:20
[2834] Hebrews 6:17-18

or outward wants: [11] Is it strong and violent temptations? [12] Is it sad and dismaying desertions? [13] Is it sharp afflictions or persecutions? [14] Or is it the very terrors and pangs of death itself? Is it any, or many, or all of these, that fills thee with discomfort, and girds thee about with sackcloth? Against all and everyone of these, this New Covenant is a most rich and precious antidote, as has been abundantly evidenced in each one of these particulars.[2835] Come hither therefore, oh you poor tossed and weather-beaten soul, who walks in darkness and has no light,[2836] learn here of this New Covenant to wait upon the Lord, and stay yourself upon your God. Come anchor in this sweet haven of peace, come lick the honey out of this rock, come draw and drink water out of these wells of salvation with joy. These New Covenant consolations are the sweetest, strongest, and most lasting consolations.

(10) **Hence finally, it is very evident, that this New Testamental Covenant approaches nearest, as in contiguity of time, so in excellency of nature, unto the celestial glory.**

The first and lowest expressure of the Covenant of Faith began in the earthly paradise;[2837] this last and highest expressure of the New Covenant will end in the heavenly paradise. This New Covenant, which is to continue until the world's end,[2838] will reach to the very borders of the heavenly country, the celestial Canaan, and of all Covenants, the sublime nature of it is most nearly elevated to the perfection of the heavenly felicity.

The three first covenants with Adam, Noah and Abraham, were suitable to the church's extreme infancy; the Old Covenant, as also those with David, and the captives in Babylon, were answerable to the church's non-age and minority; but this New Covenant is most agreeable to the church's full-age and maturity.

[2835] See General Inference 2, Property 14, and consult the places there alleged.
[2836] Isaiah 50:10
[2837] Genesis 3:15, etc.
[2838] Matthew 28:18-20; 1 Corinthians 11:26, Hebrews 13:20

Under the first three, the church was only domestic, in private families; in the next three, the church was come to be national, in that one nation of the Jews; in this last the New Covenant, the church becomes ecumenical, being generally extended to all nations of the world. In those, Christ was only promised; in this, Christ is actually performed and exhibited. In those, redemption, reconciliation, and salvation of sinners were foreshadowed; in this, all these glorious things are actually fulfilled. In those, there was much of heaven; in this, there is most of all. In this, the truth of God is most clear, the mysteries of God are most plain, the grace of God discovers itself most full and free, the gospel of God is most glorified, the people of God are most multiplied, the saints of God are most perfected, and the church of God is most completed and prepared for the eternal solemnities of her marriage with the lamb, where "the reward of virtue," (as Augustine sweetly) "will be, he that is the giver of virtue, who has promised himself, than whom nothing can be better or greater," etc. *When we shall be like him, for that we shall see him as he is* (1 John 3:2). "We shall rest and see, we shall see and love, we shall love and laud. Lo this shall be, in the end, without end."[2839]

Oh, happy New Covenant that at last will enclose the church in the bosom of God, and blissful arms of Jesus Christ! *Make haste my beloved, and be thou like to a roe, or to a young hart upon the mountains of spices* (Song of Solomon. 8:14). *And the Spirit and the bride say, come; and let him that heareth say, come: and Christ himself saith, behold I come quickly. Amen. Even so come Lord Jesus* (Revelation 22:17, 20).

1 Timothy 1:17.

FINIS.

[2839] Augustine, *The City of God*, 22.30.5

A general synopsis of the subject matters in all these four books [five volumes from Berith Press].

God's Covenants with man are unfolded in these four books:

[Volume 1 from Berith Press]

BOOK I

(1) More generally, where,
[1] God in all ages deals with his church and people by way of covenant. And why.
[2] Of the names, general nature, and distribution of God's Covenant.

BOOK II

(2) More particularly, where,

[1] Of God's Covenant of Works with the first Adam and his natural seed, before the fall. Here,
   {1} That God entered into Covenant with the first Adam and his posterity, etc.
   {2} The names, author, parties, form, and matter of this Covenant are described.
   {3} Adam had complete ability to keep this Covenant in every point.
   {4} Adam broke the Covenant of Works by disobedience.
   {5} The breach of the Covenant of Works made way for the Covenant of Faith.

[2] Of God's Covenant of Faith with the Last Adam Jesus Christ and his supernatural seed:

{1} More generally. Here are shown:

(i) That the Covenant of Works being broken in the first Adam, the Covenant of Faith was revealed in Jesus Christ the Last Adam.

(ii) What the Covenant of Faith is – the: (a) efficient, (b) parties, (c) matter, and (d) form of it. Many inferences: wherein of the conditionality of the Covenant.

(iii) The distribution of the Covenant of Faith.

{2} More particularly, namely: of (i) the Covenants of Promise, and (ii) the New Covenant.

BOOK III

(i) **Of the Covenant of Promise; in six remarkable periods of time, namely:**

(a) **From Adam until Noah. In that mother-promise of Genesis 3:14-15. Here, that this promise:**

(1) Was revealed immediately after the fall.

(2) Was revealed very imperfectly and obscurely.

(3) Was revealed in **Christ** the woman's chief seed.

(4) Revealed man's recovery in the enmity between the woman etc.

(5) Had in it, though not the name and formality, yet the nature and reality of a Covenant.

[Volume 2 from Berith Press]

(b) **From Noah until Abraham. Here are shown:**
   (1) That God – determining to drown the world, etc – covenanted to save Noah, etc.
   (2) That God, having drowned the world, covenanted never to drown it again.
   (3) That these two Covenants were a renewed discovery of the Covenant of Faith.

[Volume 3 from Berith Press]

(c) **From Abraham until Moses. Here, of:**
   (1) The federates, namely: God, and Abraham and his seed, especially Christ.
   (2) The matter of the Covenant: [1] promised mercies, and [2] repromised duties.
   (3) The form of it: [1] inward, and [2] outward.
   (4) The end of it, and 7 inferences from the whole.

[Volume 4 from Berith Press]

(d) **From Moses until David – yea, until Christ, the David. Here,**
   (1) Of the law given to Israel at Mount Sinai, more absolutely.

(2) Of the law given then as **a Covenant**, not of Works, but of Faith.
  [1] The federates: God and Israel.
  [2] The matter of it. Mercies promised; duties restipulated.
  [3] The form of it: {1} inward, and {2} outward.
  [4] The end of it. And 9 general corollaries.

(v) From David until the captivity in Babylon.

Here, of this Covenant's (a) duration, (b) author and nature, (c) federates, (d) impulsive causes and occasions, (e) matter, (f) form, (g) end, and (h) general inferences.

(vi) From the captivity until Christ.

Here, of the (a) duration; (b) author, occasion, impulsives, federates, and nature; (c) matter; (d) form; and (e) end of this Covenant – and general inferences.

BOOK IV.

(ii) Of the Covenant of Performance, namely: the New Covenant. Here are represented:

(a) The bounds or limits of its duration, of all others, most observable.

(b) The names, and general nature of it.

(c) The author, occasion, and impulsive or moving causes of it.

(d) The federate parties to it.

[Volume 5 from Berith Press]

(e) The matter of it: (1) blessings promised, and (2) duties re-promised.
(f) The Mediator, Surety and Testator of it, Jesus Christ.
(g) The form of it: (1) inward, and (2) outward.
(h) The end of it: (1) immediate, and (2) mediate.
(i) General inferences from the whole of the New Covenant.

www.ingramcontent.com/pod-product-compliance
Lightning Source LLC
Chambersburg PA
CBHW030246010526
44107CB00031B/1344/J